D1712897

Related Books of Interest

Enterprise Master Data Management

An SOA Approach to Managing Core Information

By Dreibelbis, Hechler, Milman, Oberhofer, van Run, Wolfson

ISBN-13: 978-0-13-236625-0

The Only Complete Technical Primer for MDM Planners, Architects, and Implementers

An authoritative, vendor-independent MDM technical reference for practitioners: architects, technical analysts, consultants, solution designers, and senior IT decision makers. Written by the IBM® data management innovators who are pioneering MDM, this book systematically introduces MDM's key concepts and technical themes, explains its business case, and illuminates how it interrelates with and enables SOA.

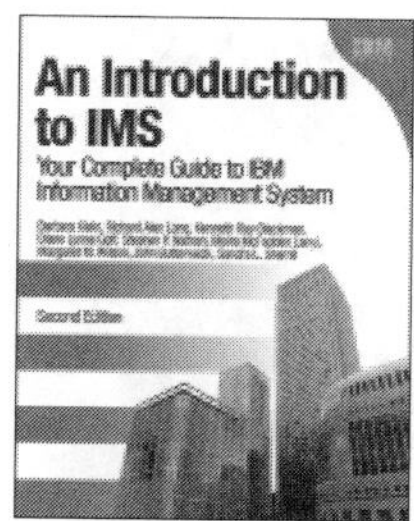

An Introduction to IMS

Your Complete Guide to IBM Information Management Systems, 2nd Edition

By Barbara Klein, et al.

ISBN-13: 978-0-13-288687-1

IBM's Definitive One-Stop Guide to IMS Versions 12, 11, and 10: for Every IMS DBA, Developer, and System Programmer

Over 90% of the top Fortune® 1000 companies rely on IBM's Information Management System (IMS) for their most critical IBM System z® data management needs: 50,000,000,000+ transactions run through IMS databases every day. What's more, IBM continues to upgrade IMS: Versions 12, 11, and 10 meet today's business challenges more flexibly and at a lower cost than ever before. In ***An Introduction to IMS, Second Edition***, leading IBM experts present the definitive technical introduction to these versions of IMS.

Sign up for the monthly IBM Press newsletter at ibmpressbooks.com/newsletters

Related Books of Interest

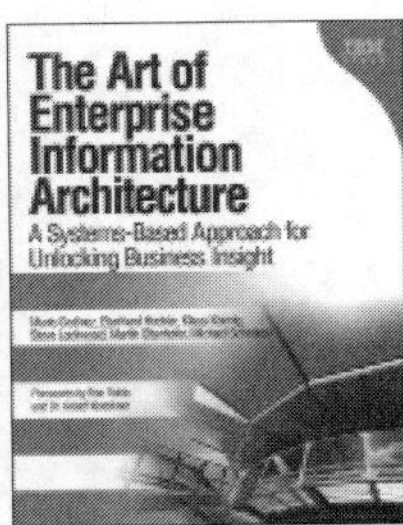

The Art of Enterprise Information Architecture

By Godinez, Hechler, Koenig, Lockwood, Oberhofer, Schroeck

ISBN-13: 978-0-13-703571-7

Architecture for the Intelligent Enterprise: Powerful New Ways to Maximize the Real-time Value of Information

In this book, a team of IBM's leading information management experts guide you on a journey that will take you from where you are today toward becoming an "Intelligent Enterprise."

Drawing on their extensive experience working with enterprise clients, the authors present a new, information-centric approach to architecture and powerful new models that will benefit any organization. Using these strategies and models, companies can systematically unlock the business value of information by delivering actionable, real-time information in context to enable better decision-making throughout the enterprise–from the "shop floor" to the "top floor."

Dynamic SOA and BPM

Best Practices for Business Process Management and SOA Agility

By Marc Fiammante

ISBN-13: 978-0-13-701891-8

Achieve Breakthrough Business Flexibility and Agility by Integrating SOA and BPM

Thousands of enterprises have adopted Service Oriented Architecture (SOA) based on its promise to help them respond more rapidly to changing business requirements by composing new solutions from existing business services. To deliver on this promise, however, companies need to integrate solid but flexible Business Process Management (BPM) plans into their SOA initiatives. ***Dynamic SOA and BPM*** offers a pragmatic, efficient approach for doing so.

Related Books of Interest

Executing SOA

A Practical Guide for the Service-Oriented Architect

By Bieberstein, Laird, Jones, Mitra

ISBN-13: 978-0-13-235374-8

This book follows up where the authors' best-selling Service-Oriented Architecture Compass left off, showing how to overcome key obstacles to successful SOA implementation and identifying best practices for all facets of execution—technical, organizational, and human. Among the issues it addresses: introducing a services discipline that supports collaboration and information process sharing; integrating services with preexisting technology assets and strategies; choosing the right roles for new tools; shifting culture, governance, and architecture; and bringing greater agility to the entire organizational lifecycle, not just isolated projects. Executing SOA is an indispensable resource for every enterprise architect, technical manager, and IT leader tasked with driving value from SOA in complex environments.

A Practical Guide to Distributed Scrum

Woodward, Surdeck, Ganis

ISBN-13: 978-0-13-704113-8

The Business of IT

How to Improve Service and Lower Costs

Ryan, Raducha-Grace

ISBN-13: 978-0-13-700061-6

Viral Data in SOA

An Enterprise Pandemic

Fishman

ISBN-13: 978-0-13-700180-4

Disciplined Agile Delivery

A Practitioner's Guide to Agile Software Delivery in the Enterprise

Ambler, Lines

ISBN-13: 978-0-13-281013-5

Outside-in Software Development

Kessler, Sweitzer

ISBN-13: 978-0-13-157551-6

Patterns of Information Management

Patterns of Information Management

Mandy Chessell
Harald C. Smith

IBM Press
Pearson plc

Upper Saddle River, NJ • Boston • Indianapolis • San Francisco
New York • Toronto • Montreal • London • Munich • Paris • Madrid
Cape Town • Sydney • Tokyo • Singapore • Mexico City

ibmpressbooks.com

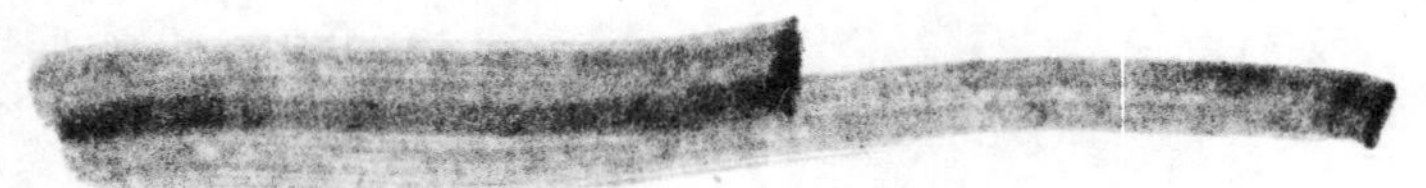

IBM Press Program Managers: Steven M. Stansel, Ellice Uffer

Cover design: IBM Corporation

Editor In Chief: Bernard Goodwin

Marketing Manager: Stephane Nakib

Publicist: Heather Fox

Editorial Assistant: Michelle Housley

Managing Editor: Kristy Hart

Designer: Alan Clements

Project Editor: Andy Beaster

Copy Editor: Karen Annett

Indexer: Lisa Stumpf

Compositor: Gloria Schurick

Proofreader: Sarah Kearns

Manufacturing Buyer: Dan Uhrig

Published by Pearson plc

Publishing as IBM Press

IBM Press offers excellent discounts on this book when ordered in quantity for bulk purchases or special sales, which may include electronic versions and/or custom covers and content particular to your business, training goals, marketing focus, and branding interests. For more information, please contact

U.S. Corporate and Government Sales
1-800-382-3419
corpsales@pearsontechgroup.com.

For sales outside the U.S., please contact

International Sales
international@pearson.com.

Library of Congress Cataloging-in-Publication Data is on file.

ISBN-13: 978-0-13-315550-1
ISBN-10: 0-13-315550-1

Text printed in the United States on recycled paper at Courier in Westford, MA.
First printing: May 2013

Some day, on the corporate balance sheet, there will be an entry which reads, "Information"; for in most cases, the information is more valuable than the hardware which processes it.

—Rear Admiral Grace Hopper

To my family and friends who have supported and encouraged me over the years, with love:
Sarah, Jane, Ray, Terri, Ben, Ella, Kay, Keith, Dan, and Chris.

—Mandy Chessell

To my family: Mary, Rebecca, Cecilia, and Paul
and my parents: Clyde and Ellen
For their love and support now and over the years.

—Harald Smith

Contents at a Glance

Table of Contents

Foreword by Rob High

In the early history of humans—when we were barely distinguishable from other animals—we protected ourselves with the construction of shelters made from branches, leaves, and mud. To suggest that these structures had architecture is being generous. But to the extent that their architectural style could be discerned at all, at best you could argue their architecture was forged from necessity and practicality. Dried mud helped keep the leaves secured and leakproof. Branches provide strength across broad spans. Leaves knitted everything together. Eons of experience and mistakes drove practices—often varying substantially from one region to another based on the available materials and climate conditions of each region. Form strictly followed function. No one, at that time, ever stopped to draw out their shelter design—critiquing it for its style and propitiousness.

Likewise, the early years of information systems implementation were driven out of necessity—leveraging the materials and practices that were available to us. Barely discernable architectures were more derived than prescribed. But, as with our ancestral laborers, we found the need to build more sophisticated and ever-larger answers to our problems. And, as before, we discovered that with a little planning, engineering, and standardized construction techniques, we could handle the task more easily. We could adapt to new functions, and we could apply form and aesthetics to the things we constructed. The results are not only more pleasing, but they are more reliable, more efficient, more economical, and more adaptable to changing conditions. There is not only derived architecture, but we can employ architecture to coerce solutions to better meet our needs.

At the heart of architecture are patterns that shape and style the materials we work with and the techniques that inform the practices of pattern adoption. Patterns form the building blocks of construction. Techniques tell us how best to select and assemble those building blocks to achieve the results we are seeking.

The idea of using patterns and techniques in the construction of information management is exactly what this book is about. Information patterns form the basis of a whole new architectural approach to systems design that, like its analog in the construction industry, is essential to assuring durability, usability, flexibility, and utility of IT solutions. The patterns presented here are not hypothetical, but rather have been forged from decades of experience in the field. They capture the bittersweet results of literally thousands of person-years of effort—trying different approaches, abandoning the ones that failed, refining the ones that showed promise, latching on to the ones that proved to work well, and promoting the ones that exceeded expectations.

The language of information patterns is a formalism of expression. It standardizes an approach to representing ideas that enables clarity and precision of communication. It allows us to exchange a common understanding of those ideas and to manipulate those ideas to create even bigger, more profound ideas. And although the basic ideas captured in the language are not new, the ability to express those ideas in a formal language is both novel and profoundly innovative. It makes it possible to unleash the value of information patterns, and build even greater value more effectively.

As the former chief architect of IBM®'s SOA Foundation, I have long advocated the use of architecture for ensuring the utility of information systems solutions. These information patterns build on the traditions of Service Oriented Architecture (SOA) and, more important, fill a critical gap in SOA by addressing the correlation between services and information in our IT solutions. In keeping with the SOA tradition, these patterns are not just the raw materials of construction for IT developers, but are essential to aligning the objectives of IT and business—driving the form of the system to both enable the business to respond quickly to changing business conditions and to even compel the business to motivate changes that will gain it a competitive advantage in its marketplace.

The use of information patterns is imperative for modern information system design. This book is a must-read and I strongly encourage you to apply these techniques in your practices.

Rob High
IBM Fellow
CTO, IBM Watson™
Former chief architect, SOA Foundation

Preface

About This Book

Information is the heart of any organization's operation. It defines who is involved, what activities are taking place, and the assets being brought to bear to create its goods and services. Managing information takes a multidisciplinary approach because it pervades every aspect of the organization's life. We must consider where information comes from; consider how it is distributed, protected, governed, and monitored; as well as ensure it is used appropriately at its destination.

From a technical point of view, a myriad of technologies have emerged to tackle different aspects of information management. There is the Service Oriented Architecture (SOA) technology that makes information available to remote systems; databases and files systems to store information; messaging technology that sends notifications between systems; extract, transform, load (ETL) technology for moving and transforming large quantities of information; federated queries; big data technologies; replication technology; data quality and metadata tools; distributed security technology; analytics; archiving processes; and many more. For the architect, the choice of technology is overwhelming and there is a strong temptation to just stick with the technology we know well. The result is that our designs can become unbalanced, with too much focus on one dimension of the problem.

This book contains architecture patterns that characterize the typical information issues associated with distributed systems. They demonstrate how the seemingly competing technologies for information management, SOA, and business process management can be blended to create an effective, interconnected, and ordered IT landscape, making it both manageable and efficient.

The patterns are built around a supply chain metaphor. Information is supplied to the organization, processed, moved around, processed some more, and then output as some form of information product, such as a report or dashboard. Through this analogy, we cover how an organization can manage its information to support its operation effectively, balancing quality, availability, breadth, precision, and timeliness with cost.

Information is not a physical asset, of course, so our notion of an "information supply chain" must extend the physical manufacturing and distribution supply chain metaphor with the recognition that information rarely moves from point to point as a discrete, whole unit. It is constantly being copied, transformed, renamed, partitioned, merged, updated, and deleted. More subtly, there are multiple versions of the "truth." People's interpretation and assumptions around the information they work with are highly contextual, and so when information is shared, it must be transformed to match the expectations and context of the new consumers before they will trust it to support their business.

Patterns of Information Management explains how information is transformed, enriched, reconciled, and redistributed along the information supply chain. The aim is to shape the way systems are integrated to create an orderly flow of information that can be reused and synchronized at key points in the processing.

A pattern-based approach is powerful because the resulting system behavior is determined by the way technologies are combined; the design choices are heavily affected by nonfunctional requirements, such as the amount of information, the arrival rates of new values, the level of quality that can be assumed, and the processing required to make the information useful. The patterns link together into a pattern language that spans from the holistic system level views for enterprise architects down to the design patterns of integration developers. The resulting pattern language enables the architect to make reasoned decisions about the applicability of each alternative approach and the inherent consequences of the choice.

Intended Audience

Patterns of Information Management is intended for enterprise architects, information architects, and solution architects who are responsible for defining how information systems should be linked together in order to synchronize, manage, and share information. Students and practitioners alike will find that the patterns create a framework in which to organize their existing experience and broaden their knowledge.

How to Use This Book

This book is principally a reference book. Chapters 1 and 2, "Introduction" and "The MCHS Trading Case Study," respectively, set the scene, explaining how the pattern language is structured and walking through some examples. It is recommended that you read both of these chapters before using the patterns.

The remaining chapters contain the pattern definitions themselves. These chapters can be used to deepen your knowledge of the topic or as a pattern reference during a particular project. Because there are so many patterns, it is not possible, or necessary, to learn all of the patterns before starting to use them in a project. The patterns are organized into small, related groups that focus on a particular aspect of information management. We suggest that you start with a pattern group that is particularly relevant to your work. Study the pattern descriptions, paying attention to the differentiating aspects of each pattern, and map them to your project.

The content can be used in various ways:

- The pattern names define a vocabulary to discuss issues and technology options related to information architecture, governance, and management. The pattern names become the nouns and verbs of your design discussions, enabling you to characterize and choose between the options available.
- The pattern icons can be used in whiteboarding sessions and for documenting design decisions in reference architectures and solution specifications.
- The pattern descriptions provide design guidance for specific information supply chains and solutions.
- The pattern language provides a foundation for setting architectural standards and reference architectures. An organization can select the patterns it wants to support and develop reference implementations for them.
- The pattern language provides material for education and training in information architecture.

As you become familiar with one group of patterns, you can turn your attention to another—iteratively growing your knowledge. The consistency built into the pattern language will accelerate your learning process and very quickly you will become proficient in a significant working set of patterns.

Structure of the Book

Patterns of Information Management is divided into the following chapters:

Chapter 1, "Introduction"

Chapter 1 is an introduction to the topic of information management and the challenges that architects face. It explains what a pattern is, the conventions we use in documenting a pattern, and how patterns are linked together to form a pattern language.

Chapter 2, "The MCHS Trading Case Study"

Chapter 2 uses a case study involving a fictitious company called MCHS Trading to illustrate how the patterns of information management can be used in a project setting. These projects cover defining an information strategy; introducing a data warehouse and management reporting; introducing master data management hubs for operational master data; improving how information is governed, monitored, and managed; exchanging information with external parties; and using predictive analytics.

Chapter 3, "People and Organizations"

Chapter 3 is the first of the pattern definition chapters. It covers patterns relating to the way an organization is operating because this has a major impact on the way that information is managed. It describes the following pattern groups:

- Information centric organizations
- Information users

These patterns help in the definition of your information strategy and information governance program.

Chapter 4, "Information Architecture"

Chapter 4 covers the nature of information and how to think about its structure, meaning, and organization. This includes patterns that describe the different life-cycle patterns of information, models, metadata, information supply chains, and the solutions you may implement to improve the management of information. It includes the following pattern groups:

- Information elements
- Information identification
- Information provisioning
- Information supply chains

These patterns help you understand and plan the overall flow of information through your organization's systems.

Chapter 5, "Information at Rest"

Chapter 5 contains pattern descriptions describing how information is accessed and stored. This includes descriptions of the different types of servers that support information management. The pattern groups in this chapter are as follows:

- Information services
- Information collections
- Information entries
- Information nodes

These patterns help to shape your thinking when deploying new capability into the IT environment, such as a new application, master data management hub, data warehouse, analytics, or reporting platform.

Chapter 6, "Information in Motion"

Chapter 6 documents the patterns for moving information between servers, including services, information routing, filtering, consolidation, and distribution. It contains the following pattern groups:

- Information requests
- Information flows

These patterns focus on how information is moved between the information nodes to satisfy the needs of their information processes.

Chapter 7, "Information Processing"

Chapter 7 describes the different types of processing that is performed on information and how it is triggered. The processes include business, movement, transformation, quality management, search, and analytics processes. It contains these pattern groups:

- Information triggers
- Information processes

These patterns help you categorize and select how information should be processed and maintained.

Chapter 8, "Information Protection"

Chapter 8 covers the patterns for protecting information, including validating, transforming, enriching, and correcting information; security; and monitoring. It includes three pattern groups:

- Information reengineering steps
- Information guards
- Information probes

Once you have your information supply chains mapped out, these patterns help you design how the information can be protected end to end.

Chapter 9, "Solutions for Information Management"

Chapter 9 covers the information solution pattern group. These patterns describe a selection of information projects that improve the information management of an organization's information systems. Solutions incorporate a set of patterns focused on addressing particular information problems, though always in context with existing information landscapes so they must integrate with, enhance, or incorporate existing systems and information.

Appendices

The appendices include a glossary of technical terms and technology types that are mapped to the relevant patterns.

What Is Not Covered

This is a design pattern language and so does not recommend specific technologies and products. It aims to describe classes of technology, where they should be used, and the consequences of using them. This book is also intended to be an overview of the information management landscape. It does not include implementation details, particularly where there is plenty of literature covering these details. Finally, there are references to information governance in the patterns. Information governance is a supporting discipline for information management that involves business controls, procedures, and related technology. It is beyond the scope of this book to cover these aspects properly.

Further Information

There is an IBM developerWorks® community for the *Patterns of Information Management* where additional details, examples, and discussions are being posted. To join, visit:
https://www.ibm.com/developerworks/mydeveloperworks/groups/service/html/communityview?communityUuid=8b999d32-11d5-4f68-a06e-6825f3c78233

This community provides you with an opportunity to ask questions about the patterns and suggest improvements.

Acknowledgments

The pattern language has been through many iterations, discussions, and workshops to get it into a state that is suitable for publishing. We would like to thank the following people who have provided help and feedback during the process.

From the EuroPLoP 2011 Pattern Writers Conference (where the INFORMATION NODE patterns were reviewed), there is our shepherd, Tim Wellhausen, and the members of the writer's workshop: Klaus Marquardt, Markus Gaertner, Andreas Fiesser, and Joerg Pechau.

IBM has provided us with an envirionment where we have been able to develop and share the material with experts from many companies, industries, and software disciplines, drawing on their years of experience delivering complex projects and systems. As a result, we received valuable feedback from many subject matter experts, including Dan Wolfson, Dougal Watt, Steve Lockwood, Kyle Brown, Loretta Mahon Smith, Mike McRoberts, Rob High, Martin Wildberger, Richard Hedges, Stephanie Hazlewood, Patrick Dantressangle, Mukesh Mohania, Ivan Milman, Lena Woolf, David Radley, Larry Yusuf, Susan Visser, Sarah Tee, Herb Berger, Prasad Vempati, Keith Enhagen, Eleomara Goncalves, and Rickey Tang.

We would also like to thank the members of Pearsons plc who have expertly guided and supported us in our first publishing effort—in particular, Bernard Goodwin and Michelle Housley.

About the Authors

Mandy Chessell

FREng CEng FBCS

Mandy has worked for IBM since 1987. She is an IBM Distinguished Engineer, IBM Master Inventor, and member of the IBM Academy of Technology Leadership Team. As the chief architect for InfoSphere® Solutions in IBM's Software Group, Mandy designs common information integration patterns for different industries and solutions.

In earlier roles, Mandy's work has focused on transaction processing, event management, business process management, information management, and model-driven development. This breadth is reflected in her invention portfolio, which to date stands at over 50 issued patents worldwide.

Outside of IBM, Mandy is a fellow of the Royal Academy of Engineering and a visiting professor at the University of Sheffield, UK. In 2001, she was the first woman to be awarded a Silver Medal by the Royal Academy of Engineering, and in 2000, she was one of the "TR100" young innovators identified by MIT's *Technology Review* magazine. In 2006, she won a British Female Innovators and Inventors Network (BFIIN) "Building Capability" award for her work developing innovative people and the BlackBerry "2006 Best Woman in Technology - Corporate Sector" award. More recently, she was granted an honorary fellowship of the Institution for Engineering Designers (IED) and she won the "2012 everywoman Innovator of the Year."

For more information on Mandy's publications, see http://en.wikipedia.org/wiki/Amanda_Chessell.

Harald Smith

Harald has worked for IBM since 2005. Harald is a software architect in IBM's Software Group specializing in information quality, integration, and governance products, and is IBM certified in delivering IBM Information Management solutions. In this role, he develops best practices, methodology, and accelerators for common information integration use cases.

Harald has 30 years of experience working with data quality products and solutions; product and project management; application development and delivery; system auditing; technical services; and business processes across the software, financial services, healthcare, and education sectors. Harald was the product manager at Ascential® Software and IBM responsible for designing and bringing the IBM InfoSphere Information Analyzer product to market as a key component in IBM's information quality portfolio. He has been issued three patents in the field of information quality and rule discovery and was recently recognized as an IBM developerWorks Contributing Author.

His publications include the IBM developerWorks articles "The information perspective of SOA design" [parts 6, 7, and 8], "Use IBM WebSphere® AuditStage in a federated database environment," "Using pre-built rule definitions with IBM InfoSphere Information Analyzer,"

"Designing an integration landscape with IBM InfoSphere Foundation Tools and Information Server" [part 1], and "Best practices for IBM InfoSphere Blueprint Director" [parts 1 and 2]. For the IBM InfoSphere Information Server documentation, Harald contributed to the "IBM InfoSphere Information Analyzer Methodology and Best Practices Guide" and "IBM InfoSphere Information Server Integration Scenario Guide"; he has also contributed to three IBM Redbooks®.

CHAPTER 1

Introduction

In software engineering, we are taught that abstraction, modularity, and information hiding are useful approaches when breaking down a set of requirements into manageable chunks for implementation. This book makes use of these principles to tackle the synchronization of information between IT systems.

Islands of Information

Most organizations use specialized IT systems called applications to run their operations. Each application supports a particular aspect of the business, either for the whole organization or a group within it. There may be applications for order taking, for billing, for distribution of goods, for management of employee data, and many more.

An application will store the information it is processing in a persistent store for later reference. This information store is often a private resource for the application. Over time, this store contains important details about the people with whom the organization is interacting, what assets they use, how, when, and why.

A healthy organization will develop and grow—and this change drives changes into its applications, affecting their function and scope. It can also lead to duplication of function:

- When two organizations merge, they can end up with at least two applications for each function.
- When a new product line or channel to market is introduced, an organization may choose to introduce a new application to support it, to avoid the possibility of disrupting the established business or to implement it faster.
- Multinational organizations find they need separate applications for different countries, or trading regions, to handle local customs and regulations.

Careful management and constant rationalization may reduce the number of applications so there is little or no overlap in function. However, an application is a complex mix of software and hardware. It takes considerable engineering effort to develop it, and so once the investment is made, an application is expected to have a long life (5–15 years). Ripping it out and replacing it can be expensive and difficult and so an organization may choose to maintain multiple applications for the same function.

When there are two applications covering the same function, information about that function is split between the two applications and is typically stored in a different format. Even when all applications support unique functions, there is still an overlap in the information that they hold. This is the information that describes the core interests of the organization, such as customers, suppliers, products, contracts, payments, assets, employees, and many more.

Over time, the private information stores of an organization's applications become islands of duplicated and inconsistent information. This affects the efficiency of an organization and its ability to operate in a cost-effective, flexible, and coherent unit.

This book seeks to address the challenge of effective information management. How does an organization improve its management of information, working with the applications it already operates, to ensure it knows what its assets are, what it is working on, what commitments it has agreed to, how well it is performing, and how it can improve its operation?

Introducing MCHS Trading

MCHS trading is a fictitious trading company used in this book to illustrate different approaches to information management. MCHS Trading sells goods through four channels: on the Internet, via mail order, via a call center, and through physical shops. Due to differences in requirements, orders are taken by three different applications: E-shop for the Internet orders, Mail-shop for mail order and the call center, and the Stores application to support the needs of the physical stores. These applications were introduced incrementally as MCHS Trading opened the new channels to its customers.

Orders are fulfilled and money is collected through the Shipping and Invoicing applications, respectively. The E-shop, Mail-shop, and Stores applications send the order details to the Shipping application, which in turn forwards them on to the Invoicing applications as soon as an order is dispatched. This is illustrated in Figure 1.1.

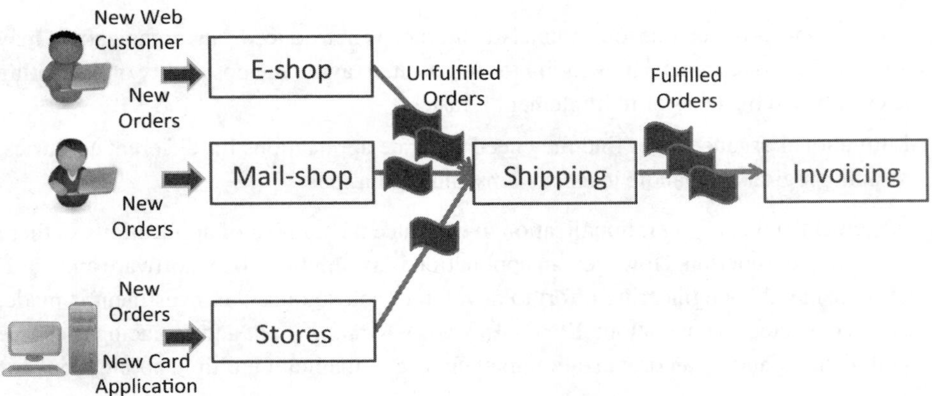

Figure 1.1 MCHS Trading's order-processing systems.

From a functional point of view, this is a rational separation of concerns. Each application has a clearly delineated set of responsibilities and the process works—customers get the goods they ordered and the correct money is collected in exchange for the goods.

However, when the information stores are added to the picture (see Figure 1.2), you can see that the details about customers, products, and orders are replicated across the systems. Why? Because this information is core to MCHS Trading's business and so every application needs it in some form or another.

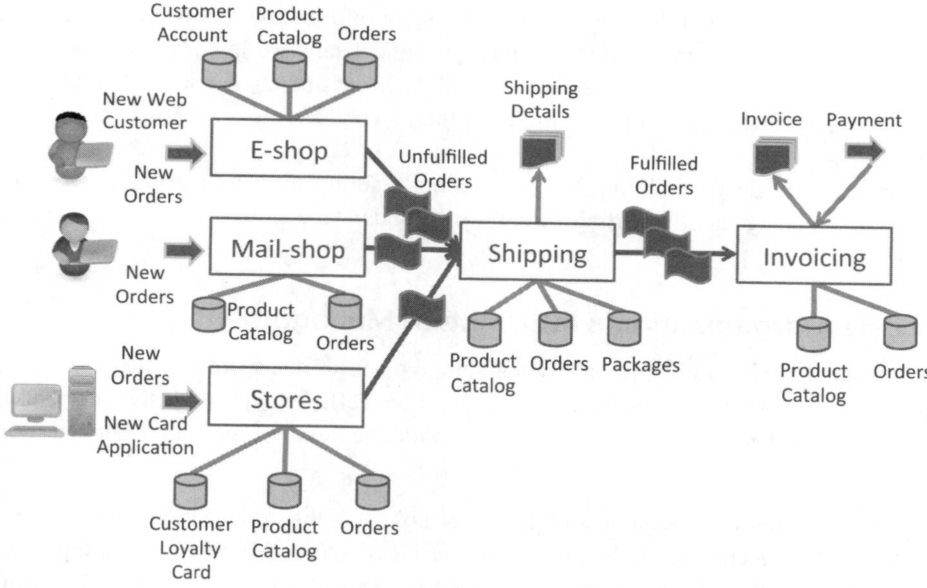

Figure 1.2 Information stores supporting order processing.

Failing to synchronize this information effectively leads to inflexibility and inefficiencies in the organization that can have an impact both internally and externally.

Consider an individual customer, Alistair Steiff. He has registered for a loyalty card, which is handled by the Stores application, and he also uses the E-shop and the mail order channel from time to time. The E-shop keeps a record of Alistair in the form of a customer account. This is different from the loyalty card account. The Mail-shop application takes Alistair's details with each order. It has no capability to maintain his details for the next time he orders something through that channel, which Alistair finds a little annoying.

Alistair experienced another issue when he moved to a new address. Although he updated his address in his E-shop account, MCHS Trading kept sending his loyalty card statements to his old address. He tried phoning MCHS Trading's call center but they could not help because they were only set up to take new orders. He had to write a letter to MCHS Trading to get the loyalty card address updated.

Within MCHS Trading, there is also frustration with the current systems. It is difficult to understand the buying patterns of its customers:

- To understand which new products would be of interest to an individual
- To understand how an individual interacts across each of MCHS Trading's sales channels

There are two issues here. First, the applications only store information that is relevant to their operation—so it is hard to see the complete picture when the details are spread among the applications. Second, applications are designed to reflect the current operational state of their work. They may keep historical data, but not in the form that is conducive to analysis of trends and anomalies.

This lack of insight is inhibiting MCHS Trading's ability to grow and there is a need to introduce new management reporting capability to understand how the business is really performing.

Improving an Organization's Information Management

The problems that MCHS Trading is experiencing are typical for many organizations. Information is distributed across multiple applications for operational efficiency, leaving the information duplicated, fragmented, and often inconsistent. As a result, the organization cannot act in a coordinated manner:

- They find it hard to get an overall picture of how well the organization is performing. This requires a consolidated view of their business activity, showing the current position, along with a historical perspective for comparison. For example, MCHS Trading would want to understand how many customers it has, what types of products its customers are interested in buying, how this is changing over time, how efficient the delivery process is, who its best suppliers are, and much more if it is to maintain its market leadership position.
- The quality of information varies from application to application. This means different parts of the organization are operating on different facts that could lead to different decisions being made for the same situation.
- The internal fragmentation of the information is often exposed outside of the organization, creating poor customer service or missed opportunities. This was Alistair Steiff's experience when he tried to change his address—he had to ensure it was updated in each application—using a different process for each one.

- External regulators are skeptical that the organization's reported results are accurate when ad hoc processes are used to create them because it is difficult to explain where the information came from and how the results were calculated.
- Information is not retained for the required amount of time—or too much information is retained for too long. Either case can inhibit the ability to find the right information in a timely manner.
- Failures in the mechanisms that move information around can corrupt the integrity of the organization's information. These failures may be errors in the information itself, which means it cannot be transferred, or errors in the implementation of the mechanism, or a failure to initiate some processing in time, resulting in missing information. These failures may not be detected for some time and can be extremely difficult to resolve.

An organization needs to maintain a strong core of information to run the business. This requires a focus on how key information is created, processed, and stored within its IT systems:

- They must *optimize where information is located relative to the workload* that is using it—ensuring copies are taken in a thoughtful way and these copies are supported with mechanisms to maintain or remove them as new information becomes available.
- *Related information should be correlated together* to create a complete picture of the organization's activities.
- *Obsolete information must be removed* to save storage and reduce the processing effort. Vital historical information needs to be retained.
- *Information must be protected* from inappropriate use, restored after a failure, and, despite the fact that most organizations have their silos and cliques, *the right information needs to be exchanged and presented to the right people at the right time.*

This is hard to achieve. Technology is often focused on providing function to the business rather than managing information. Specialist information management technology helps, but it has to be blended with the existing infrastructure. The blending process creates emergent properties.

Emergent properties are those characteristics that "appear" when components are combined together in a particular configuration—rather than being inherent properties of any one of the components. This is similar to the behavior of colors when you mix them together. If you combine blue and yellow, you get the color green. Green is an emergent property because it is not present in either the blue or the yellow—and only emerges when they are combined.

When we combine technology together, we also get emergent properties. These emergent properties may be additive, or they may override some of the components' original capabilities.

Consider two applications sited on opposite coasts of the United States. The application on the East Coast needs to regularly send information to the West Coast application. However due to the different time zones in which they operate, there is a 3-hour period of its operation when the

West Coast application is not available. It is not possible to extend the period of operation of the West Coast application—and the East Coast application is not capable of buffering the information until the West Coast application comes online.

The solution is to provide a new database that is available whenever either application is online (see Figure 1.3). The East Coast application writes information into the database. The West Coast application processes the information in the database when it becomes available.

This is a common integration approach. The database in the middle is acting as a staging area. Its effect in the integration is to expand the time window that information can be transferred between the two applications. It may also improve the resiliency of the integration because the East Coast application is no longer affected by the occasional outages of the West Coast application. However, the downside is that when both applications are available, the staging area slows down the transfer of information between the two applications because there is a small delay between the East Coast application writing the information and the West Coast application picking it up. The time it takes to transfer information between two systems is called the latency of the information transfer.

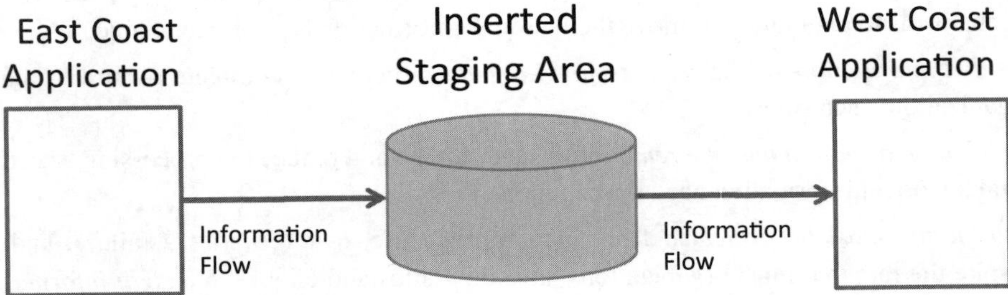

Figure 1.3 Using a staging area between two applications.

The increased availability, latency, and resilience are all emergent properties of the integration. In general, the emergent properties relate to non-functional characteristics that may not be evident until the integration is in production. This is why architects like to use tried and tested approaches where the emergent properties are well understood.

This book describes how the flow of information between applications and other systems should be designed, calling out the emergent properties as they occur.

The aim is to shape the placement of workload and information stores within the IT systems to create an orderly flow of information that guarantees the quality of the results. The material is presented as a set of connected software design patterns, called a pattern language.

Patterns and Pattern Languages

A software design pattern defines a proven approach to solving a problem. The solution described in the pattern is typically a set of components that are interacting in a particular configuration. The pattern explains why this approach works, its associated trade-offs, and resulting benefits and liabilities. It also links to other patterns that may:

- Provide an alternative approach
- Provide a complementary capability
- Describe an approach to implementing a component that is named in the pattern's solution

This linking together of related patterns creates what we call a pattern language.

Every pattern in this pattern language has a name that summarizes the solution it represents in a succinct manner. For example, there is a pattern called INFORMATION COLLECTION that describes a collection of related information. Notice that the pattern name is written using the small capitals formatting. This formatting convention is used wherever the pattern is first referenced in a section. The name of a pattern can act as shorthand for the solution during design discussions.

Choosing the terminology for the pattern names has been a challenge because the pattern language covers multiple architectural disciplines. Where possible, we have used industry standard names for the concepts and components exposed in the pattern language. However, we have found it necessary to introduce new terminology whenever there is conflicting nomenclature, or no obvious name exists.

Every pattern has an icon that can be used as a visual reminder of the pattern, particularly when whiteboarding and documenting solutions. The information collection icon is shown in Figure 1.4.

Figure 1.4 Icon for the information collection pattern.

The patterns are built on a common component model. This means that a pattern can be used as a component in the solution described by another pattern. When this occurs, the icon of the pattern is used in the solution diagram of the consuming pattern. For example, Figure 1.5

shows the solution for the staging area introduced in the previous section. It is built from a variety of pattern icons.

The meaning of the icons in the diagram, and the details of the patterns behind them, will become familiar to you as you work with the pattern language. The purpose here is to illustrate how the icon of one pattern, the information collection in this case, can be used in the solutions of other patterns.

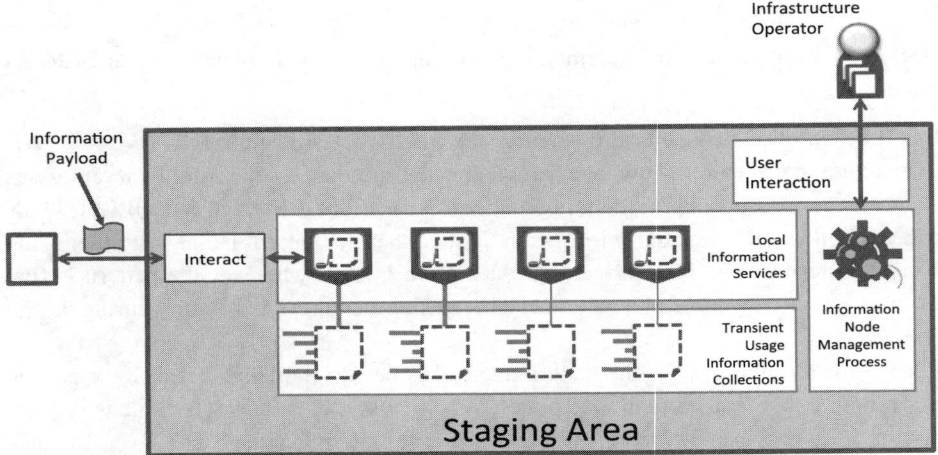

Figure 1.5 The solution diagram for a staging area showing the use of the information collection icon.

Each of the patterns of information management can be used independently. However, the real value of a pattern language is the ability to compare and contrast different approaches to resolving a situation.

The patterns of information management that are relevant to a particular situation are collected together in a pattern group. Each pattern group has a lead pattern that describes the core principles and capabilities of the group. The pattern group is named after the lead pattern. The other patterns in the pattern group enhance one or more characteristics of the lead pattern to support a more specialized situation.

You may have noticed that in Figure 1.5, the information collection icon appears slightly modified in the solution diagram with five lines coming out of the left side (as shown in Figure 1.6). The modification to the information collection icon denotes that the staging area uses specialized information collections described by the **T**RANSIENT **S**COPE pattern.

The modified icon visually represents that there is a relationship between the information collection and transient usage patterns. They are, in fact, from the same pattern group along with other patterns called **L**OCAL **S**COPE and **C**OMPLETE **S**COPE.

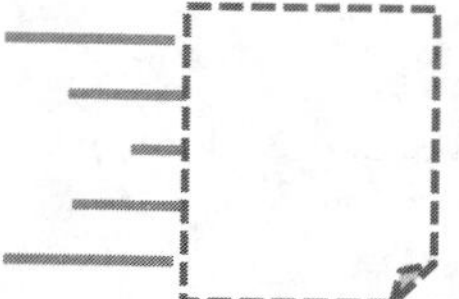

Figure 1.6 Icon for the transient scope pattern.

To make it easy to compare and contrast the patterns in a group, each group of patterns begins with a table of pattern summaries, called patlets. A patlet shows a pattern's icon, name, short problem statement, and summary of the solution. The aim of the patlets is to help you quickly discover and navigate to the pattern you need. Table 1.1 shows the patlet for the INFORMATION COLLECTION pattern, which is the lead pattern in its group.

Table 1.1 Sample Pattern Summary for Information Collection

Icon	Pattern Name	Problem	Solution
	INFORMATION COLLECTION	Information must be organized so it can be located, accessed, protected, and maintained at a level that is consistent with its value to the organization.	Group related information together into a logical collection and implement information services to access and maintain this information.

Table 1.2 shows the related scope patterns from the same group. Notice that the icons are all variations of the information collection icon.

Table 1.2 Patlet Table for the Scope Patterns in the Information Collection Group

Icon	Pattern Name	Problem	Solution
	COMPLETE SCOPE	An information process needs to perform an activity once for each instance of a particular subject area (such as a customer, product, order, invoice, shipment, etc.) that occurs within the information supply chain.	The information process needs to use an information collection that stores a single information entry for each instance of the subject area that occurs within the information supply chain. Such an information collection is said to have a complete scope.

Icon	Pattern Name	Problem	Solution
	LOCAL SCOPE	The implementations of the information processes hosted within an information node assume they are in complete control of changes to the information they use.	Provide information collections within the information node for the sole use of its information processes. These information collections will then only have information entries that are created by the locally hosted information processes. These types of information collections are said to have a local scope.
	TRANSIENT SCOPE	An information node needs to provide temporary storage for information entries that are being continuously added and removed by the information processes.	Create an information collection to temporarily store the information entries in the information node. From time to time, the information entries stored in this information collection will change, and so we say this collection has transient scope.

The detailed pattern descriptions follow the patlet tables. Many different styles and heading structures have been successfully used to describe software patterns. We have chosen to use one of the formats recommended by The Open Group Architecture Framework (TOGAF®)[1] with the following subsections:

- **Context**—The situation where it is appropriate to consider using the pattern
- **Problem**—A description of the problem that this pattern solves
- **Example**—An example of the problem
- **Forces**—The factors that make this problem hard to solve
- **Solution**—A description of solution components and how they are assembled together
- **Consequences**—The benefits and liabilities of using the solution
- **Example Resolved**—How the example described is resolved using the pattern
- **Known Uses**—References to well-known technologies and approaches that support the pattern
- **Related Patterns**—Links to other relevant patterns in the pattern language

1. http://www.togaf.info

These sections provide a way to bring together a variety of information into a well-formed structure that summarizes the essence of the pattern. Together, they enable you to make reasoned choices of approach for the solution you are building.

Basic Components in the Pattern Language

A good place to start learning about the *Patterns of Information Management* is a pattern called **I**NFORMATION **P**ROVISIONING. This describes how five basic components interact to receive, process, and produce information.

Figure 1.7 comes from the information provisioning pattern description and shows the components and how they interact. All of these relationships are many-to-many.

Notice that the information collection pattern introduced previously is shown as a component in the information provisioning pattern along with some additional patterns: **I**NFORMATION **U**SER, **I**NFORMATION **T**RIGGER, **I**NFORMATION **P**ROCESS, and **I**NFORMATION **S**ERVICE.

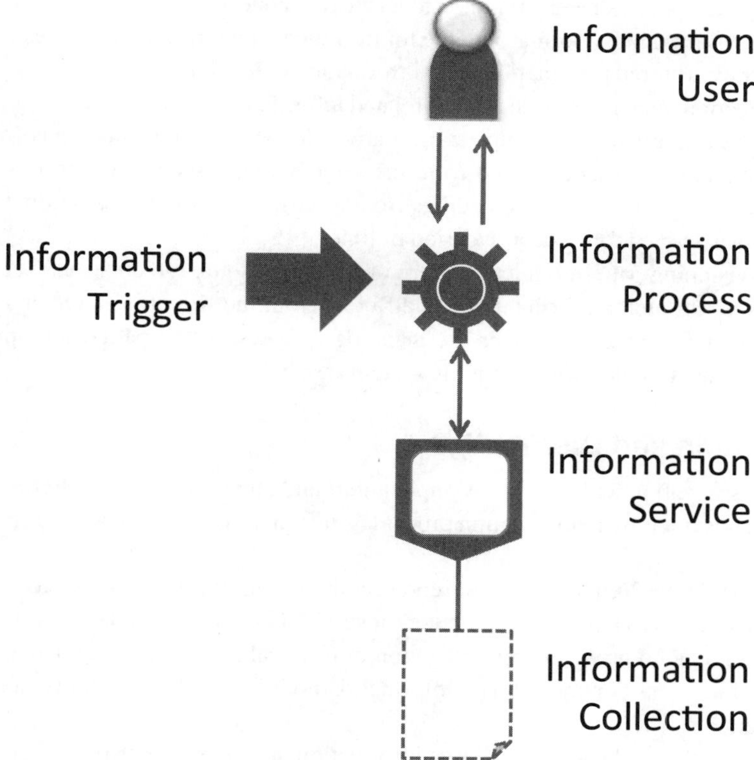

Figure 1.7 Five basic components for processing information.

The information user is a person working with the organization's information. This person may be an employee or someone outside the organization such as a customer or a supplier. Each kind of information user has his or her own requirements for the kinds of information needed, where, and when. The information user is both a consumer of existing information and a contributor of new information. The information user works with user interfaces that are controlled by information processes.

The information processes perform the automated processing of the organization. There are many different kinds of information processes—but, collectively, they are the mechanisms by which information is received, transformed, and produced in some form or another.

An information trigger starts an information process. This may be the result of an information user request, a scheduler, an event being detected, or the need for more information. The information trigger passes the information process some context information that describes why it is being started. The information process augments this context information with information from the information users and other information known to the organization.

An information process accesses any additional information it needs through well-defined interfaces called information services. An information service provides a specialized view of the information that the information process needs. It is able to locate the requested information from a variety of sources and transform it into a format suitable for the requesting information process. An information service retrieves stored information from information collections.

The information collection manages a collection of related information. Typically, the contents of an information collection relate to the same subject area. However, an information collection may contain information that was collected from the same activity, such as the results of an experiment, from the same source, such as readings from a sensor, or from the same time period, such as social media extracted for a specific period of time.

The information provisioning pattern is a lead pattern of a pattern group. It recognizes that the information a person sees through a user interface is different from the way it is stored and shows the layering of components used to manage the mapping. The rest of the pattern group describes how information is provisioned when multiple systems are involved.

Information Integration and Distribution

As already discussed, an organization will have many applications and other kinds of IT systems. Each of these systems will host their own information processes, information services, and information collections.

We use the **I**NFORMATION **N**ODE pattern to represent the general concept of a system. You may want wish to think of this as a physical computer, or server. However, with the increasing use of virtual systems and cloud provisioning, the notion of physical hardware being tied to a particular system is becoming less common. So an information node is simply an identifiable "system" that the organization runs.

The information node is the lead pattern in a large information group that describes different types of systems. The application is represented by a pattern from the group called **A**PPLI-CATION **N**ODE. The **S**TAGING **A**REA pattern is also in the same group.

The information node provides an execution environment for the information processes, information services, and information collections. Calls between these components can occur totally within the information node. However, it is also possible for information processes to access information from different information nodes. This capability is provided a specialist pattern within the information service pattern group called **R**EMOTE **I**NFORMATION **S**ERVICE.

Figure 1.8 illustrates this mechanism. The remote information service uses an **I**NFORMATION **R**EQUEST pattern to retrieve information from an information collection located in another information node. The information request pattern consists of two message flows: one from the remote information service to the information node that hosts the information to request the information, and another flowing in the opposite direction to return the requested information.

The information node that receives the request for information routes it to an appropriate information service to extract the information and return a response. In Figure 1.8, this is shown as a **L**OCAL **I**NFORMATION **S**ERVICE—that is, one that uses information collections from the same information node—but it could be another remote information service.

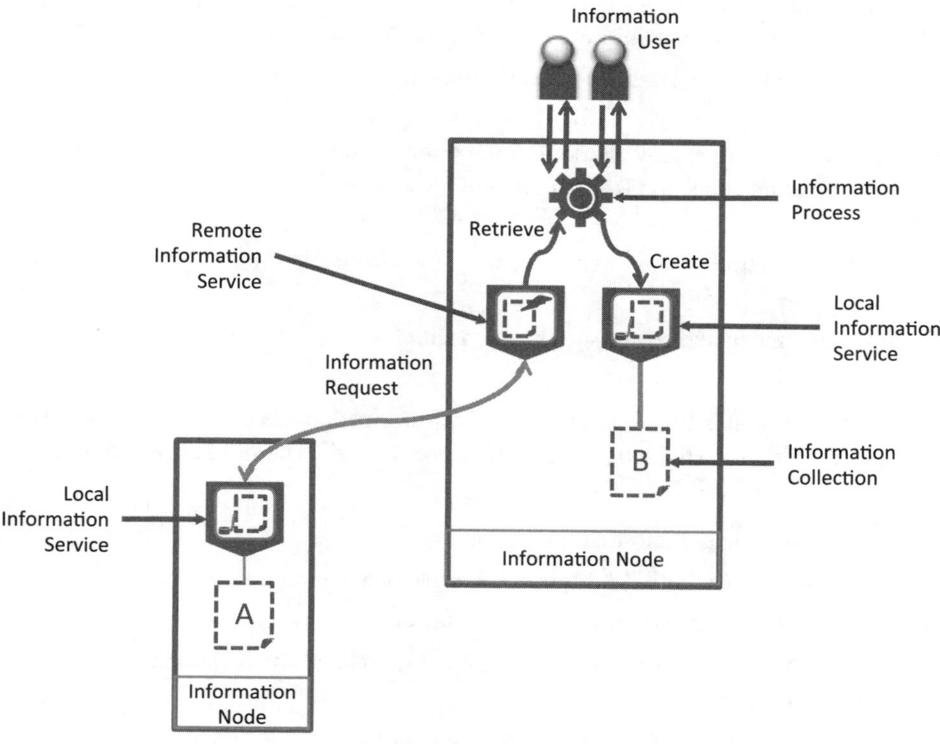

Figure 1.8 Accessing information from a different information node.

The information request pattern retrieves information from its original location on demand. This means both the calling and the called information node must be available at the same time. When information must be copied from one information collection to another—for example, for performance or availability reasons—the information flow pattern is used instead. This introduces another kind of information node called an INFORMATION BROKER that calls remote information services to extract information from one or more information collections, transform it, and store it in other information collections. The effect is that information flows between the information nodes in what we call an information supply chain.

Figure 1.9 illustrates this flow of information. The numbers on the diagram refer to these notes:

1. Here, an information process calls a remote information service to retrieve information from information collection A. Under the covers, the remote information collection uses an information request to contact the information node where information collection A is located.
2. The information process then works with some information users to update the information and store the results in information collection B.
3. Information collection B stores the information in a new entry in the information collection.
4. An information broker now starts an information process to extract the information from information collection B and transform it and save it as a new entry in information collection C.
5. Another information process starts to retrieve the information from information collection C.
6. This process may make changes to the information and update it in information collection C.

This example illustrates how multiple copies of information are created—and also how these copies quickly become slightly different from one another. The differences could be as follows:

- **Superficial—**Such as a reformatting
- **Enriching—**Where additional information is added to the original information
- **Localized—**Where updates made are only relevant to the location where they are made
- **Managed—**Where the best source of information (called the authoritative source) is well known at all times
- **Conflicting—**Where it is hard to know which information collection is the best to use or retrieve the latest information from as changes are coming in to each of the copies in an unpredictable way

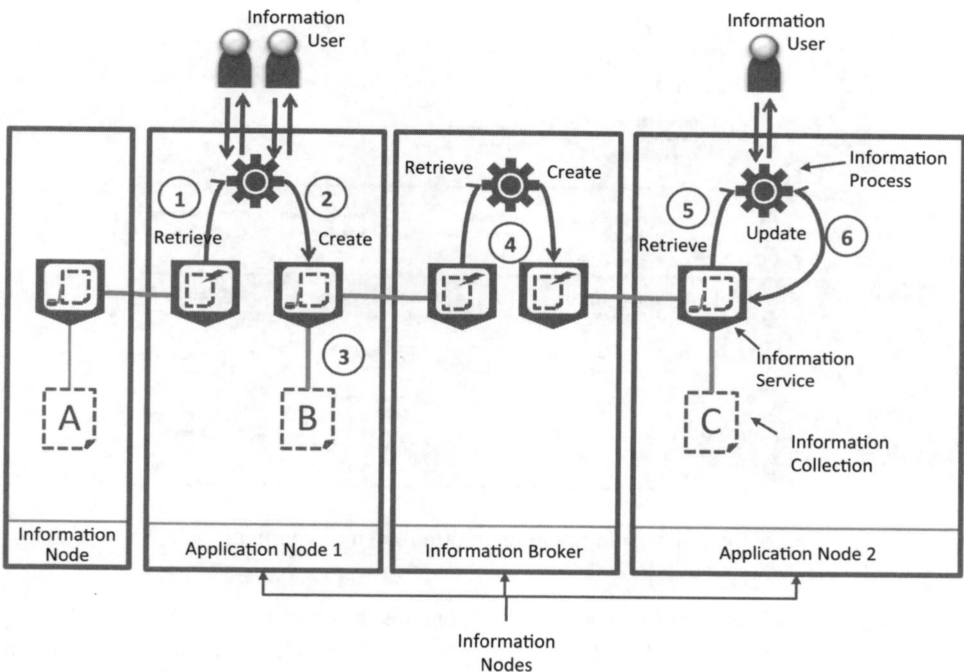

Figure 1.9 Flowing information between systems.

A well-defined information supply chain should avoid having information collections with conflicting differences in them. We aim to minimize the number of copies. Where copies are made, each should have a clear purpose and guidelines on when it should be used. Copies should be synchronized when updates are made, and where differences are unavoidable, there should be at least one copy that is known to have all of the latest information in it.

The INFORMATION SUPPLY CHAIN pattern is the lead pattern in a pattern group that describes different patterns of information movement between the information collections and how to synchronize the information to avoid conflicting differences. Designing information supply chains is a key challenge for both information architects and solution architects.

Pattern Language Structure

The pattern groups introduced in the previous sections show the breadth of factors an architect needs to consider to achieve a clean, correct, and flexible information design. At the top of the pyramid, you see the organization and the people who work within it. They drive the information strategy. The organization is supported by the information architecture, which is implemented by the information management components. This structure is summarized in Figure 1.10.

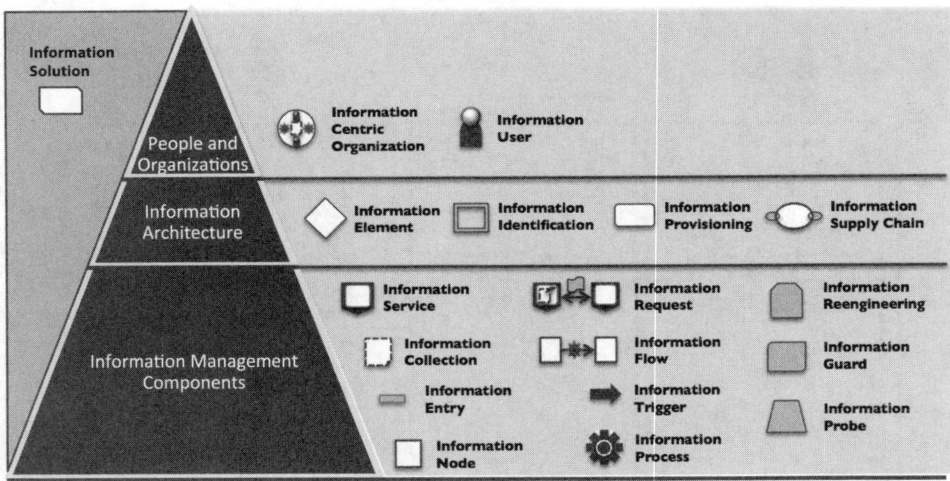

Figure 1.10 Structure of the pattern language for information management.

Chapter 2, "The MCHS Trading Case Study," contains the case study, introducing the patterns through different projects at MCHS Trading. The remaining chapters contain the pattern descriptions and are organized according to the structure in **Figure 1.10**.

Chapter 3, "People and Organizations," has the patterns for the organization and its people (see Table 1.3). These patterns include the information strategy, policy setting, and information governance.

Table 1.3 Pattern Groups in Chapter 3

Lead Pattern Name and Icon	Lead Pattern Problem Statement	Lead Pattern Solution Summary	Start Here When...
INFORMATION CENTRIC ORGANIZATION	An organization needs to make good use of its information to achieve its goals.	Make the management of information a strategic priority. Develop systems and practices that nurture and exploit information to maximum effect.	You are thinking about the holistic approach that your organization should take to information management.

Lead Pattern Name and Icon	Lead Pattern Problem Statement	Lead Pattern Solution Summary	Start Here When...
INFORMATION USER	Individuals need access to the organization's information to perform their work.	Classify the people connected with the organization according to their information needs and skills. Then provide user interfaces and reports through which they can access the information as appropriate.	You want to define what types of user roles should be supported by a new information solution.

Information architects develop an understanding of the information needs of an organization and propose best practices for how it should be structured, stored, and managed. Solution architects are responsible for developing IT-based solutions to business problems. These solutions are dependent on information and so the solution architect relies on the information architecture created by the information architect when developing a new solution. Both the information architect and the solution architect use information architecture patterns in their work. These are described in the pattern groups shown in Table 1.4, and are described in more detail in Chapter 4.

Table 1.4 Pattern Groups in Chapter 4

Lead Pattern Name and Icon	Lead Pattern Problem Statement	Lead Pattern Solution Summary	Start Here When...
INFORMATION ELEMENT	An organization is looking for the best approach to manage the many kinds of information it has.	Group together related information attributes that follow the same life cycle and manage them appropriately.	You are new to information management and want to familiarize yourself with the types of information an organization has, and how it is managed.
INFORMATION IDENTIFICATION	An organization does not know what types of information it has, where it is located, how it is managed, and who is responsible for it.	Investigate and document the information requirements and existing support available to the organization.	You want to catalog the information you have and any new requirements. The resulting information is often called metadata.

Lead Pattern Name and Icon	Lead Pattern Problem Statement	Lead Pattern Solution Summary	Start Here When...
INFORMATION PROVISIONING	An information process needs information to perform its work.	Information is supplied to the process when it starts, through its user interfaces and through stored information.	You are considering how to provide information to an information process or information user.
INFORMATION SUPPLY CHAIN	An organization needs to process information in order to fulfill its purpose. How is the flow of information coordinated throughout the organization's people and systems?	Design and manage well-defined flows of information that start from the points where the information is collected for the organization and links the flows to the places where key consumers receive the information they need.	You are designing how a particular type of information should flow between your systems.

Chapter 5, "Information at Rest," covers the way information is processed within an IT system (see Table 1.5). In this pattern language, a system is called an information node and there is a related pattern group devoted to the various types of systems.

Stored information is accessed through information services that locate the required information and format for the consumer. Information collections are logical groupings of stored information. Often the information is organized consistently within the collection. Approaches for identifying, structuring, locking, and storing information within an information collection are covered in the information entry pattern group.

Table 1.5 Pattern Groups in Chapter 5

Lead Pattern Name and Icon	Lead Pattern Problem Statement	Lead Pattern Solution Summary	Start Here When...
INFORMATION SERVICE	Some information processes need the same information, but may require it to be formatted differently.	Define well-defined interfaces to the information that meet the needs of particular consuming information processes to enable them to create, retrieve, and maintain just the information they need.	You need to decide how an information process will access the information it needs.

Lead Pattern Name and Icon	Lead Pattern Problem Statement	Lead Pattern Solution Summary	Start Here When...
INFORMATION COLLECTION	Information must be organized so it can be located, accessed, protected, and maintained at a level that is consistent with its value to the organization.	Group related information together into a logical collection and implement information services to access and maintain this information.	You need to classify how the existing stores of information are used or decide how new information should be grouped and stored.
INFORMATION ENTRY	An instance of a type of information needs to be stored in an information collection.	Structure the information collection so that it is made up of a set of information entries. Each information entry stores a single instance of the subject area. Provide capability to manage and iterate over a collection of these archetypal instances.	You are designing how information should be managed within an information collection.
INFORMATION NODE	What is the appropriate IT infrastructure to host information collections and information processes?	Related information processes and information collections should be hosted together in a server.	You are selecting the type of system to host information and its related processing.

Chapter 6, "Information in Motion," covers the information flow and information request pattern groups for moving information between information nodes (see Table 1.6).

Table 1.6 Pattern Groups in Chapter 6

Lead Pattern Name and Icon	Lead Pattern Problem Statement	Lead Pattern Solution Summary	Start Here When...
INFORMATION REQUEST	An information process needs to work with information located on a remote information node.	Open a communication link with the remote information node and synchronously exchange the information and associated commands using an agreed protocol.	You want to understand the data that flows between two communicating information nodes.

Lead Pattern Name and Icon	Lead Pattern Problem Statement	Lead Pattern Solution Summary	Start Here When...
INFORMATION FLOW	How do you implement the movement of information between two information nodes?	Use an information trigger to start an information process to control the movement of information. This information process is responsible for extracting the required information from the appropriate sources, reengineering it, and delivering it to the destination information nodes.	You are designing information integration jobs to move information between different systems.

Chapter 7, "Information Processing," covers the different kinds of information processes, along with the information triggers that start them, which are found in a typical organization's IT systems (see Table 1.7).

Table 1.7 Pattern Groups in Chapter 7

Lead Pattern Name and Icon	Lead Pattern Problem Statement	Lead Pattern Solution Summary	Start Here When...
INFORMATION TRIGGER	An information process must be started when a particular event occurs.	When the event is detected, trigger a mechanism that is able to request the initiation of the process on an appropriate information node.	You are considering how to start an information process. This information process may be providing a new business function or moving information between information collections.
INFORMATION PROCESS	An organization has to process information to support one of its activities.	Formally define and implement the processing for that activity in an information node. Ensure this information node has access to the information it needs.	You want to understand existing processing and or design new processing of information.

Another key concern for organizations with valuable information is how to protect it so it retains its quality and it is not misused or stolen. This is covered in Chapter 8, "Information Protection," (see Table 1.8).

Table 1.8 Pattern Groups in Chapter 8

Lead Pattern Name and Icon	Lead Pattern Problem Statement	Lead Pattern Solution Summary	Start Here When...
INFORMATION REENGINEERING STEP	An information process is not able to consume the information it needs, as currently exists.	Insert capability to transform the information so it is consumable by the information process.	You need to understand how information can be transformed to meet new requirements.
INFORMATION GUARD	The organization's information needs to be protected from inappropriate use and theft.	Insert mechanisms into the information supply chain to verify that the right people are only using information for authorized purposes.	You need to consider the alternatives for the security and privacy of your information.
INFORMATION PROBE	The operation of an information supply chain needs to be monitored to ensure it is working properly.	Insert probes into key points in the information supply chain to gather measurements for further analysis.	You need to plan how information management should be monitored.

The protection of information is something that must be designed holistically, considering the welfare of key information at all stages of its lifetime. It is then implemented through the deployment of small components throughout the systems, where each is responsible for protecting an aspect of the information. The patterns of information management break down the aspects of information protection into three pattern groups:

- **INFORMATION REENGINEERING STEP—**These patterns focus on maintaining the quality and format of information.
- **INFORMATION GUARD—**These patterns ensure authorized people and processes are using information for authorized purposes.
- **INFORMATION PROBE—**These patterns are used to monitor the use and movement of information. With these patterns, it is possible to detect issues in the management of information and correct it.

The information protection patterns are used as processing steps in both the information process and information service pattern groups where they transform, protect, or monitor information as it enters the organization; when it is stored; when it is sent between systems; when it is retrieved, updated, and eventually archived and deleted. Individually, they protect a single point in the processing—collectively, they protect the organization's information throughout its entire life cycle.

The final pattern group in Chapter 9, "Solutions for Information Management," covers solutions that tackle different aspects of how information management can be improved. They use the pattern groups described previously as components (see Table 1.9).

Table 1.9 Pattern Groups in Chapter 9

Lead Pattern Name and Icon	Lead Pattern Problem Statement	Lead Pattern Solution Summary	Start Here When...
INFORMATION SOLUTION	An organization recognizes there is a missing capability or a major issue with the way it manages an aspect of its information.	Create a project, or series of projects, to transform the way the information is managed by the organization's people and information systems.	You want to plan changes to your information systems to improve information management.

Summary

This chapter introduced some of the information management challenges an organization faces. Their applications provide the information processes that drive the business. These processes need access to a variety of information to perform their function. This information is distributed and duplicated among the applications and the challenge is to keep this information synchronized while ensuring it is available and suitably structured for all of the organization's needs.

This chapter also introduced the patterns of information management. The patterns of information management are a collection of software design patterns that describe best practices for blending software components together to manage the typical information management challenges that organizations face. These patterns each have a succinct name and icon for use in design discussions. Each pattern also has a tabulated short description called a patlet and a full description that explains when to use it, how it works, and the consequences of using it.

Throughout the pattern language, this book uses a fictitious company called MCHS Trading to illustrate the use of the patterns. The patterns are also grouped together around particular information management topics called pattern groups. Each pattern group has a lead pattern that describes the basic mechanism at work and the rest of the patterns in the group are variations of this basic pattern.

The first lead pattern for a pattern group that was introduced was information provisioning. This explained the layers of components used to provide information to the organization. We then went on to explain how the pattern language is structured and where each of the pattern groups are located in the book.

Now that you have seen the pattern groups in the pattern language, you can choose to navigate directly to the patterns of interest. Alternatively, Chapter 2 describes how MCHS Trading used the patterns to transform its information systems through a series of projects.

CHAPTER 2

The MCHS Trading Case Study

Examples are the best way to illustrate the complexities of information management. They provide a context in which to explore the competing requirements that must be met and how well different approaches stack up.

This chapter walks through some examples of projects at MCHS Trading that make use of the patterns for information management. There are eight projects:

- Building an information strategy
- Creating management reports
- Creating a single view of product details
- Creating a single view of customer details
- Understanding the status of orders
- Delivering information quality improvements
- Connecting MCHS Trading into a B2B trading partnership
- Exploiting predictive analytics

These projects illustrate some of the major types of capability that organizations use to improve the way their information is managed. Each case study project introduces a variety of the patterns from the patterns of information management. These projects do not cover all pattern concepts (addressed in subsequent chapters), nor do they exhaustively cover specific pattern groups, but serve to illustrate how the patterns can be used in typical information management projects.

Introduction

One of the things you have probably noticed as you wrestle with your own information projects is that there are no perfect solutions. Each choice we make has both positive and negative consequences. The patterns for information management help you understand these consequences and suggest additional steps you can take to mitigate against any effects that are unacceptable.

Chapter 1, "Introduction," introduced the fictitious trading company, MCHS Trading. Although this is a simple example, it is rich enough to cover many of the issues an organization faces. At the heart of these issues is the need for an organization to adapt to the changing world it is a part of while maintaining operational efficiency. The most constant core of the organization's existence is the information it holds. If this information core is solid and well managed, the organization can quickly detect the changing needs and adapt its processes accordingly.

The ability to move information between systems, transforming it as required, and to synchronize and consolidate different copies of the information is a key enabler of an adaptive organization. Through these mechanisms, the people using different systems see a view of the information that is specialized for their usage, but at the same time, logically consistent with the rest of the organization.

In MCHS Trading's case, the challenge is one of survival. Because it does not manufacture the goods it sells, its continued existence hinges on maintaining a loyal customer base. So the goods and services MCHS Trading offers have to be excellent and targeted to the desires of its customers; delivery has to be reliable; and customer service has to be exemplary. Strong relationships with both customers and suppliers are essential. MCHS Trading encourages suppliers to stay with it due to its valuable customer base, and draw customers back to it again and again because of the uniqueness, quality, and price of the goods and services offered.

MCHS Trading needs good information about its customers and products. Unfortunately, at the start of this story, both customer and product details are scattered throughout the systems. The organization knows this situation needs to change and so sets out on a journey to remodel its IT systems to support its plans for the future.

The first step is to define MCHS Trading's strategy for information...

Building an Information Strategy

MCHS Trading wants to become an **I**NFORMATION **C**ENTRIC **O**RGANIZATION. This is an organization that functions around a strong core of information. Being an information centric organization is not an end state. Instead, it is a state of mind—where everyone knows that information and its management matters for the ongoing success of the organization. The heart of an information centric organization is its **I**NFORMATION **S**TRATEGY. This lays out the *why*, *what*, and *how* the organization will manage information.

The *why* section covers the business imperatives that drive MCHS Trading to be information centric. This helps focus the effort on activities that deliver value to the organization. For MCHS Trading, the business imperatives laid out in its information strategy include the following:

- Exemplary customer service, where an individual customer experiences a continuous and coherent "conversation" with the organization, no matter whom he or she talks to
- Accurate, complete, and reliable information about an interesting range of products sourced from responsible and efficient suppliers
- Privacy and security of all personal information retained by the organization
- Efficient delivery of orders through a transparent supply chain

The *what* section covers the type of information that MCHS Trading must manage to deliver on its business imperatives. This includes the subject areas to cover, which attributes within the subject area need to be managed, the valid values for these attributes, and the management policies (such as protection and retention) that the organization wants to implement. MCHS Trading identifies its key subject areas as follows:

- **Customer**—Information about the individuals and organizations it sells to
- **Supplier**—Information about the organizations it buys goods from
- **Product**—The products and product bundles it sells
- **Stock**—The physical goods it has in the warehouse
- **Orders**—The orders for products its customers are making
- **Finance and Sales**—The summary of financial expenses (the cost of acquiring goods for sale) and financial income (the sales from orders by its customers) that reflect the financial health of the organization

If MCHS Trading can rely on this information, and the relationships between them, it has a sound information base to work with. These subject areas are documented in the **S**UBJECT **A**REA **D**EFINITION pattern.

Finally, the *how* section is described using **I**NFORMATION **M**ANAGEMENT **P**RINCIPLES. These principles provide the general rules for how information is managed by the information systems and the people using them, along with how information flows between them.

An organization's information strategy is a living document. It may start with a narrow focus, covering only part of an organization's information use. Then, over time, it can be gradually expanded to cover all of the core systems of the organization.

As MCHS Trading lays out its strategy, it realizes that its information systems need to change. The next few sections take you through the projects MCHS Trading implements to improve the way its information is managed. The resulting architectures it implements are captured in the **I**NFORMATION **S**OLUTION patterns. The method for implementing these solutions starts with the same basic questions:

- What requirements and processes must the solution support?
- What information must these processes deliver and to whom?
- What information do these processes need?
- Where is this information located and who owns it?
- How is this information managed?
- How are the processes provisioned?
- How is the solution monitored?
- How is the solution secured?

These questions help tease out the requirements for the solution and select the appropriate patterns. Then the information infrastructure can be designed to support these patterns. The first project focuses on producing management reports.

Creating Management Reports

Management reports are often one of the earliest information solution projects that an organization tackles. They provide consolidated views of an organization's information with a historical perspective. Justifying the value of these reports to business stakeholders is straightforward because they are typically the main beneficiaries.

MCHS Trading considers its reporting needs. Each of its main lines of business wants reports that show how well it is performing. They want to know which products are selling, the types of customers they are selling to, the reliability and quality of their suppliers, the timeliness of their delivery service, and how money is collected and spent.

Each team has a unique perspective on what is the most important type of information to focus on. The marketing team wants to know how the products are selling, the customer support team wants to know how loyal and satisfied its customers are, the finance team wants to understand profitability, and so on.

Reports come in different types. For example:

- How are certain values changing over time?
- How does information of this type relate to information of another type?
- Which are the best or worst performing aspects of an operation?

The reports also have different timelines—hourly, daily, weekly, monthly, and annually. The information is, therefore, summarized according to multiple different criteria for each focus area.

MCHS Trading realized that it needed a dedicated **P**ERFORMANCE **R**EPORTING information solution to support its requirements. This introduces a new information node called the Decision-Center. The Decision-Center's primary purpose is to host specialist **I**NFORMATION **R**EPORTING **P**ROCESSES.

An information reporting process is responsible for accessing the information for the report and displaying it in useful forms (charts, graphs, tables, and dashboards) to enable an information user to explore and understand the information it is displaying. Ideally, this process is provisioned with the information for each report in a structure that matches how information is to be displayed. However, because most reporting platforms allow people to define new reports, it may be using more generic structures designed for many types of reports.

Given the large number of reports needed by an organization, each utilizing different subsets of information, a compromise must be struck between storing copies of the information in exactly the right format for each report, or storing a shared, canonical version of the information and reformatting it dynamically when the report is to be produced. Thus, the information needed to support the Decision-Center was not available directly from any of its existing systems. The organization must create a consolidated view of the information managed by its applications.

For many organizations, provisioning their reporting processes is a multistep process that is described in the **H**ISTORICAL **S**YSTEM OF **R**ECORD information solution.

Figure 2.1 shows how this works.

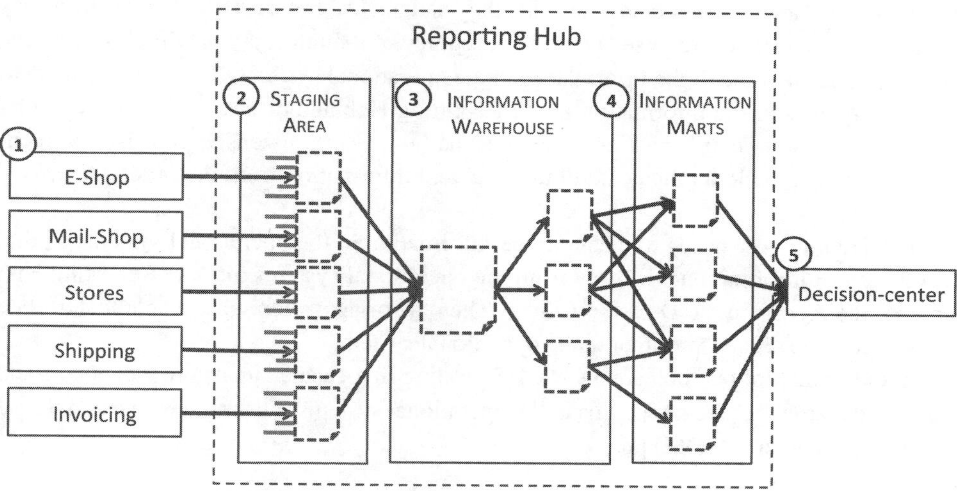

Figure 2.1 Provisioning information for management reports.

The numbers on the diagram in Figure 2.1 refer to these notes:

1. These are the operational systems that run the day-to-day business.
2. **I**NFORMATION **F**LOWS copy information from the operational systems into **S**TAGING **A**REAS ready to be imported into the information warehouse. The information flows are focused on retrieving information from the operational systems with as little overhead as possible.
3. More information flows take the information from the staging areas and run **I**NFORMATION **R**EENGINEERING **S**TEPS to correct, enrich, correlate, and consolidate the information into a coherent set of information collections in the **I**NFORMATION **W**AREHOUSE. These information collections include a historical record of how the information values have changed over time. Older information entries may be summarized when the fine-grained details are no longer needed.

4. Information flows then take copies of different subsets of the information and populate the **INFORMATION MARTS** for the different teams.
5. The information marts are used by the Decision-Center to create the reports as required. The tables in the information marts are either accessed directly or through precalculated views.

When the Decision-Center goes into production, it is hailed as a big success. The reports give the management teams views of their operations that they had not had before. However, as the weeks and months go by, questions are raised about the accuracy of the information within the reports. They don't seem to tie up with the information in the operational systems. The IT team starts to investigate the quality of the information in the Reporting Hub and discovers that the information flows that provision its information collections had to perform extensive information reengineering steps to reconcile duplicated and uncorrelated information from the order-processing systems.

MCHS Trading now needs to clean up the information in the operational systems so that the same quality of information will flow from the operational systems into the Reporting Hub and then onto the reports in the Decision-Center. Then the organization will be able to correlate the information in the reports with that in the operational systems.

The projects that follow look at how MCHS Trading first cleaned up its product details and then progressed on to the customer details in the operational systems. These are both examples of Master Data Management (MDM) projects.

Creating a Single View of Product Details

Product details are an important type of information for MCHS Trading. They describe the goods and services that MCHS Trading is offering to its customers. If these details are incorrect, they can cause customer dissatisfaction, or even litigation.

Product details are an example of an **INFORMATION ASSET**. An information asset describes a core concept of the business, such as an organization, person, real-world concept or object, product, or physical asset. It often has a long lifetime and, relatively speaking, is read many more times than it is updated. It is used as reference data throughout the organization and, as a result, is often duplicated across multiple information nodes.

A quick scan of MCHS Trading's systems shows product details are located in all of the order-processing applications. (See Figure 2.2.)

When product details change, or products are added or removed from any of the sales channels, consistent updates must be made across these applications or the end-to-end process may not work.

In MCHS Trading's case, the products offered through each of the sales channels are largely the same. Each application has its own information processes for maintaining the product details stored in its local information collections. When the product catalog is updated, these changes are manually entered into each application to update its local information collection. We call this **A**PPLICATION **P**RIVATE **P**ROVISIONING.

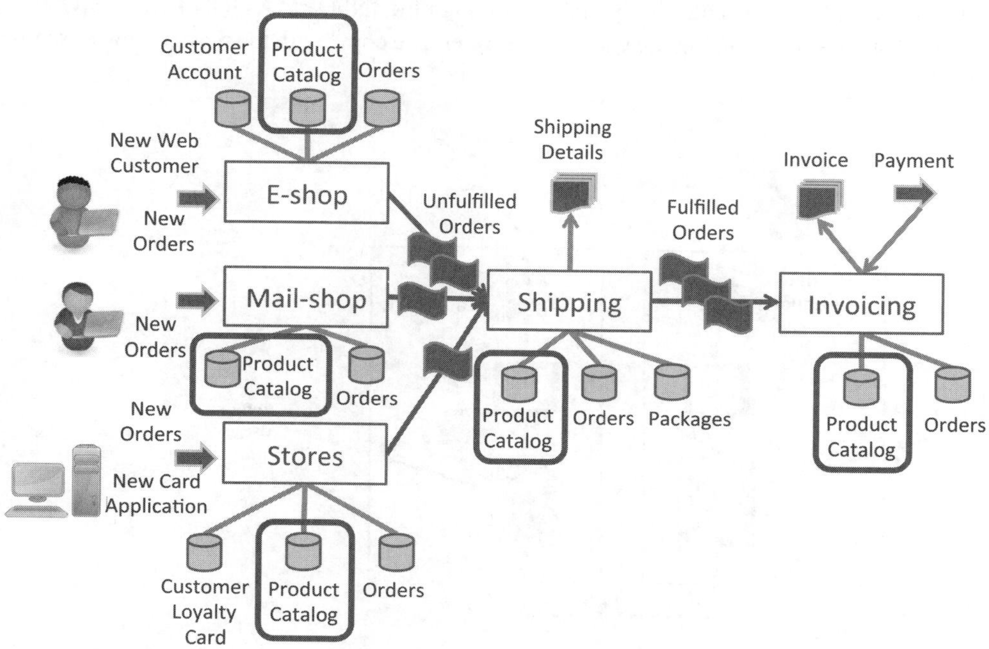

Figure 2.2 MCHS Trading's product catalogs.

As long as no mistakes are made, the current approach works—although it becomes very labor intensive when the product catalog is given a major refresh at the start of each season.

MCHS Trading wants to centrally manage and store its product details. The organization is currently using spreadsheets to define the updates that are emailed to one another. It is hard to know who has the latest version because it must be emailed between many teams. If the maintenance of the product details is centrally managed, then when changes are made, they can be automatically distributed to all of the other systems that need them.

The first challenge is to identify which information collection will store the centralized copy of the product details. As Figure 2.2 shows, there are five information collections to choose from. In the existing approach, each of these information collections is maintained directly by local information processes. These information processes are characterized as having **M**ASTER **U**SAGE of the information collections because they make changes to the information.

At the end of the project, the aim is to have just one master usage information collection for product details, and the other information collections will follow the **R**EFERENCE **U**SAGE pattern. Reference usage means that the information collection is used in a read-only mode by the core business applications, and is only updated through the **I**NFORMATION **P**ROVISIONING processes that are synchronizing the values in the reference copy, with the master copy as seen in Figure 2.3.

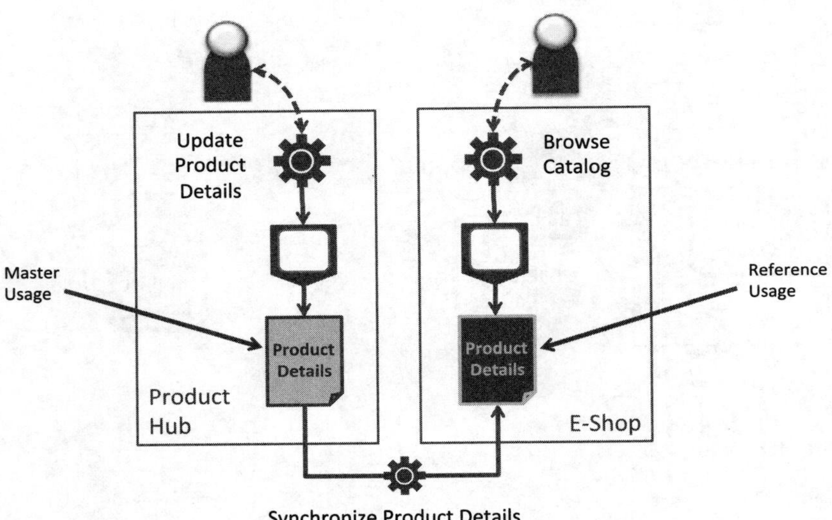

Figure 2.3 Synchronizing product details from a master usage information collection to a reference usage information collection.

For this to work, the single master copy must be a superset of the information in the other collections—both in terms of the **coverage** of the attribute values it stores and the **scope** of the instances it contains.

When we think of the scope of an information collection, there are three basic patterns. First, there is **C**OMPLETE **S**COPE. This is where the information collection contains information entries covering all possible instances that are needed. For example, in MCHS Trading's case, this would be the details all of the products that it sells. The second pattern is **L**OCAL **S**COPE. An information collection with local scope is one that stores only the instances that are meaningful to the information processes using it. For example, the product catalog in the E-Shop application only contains products that are sold through the web channel. This is local scope. The Shipping application has a product catalog for all of the products sold by MCHS Trading by any of the channels. This information collection has complete scope.

The third scope pattern is called **T**RANSIENT **S**COPE and this is used for temporary information collections where instances are coming and going continuously as they are processed. These types of collections are introduced in information stores such as **S**TAGING **A**REAS that are used when copying and transforming information.

In addition to scope, we need to consider the coverage of the attributes that an information collection stores. There are four basic coverage patterns:

- **COMPLETE COVERAGE**—All identified attributes for the subject area are present.
- **CORE COVERAGE**—The attributes that describe the different ways an instance is identified are present.
- **EXTENDED COVERAGE**—The attributes that describe the principle characteristics of an instance are present.
- **LOCAL COVERAGE**—Only the attributes needed by the consuming information processes are present. As a result, not all of the core attributes are present.

The definition of coverage is relative to the **S**UBJECT **A**REA **D**EFINITION. An information collection may also have attributes that are not included in the subject area definition. These attributes contain private information for the local information processes. They would never be shared across the information supply chain and so are not relevant to the analysis.

Finally, the single master copy must also support the same (or a stricter) set of validation rules (**V**ALID **V**ALUES **D**EFINITION) as the reference copies. Deciding what these rules are can take some coordination between the interested parties so allow time for this discussion.

MCHS Trading needs an information collection with complete coverage to act as the centralized master copy. Table 2.1 summarizes the classification of the product details information collections in MCHS Trading's applications. The icon in the table comes from combining the icons of the selected patterns.

Table 2.1 Usage, Scope, and Coverage for Product Information Collections

Host Application	Usage	Scope	Coverage	Icon
E-Shop	**M**ASTER **U**SAGE	**L**OCAL **S**COPE	**L**OCAL **C**OVERAGE	
Mail-Shop	**M**ASTER **U**SAGE	**L**OCAL **S**COPE	**L**OCAL **C**OVERAGE	
Stores	**M**ASTER **U**SAGE	**L**OCAL **S**COPE	**L**OCAL **C**OVERAGE	

Host Application	Usage	Scope	Coverage	Icon
Shipping	MASTER USAGE	COMPLETE SCOPE	EXTENDED COVERAGE	
Invoicing	MASTER USAGE	COMPLETE SCOPE	LOCAL COVERAGE	

As you can see, the closest match is the Shipping application, although it is not perfect. When the team investigates what it will cost to extend it so it has complete coverage, it discovers that it is cheaper to buy a packaged application that specializes in defining product details. This would bring efficiencies to the Merchandising Department that maintain the product catalog as well as provide a master copy for product details.

Figure 2.4 is an example of the types of processes that will be supported by the Product Hub. This is a COLLABORATIVE EDITING PROCESS where different people are responsible for each step in the process. Together, these steps gradually build up the values that make up a complete description of a product.

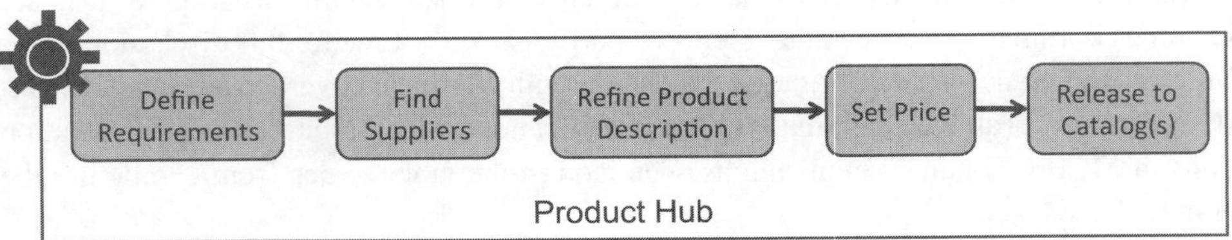

Figure 2.4 Collaborative editing process for introducing a new product in the Product Hub.

When the new Product Hub application is in place, it will act as the single master copy of the product catalog. As the updates are finished, they will be sent to each of the applications that host product details. The local information processes that used to maintain the product details information collections in these applications are decommissioned because these information collections are now reference copies.

What remains to be decided is how the product details will flow from the Product Hub to the other applications. With this design, MCHS Trading is implementing what is called a CASCADING INFORMATION SUPPLY CHAIN. This keeps the information synchronized in one direction. The part of this supply chain that distributes product details to the order-processing applications is implemented using MIRRORING PROVISIONING. (See Figure 2.5.)

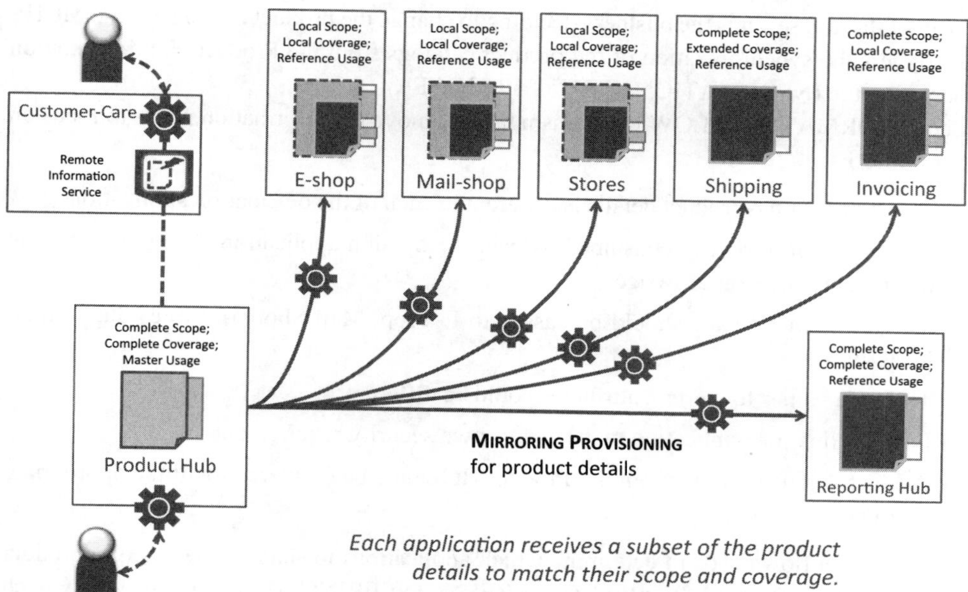

Figure 2.5 Using mirroring provisioning to synchronize product details.

There are two aspects to consider when implementing mirroring provisioning: What is the trigger that initiates the flow of information when it changes (this is called an INFORMATION TRIGGER) and what is the mechanism that moves the information once triggered (called an INFORMATION FLOW)?

Triggering information provisioning can be: a manual process (see MANUAL TRIGGER); automatically scheduled (see SCHEDULED INFORMATION TRIGGER); triggered from the information process inside the Product Hub application that makes the changes to the product details (see INFORMATION SERVICE TRIGGER); or triggered off of the changes to the product details information collection (see INFORMATION CHANGE TRIGGER).

The trigger chosen will determine when the updates are synchronized with the downstream applications and so it must match the needs of the business. In this example, MCHS Trading releases product updates to its channels in batches, either because it has on-boarded a new supplier, enabling an increase in the range of goods and/or services offered, or when they are doing a new season refresh. Both of these types of changes are planned and coincide with a marketing campaign. Outside of these changes, there are ad hoc updates to an individual product's description because an error is found in it or a supplier changes the specification.

In all of these cases, it is the business deciding to change the product catalog, and so MCHS Trading triggers the synchronization of the product catalogs from the Product Hub information processes using the INFORMATION SERVICE TRIGGER.

The INFORMATION FLOW mechanism used to move the information needs to focus on a number of details:

- The format of the product details is different in each of the destination applications.
- The subset of attributes consumed by each destination application is slightly different due to their different coverage.
- Not all product details should be passed to E-Shop, Mail-Shop, or Stores due to their local scope.
- The code values for certain attributes could be different.
- Each destination application may have its own security requirements.
- Product details sent out from the Product Hub must be delivered to all the appropriate destinations.

So, the information flow needs to determine which applications to send the details of a product to, and then slightly different INFORMATION REENGINEERING STEPS are needed for each of the selected destinations.

MCHS Trading decides to use the PARTITIONED DISTRIBUTION pattern because this supports the transformation of a different subset of information to each of the destinations.

Partitioned distribution is implemented in an INFORMATION BROKER information node. The information broker uses information collections with TRANSIENT SCOPE to act as a temporary store for each destination application. This could be hosted in a STAGING AREA or a QUEUE MANAGER. An INFORMATION DEPLOYMENT PROCESS, hosted in the information broker, takes the batches of product details and copies them into the transient information collections that each correspond to the appropriate destination applications. It uses values from the product details to determine which destinations are valid for each product description. As product details are added to a particular transient information collection, another information deployment process is triggered using the INFORMATION CHANGE TRIGGER. This process removes each individual product details entry from the transient information collection that triggered it, transforms it into the desired format for its destination, and delivers it. (See Figure 2.6.)

Once the information processes in the information broker are in place, product details can be maintained in a single place and the resulting updates are distributed to the applications that need them.

This project is captured in the CENTRALIZED MASTER information solution pattern. It illustrates the ideal solution for shared information where there is a single master copy that is used as a source of information for all of the other copies.

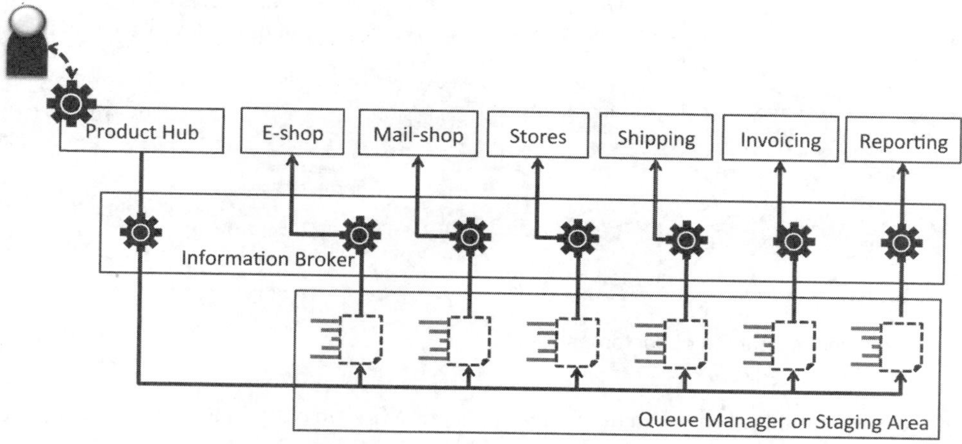

Figure 2.6 Using partitioned distribution to implement mirroring provisioning.

The next project looks at creating a single view of customer details. This is a more difficult project. It is not possible to consolidate all of the updates to a single master information collection as customer details are captured on the fly in many places during normal operations. Changes will need to be synchronized between the applications, on a peer basis, rather than a master-reference arrangement described above.

Creating a Single View of Customer Details

Like product details, customer details are INFORMATION ASSETS. They describe objects in the real world—namely, people. Information about people is harder to deal with than product details because individuals can be whimsical, using different contact details for different circumstances, and any contact information about them is often volatile. People do not have unique identifiers either—although IT systems typically try to assign one. As a result, matching a person to his or her stored information—and keeping that stored information up to date—can be a challenge.

At the start of MCHS Trading's single view of customer project, customer details are mastered in both the E-Shop and Stores application. Snapshots of a customer's information are also included with each order record as it flows between the applications. (See Figure 2.7.)

Both the customer details information collections in E-Shop and Stores have LOCAL SCOPE and LOCAL COVERAGE. E-Shop stores the details of people who have registered for an account with E-Shop. Stores hold details of people who have an MCHS Trading store card. Neither information collection is suited to holding the complete scope of customer details because the consuming information processes assume the local scope. This is best illustrated with an example.

Figure 2.7 Possible sources of customer details.

If the information processes in the Stores application find an entry in their customer details information collection, they assume it represents a person with a store card and would, for example, attempt to generate a statement, or send marketing material relating to the store card to that individual. If we had added details for an E-Shop customer to the Stores' information collection, either the information process is going to fail due to missing card details, or the individual customer is going to get some curious mail from the company.

Just simply combining the contents of these two information collections will not create an information collection with complete scope either:

- A person may appear in only one collection because he or she either uses the E-Shop or has a store card.
- A person may appear in both collections because he or she has both a store card and is registered with the website. The information in each system may not be consistent because it was created at different times and has gone through different validation processes.
- Individuals may be registered in either collection multiple times, just because they can. There is nothing in place to prevent this.
- A person may be a high-value customer of MCHS Trading and appear in neither information collection because he or she always uses either mail order or phone order. In this case, the person's details are only stored by the Mail-Shop with any order made.

The result is that MCHS Trading really does not know who its customers are, or even how many customers it has. When it comes to executing its order-processing business, this is not an issue. However, it is limiting the ability to build customer loyalty and grow revenue.

This situation is very common where systems have been built around products, channels, or accounts. If the organization simply needs to understand who its customers are, and what they bought, for historical analysis, this can be achieved by periodically extracting the customer details from each system and correcting, enriching, matching, merging, and transforming the information into a coherent information collection for analysis. This is the approach MCHS Trading took when it added a Reporting Hub to gather historical information for analysis. This Reporting Hub is fed customer information directly from E-Shop, Mail-Shop, and Stores. The customer details are transformed and merged to provide a historical view of the customer base. (See Figure 2.8.)

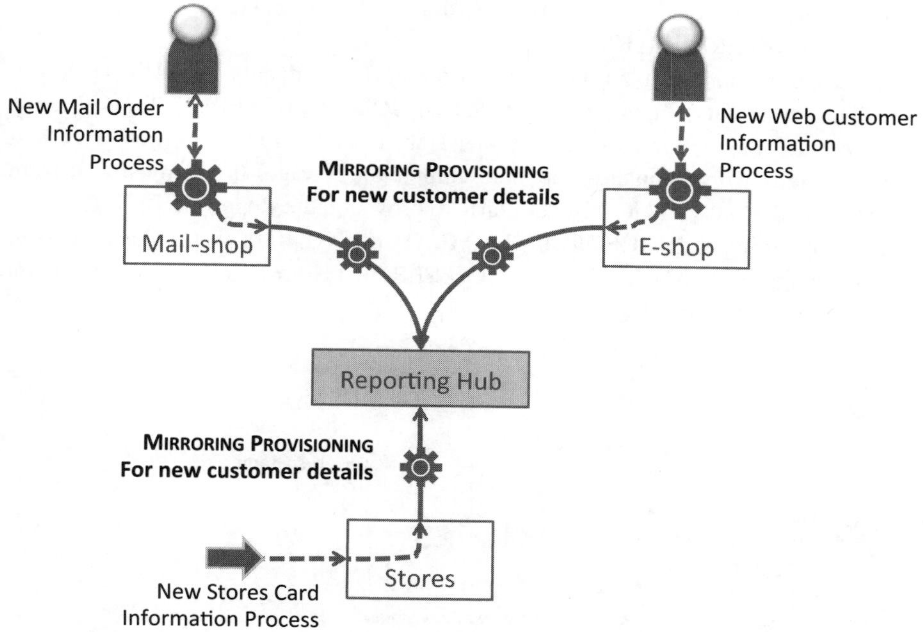

Figure 2.8 Merging customer details directly into the Reporting Hub.

MCHS Trading wants more than this. The organization wants to have a customer detail information collection with complete scope for operational use, as part of a program to provide consistent, high-quality service to its customers. This includes a loyalty program and more detailed information about the state of orders and payments.

As with product details, MCHS Trading decides to add a new information node to hold the customer information collection with complete scope. This information node is an INFORMATION ASSET HUB, which is a specialized server for managing information assets. Information asset hubs provide application-independent information for operational systems. The information processes associated with the information asset hub are constantly verifying, matching, merging, and enriching the information assets based on the combined best knowledge of all of the connected systems. The aim is to create an authoritative source for the information asset. This information can then be distributed to other information collections.

Using an information asset hub provides an organization with a neutral place to store information assets that have broad applicability across the organization. Because its focus is purely to manage the information, it is not affected by changes in the consuming information processes. It may also be used to audit the effective use of this information in a centralized manner.

The information collections in an information asset hub may have **M**ASTER **U**SAGE, **H**YBRID **U**SAGE, or **R**EFERENCE **U**SAGE.

Reference usage maintains a read-only copy of the customer details and is the easiest to provision. The diagram shown in Figure 2.9 illustrates the **G**OLDEN **R**EFERENCE information solution. The information asset hub (called Customer Hub) has a reference information collection for customer details with complete scope and complete coverage. It is provisioned from E-Shop, Mail-Shop, and Stores, and it is used, in turn, to provision the Reporting Hub. The Customer Hub is also supporting **S**ERVICE **O**RIENTED **P**ROVISIONING. This provides access to customer details through **R**EMOTE **I**NFORMATION **S**ERVICES for another new application called Customer-Care. (See Figure 2.9.)

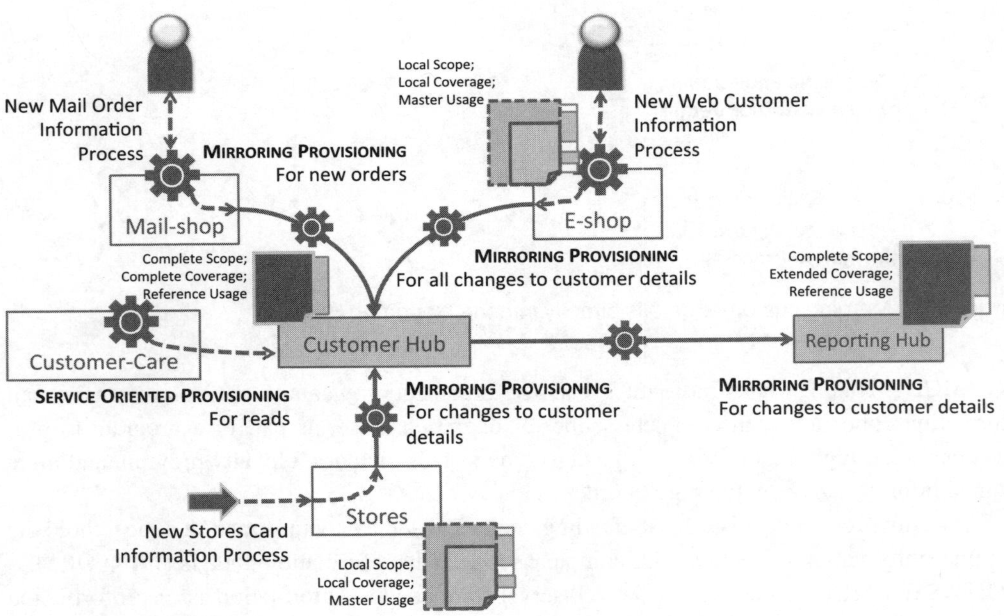

Figure 2.9 Adding a Customer Hub.

Although this approach has the merit of simplicity, it does not serve the vision that MCHS Trading has for its new Customer-Care application. MCHS Trading wants to be able to update a customer's contact details from a single place and store additional attributes relating to the loyalty program.

If the customer information collection in the Customer Hub had hybrid usage, new attributes could be added to the customer details information collections in the Customer Hub and Reporting Hub. However, the attributes shared with other applications would still be read-only and it would not provide a single point from which to update all customer details. This logic would have to be encoded in the Customer-Care application to ensure it updated the appropriate information collections in all the other applications when a change was made.

So the decision is made to have a master usage information collection in the Customer Hub. This enables the new loyalty card function to be rolled out in the Customer-Care application and the subsequent withdrawal of the store card managed by the Stores application. The Customer-Care application will provide a web-based interface for managing customer details both in the stores and in the call center.

With this approach, the flow of information between the applications and the Customer Hub now differs for each type of operation (create, update, delete).

First, let's consider how new customer details are created. This could happen in the following ways:

- When a person registers for a new E-Shop account
- When a person applies for a new loyalty card via the Customer-Care application
- When a person makes his or her first order through the Mail-Shop channels

Details about the new customer have to be shared with the Customer Hub. The Mail-Shop user looks up each customer he or she takes an order for using the Customer-Care interface and manually registers new customers through Customer-Care.[1] Customer-Care uses an information service to add the customer to the Customer Hub directly. Details about new customers registering through E-Shop are published and sent to the Customer Hub using an information flow.

When an application attempts to add a new customer, it is possible the Customer Hub already has information about this person from a different channel, and this existing customer is just creating a new account for a different channel. When this happens, the new information must be merged into the existing customer details entry. (See Figure 2.10.) Notice there is no flow of information from the Customer Hub to E-Shop. This is because E-Shop has local scope and only stores information about customers who register an account through its interface.

1. This is an awkward solution for the Mail-Shop user, and could be the source of errors, but it is only a temporary measure. There are plans to replace Mail-Shop with a new application called M-Shop that extracts and maintains customer details directly though the Customer Hub information services.

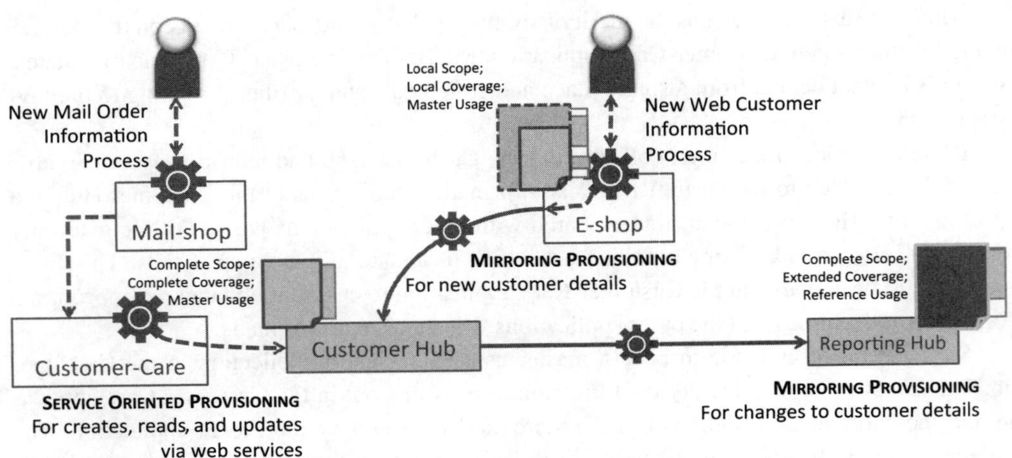

Figure 2.10 Adding new customer details.

Existing customer details can be changed through the following routes:

- When a person updates his or her account information in E-Shop
- When a person creates an order through the mail-order channel and uses different personal information, such as a new address
- When a person calls the call center, either to make a new order or to request an update

The impact of an update is more widespread because the update must be distributed to all systems that store those customer details directly and, potentially, to any information collection holding an active order for that customer. (See Figure 2.11.)

Deletes can occur either from Customer-Care or from E-Shop. When the customer is removed through the Customer-Care application, he or she is also removed from E-Shop. Removing an account from E-Shop is an update to the customer details record to remove the account. (See Figure 2.12.)

The conclusion to draw from this exercise is that whenever there are multiple master information collections that need to be kept in synchronization, a great deal of thought is required to get the flow of information correct—and this analysis has to be done on an operation-by-operation basis. On the other hand, MCHS Trading has gained an authoritative source of customer details and the ability to provide better customer service as a result.

The information solution pattern used by MCHS Trading for managing customer details is called SYNCHRONIZED MASTERS. In the next project, MCHS Trading wants to build out its new Customer-Care application to support the tracking, updating, and canceling of orders.

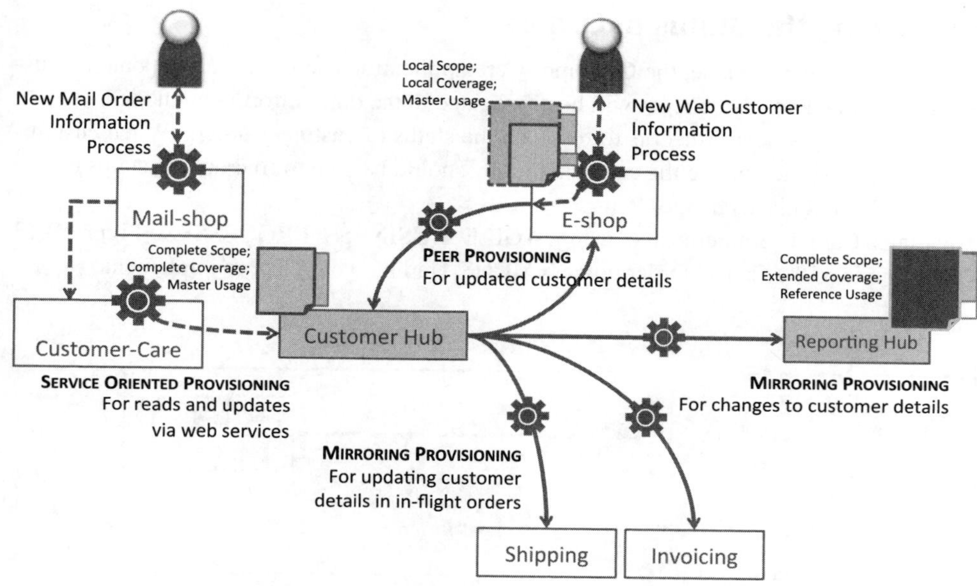

Figure 2.11 The impact of updating customer details.

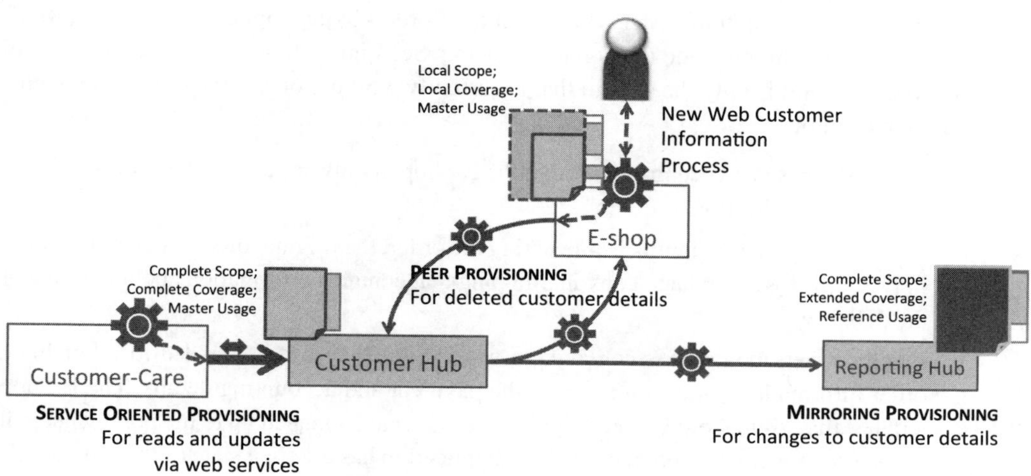

Figure 2.12 Deleting customer details.

Understanding the Status of Orders

With the Customer Hub in place, the Customer-Care application can review and update all customers' information, and any changes will be propagated to the other information nodes.

MCHS Trading's next project is to focus on the status of customer orders. When customers log in to E-Shop or telephone the call center, they should be able to find out the status of any outstanding order and make changes to it.

Customer-Care is implemented using **A**GILE **B**USINESS **P**ROCESSES. Figure 2.13 shows an example of the Cancel Order process MCHS Trading would like to implement.

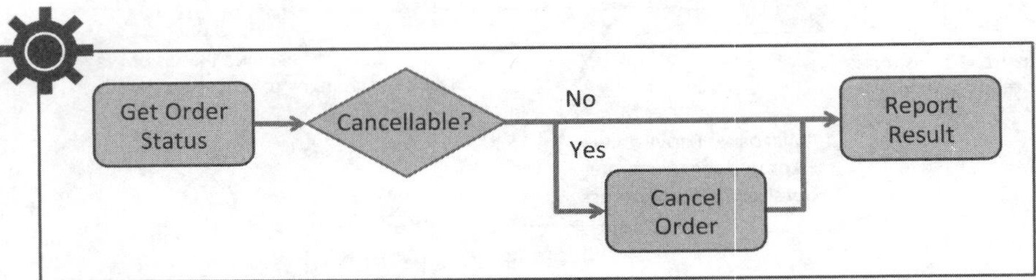

Figure 2.13 Cancel Order agile business process.

With the current solution, orders flow from their order-taking application (E-Shop, Mail-Shop, and Stores) to Shipping and then on to Invoicing. See Figure 2.14. Orders are stored in all of these systems, but it is only the system that is currently working on an order that has the current state. For example,

- If an order has just been made through the E-Shop, it only appears in the E-Shop's order information collection.
- A little later, when Shipping is processing the order, the original order will still be stored in E-Shop, plus an updated copy in Shipping that contains information about the state of the delivery.
- Finally, when the order is delivered, a new copy of the order is added to Invoicing's order information collection to cover the payment and accounting details. The E-Shop still has the original order, and Shipping knows what happened up to the point where all of the goods were delivered, but neither application has the final state of the order.

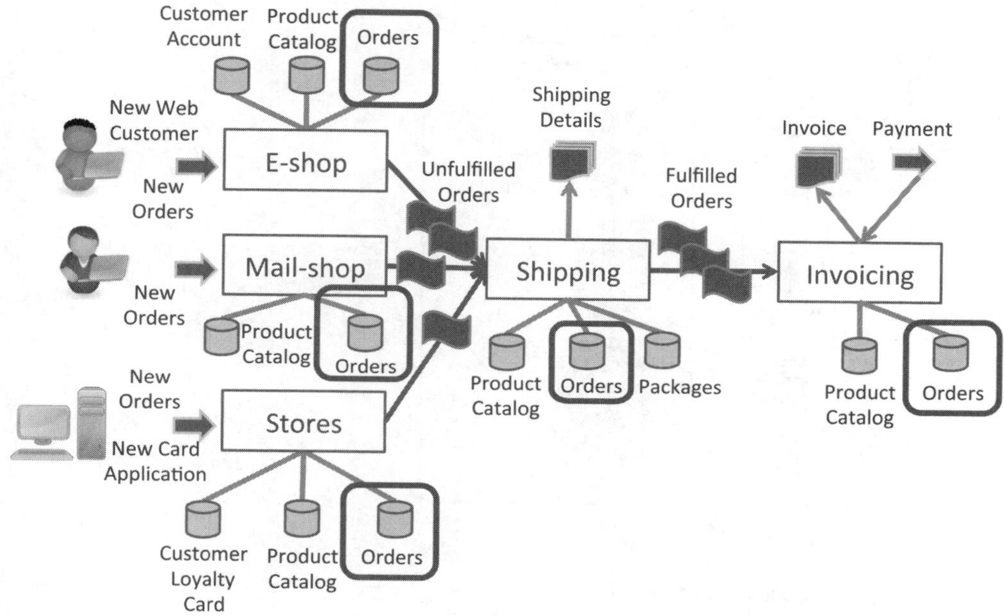

Figure 2.14 Location of order details.

Another interesting aspect of this situation is that each information node maintains different attributes about the order to suit the type of work it is doing. Typically, these are additional attributes. Figure 2.15 illustrates this. Basic details of the order are created by E-Shop and are sent to Shipping. Shipping does not change these attributes. Instead, it extends the information entry with new attributes to capture the shipping and warehouse details—resulting in a HYBRID USAGE information collection.

Invoicing also has a hybrid usage information collection for orders, but the additional attributes it has are related to payments.

In all cases, the way each information node manages the order details follows the INFORMATION ACTIVITY pattern. The information entry is created when work starts, it is updated while work is going on, and no further updates are made once work is completed. The complication is that the entire order-processing business transaction is spread across a number of information nodes and none of them have the complete picture. As a result, implementing Cancel Order is going to be a challenge.

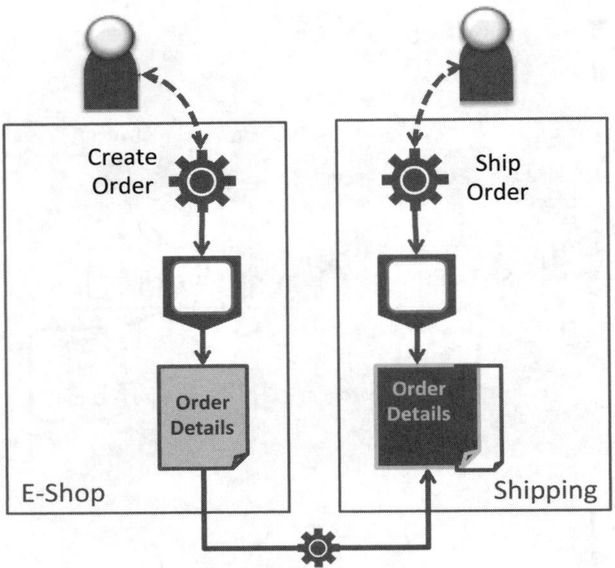

Figure 2.15 E-Shop has a master usage collection and Shipping has a hybrid usage collection.

MCHS Trading chooses to host the consolidated view of its customers' orders in a new INFORMATION ACTIVITY HUB information node called Order-Tracking. It is fed with events from all of the information nodes involved in order processing. Thus, Order-Tracking is able to accumulate the order status and all of the attributes from each of the order-processing nodes. The result is a complete picture of the order-processing business transaction as if it were running all against a single information collection. (See Figure 2.16.)

With Order-Tracking in place, the Cancel Order information process can be implemented using an information service call to Order-Tracking—to find out the current status—and, if appropriate, a call to Shipping to cancel the order. (See Figure 2.17.) It also provides a central place for running analytics and providing information to the Reporting Hub.

At this point, you have probably noticed that there is a consistent approach emerging. MCHS Trading has created shared repositories of information that support integrated views of its operations while allowing the existing applications to continue operating. These repositories provide consistency across multiple channels. They are also an ideal place to invest in improving information quality.

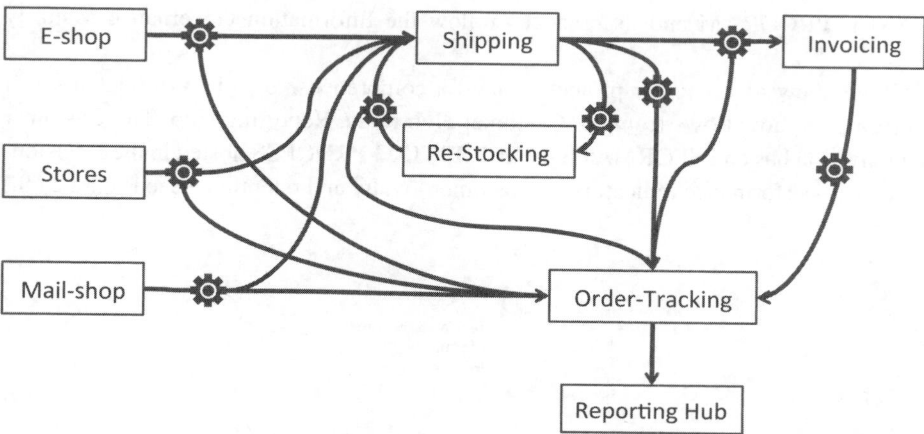

Figure 2.16 Events flowing to Order-Tracking.

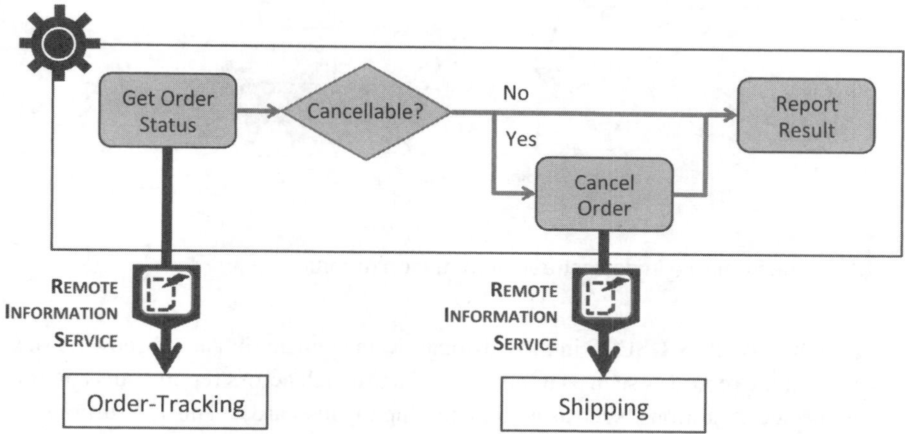

Figure 2.17 The Cancel Order process with calls to Order-Tracking and Shipping.

Delivering Information Quality Improvements

Up until this point, MCHS Trading has been creating the infrastructure to support consolidated stores of its shared information. Now it turns to implementing specific information quality improvements. Information quality management is a key discipline within an INFORMATION

GOVERNANCE PROGRAM and its practices follow the Information Governance Maturity Model.[2]

The Single View of Customer project ensured a comprehensive and consolidated set of customer information now flows from the Customer Hub to the Reporting Hub. The Customer Management division has an INFORMATION REPORTING PROCESS hosted in the Decision-Center to track key performance indicators for customer loyalty and retention. (See Figure 2.18.)

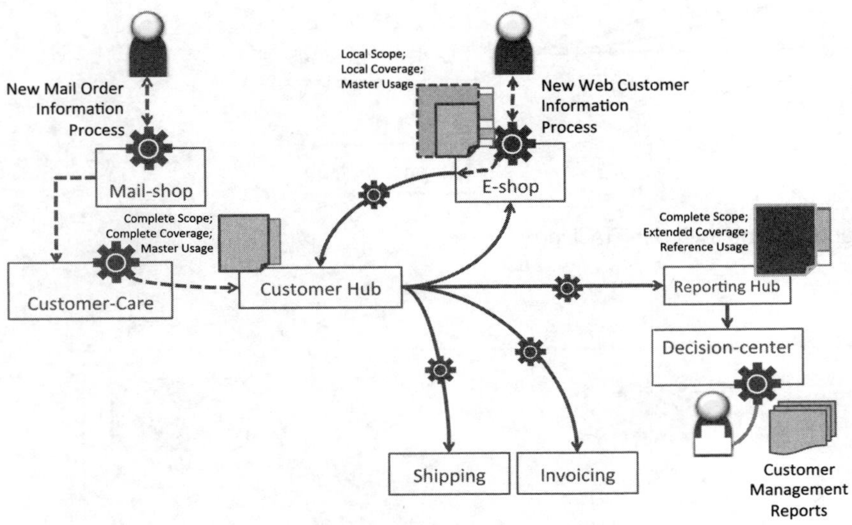

Figure 2.18 Issues emerge in downstream information reporting.

The INFORMATION USERS in the Customer Management division discover issues with the information in the reports—such as totals that did not match across reports, missing information, and unexpected conditions (such as minors holding loyalty cards). This is a surprise, considering MCHS Trading's investment in the Customer Hub already. The problem is that if incorrect information is entered in Mail-Shop, Customer-Care, or E-Shop, it is simply consolidated and distributed straight into the reports.

For MCHS Trading to effectively manage its customers and get a solid return on investment from the Customer Hub, it needs to identify the information quality issues and address them at the source, before they are distributed through the customer details information supply chain.

Information quality improvements require a collaborative effort between the business units and IT, particularly because the INFORMATION OWNERS in the order-taking systems insist

2. IBM Data Governance Maturity Model, http://www-935.ibm.com/services/uk/cio/pdf/leverage_wp_data_gov_council_maturity_model.pdf, **pg.8.**

that their information is of sufficient quality—after all, as they note, "aren't orders being processed and delivered on time?"

Information quality must be treated like any other business function: It has specific objectives and time frames, a scope, appropriate tasks, and a set of deliverables. MCHS Trading does not have any existent INFORMATION QUALITY PROCESSES in place beyond the functioning of its basic applications. MCHS Trading is also not yet certain where and how to implement these processes.

The first information quality project runs an INFORMATION PROFILE TRACKING PROCESS against all of its primary customer details repositories to establish a series of quality baselines for each source that can be subsequently utilized for tracking and trend analysis.

This information profiling captures and summarizes the actual data content in terms of its structure and values. The initial INFORMATION VALUES PROFILES produced are used in conjunction with other INFORMATION IDENTIFICATION patterns, such as SUBJECT AREA DEFINITION, SEMANTIC TAGGING, and SEMANTIC MAPPING to build up a picture of the quality of the customer details in each system. (See Figure 2.19.)

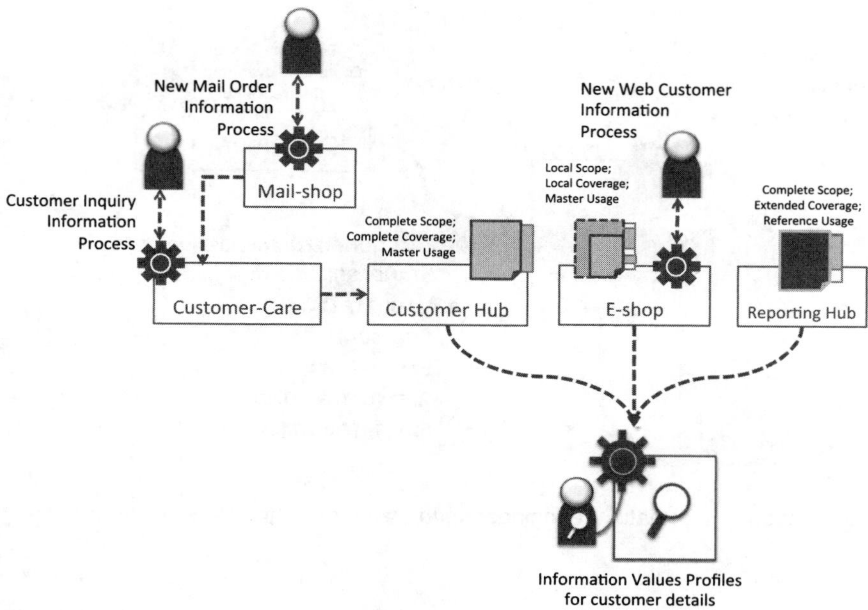

Figure 2.19 Information identification applied to all customer sources.

MCHS Trading discovers significant issues related to the E-Shop system. E-Shop is a packaged application and, due to system limitations, certain fields have been reused for different purposes or contain multiple contents. There is limited validation of the information a customer enters. Coupled with cryptic and poorly understood fields, the mapping and subsequent delivery of the information from the E-Shop systems to the Customer Hub is incorrect. MCHS Trading takes the following steps:

- Correct and improve the mapping and delivery of the data from E-Shop to the Customer Hub in the existing **I**NFORMATION **F**LOW. Improve the **I**NFORMATION **D**EPLOYMENT **P**ROCESS that transforms the E-Shop information to the format for the Customer Hub with the addition of specific **I**NFORMATION **R**EENGINEERING **S**TEPS, such as **S**TANDARDIZE **D**ATA to replace varied entries with standardized values, **V**ALIDATE **D**ATA to catch unexpected values, **C**ORRECT **D**ATA where certain exceptions can be replaced, **E**NRICH **D**ATA such as address verification, **R**ESTRUCTURE **D**ATA to align to target formats, and **S**EPARATE **E**NTRIES to create multiple records where repeating data occurs. (See Figure 2.20.)

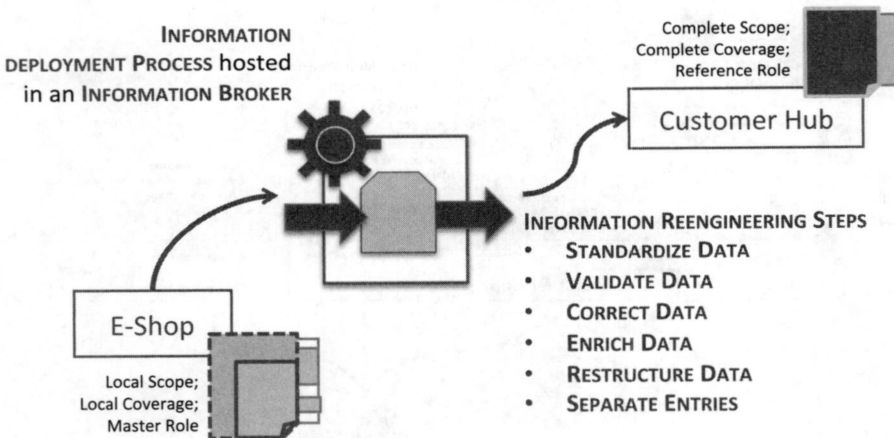

Figure 2.20 Application of information reengineering to standardize and cleanse information from E-Shop.

- Correct and improve the data already in the Customer Hub and the Reporting Hub. This could be a one-time process to clean up the existing values, followed by the deployment of an **E**VER-GREENING **P**ROCESS operating on the Customer Hub to maintain the values going forward. The ever-greening process utilizes and reuses the same steps as in the information deployment process from the E-Shop to ensure ongoing consistency and quality. (See Figure 2.21.)

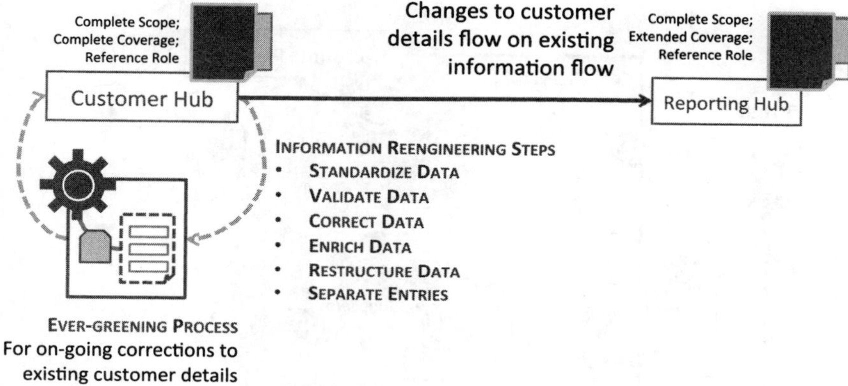

Figure 2.21 Application of ever-greening and information reengineering to improve downstream nodes.

- Implement an INFORMATION PROFILE TRACKING PROCESS to continuously collect and utilize the INFORMATION VALUES PROFILES.
- Add an INFORMATION MONITORING PROCESS to ensure that the E-Shop system does not start generating and delivering new issues. This process may form an ancillary information supply chain of quality data that also flows to the Reporting Hub, adding another dimension of insight there.

Resource constraints typically limit the ability to deliver all information quality projects simultaneously, so MCHS Trading must prioritize the initiatives. As organizations such as MCHS Trading increase their maturity in information governance and information quality, such processes are incorporated into other implementation projects and become embedded into key parts of the information supply chains.

Connecting MCHS Trading into a B2B Trading Partnership

We've looked at the introduction of a Product Hub to serve as the single master copy of the product catalog. This application now controls the flow of product details to the order-processing applications as well as the Shipping and Invoicing applications.

MCHS Trading does not exist in a vacuum. The product catalog with associated product details is based on information provided by suppliers. These are the products that MCHS Trading acquires and then sells to customers. MCHS Trading interacts with these suppliers by reviewing their catalogs, ordering from those catalogs, and paying for the products ordered in the same manner that customers interact with MCHS Trading. (See Figure 2.22.)

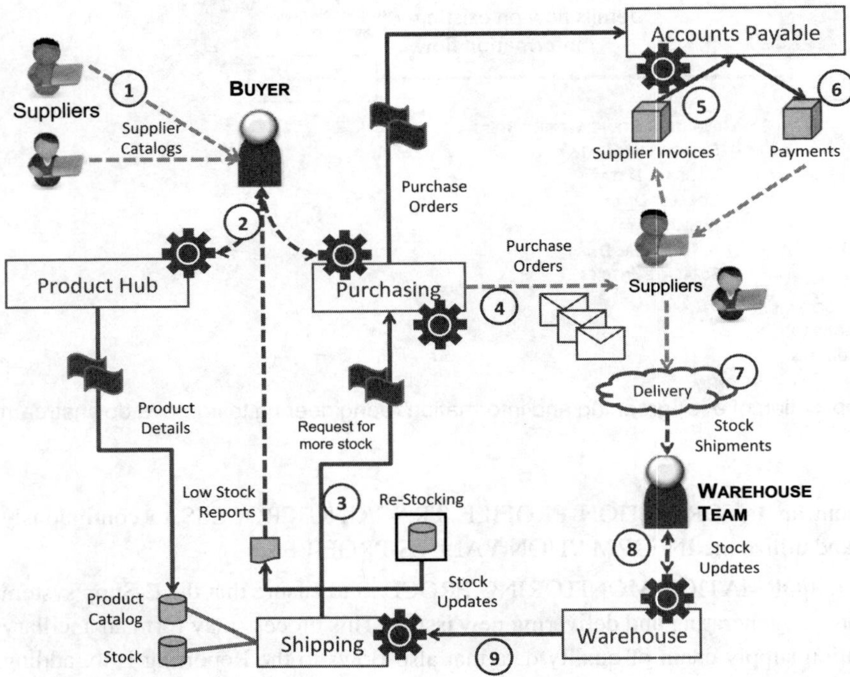

Figure 2.22 Interacting with suppliers.

The numbers on the diagram in Figure 2.22 refer to these notes:

1. The buyer receives supplier catalogs from suppliers and identifies products to add to the product catalog.
2. The buyer updates the Product Hub application with new product details—these are distributed to the order-processing systems, including Shipping.
3. When Shipping detects low stock, it sends supplier orders to the Purchasing application, which generates purchase orders, and updates the Accounts Payable application.
4. Mail purchase orders to the suppliers.
5. Receive invoices from suppliers and match the invoices to the purchase orders in the Accounts Payable application.

6. Issue payments to the suppliers for products ordered.
7. The suppliers ship the ordered stock.
8. The warehouse receives stock and the associated bills of lading from the suppliers.
9. Send stock inventory updates into the Shipping application, including updates to the Re-Stocking information store used by Customer-Care.

The interaction between the buyers and supplier is currently manual. Some interactions are INFORMATION FLOWS, but these are point-to-point, separate from all other processing and are surrounded by considerable manual effort involving paper-based input and output. MCHS Trading and its suppliers want to speed this up in two ways. When the suppliers update their product details, they want to send them to MCHS Trading electronically. When MCHS Trading needs to order more stock, it wants to exchange purchase orders and invoices electronically.

It is possible to connect MCHS Trading's systems directly with all its suppliers. However, because each organization is an independent legal entity, with its own governance rules, all parties are keen to operate a protected gateway where details of all information exchanged are secured and audited.

The gateway is implemented using a specialized Electronic Data Interchange (EDI) INFORMATION BROKER designed for business partners to exchange information. The information broker is named Supplier-net as it is the gateway that is connecting MCHS Trading to its supplier network, as seen in Figure 2.23.

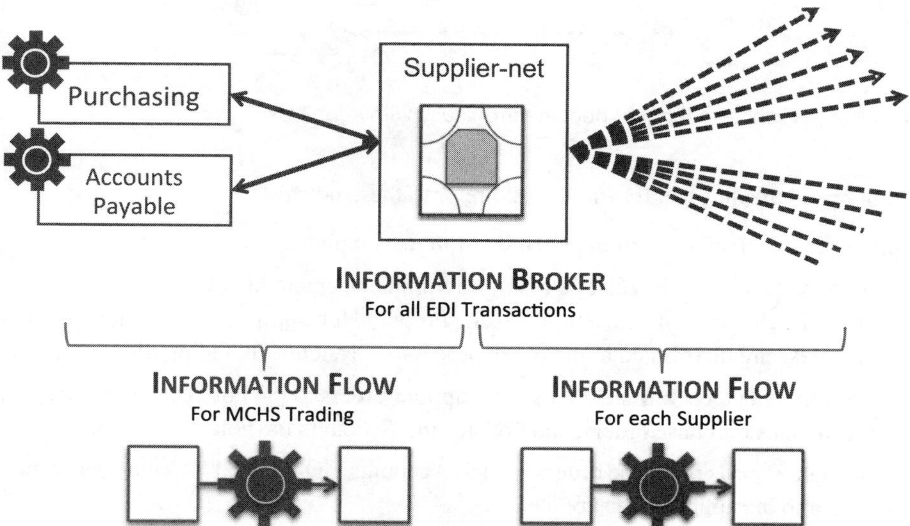

Figure 2.23 Introducing an information broker to control information flows to suppliers.

When Supplier-net is in place, the interaction is much more efficient. The flows are illustrated in Figure 2.24.

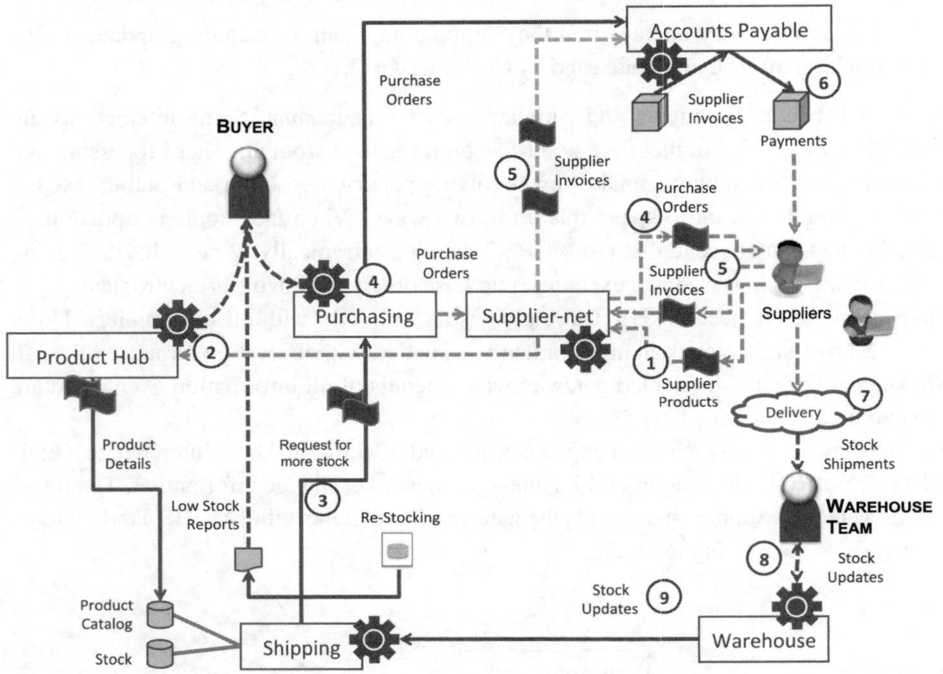

Figure 2.24 Using Supplier-net to connect electronically with suppliers.

The numbers on the diagram for Figure 2.24 refer to these notes:

1. Supplier-net received new product details from the suppliers.
2. The buyer receives new product details from Supplier-net and identifies products to add to the product catalog. The buyer updates the Product Hub application with new product details—these are distributed to the order-processing systems, including Shipping.
3. When Shipping detects low stock, it sends supplier orders to the Purchasing application, which generates purchase orders, and updates the Accounts Payable application.
4. Purchasing forwards purchase orders both to Accounts Payable and Supplier-net, which sends them to the appropriate suppliers.

5. Supplier-net receives invoices from suppliers and forwards them to Accounts Payable, where they are matched to the purchase orders.
6. Accounts Payable issues payments to the suppliers for products ordered.
7. The suppliers ship the ordered stock.
8. The warehouse receives stock and the associated bills of lading from the suppliers.
9. Send stock inventory updates into the Shipping application, including updates to the Re-Stocking information store used by Customer-Care.

With this processing in-place, MCHS Trading has significantly enhanced its collaboration in order management, invoice reconciliation, and payment processing with its suppliers, reducing paperwork and manual effort to process.

This project is an example of a **P**ARTNER **C**OLLABORATION information solution. This solution not only improves MCHS Trading's interaction with existing suppliers, but it also expands the capacity to manage many more suppliers, resulting in a broader and more exciting product range to delight and retain customers.

MCHS Trading continues to look at improving its stock management through predictive analytics.

Exploiting Predictive Analytics

Employees of MCHS Trading make decisions every day: whether to expand into a new product line, what products to buy and stock, how many items of a product to buy, whether to reorder and restock a product, or whether a new supplier can provide the same or a similar product in sufficient quantity and at the same quality. Information in various forms may trigger or be utilized in these decisions. However, it is often unavailable, late, or hidden within other data.

MCHS Trading spent considerable time and effort to improve its supplier interaction. Suppliers receive their orders faster, the products to sell are received sooner in the warehouses, and there is substantially reduced paperwork. Despite this effort, MCHS Trading still does not have good control over its product inventory. In some instances, it has far too much inventory such as goods ordered in bulk after a high sales quarter that are still sitting in the warehouse. In other instances, there always seems to be a shortfall of goods in stock, resulting in lost sales and customer complaints. MCHS Trading wants to improve its ability to predict which products to order when and in what quantity.

Figure 2.25 highlights MCHS Trading's current activity in product inventory management.

The numbers on the diagram refer to these notes:

1. When Shipping detects it is low on stock, it requests more from purchasing.
2. The buyer requests more stock, which sends order requests to Supplier-net.
3. Purchase orders go to suppliers.
4. Suppliers deliver products to the warehouse operations.
5. Warehouse updates the stock inventory in the Warehouse applications.

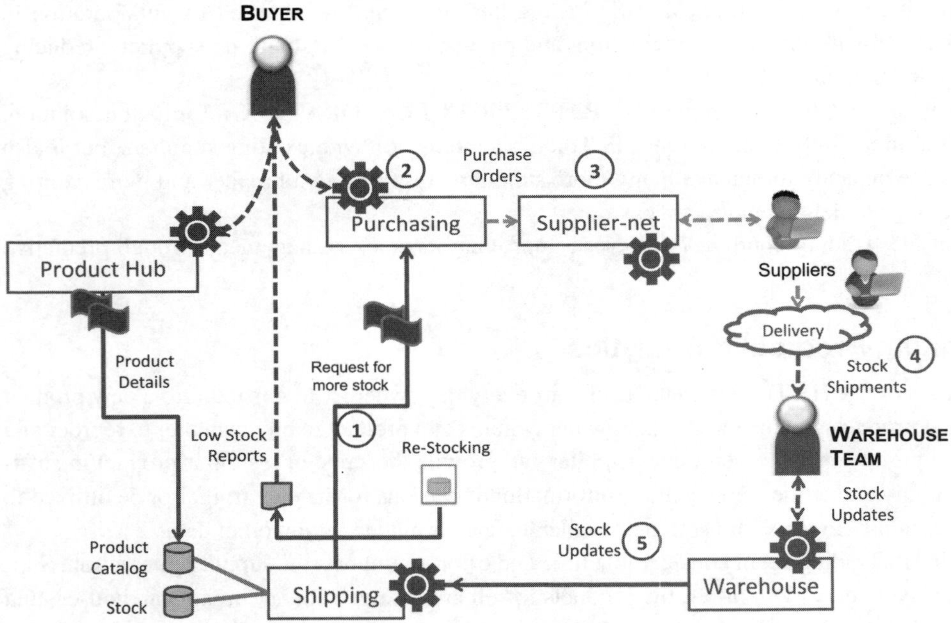

Figure 2.25 The information supply chain for stock details.

The information used in the process shown in Figure 2.25 is incomplete, though, from the buyer's perspective. The product details only contain the basic descriptive content on the product, and the inventory reports only note the last update and current inventory quantities. The buyer also reviews product sales reports (to assess customer demand for the product by month and quarter) and customer satisfaction reports (to assess quality of the product), when those are available, before initiating a reorder request (a manual entry into the Product Hub). (See Figure 2.26.)

Instead of looking at this view as a series of isolated details and reports coming into the buyer, it can be recast as the intersection of a series of INFORMATION SUPPLY CHAINS, each containing some product-related content that the buyer must integrate together before manually triggering the request to the supplier. (See Figure 2.27.)

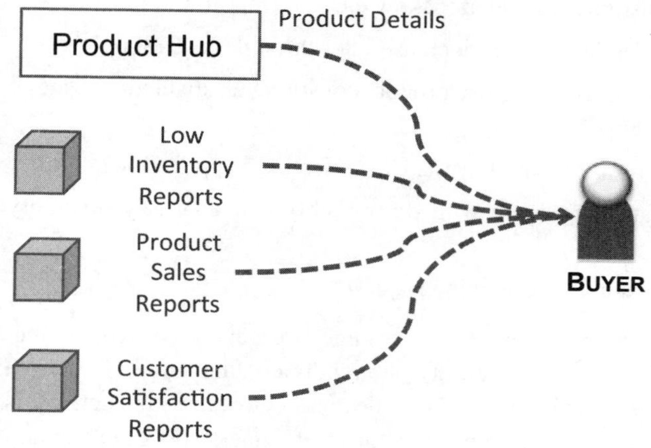

Figure 2.26 Information relevant to stock levels for the buyer.

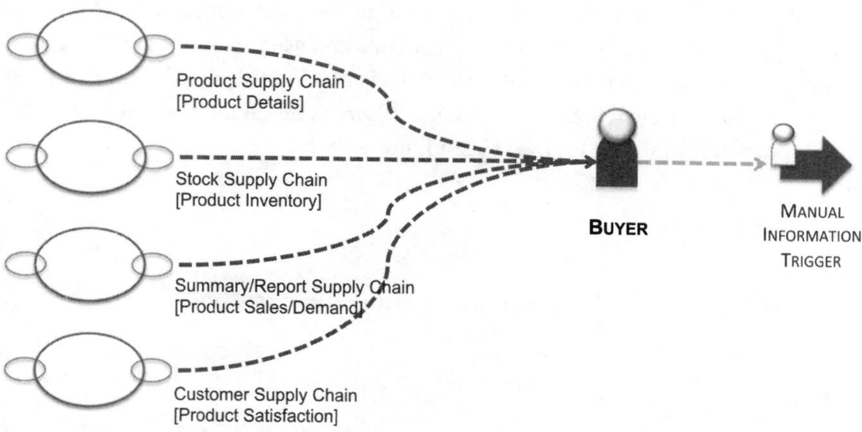

Figure 2.27 An information supply chain perspective for the buyer.

The burden here is on the individual buyer with his or her experience and skill to ensure the information is gathered in a timely fashion, organized, correctly linked together, and appropriately analyzed. They must be able to answer these types of questions:

- Do the quarterly sales reports flatten or hide the seasonal demand and purchase of the products?

- Did one large order by one customer last quarter skew the sales report?
- Did bad weather impact sales in the stores or increase sales through the E-Shop?
- Do a number of customer returns of a specific product constitute a satisfaction issue or just purchases of the wrong item?
- Were any details about the returns captured by the Customer-Care application?
- How does the sales information compare with the monthly and quarterly inventory stock reports?
- How quickly did suppliers respond to restocking requests?

MCHS Trading only has a limited number of buyers. As the volume of products stocked, number of suppliers, and customer care details increase, the ability of an individual buyer to sift through the quantity of information needed for an effective decision decreases. Because this activity is at the core of MCHS Trading's business, in order to meet its business imperatives of exemplary customer service and efficient delivery of a wide range of products, MCHS Trading wants to improve its ability to handle and utilize its information.

MCHS Trading looks to automate this decision-making process through an **O**PERATIONAL **A**NALYTICS information solution that can take the feeds of information from these diverse information supply chains, analyze the related contents and use predictive analytics models to determine likely needs, and generate one of several decisions, such as discontinue the product, reorder the product, flag for customer care response (such as an email regarding expected product availability), or send for manual review. (See Figure 2.28.)

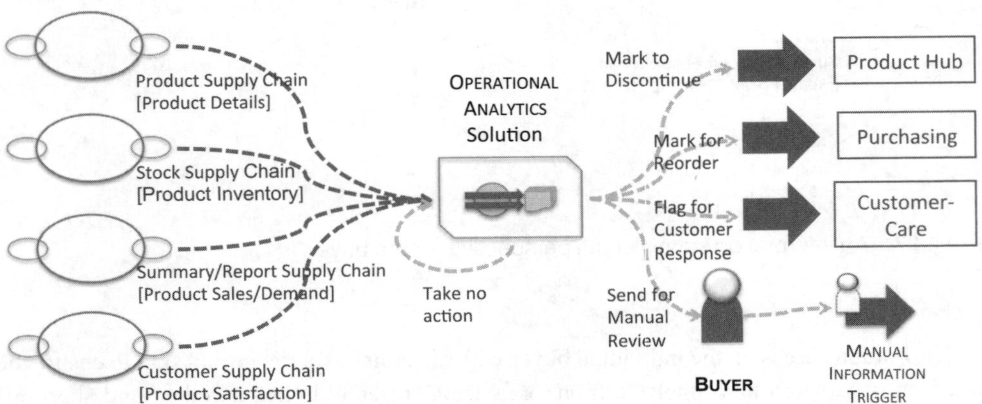

Figure 2.28 Introducing an operational analytics solution into the restocking decision.

The decisions or events coming from the operational analytics solution are translated into INFORMATION TRIGGERS that kick off INFORMATION PROCESSES within the downstream applications, such as Product Hub, Supplier-net, or Customer-Care. The buyer is not removed from the picture, but his or her time is freed from common events (sorting through and correlating reports), and his or her role is shifted to focus on more complex cases, such as looking for a new supplier for a given product where customer complaints have increased and sales have declined.

Implementing such an operational analytics solution requires a deeper view into the patterns needed to support the solution and the forces, which will impact the implementation. There are three perspectives that make sense to consider at this point: an information processing perspective; an information at rest perspective (looking at the information collections and nodes that both supply information and support the processing); and an information in motion perspective (looking at the necessary information provisioning to make the information collections available to the processing).

At the center of the operational analytics solution is a set of information processes, which, in essence, replace the manual steps performed by the buyer. Currently, the buyer works through a series of reviews and decisions:

- Which product has low inventory?
- What is the recent and past sales history? (For example, are there seasonal variations?)
- Was customer review of the product favorable?
- How responsive and reliable is the supplier?

The new solution needs to incorporate these process steps, responding to these questions and generating the right events or triggers for subsequent work, as shown in Figure 2.29.

Triggered by the low inventory report, the new Decision to Buy (or reorder) process must:

- Obtain monthly and quarterly sales information.
  - Identify sales patterns and trends, including anomalies.
  - If trends are not conclusive, evaluate whether to send to the buyer.
- Obtain customer reviews of the product.
  - Identify positive and negative customer feedback.
  - If positive, create the reorder request and trigger a process in the Supplier-net application.
  - If negative, continue processing, but also check whether to inform the buyer.

- Obtain product and supplier details.
  - Identify supplier responsiveness.
  - If positive, then potentially discontinue the product (poor product) or take no action.
  - If negative, continue processing, but also check whether to inform the buyer.
- Obtain the list of alternate suppliers.
  - Evaluate and select an alternate supplier.
  - If a supplier is selected, create a new purchase order and trigger a process in the Supplier-net application.
  - If no supplier is identified, route to the buyer.

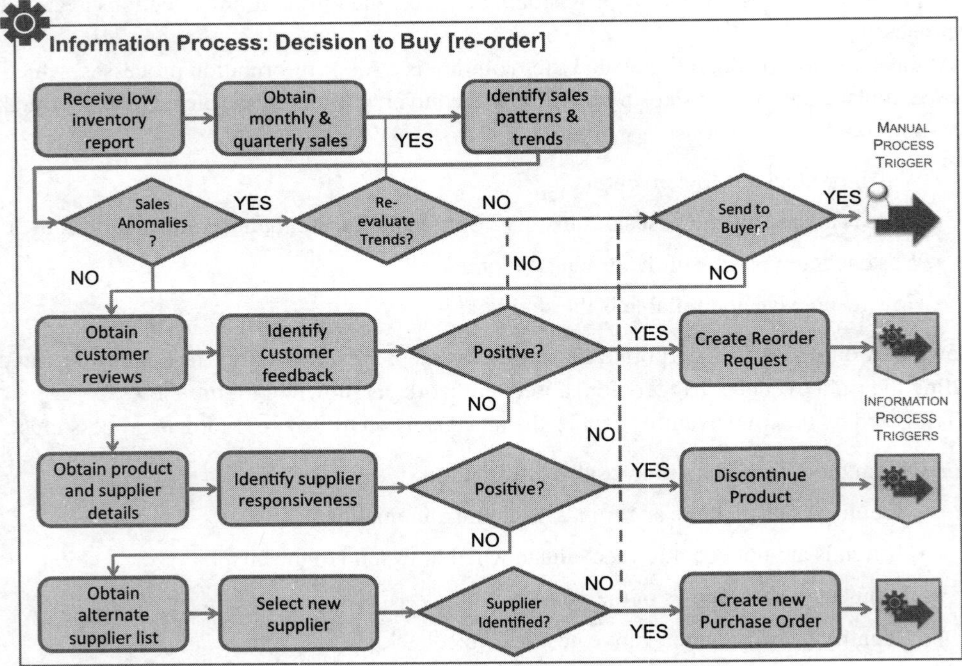

Figure 2.29 The information process for reordering stock.

Additional steps, decisions, and triggers may be needed as MCHS Trading refines its business requirements.

Potentially, these steps may be addressed within a **P**ACKAGED **A**PPLICATION **P**ROCESS, assuming one is available and meets the needs of the business. However, there will be a cost associated with a packaged application, and the business model within it could limit MCHS Trading's processing or ability to adapt to changing business needs. The organization's INFORMATION STRATEGY intersects with its business strategy at this point and must take into account the forces and limited resources available.

Alternately, and in line with the desire for more predictive analytics, these steps could be addressed by an INFORMATION DECISION MODEL. Such a process incorporates business rules and decisions that can be tailored to the changing needs of MCHS Trading, including the ability to incorporate additional predictive analytics.

Key forces and decision factors for MCHS Trading are business agility, cost, and integration with other analytical processes.

One reason MCHS Trading desires integration with other analytical processes has to do with the challenges for individual buyers to identify patterns and data correlations across a diverse range of inputs. MCHS Trading believes that specific customer demographic groups purchase specific types of products in predictable ways, perhaps following new consumer trends or trendsetters. MCHS Trading needs to connect its customer demographics with ordering, shipping, daily sales (rather than quarterly or monthly summaries), and Product Hub details to see where correlations occur.

To achieve this, it embeds an INFORMATION PATTERN DETECTION PROCESS as part of the step to identify sales patterns and trends. The result of this is a different decision point—instead of looking for sales anomalies, which might feed back into the sales review step, the process now looks for rapidly emerging sales trends (as well as anomalies) that indicate an immediate reorder is due even without more detailed customer feedback. (See Figure 2.30.)

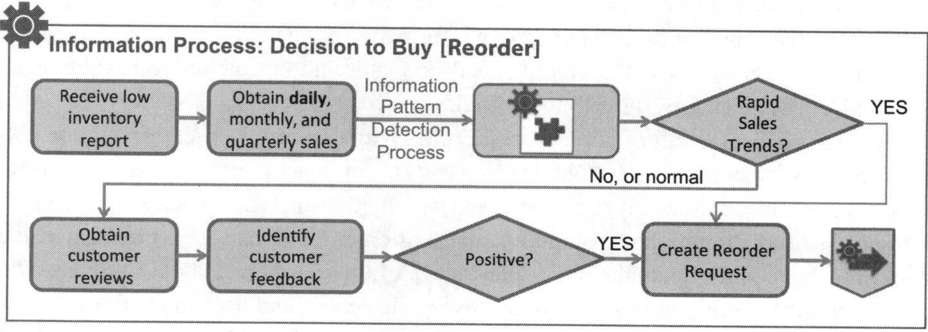

Figure 2.30 Introducing an information pattern detection process for sales trends.

The customer feedback step may be enhanced as well. MCHS Trading largely works with flags (specific INFORMATION ELEMENTS) that are delivered from its Customer-Care application. However, there is more content contained in the descriptive fields that the customer care representatives enter. Customers are also adding product reviews right onto the E-Shop website with ratings and free-form comments. MCHS Trading also knows that other websites could be mined for related product information. Putting all these pieces together would give richer insight into the overall customer experience. MCHS Trading adds another INFORMATION PATTERN DETECTION PROCESS as part of the step to identify customer feedback. (See Figure 2.31.)

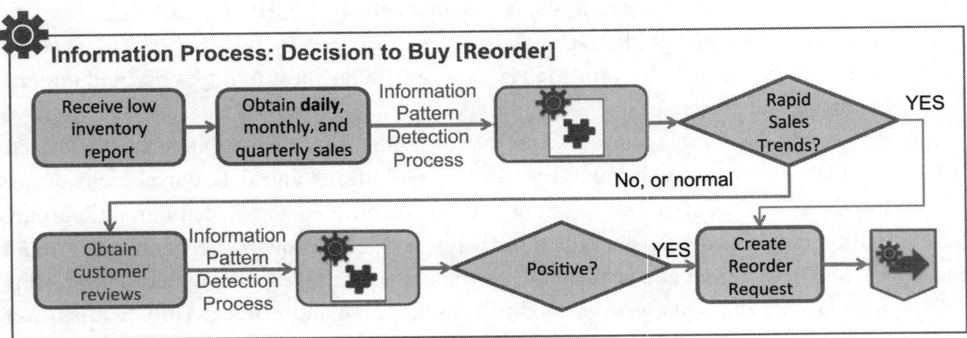

Figure 2.31 Adding an information pattern detection process for customer reviews.

Other steps need to incorporate relevant INFORMATION DECISION DEFINITION PROCESSES as well, which combine business rules with the results of the pattern discovery and detection processes in order to achieve greater agility in the decision-making processes. The buyers can now build, shape, and refine these rules as they see what is producing effective decisions for restocking and what is not, or as they have more information available.

Beyond this process view, MCHS Trading needs to factor into this picture its requirements for the INFORMATION COLLECTIONS to be used.

The initial trigger for the information process comes with or references an information collection for the Stock subject area. Each "Obtain" step adds or references one or multiple information collections for additional relevant data. Because the predictive analytics processing is outside the applications, such as Product Hub, Shipping, and Customer-Care, and it requires extensive processing power that could impact the day-to-day usage of those applications, it needs its own information collections specifically for pattern discovery, detection, and decision making.

The information collections may be represented as shown in Figure 2.32 where the internal collections are provisioned from the key external information collections. Decisions about which collections to provision from are driven by requirements within the predictive analytics process, regarding scope, coverage, and usage roles.

For instance, the reorder decision needs all the primary stock information related to products. So the expectation is that this information will have COMPLETE SCOPE. However, it only requires a specific set of information elements, so CORE COVERAGE is acceptable, and the processing only needs a read-only copy, so it serves in a REFERENCE USAGE. (See Figure 2.32.)

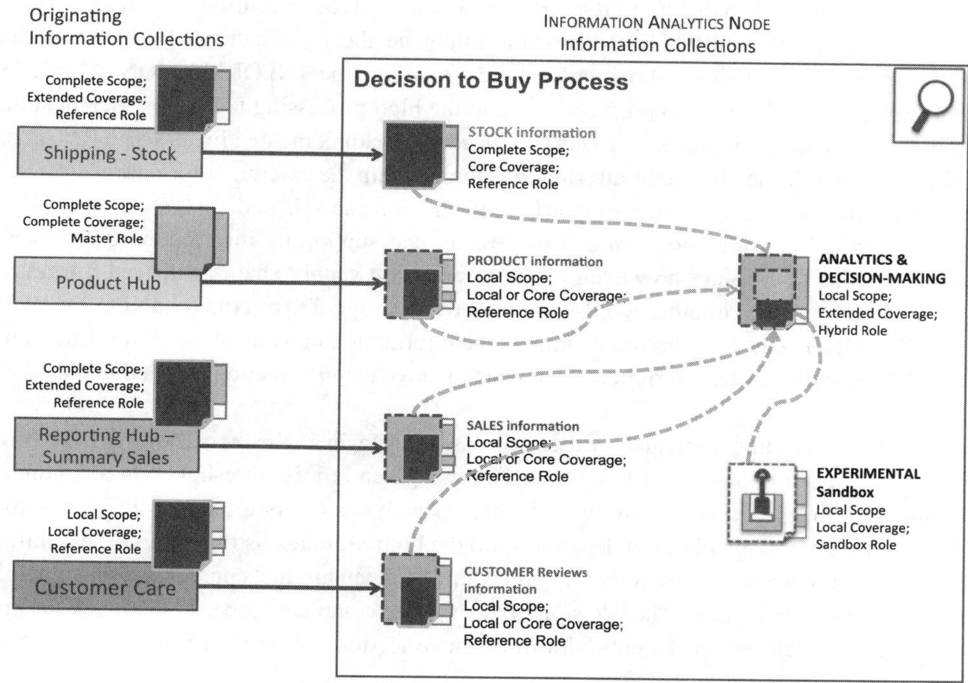

Figure 2.32 Incorporating information collections into the predictive analytics information node.

Also within the information process, there will be collections serving the core analytics and decision making as well as experimental modeling.

For the analytics, there will be information specific to the decision-to-buy process (business rules, models, etc.) as well as the additional attributes contributed by several information supply chains. This means that the analytics information collection will take on a HYBRID USAGE. The analytics process will be in complete control of the decision making, so it will have a LOCAL SCOPE. And because the processing must produce information for downstream consumption (and will store its decisions for use in subsequent analysis), the analytics information collection has EXTENDED COVERAGE.

Experimental modeling also occurs as part of the information process and requires information collections that will not impact the core decision making. These information collections have a **S**ANDBOX **U**SAGE, and they have **L**OCAL **C**OVERAGE only because the results are not needed downstream. Further, they only last for a given time, so they have a transient scope.

A remaining question in regard to these information collections is what is the appropriate type of information node on which to host them? There are information nodes that host business applications such as an **A**PPLICATION **N**ODE. If the analytics occurred as part of a **P**ACKAGED **A**PPLICATION **P**ROCESS, then this might be the right pattern. However, because MCHS Trading is adopting a broader analytics solution, the **I**NFORMATION **A**NALYSIS **N**ODE will provide the best support, dedicated to the high processing load and efficient storage required by the analytical processes. This may need to be supplemented by an **I**NFORMATION **M**INING **S**TORE if the volume of information coming from the external information collections is high enough to impact the processing on the information analysis node.

With initial considerations around processing and supporting information collections in mind, it remains to consider how each of the information supply chains will feed information to the analytics process: in other words, what are the appropriate patterns for **I**NFORMATION **P**ROVISIONING, what triggers should initiate the information movement (the **I**NFORMATION **T**RIGGERS), and what are the right mechanisms to move the information (the **I**NFORMATION **F**LOWS).

In MCHS Trading's manual reorder process, the trigger is the arrival of the Low Inventory report. The list of stock that has passed below a given reorder threshold could continue to drive the analytics processing. However, the use of analytics offers the opportunity to account for factors such as seasonally high demand, sporadic high-volume customer purchases, shifts of purchases from one product to another, relationships between products purchased, and emerging or declining product demand. The decision to incorporate complete scope for the Stock information implies that delivery of the entire information collection (rather than just low stock items) will be the new trigger.

MCHS Trading needs to use the **M**IRRORING **P**ROVISIONING pattern for the Stock information to keep the information collections synchronized on at least a daily basis. The same pattern is used for Daily, current Monthly, and current Quarterly Sales information. Because the prior Monthly and Quarterly Sales information is only changed to reflect unusual events, the **S**NAPSHOT **P**ROVISIONING pattern is satisfactory for those details. Both the Product and Customer Review information should use the **M**IRRORING **P**ROVISIONING pattern to ensure consistent synchronization of information collections necessary for useful analytics and decision making. (See Figure 2.33.)

From this point, MCHS Trading starts drilling into the specific provisioning patterns to identify the correct **I**NFORMATION **T**RIGGERS and **I**NFORMATION **F**LOWS.

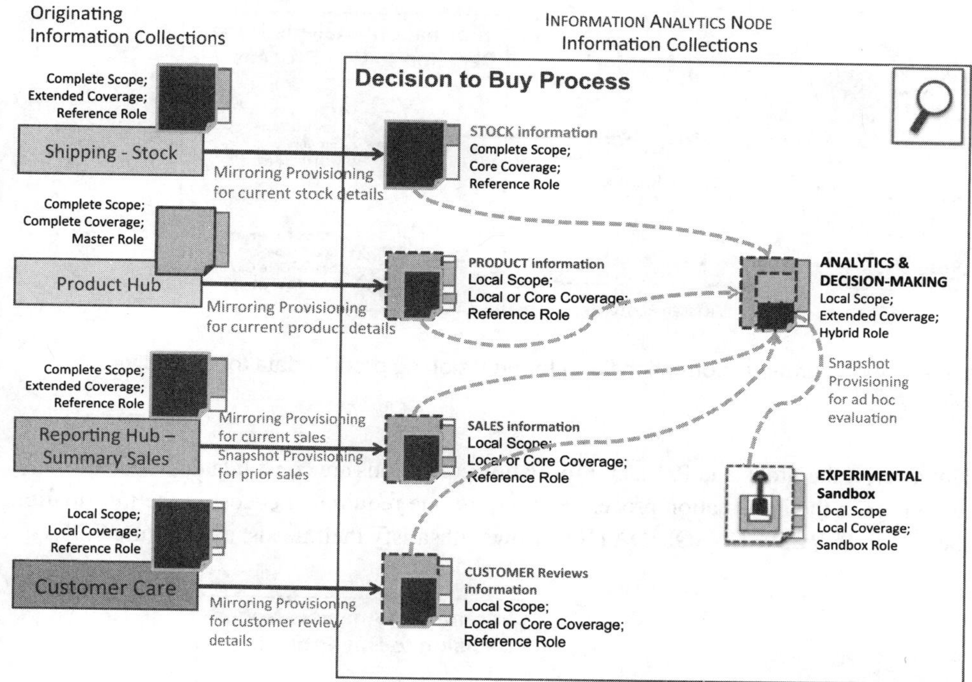

Figure 2.33 Provisioning of collections within the predictive analytics solution.

For instance, while the initial configuration of this information process has distinct information collections for Stock and Product, as they both carry product-related information elements and have common information keys, it may be cost effective to consolidate these into one INFORMATION COLLECTION. This does not alter the provisioning patterns used (the information is still mirrored), but may result in very different flows.

Consider that the Shipping application does not have the capability to be modified to provision the analytics solution's Stock information. The Product Hub application does have the ability to provision another downstream application (just as we've seen it provision the Shipping and Supplier-net applications). The analytics solution is designed to handle processing from internal information collections (known to its processes), but not from external proprietary applications.

Based on the information collections initially outlined, there needs to be a STAGED ROUTING FLOW from Shipping into Analytics while only a FILTERED ROUTING FLOW from Product Hub into Analytics. (See Figure 2.34.)

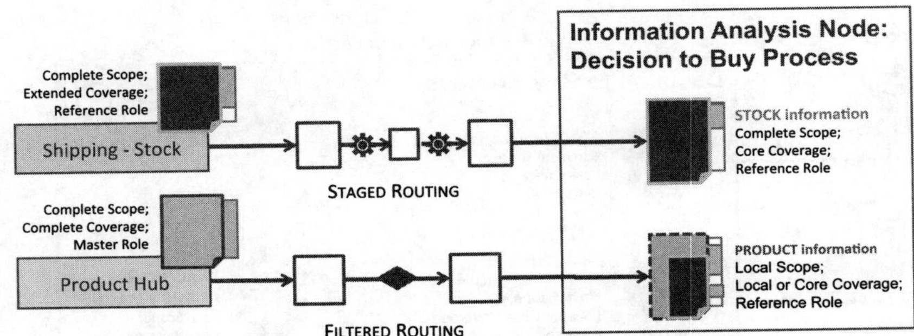

Figure 2.34 Incorporating information flows for provisioning product data for predictive analytics.

However, if the Stock and Product information collections are consolidated, reducing some of the workload in the information process and the storage requirements/cost in the information node, then a **FILTERED CONSOLIDATION** flow will satisfy their needs. (See Figure 2.35.)

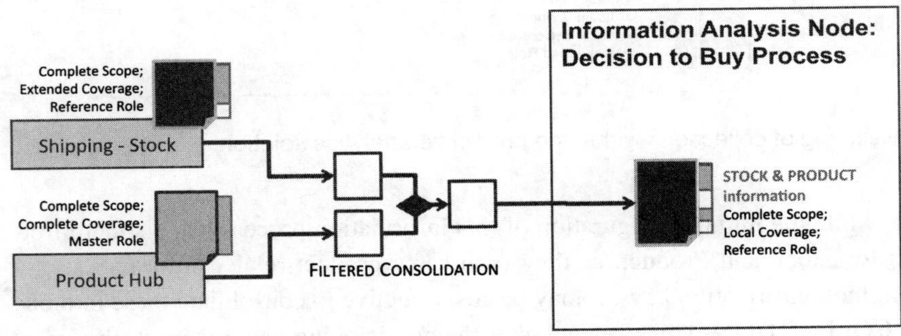

Figure 2.35 Consolidating information flows for Product and Stock information.

Thus, the shift from a manual reordering process to an approach driven by predictive analytics has a series of consequences to the broader information management strategy and underlying information supply chains. Whereas previously a buyer's consumption of the information from four distinct supply chains was somewhat haphazard, this information is now formalized into specific information collections relevant to the decision-to-buy information process. Decisions on how and where to host these information collections create provisioning requirements, and the forces and limitations of the processes along the information supply chain create or mandate other additional requirements (new staging areas, new information processes, additional information nodes, etc.).

Summary of Case Study

In this case study, MCHS Trading has built out the ability to report on the state of the business, to manage information about the products they sell, to have greater control over their stock management, and to provide comprehensive customer service. All of these new capabilities have a direct impact on the success of the organization, even though many of these changes are deployed behind the scenes using middleware.

The MCHS Trading case study introduces a variety of the patterns from the patterns of information management. The chapters that follow cover all of the patterns in more detail. Figure 2.36 shows how the pattern groups are organized into chapters. The numbers on the diagram represent the chapter number where the pattern groups are located.

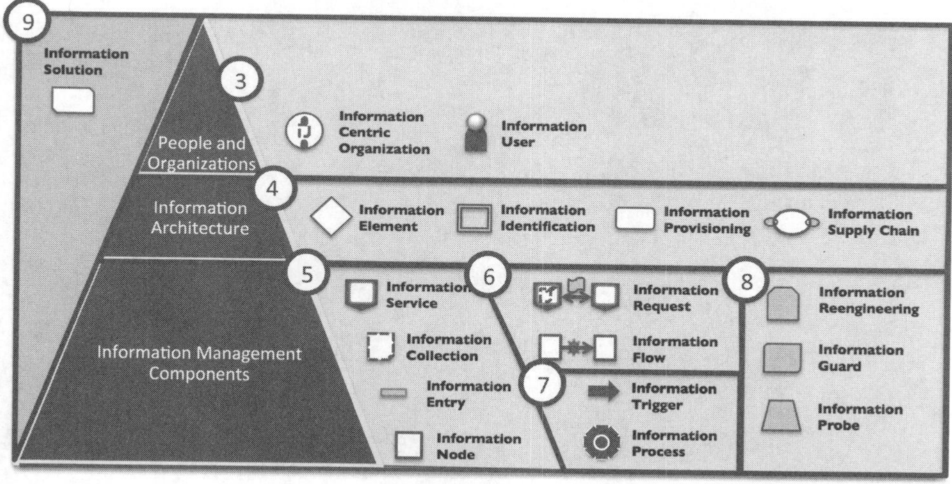

Figure 2.36 Pattern groups and their chapters.

CHAPTER 3

People and Organizations

The key to good information management is not technology. It is the attitude, culture, and behavior of the organization that is using the information. Information technology can only provide the mechanisms to automate the routine aspects of the organization and deliver the right information to the right people when appropriate. It is still up to the individuals receiving the information to use it appropriately.

So how should an organization operate to create an environment that fosters good information management? This chapter covers two pattern groups that focus on the formulation of approach, strategy, and governance for information management and the people involved in the process. These are the INFORMATION CENTRIC ORGANIZATION pattern group and the INFORMATION USER pattern group (see Figure 3.1). We start with the activities that the organization must perform to set up the framework for information management.

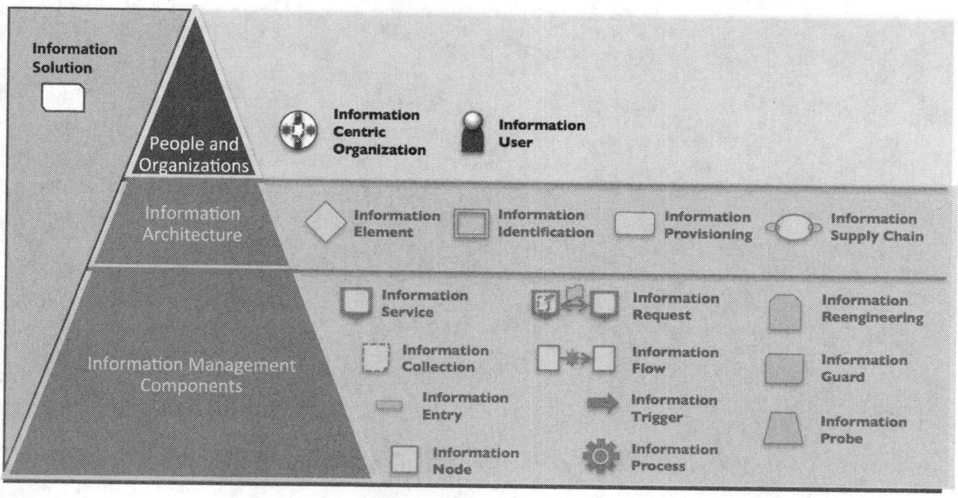

Figure 3.1 People and organizations pattern groups in the context of the pattern language.

Information Centric Organization Patterns

An *information centric organization* is an organization driven from high-quality, complete, and timely information that is relevant to its goals.

This section covers some of the mechanisms that help an organization maintain its focus on information. The INFORMATION CENTRIC ORGANIZATION pattern describes the characteristics of such an organization. The INFORMATION MANAGEMENT OBLIGATION pattern documents a regulation or a policy that the information management must conform to. The INFORMATION MANAGEMENT STRATEGY pattern describes how to define the approach to information management. The INFORMATION MANAGEMENT PRINCIPLE pattern describes the general rules that enterprise architects and solution architects should keep in mind when designing changes to the information management capability of the organization and the INFORMATION GOVERNANCE PROGRAM covers how information management controls are maintained. These patterns are summarized in Table 3.1.

Table 3.1 Information Centric Organizations Summary

Icon	Pattern Name	Problem	Solution
	INFORMATION CENTRIC ORGANIZATION	An organization needs to make good use of its information to achieve its goals.	Make the management of information a strategic priority. Develop systems and practices that nurture and exploit information to maximum effect.
	INFORMATION MANAGEMENT OBLIGATION	An organization has an obligation to operate in a legal and ethical manner according to the regulations covering its type of operation. This includes the way information is managed.	Review the regulations and policies that apply to the organization, and extract and document the specific requirements that relate to information management as information management obligations that define where the requirement came from and how the organization operations comply.
	INFORMATION MANAGEMENT STRATEGY	What are the aspects of an organization's information management that it should focus on to develop a strategy to become more information centric?	Define an information strategy that lays out the *why*, *what*, and *how* the organization will manage information.

Icon	Pattern Name	Problem	Solution
	INFORMATION MANAGEMENT PRINCIPLE	An organization has not defined how information should be managed.	Agree the underlying general rules that define how information shall be used, maintained, and/or protected.
	INFORMATION GOVERNANCE PROGRAM	An organization is experiencing quality and management issues with its information or must ensure compliance to regulations and policies.	Appoint an **INFORMATION GOVERNOR** to set up and run an information governance program.

These patterns link together to guide the organization in its information management practices.

Figure 3.2 shows a possible approach. Every organization is different, so approaches will vary. For large organizations, these activities may be driven from within each business unit. The important point is that the management and use of information has focus from strategy through to operations and is centered on supporting the organization's primary objectives.

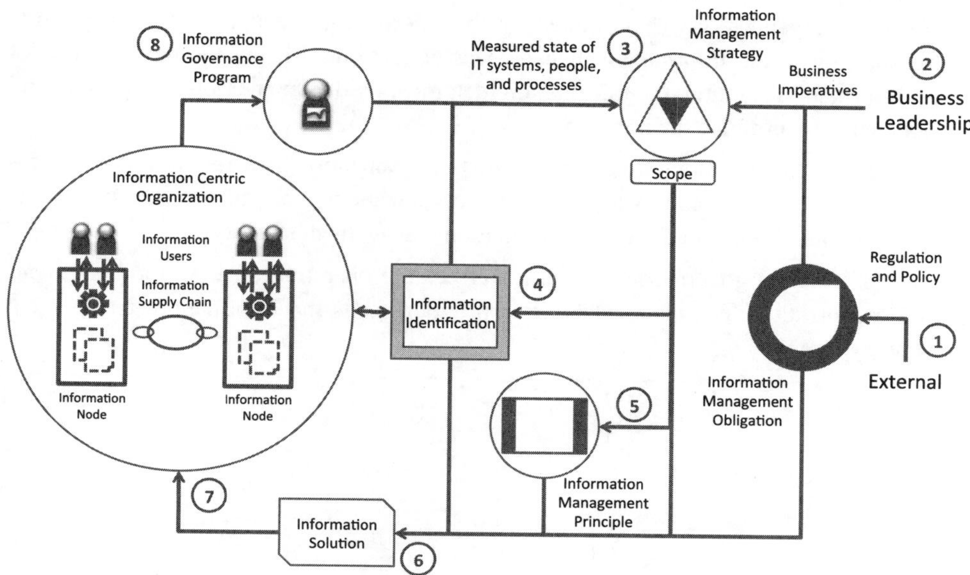

Figure 3.2 Interacting patterns in an information centric organization.

The numbers on the diagram in Figure 3.2 refer to these notes:

1. The organization reviews the current regulations and policies to determine which affect information management and what the internal response will be to these regulations. These are documented in the information management obligations.
2. The business leadership adds to these requirements with their vision for the organization's future in the form of business imperatives.
3. The business imperatives and information management obligations, together with the current measured state of the existing organization, are used as input to develop the information management strategy. This lays out how the organization is going to manage information. Often the strategy starts with a very small scope—such as a single subject area within one or two key systems—and then expands its focus as the organization builds skills and sees the benefits.
4. The information identification patterns provide much of the information that describes the current state of the organization. This documentation is continuously maintained and expanded as the organization changes and the scope of the information management strategy grows.
5. Information management principles are developed to support the information management strategy and are used as input into the information solutions.
6. The information solutions expand and improve the information management capability of the organization. They implement the information management strategy while conforming to the information management obligations. During the development of an information solution, the information identification documentation is expanded and updated to incorporate the new capability.
7. The information solutions are deployed into the organization's operations and new measurements are generated to validate that the organization is making progress in delivering the requirements set out in the information management strategy.
8. The information governance program oversees the operation of the information centric organization. The insight from this program feeds the information management strategy.

Information Centric Organization

Context

An organization exists for a purpose. It has targets to achieve and long-term aspirations.

Problem

An organization needs to make good use of its information to achieve its goals.

This seems a simple, obvious statement, but in practice it is very hard to achieve. Information is not a physical thing that can be controlled. It is ever changing and conveys different meanings depending on the context in which it is used. The absence of information can be as misleading as information that is out of date or just plain wrong. Too much information can be overwhelming and unhelpful.

It costs money to store and maintain information. Some information is required for regulatory reasons and keeping some types of information, such as personal information, imposes legal responsibilities to keep it safe and to retain it for a specified period of time. The management of information must be purposeful and continuous.

How does an organization collect, maintain, and distribute the right information to support its activities?

Example

MCHS Trading is a trading company that has four channels to market for the goods and services it offers: physical stores, an Internet site, mail order, and a customer call center where people can phone in orders.

MCHS owns a number of applications, each supporting different parts of the business. Information must flow between its order taking, shipping, and invoicing applications to receive and fulfill customer's orders. Any failures in this flow of information could affect the organization's ability to serve its customers, or collect money for goods sent out.

Forces

- **Conflicting business imperatives and obligations**—The same information may be subjected to conflicting requirements across different lines of business or from diverse obligations.
- **Information not seen as an asset**—Information is considered secondary or merely supportive to the "real" business.

- **No one takes ownership**—Ownership of information implies responsibility for its management and many individuals or groups do not want responsibility for what they can't control.
- **Information not tracked or measured**—The organization has limited insight into what information is being stored, how it is being managed, and where and how it is being used.
- **Limited means to ensure information management practices are understood**—The organization does not have clear or effective channels to ensure everyone understands how information is managed.
- **Duplicated information**—The same information may be stored in many places in an organization's systems.
- **Many formats for each type of information**—Each copy of information tends to have its own unique format and there are differences in validation rules and the use of the information.
- **Inconsistent information**—The set of valid values for an information attribute may not be consistent throughout the organization.
- **Information comes from many sources**—An employee receiving new information may not be a direct user of any of the information processes within the information supply chain.
- **People make mistakes**—They may enter incorrect information into a user interface, either through lack of attention, lack of training, or because the values they have are not correct.
- **Information quality varies**—Information coming in from outside of the organization can arrive through many channels and can have differing levels of quality.
- **Access and privacy controls require constant scrutiny**—Information is regularly distributed and dispersed through the organization for varied uses, often with insufficient controls.
- **Storage costs money**—Each copy of information costs money to store and maintain.

Solution

Make the management of information a strategic priority. Develop systems and practices that nurture and exploit information to maximum effect.

This does not mean information is kept for no reason. The essence of information management is to only keep information that is necessary for the running of the organization and to manage it throughout its life cycle—from creation, through maintenance, and eventual archival and deletion.

The characteristics of an information centric organization are as follows:

- Appropriate information is delivered to individuals as and when they need it to perform their jobs.
- Information is protected and only available to those who need it.
- The organization can demonstrate that it is meeting its legal and ethical obligations (see INFORMATION MANAGEMENT OBLIGATION).
- Information is only kept as long as it is needed. After that, it is destroyed.
- The use of information and any opportunities to make use of new sources of information are actively sought to continuously improve the organization's effectiveness.

Delivering these characteristics requires four patterns to be in place:

- An INFORMATION GOVERNANCE PROCESS ensures information has an owner and people have a clear understanding of their responsibility toward the management and protection of information.
- INFORMATION PROVISIONING ensures INFORMATION PROCESSES operate on information from authoritative sources.
- Information is moved between systems (INFORMATION NODES) along well-defined and managed pathways called INFORMATION SUPPLY CHAINS.
- Information is managed appropriately throughout its life cycle according to the kind of INFORMATION ELEMENT it is.

Consequences

- **Benefits**—An information centric organization knows what actions it is taking, where, when, by whom, and why.
- **Liabilities**—Becoming an information centric organization requires a willingness to constantly review, refine, and develop the breadth and depth of information available to decision makers in the organization because the world, and its expectations, are continuously changing as people become more sophisticated in their use of information. It also requires the organization to see information as not only important, but also as a strategic asset, and not simply as an adjunct to the business.

Example Resolved

In MCHS Trading, order records are created in the order-taking applications and passed to the Shipping application. The Shipping application controls the dispatch of goods. When all of the goods on the order are sent to the customer, a copy of the order record is sent to the Invoicing application. The Invoicing application controls the process for invoicing the customer and collecting the payment. This is shown in Figure 3.3.

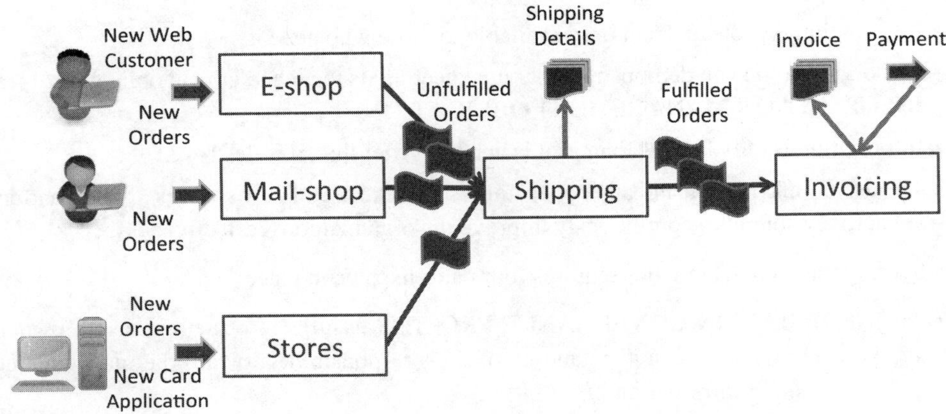

Figure 3.3 Handling of order records.

Each information node (application) supporting the order-processing activity maintains an information collection of order records. These records reflect the work performed on the order within the information node. When the work for an order moves to a new information node, the order record in the original information node is no longer updated.

Each information node also needs information collections that describe the customers and products that are referenced by the orders. Additional information processes must maintain this information and distribute any changes because the values should be consistent in each information node. When MCHS Trading embarked on becoming an information centric organization, the update of customer and product details was handled manually in each information node. It also had no ability to create management reports on customer trends and which products were the most profitable. MCHS Trading created an INFORMATION GOVERNANCE PROGRAM and implemented a number of INFORMATION SOLUTIONS to improve how it was managing information, including the following:

- CENTRALIZED MASTER for product details
- SYNCHRONIZED MASTERS for customer details
- DISTRIBUTED ACTIVITY STATUS for order processing
- HISTORICAL REPORTING for their management reports
- PARTNER COLLABORATION to connect to their suppliers to replenish the stock

The result is an efficient and effective management and distribution of information between its systems. Figure 3.4 summarizes many of MCHS Trading's information supply chains.

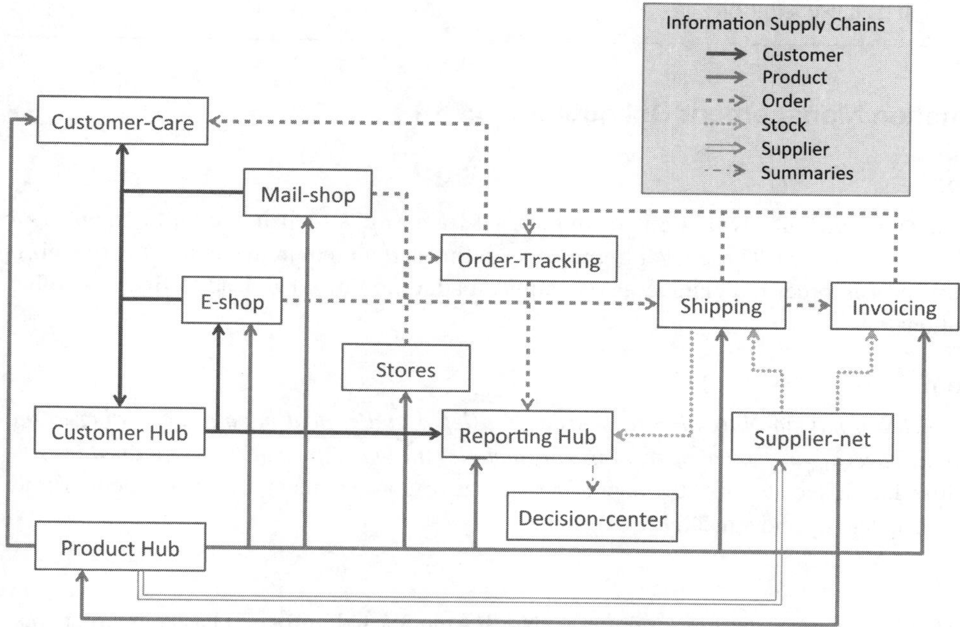

Figure 3.4 MCHS Trading's key information supply chains.

Known Uses

In many industries, we see successful organizations making information a key asset and using it to deliver better value and customer service by treating people and issues in a holistic way. The business leadership in an organization is responsible for driving focus on information within the business strategy and plan. This is referred to as their **Information Agenda**.

Related Patterns

The definition of what it means for an organization to become information centric is laid out in an **I**NFORMATION **M**ANAGEMENT **S**TRATEGY. The strategy supports the organization's business imperatives and is guided by the organization's **I**NFORMATION **G**OVERNANCE **P**ROGRAM. This controls and monitors the use and management of information within the organization. The **I**NFORMATION **I**DENTIFICATION patterns describe how to document the information in use in the organization. The **I**NFORMATION **M**ANAGEMENT **O**BLIGATION describes how to assess and manage requirements from regulations and other legal frameworks. Implementing **I**NFORMATION **S**OLUTIONS will change the IT infrastructure to improve the management of information. **I**NFORMATION **M**ANAGEMENT **P**RINCIPLES guide the development of these solutions.

Information Management Obligation

Context

An organization operates within one or more legal frameworks (depending on the number of countries it operates in). These legal frameworks define certain requirements that the organization must meet in order to continue its operations. Failure to do so can lead to fines and other prosecutions.

Problem

An organization has an obligation to operate in a legal and ethical manner according to the regulations covering its type of operation. This includes the way information is managed.

How does it keep track of the regulations and its response to them, in order to demonstrate it is operating legally and ethically?

Example

MCHS Trading operates its stores throughout North America and Europe. It has an Internet presence, which means it is selling to people from all over the world. The goods that it sells come from small-scale producers who are located in many difference countries. How can it be sure that it is managing the information that supports its operation correctly? Different countries have different accounting, privacy, import/export rules to name but a few of the regulations it needs to respect.

Forces

- **An organization is a collection of freethinking individuals**—Their actions when working on behalf of the organization must be in compliance with the regulations. However, very few will have read these regulations, or could really understand them if they tried and rely on specialized education and guidance from co-workers and the information systems they use to operate in the right way.

- **Many industries are seeing a growth in the number of regulations that apply to them**—These regulations overlap in content, and where an organization spans the boundaries of different legal frameworks, it can find itself subject to conflicting regulations.
- **It is not enough to be compliant with a regulation**—An organization must be able to demonstrate its compliance. This means that everyone in the organization should comply with the regulations in a consistent way and keep records of this compliance.

Solution

Review the regulations and policies that apply to the organization and extract and document the specific requirements that relate to information management as information management obligations that define where the requirement came from and how the organization operations comply.

The aim of this exercise is threefold:

- To understand what is required.
- To document what is required in a language that is meaningful to the organization.
- To make decisions on how the organization will conform, or not, as the case may be. This way, the organization is purposeful in its response to the regulations and individuals understand what they need to do.

Regulations evolve over time and are created for specific purposes by different groups of people. There is often duplication and inconsistency within the regulations. The clauses of the regulations need to be linked to similar and contradicting clauses from other regulations. Then a response to each of the uniquely identified requirement or obligation is created. This will define how the organization will implement the obligation and also provide the evidence that it is doing so. See Figure 3.5.

Consequences

- **Benefits**—The organization develops a cost-effective response to the regulations it must comply with.
- **Liabilities**—Reading and reviewing regulations takes time. It needs tools that can contain the regulations and link to the organization's interpretation and response. Often there are industry bodies that can provide guidance on how to implement the regulations within the industry.

The cost of implementing a regulation may be greater than the cost of noncompliance.

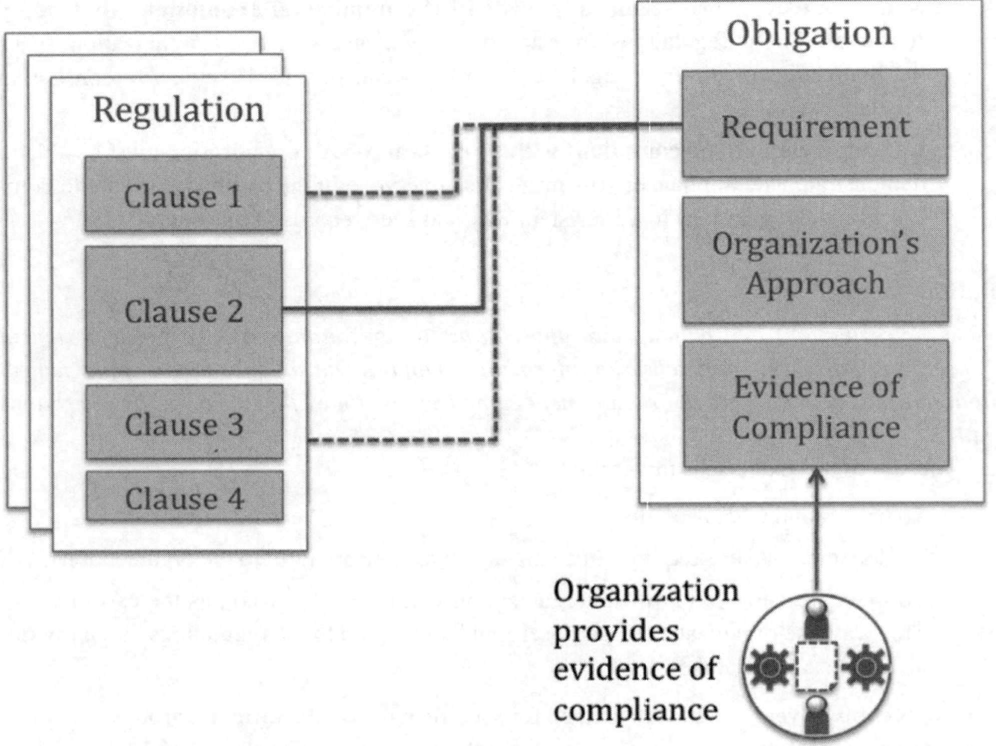

Figure 3.5 Information management obligations.

Example Resolved

MCHS Trading has a department dedicated to understanding and defining how the organization will respond to the many regulations it is subject to, such as tax, import/export regulations, health and safety, privacy, vendor regulations, and many more. This department reports to the chief operating officer (COO).

Known Uses

The responsibility for reviewing regulations and defining the response is usually centralized in a business controls operation. These people also drive the documentation and auditing of compliance within the organization.

Tools exist to manage and document regulations. A common name for them is the **Inventory of Obligations**. The regulations and responses associated with the regulation may be referenced in an Enterprise Content Management system, or captured and stored in a *wiki* (a commonly accessible and online reference site within the organization). Audit, Legal, and Risk Management functions within an organization are generally responsible for the review, response, and monitoring of these obligations.

Related Patterns

The **I**NFORMATION **G**OVERNANCE **P**ROGRAM is responsible for the implementation of many of the obligations relating to the management of information.

Information Management Strategy

Context

An organization wants to become an **I**NFORMATION **C**ENTRIC **O**RGANIZATION.

Problem

What are the aspects of an organization's information management that it should focus on to develop a strategy to become more information centric?

Many organizations recognize that trusted information is a key to their success. However, they have a lot of information and changing everything at once is neither feasible nor necessary because some types of information are more important than others. The organization needs to define a strategy that lays out its approach.

Example

How does MCHS Trading become an information centric organization? What type of information should it focus on? What solutions should it invest in? What else needs to change?

Forces

- **Business strategy—**An organizations has a strategy that defines how it will produce/acquire and sell goods or services in order to achieve a profit within constraints, options, or directions.
- **Limited resources—**An organization has limits in terms of money, physical resources, and human resources that it can apply to its information management strategy.
- **Limited ability to absorb change—**The resources in an organization have a finite ability to handle change at a given point or for a given period of time.
- **Variety of information—**An organization has many kinds of information—of varying value and quality.

- **Duplicated information**—The same information may be stored in many places in an organization's systems.
- **Many formats for each type of information**—Each copy of information tends to have its own unique format and there are differences in validation rules and the use of the information.
- **Inconsistent information**—The set of valid values for an information attribute may not be consistent throughout the organization.
- **Information comes from many sources**—An employee receiving new information may not be a direct user of any of the information processes within the information supply chain.
- **People make mistakes**—They may enter incorrect information into a user interface, either through lack of attention, lack of training, or because the values they have are not correct.
- **Information quality varies**—Information coming in from the outside of the organization can arrive through many channels, and have differing levels of quality.
- **Storage costs money**—Each copy of information costs money to store and maintain.

Solution

Define an information strategy that lays out the why, what, *and* how *the organization will manage information.*

An information management strategy defines the goals and road map for developing and improving the collection, use, and management of information.

The *why* section covers the business imperatives that drive the need to be information centric. This helps focus the effort on activities that deliver value to the organization.

The *what* section covers the type of information that MCHS Trading must manage to deliver on its business imperatives. This includes the subject areas to cover, which attributes within the subject area need to be managed, the valid values for these attributes, and the management policies (such as protection and retention) that the organization wants to implement.

Finally, the *how* section is described using INFORMATION MANAGEMENT PRINCIPLES that provide the general rules for how information is to be managed by the information systems and the people using them along with how information flows between them.

Consequences

- **Benefits**—Developing an information management strategy creates a set of objectives for the organization, which guides the investment in information management technology and related solution that support the business. Starting with the business imperatives ensures the information management strategy is aligned with the needs of the organization, making it easier to demonstrate its relevance and value.

- **Liabilities**—An information management strategy needs sponsorship from the business—without it, the actions it recommends will not be implemented. The stakeholders in the organization need to support efforts to align projects with the strategy and ensure the information governance program is empowered to support it.

Example Resolved

MCHS Trading has the following business imperatives that are relevant to the information management strategy:

- Exemplary customer service, where an individual customer experiences a continuous and coherent "conversation" with the organization, no matter whom they talk to
- Accurate, complete, and reliable information about an interesting range of products sourced from responsible and efficient suppliers
- Privacy and security of all personal information retained by the organization
- Efficient delivery of orders through a transparent supply chain

MCHS Trading identifies the following subject areas of information that it should focus on.

Known Uses

An enterprise architecture team developing a shared approach to IT for the organization often creates the information management strategy, typically in the form of an IT strategy and an enterprise architecture. It helps them think through where they should invest to deliver the best value for the organization.

Related Patterns

The SUBJECT AREA DEFINITION describes a subject area identified in the information management strategy.

The INFORMATION MANAGEMENT PRINCIPLE defines guidelines for the INFORMATION SOLUTIONS that are commissioned to implement the information management strategy.

Information Management Principle

Context

An organization is defining its information management strategy.

Problem

An organization has not defined how information should be managed.

As a result, every IT project makes an independent decision on how they collect, manage, store, and use information. Over time, the variety of approaches leads to high maintenance costs and requires complex integration software to connect all of the systems together.

Example

MCHS Trading is looking to improve how its information nodes manage information and need to develop guidance on how the technical teams should develop this new capability.

Forces

- **Variety of technology—**Many types of technology and vendors offering information management solutions. Which ones should be used, when, and in which combination?
- **Variety of patterns for information management—**Which style of information management should be used and under what circumstances?
- **Rapid shifts in technology and skill requirements—**Changes in technology and the skill sets to use the new technology require regular review to ensure they are addressed by the defined principles.
- **Acquisition of new business and resources—**Mergers, acquisitions, and initiation of new business lines bring together teams working from different core sets of principles. The differing principles must be merged, aligned, or resolved.
- **Limited skill and resource—**Many organizations have a fixed pool of IT staff, have limitations in training that staff, and have a limit as to how many different types of technology it can support.

Solution

Agree on the underlying general rules that define how information shall be used, maintained, and/or protected.

These general rules are called information management principles and they are a core element of the INFORMATION MANAGEMENT STRATEGY of an organization:

They are used to capture the core beliefs and approaches defining how the organization will utilize and deploy both business and information technology assets and resources to support the information supply chains.

Each principle is defined with a short description, the reasons (purpose) for adopting the principle, and a list of implications for the organization:

- The purpose statements provide a basis for justifying all proposed decisions and related activities.
- The implication statements provide an outline of the key tasks, resources, and potential costs to the business of implementing the principle. They also provide valuable inputs to future transition initiative and planning activities.

Once approved, information management principles are often refined into policies and rules that are specific to different parts of the organization. They are embedded in the operation of processes across the organization and measured through metrics defined by the information governance program.

Consequences

- **Benefits**—Information management principles provide an effective framework within which the business can start to make conscious decisions about the business, its management style and structure, and how its information infrastructure.
- **Liabilities**—Information management principles are only effective if they are enforced across the organization. This requires buy-in at multiple levels of the organization.

Example Resolved

MCHS Trading defines the following set of information management principles to guide its information solutions. Here are some examples:

Information is an asset. It has value, and cost, to the organization and should be captured, managed, stored, used, and disposed of according to well-defined and cost-effective procedures that ensure it is available to the appropriate person at the right time and at a sufficient level of quality.

Purpose:

- Raises awareness and motivates leaders to focus effort on the effective management of information—from creation to destruction.
- Prevents incorrect or inconsistent information from inhibiting decision making.

Implications:

- Individuals who use the organization's information must be aware of their responsibilities toward the information that they handle.
- Consideration of the management of information is an important part of any IT project.
- The organization should create a model of the cost and value of its information to help steer investment in its information management capability.

Information is shared. It should be captured, stored, and managed in a way that will allow appropriate sharing across the organization based on business need and security rules. It should be validated as it is captured and it should flow between applications along well-defined information supply chains.

Purpose:

- Reduces the number of independent copies of information that must be kept synchronized.

Implications:

- The organization should agree on what information is important to share and how it should be managed.
- The IT part of the organization should invest in skills and projects to enable it to actively manage the sharing of information between information collections.

Information is identified. The core types of information that are of critical importance to the organization are defined in a subject area definition and preferred structures for managing this information are documented in information models. The management and distribution of this type of information is handled through an information supply chain.

Purpose:

- Ensures consistent view and use of information throughout the organization
- Increases the consistency of how this type of information is stored in the information collections and transmitted between the information nodes

Implications:

- One or more individuals must be given responsibility to maintain the descriptions and models of this type of information.
- The subject area definition and information models should be used in decision making and the development of new information solutions.

Information is governed. An information governance program is responsible for governing how each type of information should be managed, protected, and used. This program defines the rules, communicates them to affected parts of the organization, reviews and grants exceptions to the rules where appropriate, audits compliance, and refines the rules to meet new business requirements.

Purpose:

- Provides a focal point for defining and enforcing policies related to the management of information.

Implications:

- The organization needs to appoint an Information Governor and provide him or her with the appropriate sponsorship to be able to make the necessary changes to the way people work, and to commission changes to the information nodes that manage the information.

Information is protected. Information is protected from inappropriate use, only available to authorized users, and recoverable.

Purpose:

- Ensures information is only used by authorized people and does not leak out of the organization.
- Ensures the privacy of any person's details stored by the organization.
- Protects the organization's information from theft or malicious attack.
- Ensures the organization's information is recoverable in the event of a disaster.

Implications:

- Individuals within an organization need a unique identity (user account/password) so that all of the activity they perform using the information nodes is attributable.
- Individuals need well-defined roles that determine which information they have access to.
- Individuals need to understand their roles in protecting the information they do have access to.
- There must be good information management practices around the information nodes to ensure their information collections are properly maintained and backed up.

Information is measured. The quality, volume, consistency, usage, and redundancy of information is measured on a regular basis, and continuous improvement is made to the management of information to ensure these measures are trending in a positive direction.

Purpose:

- Enables fact-based decision making for information management.
- Ensures consistent view and use of information throughout the organization.
- Improves the coordination and integration between information nodes.
- Prevents incorrect or inconsistent information from inhibiting decision making.

Implications:

- The IT infrastructure is instrumented with information probes to collect the measurements.
- Operational management takes the time to review the measurements and take action if the indicators are moving in the wrong direction.
- There is continuous investment in the IT infrastructure that supports the management of information.

Known Uses

The notion of identifying "principles" is a common approach used by architects to define a framework of rules that will govern the projects within their domain. These principles comprise part of an enterprise architecture.

Related Patterns

Information management principles support an **I**NFORMATION **M**ANAGEMENT STRATEGY.

Information Governance Program

Context

An organization is concerned with the efficient and accurate use of information.

Problem

An organization is experiencing quality and management issues with its information.

They want to find a reliable and repeatable resolution to this issue.

Example

A customer calls the MCHS Trading call center to inform the company that he changed his address. Nothing is done about it and MCHS Trading continues to use the old address—much to the annoyance of the customer.

Forces

- **Variety of information—**An organization has a lot of different types of information—of varying value and quality.
- **No single version of the truth—**Information is often duplicated and inconsistent when looking across the information nodes.

- **Decentralized ownership of information**—Different copies of information tend to be owned by different groups/teams within the organization.
- **No common definitions for information**—There are different perspectives on what is valid and relevant to different groups/teams within the organization.
- **Unknown content**—The knowledge of what type of information is held by an IT system may be lost.
- **Poorly communicated or understood principles**—The principles on which to act in regard to information are not provided or clarified for those who work with the information.

Solution

Appoint an INFORMATION GOVERNOR *to set up and run an information governance program.*

Information governance requires a two-way exchange of information enabling the governance board to set policy, communicate requirements, and then receive requests for exceptions and amendments to the policies. Comprehensive monitoring and metrics to demonstrate both compliance and value delivered by the program must back this up.

The leader of the governance program is called the INFORMATION GOVERNOR. This role chairs a governance board that decides on the information subject areas that require special care and the INFORMATION MANAGEMENT PRINCIPLES (policies, impact, and outcomes) by which this information will be governed.

INFORMATION OWNERS are identified for each of the key information nodes and/or processes that use this type of information and they appoint INFORMATION STEWARDS to monitor the quality of the information and remediate any issues. There are five main activities in an information governance program:

- **Managed communication**—Ensuring people understand their role in information governance
- **Managed vitality**—Keeping the governance program up to date and relevant to the organization
- **Managed feedback**—Measuring and reporting on the effectiveness of the governance program
- **Managed exception**—Enabling people to request an exemption from following the governance program for a particular circumstance
- **Managed compliance**—Particular procedures that enforce the requirements of the governance program

These activities describe how the governance team interacts with the other teams in the organization that are responsible for the information being governed. They are supported by information management functions that support the measurement, reporting, enforcement, and remediation of issues with governed information.

Consequences

- **Benefits**—An information governance program provides a focal point for coordinating the management of shared information.
- **Liabilities**—The information governance program will cause additional work for some teams, who may not necessarily reap the benefit. The information governance program needs executive sponsorship and must routinely demonstrate that it is delivering value. As such, starting small, demonstrating success, and then growing scope is often an effective strategy. The information governance program has to listen for and adapt to the changing priorities of the organization to maintain its relevance. Finally, it has to have teeth; otherwise, once teams realize nothing happens when they are noncompliant, they tend to deprioritize their compliance work.

Example Resolved

Whenever MCHS Trading receives a change of address for a customer, it must be captured, the address validated and standardized so all the relevant fields are completed, and then it must be distributed to the Customer Hub, E-Shop, and Stores applications. The customer address for in-flight orders is unchanged.

Prior to the introduction of the Customer-Care application, this process was ad hoc and very error-prone. MCHS Trading recognized that its current systems make it very difficult to ensure that a change to a customer's details is made reliably and consistently to all copies of this information. Worse still, its employees had come to accept there is nothing that they can do about it. Therefore, a governance program is set up for customer details. The team assigned to this program first focuses on how customer details are managed by the information nodes. It discovers each system has its own copy of this information and there is no synchronization. The team commissions a number of projects to create an **I**NFORMATION **S**UPPLY **C**HAIN for customer details. This includes a new Customer-Care application where customer-facing employees can request changes to customer details. This includes changing contact details as well as issues, complaints, and special requests. The team also provides training to all employees who work with customer details for its responsibilities toward its quality. Finally, the team adds regular monitoring and reporting on how the quality of customer details is changing over time.

Known Uses

Information governance programs (sometimes called data governance programs) are common in large organizations where the number of systems typically is more than an individual can oversee. Typically, an organization implements information governance in a staged manner, gradually increasing its level of information governance maturity (see http://www-935.ibm.com/services/uk/cio/pdf/leverage_wp_data_gov_council_maturity_model.pdf).

Related Patterns

The INFORMATION IDENTIFICATION patterns describe the information (metadata, rules, and policies) that should be gathered to support a governance program. The INFORMATION SOLUTION patterns describe improvements to the way information is managed. The INFORMATION SUPPLY CHAIN pattern describes how to structure the flow of information between information nodes.

Information User Patterns

The information user patterns describe the key user roles involved in an information supply chain. They are provided to show how individuals interact with the information supply chain. The generic INFORMATION USER pattern is shown first in Table 3.2 and are followed by summaries of more specialist users.

Table 3.2 Information User Pattern Summary

Icon	Pattern Name	Problem	Solution
	INFORMATION USER	Individuals need access to the organization's information in order to perform their work.	Classify the people connected with the organization according to their information needs and skills. Then provide user interfaces and reports through which they can access the information as appropriate.

Information User

Context

There is an organization. It exists to fulfill a purpose and employs people to perform activities that contribute to that purpose.

Problem

Individuals need access to the organization's information in order to perform their work.

Each individual's information need is specific to the work he or she is performing. It must be delivered in the right context, and at the right time, to support his or her work. An individual may also have new information to contribute. The organization must make it easy for the individual to provide this information and also validate that it make sense.

Example

An MCHS Trading employee is talking to a customer on the order help line. The employee needs to retrieve information about the customer, answer queries about any orders the customer has, and make a record of the conversation. The employee may also need to update information about the customer, such as a change of address, phone number, or email account.

Forces

- **Information must be protected from inappropriate use**—For example, information about individuals should be treated as private. Financial results, or information that gives an organization a competitive advantage, must only be revealed to employees who are privileged to receive it.
- **The value and meaning of information depends on perspective**—Individuals across the organization will need different types of information, with different levels of precision, accuracy, and currency.
- **Information has multiple interpretations**—Information about the same object, person, organization, activity, result, event, or concept exists in many forms and is not always consistent.
- **Poorly communicated or understood principles**—The principles on which to act in regard to information are not provided or clarified for those who work with the information.
- **Knowledge is recorded locally**—Individual users working with information do not consistently record details where other users can access and understand it.

- **Rapid turnover of resources**—Regular change in information users may disrupt the flow and understanding of information as well as the principles that govern it.
- **Multiple points of user entry with differing roles**—Systems, applications, processes, and information stores do not necessarily have consistent implementations of user roles. Consequently, users may have overlapping and potentially conflicting roles in their work.

Solution

Classify the people connected to the organization according to their information needs and skills. Provide common channels of communication and knowledge sharing about information. Then provide user interfaces and reports through which they can access the information as appropriate.

The classification of individuals interacting with an organization's IT systems is typically expressed as user roles. A user role expresses a person's responsibilities and goals, his or her skills, the tasks he or she needs to perform, the information he or she is working with when performing tasks, and where he or she needs to get information to perform his or her role.

INFORMATION PROCESSES provide IT support for the tasks a person performs. The information is displayed and accepted through user interfaces, such as web browsers, mobile devices, and the more traditional laptops or computer terminals. An information process drives sequences of interactions between the individual and the IT systems, enabling him or her to select the task he or she wants to perform and then stepping through screens that allow the individual to retrieve, change, and add information. The information process may support the work by performing calculations or bringing significant facts to the individual's attention.

Behind the scenes, the information process is interacting with the information supply chain through INFORMATION SERVICES that are responsible for retrieving and updating the INFORMATION COLLECTIONS as appropriate. The information collections persist the information in case of system failure. See Figure 3.6.

Consequences

- **Benefits**—Identifying the user roles of individuals using an organization's IT systems enables the organization to control what information is made available to whom and under which circumstances. This can be very helpful and reduce the effort to demonstrate that the organization is compliant with regulations related to information production and use.

  This type of analysis can simplify the work of many individuals because they only have to learn how to perform the tasks relevant to their role, rather than having to understand a much broader view of the organization's operation.

- **Liabilities—** Hard-coding the tasks and type of information made available to groups of people in the information processes can create inflexibility in the operation of the organization.

Each person using an organization's information must be aware of his or her responsibilities for appropriate management of this information.

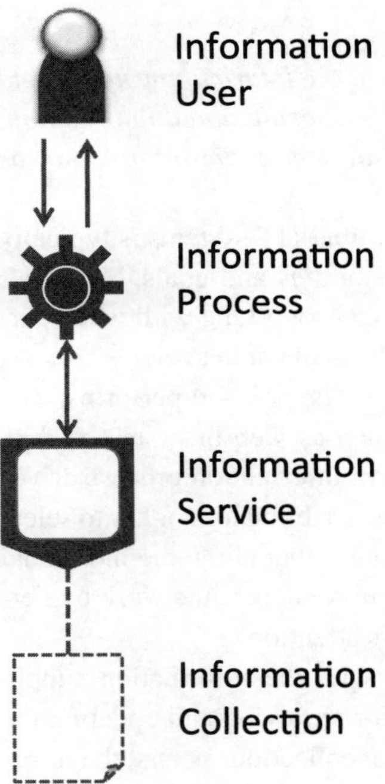

Figure 3.6 Information users and their interaction with information.

Example Resolved

The MCHS Trading employee talking to the customer on the telephone uses the Customer-Care application. This application incorporates information processes to retrieve customer details along with related orders and make changes as necessary. These information processes are designed to support the Customer Support Representative user role.

Known Uses

Documenting user roles is a common practice for user experience practitioners. These user roles can be described as text or more formally in models (see http://www.ibm.com/developerworks/library/ar-usermod1/).

Most user interfaces are provided from applications that implement the majority of information processes. These are also flexible approaches to supporting user roles using Business Process Management technology that works from a model of how the process should operate. This model defines the tasks a user of a particular role will perform. For example, see the HumanActor element in the Open Group's SOA Ontology (http://www.opengroup.org/soa/source-book/ontology/human_task.htm).

User roles are often used to control access to systems. A user registry, such as the Lightweight Directory Access Protocol (LDAP), defines what operations are permissible on the information. Then individuals are assigned to the roles. When an individual logs on to an information system, his or her identity is checked to discover which roles, and as a consequence, which operations/information access are permitted. Individual applications and databases incorporate their own specific security, which may or may not utilize common user registries.

User roles form part of the broader strategy for information security.

Related Patterns

Information users are supported in their work by INFORMATION PROCESSES. They are able to start an information process directly using a MANUAL INFORMATION TRIGGER.

The IDENTITY VERIFICATION pattern is used to ensure an individual is who he says he is. Once his or her identity has been established, the user role and corresponding access can be determined. Other INFORMATION GUARD patterns may be used to further constrain information users, such as ensuring SEPARATION oF DUTIES.

INFORMATION PROBES may be used to monitor and record the activities of information users.

Variations of the Information User Pattern

The pattern summaries in Table 3.3 describe more specialized types of users who have special roles around information management. These are not all of the roles that will exist in an organization, but they represent key roles that impact information management.

Table 3.3 Information User Specialized Patterns Summary

Icon	Pattern Name	Problem	Solution
	INFORMATION WORKER	The organization needs people to organize, manage, and operate its core business activity.	Appoint individuals who are responsible for the manual steps in the core business activity. Create user interfaces and access rights to provide these individuals access to the information supply chain through the information processes.
	INFORMATION STEWARD	Not all activity that ensures information quality can be automated, nor does it fit neatly into the organization's information processes.	Appoint an individual to coordinate the manual activity necessary to monitor and verify that an information collection is meeting agreed quality levels. Create user interfaces and access rights to involve this individual in information quality processes such as the exception management process.
	INFORMATION GOVERNOR	There is no obvious point of control in an organization to ensure people treat information as an asset.	Appoint an individual to coordinate the definition of policies related to information governance and their implementation.
	INFORMATION OWNER	An information collection needs investment to ensure its contents are of acceptable quality to support the organization's activities.	Appoint an individual to be the owner of the information collection who is responsible and accountable for ensuring it is capable of supporting the organization's activities.
	INFORMATION AUDITOR	An organization needs to demonstrate it is operating legally, ethically, and effectively.	Appoint an individual or team of individuals to review key aspects of how the organization is actually operating and compare it with agreed processes.

Icon	Pattern Name	Problem	Solution
	DATA QUALITY ANALYST	The actual information values that are flowing through the information supply chain needs to be monitored and assessed.	Appoint an individual to monitor and analyze the state of the information flowing through the information supply chain.
	BUSINESS ANALYST	An organization needs to improve how it operates.	Appoint an individual to analyze the way people are working, understand where the processes can be improved, and define new procedures, rules, and requirements for the IT systems.
10001 01010 00100 01010 10001	DATA SCIENTIST	An organization needs to understand how it can improve its operational efficiency and customer service.	Appoint an individual to analyze the information that the organization is collecting in order to understand patterns of success.
	INFRASTRUCTURE OPERATOR	The systems that support the information processes of an organization need to be available and operating correctly.	Appoint an individual responsible for starting, maintaining, and monitoring the systems that support the information supply chain.

Summary

Technology alone is not sufficient to ensure the quality, consistency, and flexibility of an organization's information. The attitudes and skills of an organization is a major determination of the success of an information management program.

The patterns in this section discuss some of the activities and roles that an organization establishes to set the strategy and enable the right behavior in everyday operations. The next chapter considers how the organization's information, and the systems that manage it, should be architected to deliver the right information to the right people at the right time.

CHAPTER 4

Information Architecture

As we consider the information requirements for an organization, there are some patterns that help classify, design, and document which information is needed, how it is used, and where it is located. Collectively, the results of this activity are called the information architecture. The information architecture is a living description of the information in use by the organization.

First, there is the INFORMATION ELEMENT group of patterns. They classify the life cycles of information in use by the organization and, consequentially, the approach that is appropriate to manage them.

Then, we have the INFORMATION IDENTIFICATION patterns that cover the models, schema, and metadata that are used to describe information structure and how it is managed.

Next are the INFORMATION PROVISIONING patterns that describe different approaches to making information available to an information process.

Finally, there is the INFORMATION SUPPLY CHAIN pattern group that describes how a particular kind of information can be synchronized end-to-end among the IT systems (INFORMATION NODES) used by the organization.

Figure 4.1 shows these patterns in the context of the patterns of information management.

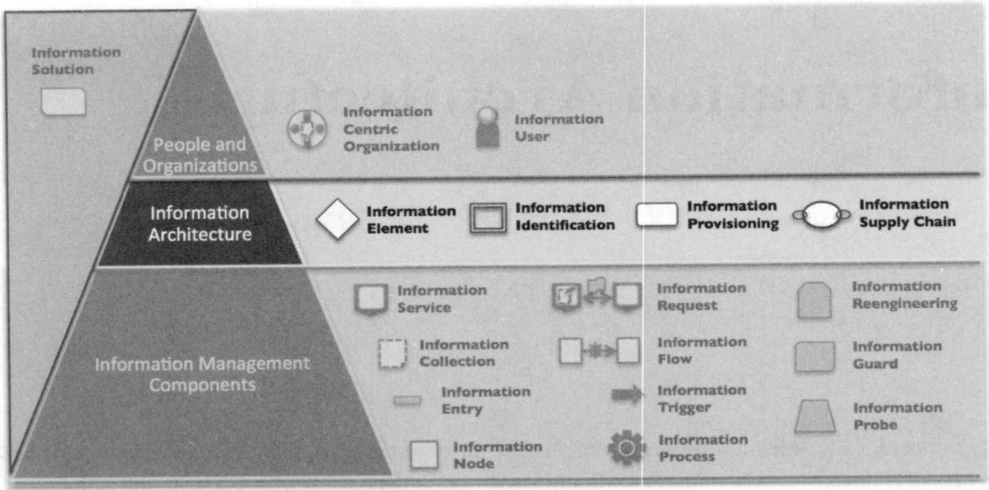

Figure 4.1 Information architecture pattern groups in the context of the pattern language.

Information Element Patterns

There is a wide variety of information held by an organization. Information differs in subject area, in format, in reliability, in location. All of these aspects matter when it comes to information management. However, there are some fundamental information patterns that influence many of the decisions we make as architects because each pattern needs a different information management approach.

The **I**NFORMATION **E**LEMENT shown in Table 4.1 describes the general concept of a particular kind of information.

Table 4.1 The Information Element Pattern Summary

Icon	Pattern Name	Problem	Solution
◇	INFORMATION ELEMENT	An organization is looking for the best approach to manage the many kinds of information it has.	Group together related information attributes that follow the same life cycle and manage them appropriately.

Information Element

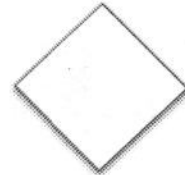

Context

Managing the information needs of an organization can seem overwhelming. There are many types of information, located in different places, and managed using different technologies. Where do you start?

Problem

An organization is looking for the best approach to manage the many kinds of information it has.

The organization wants to focus on the most important kinds of information and manage that efficiently and effectively. It knows there are different types of information management technology (such as master data management hubs, information quality tools, data warehouses, information integration tools) that can help, but it is not obvious how to map them to the information nodes (systems) and subject areas (topics) the organization has and show how they deliver value to the business.

Example

The purpose of the MCHS Trading organization is to sell goods to its customers. This activity needs information about its customers, products, the orders taken, and the money received, among other things. How should this information be managed?

Forces

Information management must handle the variety of information and its needs change:

- **An organization's information needs are complex—**The information held by an organization is complex with many competing requirements.
- **The world is constantly changing—**Information needs to be kept up to date.
- **Information is duplicated—**Information about the same object, person, organization, activity, result, event, or concept exists in many forms and is not always consistent.
- **When information is updated, the changes must be synchronized with all copies—**Without this synchronization, the copies become inconsistent.
- **Some information is more valuable than others—**It makes sense to focus on the most valuable and delete the information that has no value at all.
- **The value of information changes over time—**How do you know when it is no longer required?
- **The value and meaning of information depends on perspective—**Individuals across the organization will need different kinds of information, with different levels of precision, accuracy, and currency.
- **Some information is mandatory—**Information that must be produced for legal regulations often also requires a proof that it is correct.

Solution

Group together related information attributes that follow the same life cycle and manage them appropriately.

In information management, we think about the organization's information as a set of linked information elements. An information element is a collection of attributes that relates to a specific object, person, organization, activity, event, result, or concept.

An information element can be any size—from a few bytes representing a reading from a sensor, to details about a person, to a document describing how to fix an engine, to a multigigabyte result of a scientific simulation.

No matter what the size of an information element, its important characteristic is that the information within it follows the same life cycle—so we can manage the content of an information element in a consistent way.

The specifics of an information element's life cycle will depend on the INFORMATION PROCESSES that are manipulating it, but, in general, the information element will follow one of the following patterns:

- **INFORMATION ASSET**—The record of a core component or asset of the business, such as an organization, person, real-world concept, object, product, or physical assets. The lifetime of an information asset is typically of long duration and its values change slowly. Many information processes throughout the organization use this information so there are many copies that need to be synchronized.
- **INFORMATION ACTIVITY**—The record of an activity that the organization is performing or monitoring. The information activity element is created when the activity starts. As the activity progresses, more information is added to it to reflect the current state of the work. When the activity completes, the information activity element is no longer updated, but can be kept for reference. Eventually, it is deleted. Key attributes within an information activity may be INFORMATION LINKS to information assets and information events.
- **INFORMATION EVENT**—The record of an event that has occurred. This would include when, where, and in what context the event occurs. Information event elements typically do not change in their core values once they are created, although other information elements may be linked to it to describe the context in which the event occurred and any action taken as a result.
- **INFORMATION PROCESSING VARIABLES**—Private information values used by an information process as it executes. These values describe the context in which the process was started and in which information is being gathered from the information users of the information process. Some values are implicit in the code that drives the information process. Often the initial values of these information processing variables come from an information event that triggered the process to start. It is augmented with

information from the information users and it, in turn, populates an information activity, which is the persisted information about the work that the information process is supporting.

- **INFORMATION PAYLOAD**—Information values packaged up for sending over the network. Information payloads have a short lifetime. At the start, they reflect the originator's view of the information. As it flows through the network, it may be transformed and enriched to match the needs of the destination(s).
- **INFORMATION LINK**—Attributes that provide the information necessary to identify and retrieve values from a specific information entry stored in a different information collection. The information link is typically stored as an attribute in another information element and the information processes managing the hosting information element control its lifetime. So the life cycle of an information link is different from the information entry it represents—creating some interesting challenges.
- **INFORMATION METRIC**—Information values that have been derived from other values to illustrate how well the organization is performing in a particular aspect of its operation. Information metrics are constantly refreshed, but maintain a historical record of their values to allow point-in-time queries.
- **INFORMATION CODE**—A representation of an information value. Sets of related information codes are grouped together into code tables and are used to govern the values used in an information attribute.
- **INFORMATION SUMMARY**—Summarized information kept for historical analysis. It is updated periodically as time passes because more values become available for summarization.

Information about a subject area (topic) is not restricted to a single kind of information element. For example, consider the customer details subject area. When information is being collected to register a new customer, customer details are collected in information process variables and then possibly stored in an information activity if this is an auditable process. When the customer is established, his or her details will be managed as an information asset. When information about a customer is sent between information nodes, it is stored in an information payload. An order may link to customer details using an information link and, finally, customer details may appear in information summaries and information metrics for reporting purposes.

This example illustrates the importance of identifying and classifying the information elements because these are the strongest indicators of how each piece of information should be managed.

Also notice that information elements reference one another and some elements are created from others. As a result, errors should be removed from information as early as possible because they can rapidly become proliferated to multiple information collections, which in turn impacts multiple information processes. In addition, we must consider the following:

- How we manage different information elements that may nominally carry the same information but are located in different places and hosted by different technology
- How we maintain relationships between different kinds of information elements when each has its own independent life cycle

Some answers to these questions can be found in the pattern descriptions for the specialized information elements and their related patterns.

Consequences

Benefits:

- Understanding the information elements associated with the information processes of an organization helps to ensure the information is properly managed throughout its life cycle.

Liabilities:

- Organizations typically have limited budgets for information management. The temptation is to categorize all of the information it manages—taking time and resources and yielding limited value. It is important to focus on the information that supports the most critical information processes for the organization. Once this is properly categorized and managed, the next focus should be on removing the information that either has no value, or represents a liability because it is inaccurate or obsolete.

Example Resolved

In order to sell goods to its customers, MCHS Trading manages information elements relating to its customers, the products it sells, and the orders that have been placed. MCHS Trading also needs to create invoices, packing lists, and process payments.

Figure 4.2 shows where this information is located and the type of life cycle it belongs to. Notice that even for this fairly simple use case, there is a lot of information required and it is duplicated across many of the INFORMATION NODES (systems). Each copy is likely to be structured differently.

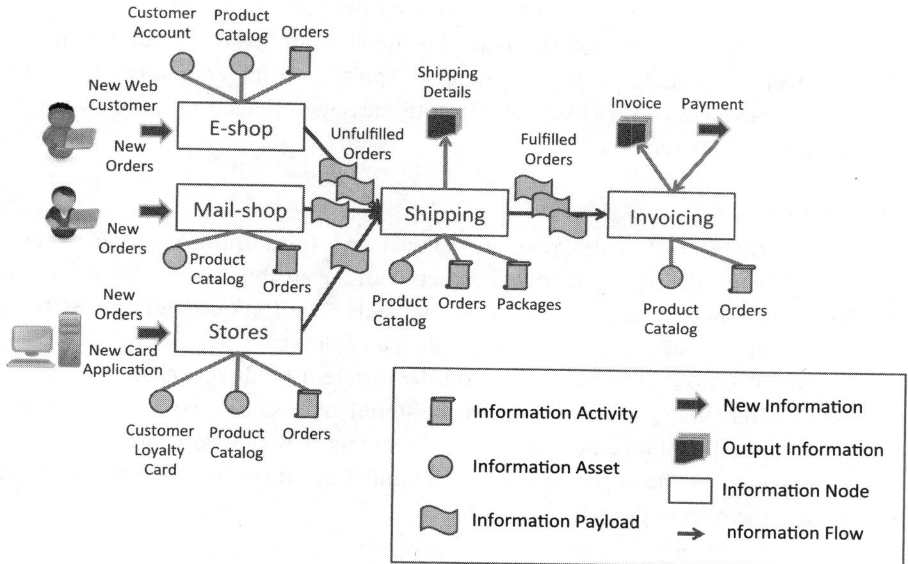

Figure 4.2 Examples of information elements in MCHS Trading's information nodes.

Known Uses

The generic concept of an information element is defined during the logical modeling of information structures. Groups of related attributes—for an object, for example, or an entity or a table—are referred to as model elements.

Aspects of an organization's information are classified into different kinds of information elements whenever an investment is being considered. This could be during the formation of the INFORMATION STRATEGY, when an INFORMATION GOVERNANCE PROGRAM is being set up or extended, or at the start of an INFORMATION SOLUTION. Further information elements are identified as these projects progress.

Practitioners recognize the different kinds of information elements, identifying and cataloging their occurrences whenever they are found, and using specialized technology to manage them. Associated practices on how to manage each kind of information element have also been developed. These are documented in the pattern descriptions for each kind of information element. However, to illustrate the point here, consider the INFORMATION ASSET pattern. This type of information element is often referred to as master data. Master data is managed using the Master Data Management (MDM) practices and there are specialized MDM technologies to manage this information. Now consider the INFORMATION LINK pattern. There are standards developed around this type of data such as the World Wide Web Consortium (W3C)'s uniform resource locator (URL) and Open Services for Lifecycle and Collaboration (OSLC). These standards have best practices and specialized technology to manage them. Finally, consider the INFORMATION PAYLOAD. To Enterprise Application Integration (EAI) practitioners, this is called a message, and it is supported using message-oriented technologies such as queues and publish-subscribe services.

Related Patterns

A SUBJECT AREA DEFINITION describes the subject area for an information element. An INFORMATION MODEL describes the logical structure of the attributes within an information element and the relationships between information elements. The INFORMATION SCHEMA describes an implementation structure for an information element.

The sections that follow give more detail on the different kinds of information element identified above. Different kinds of information can be stored in the same repository (information collection) and are often linked together—despite the fact that they typically have different life cycles. We need to recognize the occurrences of each kind of information within an information collection to manage them appropriately.

Entity-Level Information Elements

The patterns in Table 4.2 describe particular kinds of information elements that represent the attributes of an entity that the organization wants to manage (such as details of a person, place, object, event, activity, and more). We call them entity-level information elements. They are found in INFORMATION NODES. They are typically stored as an INFORMATION ENTRY in an INFORMATION COLLECTION. Each kind of entity-level information element has a different pattern in their life cycle that requires a different approach to managing and synchronizing it.

Table 4.2 Entity-Level Information Elements

Icon	Pattern Name	Problem	Solution
	INFORMATION ASSET	An organization needs to retain information it knows about the goods and services it offers, the assets it has, and the relationships it maintains with other parties (people and organizations).	Centrally manage this information and synchronize changes with other copies.
	INFORMATION ACTIVITY	An organization must track its activities to ensure it keeps its promises to deliver value and, as a consequence, receives appropriate recognition.	Manage this information close to the information processes that are supporting the activity and distribute read-only copies once the activity is complete.

Icon	Pattern Name	Problem	Solution
	INFORMATION EVENT	Something significant has occurred and the organization needs to react to it.	Store the event for audit purposes and send a read-only copy to the parties that must react to the new situation.
	INFORMATION PROCESSING VARIABLES	An information process needs access to information about how and why it was started and any work-in-progress values it has.	The information process maintains this information in memory while it is running. This includes links to relevant entries in the information collections. It stores any new values into the appropriate information collections before it completes.
	INFORMATION SUMMARY	Detailed information that is collected and used in the short term has decreasing value as time passes.	Combine the detailed operational data into summaries that retain enough detail for historical analysis, without recording the fine-grained detail of every activity.

Information Asset

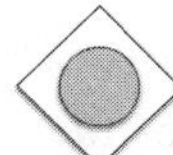

Context

The way an information element is managed depends on what it represents and how it is used.

Problem

An organization needs to retain information it knows about the goods and services it offers, the assets it has, and the relationships it maintains with other parties (people and organizations).

This type of information describes the physical world. It provides the background information for many of the activities in the organization. It enables the organization to document the complex interaction it has with the physical world. What are the information management approaches required to manage this type of information?

Example

MCHS Trading needs to maintain a product catalog and details of customers who have registered with the E-Shop or have a store card.

Forces

- **Widely distributed information—**This type of information is needed in many of the information processes used by the organization because it describes the key concerns of the organization.
- **Slowly changing—**This type of information changes in a slow and continuous manner.
- **Inconsistent validation—**The set of valid values for an information element may not be consistent throughout the organization.
- **Varying coverage—**Not all parts of the organization use the same subset of attributes about the type of information.

Solution

Purposefully maintain as little information as possible about the physical world and actively coordinate how this information is updated and distributed.

This type of information is called an information asset because it has enduring value across many activities of the organization and needs to be managed and maintained to preserve its value.

Within an information collection that contains information assets, there would be:

- An identifier, typically assigned by the organization
- Some basic attributes that the asset is known by outside the organization
- Information values that are shared by many of the other copies of this information
- Information values that are unique to this copy

The state of the physical world is outside of the control of the organization. Even when it describes physical assets that the organization owns, it cannot be sure when it will break, or be needed by someone. This means it takes a proactive approach to keep this information up to date. Such updates need to be distributed among all of the copies.

The principles for managing information assets are as follows:

- Maintain only the information that has value to the organization. This requires coordination between each part of the organization using this information to define what is really required. There will be differences in scope, precision, and vocabulary so these negotiations can take time and, inevitably, flexibility is required.
- Pay special attention to how individual instances are uniquely identified and mapped to the physical world.
- Be realistic about the rate of decay of this information and take steps to refresh the values when appropriate.
- Look for mechanisms that will allow you to automatically refresh the information from external sources.

- Minimize the places where this information is maintained.
- Coordinate the synchronization to other, reference copies.

Consequences

Benefits:

- Consistently managing your information assets creates an organization that is acting in a consistent manner with respect to the physical world objects, people, and assets they represent. It is also able to react to change because information remains stable even though the information processes will change.

Liabilities:

- Consistently managing information assets needs a mature organization that is willing to collaborate and agree how this information should be managed and paid for. We call this an INFORMATION CENTRIC ORGANIZATION.

Example Resolved

MCHS Trading maintains its product catalog in a single application called Product Hub. Once updates are made, read-only copies of the product descriptions are distributed to the other applications that need the product details using MIRRORING PROVISIONING.

The story for customer details is more complex because both the Stores and the E-Shop maintain their own customer details. The Mail-Shop applications only take a customer's details as part of an order. MCHS Trading installed a Customer Hub (INFORMATION ASSET HUB pattern) to act as the consolidated master for customer details that synchronizes updates between itself, E-Shop, and Stores using PEER PROVISIONING.

Known Uses

Information assets are often referred to as **master data** in operational systems and **dimensional data** in data warehouse and business intelligence systems. The approach used to manage this type of information is called Master Data Management (MDM).

Related Patterns

Information assets can be centrally managed in an INFORMATION ASSET HUB. This is a specialized INFORMATION NODE that actively manages the quality of the information assets stored within it,

The information assets are stored as INFORMATION ENTRIES in an INFORMATION COLLECTION. The information collection patterns provide details of how to classify the role, scope, and coverage of an information collection.

The INFORMATION KEY patterns describe approaches to uniquely identifying information assets.

Synchronizing between the information collections can be done using MIRRORING PROVISIONING if synchronizing from a master to a reference, or between reference copies, and using PEER PROVISIONING if between masters.

Information Activity

Context

The way an information element is managed depends on what it represents and how it is used.

Problem

An organization needs to keep track of its activities to ensure it keeps its promises to deliver value and receives appropriate recognition.

This information is sometimes referred to as the transaction record of the activity and is used to record the decisions and actions of the information processes that are supporting the activity. Once the activity is complete, the organization may need to understand why a decision was made—or why an activity resulted in a particular outcome. Typically, this analysis happens some time after the event and the values of related information assets may have changed since the work was carried out.

Example

MCHS Trading must keep track of the orders it has accepted to make sure it delivers the goods as promised and collects appropriate payment. Once the order is shipped, MCHS Trading needs to know the actual name and address of the customer that was associated with a particular order in case there is an issue with the delivery. This is particularly important when a customer changes his or her address—was the order associated with the old address or the new one?

Forces

- **Activity is distributed**—Not all of the activity to fulfill a business commitment occurs at the same time, place, or through a single information process.
- **Intermittent failures occur**—One or more information nodes may fail while an activity is partially complete. The information supply chain needs to recover and continue with the activity.
- **Historical information is required**—Not all information nodes are able to support temporal queries and so this historical information must be stored away from the originating information collection.

Solution

Create a record of each activity with information about the environment in which the activity took place.

An information activity is a stored record of a business activity. While the activity is in progress, one or more information processes that are supporting the business activity maintain it.

The information held within an information activity typically includes the following:

- Links to the information assets that are involved in the activity
- Links to the information events that are relevant to the activity
- Details of the steps that have been processed so far and the current state of the activity

The information activity is typically persisted as an information entry in an information collection.

When the information process is complete, the information activity is marked as complete and this final update is persisted to the information collection. The information activity is not updated again. It may be retrieved at a later time to understand how the activity was processed.

When the information activity is no longer needed for reference, it can be either deleted or archived to free up operational storage.

Consequences

Benefits:

- The information activity pattern provides an elegant solution for storing the values associated with an information process along with its current state.

Liabilities:

- When an information process spans multiple information nodes, the out-of-date information activities are left on the information nodes that have completed their processing. Knowledge of the structure of the information process is needed to chase down the most up-to-date copy of the information activity.
- At some point in time after the information process instance has completed, the information supply chain must either archive or delete the information activity because the number of information activities grows over time.
- Storing the information activities once the information process is complete results in lot of additional information being kept for the rare occasion when it is necessary to investigate the processing or a particular piece of work. So the ability to understand a complete picture in these circumstances needs to be weighed against the increase in information being stored.

Example Resolved

When one of the MCHS Trading order-taking applications—E-Shop, Mail-Shop, or Stores—takes an order, it creates an information activity to represent the order.

Order information stored by MCHS Trading's applications always includes details of the customer's name, address, and customer number. It also includes the date and time the order was taken and the channel used. This means that there is a permanent record of where the goods were sent, even if the customer changes address at a later date.

This order information is sent to the Shipping application, which packages up the ordered goods and sends them to the customer. The order information is updated with the package information and the date it was sent. Then the order information activity is sent to the Invoicing application, where an invoice is sent and the payment is received. Again, the Invoicing application records the progress of collecting the payment in the order information activity.

When the order information activity is passed to the Shipping application, the order-taking applications do not update their copy of the activity again. Similarly, when the Shipping application sends the order information activity to the Invoicing application, it no longer updates its copy. The result is that you have to query the right application to find the latest state of the order, and there are three copies of the order information activity to delete/archive when they are no longer needed.

Known Uses

An information process will use an information activity to store information about the business transaction it is processing.

In data warehouse applications, information activities are sometimes called transaction records, which are stored in fact tables in the data warehouse. These information activities may be consolidated from the various operational systems running the organization's business.

Related Patterns

An information activity typically describes the status of one or more instances of an **I**NFORMATION **P**ROCESS. It is fed from the **I**NFORMATION **P**ROCESSING **V**ARIABLES of these information processes.

Information activities can be centrally stored and maintained in an **I**NFORMATION **A**CTIVITY **H**UB.

When **D**AISY **C**HAIN **P**ROVISIONING is being used, a copy of the information activity is put into an **I**NFORMATION **P**AYLOAD, which is sent between the supporting **I**NFORMATION **N**ODES using an **I**NFORMATION **F**LOW or an **I**NFORMATION **R**EQUEST.

Information Event

Context

The way an information element is managed depends on what it represents and how it is used.

Problem

Something significant has occurred and the organization needs to react to it.

Such an event can have consequences, either immediately, or sometime later.

Example

An MCHS Trading customer phones the customer support center to notify the organization that he has changed his address.

Forces

- **Auditors require proof—**It is not enough for an organization to comply with a regulation—they need to be able to demonstrate that they are compliant.
- **Events happen in many places—**It is necessary to capture the event type, time, location, and context in which it occurred.
- **Events happen in awkward places—**The information process or individual who detects a significant event may not be the place where it can be processed.

Solution

Record the event and send it to the parties who must react to the new situation.

The record of an event is called an information event. The type of information in an information event information element includes the following:

- The type of event
- The date/time it occurred
- Who or what detected it
- The information process that was executing, plus some of its context
- Links to other related information elements
- Other relevant information values

The life cycle of an event is simple. The record of the event is created and stored. It may be retrieved, read, and copied to different locations. However, the content should never be changed from the time it is created to the time it is deleted. This means it is a true record of the event as it was detected at a particular moment in time. When the event is processed, it is linked to the information activity relevant to this processing.

Consequences

Benefits:

- Understanding and managing the important events that occur in an organization helps it plan for how it should react when certain events happen.

Liabilities:

- Events are happening all of the time. It is important to focus on those that are significant to the organization.

Example Resolved

The customer service representative creates a customer address change event information element. This causes the new customer address information process to run, which looks up the customer in the Customer Hub to discover the list of accounts that the customer has. It then updates the address first in the Customer Hub, and then in any other system that holds the customer details.

Known Uses

Information events are sometimes referred to as notifications. They are often saved to an audit log as a record of what is happening.

The **Common Base Event** standard provides a comprehensive view of the type of information that should be included in an information event: http://www.eclipse.org/tptp/platform/documents/resources/cbe101spec/CommonBaseEvent_SituationData_V1.0.1.pdf

Related Patterns

Information events typically act as **I**NFORMATION **T**RIGGERS to start an appropriate **I**NFORMATION **P**ROCESS to react to the event.

The **S**TATE **D**RIVEN **P**ROCESS is an information process that is driven by information events.

The **I**NFORMATION **E**VENT **S**TORE provides managed storage for events.

Information Processing Variables

Context

The way an information element is managed depends on what it represents and how it is used.

Problem

An information process operates in a context that defines why it was started and the existing information elements that it should be working with.

It needs easy access to the information for every step of its processing.

Example

What is the context of the New Order information process running in E-Shop?

Forces

- **Private information—**The context is an integral part of the implementation of an information process.
- **Limited lifetime—**Some of the context may only be relevant to the information process and not needed once the information process has completed.

Solution

Information values that describe the context are made available to the information process while it is running.

The information processing variables refer to the in-memory variables of an information process. It is created then the information process is initialized using values from the INFORMATION EVENT that triggered the information process.

The values in the information processing variables are displayed to INFORMATION USERS through user interfaces. As the information process progresses, its knowledge of the context in which it is running grows as it is fed new information through these user interfaces. Additional values are acquired through the INFORMATION SERVICES that access information stored in the INFORMATION COLLECTIONS.

The information process persists relevant parts of its information processing variable to an INFORMATION ACTIVITY, or other relevant information elements such as information events and INFORMATION ASSETS.

Consequences

Benefits:

- The information processing variables pattern clarifies the information that is being used by an information process. It provides a definition of the information dependencies that an information process has.

Liabilities:

- The information processing variables are lost when the information process ends—regardless of whether it succeeded or failed. Any of the information processing variables needed beyond the end of the life of the information process should be persisted into other information elements before this happens.

Example Resolved

When the New Order information process is started, it has very little knowledge of its context beyond the implicit knowledge that a potential customer wants to order something from MCHS Trading's product catalog.

The customer may be logged in to E-Shop, in which case, New Order can retrieve the logon details and map them to an information entry in the customer details information collection. The INFORMATION KEY of that entry is stored in New Order's information-processing variables.

Through its user interface, New Order guides the customer through the process of selecting the products he or she wants to order. These order items are stored in the information-processing variables.

Once the customer has selected the products he or she wants to order, New Order retrieves the address and payment details about the customer from the customer details information collection if he or she is a known customer, or invites the customer to enter the details directly. A new information entry in customer details is created if this is a new customer.

New Order creates a new information entry in the order details information collection and puts the information key of this new entry into its information-processing variables. This is the order number that will be displayed to the customer once the order is successfully completed.

This Order Details information entry is the information activity for the customer's order. The information key of the customer's details, the items ordered, and any payment details are added to this information element.

Once the order completes successfully, the New Order information process terminates and the information-processing variables are deleted.

Known Uses

In BPMN 2.0,[1] the information-processing variables are specified using data objects.

The information-processing variables typically implemented as a set of local variables within an information-process implementation. They live mainly in memory, but may be stored in an information collection to enable the information process to be restarted or recovered partway through if the information node is capable to restarting processes partway through.

Related Patterns

The INFORMATION PROCESS uses information-processing variables to manage private information about the activity it is supporting.

The permanent record of how one or more information processes supported an organization's activity is stored in an INFORMATION ACTIVITY. The information activity is populated from the information-processing variables of these information processes.

1. http://www.omg.org/spec/BPMN/2.0/

Information Summary

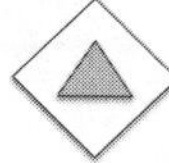

Context

The way an information element is managed depends on what it represents and how it is used.

Problem

Detailed information that is collected and used in the short term has decreasing value as time passes.

An organization needs to retain historical information to enable it to compare current operations against those in the past. However, this takes up a lot of storage.

The information recorded in the operational systems is designed to enable the organization to know exactly where they are in an activity so they can manage both the expected and unexpected events that occur in any organization.

Example

In MCHS Trading when a package is shipped, details of the packaging style, truck, batch, drivers, route, intermediary depots, weather, and a full set of timings for each stage of the journey are recorded. This is to make it possible to locate a lost shipment or prove the goods were delivered, or similar types of incidents. MCHS Trading also uses this summary to monitor the effectiveness of the delivery companies it uses.

Forces

- **It is hard to know what information you might need in the future**—The temptation is to keep it all just in case.
- **The value of information can diminish over time**—As such, it may not be cost effective to keep it forever.
- **Information must be viewed in context for it to be understood correctly**—Not everyone in an organization will use the same terminology, precision, validation rules, or have the same expectations for information quality and timeliness.
- **Storing information that is never going to be used is wasteful**—Storage costs money to buy and power to operate.

Solution

Combine the detailed operational data into summaries that retain enough detail for historical analysis, without recording the fine-grained detail of every activity.

The design of these summaries, called INFORMATION SUMMARY information elements, must reflect both the key pieces of information, plus the context in which the information was created.

Consequences

Benefits:

- Using summary information elements will reduce the storage necessary for keeping historical information. More important, designing summary information elements for this purpose means the information kept includes the context in which it was created.

Liabilities:

- It is possible that information needed in the future was not anticipated and is discarded in the summary process. Also, the summarizing logic requires an additional information process to be maintained and run.

Example Resolved

The detailed shipping information is summarized into two information elements as follows:

- A summary of the package shipment, including the following:
    1. Order number
    2. Package number
    3. Shipment date/time
    4. Delivery date/time
    5. Shipping company

- A summary of each shipping incident, including the following:
    1. Incident number
    2. Order number
    3. Package number
    4. Incident raise date/time
    5. Incident type
    6. Incident description
    7. Incident resolution type
    8. Incident completion date/time

These two types of summaries cover the minimal information about a shipment for most packages that are delivered without incident. When issues occur, additional information is kept about the shipping incident.

Known Uses

Rolling up information into summaries is common practice in data warehousing systems, less so in operational systems, which typically focus on creating the detailed information elements, such as information assets, information activities, and information events.

Related Patterns

The HISTORICAL SYSTEM OF RECORD solution makes extensive use of information summaries.

The INFORMATION SUMMARIZING PROCESS generates information summaries.

Message-Level Information Elements

The INFORMATION PAYLOAD information element shown in Table 4.3 describes how information is represented as it flows between information nodes. They are used both in INFORMATION REQUESTS and INFORMATION FLOWS.

Table 4.3 An Information Element Used to Send Information Between Information Nodes

Icon	Pattern Name	Problem	Solution
	INFORMATION PAYLOAD	Some information must be passed from one information node to another.	Package up the information into a well-defined schema that includes the context and action required in addition to the information values.

Information Payload

Context

The way an information element is managed depends on what it represents and how it is used.

Problem

An organization needs to verify that the information being passed between information nodes is being processed appropriately.

The information transmitted may be misleading or incomplete because it was created under different assumption to the information processes that will consume it at the destination. The information may be of a sensitive nature and need special protection. How does the organization ensure the appropriate information is sent between the information nodes?

Example

Orders are sent from MCHS Trading's order-taking systems—E-Shop, Mail-Shop, and Stores—for processing first by the Shipping application and then by the Invoicing application. How does MCHS Trading ensure the right information is flowing to make this processing successful?

Forces

- **Information must be processed in context—**When information is received from a remote information node, it is necessary to understand the context under which it is sent in order to process it successfully.

Solution

Package up the information into a well-defined schema that includes the context and action required in addition to the information values.

The software that manages the transfer of information between information nodes must be passed the information to send in a flattened structure called an information payload. The information payload is then inserted into a message structure for transmission.

The content of the information payload is of no interest to the networking software. However, it is of interest to the sending and receiving information nodes and its format should be explicitly defined to ensure there is clear understanding of what is being sent, and for what purpose; otherwise, it is very difficult to maintain governance over the **I**NFORMATION **S**UPPLY CHAIN.

There are three sections that are needed within the information payload:

- **The information source—**Such as where the payload is coming from, the activity that originated the information, and the information assets that are associated with this request.
- **The action required—**What should the destination information node do with this information?
- **The information values that are being sent—**These are the parameters to the action required.

Consequences

Benefits:

- The information payload defines exactly what type of information is being exchanged between information nodes.

Liabilities:

- Many information payloads are defined based on the needs of the consuming information processes. These requirements may change as the operations of the organization evolve.
- The format of the information payload may need to change as it flows between the source and the destination information nodes. There are different approaches for which part of the processing is responsible for the transformation. Three suggestions are shown in Table 4.4.

Table 4.4 Supplementary Patterns for Information Payload

Icon	Pattern Name	Problem	Solution
	SOURCE-SPECIFIC PAYLOAD	An information process that needs to send information into an information supply chain is not able to transform data.	The source information process sends the data payload in its local format. The downstream information processes transform the data as required.
	TARGET-SPECIFIC PAYLOAD	An information process that needs to receive information from the information supply chain is not able to transform incoming data.	The source information process, or an intermediate information process, needs to transform the data payload into the required format before it reaches the destination information node.
	CANONICAL-BASED PAYLOAD	An information supply chain has many information processes that each understands its own data format. How can the process of transforming data be simplified?	Use a canonical data format for as many data payloads as possible. The information processes then only need to be able to transform data between their local format and the canonical format.

Example Resolved

The information payload that represents an unfulfilled order includes the following:

- Order ID
- Order-taking system
- Order date/time
- Customer identifier
- Customer name
- Billing address

- Delivery address
- List of items ordered with price
- Total order cost
- Amount paid

Known Uses

Information payload definitions are referred to as message structures or message schemas by message-oriented middleware and request/response operation signatures, or schemas that define the parameter list by service-oriented middleware.

Related Patterns

The INFORMATION REQUEST patterns show the interaction of the information payloads when information processes in different information nodes are exchanging information.

SEMANTIC MAPPING is a useful way to ensure the right information is being included in the information payload.

Attribute-Level Information Elements

These final kinds of information elements shown in Table 4.5 still have their own life cycles, but are typically located as complex attributes in the information elements described above.

Table 4.5 Information Elements That Are Stored as Complex Attributes

Icon	Pattern Name	Problem	Solution
	INFORMATION LINK	An information entry needs to store a reference to another information entry located in a different information collection.	Store information values that identify the information node, information collection, and information entry within the collection.
	INFORMATION METRIC	An organization needs to know how well it is performing.	Maintain the results of calculations that indicate how well the organization is performing.
	INFORMATION CODE	An information attribute has a fixed set of valid values that need to be efficiently stored and verified.	Use a code value for each of the valid values. The code value is stored and translated into a string format when it is displayed to a person.

Information Link

Context

The way an information element is managed depends on what it represents and how it is used.

Problem

An organization needs to be able to link together information entries from different information collections.

The information collections may be together hosted on the same information node, or distributed across different information nodes.

Example

MCHS Trading has an Order-Tracking information node that stores an information collection of in-flight orders. Each information entry in this information collection represents details of an order. The information entry needs to link to details of the customer (stored in the Customer Hub) and the products ordered (stored in the Product Hub).

Forces

- **Independent life cycles**—The maintenance of information entries in different information collections is independent of one another.
- **Broken links**—If an information entry is deleted, all of the other information entries that have links to it now point to missing information.
- **Link-based queries**—An information service is required to retrieve the information values from the information entry that is referred to in the information link.

Solution

Create a reference for the information entry and an information service that is able to return the values from the information entry on request.

An information link is an attribute in an information entry. It contains enough information about the linked to information entry to enable an information process to retrieve the information from a well-known service. Either the original information process that requested information from the information collection, or a new information process triggered by access to the information collection is responsible for retrieving the information values from the information entry.

Consequences

Benefits:

- Information links enable the latest information to be linked together and hence reduce the need to copy information into multiple information collections.

Liabilities:

- Information links can be broken when information entries are moved or deleted.
- An information link implies there is an information service that can retrieve the information values for an information entry based on the values stored in the information link. The values are only available if the information node hosting the information service is running.

Example Resolved

The information keys for the appropriate customer and the product details are used to implement the information links.

Known Uses

Information links are typically implemented using information keys. An information link typically contains the information key of the information entry being linked to and the code of the information processes that use the information link know which information service to call in order to get further details.

There is a semantic web standard called Open Services for Lifecycle and Collaboration (OSLC) that provides explicit mechanisms for supporting distributed information links. Each information entry is represented as a uniform resource locator (URL) that points to a service provider that can serve up the information values for that entry. The information link simply calls the URL to get the information. This has the advantage that the information service logic is not hard-coded into each information process that uses the link. However, it does require stable URLs and so server names and IP addresses should not be used in the URLs. The URLs should have logical names that are resolved by a directory service.

Related Patterns

INFORMATION KEYS provide unique identifiers for information links.

The SEMANTIC INTEGRATION information solution makes extensive use of information links.

Information Metric

Context

The way an information element is managed depends on what it represents and how it is used.

Problem

An organization needs information to understand how well it is performing.

Many organizations are judged on the profit they make and the confidence that they will continue to make that profit going forward. The way this confidence is measured is not an exact science, but investors and managers look for indicators that suggest whether the organization is growing or shrinking; has unmanaged risks; is operating legally and ethically; is in a stable, growing, or diminishing market; and more intangible aspects such a public perception.

The information systems need to produce the right information to enable people to assess these indicators.

Example

MCHS Trading is unsure how well it is performing in terms of customer growth and existing customer satisfaction.

Forces

- **Some information is mandatory**—Many regulations stipulate what type of information must be produced to demonstrate compliance.
- **Information may be combined from multiple sources**—Some metrics require calculations based on information gathered from multiple sources.

Solution

Maintain the results of calculations that indicate how well the organization is performing.

These results are recorded in information indicators. These information elements record the time the calculation was made, the parameters used, the calculation used (such as the model or formula), and the results. Sometimes the parameters are complex and include a large volume of information, in which case the indicator may just contain a reference to the parameter information.

Consequences

Benefits:

- Defining indicators and then recording and tracking these values creates a focus on the performance of the organization.

Liabilities:

- When people realize they are being measured on particular criteria, they change their behavior—which can have both positive and negative consequences.

Example Resolved

MCHS Trading has decided to maintain the following information indicators to understand how well it is serving its customers:

- A count of the number of new customers who have registered with either their loyalty card or their Internet shop, E-Shop
- The average number of orders each customer is making
- A segmentation of how many customers have not made an order in the last month, in the last 6 months, in the last year
- The percentage of packages delivered without incident
- The level of satisfaction recorded by customers on receipt of their orders
- The ratio of ordered goods to returned goods

These indicators, and how they trend over time, will help MCHS Trading to access how well its business is performing.

Known Uses

Information metrics provide key information for business intelligence applications such as management reporting. They are also known as Key Performance Indicators or Key Predictive Indicators—both shortened to KPI.

Analytical processes often generate information metrics called scores.

Related Patterns

INFORMATION **P**ATTERN **D**ETECTING **P**ROCESSES often calculate information metrics.

INFORMATION **R**EPORTING **P**ROCESSES often consume information metrics.

The **R**OLL UP **I**NFORMATION **S**UPPLY **C**HAIN can provide information for a new information metric.

Information Code

Context

The way an information element is managed depends on what it represents and how it is used.

Problem

An information attribute has a fixed set of valid values that need to be efficiently stored and verified.

Example

A customer's name includes a courtesy title, such as Mr, Mrs, Miss, or Dr. How is the value for courtesy title stored in Mail-Shop's order details information collection?

Forces

- The set of valid values changes over time.
- The valid values need to be displayed in drop-down menus for information users to select.
- The valid values may need to be displayed in different languages for different audiences.
- Each information node may implement a different set of valid values for an attribute in its information collections.

Solution

Use a code value for each of the valid values. The code value is stored and translated into a string format when it is displayed to a person.

An information code is defined as a small number of attributes. The first attribute is the code value and the other values are various string representations of that code value. The information code definitions are stored in their own information collection with the code value as the primary key.

The code value is stored in information collections that are using the information code for one of its attributes.

The information processes that consume an attribute containing the code value are written in a generic fashion to access the information code definition and use the values it contains. This avoids hard-coding the values in the information process logic.

Consequences

Benefits:

- Using an information code definition simplifies the maintenance of the valid values because they can be maintained by updating the information collection rather than having to change the display and validation code.

Liabilities:

- When information flows between information collections that are using information codes, the code values need to be translated from the set used in the source to the set used in the destination. This process is called transcoding.

Example Resolved

Mail-Shop uses information codes to represent the list of valid values for the courtesy title. This is illustrated in Figure 4.3.

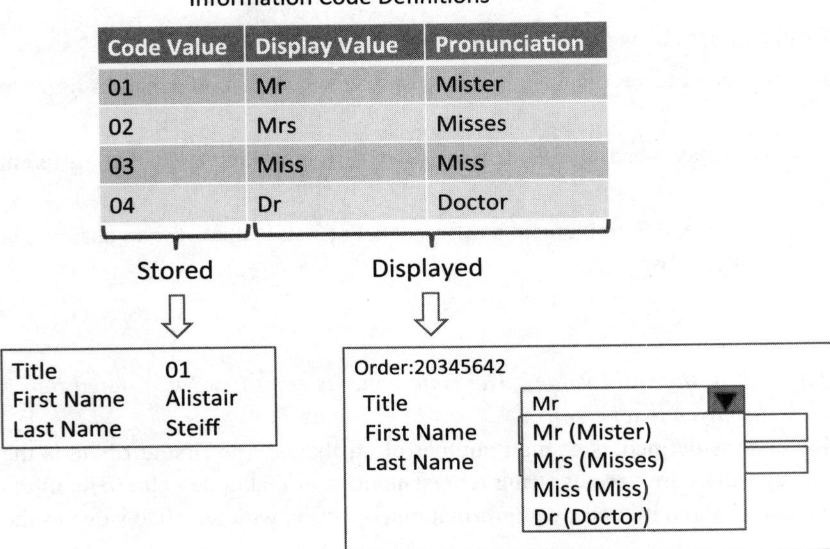

Figure 4.3 Example of using information codes for courtesy title.

Known Uses

Information codes are used in applications to define the valid values for an attribute. They appear in UML models as enumerations.

An information code is defined in a database as a row in a table where the information code value is the primary key and the other columns are the different string values.

Information codes are sometimes called reference data and the centralized management of code values and the mappings between code values in different information nodes is called Reference Data Management (RDM). Note there is a confusion of terminology here between the term reference data and the **R**EFERENCE **U**SAGE of an information collection. Reference usage is for information collections that have read-only usage by its information processes, so it has applicability beyond information codes.

Related Patterns

LOOKUP **T**ABLES are used by **I**NFORMATION **B**ROKERS to translate between the information codes used in different information nodes.

Summary of Information Elements

The information element patterns describe different life-cycle patterns found in an organization's information and the specialized practices and technologies that have evolved to manage them.

The next chapter looks at how an organization's information is classified, documented, and cataloged to provide a knowledge base for practitioners as they work to improve the information management provision for this information.

Information Identification Patterns

We like to think that the facts we know are correct—they are the truth. However, the truth is rarely absolute. It often reflects a point of view, and so we learn that to really understand the meaning of certain facts, we must understand the context around them.

An organization's information is also affected by the context in which it is collected—and this context is not always under the organization's control. For example, if the organization asked a customer for his or her email address, then, for most people, the answer given would depend on whether this request was related to work or to a leisure activity—because many people have different email addresses for each situation.

The context is typically a reflection of the activity that collected the information, the history of interaction between an individual and the organization, plus broader external influences. It can influence an information value itself, the level of precision we use in collecting the value, how sensitive it is, the degree of timeliness that is acceptable, and the length of time it is expected to be valid.

There are multiple contexts in operation at any one time. An individual has different personas and expectations for home, work, and leisure. This is true for organizations as well. Different parts of the organization are focused on different activities and may have a different context for its work. This is reflected in the information managed by the information nodes serving their part of the business.

In a standalone system, where the information collections are only used by local information processes, the context for the information within is pretty clear, and the built-in assumptions in the logic of the information processes, and the way that the people use the information is often in line with that context. But what happens when we repurpose information for new uses? For example,

- An information collection is made available to remote information processes through an information service.
- The contents of an information collection are packaged up and sent to a new copy where different information processes will use it.

In each case, how can we be sure that the new information processes understand the context around the original information collection?

The information identification pattern group covers the approaches commonly adopted to document what a piece of information is about and how it is used. The purpose is to ensure that the original context associated with information is not lost and there are no resulting misuses of information. The patterns cover the semantic definition of information, how it is structured, the validation rules that are associated with the information attributes, and summaries of the information values that are stored in various information collections owned by the organization. The lead pattern is INFORMATION IDENTIFICATION, which is shown in Table 4.6.

Table 4.6 Information Identification Pattern Summary

Icon	Pattern Name	Problem	Solution
	INFORMATION IDENTIFICATION	An organization does not know what types of information it has, where it is located, how it is managed, and who is responsible for it.	Investigate and document the information requirements and existing support available to the organization.

Information Identification

Context

An organization is documenting its information architecture as part of a program to improve its information management.

Problem

An organization does not know what types of information it has, where it is located, how it is managed, and who is responsible for it.

This affects the organization's ability to manage its information because it has no basis against which to assess success, detect issues, or drive improvement.

Example

MCHS Trading is committed to high customer service. To achieve this, MCHS Trading knows it needs to keep information about its customers and the activities that concern them. There have been some recent incidents where a customer has not received good service and this has been attributed to incorrect information about the customer or a product he or she has ordered.

To fix this, MCHS Trading must first understand the types of information it needs to keep, where it is located, and its level of quality. Then it can put measures in place to resolve any issues.

Forces

- **Different definitions—**The terminology and conventions around information may vary between different parts of the organization and IT systems.
- **People move on—**Changes in personnel over time reduce the available knowledge about an information collection.
- **Unknown content—**The contents of some information collections are not understood or clearly documented. The organization does not know whether it needs the information collection or, if it does—what levels of information management are appropriate.
- **Technical limitations—**Most IT systems are not able to supply semantic definitions of their information.

Solution

Investigate and document the information requirements and existing support available to the organization.

Information identification is an iterative process that is integrated into the organization's operational and project practices. It creates a set of information identification resources, where each resource defines an aspect of the organization's information requirements or provision. These resources are linked together and stored in a common repository so other teams can use them in future work.

There are a number of parts to information identification that are described in the following sections:

- **Defining Which Information to Manage and How—**First, it is necessary to establish the scope of the information to manage. This is in terms of its meaning, the values that are valid for this information, and the way it should be managed. This is part of establishing requirements for the project or standing team.
- **Defining How Information Is Structured—**Next, it is necessary to define how information is to be structured so it can be efficiently stored and accessed by the information processes. This is part of the design work for a project or standing team.
- **Locating the Right Information to Use—**To make use of existing information, it is necessary to know where it is so there are information identification resources that define where the different types of information are located. A team creates these resources when it creates a new information collection or investigates an existing information collection that has not been documented yet.
- **Different Reports About Information—**Finally, a project or standing team often needs to understand the characteristics of the information values that the organization has. This section defines reports on the information values for a particular type of information.

Each project or standing team is responsible for reviewing, developing, and using the information identification resources that are relevant to its work. Over time, as more teams perform information identification, these information resources expand to cover all the key information used by the organization.

Consequences

Benefits:

- Information identification creates a comprehensive and consistent definition of the information requirements and provision within an organization. This enables the organization to assess the state of its information management and drive improvements. The sharing of information identification resources reduces duplicated effort and increases the consistency of information management across the organization.

Liabilities:

- Information identification is only documentation. It must be maintained and used effectively to deliver value to the organization. Identifying, establishing, and maintaining the information identification resources takes time and requires commitment from both the business and IT parts of the organization to ensure this information is accurate and used where appropriate.

Example Resolved

MCHS Trading begins to build up a picture of the information it needs to support its customer-centric activities by creating the following information identification resources:

- A **S**UBJECT **A**REA **D**EFINITION documents the semantics of customer information, including name, address, and tax ID.
- **I**NFORMATION **L**OCATION resources are used to document the location of customer information in the information collections.
- Definition of the content, structure, and quality of the customer information is achieved through the **I**NFORMATION **M**ODEL and **I**NFORMATION **V**ALUES **P**ROFILE pattern.
- The **S**EMANTIC **T**AGGING pattern is used to ensure that the sources and content of the customer information are appropriately connected to the **S**UBJECT **A**REA **D**EFINITION.
- During design and development of a new **I**NFORMATION **S**UPPLY **C**HAIN, the **I**NFORMATION **F**LOWS that send customer information are appropriately validated through the **S**EMANTIC **M**APPING pattern.

As new information solutions are implemented, they use the previously established INFORMATION IDENTIFICATION resources and continue to extend it to cover more of the organization's information.

Known Uses

Information identification is used in the requirements gathering phases of many IT projects. It is sometimes referred to as **metadata management**. An example of an implementation of metadata management is described in:

- *Metadata Management Using IBM Information Server*, IBM Redbook, http://www.redbooks.ibm.com/abstracts/sg247939.html?Open

Related Patterns

Understanding what information is available, where it is located, and how it is managed is the first step to becoming an INFORMATION CENTRIC ORGANIZATION.

An INFORMATION GOVERNANCE PROGRAM makes extensive use of information identification resources.

Defining Which Information to Manage and How

This group of patterns in Table 4.7 defines how to describe the type of information that your organization needs to manage.

The SUBJECT AREA DEFINITION pattern provides a specification of a subject area, or topic, that an organization is keeping information about. For example, customer, product, account, order, invoice, and payment are examples of subject areas.

The VALID VALUES DEFINITION pattern defines rules for the values stored in an attribute or group of related attributes. This definition is a specification for validation rules used when new information is introduced into an information supply chain.

The INFORMATION CONFIGURATION pattern describes how the IT infrastructure is configured to support the appropriate information management behavior. Using configuration rather than hard-coding this behavior creates faster time to value and results in a more flexible infrastructure.

Table 4.7 Information Identification Patterns for Defining Information Requirements

Icon	Pattern Name	Problem	Solution
	SUBJECT AREA DEFINITION	An organization wants to document details of the information it keeps about a particular topic.	Describe the types of information values associated with the topic, and link them to definitions of how they are structured and where they are used.
	VALID VALUES DEFINITION	An organization wants to maintain consistency in the values that are allowed in a particular attribute across multiple information collections.	Define a rule or set to characterize the valid values allowed for the attribute in an implementation independent format. Use this definition as a requirement for all projects that implement an information collection that includes this attribute.
	INFORMATION CONFIGURATION	An organization wants to be able to modify the way that information is managed on an ongoing basis.	Deploy configuration at each of the key points of variability in the information processes that control how the information is managed. Provide the ability for appropriate information users to change and redeploy this configuration to modify how the information is managed.

Subject Area Definition

Context

An organization is documenting its information architecture as part of a program to improve its information management.

Problem

An organization wants to document details of the information it keeps about a particular topic.

This definition is focused on the semantics (meaning) of this information, rather than the implementation. The aim is to create something that the information users will understand and can agree that this is the type of information they need.

Example

MCHS Trading is focusing on the management of its customer information. The first question it asks is: What type of customer information does it need?

Forces

- **Information requirements are unclear**—The organization does not have a clear definition of the information needs of each group within the organization.
- **Inconsistent definitions**—Typically, each group has a slightly different set of requirements and/or terminology to describe its information needs and usage.
- **Local coverage of information**—Applications typically only store the subset of attributes that they need to perform their specific processing.
- **Semantic drift and quality erosion**—The meaning of terms, attributes, and information values gradually change over time. This change can occur at different rates in different parts of the organization.

Solution

Describe the types of information values associated with the topic, and link them to definitions of how they are structured and where they are used.

This description of a topic area is called a subject area definition. It consists of terms with a textual definition describing what it means and where is it used. The terms may be classified into related groups and linked together to show related concepts, synonyms, and antonyms.

This subject area definition becomes the authoritative source of documentation for the terminology in use in the organization and a nontechnical view of the information needs of the organization.

Consequences

Benefits:

- The subject area definition clarifies the meaning of information required by the organization.

Liabilities:

- Establishing and maintaining a subject area definition can be time consuming and requires commitment by the organization across and including business and technical teams.
- For a large organization, it may not be practical to create subject area definitions to cover all aspects of the organization's information needs. In this case, they can be created gradually, focusing on the high-value information first and then adding to it as projects and the organization's focus requires.

Example Resolved

MCHS Trading creates subject area definitions for Customer Details, Product Details, and Order Details.

Known Uses

There are a number of approaches to implementing a subject area definition in use today. The approach used by an organization depends on how formal a definition they need.

- **Glossaries**—A glossary is an alphabetically organized set of terms and their definitions. It can be used to create standard semantic definitions of the different types of attributes used by the organization. The attribute names used are based on the vocabulary used by people in the organization.
- **Taxonomies**—A taxonomy extends a glossary in that it provides a classification scheme around the terms and their definitions. With a taxonomy, it is possible to see how the attributes are related to the subject areas. It is consumable by both business and IT professionals.
- **Data dictionaries**—A data dictionary defines the meaning of the data fields implemented in databases, files, and messages. IT professionals use it to understand what values are stored in a particular repository.
- **Ontologies**—An ontology is a formal definition of the concepts and attributes in a subject area showing how they relate together. The ontology provides the most comprehensive view of the types of information that an organization wants to store. It must be created by ontology modeling experts and can become quite complex if its scope is large. The most useful ontologies typically only cover a small number of subject areas because this is about as much complexity that a person can comprehend.

Related Patterns

INFORMATION LOCATION provides an approach to defining the location of information within the information nodes.

INFORMATION MODELS define structures for the INFORMATION ELEMENTS that store information about the subject area.

SEMANTIC INTEGRATION is a solution pattern that shows how an ontology can be used to drive a federated style of information integration.

Valid Values Definition

Context

An organization is documenting its information architecture as part of a program to improve its information management.

Problem

An organization wants to maintain consistency in the values that are allowed in a particular attribute across multiple information collections.

This will broaden the number of people and information processes that will be able to interpret the information correctly.

Example

MCHS Trading wants to establish a set of valid values to support marketing by understanding how a customer learned about the products.

Forces

- **Information processes are implemented independently**—Each information process may hard-code different information validation rules and standards. When a change is required, it can take a lot of recoding.
- **Inconsistent definitions**—Typically, each unit has a slightly different set of requirements and/or terminology to describe its information needs and usage, which means different sets of valid values may exist for the same type of information.
- **Active information maintenance**—For the valid value definitions to remain an authoritative source of information needs, they must be regularly maintained and reviewed.
- **Semantic drift and quality erosion**—Over time, employees may come to assign certain existing valid values to new conditions, even if not truly accurate. Also, there may be default values that are used to represent unknown states or values that are used to quickly process information and avoid specific conditions. All of these can change the quality of the information.

Solution

Define a rule or set to characterize the valid values allowed for the attribute in an implementation-independent format. Use this definition as a requirement for all projects that implement an information collection that includes this attribute.

The rules or sets of valid values are called valid values definitions. They define whether the value assigned to one or more attributes is an allowable value—although not that it is necessarily the correct value.

There are a number of approaches to specifying a valid values definition. For example,

- Defining a list of valid values.
- Defining a range of values.
- Ensuring a selection of related attributes are consistent.

- Defining an authoritative source that lists the valid values. This may, for example, be a set of INFORMATION CODES, or a collection or INFORMATION ASSETS, that are known to be the complete set of valid values.

Consequences

Benefits:

- Creating and maintaining a set of valid values provides the definition of key information requirements for an organization. This can be used to facilitate an information governance program. It may also drive initiatives to optimize and simplify the IT system provision for the organization by identifying what information is considered valid by the organization.

Liabilities:

- In an ideal world, there is a consistent definition of the valid values for a particular piece of information that is checked when information is received/created and honored in each system. In reality, there will be many approaches to implementing the piece of information requiring different mechanisms to validate it. In addition, not all information processes will enforce the valid values either through age, bugs, or priority.

Example Resolved

MCHS Trading creates a set of valid values for Marketing Channel:

- "C" = other customer
- "E" = email
- "M" = mail (e.g., flyers)
- "S" = social media
- "W" = website

Known Uses

Valid values definitions are typically documented either in text, pseudocode, or using a rules package. A rules package allows rules to be defined in a human-consumable format, but with enough rigor that the rules can be executed in the IT systems.

There are many commercial rules packages available. The Object Management Group (OMG) has a rules standard called Semantics of Business Vocabulary and Business Rules (SBVR).[2]

2. http://www.omg.org/cgi-bin/doc?formal/08-01-02.pdf

Related Patterns

CHECK DATA is a REENGINEERING INFORMATION STEP that will check whether information values conform to a valid values definition. The INFORMATION VALUES PROFILE can report on the effectiveness of the information validation.

Information Configuration

Context

An organization is documenting its information architecture as part of a program to improve its information management.

Problem

An organization wants to be able to modify the way that information is managed on an ongoing basis.

The organization needs to set, control, and adjust processing thresholds, timing intervals, and similar parameter values.

Example

MCHS Trading wants to periodically tune the parameters of its automated matching of customer information from different information nodes to control the number of CLERICAL REVIEW PROCESSES generated for its INFORMATION STEWARDS by the INFORMATION MATCHING PROCESS.

Forces

- **Hard-coded behavior**—Many information processes have hard-coded implementations that require a code change to alter their behavior.
- **Validation of behavior**—No matter how it is specified, the behavior of an information process needs to be verified to ensure it is meeting the needs of an organization.

Solution

Deploy configuration at each of the key points of variability in the information processes that control how the information is managed. Provide the ability for appropriate information users to change and redeploy this configuration to modify how the information is managed.

A place in an information process where externally defined values are used to control its behavior is called a **point of variability**. The externally defined values are called the information configuration.

The information configuration values are set through the configuration user interfaces of an information node or information process, or through external rules packages that are called during the execution of the information processes.

When the information process reaches a point of variability, it retrieves and interprets the information configuration to determine the next step to take.

Consequences

Benefits:

- Using information configurations rather than hard-coded logic in its information processes provides an organization with more control over the behavior of its information processes on an ongoing basis.

Liabilities:

- Retrieving and interpreting information configuration can slow down the execution of an information process. If the information configuration values are changing slowly, they could be cached in memory and only refreshed when either the information process starts or the information node hosting the information process is restarted.

Example Resolved

MCHS Trading utilizes an **I**NFORMATION **M**ATCHING **P**ROCESS within its Customer Hub to match customer records from different information nodes together. This matching process has an information configuration that controls the matching process—including determining the thresholds where an information steward is required to verify the match. As its confidence with the effectiveness of matching configuration grows, MCHS Trading tunes the matching thresholds to specific levels to maximize high-quality matches and minimize manual review of common exceptions.

Known Uses

Information configuration is often used to allocate processing resources to an information process—such as a pointer to a persistence store, or memory or storage space. It is also used to set thresholds for when something happens—such as how long since it was last accessed should an information entry in an information collection be archived.

This configuration can also determine the way information is classified, which in turn determines which logic path it is processed on by the information process. For example, the configuration may determine the characteristics of a high-value customer, which may affect the way one of the orders is processed.

Related Patterns

INFORMATION **P**ROCESSES use information configuration to control their operation.

Defining How Information Is Structured

These patterns in Table 4.8 cover how information is structured.

Table 4.8 Defining How Information Is Structured

Icon	Pattern Name	Problem	Solution
	INFORMATION MODEL	Individuals in an organization need to discuss and document how information for a particular purpose is or will be structured.	Use a modeling language to create a well-defined logical model of the information elements, the attributes they contain, and the relationships between these elements.
	INFORMATION SCHEMA	An information process needs to understand how the attributes within an information element are structured in order to process it correctly.	Define a description of the structure of the information element that is both machine readable and human readable.

Information Model

Context

An organization is documenting its information architecture as part of a program to improve its information management.

Problem

Individuals in an organization need to discuss and document how information for a particular purpose is or will be structured.

This helps identify that attributes are stored, the kinds of information elements involved, and the way pieces of information are related to one another.

Example

MCHS Trading wants to create a Reporting Hub that supports a range of management decisions based on orders, sales, and stock inventory.

Forces

- **Inconsistent definitions**—Typically, each unit has a slightly different set of requirements and/or terminology to describe its information needs and usage, which means different sets of information elements must be reconciled for an effective information model.

- **Active information maintenance**—For the information model to remain an authoritative foundation of information needs, it must be regularly reviewed, maintained, and utilized. The most effective way to achieve this is to make the use and maintenance of the information model a part of selected employees everyday jobs.
- **Semantic drift and quality erosion**—Over time, employees may come to utilize certain information elements for purposes other than what was intended in the information model. Such use changes the context and quality of these elements in processing across the information supply chain and creates risk in effective use of the information model for subsequent applications.
- **Information volume**—The number of information elements to model, or the number of information models to maintain, may overwhelm the people performing the tasks.

Solution

Use a modeling language to create a well-defined logical model of the information elements, the attributes they contain, and the relationships between these elements.

Consequences

Benefits:

- The modeling process helps the team to think through the type of information it needs to capture.

Liabilities:

- The model needs to be kept up to date with the changes to the systems or it becomes useless. This takes governance in the software development life cycle.
- An information model only covers the static structure of information. It does not cover the dynamic aspects, such as when the information is available, or the level of quality and precision that is needed. This must be specified elsewhere in VALID VALUES DEFINITIONS and state machine models.

Example Resolved

MCHS Trading reviews the information elements from the information collections in the Customer Hub, Shipping, Invoicing, Purchasing, and Accounts Payable applications. It uses a modeling tool to establish an initial information model focused on sales of products to customers that includes sales details (as well as summaries by week, month, quarter, and year) and product cost per unit.

This information model is connected to the SUBJECT AREA DEFINITION to ensure that the information elements used in the model are clearly understood and is used to generate the INFORMATION SCHEMA for the Reporting Hub used by the report developers.

Known Uses

Information modeling is a well-established practice for relational database construction, and is a primary activity in designing and developing information processing to store information collections. Usage includes the following:

- Integrating multiple applications that contain pieces of information collections
- Acquiring and merging (or consolidating) new data sources into existing information models
- Designing, developing, and integrating into a data warehouse, data mart, or Master Data Management system

There are many types of information models, such as the following:

- Entity-relationship data models are used to describe how information is persisted in a database or file.
- UML class diagrams are used to describe how information is structured in applications, information processes, and information services.
- An ontology model is used to describe the concepts and the relationships between them in a subject area.

Related Patterns

An information model describes the structure of an INFORMATION ELEMENT or an INFORMATION ENTRY.

Information Schema

Context

An organization is documenting its information architecture as part of a program to improve its information management.

Problem

An information process needs to understand how the attributes within an information element are structured in order to process it correctly.

Example

MCHS Trading wants to create a Reporting Hub that supports a range of management decisions based on orders, sales, and stock inventory.

Once the INFORMATION MODEL for the Reporting Hub is defined, it needs to be translated into a technical form usable by the information processes that will store information in the Reporting Hub and those that will report on the contents.

Forces

- **Information requirements are unclear**—The organization does not have a clear definition of the information needs of each unit within the organization.
- **Inconsistent definitions**—Typically, each unit has a slightly different set of requirements and/or terminology to describe its information needs and usage, which means different sets of information elements must be reconciled for an effective information model and its associated information schema.
- **Active information maintenance**—For the information schema to remain usable by the information processes, it must be regularly reviewed, maintained, and utilized. The most effective way to achieve this is to make the use and maintenance of the information schema a part of selected employees everyday jobs.
- **Ad hoc change**—For information schemas to remain effective, they need to remain aligned with their associated information models. Ad hoc changes to the information schemas to quickly address problems result in schemas that are no longer aligned to their information models.
- **Semantic drift and quality erosion**—Over time, employees may come to utilize certain information elements for purposes other than what was intended in the information model and its associated information schemas. Such use changes the context and quality of these elements in processing across the information supply chain and creates risk in effective use of the information schema for information processing.
- **Information volume**—The number of information models to maintain and translate into schemas, or the number of ad hoc changes needed to schemas, may overwhelm the employees performing the tasks.

Solution

Define a description of the structure of the information element that is both machine readable and human readable.

Consequences

Benefits:

- The structure of the information is in a form that is both machine and human readable.

Liabilities:

- The schema must be updated when the information needs changes. Some teams are tempted to store information in available attributes that were designed for different values rather than update the schema.

Example Resolved

MCHS Trading uses a standard database management software (DBMS) product for its Reporting Hub. Its information modeling tool can automatically generate the scripts in the form needed by the DBMS to create an information schema.

This information schema is connected to the **S**UBJECT **A**REA **D**EFINITION based on the information model to ensure that the information elements incorporated are clearly understood by application and report developers.

Known Uses

Information schema generation is a well-established practice for relational database construction, and is a primary activity in designing and developing information processing to store information collections. Usage includes the following:

- Integrating multiple applications that contain pieces of information collections
- Acquiring and merging (or consolidating) new data sources into common information schemas
- Designing, developing, and integrating into a data warehouse, data mart, or Master Data Management system

Related Patterns

An information schema describes the structure of the implementation of an **I**NFORMATION **E**LEMENT or an **I**NFORMATION **E**NTRY.

Locating the Right Information to Use

These patterns shown in Table 4.9 describe the context in which information is being used.

Table 4.9 Information Identification Patterns for Locating Related Information

Icon	Pattern Name	Problem	Solution
	INFORMATION LOCATION	An organization does not know where its information is located, how well it is managed, and who owns it.	Create a description of the information collections hosted by the organization's information nodes and who is responsible for them. Link this definition to the appropriate subject area definitions.
	SEMANTIC TAGGING	An organization does not understand the meaning of the attributes within a data payload.	Use a subject matter expert to analyze and identify the meanings of the attributes. Document the meanings with their associated subject area. Link the meanings to the attribute definitions.

Icon	Pattern Name	Problem	Solution
	SEMANTIC MAPPING	An organization does not understand the relationship between attributes in two different information models.	Use semantic tagging to guide the mapping process.

Information Location

Context

An organization is designing how information must flow along an information supply chain.

Problem

An organization does not know where its information is located, how well it is managed, and who owns it.

Example

Certain customer demographic information falls under specific data privacy and reporting policies, such as date of birth, gender, and credit rating. Where is this information located?

Forces

- **Unknown data contents—**The location, content, format, ownership, and quality of the data in each system are not well understood.
- **Information governance—**Information governance is a priority for the organization.
- **Rapid organizational change—**New business and information initiatives need to rapidly identify how to obtain the required information.

Solution

Create a description of the information collections hosted by the organization's information nodes and who is responsible for them. Link this definition to the appropriate subject area definitions.

This definition should detail the name of the information node, who owns it, and the information collections it hosts. It should also detail the types of usage patterns that the information processes use and an estimate of the number of INFORMATION ENTRIES each information collection contains.

Consequences

Benefits:

- Once the provisioning inventory is complete, it needs to be maintained as systems are updated over time.
- This provisioning inventory may be used as a resource to understand where data is located during the development of an information supply chain.

Liabilities:

- Establishing and maintaining an inventory for information provisioning can be time consuming and requires commitment by the organization across and including business and technical units.

Example Resolved

Review the information collection in each information node and in the case of MCHS Trading's Stores Account customer demographic information, the contents of the information collection must be identified, appropriately tagged, and then designated for use in a provisioning inventory:

- Create the inventory of the Stores application, including the Account and Account Reference tables.
- Create an INFORMATION VALUES PROFILE to discover and analyze the data fields in the Stores application that are not clearly understood or documented.
- Establish business terms for Date of Birth, Gender, and Credit Rating through the SUBJECT AREA DEFINITION.
- Connect the Information Location entry for fields ACBDT, ACGCD, and ARCRT to the core business concepts through SEMANTIC TAGGING to ensure that the sources and content of the customer information are appropriately connected to the SUBJECT AREA DEFINITION.
- Identify the same or associated data for INFORMATION PROVISIONING through INFORMATION LINEAGE.

Known Uses

Information identification is a primary activity in managing information collections and moving data from one information collection to another. Usage includes the following:

- Integrating multiple applications, which contain pieces of information collections
- Acquiring and merging (or consolidating) new data sources

- Populating and maintaining information collections stored in a data warehouse, data mart, or Master Data Management hub
- Transforming and delivering messages from incoming information nodes to operational applications

Related Patterns

The information identification patterns—**S**UBJECT **A**REA **D**EFINITION, **I**NFORMATION **V**ALUES **P**ROFILE, and **S**EMANTIC **T**AGGING—can supplement the location definition.

Semantic Tagging

Context

An organization is designing how information must flow along an information supply chain.

Problem

An organization does not understand the meaning of the attributes within a data payload.

The business or semantic context of the data elements is not well understood or does not align with expected content.

Example

MCHS Trading maintains an information collection for Account data as part of the Stores system with associated customer information where there may be multiple accounts based on unique store location for any given customer. The system is an older application and while different individuals have understood the use of certain fields over time, the field names are quite cryptic and many individuals familiar with the system have left the organization. Aside from sporadic emails, there is nothing to connect the fields with their actual purpose. Even information found through data profiling may quickly be lost, such as the following:

- The ACXDT field in the Account table does contain dates, but only contains dates when the associated Account status field equals 'Canceled' indicating this is the Account Cancellation date.
- The ACMNM field in the Account table contains a mixture of names, cryptic 8-character alphanumeric values, and questions. This information not only needs to be segregated, but likely falls under new governance and data privacy requirements.
- The ACTID field in the Account table does contain tax identifiers though in a mixture of formats as well as many default values and other duplicated values, which must be accounted for in subsequent usage.

Forces

- **Information governance—**Information governance is a priority for the organization.
- **High cost/risk—**Incorrectly applied data in an information supply chain has a cost or risk to the business in the design, development, delivery, or management of that supply chain.
- **Unknown data contents—**The content, validity, and reasonableness of the data in each system is not well understood in its business context.

Solution

Use a subject matter expert to analyze and identify the meanings of the attributes. Document the meanings with their associated subject area. Link the meanings to the attribute definitions.

Apply automated data classification to identify potential semantics of each data element. Discover underlying sensitive and critical data elements. Assess data content, metadata definitions, and data lineage to link (or tag) data elements with their associated business terms to assign business context. Add additional links or tags as new systems are inventoried and additional data is profiled.

Consequences

Benefits:

- Once the semantic tags are created, they should be regularly reviewed for updates as systems, data, and semantics change over time.
- The semantic tags may be used as a resource to understand data structure, content, and quality during the development of an information supply chain.

Liabilities:

- If there are many different terms and information nodes within the information supply chain, the burden of creating and managing semantic tagging can be high.
- Establishing and maintaining a metadata collection of information terms for use in semantic tagging can be time consuming and requires commitment by the organization across and including business and technical units.

Example Resolved

In the case of MCHS Trading's account information, data stewards take advantage of a business glossary storing SUBJECT AREA DEFINITIONS where they can assign relationships and semantically tag the assets stored in a metadata collection:

- **I**NFORMATION **V**ALUES **P**ROFILE software that includes automated data classification tags the fields in the metadata collection with rough detail: The ACXDT field in the Account table is a Date; the ACMNM field in the Account table contains mixed Text; the ACTID field in the Account table contains a high percentage of tax identifiers, specifically Social Security numbers.
- Data analysts use the metadata collection, including the detailed analysis from an information values profile, to conduct a data-driven tagging and annotation to ensure greater accuracy in semantic tagging.
- Data stewards add labels to both the business glossary and known assets to facilitate further semantic tagging, and assign assets to glossary terms: The ACXDT field is assigned to the Account Cancellation Date term; the ACMNM is assigned to the Account Maiden Name term as well as the Account Password Reset term given the additional data present; and the ACTID field is assigned to the Account Tax Identification term.

Known Uses

Information identification is a primary activity in managing information collections and moving data from one information collection to another. Usage includes the following:

- Integrating multiple applications that contain pieces of information collections
- Acquiring and merging (or consolidating) new data sources
- Populating and maintaining information collections stored in a data warehouse, data mart, or Master Data Management system
- Transforming and delivering messages from incoming information nodes to operational applications

Related Patterns

The **S**UBJECT **A**REA **D**EFINITION**, I**NFORMATION **L**OCATION**,** and **I**NFORMATION **V**ALUES **P**ROFILE patterns can provide information on which data to tag with appropriate semantics. The **S**EMANTIC **M**APPING pattern can apply additional semantic tags through mapping relationships or can leverage semantic tags to determine mapping relationships.

Semantic Mapping

Context

An organization is designing how information must flow along an information supply chain.

Problem

An organization does not understand the relationship between attributes in two different data payloads.

The relationship of business or semantic terms to data elements is not well understood or does not provide sufficient insight in identifying and mapping information along the information supply chain.

Example

MCHS Trading is integrating account, demographic, and customer information from the Stores systems into its Customer Hub for downstream reporting. There are inconsistencies in data content and format across the systems and the developers of the Customer Hub do not understand which fields relate to which other fields. Without clear semantic relationships across data, prior projects have seen the following:

- The ACMNM field in the Account table was interpreted as a middle name field when it actually contains maiden name, resulting in incorrect customer names and failed attempts to correctly match customer data.
- The ACXDT field in the Account table was interpreted and used as the account creation date when it is actually the account cancellation date.
- The ACTID field in the Account table was interpreted as a customer ID when it is actually the tax identifier and incorrectly mapped to the customer ID in downstream systems.

Forces

- **Information governance**—Information governance is a priority for the organization.
- **High cost/risk**—Incorrectly mapped data because of semantic mismatches in an information supply chain has a cost or risk to the business in the design, development, delivery, or management of that supply chain.
- **Information requirements are unclear**—The relationship or mapping of the business semantics is not well understood in its relationship to the information supply chain.

Solution

Use semantic tagging to guide the mapping process.

Discover semantic mappings based on similarity of related terms, lexically similar metadata, data element relationships, and data lineage relationships. Apply additional semantic mappings across the discovered relationships.

Consequences

Benefits:

- The semantic mappings may be used as a resource in establishing the connections between information and data elements in the design and development of the information supply chain.
- Once the semantic mappings are created, they should be regularly reviewed for updates as systems, data, and semantics change over time.

Liabilities:

- If there are many different terms and information nodes within the information supply chain, the burden of creating and managing semantic tagging necessary for semantic mapping can be high.
- Establishing and maintaining a metadata collection of information terms for use in semantic mapping can be time consuming and requires commitment by the organization across and including business and technical units.

Example Resolved

In the case of MCHS Trading's integration of account, demographic, and customer information from the Stores systems into its Customer Hub for downstream reporting, MCHS data analysts have utilized the SUBJECT AREA DEFINITIONS and associated assets tagged with the terms in a metadata collection to enhance their mapping process:

- Data analysts and data stewards have tagged the ACMNM field in the Account table as maiden name in their metadata collection.
- The ACXDT field in the Account table is tagged as the account cancellation date.
- The ACTID field in the Account table is linked to the tax identifier with annotations to indicate it is not for use as a customer identifier.
- Data analysts use SEMANTIC MAPPING as part of their mapping specification process to discover similar fields with the same semantic tag in the new Customer Hub and the Reporting Hub.
- Where fields are not yet semantically tagged, the data analysts use the results from an INFORMATION VALUES PROFILE to review data contents and formats, explore overlaps across data sources, and suggest or recommend additional semantics in the SUBJECT AREA DEFINITIONS of the metadata collection.
- Where fields are linked in the mapping specification but only one of the fields contains the SEMANTIC TAGGING, the data analysts push the linkage into the metadata collection as new SEMANTIC MAPPING.

- The mappings created and captured in the metadata collection establish INFORMATION LINEAGE patterns, which enable more semantic mapping in the future.

Known Uses

Information identification is a primary activity in managing information collections and moving data from one information collection to another. Usage includes the following:

- Integrating multiple applications that contain pieces of information collections
- Acquiring and merging (or consolidating) new data sources
- Populating and maintaining information collections stored in a data warehouse, data mart, or Master Data Management system
- Transforming and delivering messages from incoming information nodes to operational applications

Related Patterns

The SUBJECT AREA DEFINITION, INFORMATION LOCATION, and INFORMATION VALUES PROFILE patterns can provide information on which data to tag with appropriate semantics.

The SEMANTIC TAGGING pattern can apply semantics to data through automated classification or discovery or via direct assignment, which can then be used to achieve SEMANTIC MAPPING.

The INFORMATION VALUES PROFILE pattern can add additional data elements, including detail on content and structure to the process of SEMANTIC MAPPING.

The information identification pattern INFORMATION LINEAGE can indicate where other occurrences of the same data exist, even where the field names differ, or where the data comes from or goes to, based on current process flows.

Different Reports About Information

This final group of patterns shown in Table 4.10 covers different types of reports on the organization's information.

Table 4.10 Information Identification Patterns for Reports

Icon	Pattern Name	Problem	Solution
	INFORMATION VALUES REPORT	An organization wants to review the values of some of its information.	Create a report that shows the information values of interest, typically with related summaries and metrics.

Icon	Pattern Name	Problem	Solution
	INFORMATION VALUES PROFILE	An organization does not know what type and level of quality of data is located in a particular information store.	Use a data-profiling tool to understand the types of data stored and range of values these types are set to.
	INFORMATION LINEAGE	An organization does not know where the information located in an information store could have come from.	Review design documentation, metadata, and existing system configuration and behavior to build up a picture of the information supply chain to the information store.

Information Values Report

Context

An organization is using the information it is managing and wants to assess its content.

Problem

An organization wants to review the values of some of its information.

The organization needs this information collated and summarized to help it understand the relevance and significance of the values it is reviewing in order to understand a particular situation.

Example

As part of its annual sales review, MCHS Trading needs reports by product type and brand that indicate how well such items have sold over the past year.

Forces

- **Relevant information is dispersed**—Often the information that an information user needs to make a decision is dispersed among different information collections.
- **Processing overhead**—Collating and summarizing information from multiple sources can require a fair amount of processing power. If a report is required frequently, it requires special provision to reduce the overhead.
- **What does it mean?**—Information from different parts of the organization may be collected with different assumptions that may create misleading results when they are consolidated together.
- **The effect of failures**—A failure in the information supply chain that provisions an information values report can cause misleading values in the report.

Solution

Create a report that shows the information values of interest, typically with related summaries and metrics.

An information values report provides summaries of some related information values. Information users use them to assess the state of the organization, the behavior of the teams and IT systems, along with the health of the business.

Information values reports are created by **I**NFORMATION **R**EPORTING **P**ROCESSES. These processes pull information together from multiple information collections to assemble the report contents.

Reports that are produced frequently typically have their own information collections that have been provisioned solely to support the needs of the report.

Consequences

Benefits:

- Consistent representation of information collections ensures that the information values reports have consistent meaning and can be effectively utilized to drive key business decisions and performance indicators.

Liabilities:

- In identifying information and information values, there is the possibility that information may be lost, incorrectly identified, or misapplied in the information nodes resulting in incorrect or invalid reports.
- If there are many different information nodes and data flows within the information supply chain, the burden of choosing the right information node for correct communication can be high. Decisions based on the wrong information can have significant negative consequences for the organization.

Example Resolved

For MCHS Trading's sales review, several ad hoc information values reports are created against the new Reporting Hub. One report shows the values for product type; one report shows the values for brand. In each case, the reports summarize total number of items sold, total gross sales, and total net sales by month, quarter, and year for the respective values.

The MCHS Trading buyers will note product types and brands with no sales or declining sales for discontinuation.

Known Uses

Information values reporting is supported by most applications to show the operational state of the aspect of the business. Business intelligence and specialized reporting packages provide more sophisticated information values reports that have been created from consolidated information collections such as data warehouses and data marts.

Related Patterns

An INFORMATION **R**EPORTING **P**ROCESS generates an information values report. It makes extensive use of INFORMATION **S**UMMARY and INFORMATION **M**ETRIC information elements. This is explained in the **P**ERFORMANCE **R**EPORTING information solution.

INFORMATION **W**AREHOUSES and INFORMATION **M**ARTS provide good sources of information for information values reporting.

The **S**UBJECT **A**REA **D**EFINITION pattern can provide information on the business definitions and usage to facilitate the right information identification in support of information values reporting.

The INFORMATION **V**ALUES **P**ROFILE pattern can provide information in advance of reporting on the contents of a given information collection, helping to ensure that quality issues are identified and resolved.

Information Values Profile

Context

An organization is using the information it is managing and wants to assess its content.

Problem

An organization does not know what type and level of quality of data is located in a particular information store.

Example

MCHS Trading maintains an information collection for Account data as part of the Stores system with associated customer information where there may be multiple accounts based on unique store location for any given customer. The system is an older application and due to system limitations certain fields have been reused for different purposes or contain multiple contents. Further, the field names are quite cryptic and many individuals familiar with the system have left the organization:

- It is believed that a field in the Account table called ACXDT contains the Account Activation date, but documentation has been lost.
- A field in the Account table called ACMNM is thought to store the customer's middle name for purposes of data consolidation to the Customer Hub but has caused errors during testing.
- The field in the Account table called ACTID is thought to store the tax identifier but seems to have inconsistent usage.

Forces

- **Rigid information processes—**The data structures used with each information node cannot be easily changed (this is particularly true when the information originates from or is flowing to third parties, such as government agencies or existing or packaged applications).
- **Unknown data contents—**The location, content, format, ownership, and quality of the data in each system are not well understood, preventing applicable rules and policies from being applied appropriately.
- **Information governance—**Information governance is a priority for the organization.
- **Rapid organizational change—**New business and information initiatives need to rapidly identify how to utilize the available information.

Solution

Use a data-profiling tool to understand the types of data stored and range of values these types are set to.

Data profiling typically occurs as a key step of information identification within an information supply chain initiative to provide data-driven understanding of the format, content, and quality of the actual data.

Consequences

Benefits:

- Consistent representation of information collections is achieved in the target information node without requiring modification of the source information node.
- Information collections are enriched with associated and relevant information.
- Reengineering data dynamically whenever it is moved along the information supply chain means the information nodes are free to structure their information collections to suit their internal needs.

Liabilities:

- In identifying information, there is the possibility that information may be lost, incorrectly identified, or misapplied in the information nodes.
- If there are many different information nodes and data flows within the information supply chain, the burden of information identification can be high.

Example Resolved

In the case of MCHS Trading's Stores application information, data profiling reveals key data considerations for each field that is captured, analyzed, and reported:

- The ACXDT field in the Account table does contain dates, but only contains dates when the associated Account status field equals 'Cancelled' indicating this is the Account Cancellation date.
- The ACMNM field in the Account table contains a mixture of names (that in some cases matches last name where the gender is female, suggesting it was originally a maiden name field), cryptic 8-character alphanumeric values (suggesting it stores some customer passwords), and questions (such as "What is the name of your first pet?" indicating it is used to hold password prompts). This information not only needs to be segregated, but likely falls under new governance and data privacy requirements.
- The ACTID field in the Account table does contain tax identifiers though in a mixture of formats (some with hyphens, some without) as well as many default values ('999999999') and other duplicated values that must be accounted for in subsequent usage.

Known Uses

Information identification is a primary activity in managing information collections and moving data from one information collection to another. Usage includes the following:

- Integrating multiple applications that contain pieces of information collections
- Acquiring and merging (or consolidating) new data sources
- Populating and maintaining information collections stored in a data warehouse, data mart, or Master Data Management system
- Transforming and delivering messages from incoming information nodes to operational applications

Related Patterns

The **S**UBJECT **A**REA **D**EFINITION pattern can provide information on the business definitions and usage to facilitate information identification.

The **S**EMANTIC **T**AGGING and **S**EMANTIC **M**APPING patterns can provide information on the relationship between the data and relevant business terms and definitions.

The information identification pattern **I**NFORMATION **L**INEAGE can indicate where other occurrences of the same data exist, even where the field names differ, or where the data comes from or goes to.

The **I**NFORMATION **P**RINCIPLE and **I**NFORMATION **L**OCATION patterns may provide policy and usage information to inform how this data source should be managed and maintained.

Information Lineage

Context

An organization is using the information it is managing and wants to assess its content.

Problem

An organization does not know where data located in an information store could have come from.

Existing data flows and relationships are not well understood or do not align with expected flows.

Example

MCHS Trading is attempting to understand the flow of data from the Stores systems as it builds its Customer Hub for downstream reporting. However, the lineage into the Order, Inventory, and Shipping systems is not recorded. Therefore, they cannot readily establish the following:

- Which fields are used to drive order fulfillment?
- Which customer data has precedence in the order?
- What is the origin of data on business reports?
- Which fields are critical to the upcoming Customer Hub and reporting initiatives?

Forces

- **Information governance—**Information governance is a priority for the organization.
- **High cost/risk—**Incorrectly applied data in an information supply chain has a cost or risk to the business in the design, development, delivery, or management of that supply chain.
- **Poorly understand information flows—**The flow and relationship of the data in and across each system in the information supply chain is not well understood or is no longer correctly described.

Solution

Review design documentation, metadata, and existing system configuration and behavior to build up a picture of the information supply chain to the information store.

Incorporate existing information supply chains into a metadata collection and review the associated data lineage. Discover underlying information flows and relationships, including information store and data mapping. Identify those data domains and elements that should be profiled and monitored.

Consequences

Benefits:

- Once the metadata collection is complete, or new information supply chains are built, it should be periodically updated as systems change over time.
- The data lineage may be used as a resource to understand data flows and relationships during the development of an information supply chain.

Liabilities:

- If there are many different processes and information nodes within the information supply chain, the burden of creating, managing, and understanding the data lineage can be high.
- Establishing and maintaining a metadata collection of information assets for use in data lineage can be time consuming and requires commitment by the organization across and including business and technical units.

Example Resolved

In the case of MCHS Trading's movement of Stores Account information into the Customer Hub, the bulleted activities are implemented as part of an information pathway:

- Data sources are captured in the metadata collection as part of the **S**UBJECT **A**REA **D**EFINITION.
- Process flows are added into the metadata collection linking one data source to another, either automatically as processes or jobs are implemented or manually when capturing older, existing processes or jobs.
- Ongoing executions of process flows add operational metadata to the **I**NFORMATION **L**INEAGE.
- **S**EMANTIC **T**AGGING allows users to build different views of the **I**NFORMATION **L**INEAGE in order to identify data usage in reports, as well as identify impacts of potential changes to the information supply chain.

Known Uses

Information identification is a primary activity in managing information collections and moving data from one information collection to another. Usage includes the following:

- Integrating multiple applications that contain pieces of information collections
- Acquiring and merging (or consolidating) new data sources

- Populating and maintaining information collections stored in a data warehouse, data mart, or Master Data Management hub
- Transforming and delivering messages from incoming information nodes to operational applications

Related Patterns

The INFORMATION LOCATION and SUBJECT AREA DEFINITION patterns can provide information on new metadata to incorporate into the data lineage views. The INFORMATION VALUES PROFILE, SEMANTIC TAGGING, and SEMANTIC MAPPING patterns can supplement the data lineage.

Summary of Information Identification

The information identification patterns describe the types of documentation that is useful to record your organization's information architecture. Next is the information provisioning patterns that describe how information is supplied to information processes.

Information Provisioning Patterns

Consider an information process running in an information node. How is information supplied to this process? That is the question that the information provisioning patterns seek to answer.

The most appropriate approach to information provisioning is dependent on a number of factors:

- What is the best source, or sources, of information?
- Where is this source located? Can the information be used directly in its current location or does it need to be moved or copied?
- How many other information processes need the same information and where are these information processes located?
- How much information is required? How large is the collection of information that is to be provisioned? Any copies will take up storage and there will need to be an initial load of the new collection to set it up. If we create a new copy, how long will it be needed for the initial load?
- How frequently does this information change? Any modifications to the original collection(s) may have to be sent to any copies. How much information will be flowing on an ongoing basis?
- What are the regulations and company policies that affect this information? For example, are there privacy, security, and other legal constraints affecting the distribution of this information?

- Will the information need to be transformed, enriched, or corrected in some way? How will that be achieved? Where is the most effective place to do this?
- How reliable does the synchronization of the collections need to be? Is it acceptable if some of the updates are lost due to an outage—or must the synchronization be perfect? What time lag is acceptable for changes to be reflected in the copies?
- How will the provisioning be triggered? Is this a business decision, which must be coded in the appropriate information process, or can the infrastructure detect particular events and trigger provisioning as a result?

The combination of these factors affects the style of provisioning required.

The basic mechanisms for information provisioning are fairly straightforward and are covered in the **I**NFORMATION **P**ROVISIONING pattern. See Table 4.11.

Table 4.11 Information Provisioning Pattern Summary

Icon	Pattern Name	Problem	Solution
	INFORMATION PROVISIONING	An information process needs information to perform its work.	Information is supplied to the process when it starts, through its user interfaces, and through stored information.

This pattern is then followed by specialized provisioning patterns targeted at different situations:

- **Localized provisioning**—Where information sharing is left to the **I**NFORMATION **U**SERS
- **Process-level provisioning**—Where information is provisioned through the **I**NFORMATION **T**RIGGERS
- **Service-level provisioning**—Where provisioning is controlled in the **I**NFORMATION **S**ERVICES
- **Collection-level provisioning**—Where information is synchronized between the **I**NFORMATION **C**OLLECTIONS

Information Provisioning

Context

An organization requires an information process to support one of its activities, and information must be provided to the process.

Problem

An information process needs information to perform its work.

An information process operates in a context. This context is the information that describes how and why it was started, whom it is working for, the resources available to it, and how it relates to past events and activities. How is this information process provisioned with the contextual information it needs?

Example

The Mail-Shop application is responsible for recording new orders. Where does the new order information come from? How is the order processed?

Forces

- **The same information is needed multiple times**—Individuals do not want to repeatedly type in the same information.
- **Valid values vary**—The definition of which are valid values for an attribute in a subject area may not be consistent throughout the organization.
- **Information costs money to store and maintain**—Multiple copies multiply the cost.
- **Information needs to be shared between processes**—Although each process is probably using different subsets of the information and may want it formatted differently.
- **Reformatting takes processing effort**—Collating and reformatting the same piece of information on the fly, over and over again, is inefficient.

Solution

Information is supplied to an information process when it starts, through its user interfaces, and through stored information.

See Figure 4.4.

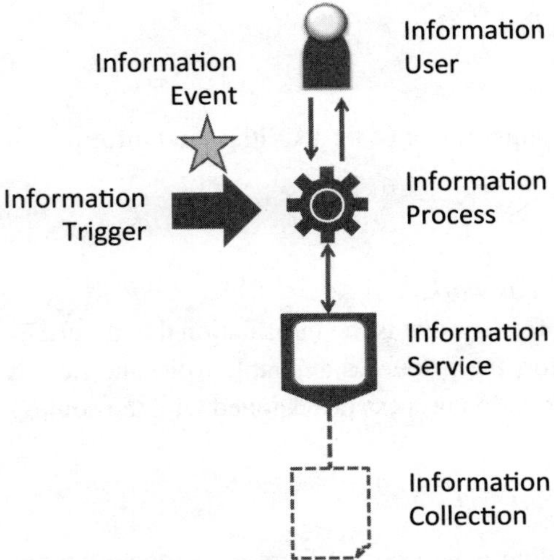

Figure 4.4 Provisioning an information process.

An INFORMATION TRIGGER starts an information process. This trigger may have an INFORMATION EVENT associated with it, which is passed to the information process when it starts. This is the first piece of information that the information process receives and typically describes the context in which it was invoked.

Once running, the information process may have one or more user interfaces that are used to interact with its information users. A user interface represents a key opportunity to receive new information—and to deliver valuable information to the organization. It is also a place where incoming information needs rigorous validation, while outgoing information must only be delivered to the right information users.

Finally, an information process may work with stored information. This is made available to it through INFORMATION SERVICES. An information service will produce information for an information process on request. It will allow the information process to create, update, and delete information as well. Typically, an information service supports information from a particular subject area and so it is common for an information process to work with multiple information services.

The information service is responsible for locating the stored information and hiding the details of this mechanism from the information process. Ultimately, the information is stored in one or more information collections. However, the precise location and format of the information is hidden from the information process.

The mechanisms required to support the work of the information services are where the complexity of information management lies. These different mechanisms are explained in detail by the specialized information provisioning patterns that follow. The choice of provisioning pattern is typically a compromise between providing local information structured exactly to the needs of the information process and reducing the number of copies of the same information kept in the organization's information nodes.

Consequences

Benefits:

- Information provisioning provides a well-defined approach to supplying information to the organization's information processes.

Liabilities:

- In an ideal world, there would only be one copy of each type of information stored by the organization. However, this is rarely feasible because information processes can have slightly different information needs to one another. As a result, information provisioning has to become more sophisticated, creating multiple copies of the information and potentially synchronizing these copies through multiple stages of processing in order to meet all of the needs of the organization.

Example Resolved

When a customer phones the mail order help line, the customer service representative triggers a new order information process in the Mail-Shop application. This takes the customer service representative through a series of screens requesting information about the customers, the goods they want to order, their payment details, and the delivery address. These values are stored in an information collection when the process is complete and the customer confirms the order.

Known Uses

Information provisioning is a continuous and active part of every IT system.

Related Patterns

The patterns that follow are specializations of the information provisioning pattern. Together they form the linkages between the information collections and the information processes that implement the INFORMATION SUPPLY CHAIN.

The INFORMATION IDENTIFICATION patterns describe how to document the sources of information for information provisioning.

The INFORMATION FLOW patterns describe how information is moved and delivered within a specified provisioning pattern.

Localized Provisioning

The INFORMATION PROVISIONING pattern introduced the basic mechanisms that supply an information process with information.

For many organizations, information provisioning is essentially localized within each INFORMATION NODE. Any sharing of information is via people (speech, printouts, email). This is the default situation if no measures are taken to integrate the information nodes together to automate the sharing of information. It works for a small organization where people know one another but can create silos of operation as the organization grows. This is shown in Figure 4.5.

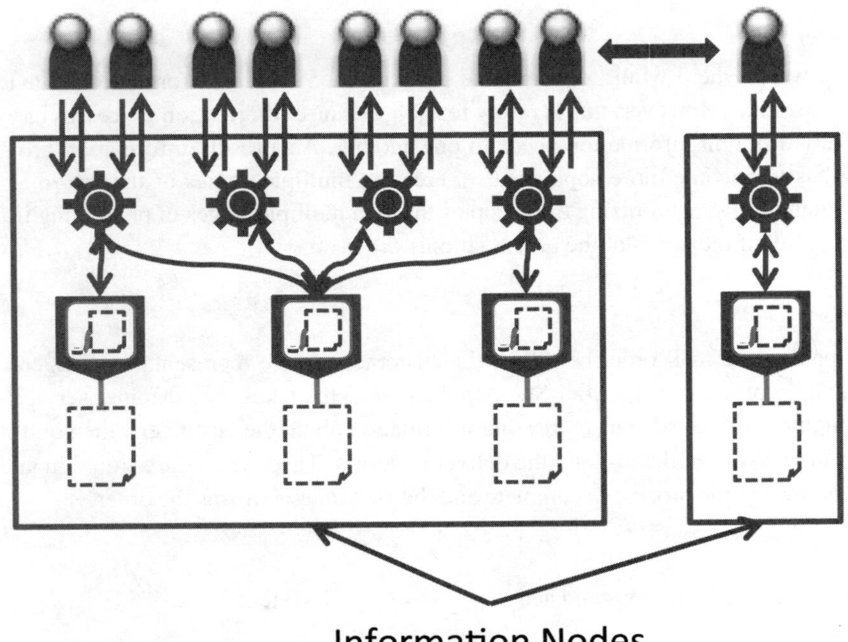

Figure 4.5 Localized provisioning.

In the patterns, we have two examples of this style of provisioning, as shown in Table 4.12.

Table 4.12 Localized Provisioning Patterns Summary

Icon	Pattern Name	Problem	Solution
	USER PRIVATE PROVISIONING	An information user needs to perform an ad hoc piece of work using the information he or she has in his or her private work-space.	Provide the ability to run an information process and store the results in the information user's private workspace.
	APPLICATION PRIVATE PROVISIONING	The information processes within an information node need independent control of the information collections that they are using.	Locate the information collections in the same information node as the information processes. The local information processes are responsible for maintaining these information collections on a day-to day basis.

Both of these patterns provide targeted support for small groups of people working together. As a result, they are the most prevalent approaches to information provisioning in any size of organization and are unlikely to be eliminated. Instead, these approaches are augmented with other types of information provisioning that distribute and synchronize the information they maintain with information from other parts of the organization.

User Private Provisioning

Context

How is information supplied to an information process?

Problem

An information user needs to perform an ad hoc piece of work using the information he or she have in his or her private workspace.

Not all work in an organization is planned. Sometimes ad hoc requests are made to an information user. They need IT facilities that are flexible enough to allow them to process ad hoc data and retain the results.

Example

An information user has a new idea for a customer offering and wants to develop it further before sharing it with others.

Forces

- **Ad hoc activity needs ad hoc provisioning—**It is impossible to anticipate exactly what the information is required for an ad hoc activity.
- **Keeping early drafts private—**Often information users want to keep information private to them, particularly in the early stages of a project when various aspects are still fluid.
- **Centralized provisioning—**The IT-provided systems tend to automate the commonly occurring, business-critical, and consistently defined activities as information processes.

Solution

Provide the ability to run an information process and store the results in the information user's private workspace.

This information process may be running on the information user's personal computer, smart device, or a centrally managed information node.

Consequences

Benefits:

- This type of provisioning creates a flexible environment where information users can support ad hoc requests.

Liabilities:

- This type of provisioning results in information that could be important to the organization being stored in an ungoverned manner. It relies on the judgment of the information user to know how to protect the information and when to share it. Often, when sharing occurs, it is also in an ungoverned manner via emails and shared storage.

Example Resolved

A buyer in the Merchandising Department at MCHS uses a process in the Product Hub to download (copy) a set of products and its details to a local file and populates the information in her spreadsheet. She adds additional information out of several supplier catalogs to the spreadsheet and performs analysis on the information there.

Known Uses

This pattern is in operation when people use desktop applications such as word processing and spreadsheets. It is good for locally optimizing the work of an individual but has negative consequences on governing and sharing the information people use and create.

Related Patterns

If the results of such ad hoc activity need to be shared among a team—or further—consider the USER SHARED PROVISIONING.

If the activity supported by this type of provisioning is, in fact, critical to the business, or occurring frequently, then consider supporting it directly with a specialized INFORMATION PROCESS that is using a more managed form of provisioning.

Application Private Provisioning

Context

How is information supplied to an information process?

Problem

The information processes within an information node need independent control of the information collections that they are using.

This may be because it is to be deployed into many different environments and cannot depend on other sources of information for its ongoing operation.

Example

The E-Shop application is a packaged application for providing web-based catalogs and ordering. The application is sold by a vendor to many organizations and needs to be able to operate independently of other systems because there is no knowledge of what will be available in each deployment.

Forces

- **An information process is dependent on all of the information collections it uses—** These information collections are only available if the information nodes that host them are operational.
- **No application is truly an island—**It needs to receive up-to-date information about other activities in the organization. Also, other information nodes need the information that it possesses.

Solution

Locate the information collections in the same information node as the information processes. The local information processes are responsible for maintaining these information collections on a day-to day basis.

See Figure 4.6. An information node where the information processes are locally provisioning with their own private information collections is often referred to as an application.

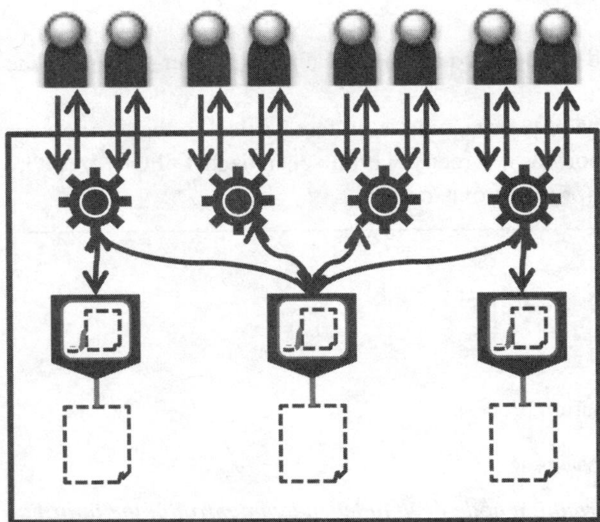

Figure 4.6 Private provisioning for an application.

Consequences

Benefits:

- An information node with this type of provisioning can be deployed into many environments.

Liabilities:

- An information node using only this style of provisioning does not share information with other information nodes. The information sharing happens between people, through conversations, printouts, memory keys, and emailing snapshots of data between groups of people. The result is that the sharing of information is not governed and teams can become dependent on an extracted snapshot of data that has an unknown provenance; it is not backed up nor protected in any way.
- Organizations running many applications invest in synchronizing and distributing information between them. The better application packages recognize this requirement and provide interfaces to facilitate additional information provisioning.

Example Resolved

When first installed, the E-Shop application had its own information collections for storing customer accounts, the product catalog, and orders from customers. All of its locally hosted information processes use these local collections.

Known Uses

Most applications and commercial software packages are written to use their own private information collections.

Related Patterns

More information about the makeup of an application is described in the APPLICATION NODE pattern.

Information collections that are used in this style of provisioning typically have MASTER USAGE, LOCAL SCOPE, and LOCAL COVERAGE. The information collections may be initially populated from other information sources using SNAPSHOT PROVISIONING.

Once up and running, an information node using application private provisioning may be connected to the organization's information supply chains to exchange information with other applications. The other information provisioning patterns cover how this might be done. For example, CONSOLIDATING INFORMATION SUPPLY CHAINS utilize MIRRORING PROVISIONING to pass information from one information collection to another.

Process-Level Provisioning

Process-level provisioning occurs when information processes pass work to another using an INFORMATION TRIGGER. The information trigger is used to start an information process. It carries with it an INFORMATION EVENT, which will provide context information to the newly started process. Using this mechanism, work can be coordinated between independent information nodes with little change to their existing operation. See Figure 4.7.

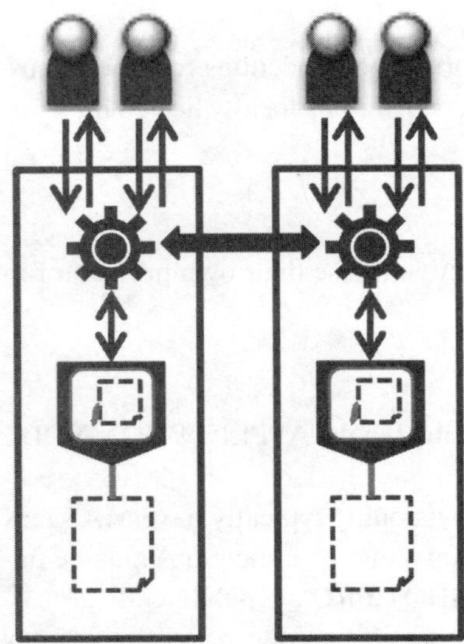

Figure 4.7 Provisioning between processes.

There is one process-level pattern in this pattern language, called DAISY CHAIN PROVISIONING. See Table 4.13.

Table 4.13 Process-Level Provisioning Patterns Summary

Icon	Pattern Name	Problem	Solution
	DAISY CHAIN PROVISIONING	A single business transaction is supported end-to-end by information processes from multiple information nodes. How is this work coordinated?	Pass control of the work for the business transaction between the information processes in a similar way that a baton is passed between runners in a relay.

Daisy Chain Provisioning

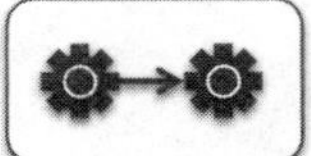

Context

How is information supplied to an information process?

Problem

A single business transaction is supported end-to-end by information processes from multiple information nodes. How is this work coordinated?

This often occurs when the organization has many specialized applications. Each application implements part of the required processing and then needs to initiate another information process to continue the work.

Example

When the E-Shop application creates a new order, it must be passed to the Shipping application to fulfill the order.

Forces

- **Applications are typically implemented in an independent fashion**—Particularly packaged applications because they are to be sold into many organizations and need to operate independently.
- **Organizations operate in silos**—As organizations grow, they need to be split into independent operating units to make the work manageable. Applications are often implemented to support just one part of an operating unit. The people working within the operating unit are specialists and are unaware how the rest of the organization operates.
- **Information processes are implemented with assumptions on how their information is managed**—For example, E-Shop may assume a person with an entry in its customer details information collection is registered to use the E-Shop application. These assumptions limit how much information can be consolidated and changed.
- **Applications may not be easy to integrate with other systems**—For example, they may not have externally callable interfaces to provide access to the information processes and information collections. As such, integration middleware is needed to connect them to the organization's information supply chains.

Solution

Pass control of the work for the business transaction between the information processes in a similar way that a baton is passed between runners in a relay.

The original information process should raise an information event to trigger the new information process. This event is raised through a TRIGGERING INFORMATION SERVICE.

Figure 4.8 shows how this works.

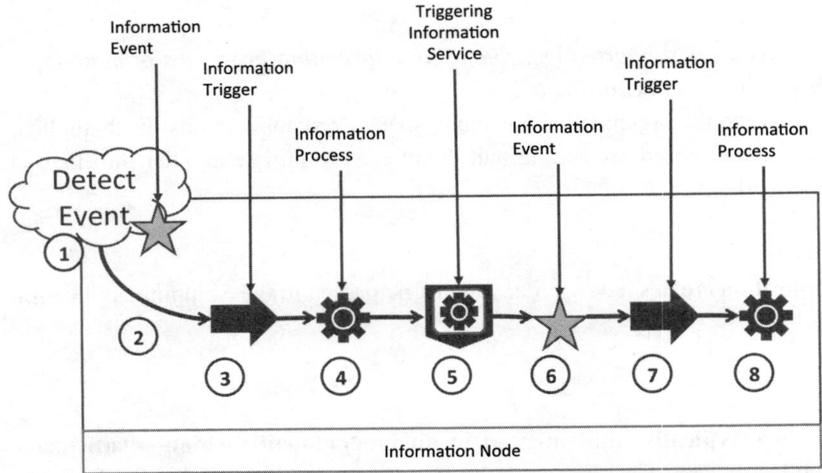

Figure 4.8 Daisy chain provisioning of information processes.

The numbers on the diagram of Figure 4.8 refer to these notes:

1. When a new business transaction is detected, an **I**NFORMATION **E**VENT is raised.
2. The **I**NFORMATION **T**RIGGER detects this information event.
3. The information trigger starts the first information process.
4. The information process runs to completion.
5. It calls a **T**RIGGERING **I**NFORMATION **S**ERVICE for the subsequent processing.
6. The information service raises another information event for the next step to begin.
7. This, in turn, creates another information trigger to initiate the next information process.
8. The triggering of the sequence of information processes continues until the business transaction is complete.

Often, the information processes supporting the business transaction are hosted in different information nodes. This case is shown in Figure 4.9.

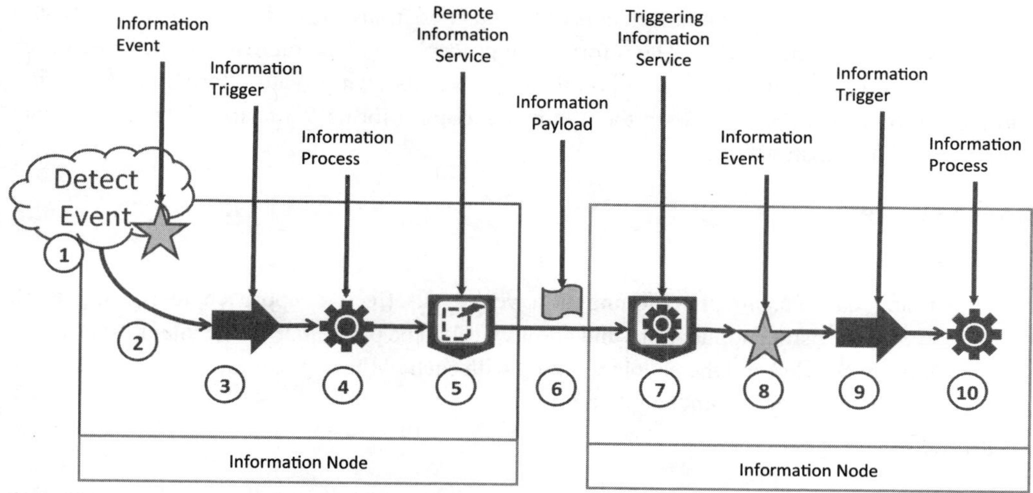

Figure 4.9 Daisy chain provisioning of information processes on different information nodes.

The sequence is very similar. The numbers on the diagram in Figure 4.9 refer to these notes:

1. When a new business transaction is detected, an **I**NFORMATION **E**VENT is raised.
2. The **I**NFORMATION **T**RIGGER detects this information event.
3. The information trigger starts the first information process.
4. The information process runs to completion.
5. It calls a **R**EMOTE **I**NFORMATION **S**ERVICE to initiate the next step.
6. The remote information service uses an **I**NFORMATION **P**AYLOAD to send the request to the next information node.
7. Receipt of the information payload invokes a **T**RIGGERING **I**NFORMATION **S**ERVICE.
8. The triggering information service converts the information payload into an information event.
9. This, in turn, creates another information trigger to initiate the next information process.
10. The triggering of the sequence of information processes continues until the business transaction is complete.

In both cases, important context information must be passed to the information processes. This is the role of the information event and the information payload structures. While the information process is running, the context is stored in **I**NFORMATION **P**ROCESSING **V**ARIABLES.

The context typically contains details of the business transaction, intermediate results, and references to stored information. The information processes may be referring to the same information collections, but it is most common that each has its own private information collection and the information passed between them is just enough information to locate the appropriate locally stored information.

Consequences

Benefits:

- Using daisy chain provisioning is a very cost-effective approach to passing work between existing applications and allows work to be parallelized. The integration is very loosely coupled and the people working with each of the applications are not affected by the operation of the other applications.

Liabilities:

- It may be hard to trace where a piece of work has got to—or to correct the information about it once it has left the first application. Typically, an investigator has to query each application in turn to understand what processing has occurred.
- This style of provisioning is often used between information nodes whose information processes were designed to use APPLICATION **P**RIVATE **P**ROVISIONING. This means that each step in fulfilling the business transaction is executed using different information collections. These information collections must be kept synchronized to ensure consistent behavior throughout the business transaction.
- If an information process is unavailable, the passing of work will fail and part of the business transaction will not run.

Example Resolved

The E-Shop application was not designed with integration in mind. The implementation of the New Order information process does not include a trigger to kick off any order-fulfillment process. It has its own information processes that require an information user to repeatedly query for new orders. MCHS Trading's operations are too extensive to make that approach practical and it needs to automate the fulfillment of orders as much as possible. This includes automatically triggering the Shipping application to ship the goods. This triggering is driven when E-Shop writes the new order in its order details information collection.

Each new order results in a new **I**NFORMATION **E**NTRY in the order details information collection. When the information entry is written, it creates an event that results in an **I**NFORMATION **C**HANGE **T**RIGGER. This information change trigger issues a **R**EMOTE **I**NFORMATION **S**ERVICE to copy details of the order to an **I**NFORMATION **P**AYLOAD and send it to an **I**NFORMATION **B**ROKER. The information broker transforms the information payload into a format suitable for Shipping and passes it to a **QUEUE MANAGER**. The queue manager's role is to safeguard the information payloads for the periods when the Shipping application is not available. It will pass the information payload to the Shipping application as soon as possible. When Shipping receives the information payload, it starts to fulfill the order.

Known Uses

Daisy chain provisioning is often referred to as Enterprise Application Integration (EAI). EAI uses distributed messaging to pass work between applications.

Related Patterns

The **INFORMATION TRIGGER** patterns cover the different mechanisms for triggering an information process.

The **AGILE BUSINESS PROCESS** pattern offers an alternative approach by implementing an information process that spans the capability of multiple applications. It acts as a centralized coordinator of the work, keeping track of where the work is, and initiating new work when a previous piece has finished.

The **DISTRIBUTED ACTIVITY STATUS** information solution describes how to monitor the status of a business transaction that is supported with daisy chain provisioning.

Service-Level Provisioning

INFORMATION SERVICES are the means by which information processes access stored information. The information services are implemented to support information content and structure that is targeted to the needs of the consuming information processes, rather than the specific way that the information is stored. Information services may rename attributes; reformat data types; select and combine information from multiple information collections, both local to the information process and remote. In short, information services provide comprehensive capabilities to provision information on demand, directly from where this information is stored.

The patterns in Table 4.14 illustrate some of the ways that information services can support the provisioning of information.

Table 4.14 Service-Level Provisioning Patterns Summary

Icon	Pattern Name	Problem	Solution
	USER SHARED PROVISIONING	A team of information users is working together to perform an ad hoc project.	Provide an information node that can store a variety of information under the control of the team members.

Icon	Pattern Name	Problem	Solution
	SERVICE ORIENTED PROVISIONING	An information collection is too big, too sensitive, too valuable, and/or changing too rapidly to be copied to other information nodes.	Provide information services for the information collection to enable information process to access it, irrespective of the information node they are located in.
	LINKED INFORMATION PROVISIONING	An entry in an information collection needs to reference an entry in another (possibly remote) information collection.	Store a reference to the entry, which includes the location for its information collection and the identifier of the entry within it.
	CACHE PROVISIONING	A critical information collection may occasionally be offline or not able to provide information fast enough for the consuming information processes.	Keep a relevant subset of information for the consuming information processes in memory and refresh it as appropriate.

User Shared Provisioning

Context

How is information supplied to an information process?

Problem

A team of information users is working together to perform an ad hoc project.

As a result, the information they are using and creating will need to be shared among them. The team needs to control how this information is organized, which information is available to people outside of the team and when this happens.

Example

MCHS Trading decides to acquire another company to expand its distribution capability. It needs to perform analysis of how this will affect its existing offerings, how this will be financed, how the organization will be structured, and create communications for various audiences—all before the acquisition goes ahead.

Forces

- It is impossible to anticipate exactly what information is required for an ad hoc activity.
- Often, information users want to keep information private to them, particularly in the early stages of a project when various aspects are still fluid.

- The IT-provided systems tend to automate the commonly occurring, business-critical, and consistently defined activities as information processes.

Solution

Provide an information node that can store a variety of information under the control of the team members.

Typically, the information being generated is in the form of documents and spreadsheets. It needs to be organized so it can be reviewed and commented upon. Multiple versions of this information will be created as the team's thoughts mature.

Consequences

Benefits:

- This approach allows a level of sharing, management, and protection of the information being produced by the team, without restricting the type of information it can produce.

Liabilities:

- The structure and organization of the information is left to the team's discretion, which can make it hard to harvest the information for future projects.

Example Resolved

The financial analysts at MCHS Trading create reports from the Reporting Hub and store them in a shared information node. They obtain reports from the other company as part of their due diligence and bring the information together in a set of shared spreadsheets in which they perform their financial analysis. From their results, they build documents and presentations that are also stored in the shared information node.

Known Uses

This pattern describes the use of collaboration technology, such as network file systems, wikis, blogs, and document repositories.

Related Patterns

This type of provisioning is often associated with INFORMATION COLLECTIONS that use the TAGGED MEDIA STRUCTURE.

Service Oriented Provisioning

Context

How is information supplied to an information process?

Problem

An information collection is too big, too sensitive, too valuable, and/or changing too rapidly to be copied to other information nodes.

Example

MCHS Trading's E-Shop application is responsible for capturing customer orders through the Internet. However, in order for a customer to place an order, the application must obtain the stored payment details about the customer and the order codes from the product details. This information is not stored in the E-Shop application.

Forces

- **Independent implementations**—Packaged applications in particular have distinct implementations because they are to be sold into many organizations and need to operate independently, and, therefore, have distinct and different information services from those built within an organization.
- **Inconsistent information definitions**—Lack of clear understanding of information across the information supply chain can impact effective service definition or the selection of the right information collection to use.
- **Assumptions on how information is requested and delivered**—The assumptions/models incorporated when services are introduced may limit how much information can be integrated, consolidated, utilized, and changed within an information process.
- **Difficulty integrating with other systems**—For example, a set of information services may not have externally callable interfaces to provide access to the information processes and information collections with which they work. As such, specialized integration middleware is needed to connect them to the organization's information supply chains.

Solution

Provide information services for the information collection to enable information processes to access it, irrespective of the information node they are located in.

See Figure 4.10.

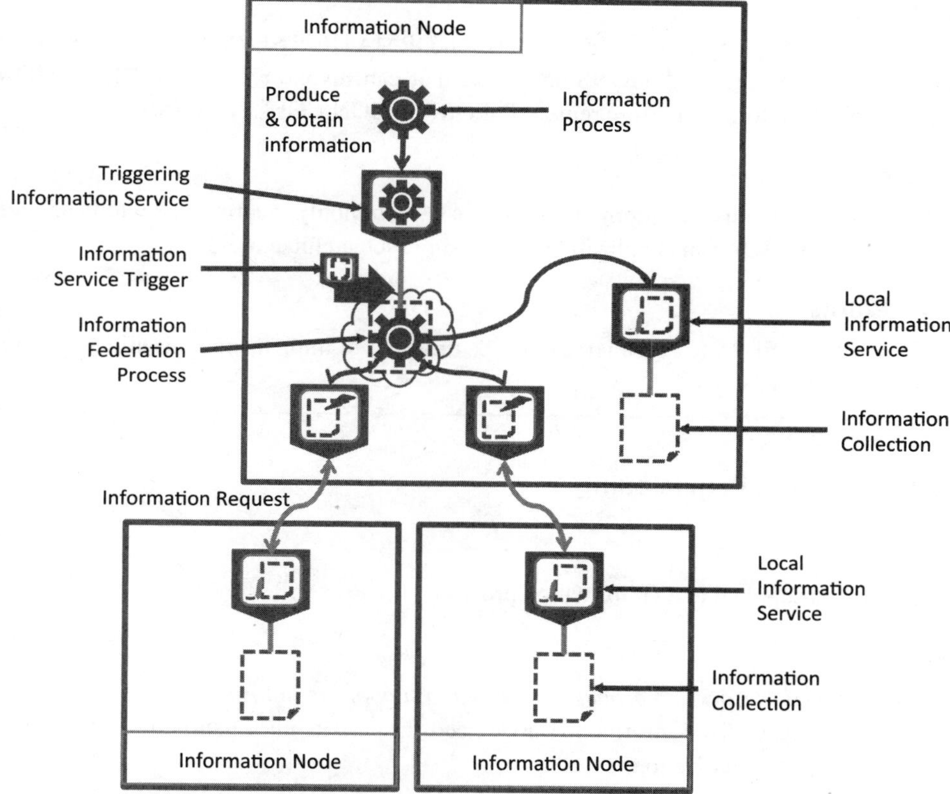

Figure 4.10 Interaction in service oriented provisioning.

Consequences

Benefits:

- This approach allows a level of sharing, management, and protection of the information being utilized by different information processes, without requiring the movement of all information to a specific information node and ensuring that the information used is the most current information.

Liabilities:

- The structure and organization of the information is based on the requirements of the local information nodes, which can make it hard to integrate the information. The information services must be standardized, cataloged, and managed to ensure consistency of use across the different information nodes and processes that call them, and to reduce the cost of maintaining them.

Example Resolved

MCHS Trading's E-Shop application incorporates INFORMATION SERVICES that work with local INFORMATION COLLECTIONS and those that can invoke remote INFORMATION SERVICES to obtain information from remote INFORMATION COLLECTIONS.

Known Uses

This pattern describes the use of information services as commonly incorporated within service oriented architectures (SOA) and applications built using such architectures.

Related Patterns

The INFORMATION SERVICES patterns describe the types of implementations utilized within the provisioning pattern.

Linked Information Provisioning

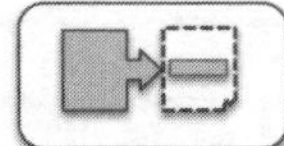

Context

How is information supplied to an information process?

Problem

Data from distributed sensors and probes is required to support an information process.

An entry in a specialized information node needs to pass its information to another (possibly remote) information collection.

Example

The MCHS Trading warehouses receive product stock from various suppliers. The warehouses have implemented bar-code scanners to record the shipments received and reduce manual error. The bar-code scanners have limited memory and storage and cannot serve as INFORMATION NODES that house INFORMATION COLLECTIONS, though they link to an INFORMATION NODE that does log all transactions. MCHS Trading needs to connect this information to other applications.

Forces

- **Minimal information storage—**Sensors, probes, and related devices receive and transmit information in high frequency, but may not support storage of significant amounts of information.
- **Difficulty integrating with other systems—**Sensors and similar devices have unique operating systems and may not readily connect with other systems or applications.

- **High information volume and/or frequency**—The information process and information collection into which the information is delivered must be able to meet the volume/frequency of the incoming information.

Solution

Deliver and store a reference to the entry, which includes the location for its information collection and the identifier of the entry within it.

Receive the data from the source and store it, including references to the source INFORMATION NODE. Perform a first pass on the data as close to its source as possible with an aim to cleanse and add context to it. Then pass the data to a centralized information collection where information processes can build up the big picture.

Consequences

Benefits:

- High volume and high frequency information can be recorded, forwarded, and collected where it can be utilized by other applications.

Liabilities:

- Information will be limited by what the sensor or other device can record. Certain types of devices are susceptible to "noise," in which case such noise will be forwarded and stored as well as legitimate information. This may have significant consequences when other applications attempt to use the information.

Example Resolved

MCHS Trading establishes an INFORMATION NODE containing an INFORMATION COLLECTION to record the shipment's bar-code information. The node is directly linked to the bar-code scanner application, which sends the information entries into the collection. Other applications such as the Shipping and Purchasing applications can now connect to this INFORMATION COLLECTION through other regular provisioning patterns.

Known Uses

Initial receipt of information coming from devices such as sensors, probes, and scanners utilize this pattern.

Related Patterns

Deliver and store the information in a STAGING AREA (a cache) if the target is not consistently available. The CACHE PROVISIONING pattern can then be utilized by consuming applications when needed.

Where higher volumes of information preclude handling through a simple cache, an INFORMATION MIRROR STORE can be loaded via an INFORMATION BROKER.

Cache Provisioning

Context

How is information supplied to an information process?

Problem

A critical information collection may occasionally be offline or not able to provide information fast enough for the consuming information processes.

How does a consuming information process continue to operate?

Example

MCHS Trading's E-Shop application is responsible for capturing customer orders through the Internet. The E-Shop is expected to be available twenty-four hours per day, seven days a week (24/7) for customers to place their orders, but the applications handling the customer and product details required for the orders are offline at scheduled intervals to address daily processing requirements.

Forces

- **Information collections are not always available**—The information collections from which the information is obtained are not accessible.
- **Information values change over time**—Any copies of information need to be kept synchronized with the master usage information collection.

Solution

Keep a relevant subset of information for the consuming information processes in memory and refresh it as appropriate.

The area where the information is held in memory is called a cache. There are two approaches for provisioning the cache:

1. An additional information provisioning process pre-populates the cache with all of the information from the information collection and copies the latest values from the critical information collection into the cache as they become available. The consuming information processes accesses the cache whenever it wants some information.
2. The consuming information process calls an information service. The information service checks to see if the requested information is in the cache. If it is (and has not been in the cache too long and become stale), this value is used; otherwise, the requested values are retrieved from the information collection. They are then placed in the cache and returned to the requester.

Consequences

Benefits:

- Continuous operational processing can be maintained.

Liabilities:

- Information processes may not have current information available, if there is delay updating the cache.

Example Resolved

The E-Shop application incorporates specific services that poll the customer and product INFORMATION COLLECTIONS at periodic intervals and stores the results in a local cache. When the E-Shop application fails to directly connect to its targeted INFORMATION COLLECTION, it triggers an alternate information process that provisions the calling information process from the cache.

Known Uses

Cache provisioning is often used to speed up the access of slowly changing information, such as images for web pages or user profile attributes. The first time the information is requested, it is read from the information collection and added to the cache. It stays in the The cache may be located in the web server, or further out in an edge-of-network server.

Related Patterns

Where the volatility of information is low, utilize one of the collection-level provisioning patterns to populate local INFORMATION COLLECTIONS.

Collection-Level Provisioning

It stands to reason that information stored in a remote information node will take longer to retrieve than information stored in the local information node. If the information is only needed on an ad hoc basis, or is changing rapidly, this increased latency is tolerable. However, if the same remote information is needed repeatedly, or needs extensive reformatting to consume it, or is not retained or managed appropriately for the local node's requirements, then it may be necessary to copy the information to a local information collection. This is the goal of the collection-level provisioning patterns shown in Table 4.15.

Table 4.15 Collection-Level Provisioning Patterns Summary

Icon	Pattern Name	Problem	Solution
	SNAPSHOT PROVISIONING	A team needs its own copy of some information for analyzing or for experimenting with.	Schedule an information flow from each of the source information collections to transfer the information to an information collection that will contain the snapshot of information.
	MIRRORING PROVISIONING	When a new information process is introduced, or updated, the reference information it requires is not always available at a suitable class of service.	Create new information collections for the information process and regularly provision them from other sources of information.
	PEER PROVISIONING	An organization needs to keep the information in multiple master information collections synchronized.	Each time an information entry in any of the information collections changes, the updated information values are sent to the other collections.
	EVENT-BASED PROVISIONING	An information process needs to keep track of when particular events occur, either locally or in other parts of the organization.	Collect together the events into a well-known information collection that the information process can access.
	RECOVERY PROVISIONING	The infrastructure supporting an information collection may fail. How do we restore the information to the information supply chain?	Maintain an ongoing backup copy that is physically separate and secure. Ensure there is an alternative infrastructure to host the restored collection.

Snapshot Provisioning

Context

How is information supplied to an information process?

Problem

A team needs its own copy of some information for analyzing or for experimenting with.

Often, this is for a specific project where the team wants to make experimental changes to aspects of the information to understand the effects. By using a copy, the team can perform the experiments without disrupting the existing business.

Example

MCHS Trading decides to acquire another company to expand its distribution capability. It needs to experiment with the way that the stores and sales teams will be organized after the acquisition.

Forces

- Each application typically has its own unique data formats that must be supported by the provisioning process.
- Information is not always captured in the form that is useful for processing.
- When information is shared among multiple information processes, each information process is affected by the work of the others. While an information process is partway through a set of related updates, the affected information entries are typically locked so the other information processes do not see the partially completed changes. This works well for changes that take a few seconds. Anything longer than that needs an alternative approach.

Solution

Schedule an information flow from each of the source information collections to transfer the information to an information collection that will contain the snapshot of information.

When the team has finished with this copy of the information collection, it can be deleted. Alternatively, its contents can be replaced periodically to refresh the values. See Figure 4.11.

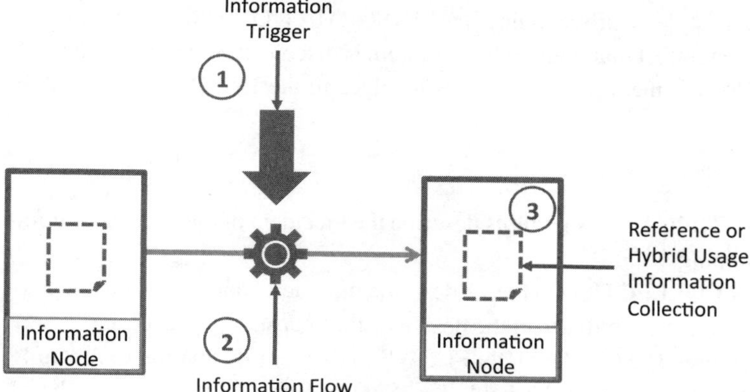

Figure 4.11 Scheduling an information flow to provision a snapshot collection.

Consequences

Benefits:

- This style of provisioning allows experimentation without disrupting the existing business.

Liabilities:

- This style of provisioning creates a copy of information that must be protected as if it were the original version. Particularly, when the team has finished with it, it must be destroyed appropriately.

Example Resolved

The acquisition team is given a snapshot of the sales and stores information so that the team can try different organizations to determine the best one.

Known Uses

This style of provisioning is used to support projects that need information for a finite period of time or to seed the information collections of a new application. Sometimes the provisioning is into a spreadsheet, stored in an information user's private workspace. Alternatively, the snapshot could be located on a managed information node.

Note that snapshot provisioning is also common when replacing an operational system where the old and new systems are to run in parallel for a period of time. The snapshot is generally run once to populate the new system, and then both systems are supported by INFORMATION FLOWS with the same style of provisioning until INFORMATION USERS are satisfied with the results in the new system. At that point, the old system is disconnected from the INFORMATION SUPPLY CHAIN, and the new system takes its place in the INFORMATION SUPPLY CHAIN.

Related Patterns

The INFORMATION IDENTIFICATION patterns describe the metadata of the sources of information for snapshot provisioning.

The INFORMATION COLLECTION patterns describe the roles, scopes, and coverage of information collections. These factors will affect the design of the snapshot provisioning.

Snapshot provisioning uses INFORMATION FLOWS to deliver information to the information collection where the snapshot is to be held. The flow of information is started by an INFORMATION TRIGGER, which starts an INFORMATION FLOW to transport (and typically transform) the information to where it needs to be. The INFORMATION FLOW is likely to include INFORMATION REENGINEERING STEPS if changes to the INFORMATION ELEMENTS are needed.

Mirroring Provisioning

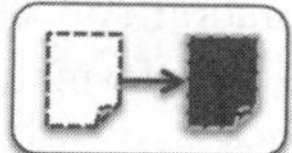

Context

How is information supplied to an information process?

Problem

When a new information process is introduced, or updated, the stored information it requires is not always available at a suitable class of service.

Typically, this may be because the changes are being made to an information collection with **M**ASTER **U**SAGE and they are being distributed to a related information collection with the **R**EFERENCE **U**SAGE.

If the information is not synchronized, some, or all, of the information processes will be working with out-of-date information.

Example

MCHS Trading has product information in the following systems: E-Shop, Mail-Shop, Stores, Shipping, Invoicing, and Reporting Hub. This product information needs to be synchronized with the master copy of the product catalog that is maintained in the Product Hub application.

Forces

- **Unique data requirements**—Each application typically has its own unique data formats that must be supported by the provisioning process.
- **Offline working**—An information process needs occasionally to work offline from one of its reference information collections and needs to keep a relevant subset of information for the information process in memory and refresh it as appropriate.
- **Need for rapid data access**—Local information collections, designed specifically for an information process, typically provide the fastest access to the information for that information process.

Solution

Create new information collections for the information process and provision them from other sources of information.

The mirroring provisioning pattern copies information between **I**NFORMATION **C**OLLECTIONS in order to simplify the work of one or more information processes. For example, the information provisioning mechanism may copy information so it is local to a consuming information process for faster access, to consolidate and correlate the information from multiple places so a complete view is available, or reformat the information to match the queries used by the information process.

Whenever a change is made to the source information collections, trigger an information flow to transmit the changes to each of the destination information collections. This is shown in Figure 4.12.

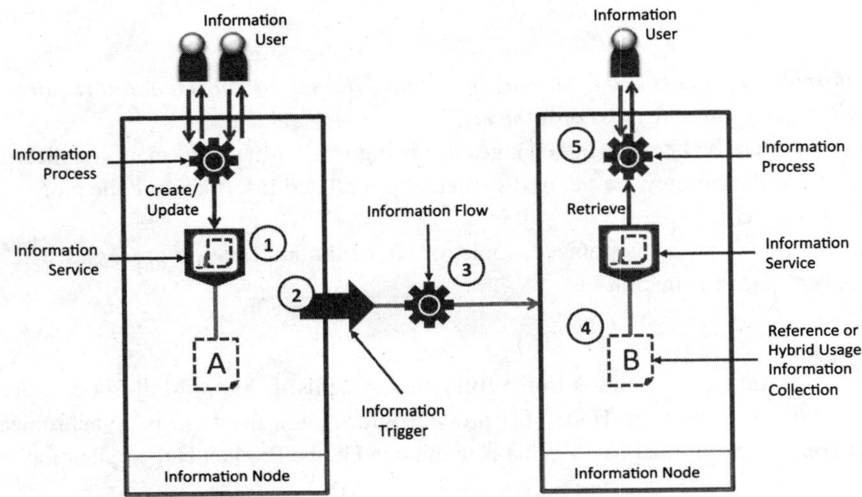

Figure 4.12 Mirroring an information collection into other information nodes.

The numbers on the diagram in Figure 4.12 refer to these notes:

1. An information process changes information in the source information collection.
2. This change triggers an information flow.
3. The information flow transforms and transports the information to one or more destinations.

Mirroring provisioning is usually designed in three phases:

1. The initial load of the new information collection(s). This copies all of the existing values into the new information collections. Often, specialized techniques for bulk-loading data into the persistent storage are required to complete the initial load in a reasonable time.
2. The synchronization of subsequent changes to the source information collections with the copies. This processing is sometimes called the *delta load* if it is batch or "trickle-feed" if it is real time. It is necessary if the copy is to reflect the current state of the

information over a sustained period of time. Typically, the implementation of this synchronization is different from the initial load—the triggering process must be more selective, ensuring the appropriate information is sent at the right time. The transport mechanism is often different—optimized for smaller, frequent transfers of a variety of information payloads.

3. The decommissioning of the copies when they are no longer needed. A phase that is often forgotten about in the rush to create the new copy. This copy will have information processes dependent on it—but for how long? When does the organization know it can remove the copy? How will it be done?

INFORMATION **F**LOWS are used to implement the initial load and the subsequent trickle-feed. They are either passed the information, or they extract it from the original information collections. They then may perform a number of **I**NFORMATION **R**EENGINEERING activities on it, before delivering it to the destination information collections.

The choice of information flows required will depend on the type of information provisioning. These are described in the information patterns that follow.

Decommissioning is essentially a delete process, although many organizations move the contents to an archive in case the information collections need to be restored.

Consequences

Benefits:

- Mirroring provisioning (1) enables new information processes to be introduced by the organization that have slightly different information needs to the existing information processes; (2) can move information to more cost-efficient information nodes for certain types of processing.

Liabilities:

- Mirroring provisioning can create copies of information that need to be stored and maintained. It is important to ensure these copies are properly secured and deleted once no longer needed.
- Ideally, the information collections that are being provisioned using mirroring provisioning will have **R**EFERENCE **U**SAGE or **H**YBRID **U**SAGE by the information processes that use them. Any updates made to the copy may be lost as a result of new information being received through the trickle-feed. Also, understanding which collection has the best set of values becomes problematic if there are multiple information collections for the same subject area that have **M**ASTER **U**SAGE.
- Care must be taken to ensure the meaning of the information at the originating information node matches the intended use in each of the destinations.

Example Resolved

An INFORMATION PROCESS TRIGGER fires whenever there are new product details to distribute and that action triggers a PARTITIONING DISTRIBUTION information flow. See Figure 4.13.

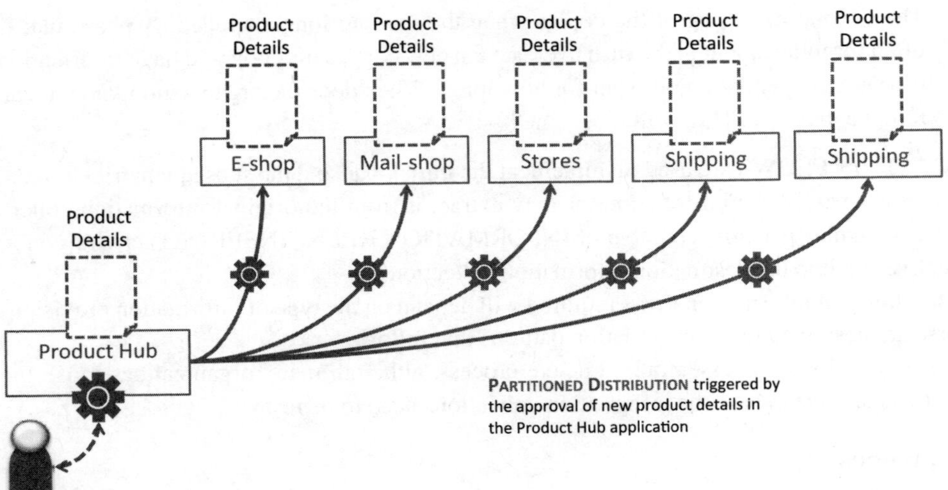

Figure 4.13 Using partitioned distribution to support the mirroring of information.

Known Uses

Mirroring provisioning is used extensively in data warehouse and analytical applications. It often is a mechanism that is used to keep operational systems synchronized or to migrate information between versions of the same application.

Related Patterns

The INFORMATION IDENTIFICATION patterns describe the metadata needed to locate the sources of information for mirroring provisioning.

The INFORMATION COLLECTION patterns describe the roles, scopes, and coverage of information collections. These factors will affect the design of the mirroring provisioning.

The INFORMATION TRIGGER patterns describe approaches to ensuring the provisioning information processes run frequently enough to keep the information collection in step.

The INFORMATION FLOW patterns are used to implement both the initial load and the trickle-feed for mirroring provisioning. They in turn use information processes to drive the movement and reengineering of information. See these information processes for examples of this processing:

- INFORMATION **D**EPLOYMENT **P**ROCESS
- INFORMATION **R**ELOCATION **P**ROCESS
- INFORMATION **R**EPLICATION **P**ROCESS
- INFORMATION **F**EDERATION **P**ROCESS
- INFORMATION **S**ERVICE **P**ROCESS
- INFORMATION **Q**UEUING **P**ROCESS
- INFORMATION **B**ROADCASTING **P**ROCESS
- INFORMATION **S**TREAMING **P**ROCESS
- INFORMATION **S**UMMARIZING **P**ROCESS

The **A**RCHIVING **P**ROCESS is typically used when decommissioning a provisioned information collection.

Peer Provisioning

Context

How is information supplied to an information process?

Problem

An information supply chain needs to keep the information in multiple master information collections synchronized.

This situation arises when the same kind of information must be collected from multiple sources and this information is stored close to where it is collected.

Example

MCHS Trading has multiple sources of input for customer data: the Stores, the Mail-Shop, the E-Shop, and the new Customer-Care application. The customer details have been consolidated into a Customer Hub, but because the E-Shop application is a primary entry point for customers, it receives updates through its own Customer Master, distinct from the Customer Hub. For effective customer service, MCHS Trading must ensure that updates to the Customer Hub reach the E-Shop and those from the E-Shop are applied into the Customer Hub.

Forces

- **Multiple points of origination—**Where multiple applications originate change, these must be synchronized across all the applications to ensure that the most recent information is available everywhere and not repeatedly overlaid by out-of-date information.

- **Unique data requirements**—Each application typically has its own unique data formats that must be supported by the provisioning process.
- **Need for rapid data access**—Local information collections, designed specifically for an information process, typically provide the fastest access to the information for that information process.
- **Impact of latency**—In some industries, there is no or little tolerance for latency in distributing the changes to the data.

Solution

Each time an information entry in any of the information collections changes, the updated information values are sent to the other collections.

If there are only two **I**NFORMATION **C**OLLECTIONS to synchronize, then **M**IRRORING **P**ROVISIONING can be used flow updates made to one of the information collection on to the other so the information is flowing in both directions.

As the number of information collections involved increases, this approach leads to multiple point-to-point solutions with increasing risk of inconsistent change and delivery. A second approach is for each to push the new information into a **Q**UEUE **M**ANAGER running an **I**NFORMATION **B**ROADCASTING **P**ROCESS that distributes the updates to the other information nodes.

Consequences

Benefits:

- The most current information is available in all applications, although such information comes from many distinct points of entry.

Liabilities:

- Changes that are propagated to a peer should not cause a return flow back to the originator—causing a continuous loop of updates. As a result, the trigger for the synchronization typically cannot be driven from the detecting changes in the information collections (see **I**NFORMATION **C**HANGE **T**RIGGER).
- There may be race conditions where the same attribute is updated in two places with different values—which one is kept?
- Peer provisioning may be synchronizing information collections that have different scopes and coverage. The provisioning process should only introduce new information entries into a destination information collection if it makes sense with respect to the scope of this information collection. The provisioning process may have to retrieve attributes from an additional information collection if the coverage of a destination information collection is broader than the coverage of the source information collection.

Example Resolved

MCHS Trading only needs to keep its Customer Hub and E-Shop application synchronized, but it also wants to leave room for possible changes (such as acquisitions of new business lines) in managing its customer details. Each information node is allocated a queue on a **Q**UEUE **M**ANAGER. When a change is made to customer information on either information node, it triggers an **E**VENT **I**NFORMATION **R**EQUEST to copy details of the change into the appropriate queue.

An **I**NFORMATION **B**ROKER picks up the resulting **I**NFORMATION **P**AYLOAD from the queue. Customer Hub has **C**OMPLETE **S**COPE so all information payloads from E-Shop are transformed and passed to Customer Hub. E-Shop has **L**OCAL **S**COPE so only information payloads that are related to existing **I**NFORMATION **E**NTRIES in E-Shop's customer information collection are transformed and passed to E-Shop. Otherwise details of customers using other channel would find their way into E-Shop's customer data, which would cause errors in the E-Shop information processes.

Known Uses

Peer provisioning is used extensively in applications handling master data or where operational systems must be synchronized.

Related Patterns

The **S**YNCHRONIZED **M**ASTERS solution pattern utilizes peer provisioning.

The **I**NFORMATION **I**DENTIFICATION patterns describe the metadata needed to locate the sources of information for peer provisioning and how closely the information collections are aligned.

The **I**NFORMATION **C**OLLECTION patterns describe the roles, scopes, and coverage of information collections. These factors will affect the design of the peer provisioning.

The **I**NFORMATION **T**RIGGER patterns describe approaches to ensuring the provisioning information processes run frequently enough to keep the information collections synchronized with minimal latency.

The **I**NFORMATION **F**LOW patterns are used to implement both the initial load and the ongoing delta changes for peer provisioning. They in turn use information processes to drive the movement and reengineering of information. See these information processes for the most common examples used in peer provisioning of this processing:

- **I**NFORMATION **S**ERVICE **P**ROCESS
- **I**NFORMATION **Q**UEUING **P**ROCESS
- **I**NFORMATION **R**EPLICATION **P**ROCESS
- **I**NFORMATION **R**EDEPLOYMENT **P**ROCESS

As the need for information transformation increases between the **I**NFORMATION **N**ODES, there is greater need for a robust intermediary that we see in the **H**UB **I**NTERCHANGE **I**NFORMATION **S**UPPLY **C**HAIN pattern.

Event-Based Provisioning

Context

How is information supplied to an information process?

Problem

An information process needs to keep track of when particular events occur, either locally or in other parts of the organization.

Example

MCHS Trading wants to monitor the comments that people are making about its products on social media so that it can react to them in a timely manner whenever appropriate.

Forces

- **Minimal reaction time to events is required—**If an information process needs to react to events as they are happening, the information gathering and processing must be as close to real time as possible.

Solution

Collect together the events into a well-known information collection that the information process can access.

As these facts and events are discovered, details of them are sent using **E**VENT **I**NFORMATION **R**EQUESTS to a common information collection that is available to the information process.

Consequences

Benefits:

- This pattern supports the processing of huge quantities of incoming data, which is extremely vital for managing information from real-world sensors and networks.

Liabilities:

- Care must be taken to save all of the information necessary for downstream information processes. In addition, some thought should be given to being able to demonstrate that the processing within the streaming provisioning is working correctly.

Example Resolved

MCHS Trading has set up a feed from a number of social media sites and uses an **I**NFORMATION **S**TREAMING **P**ROCESS to parse the text and detect when people are commenting on either the company or selected products. When these entries are detected, events are sent to the customer call center detailing the source.

Known Uses

Monitoring of information utilizes event-based processing and occurs in situations such as social media feeds, operational health monitoring, or information quality remediation processes.

Related Patterns

The **I**NFORMATION **P**ROBE patterns describe the detection and capture of events in **I**NFORMATION **N**ODES.

The **I**NFORMATION **T**RIGGER patterns describe how events may initiate subsequent actions, such as **I**NFORMATION **R**EQUESTS or **I**NFORMATION **P**ROCESSES.

Recovery Provisioning

Context

How is information supplied to an information process?

Problem

The infrastructure supporting an information collection may fail. How do we restore the information to the information supply chain?

Example

One stormy night, there is a power outage and the E-Shop application suffers a disk head crash. How does the MCHS Trading team recover the situation?

Forces

- **Failures may happen at any time**—An unusual incident can create a cascading series of failures.
- **Constant change of information**—Information that is critical to an organization's operation is often changing all of the time.

Solution

Maintain an ongoing backup copy that is physically separate and secure. Ensure there is an alternative infrastructure to host the restored collection.

Recovery provisioning is enabled through backup/restore routines. It takes planning to work though all of the permutations of possible failures from a simple accidental delete of information, to hardware failure, or an incident at the physical location of the information nodes, which prevents their use. The plans should consider how to act if the situation is either temporary or permanent. Finally, an organization must practice its responses to different types of incidents to ensure all recent changes to teams, systems, and working practices are covered in the plans.

Example Resolved

MCHS Trading replaces the failed drive and restores E-Shop's information collections from its backup that fortunately finished about an hour before the storm started.

Consequences

Benefits:

- Having backup collections and processes helps to ensure successful recovery from unanticipated disasters or from planned maintenance.

Liabilities:

- Backups need to be regular and managed in order to be successful, particularly as part of a disaster recovery plan, a common managed activity. Backups require storage, which adds cost, whether onsite or offsite. Disaster recovery plans and backups also require periodic review and tests to ensure effectiveness.

Known Uses

Recovery provisioning is used after an incident that takes away the information normally available to an information process.

Related Patterns

Recovery provisioning should be used with all information collections that have either MASTER USAGE or HYBRID USAGE.

Summary of Information Provisioning

The information provisioning patterns describe how information is supplied to information processes. This may involve moving information between information collections. The patterns that describe how information flows between information collections are described by the INFORMATION SUPPLY CHAIN patterns.

Information Supply Chain Patterns

Using the terminology of a supply chain, the purpose of an "information" supply chain is to produce one or more related "information products" (for example, reports, documents, web pages, or stored collections of information) from the information supplied to it. The information products must be delivered to their consumers at the right time and through the appropriate channels.

An information supply chain defines the end-to-end view of how information of a certain type, or for a certain purpose, is delivered to where it is needed. An organization will have many information supply chains supporting its business—each one designed to fulfill a particular purpose.

The INFORMATION SUPPLY CHAIN pattern shown in Table 4.16 describes the basic mechanism of an information supply chain.

Table 4.16 Information Supply Chain Pattern Summary

Icon	Pattern Name	Problem	Solution
	INFORMATION SUPPLY CHAIN	An organization needs to process information in order to fulfill its purpose. How is the flow of information coordinated throughout the organization's people and systems?	Design and manage well-defined flows of information that start from the points where information is collected for the organization and links them to the places where key consumers receive the information they need.

Information supply chains are described in terms of linked INFORMATION COLLECTIONS that show how information flows between them. The aim is to clarify where responsibility for keeping the information up to date is located and the influence that those changes have on other information collections due to the distribution of information between the information collections.

This activity highlights inefficiencies in the information flow and places where updates are missing.

The supply chain analogy helps in the strategic planning for the information systems, the design of the integration logic, and in the day-to-day operations. It helps to maximize the benefit of any processing on the information and minimize the inefficiencies, particularly in the one major aspect where information supply chains differ from physical manufacturing supply chains. Information can be duplicated very easily. The expense comes in storing, synchronizing, managing, protecting, and recovering the information. So the aim is to create a well-ordered flow, which places the processing in the most optimal place and reduces the number of times information is duplicated. Once the information is duplicated, we minimize the amount it is processed, trying to keep it as a read-only reference copy.

Operationally, quality checks and monitors can be introduced at strategic points in the information supply chain to ensure the right processing is occurring and that information is transformed in a manner that maintains consistency and integrity across the information nodes.

Information Supply Chain

Context

An organization is a complex mix of people and assets, cooperating and interacting with the world around it to fulfill its purpose.

Problem

An organization needs to process information in order to fulfill its purpose. How is the flow of information coordinated throughout the organization's people and systems?

The volume and quantity of information needed to operate even a small organization is much more than any one individual can comprehend. So work and information is divided up into manageable chunks. These chunks need to coordinate and share information. The interactions are complex with many opportunities for error.

How do we coordinate the sharing of information in a reliable, timely, and cost-effective way?

Example

MCHS Trading owns a number of applications, each supporting different parts of the business. Information must flow between its order-taking, Shipping, and Invoicing applications to receive and fulfill customers' orders.

Any failures in this flow of information could affect the organization's ability to serve its customers or collect money for goods sent out.

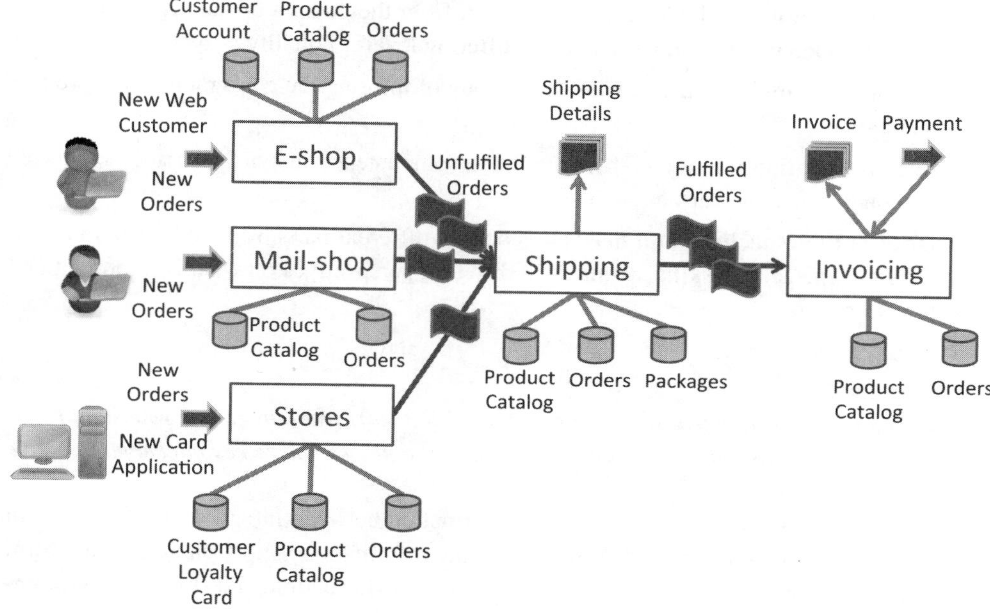

Figure 4.14 Order-processing systems at MCHS Trading.

Forces

- **Duplicated information**—The same information may be stored in many places in an organization's systems.
- **Variety of information formats**—Each copy of information tends to have its own unique format and there are differences in validation rules and the use of the information.
- **Inconsistent definition**—The set of valid values for an information attribute may not be consistent throughout the organization.
- **Disconnected information supply**—An employee receiving new information may not be a direct user of any of the information processes within the information supply chain that manages this type of information.
- **People make mistakes**—Someone may enter incorrect information into a user interface, either through lack of attention, lack of training, or because the values he or she has are not correct.

- **Multiple channels**—Information coming in from the outside of the organization can arrive through many channels and have differing levels of quality.
- **Storage and maintenance costs**—Each copy of information costs money to store and maintain.
- **Synchronization latency**—There is always some latency in synchronizing new information between the various copies.
- **Different perspectives and needs**—People in different parts of the organization have different specialized skills, resulting in different perspectives on what is important and the information they need.

Solution

Design and manage well-defined flows of information that start from the points where information is collected for the organization and links them to the places where key consumers receive the information they need.

An information supply chain is a flow of information between information collections in order to convert information received from outside the information supply chain into the form that is needed by its information users. The movement, transformation, and storing of information in the information collections is the responsibility of the information processes.

The type of information within an information supply chain is typically information from a particular subject area (topic) or information for a particular process. This information is transformed between the different kinds of INFORMATION ELEMENTS as it flows along the information supply chain.

Consider Figure 4.15. The start of an information supply chain is where the organization receives new information either from people or external systems that is needed for it to fulfill its goal. It combines this "information supply" with the built-in capability/knowledge of the organization to produce the information products.

INFORMATION PROCESSES inside the information supply chain are responsible for processing information to build the information products. There are many types of information processes in the information supply chain, each with their own responsibilities to receive, transform, and move information around.

INFORMATION NODES are the systems that host the information processes. They also host the storage of information in what are called INFORMATION COLLECTIONS.

Information processes may need to access information stored in information collections that are hosted on different information nodes. INFORMATION PROVISIONING provides the mechanisms to connect the information processes to the information they need.

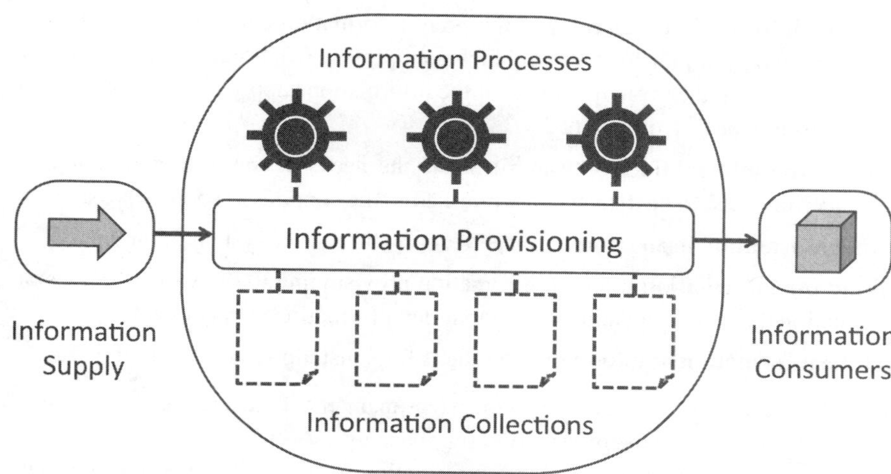

Figure 4.15 Information Supply Chain solution components.

The information within the information supply chain must be protected from carelessness, theft, accident, and improper use. It is protected using three groups of patterns:

- **I**NFORMATION **R**EENGINEERING—Defines the types of processing that improves the quality of the information
- **I**NFORMATION **G**UARD—Defines ways to ensure information is only used for its intended purpose
- **I**NFORMATION **P**ROBE—Measures that information is what it should be, where it should be, and when it should be

These capabilities are applied within the information provisioning part of the information supply chain. The descriptions for these patterns explain how they are used.

Information supply is one of the key points of vulnerability of the information supply chain. It provides the opportunity to receive bad information. It also runs the risk of missing information that is vital to the correct working of the organization.

Managing the information supply is hard because information is supplied to the organization through many different routes. For each route, it is important to understand the context under which the data is captured because this will affect the assumptions that can be made about the values and where it is appropriate to use it in the information supply chain.

In broad outline, the information supply chain has the following parts:

- **Capture the information** preferably at the point information enters the organization. This is typically (a) through an externally facing employee, (b) through an external user interface, (c) from another system outside of the information supply chain, or (d) from a sensor monitoring the environment.
- **Reengineer the information** to ensure it meets the needs of the information supply chain. Any errors need to be detected and returned to the supplier as soon as possible.
- **Store the information** in an information collection—in case of system failures.
- **Distribute the information** through information provisioning to the various copies of the information that needs updating throughout the information supply chain.
- **Export the information** as information products for consumption by external parties.

These steps should be present and executed in a consistent manner for each of the routes that a particular type of information enters the information supply chain.

When an information supply chain produces information for a consumer, it goes through the following steps:

- The recipient connects to the information supply chain at the appropriate point.
- Information guards ensure the recipient is allowed to receive the information.
- The information is gathered from the information collections and an information product is created.
- The information product is exported from the information supply chain to the recipient. A record of the export may be stored.

Some information products require information to be gathered from multiple remote information collections. Then it must be restructured, aggregated, and analyzed before the information product can be created.

Information collections store the values for the information product where the processes needed to create it are involved, or the product is used repeatedly. When the information product is requested, it can be quickly generated from this information collection alone. This not only saves work, it also provides useful information for auditors to understand who knew what information at any one time.

Within the information supply chain, updates to the stored information are received from the information processes and information is moved between the information collections. The usage of these information collections along the information supply chain should ensure the **M**ASTER **U**SAGE information collections are at the start, then the **H**YBRID **U**SAGE information collection and the **R**EFERENCE **U**SAGE in the middle and **S**ANDBOX **U**SAGE collections in the leaf nodes. This is described in Figure 4.16.

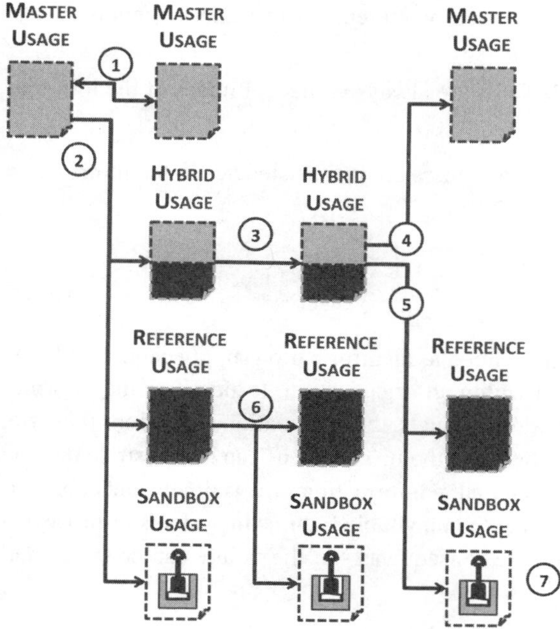

Figure 4.16 Usage of information collections along an information supply chain.

The numbers on the diagram for Figure 4.16 refer to these notes:

1. All information collections in the information supply chain with master usage should be synchronized, typically with PEER PROVISIONING.
2. A master usage information collection can be used to provision hybrid and reference usage information supply chains, typically with MIRRORING PROVISIONING, and sandbox usage information collections, typically with either mirroring provisioning or SNAPSHOT PROVISIONING.
3. A hybrid usage information collection can feed another hybrid usage information collection. All of the attributes sent should be reference values in the downstream information collection that have been enriched with additional master usage attributes.
4. A hybrid usage information collection may feed a master usage information collection as long as the master usage information collection only stores attributes that are mastered by the hybrid information collection.
5. A hybrid information collection can also feed a reference usage and a sandbox usage information collection.

6. A reference information collection can feed a reference usage and a sandbox usage information collection.
7. The sandbox usage information collections are always in the leaf nodes of the information supply chain.

If you see different patterns of usage, it is a sign that there are inconsistencies in the information supply chain.

Consequences

Benefits:

- Analyzing the end-to-end flow of information as an information supply chain highlights how information is created and used within an organization. It identifies the information processes that create the information products, the information collections they use, and how information is provisioning between them. This focus can demonstrate that the organization is working effectively because the information flow is timely and appropriate. This understanding also ensures that the inevitable failures in systems or processes can be dealt with effectively because the consequences of the failure can be traced and corrected.

Liabilities:

- An organization gets the information it deserves. Good design of the information supply chain provides the basic mechanisms, but if there is no governance around information, meaning an individual is not incented to treat information quality as an important part of his or her role, much of the value is lost. There is more detail on the information governance in the **I**NFORMATION **G**OVERNANCE **P**ROGRAM pattern.
- Most information supply chains need to include applications because these systems act as key sources of the latest information. However, these systems are not always built with information provisioning in mind and they must be connected into the information supply chain with care so this additional processing does not detract from their main mission.
- Connecting an existing system to the information supply chain means that the downstream systems become dependent on it, which may make it harder to upgrade and enhance it in the future.
- The validation rules for information located in an information node within the information supply chain must be compatible with the rules in force downstream of it or information values will not be able to flow all of the way along the information supply chain.

Example Resolved

MCHS Trading has five information supply chains that are critical to its business, as shown in Figure 4.17:

- **Customer**—Synchronizing and collating information about their customers
- **Product**—Maintaining and distributing information about the products they are selling
- **Order**—Sending details of the orders to process between the order-processing information nodes
- **Stock**—Requesting new stock from suppliers
- **Summaries**—Collating and summarizing the state of the business

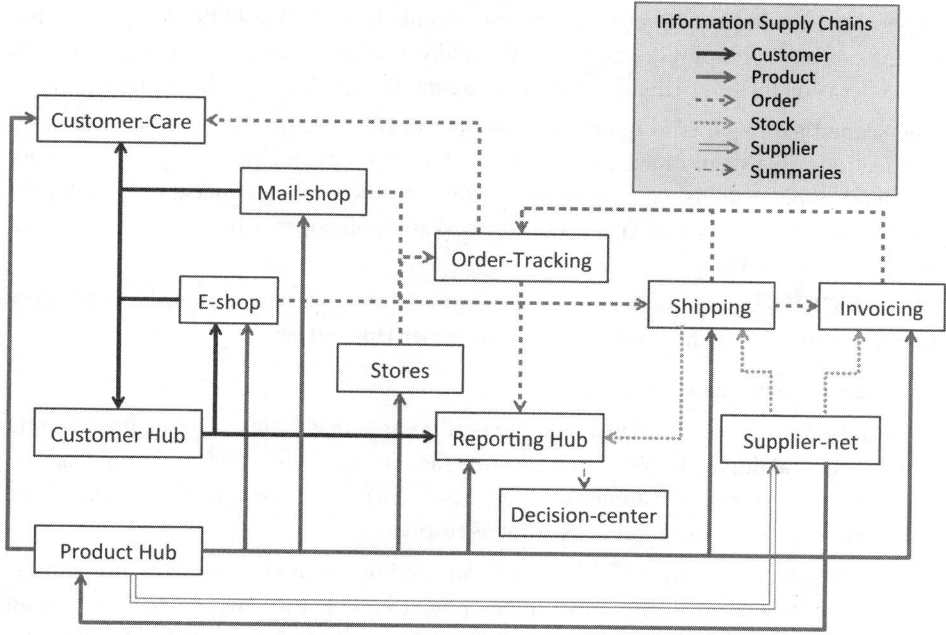

Figure 4.17 Information supply chains at MCHS Trading.

Each was designed and improved independently. However, you can see that they share components such as information nodes and information collections.

Looking at the customer information supply chain in more detail, you can see that it originates from a new application called Customer-Care. An MCHS Trading employee is able to enter new details for a customer through Customer-Care's user interface and validate that the details are complete and correct. If the customer is present, he or she can also perform a validation of the other contact details, request a loyalty card, and answer questions about the status of orders or other inquiries. All changes are sent to the Customer Hub to update the master customer record.

The Customer Hub would also receive updates from the E-Shop application when the customer changes his or her contact details directly through the E-Shop website.

New customer details received through the Mail-Shop application are more problematic because they are captured in the context of making an order, rather than the customer explicitly informing MCHS Trading that his or her details have changed. MCHS Trading needed to make a policy decision as to how it wanted to handle this case:

1. The safest approach is to ask the customer explicitly at the time of ordering if the address given is a permanent residence. This changes the implicit change of address into an explicit request. It would require changes to the mail order forms and the Mail-Shop application would have to retrieve customer details from the Customer Hub so that the customer service employee can verify the address information on the order while the customer is on the line. This approach is using the UNIQUE ENTRIES pattern.
2. The second approach is to ignore all customer details entered through the Mail-Shop application. This would mean the Customer Hub only maintains details of customers that have either established a relationship with MCHS Trading either through a Stores card or an E-Shop account. This is the cheapest solution but may have knock-on effects for the Reporting Hub.
3. Third, MCHS Trading could assume the card address received in an order is the customer's permanent address and have the Customer Hub either:
   - Update the new value directly.
   - Create a new customer record with the new address that is linked to the original one as a potential duplicate. When the customer next makes contact with MCHS Trading, either the E-Shop or Customer-Care application asks the customer to validate his or her address so that the address question is resolved.

This discussion illustrates how important it is to understand the context in which information is collected and where they are mismatches with the context in which it is to be used, there is an INFORMATION MANAGEMENT PRINCIPLE set out describing how it should be handled. This information principle would have to apply consistently across the information supply chain.

Once the customer master is updated, the Customer Hub distributes the changes to the Reporting Hub and, if necessary, to the E-Shop application.

The flow of information along the customer information supply chain is maintained using MIRRORING PROVISIONING.

Known Uses

An information supply chain is created whenever systems are integrated so information is flowing between them. Each information supply chain is focused on achieving a particular goal:

- Synchronizing information of a particular subject area, such as Customer Details
- Consolidating information that supports a particular information product, such as a regulatory report
- Supplying an information process, such as analytics
- Supplying information to a group of people with specialist skills, either for a project, or an ongoing basis

Often these information supply chains are implemented by a single project and may not take a holistic view of the organization's information as suggested by this pattern.

Related Patterns

The solution for this pattern has already referenced a number of patterns that describe the different aspects of the information supply chain. These patterns give more details of how these capabilities work and link to one another. They also cover the many variations that exist in real-world organizations. The principle patterns are as follows:

- INFORMATION PROCESS
- INFORMATION COLLECTION
- INFORMATION PROVISIONING
- INFORMATION NODE

Most information supply chains support a single subject area, as specified by a SUBJECT AREA DEFINITION. It supports the transformation of information from this subject area through the various kinds of INFORMATION ELEMENTS.

Variations of the Information Supply Chain Pattern

The variations of the information supply chain pattern shown in Table 4.17 consider how information is supplied to different organizational structures. These organizational structures affect the ownership of information, where it is created and updated, and how it is consumed.

Table 4.17 Types of Information Supply Chains Patterns Summary

Icon	Pattern Name	Problem	Solution
	CASCADING INFORMATION SUPPLY CHAIN	Information that is centrally maintained must be distributed to other parts of the organization.	Distribute read-only copies of the information to other information nodes and synchronize these copies whenever values change in the centrally controlled information.
	HUB INTERCHANGE INFORMATION SUPPLY CHAIN	Information that has distributed ownership among peer organizations must be managed and shared.	Consolidate the information into new information collections (often hosted in a new information node) and then distribute the consolidated information from there.
	SINGLE VIEW INFORMATION SUPPLY CHAIN	An organization requires a real-time consolidated view of information that is managed through distributed operation and ownership.	Consolidate information into coherent information collections that provide appropriate information services to collectively meet the information requirements.
	CONCENTRATING INFORMATION SUPPLY CHAIN	Information must be provided for centralized control of distributed activity.	Perform a first pass on the data as close to its source as possible with an aim to cleanse and add context to it. Then pass the results to centralized information collections where information processes can build up the big picture.
	HIERARCHICAL INFORMATION SUPPLY CHAIN	Information must be exchanged between centralized and decentralized parts of an organization.	Design a multiway synchronization where each information node flows changes to the values it masters to the other information nodes that maintain a reference copy.
	PEER EXCHANGE INFORMATION SUPPLY CHAIN	Independently operating organizations need to share information among one another.	Each organization is responsible for broadcasting all changes to its peers, who are then responsible for incorporating these changes in their information collections.

Cascading Information Supply Chain

Context

An organization needs to process information in order to fulfill its purpose. How is the flow of information coordinated throughout the organization's people and systems?

Problem

Information that is centrally maintained must be distributed to other parts of the organization.

More specifically, there are other information nodes that host read-only information collections of the same subject area and these information collections need to be kept synchronized with the centrally maintained information.

Example

MCHS Trading has introduced a Product Hub application for creating the definition of the goods and services it offers to its customers. These product definitions need to be distributed to the order-taking systems: E-Shop, Mail-Shop, and Stores, plus the Shipping and the Invoicing applications.

Forces

- **Different information formats**—Each information collection will probably store information from the same subject area in its own private format.
- **Different subsets of information**—Each information collection will have its own scope of information entries and coverage of attributes.
- **Different availability**—The information nodes may be available at different times.
- **Different keys**—The information collection may use different approaches to identifying their information entries.

Solution

Distribute read-only copies of the information to other information nodes and synchronize these copies whenever values change in the centrally controlled information.

This information supply chain assumes there is a single place in the organization where information values from a subject area are maintained (created, updated, deleted). This information collection, called the centralized master, can be maintained by:

- Information processes hosted on the same information node
- Information processes hosted on another information node, but accessing through remote information collections

Other information nodes may host these values, but they are read-only reference copies of the centralized master that are synchronized using collection-level INFORMATION PROVISIONING.

The simplest form of this information supply chain is where all of the attributes for the subject area are maintained and then distributed from a single information collection. However, the information supply chain may be multilevel where downstream information nodes may add additional attributes before cascading the information further.

Figure 4.18 illustrates the cascading information supply chain.

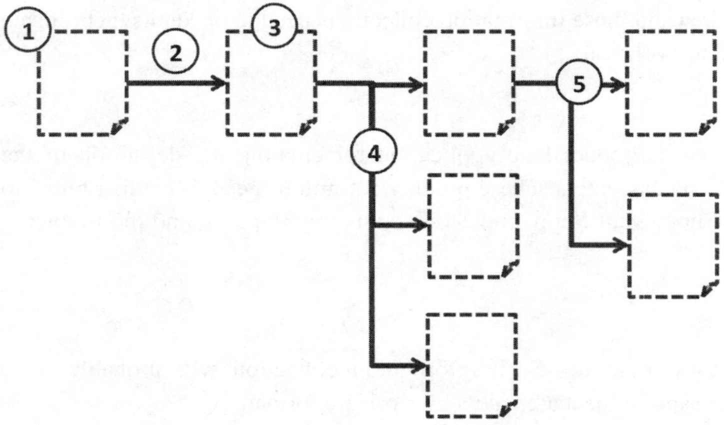

Figure 4.18 Cascading Information Supply Chain solution.

The numbers on the diagram in Figure 4.18 refer to these notes:

1. At the head of the information supply chain, information is collected together and stored in an information collection.
2. The information is distributed to one or more downstream information nodes, where it is stored in local information collections.
3. The information received is read-only, but an information node may add attributes to each information entry.
4. These additional attributes may be distributed with the original information.
5. No matter how many times the information is distributed, no received values can be changes—only new attributes added.

Consequences

Benefits:

- This information supply chain is the easiest to coordinate because all updates are happening in one copy of the information—in the single source. Therefore, there is only one place where the quality of the information needs to be assured and because all copies are derived from a common base, there is good consistency between them.

Liabilities:

- The systems on the receiving end of this information supply chain must not make changes to the information they receive because:
  - It breaks the consistency of the information supply chain because there is no mechanism to distribute these changes back to the other systems.
  - These changes are likely to be overwritten at some point when updates from the upstream systems are received.

  As a result, any information processes in these downstream systems that make changes to the information collections must be disabled.

Example Resolved

See Figure 4.19.

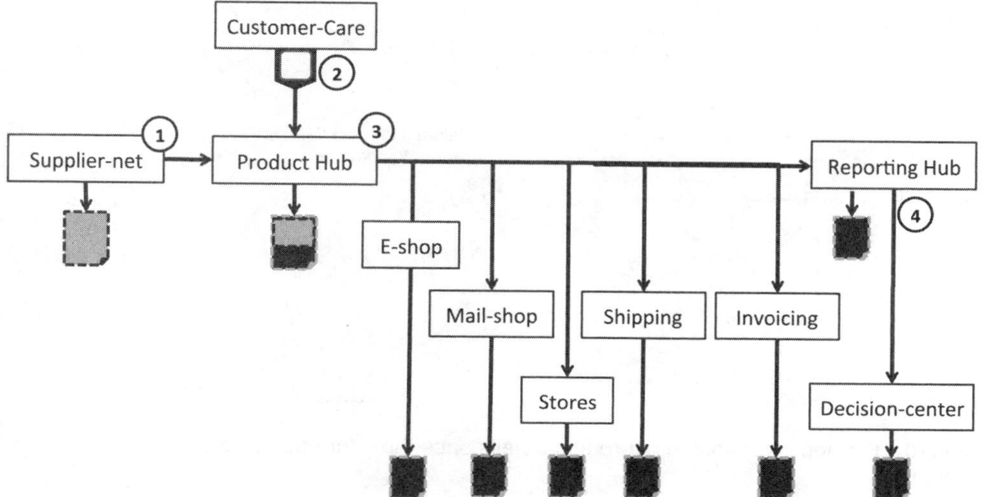

Figure 4.19 Product details cascading though MCHS Trading's information nodes.

The numbers on the diagram in Figure 4.19 refer to these notes:

1. Product details from the suppliers are supplied to MCHS Trading via the Supplier-net gateway and are sent to Product Hub.
2. The Product Hub is used to define additional information about the product to make it suitable for the MCHS Channels. The Customer-Care application uses an information service to query the product details in the Product Hub whenever they are needed.
3. MCHS Trading use MIRRORING PROVISIONING to synchronize the product details from Product Hub to E-Shop, Mail-Shop, Stores, Shipping, Invoicing, and Reporting Hub. Notice that each of these applications has a different scope and coverage so the provisioning must filter and transform the information differently for each of the destinations.
4. The Reporting Hub sends summaries of the product details to different information marts in the Decision-Center.

The E-Shop and Mail-Shop applications both have information processes that allow an information user to maintain their product details information collection. These information processes are disabled once the product details information supply chain is in place. See Figure 4.20.

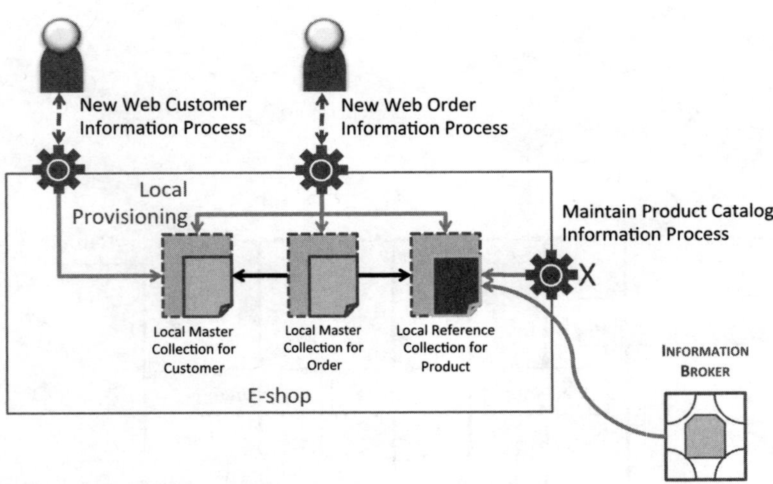

Figure 4.20 E-Shop provisioning of product details once the information supply chain is operational.

Known Uses

This pattern is used whenever it is possible to centralize information and publish read-only copies to other systems that need the information stored locally.

It is also used to populate an INFORMATION WAREHOUSE and related INFORMATION MARTS and INFORMATION CUBES.

Related Patterns

The CENTRALIZED MASTER information solution uses the cascading information supply chain.

Hub Interchange Information Supply Chain

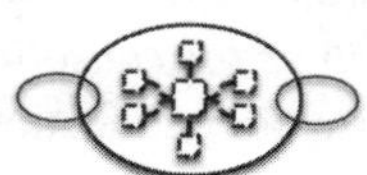

Context

An organization needs to process information in order to fulfill its purpose. How is the flow of information coordinated throughout the organization's people and systems?

Problem

Information that has distributed ownership among peer organizations must be managed and shared.

This means that information from the same subject area is located in a variety of information nodes owned by different parts of the organization. This information must be collated and distributed as a consistent view of information among these information nodes.

Example

Loyal and satisfied customers are a key reason MCHS Trading has been so successful over the years. However, the rising number of channels that provide service to their customers has led to a fragmentation of the information about their customers. How do they enable the different channels to continue to operate independently while sharing a consistent view of their customers?

Forces

- **Unsuitable formats—**The format of the same information in different information nodes is typically different.
- **Different scopes and coverage—**The scope and coverage of the information collections in each information node is probably different. **Note:** Scope and coverage are concepts covered in the INFORMATION COLLECTION patterns.
- **Inadequate availability—**The availability of the different information node will vary because the operating times of different parts of the organization are different.

- **Uncorrelated information**—Information about the same instance is rarely correlated between the different sources of information. For example, information about a particular person may appear in more than one information node and the information keys used to identify the person are likely to be different in each source.
- **Inconsistent information**—Information about the same instance is rarely consistent between the different sources of information. For example, information about a particular person may appear in more than one information node and the information values stored could vary between each source.

Solution

Consolidate the information into new information collections (often hosted in a new information node) and then distribute the consolidated information from there.

The new information collections form a hub that is used to synchronize the information. They are often hosted in a new information node because it must be available whenever any of the existing information nodes need it and this is easier to achieve if the hosting node is only managing information. See Figure 4.21.

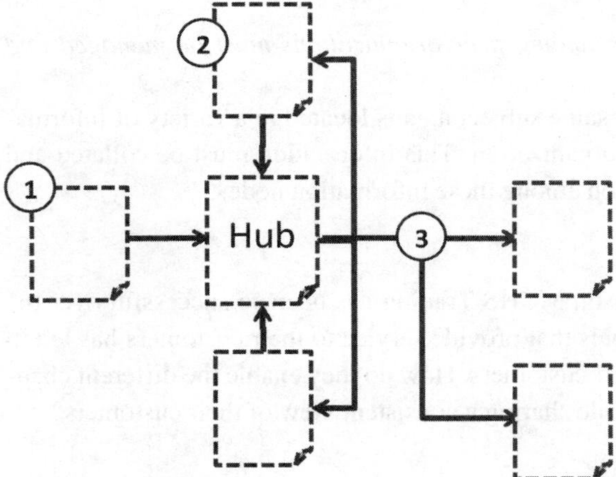

Figure 4.21 Hub interchange information supply chain.

The numbers of the diagram in Figure 4.21 refer to these notes:

1. Some information collections are feeds to the hub. These are master usage information collections and receive no updates to that information from the hub. The hub may treat these values as reference values, or it must be reconciled between any new values that come from these sources and those stored in the hub.

2. Some information collections are synchronized with the hub. New values are exchanged in either direction.
3. Some information collections receive updates from the hub. These values should be treated as reference values in order to have a synchronized information supply chain.

Before the hub can be used, it must be loaded with the information that is to be shared between the existing information nodes. This loading process will cleanse, correlate, and consolidate the information together so there is a single consolidated view of the information.

Once the single consolidated view of the information is available, the organization may choose to synchronize these values back to the original information nodes. This can potentially create a lot of churn in the original information nodes if the quality of their information is poor. However, the benefit is that all of the information nodes begin with consistent information.

Once the hub is operational and any initial information synchronization is complete, a variety of INFORMATION PROVISIONING approaches are used to keep all of the information collections synchronized among the participating information nodes as information is created, retrieved, updated, and deleted. For example,

- INFORMATION SERVICES are used to supply information from the hub to information processes on demand. These information processes may be business information processes supporting the organization's work directly or provisioning information processes that are synchronizing information with other information collections.
- MIRRORING PROVISIONING is used to pass new information to the hub from information collections that are just acting as a source of information for the hub.
- Mirroring provisioning is also used to distribute new information to information collections that are only destinations for the hub.
- PEER PROVISIONING is used to synchronize information both to and from the hub and another information collection.

The synchronizing of information between the hub and the other information nodes can be done immediately when a change occurs, or batched up and delivered periodically.

Consequences

Benefits:

- The hub provides a place to consolidate and correlated distributed information into a canonical form before it is distributed. It provides the means to decouple the sources from the destinations. It also provides a point to run analytics and other monitoring against the information.

Liabilities:

- You have introduced another copy of the information that needs to be managed. As such, it needs an owner who will sponsor ongoing development and maintenance of the hub so that it continues to meet the needs of the destinations.
- As information is distributed from the hub, care must be taken to respect the scope and coverage of the destination information nodes to ensure they are not affected by the availability of more information than they were designed to handle.

Example Resolved

MCHS Trading introduces an **I**NFORMATION **A**SSET **H**UB called **Customer Hub** to manage its customer details. See Figure 4.22. This is kept synchronized through **P**EER **P**ROVISIONING with the **E-Shop** application (1). At the same time, the loyalty card for the physical stores is upgraded to cover all channels and support for it is transferred to a new information node called **Customer-Care** (2). Customer-Care uses the **I**NFORMATION **S**ERVICES of the Customer Hub directly to get access to customer details because it needs to access information about all customers irrespective of the channel they use. Any changes to customer details are sent from the Customer Hub to the Reporting Hub (3).

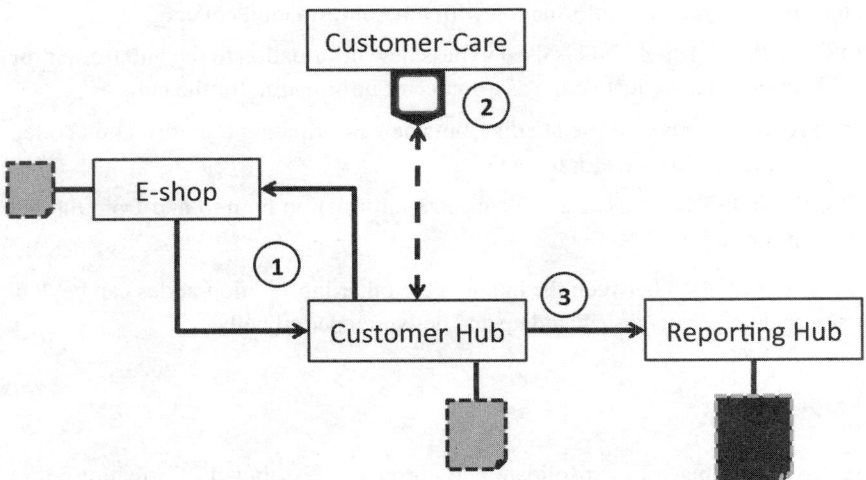

Figure 4.22 The Customer Hub at MCHS Trading.

Known Uses

This pattern is used to synchronize information with a Master Data Management (MDM) hub or operational data store.

Related Patterns

The **I**NFORMATION **A**SSET **H**UB and **O**PERATIONAL **S**TATUS **S**TORE information nodes can host the hub component described in this pattern. The following information solutions implement a hub interchange information supply chain:

- **I**NFORMATION **R**EGISTRY
- **G**OLDEN **R**EFERENCE
- **S**YNCHRONIZED **M**ASTERS

Single View Information Supply Chain

Context

An organization needs to process information in order to fulfill its purpose. How is the flow of information coordinated throughout the organization's people and systems?

Problem

An organization requires a real-time consolidated view of information that is managed through distributed operation and ownership.

A new information process can introduce requirements for a new information collection. The information that belongs in this information collection exists, but is currently located in a multitude of information nodes. How can this information be accessed and correlated to answer real-time information service queries from the information process?

Example

When a customer calls the MCHS Trading customer care center, the customer service representative needs to understand who the customer is, his or her history of interaction with the organization, and in-flight/recent orders. This information is located in multiple information nodes, including E-Shop, Mail-Shop, Stores, Shipping, and Invoicing.

Forces

- **Real-time access**—The information process needs up-to-date information in real time but this information is dispersed among a variety of information collections.
- **Information does not meet requirements**—The format and consistency of the information in the sources is not necessarily consistent with the requirements of the information process.
- **Multiple element types**—A consolidated view typically includes multiple types of information elements. The core is often an INFORMATION ASSET that is linked to multiple types and instances of INFORMATION ACTIVITIES and INFORMATION EVENTS, which in turn may link to other types of information assets. Each type of element may be located in a different information collection and they must be retrieved and linked together to support the single view.
- **Incompatible availability**—The availability of the information sources is not necessarily compatible with the needs of the single view consumers.

Solution

Consolidate information into coherent information collections that provide appropriate information services to collectively meet the information requirements.

The on-demand information supply chain is based around an INFORMATION COLLECTION that meets the needs of the consuming information processes. This information collection is implemented with an INFORMATION FEDERATION PROCESS that calls information services of a set of information collections that provide the information for the virtual information collection. Some of these information collections are located in existing information nodes and others are created especially to support this information supply chain. These new information collections are synchronized with other existing information nodes using either MIRRORING PROVISIONING or PEER PROVISIONING. The single view information supply chain is illustrated in Figure 4.23.

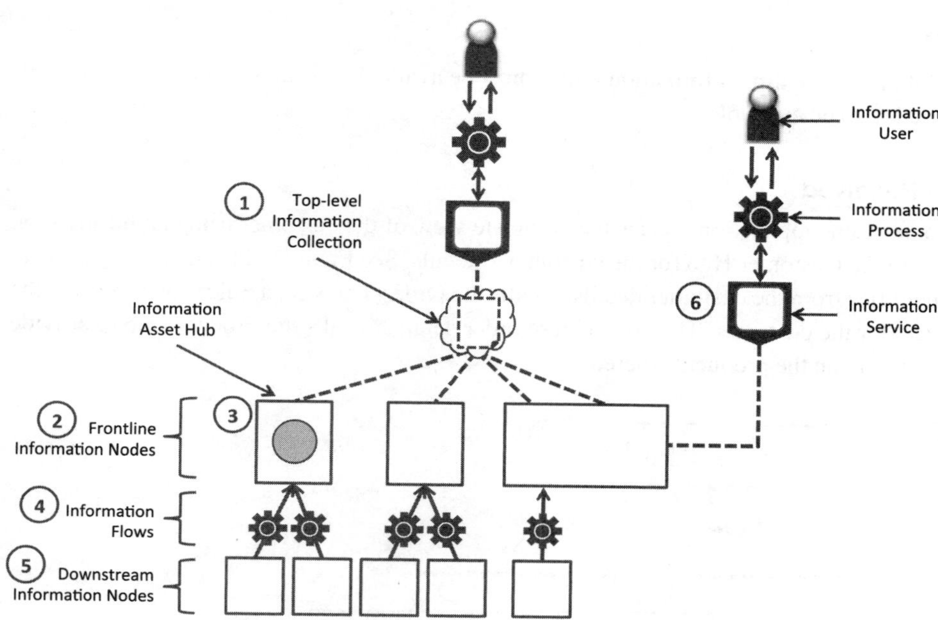

Figure 4.23 Single View Information Supply Chain solution.

The virtual information collection at the root of the information supply chain is labeled (1) and supports the federated views of the information. Behind it are the frontline information nodes (2) that host the information services that collectively support the virtual information collection. They are called each time the top-level information service is called.

These types of information supply chains often need a consolidated view of key INFORMATION ASSETS among the frontline information nodes, which is why you see an INFORMATION ASSET HUB at position (3).

Downstream information nodes (5) may feed the frontline nodes using INFORMATION FLOWS (4).

Both the frontline and downstream information nodes are still accessed directly (6). The information they see is a partial view of the same information exposed through the single view information supply chain.

Consequences

Benefits:

- The information processes using the virtual information collection are reusing information stored in existing information collections.

Liabilities:

- All of the frontline information nodes must be available for the virtual information collection to be available.

Example Resolved

The Customer-Care application creates the complete view of the customer using an information service call to the Customer Hub for the customer's details. See Figure 4.24. Then using the customer's identifier from the customer details, it calls the Order-Tracking application to extract the recent orders for the customer. Then from these order details, it calls the Product Hub to provide more information on the products ordered.

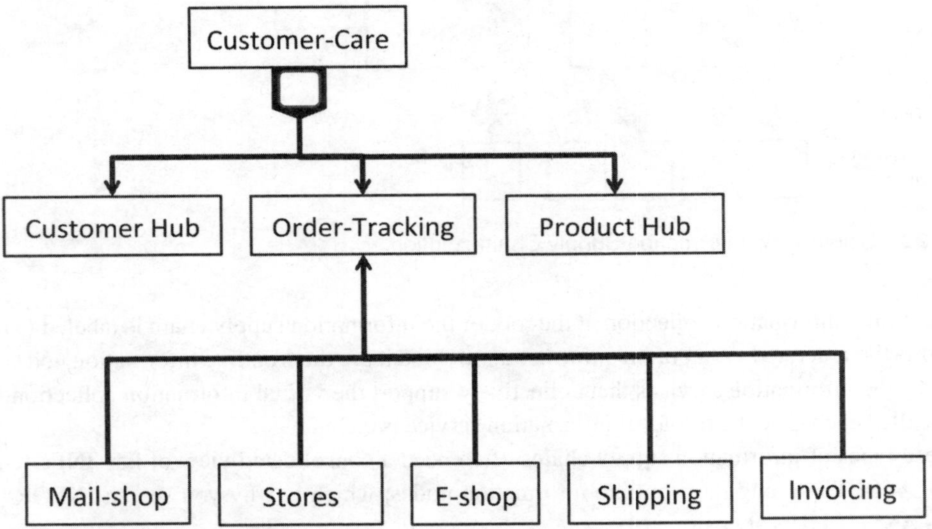

Figure 4.24 Single view of MCHS Trading's customers.

Known Uses

This approach is used to create consolidated views of customer details for websites and predictive analytics scoring.

Related Patterns

An **I**NFORMATION **A**SSET **H**UB is usually one of the frontline information nodes.

A **T**RIGGERING **I**NFORMATION **S**ERVICE provides the implementation of the virtual information collection. It typically triggers an **I**NFORMATION **F**EDERATION **P**ROCESS.

Consolidating Information Supply Chain

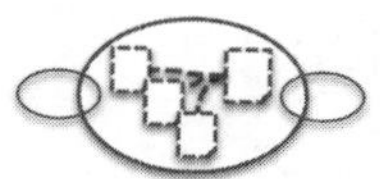

Context

An organization needs to process information in order to fulfill its purpose. How is the flow of information coordinated throughout the organization's people and systems?

Problem

Information must be provided for centralized control of distributed activity.

Example

MCHS Trading wants to centrally monitor that its information supply chains are working properly. For example, it wants to know that orders are being fulfilled on time, that product descriptions are correct, and that customer information is up to date. How does MCHS Trading achieve this?

Forces

- **Information has a context—**This must be captured and preserved if the information is moved to a new location.

Solution

Perform a first pass on the information as close to its source as possible with an aim to cleanse and add context to it. Then pass the results to centralized information collections where information processes can build up the big picture.

The effect is that the scope of the information collections increases as the information moves further down the information supply chain. See Figure 4.25.

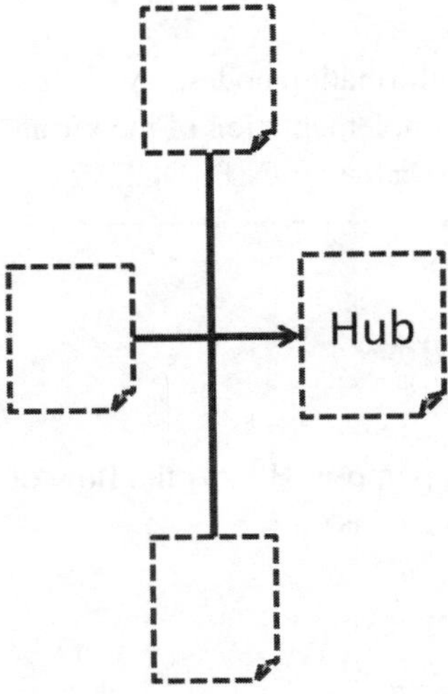

Figure 4.25 Consolidating Information Supply Chain solution.

Consequences

Benefits:

- This type of information supply chain efficiently collates and consolidates information from information collections that are distributed throughout an organization's information nodes.

Liabilities:

- The process of collating and consolidating the information may introduce a delay before the information is analyzed. Where events need to be evaluated within minutes, it may be better to use a SINGLE VIEW INFORMATION SUPPLY CHAIN.

Example Resolved

MCHS Trading set up INFORMATION PROBES at each of its information nodes to monitor the information processes that contribute to its information supply chains. Each information probe writes the events it detects to a local INFORMATION EVENT STORE. Periodically, new events are extracted from the information event store and sent to their central operations console. Events more than 3 days old are removed from the event stores.

This use of a consolidating information supply chain is often time critical. Its aim is to gather information from a wide range of sources and consolidate them into a central location where the values can be processed in near-real-time, while also allowing historical analysis of the information. See Figure 4.26.

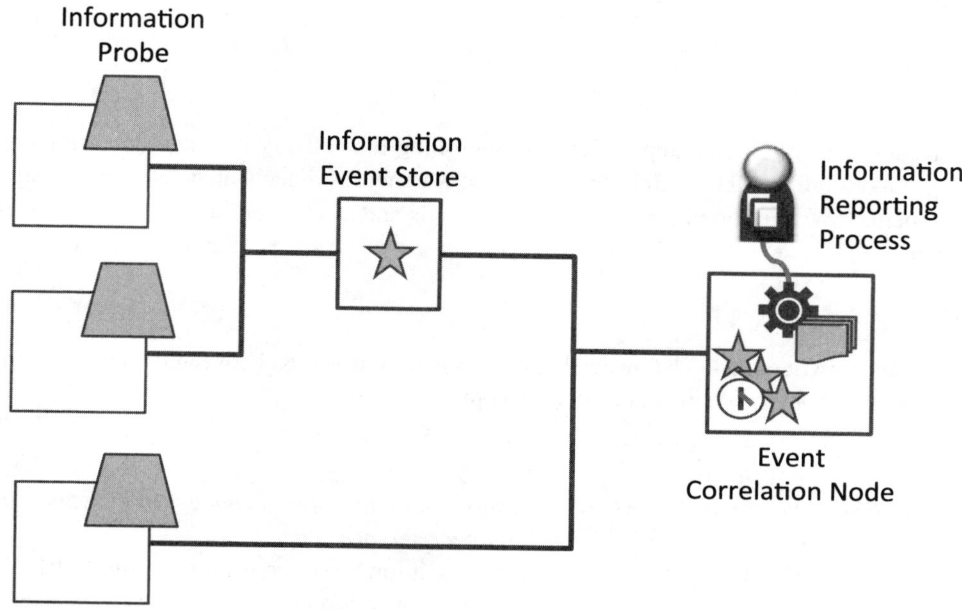

Figure 4.26 Monitoring and collecting events at MCHS Trading.

Known Uses

Consolidating information supply chains are used to support centralized monitoring solutions where information is captured in highly dispersed locations and then consolidated into a central monitoring point. It is sometimes referred to as a *fan-in* style of integration. The way that events are moved through the information supply chain is sometimes referred to as *store and forward*.

Related Patterns

The INFORMATION MONITORING solution makes use of a consolidating information supply chain.

Hierarchical Information Supply Chain

Context

An organization needs to process information in order to fulfill its purpose. How is the flow of information coordinated throughout the organization's people and systems?

Problem

Information must be exchanged between centralized and decentralized parts of an organization.

Example

MCHS Trading has a Shipping application for controlling the delivery of orders to customers and stores. Goods are distributed from three physical warehouses. Each warehouse runs a stock control system. How is information about product details and stock coordinated between these four systems?

Forces

- **Shared ownership**—The ownership of information is shared between the information nodes, although each maintains its own copy.

Solution

Design a multiway synchronization where each information node flows changes to the values it masters to the other information nodes that maintain a reference copy.

The hierarchical information supply chain uses information collections with **H**YBRID **U**SAGE. The strategy is that for each value, there is only one information node that is responsible for updating it (**M**ASTER **U**SAGE), while the others read it (**R**EFERENCE **U**SAGE).

Figure 4.27 illustrates the pattern.

The numbers on the diagram in Figure 4.27 refer to these notes:

1. The hierarchical information supply chain is split into two levels: the top-level node and then subordinate nodes.
2. When information changes in one level, it is made available to the other level. In the diagram, this is shown using mirroring provisioning, which will copy the information from one level to another. An alternative is to use **V**IRTUAL **I**NFORMATION **C**OLLECTIONS that use **I**NFORMATION **S**ERVICES to exchange information as it is requested.

This pattern can repeat through additional levels, but it can get increasingly hard to apportion ownership of the information values, as the tree gets deeper.

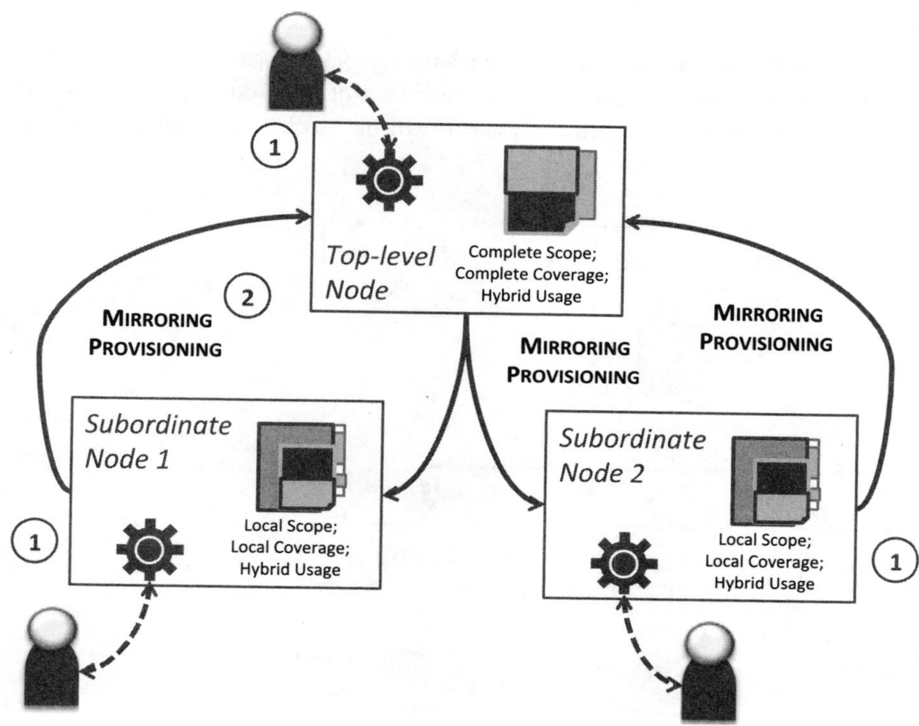

Figure 4.27 Hierarchical Information Supply Chain solution.

Consequences

Benefits:

- This pattern establishes clear ownership rules that lead to a simple synchronization approach.

Liabilities:

- There is no synchronization between the leaf nodes.

Example Resolved

The Shipping and stock management systems each have a stock information collection that has **H**YBRID **U**SAGE. The Shipping application is the owner of the product attributes within these collections, and the stock management systems own the stock level. This is shown in Figure 4.28.

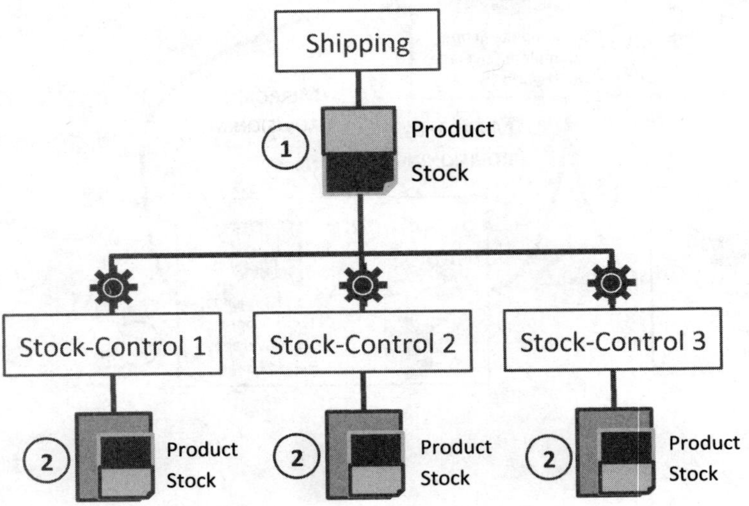

Figure 4.28 Stock information management.

The numbers on the diagram Figure 4.28 refer to these notes:

1. When product details change, they are updated in the Shipping collection and then the new values are copied into the stock management system's information collection where they have reference usage.
2. When one of the warehouses ships a package to a customer, its local stock level is reduced. This change is not relevant to any of the other stock management systems, but it does need to be reflected in Shipping. MCHS Trading had two choices to do this: either to use **M**IRRORING **P**ROVISIONING to sent the new value from the stock management system to Shipping, or to use a **R**EMOTE **I**NFORMATION **S**ERVICE call from Shipping to retrieve the latest values whenever they are needed. MCHS Trading opted to use the information service call approach because the stock values were changing much more frequently than the Shipping application queried the values.

Known Uses

This type of information supply chain is useful for providing a headquarters view of decentralized operations. Here is an example for customer details. The company chooses which level that they will introduce all new customers at and how the ownership of attributes is distributed. See Figure 4.29.

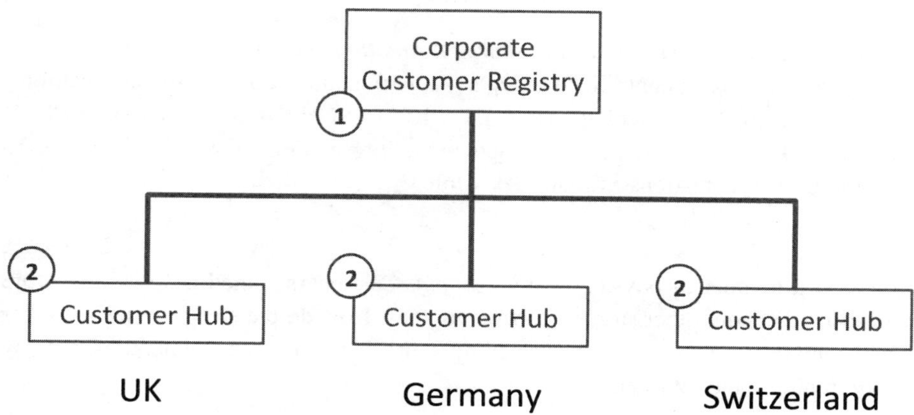

Figure 4.29 Hub of hubs example.

The numbers on the diagram **Figure 4.29** refer to these notes:

1. Introducing customers at the headquarters level ensures a single consistent view of the customer across the organization, and simplifies the centralized coordination when details of a new customer must be checked to ensure they meet any regulatory criteria. For example, under anti-money laundering (AML) legislation banks must validate the identity of a person opening a new account.
2. Introducing customers in the decentralized parts of the organization means that only the headquarters view sees the consolidated view of the customer (they would need to use a **H**UB **I**NTERCHANGE **I**NFORMATION **S**UPPLY **C**HAIN to achieve that).

Related Patterns

The **H**YBRID **U**SAGE pattern provides more information on how ownership of an information collection can be shared between information nodes.

Peer Exchange Information Supply Chain

Context

An organization needs to process information in order to fulfill its purpose. How is the flow of information coordinated throughout the organization's people and systems?

Problem

Independently operating organizations need to share information among one another.

In this scenario, there is no centralized group to support a hub to coordinate the synchronization of information (compare this with the **H**UB **I**NTERCHANGE **I**NFORMATION **S**UPPLY CHAIN). Each organization needs to be able to update the information and for these changes to be available to all other organizations as soon as possible.

Example

MCHS Trading has a number of physical stores (shops). Customers sometimes visit one store and ask for information about other stores in different areas. How do the stores keep each other informed of local news for each store, such as opening hours, location, related amenities, holiday cover, staff opportunities, and rotations?

Forces

- **Disparate copies**—Information that is duplicated across multiple systems is often stored in different formats with different validation rules and currency.

Solution

Each organization is responsible for broadcasting all changes to its peers, who are then responsible for incorporating these changes in their information collections.

This could be achieved with an **I**NFORMATION **B**ROADCAST **P**ROCESS running in a **Q**UEUE **M**ANAGER. The peers in the exchange would have to agree to a canonical format that information payloads would follow and be responsible for translating between their internal format and the canonical format.

Figure 4.30 illustrates the peer exchange information supply chain.

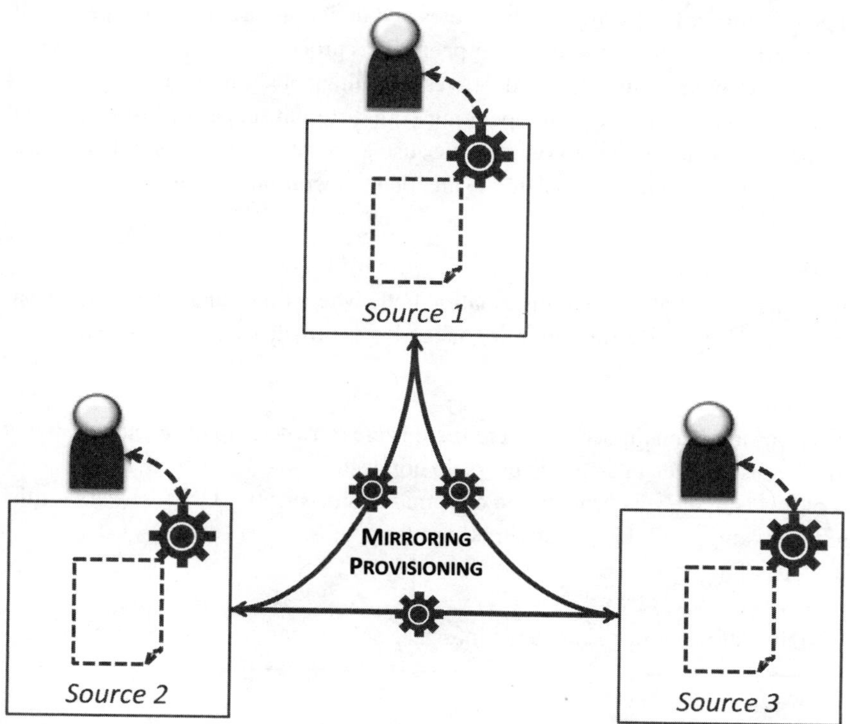

Figure 4.30 Peer Exchange Information Supply Chain solution.

Consequences

Benefits:

- No centrally funded hub is required.
- Each source system has its own copy of the information and so can continue operating even if the network or one of the peer systems is unavailable.

Liabilities:

- As the number of peers increases, the number of information exchanges increases. This can become expensive as the formats and information standards are likely to be different, too.
- The peers in the exchange need to operate in total trust that all information is being shared and that it is only being used for the intended purposes.

- Any change to information—particularly creates and updates—are made independently by each peer and then replicated to the other peers. This process creates possibilities that changes are made (creates, updates, and deletes) simultaneously in different peers that need to be reconciled. If the peers are operating with different scopes of instances, then the reconciliation process is more complex because a create operation or delete operation in one peer may need to be translated to an update operation in another.

Example Resolved

The MCHS Trading stores each have a local information node where they can maintain information about the local store. When this information is changed, it is broadcast to the other stores.

Known Uses

This type of information supply chain occurs where there is clear ownership of resources so that incompatible simultaneous updates in different peers do not occur.

An example of this is in the synchronization of domain name system (DNS) servers for the Internet. There are few examples of this pattern in business systems.

Related Patterns

PEER PROVISIONING defines how to exchange information between peer information nodes.

Summary of Information Supply Chains

The information supply chain patterns describe different schemes for synchronizing the same kind of information between systems in an orderly manner so that ownership and content are clear. They are useful when:

- Trying to understand the way systems have been integrated in the past. This can seem a daunting task, and the information supply chain patterns help to tease apart the different information flows and how they work together.
- Extending an existing distribution of information to incorporate new systems.
- Designing new integration flows between systems to provision new information processes.

Summary

The patterns in this chapter focus on documenting the information architecture for an organization. A key part of this is classification. The information element patterns provide a classification scheme that describes the life cycle of common kinds of information. From these patterns, it is possible to select appropriate information management patterns. The information identification patterns describe approaches to describing the meaning, structure, content, and location of these kinds of information in the organization's systems. The information provisioning patterns describe how an information process might be supplied with information and the information supply chains describe the possible lineage of this information.

A detailed, accurate, up-to-date architecture of all of an organization's information is hard to achieve because an organization is complex and dynamic. On the other hand, without some form of architecture to guide the development of new capability, it is unlikely that there will be any coherence to an organization's information. It is important to take a pragmatic approach when it comes to information architecture:

- Focus on the information that is of high importance to the organization.
- Involve people from both the business and IT in the review and maintenance of the information architecture.
- Automate the collection of descriptive information about the organization's use of information.
- Review and refine the architecture at regular intervals with key stakeholders.
- Report improvements and breaches through the INFORMATION GOVERNANCE PROGRAM.

In many respects, the success of the information architecture and the information governance program are linked. The information architecture provides the blueprint of the intended information use and how it flows through the systems. The information governance program ensures this is the case and provides the evidence that drives improvement and investment where appropriate.

CHAPTER 5

Information at Rest

The information at rest patterns describe how information is accessed and stored. There are four levels to this:

- At the top are the INFORMATION SERVICES. They provide information processes with a well-defined interface to access stored information. The information services call information collections.
- INFORMATION COLLECTIONS are stored collections of related information.
- This information is typically organized into well-defined structures that are represented by the INFORMATION ENTRY patterns. These structures could hold all types of information, including numeric binary, text, documents, and media such as video and audio and so covers both what has traditionally been called *structured data* and *unstructured data*.
- Finally, there are the servers that host the information processes, information services, and information collections. These are described by the INFORMATION NODE patterns.

Collectively, the information at rest patterns describe the conditions under which your organization's information is managed. They appear in the information management components part of the pattern language, as shown in Figure 5.1.

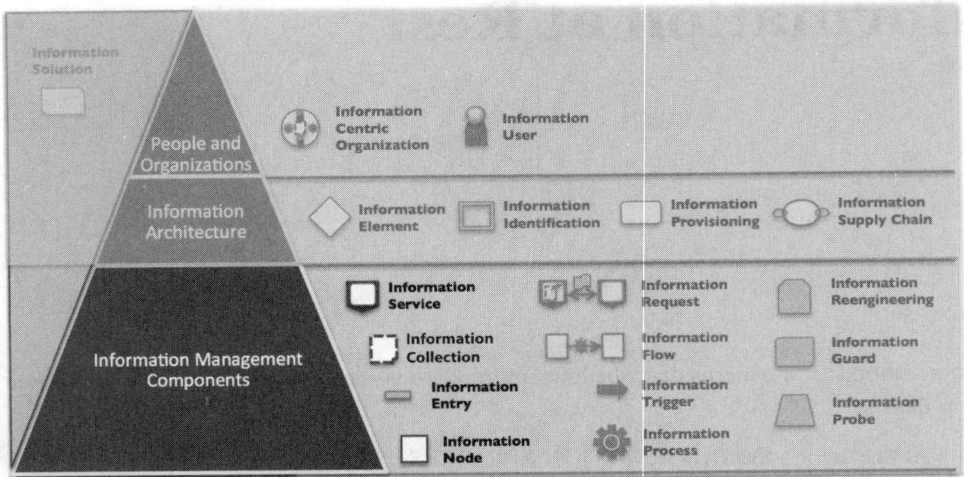

Figure 5.1 Information at rest patterns in the context of the pattern language.

Information Service Patterns

The information service patterns describe the mechanisms to connect an information process with the actual information stored in one or more information collections. The information service is the information processes' interface to the information and controls what information is returned, where it came from, how the attributes are named, and its structure. See Figure 5.2.

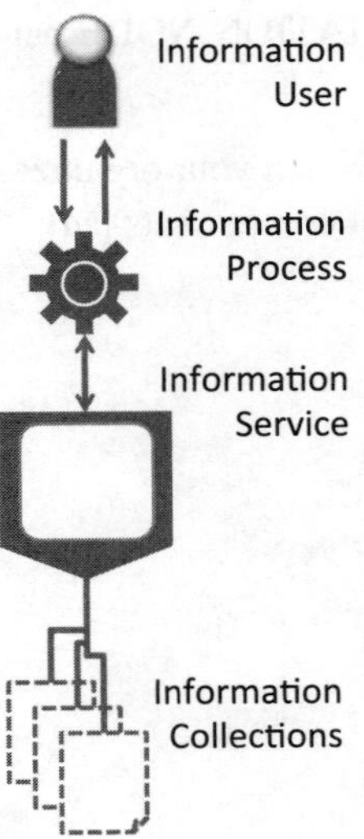

Figure 5.2 Information services access information collections when called by an information process.

You may be wondering why we introduce a layer in between the information process and the information collection. The reasons are both for consumability and governance.

The software developer of an information process is focused on supporting a specific part of the business. The temptation is to create a new information collection just for this process because the information is then just what is needed. This is the start of another information silo. There is no issue if the information it stores is unique to this information process. However, many information processes need information about the key elements of the business—customers, products, accounts, contracts and orders, employees, partners, and many more. Creating new information silos in these subject areas creates fragmented, inconsistent, and duplicated information.

In an attempt to avoid this, an extreme approach could be to say that such shared information should be centralized and accessed through a single canonical interface. This canonical interface quickly becomes complicated and it has to handle every variation and special case that exists in an organization.

The information service is a compromise between these two extremes by providing an abstraction layer that separates how information is consumed from how it is stored.

The information services deliver information in a form that is convenient for the software developer of an information process to consume—both in terms of the structure and the naming of the attributes. This reduces the chances that the developer of an information process will mistakenly use information incorrectly. The information services map that interface onto the best sources of the information. Because the relationship from information services to information collection is many-to-many, the information services increase the sharing of information and contain valuable knowledge about how canonically structured stored information is consumed by the information processes.

The top-level **INFORMATION SERVICE** pattern shown in Table 5.1 describes the general mechanism of an information service. This is followed by the other patterns in the group that cover different implementation approaches for an information service.

Table 5.1 Information Service Pattern Summary

Icon	Pattern Name	Problem	Solution
	INFORMATION SERVICE	Some information processes need the same information, but may require it to be formatted differently.	Establish well-defined interfaces to the information that meet the needs of particular consuming information processes to enable them to create, retrieve, and maintain just the information they need.

Information Service

Context

An organization requires an information process to support one of its activities. This information process is using stored information.

Problem

Some information processes need the same information, but each requires it to be formatted differently.

The difference in the formatting may be structural—or formatted for a different vocabulary. For example, consider an information collection that contains entries for people that are linked to other collections containing details such as address and contract. This information could be consumed in the following ways:

- All people and the contracts they have with the organization
- Each sales area and the people who live within it
- All employees (these are people with an employment contract)

The first two examples are structural changes; the last one takes a subset of the information and renames it from information about people to information about employees.

Example

MCHS Trading's E-Shop application is taking customer orders through the Internet. It has three main information processes:

- **Login**—To identify a customer. This needs access to the stored customer details to verify the customer's account details.
- **Browse Catalog**—To allow the customer to search and view the details of products offered for sale. This requires access to the stored product details.
- **New Order**—To make an order for products from MCHS Trading. This is using the stored payment details about the customer, order codes from the product details, and stored details of a new order.

These processes are making use of three information collections: customer details, product details, and order details in a variety of ways. How should the information processes access these information collections?

Forces

- **Specialized information collections are the fastest—**Information collections designed specifically for an information process, and stored locally in the same information node as the information process, typically provide the fastest access to the information for the information process.
- **Information copies add cost—**Every copy that is made of some information values costs money to store and maintain.
- **Inline transformation is transient—**If transformed information is not stored, then the transformation must be redone each time the information is needed in that format. This makes sense if the information values are changing rapidly, they must be current, or the transformations are minimal. However, when the information values are fairly static or the transformations necessary are complex, collating and reformatting the set of information values on the fly over and over again is inefficient.
- **Inconsistent terminology for the same information—**Different parts of an organization may use inconsistent terminology from each other. This terminology difference may derive from a different heritage, skill sets, or decentralized operation.

Solution

Define well-defined interfaces to the information that meet the needs of particular consuming information processes to enable them to create, retrieve, and maintain just the information they need.

This interface includes actions (operations) with parameters where information is passed in and out. Each parameter is defined as a structure with one or more attributes that are named according to the requirements of the consuming information process. This structure is used on the programming interface of the INFORMATION SERVICE. When the consuming information process interacts with the information service, the information is formatted as defined by the view.

An information service provides one or more operations on the interface. Each operation performs a well-defined function. Typically, the operations are related and focus on providing access to a particular type of information. The operations could include the following:

- **Create—**Add new information to the information collections.
- **Retrieve one—**Retrieve a discrete instance of information.
- **Retrieve cursor—**Retrieve a related set of information instances that can be stepped through one at a time.
- **Retrieve collection—**Retrieve a related set of information instances altogether.
- **Update—**Change specific information values.

- **Delete**—Either remove the information from the information collection or mark it as removed so the information processes can no longer use it.

The implementation of an operation shown in Figure 5.3 makes use of the information protection pattern groups described in Chapter 8, "Information Protection." The **I**NFORMATION **P**ROBES can record the request and the response or monitor for exceptional conditions. An **I**NFORMATION **G**UARD validates that the information process is allowed to access the information on the request, and another information guard may prune or mask the results on the response. **I**NFORMATION **R**EENGINEERING **S**TEPS transform the request before calling the information collection, and transform the result to create an appropriate form for the information process.

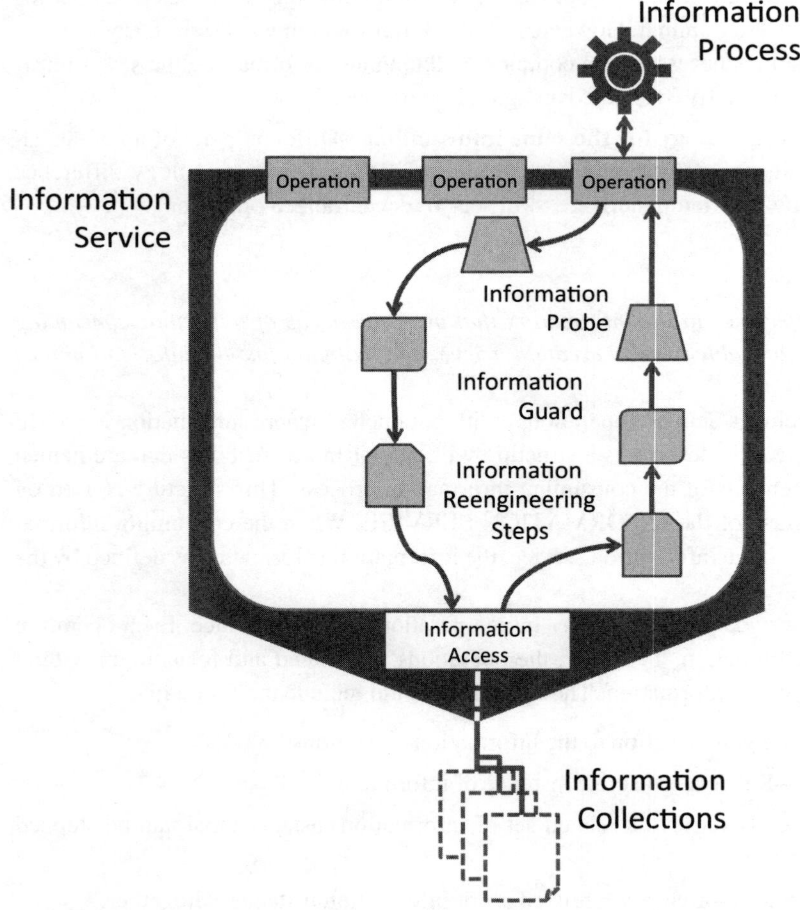

Figure 5.3 Inside an information service.

The precise mechanism used by the information service to access the information collection is described by the information service implementation patterns:

- LOCAL INFORMATION SERVICE
- REMOTE INFORMATION SERVICE
- TRIGGERING INFORMATION SERVICE

Consequences

Benefits:

- Software developers who are writing new information processes are more likely to use stored information appropriately because the information service formats it for their needs.
- The information processes are isolated from the provisioning mechanism used to supply the information through the information service. This creates opportunities to consolidate and improve the information "behind the scenes" without affecting the implementation of the information processes.
- Information collections can use a canonical form with a more complete scope and coverage than local programmers need. The information services expose useful subsets of this information, making them consumable to a broader set of information processes.

Liabilities:

- If information services are not properly defined, cataloged, and communicated, redundant and inconsistent information services can be created, making it difficult to understand which to use and when.
- Using this pattern may result in additional latency if the format of the information as it is stored is very different from the format that is used by the information services. This can become a significant and unnecessary overhead for a popular information service if the information values are relatively static and suggests the need for a REFERENCE USAGE copy of the information for these information collections.

Example Resolved

MSCH Trading's E-Shop application provides six information services to support its three main information processes:

- **Verify customer**—Compares the customer's input with the stored account details from the customer details collection
- **Get payment details**—Retrieves details of the customer's preferred payment method

- **Search catalog**—Returns a list of products that matches a search criterion
- **Get product details**—Retrieves descriptive details of selected products from the product details information collection
- **Get order code**—Retrieves the product codes used in the warehouses
- **Create order**—Adds a new entry in the Order Details information collection

This is illustrated in Figure 5.4.

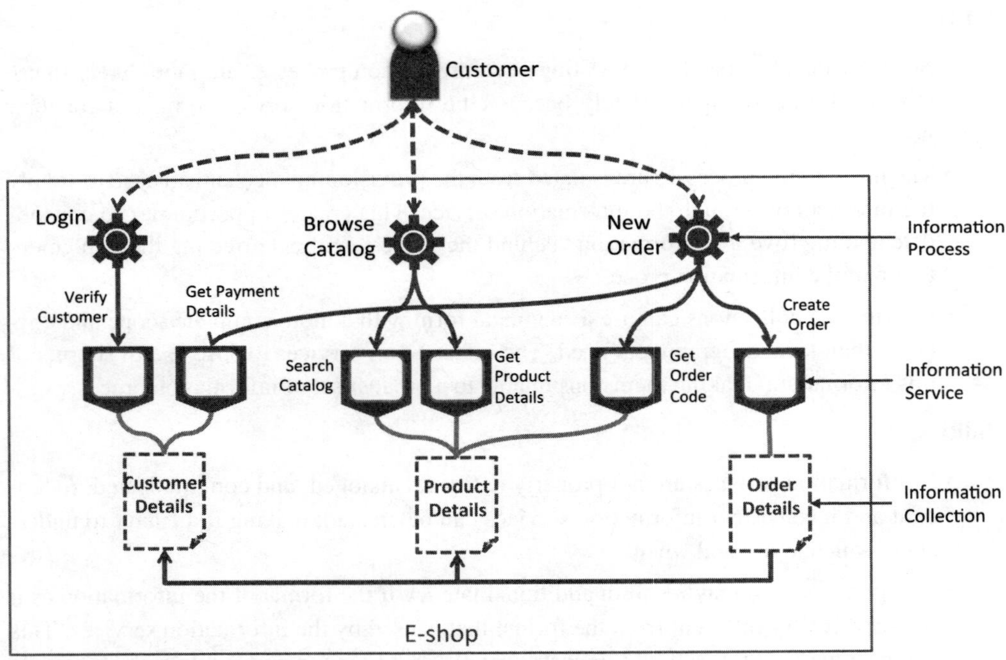

Figure 5.4 Information services in the E-Shop application.

Known Uses

There are many technologies that provide interfaces to information. For example, databases offer SQL interfaces, such as Open Database Connectivity (ODBC) and Java Database Connectivity (JDBC). Application servers offer remotely callable interfaces such as web services and Representational State Transfer (REST) interfaces. Such an interface is an information service if the interface is a well-defined contract for working with information that is offered to consumers. This interface may very closely resemble the way the information is stored, or an abstraction of it.

Related Patterns

Information services provide the means to implement service level provisioning patterns, including USER SHARED PROVISIONING, CACHE PROVISIONING, and SERVICE-ORIENTED PROVISIONING.

The INFORMATION MODEL and INFORMATION SCHEMA patterns describe definitions of information structures.

Information Service Implementation Patterns

All information services provide well-defined information interfaces for the information processes. The variations of this basic pattern shown in Table 5.2 describe how the access to the information collections is implemented. There are three patterns: Information is accessed within the local information node, via an information request, or it is constructed from multiple sources.

Table 5.2 Information Service Implementation Patterns

Icon	Pattern Name	Problem	Solution
	LOCAL INFORMATION SERVICE	The information requested by an information process is located in an information collection hosted on the local information node.	Interact directly with the local information collection whenever the information process calls the information service.
	REMOTE INFORMATION SERVICE	The information requested by an information process is stored in a different information node.	Issue an information request to call an information service hosted in an information node that has access to the required information.
	TRIGGERING INFORMATION SERVICE	The information requested by an information process is dispersed among multiple information collections.	Partition the request into calls to other information services that between them have access to the requested information—then combine and return the results.

Local Information Service

Context

An information process is using an information service. How is this information service accessing the information from the information collections?

Problem

The information requested by an information process is located in an information collection hosted on the local information node.

How does the information service retrieve and maintain the information requested by the information processes?

Example

The MCHS Trading E-Shop application has a login information process that needs to access information about a customer's account in order to validate that customer's identity and operate according to the predefined preferences.

Forces

- **Different structures of information**—The structure of the information that is stored may be different from the needs of the information process.
- **Specialized information collections are the fastest**—Information collections designed specifically for an information process, and stored locally in the same information node as the information process, typically provide the fasted access to the information for the information process.
- **Information in motion needs protection**—As information is requested within an information node, it needs protection to ensure it is not intercepted and either stolen or changed in an unauthorized way.
- **Information copies add cost**—Every copy that is made of some information values costs money to store and maintain.

Solution

Interact directly with the local information collections whenever the information process calls the information service.

Every information collection provides a basic interface for retrieving and maintaining the information it retains. The information service uses this interface to access the stored information. See Figure 5.5.

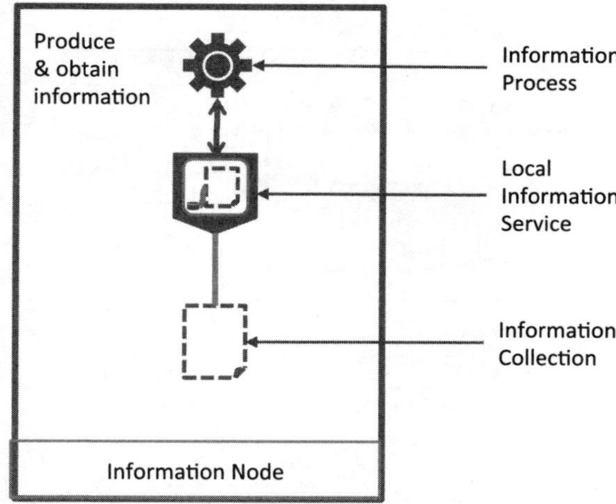

Figure 5.5 Local Information Services.

Consequences

Benefits:

- With this pattern, the information collection and the information processes using it are located in the same information node. This is typically the fastest way to supply information and typically the information collections are styled to favor the needs of the local information processes.

Liabilities:

- If an organization only uses local information services, shared information must be copied into information collections located in each information node to ensure it is local to all of the information processes that need it. This results in high cost of moving, storing, and managing the copies.

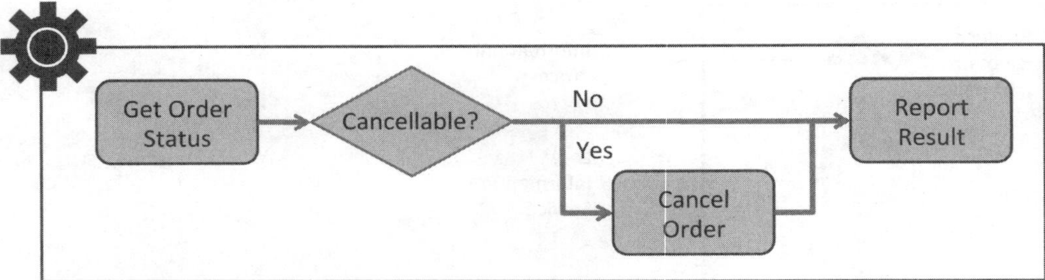

Figure 5.6 Local Information Services

Example Resolved

The login information process calls the verify customer information service that, in turn, calls the customer details information collection to retrieve the stored details about the customer. The login process then compares the results with the input from the customer and acts accordingly.

Known Uses

Local information services are interfaces that are private to the information processes within the local information node. An information node may be implemented with multiple server processes. For example, it could be implemented with an application server and a database where the processes may be making network requests to access the stored information. However, only the locally hosted information processes need to be changed when the information service changes.

Related Patterns

This is an information access implementation pattern for an **I**NFORMATION **S**ERVICE.

Local information services patterns are used in localized provisioning patterns, such as USER **P**RIVATE **P**ROVISIONING and **A**PPLICATION **P**RIVATE **P**ROVISIONING.

Remote Information Service

Context

An information process is using an information service. How is this information service accessing the information from the information collections?

Problem

The information requested by an information process is stored in a different information node.

The information values are changing rapidly and there is a strong desire not to create a local copy of the information for the information process because of the cost of keeping it synchronized with the original information collection. How is this information supplied to the information process?

Example

MCHS Trading plans to add the ability for an E-Shop customer to cancel an order that has not yet been shipped. The Cancel Order information process in the Customer-Care information node will implement this capability using the process in Figure 5.7. How is information supplied to this information process?

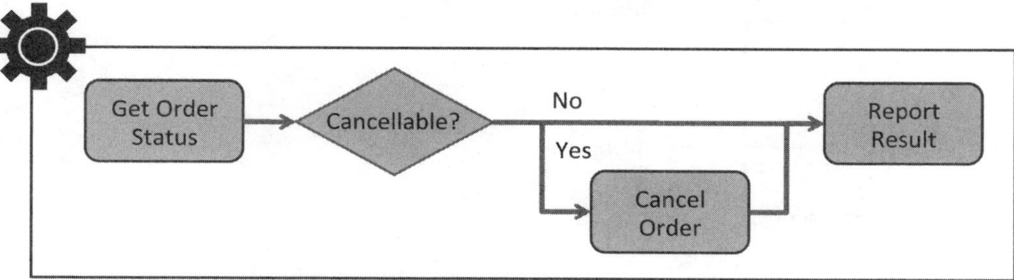

Figure 5.7 The Cancel Order information process.

Forces

- **Information nodes are not always available**—The information collection hosted on a remote information node may not be available when the information process requires information.
- **Redundant information nodes add cost**—When the information process requires an information collection and the primary information node is unavailable, a redundant or mirror node may be required, resulting in additional storage costs.
- **Communication costs**—It takes time to transfer information from one information node to another.
- **Information in motion needs protection**—As information is transferred between information nodes, it needs protection to ensure it is not intercepted and either stolen or changed in an unauthorized way.
- **Closed application information**—Many applications have information collections that store information in proprietary formats that cannot be easily accessed outside of the application.

Solution

Issue an information request to call an information service hosted in an information node that has access to the required information.

An **I**NFORMATION **R**EQUEST is a pattern that describes how to package up a request for an information service and send it to another information node to execute. The information request then packages up the results and sends them back to the local information service. See Figure 5.8.

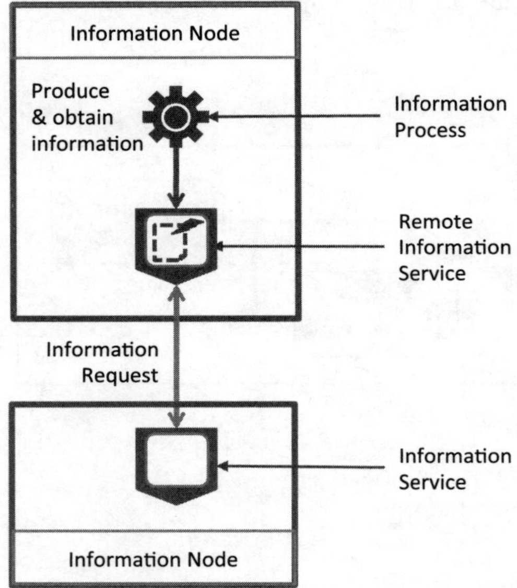

Figure 5.8 Remote information service.

In most cases, the remote information service uses **I**NFORMATION **C**ONFIGURATION to determine the network location of the information service it must call. This configuration is typically static—either hard-coded in the remote information service or read from configuration at startup. In circumstances where this linkage needs to be more flexible, it is possible to have a dynamic registry of information services that the remote information service contacts to looks up the network information each time it issues an information request.

Consequences

Benefits:

- Remote information services allow information processes to work with authoritative information located on remote information nodes. They can also be used to initiate work in other information nodes and/or to distribute workload among a cluster of similar information nodes.

Liabilities:

- The information node that hosts the information collection may be unavailable when the information process calls the information service. The information service should log that the information collection is not available and the information process should fail gracefully when this occurs. Or for critical information processes, there may be a requirement for an alternate information node to be available.

Example Resolved

The Cancel Order information process shown in Figure 5.9 uses information services to connect directly with the information it needs.

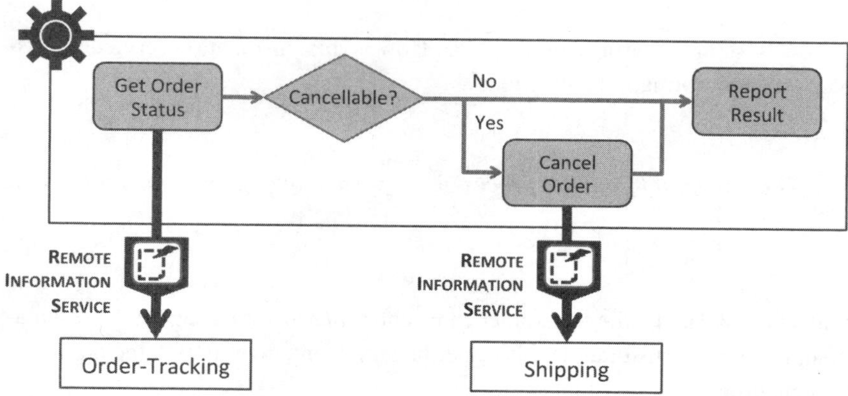

Figure 5.9 Cancel Order information calling remote information services.

Known Uses

Remote information services are available through many types of technology. Here are some examples:

- Remote procedure calls supported by standards such as Java Enterprise Edition (JEE)
- Web services technology
- RESTful interfaces
- Linked data interfaces such as Open Services for Lifecycle and Collaboration (OSLC)
- Remote interfaces to databases such as Open Database Connectivity (ODBC) and Java Database Connectivity (JDBC)

Related Patterns

This is an information access implementation pattern for an **I**NFORMATION **S**ERVICE.

INFORMATION **B**ROKER information nodes make extensive use of remote information services when executing an **I**NFORMATION **F**LOW.

DAISY **C**HAIN **P**ROVISIONING uses a remote information service that calls a **T**RIGGERED **I**NFORMATION **S**ERVICE to pass context information to the next information process and to start it running.

Triggering Information Service

Context

An information process is using an information service. How is this information service accessing the information from the information collections?

Problem

The information requested by an information process is dispersed among multiple information collections.

Example

When a customer calls the MCHS Trading customer care center, the customer service representative needs to understand who the customer is, his or her history of interaction with the organization, and in-flight/recent orders.

Forces

- **Inline transformation is transient**—If transformed information is not stored, then the transformation must be redone each time the information is needed in that format. This makes sense if the information values are changing rapidly, they must be current, or the transformations are minimal. However, when the information values are fairly static or the transformations necessary are complex, collating and reformatting the set of information values on the fly over and over again is inefficient.

- **Dispersed information is inconsistent**—Combining information from disparate information collections takes care to ensure proper correlation is made as the information is brought together. The effort required to do this may be too much to do on demand—particularly when it requires human judgment to handle the edge cases.

Solution

Partition the request into calls to other information services that between them have access to the requested information—then combine and return the results.

The triggered information service calls an INFORMATION SERVICE TRIGGER to start or invoke an INFORMATION PROCESS. This information process is responsible for calling the multiple information services and combining the results. See Figure 5.10.

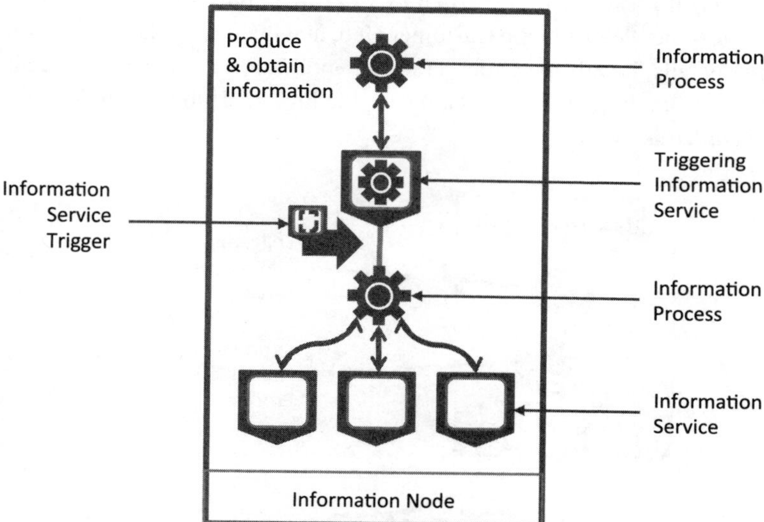

Figure 5.10 Triggering information service.

Consequences

Benefits:

- The triggered information service can be used to correlate information from multiple sources together. It can also initiate work in another information node.

Liabilities:

- The information services may use different security models, requiring the information process to switch security credentials for each call. These security credentials need to be managed securely for the information process's exclusive use so others cannot acquire or make use of them.
- The triggered information service is only available if all of the sources it calls are available. For critical information services, alternate information collections may be required, resulting in additional storage cost.

Example Resolved

The information process shown in Figure 5.11 calls a triggered information service to create the complete view of the customer. It uses an **I**NFORMATION **F**EDERATION **P**ROCESS to call the information service for customer details in the Customer Hub, and then using the customer's identifier from the customer details, it calls the Order-Tracking application to extract the recent orders for the customer. Then, from these order details, it calls the Product Hub to provide more information on the products ordered.

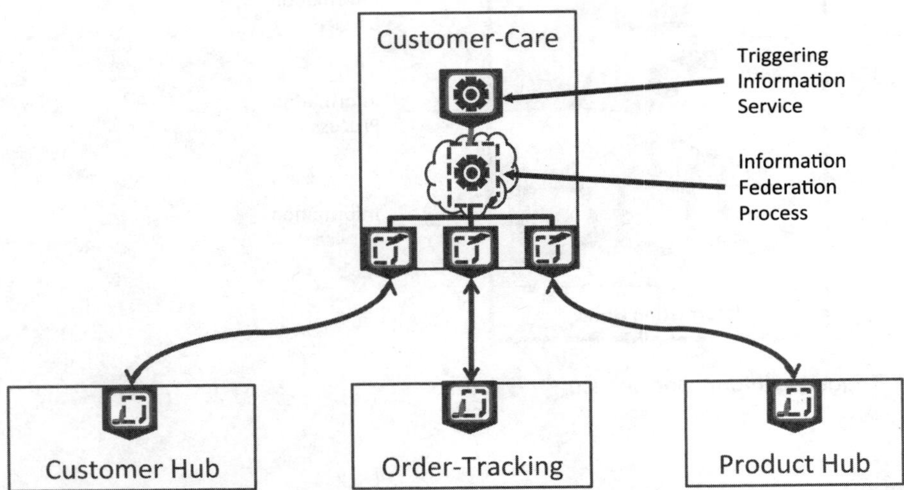

Figure 5.11 A triggering information service in Customer-Care.

Known Uses

Triggering information services are used in federating technologies to pull together information from multiple sources.

Related Patterns

This is an information access implementation pattern for an INFORMATION SERVICE.

DAISY CHAIN PROVISIONING uses a REMOTE INFORMATION SERVICE that calls a triggered information service to pass context information to the next information process and to start it running.

A VIRTUAL INFORMATION COLLECTION uses triggered information services to federate information from multiple information collections.

Summary of Information Services

The information service pattern group describes a set of patterns for providing an abstraction layer for information that is distributed across multiple information nodes.

Information Collection Patterns

This section focuses on how information is stored within an INFORMATION NODE. The primary pattern is called the INFORMATION COLLECTION.

The information collection pattern shown in Table 5.3 is a logical collection of related information that is managed together as a group. Often, the information collection consists of instances of information of the same type, but not always. It may be information relating to a single event, or collected from the same location over a period of time. The important point is that there is a simple, documented explanation as to why this information is considered a related collection because it is used to determine which information processes should work with it.

Table 5.3 Information Collection Pattern Summary

Icon	Pattern Name	Problem	Solution
	INFORMATION COLLECTION	Information must be organized so it can be located, accessed, protected, and maintained at a level that is consistent with its value to the organization.	Group related information together into a logical collection and implement information services to access and maintain this information.

Although the concept of an information collection is simple, it is the source of much of the complication in managing information within an organization. First, there are many ways to implement it and, within a single organization, many of these options will already be deployed somewhere in the organization's systems. Second, information is not always stored in a convenient location for the information processes that use it. It may be dispersed or duplicated, and is often inconsistently represented amongst multiple information nodes. So it becomes a challenge to locate the right information and keep it synchronized.

Designing an effective approach to synchronizing multiple copies of the same information requires the end-to-end thinking that is described by the **I**NFORMATION **S**UPPLY **C**HAIN pattern. One of the key steps in designing an information supply chain is to classify the information collections according to four criteria: the location, the usage, the scope, and the coverage. These classifications are defined as specializations of the information collection and are described in the patterns that follow.

Once you have an idea of the information collections in your information supply chain, the **I**NFORMATION **N**ODE patterns describe different approaches to hosting them, the **I**NFORMATION **S**ERVICE patterns describe how information processes can access them, and the **I**NFORMATION **P**ROVISIONING patterns describe how they should be linked together in an information supply chain.

Information Collection

Context

An organization uses a wide variety of information to support its activities. This information must be easy to locate, manage, and protect.

Problem

Information must be organized so it can be located, accessed, protected, and maintained at a level that is consistent with its value to the organization.

Not all information has equal value to the organization. The type of information, how it is used, and the context in which it is used will affect the types of access and the level of availability, management, and protection required.

How should information be organized so that an information process can locate the right information and the appropriate mechanisms can be applied to the management and protection of the information behind the scenes?

Example

The MCHS Trading E-Shop application has to manage details of many different customers and the orders they are making. How should this information be organized?

Forces

- **Information is subject to obligations**—Information collections must be aligned to information management obligations in the form of governmental regulations, legal requirements, or organizational governance.
- **Information nodes are not always available**—Information processes, hosted in information nodes, manage information for an organization. The hosting information nodes are not always available. They may be shut down for regular maintenance or may fail at unexpected times.
- **Information collections may be accessed from remote information nodes**—Information processes hosted on different information nodes may need access to the same information. As such, information must be accessible from a remote information node.
- **Information users and processes have different needs for information**—Information users and processes need similar, but often subtly different, information. These distinctions create variations through an information supply chain, or even produce new information supply chains.

Solution

Group related information together into a logical collection and implement information services to access and maintain this information.

An information collection is a group of related information that is managed together. Often, an information collection supports information related to a single subject area, such as customer details; however, this is not essential. An information collection may contain information about a single event or information gathered from a single location.

An information collection must be accessible to an information supply chain. See Figure 5.12. Specifically, INFORMATION PROCESSES use INFORMATION SERVICES to locate and access the information collections. These information services provide operations to retrieve, create, update, and delete information in the information collection.

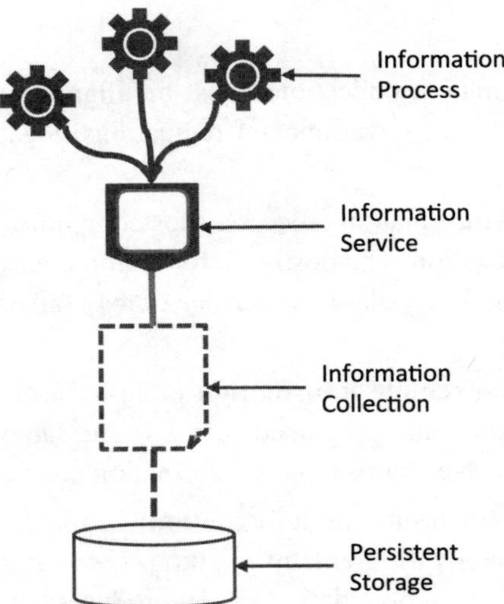

Figure 5.12 An information collection's relationship to other patterns.

An information collection must be stored somewhere to make sure it is not lost when the information nodes are restarted. It can be stored in a single information node (**P**HYSICAL **I**NFORMATION **C**OLLECTION) or partitioned across multiple information nodes (**V**IRTUAL **I**NFORMATION **C**OLLECTION).

Within an information supply chain, an information collection will be used in a particular way by the information processes. Understanding how the information collection is to be used, by which processes, and the location of these processes is necessary to decide on the appropriate style of **I**NFORMATION **P**ROVISIONING to use. The usage patterns for an information collection are described in the following patterns:

- **M**ASTER **U**SAGE
- **R**EFERENCE **U**SAGE
- **H**YBRID **U**SAGE
- **S**ANDBOX **U**SAGE

An information collection also has a scope that defines the proportion of unique instances it maintains with respect to the total number existing for the subject area. The choices are described in the following patterns:

- **L**OCAL **S**COPE
- **C**OMPLETE **S**COPE
- **T**RANSIENT **S**COPE

Finally, it has a coverage pattern for the attributes it contains relative to the SUBJECT AREA DEFINITION:

- LOCAL COVERAGE
- CORE COVERAGE
- EXTENDED COVERAGE
- COMPLETE COVERAGE

In summary, an information collection describes stored information that is related in some way. Information processes use information services to access the information collection and the usage, scope, and coverage patterns classify their approach.

Consequences

Benefits:

- The information collection pattern describes a simple concept for thinking about the information stored within the information nodes of an information supply chain. In particular, it identifies the location of information about a particular subject area and its scope and usage. This knowledge is invaluable in the understanding and planning of effective information supply chains.

Liabilities:

- The volumetrics for the information collection (includes details such as the size of the information store, average number of entries, number of requests to either read or update the information, availability times, and reliability) will affect the sophistication of capability necessary to implement the information collection.
- The same type of information may be managed by more than one information node. There is no guarantee that each information node will implement its information collections in the same way. The attribute structures, valid values, level of quality, and supported operations may all be different. These differences will need to be uncovered and tackled when building an information process that implements the logic to synchronize the information between these information collections.

Example Resolved

Within the MCHS Trading E-Shop application, there are three information collections: one for customer details, one for orders made, and once for the products that are on sale through the website. Figure 5.13 summarizes the usage and scope of these. Also note that there are relationships from order details to both the customer details and product details.

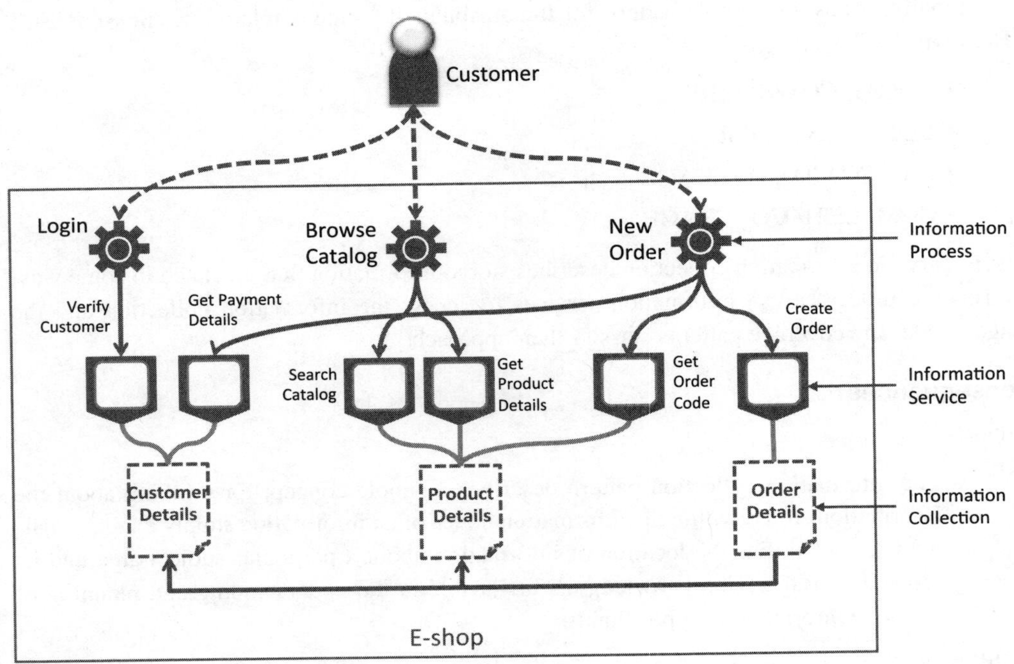

Figure 5.13 Usage and scope of information collections in the E-Shop.

Known Uses

The majority of IT systems, particularly applications, keep information in persistent storage such as files, databases, or content management systems. Here are some examples of information collection implementations:

- An information collection could be implemented in a file where each row stores an information entry and the values of the entry's attributes are delimited by a special character (e.g., a comma-separated value or .csv file).
- An information collection could be implemented in a file where each information entry is stored as a different XML document, or fragment.
- An information collection could be implemented in a database using one or more linked tables. The information entry would be stored in one or more rows of these tables.
- An information collection could be a directory of documents, images, and/or video stored on a file system.
- An information collection could be a collection of documents, images, and/or video stored in a content management system.

Related Patterns

An information collection is located in an INFORMATION NODE. Information collections are accessed by INFORMATION PROCESSES using INFORMATION SERVICES.

The INFORMATION ENTRY describes how to provide structure to an information collection.

Information collections may be copied and synchronized during INFORMATION PROVISIONING.

The information within a collection may follow different life cycles from one another. These life cycles are covered in the INFORMATION ELEMENT patterns.

The content and structure of the information collection may be captured, recorded, and tracked through INFORMATION IDENTIFICATION.

Location of Information

The contents of an information collection must be stored somewhere to ensure the information is preserved even if its hosting information node is restarted. The information processes that use the information collection are unaware how this achieved because they are insulated from the details by the information services.

Typically, the entire information collection is stored within a single information node. This is described by the PHYSICAL INFORMATION COLLECTION pattern. A single location for an information collection makes it easier to ensure the entire information collection is managed consistently and is either completely available, or completely unavailable—because partial availability can lead to misleading results.

The alternative is the VIRTUAL INFORMATION COLLECTION, where the contents of the information collection are partitioned and stored in different information nodes. The information services call information processes to assemble the information on request. Table 5.4 summarizes these patterns.

Table 5.4 Information Collection Location Patterns

Icon	Pattern Name	Problem	Solution
	PHYSICAL INFORMATION COLLECTION	The information hosted by an information node must be retained even if the information node is shut down and restarted.	Provide persistent storage to the information node where related information can be stored.

Icon	Pattern Name	Problem	Solution
	VIRTUAL INFORMATION COLLECTION	Some related information needed by an information process is dispersed among a number of information collections hosted on different information nodes.	Create an information service to represent the desired collection of information and use information processes to obtain and maintain the distributed information whenever requests are made to the information service.

More details of how these approaches work, where they are used, and the consequences of doing so are described in the following full pattern descriptions.

Physical Information Collection

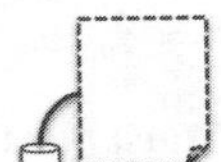

Context

An INFORMATION COLLECTION is hosted on an INFORMATION NODE. This means that the INFORMATION NODE is responsible for managing and protecting the information within the collection.

Problem

The information hosted by an information node must be retained even if the information node is shut down and restarted.

Example

The MCHS Trading E-Shop application has to manage details of many different customers and the orders they are making. This information must be preserved even if the E-Shop fails or is restarted for maintenance.

Forces

- **Even the best-run information node fails from time to time**—When the information node fails, the information that it was working with will be lost if it is not written to persistent storage. Even if the information node does not fail, it needs to be shut down from time to time for maintenance. How should the information node preserve the information it is responsible for over a shutdown and restart? How should this preserved information be organized so it can be retrieved and maintained?
- **Increasing requirements produce a complex information collection**—An information supply chain is much easier to manage if there is a single place where information about a particular subject area is created, updated, and deleted. However, different

information processes need different subsets of information. The more information processes use an information collection, the more complex each information entry within the information collection becomes and the bigger the impact of any change to the information collection.

Solution

Provide persistent storage to the information node where the entire information collection can be stored.

The information collection and persistent storage are located within the boundaries of an information node. See Figure 5.14. Information processes located within the same information node use a **L**OCAL **I**NFORMATION **S**ERVICE to access the information. Information processes located in other information nodes use a **R**EMOTE **I**NFORMATION **S**ERVICE to access the information collection.

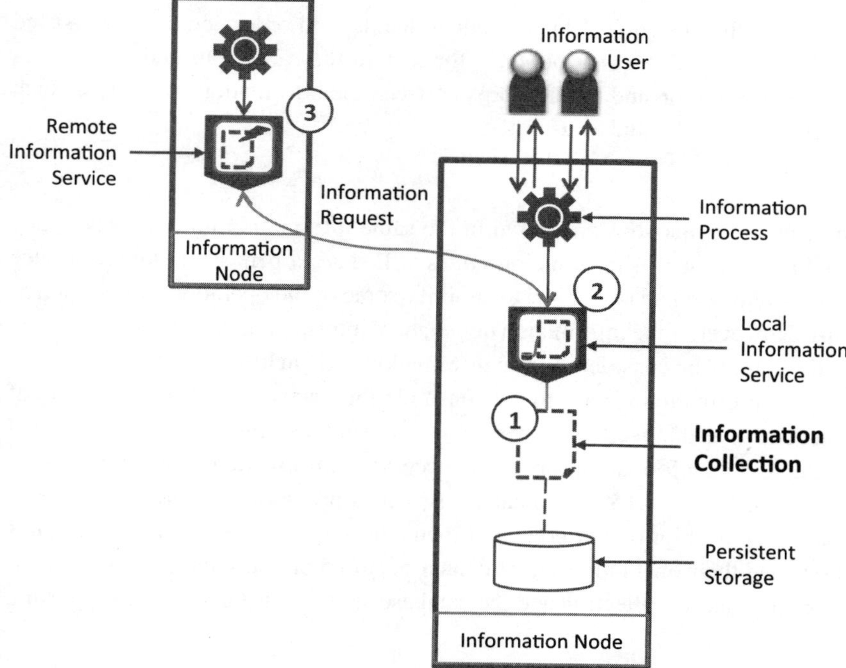

Figure 5.14 Collocation of information collection and persistent storage in an information node.

Consequences

Benefits:

- Persisting the information for a collection within the information node that hosts the information collection makes the responsibilities for managing the information very clear. Investments can be made that are in line with the value of the information and appropriate people in the organization can be made accountable for its proper management.

Liabilities:

- An organization will have many information nodes. With each information node persisting its own information collections, there will be inconsistencies in how the information is protected and managed, and potentially additional storage costs.

Example Resolved

In the E-Shop application, the customer details, product details, and order details are persisted in a database as database tables. There is a root table for each of the collections and other tables holding supplementary information and relationships between the information collections, such as the relationship between an order and a customer.

Known Uses

The majority of information collections are stored in the same information node in which they are managed. Sometimes, a group of information nodes will share a persistent storage service (such as a shared file system or database server) to simplify some of the operations tasks, such as backup and archiving. However, if the information nodes share information in this persisted store, then the persistent store should be considered as an information node in its own right because it is effectively providing an information service to the consuming information nodes. Ownership of the information collection is also moved to the persistent store and the original consuming information nodes are using remote information services to access the information collection.

This is illustrated in Figure 5.15. If a database server is providing a shared database to multiple applications, it is an information node and owns the information collections it stores (1). If the applications had their own independent database, stored on the same database server, then each has its own information collection and the database server is just part of the supporting infrastructure (2).

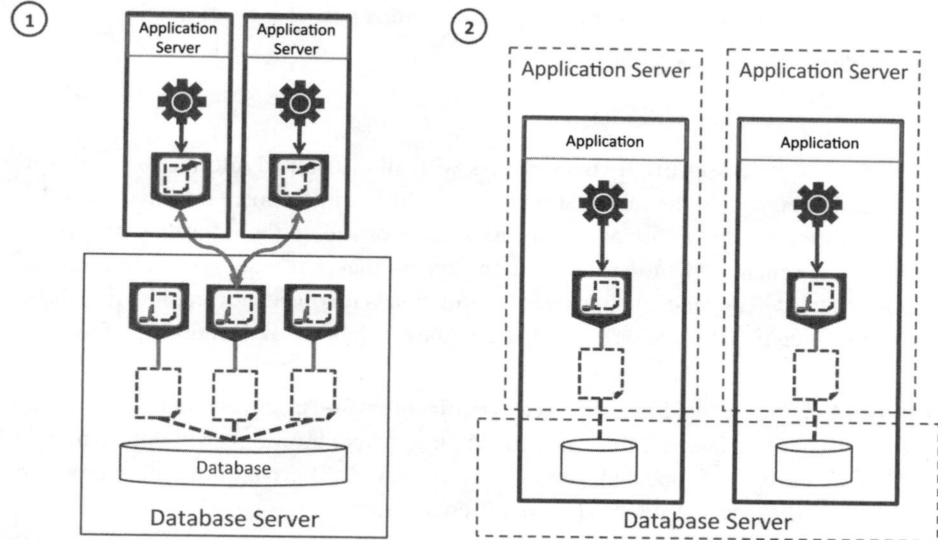

Figure 5.15 Shared database versus independent database.

The difference between the two scenarios is the point of control. In many organizations, the information node is the control point for ownership, investment, staffing, and change. Where information is shared, changes to the information must be coordinated between the consumers, but at the end of the day, it needs a single owner.

Related Patterns

LOCAL PROVISIONING is based around the idea that all information processes located on an information node should have physical information collections so the information node can operate completely independently from other information nodes.

Virtual Information Collection

Context

An organization has many information nodes, each hosting information collections.

Problem

Some related information needed by an information process is dispersed among a number of information collections hosted on different information nodes.

This information needs to be gathered together, correlated, and presented to the information process in a usable form. Depending on the requirements for the information collection, there may be additional need for restructuring and standardization of the information from the different collections.

Forces

- **Information processes are dispersed**—As with all distributed information situations, the question is, should the information be consolidated into a local information collection in advance of the information process's need, or should the information be pulled together on demand when the information process makes a request to an information service? This will depend on how much information is involved, how rapidly it is changing, how much transformation is needed, and the availability of the hosting information nodes.
- **Information processes have different requirements**—An information supply chain is much easier to manage if there is a single place where information about a particular subject area is created, updated, and deleted. However, different information processes need different subsets of information in different structures.
- **Sharing can increase semantic complexity**—As more information processes use a virtual information collection, there is greater need for clear semantic understanding of all information entries within the information collection and the relationships between those information entries.

Example

The Shipping application is supporting three physical warehouses. The warehouses coordinate the distribution of goods and are located at strategic places to give MCHS Trading a fast and efficient distribution capability. Each warehouse runs its own stock management system that keeps track of local stock levels and coordinates orders and deliveries from its suppliers. The Shipping application is responsible for allocating the orders among the warehouses. It needs to know the stock levels in each warehouse to ensure it is making the best allocation. How does it know the stock levels of the items listed in an order when the stock levels are kept in the stock management systems located in each of the warehouses?

Solution

Create an information service to represent the desired collection of information and use information processes to obtain and maintain the distributed information whenever requests are made to the information service.

This pattern is also known as a federated view. The caller of the top-level information service is unaware that the information collection is dispersed. The mechanism that pulls the information together is hidden behind the top-level information service.

This mechanism is configured with details of where the information collections are located, how to access them, and the transformations and mappings required to stitch together the information from the different sources in response to the calls to the virtualized information service.

Consequences

Benefits:

- This pattern avoids creating another copy of the information required to provision the information process.

Liabilities:

- This pattern creates operational dependencies between the information node where the virtual collection is logically hosted and the information nodes whose information services are called to satisfy requests to the virtual collection.
- This pattern assumes that the semantics and the level of quality of the information collections it is federating are equivalent and the effort to match information across them is suitable for real-time invocation.

Example Resolved

The stock management system in each of the warehouses supports an information service that can return the stock levels and estimated time to deliver an order. The Shipping application has an information service that calls each of the stock management systems and returns the aggregated stock levels, best delivery time, and warehouse to use.

Known Uses

There are three basic types of technology used to provide a virtualized information collection illustrated in Figure 5.16. They are sometimes called information federation technologies.

Database-level federation (1) is typically implemented in a database server and provides an SQL interface to a set of virtual tables. When an SQL request is made, the request is broken up and pushed down to the databases that are actually storing the information.

Service-level federation (2) triggers an information process to call the services of the information collections that are storing the information and then collate the results to pass back to the caller.

Both database-level federation and service-level federation are well-established techniques for creating a virtual information collection. There is a third approach that is being explored by a number of organizations that is called semantic federation (3). The **S**EMANTIC **I**NTEGRATION solution pattern describes this approach in more detail.

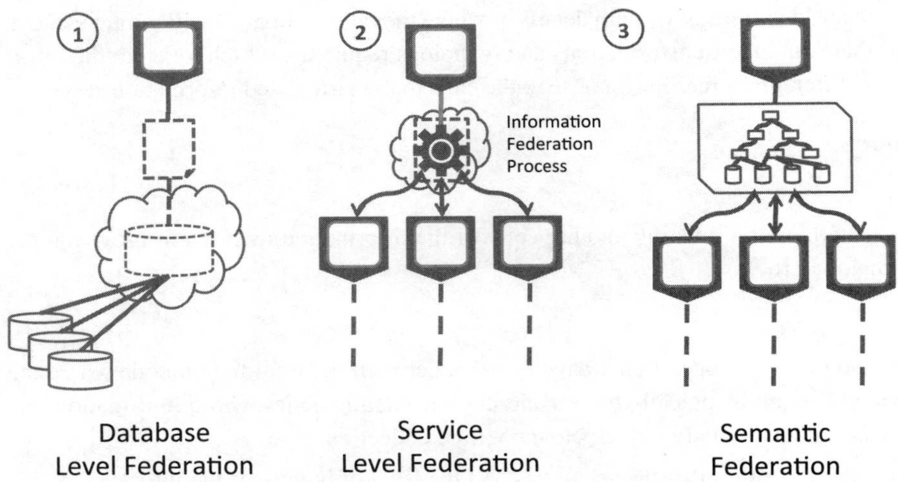

Figure 5.16 Federation techniques for virtual information collections.

Related Patterns

The TRIGGERED INFORMATION SERVICE pattern provides more detail on how service federation works. The INFORMATION FEDERATION PROCESS is typically used to create the virtual collection.

The SEMANTIC INTEGRATION solution pattern describes how semantic federation works.

The SINGLE VIEW INFORMATION SUPPLY CHAIN is headed by a virtual information collection.

Usage of an Information Collection

The four usage patterns shown in Table 5.5 describe the types of operations that the information processes are performing on an information collection. These patterns help you classify the role that the information collections are playing in the information supply chain and how critical they are to your operation.

Table 5.5 Information Collection Usage Patterns

Icon	Pattern Name	Problem	Solution
	MASTER USAGE	A group of related information processes must maintain up-to-date information.	When these information processes run, they update the information in the appropriate information collection directly, as part of their processing logic. As a result, the values stored in the information collections represent the latest status known to these processes.
	REFERENCE USAGE	A group of related information processes requires a reference copy of information that is maintained elsewhere.	Create a read-only copy of the information from an appropriate information collection and locate it where it is accessible to the new information processes. Use information provisioning to keep this copy in synchronization with the original.
	HYBRID USAGE	A group of related information processes requires access to information about a subject area that is broader than the attributes they are able to manage locally.	Create an information collection that supports all of the attributes needed by the local information node. Maintain as many attributes as possible through local processing and supply the other attributes, as read-only copies, from other information collections.
	SANDBOX USAGE	A group of related information processes used for a project needs to make experimental changes to the organization's information.	Commission and provision a set of information collections that are suited to support the needs of the project. During the project, the team is able to run the workloads and make the changes to the information as and when they need to. At the end of the project, these information collections are deleted.

Master Usage

Context

Information collections are storing information throughout the information supply chain. Some information collections will store the same type of information and need to be synchronized. You want to understand the best way to keep them synchronized. This is dependent on the behavior of the information processes using it.

Problem

A group of related information processes must maintain up-to-date information about a subject area.

This means they are creating, retrieving, updating, and deleting information entries in the information collection.

Example

MCHS Trading's E-Shop application needs to store details of the people who have registered accounts. This customer profile contains information about the individual's name, address, payment information, and other web preferences.

Forces

An information supply chain is much easier to manage if there is a single place where information about a particular subject area is created, updated, and deleted. However, different information processes need different subsets of information. The more information processes use an information collection, the more complex each information entry within the information collection becomes and the bigger the impact of any change to the information collection.

Solution

When these information processes run, they update the information in the appropriate information collections directly, as part of their processing logic. As a result, the values stored in the information collections represent the latest status known to these processes.

An information collection used in this way is said to be playing the master usage in the information supply chain. Multiple information processes would use such an information collection as their primary source of information. The information services that these processes use to maintain the information collection would include create, retrieve, update, and delete operations.

Information collections playing the master usage are often used as a source of information to distribute to other information collections in the information supply chain.

Information collections playing the master usage typically reside in the same information node as the information processes that are using them. However, this is not essential because information collections can be accessed from a remote information collection via a **R**EMOTE **I**NFORMATION **S**ERVICE. See Figure 5.17.

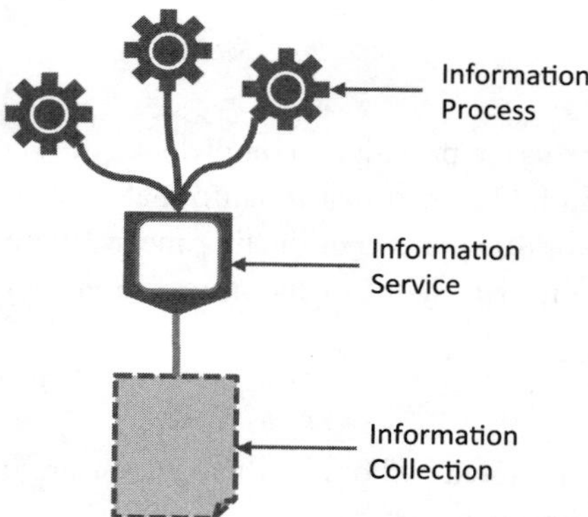

Figure 5.17 Master usage information collection.

Example Resolved

E-Shop has a master usage information collection to maintain customer details. See Figure 5.18.

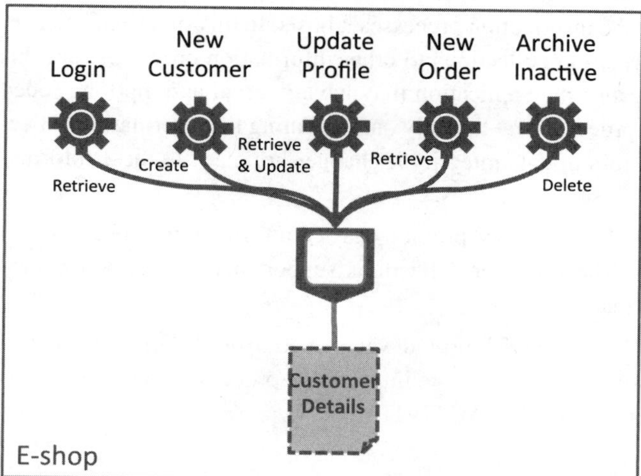

Figure 5.18 Master usage customer details information collection in E-Shop.

Consequences

Benefits:

- An information collection performing the master usage provides a complete set of services to the information processes that are using it. The fact that the information processes update the information inline with the work they are coordinating means these types of information processes represent the up-to-date status of the information processes.

Liabilities:

- New information needs to be validated before it is stored and/or distributed to ensure it does not contaminate other parts of the information supply chain.
- Any changes to the information in the information collection should be distributed to other copies of the information located throughout the information supply chain.

Known Uses

There are three common uses of this pattern:

- It is typical for an **A**PPLICATION **N**ODE to provide master information collections that are used exclusively by the information processes it hosts. In this situation, it is possible to open up these information collections to other information processes, but this must be done with care because the application may have internal assumptions coded that assume its information processes are the only ones updating the information collections. The result could be a loss of data integrity if changes are made to these information collections that violate these assumptions.
- An **I**NFORMATION **A**SSET **H**UB may provide master information collections for **I**NFORMATION **A**SSETS. These master collections support many information processes hosted by other information nodes.
- An **I**NFORMATION **A**CTIVITY **S**TORE provides information collections with a master usage for recording the status of one or more information processes that are processing a particular type of **I**NFORMATION **A**CTIVITY.

Related Patterns

Contrast the master usage pattern with the **R**EFERENCE **U**SAGE and **H**YBRID **U**SAGE patterns.

An information collection with master usage should have **R**ECOVERY **P**ROVISIONING enabled.

Reference Usage

Context

Information collections are storing information throughout the information supply chain. Some information collections will store the same type of information and need to be synchronized. You want to understand the best way to keep them synchronized. This is dependent on the behavior of the information processes using it.

Problem

An organization wants to centralize the management of information, but information processes located on different information nodes still need their own local copy of the information.

Reasons for this include (1) the format of the information is not convenient, (2) the performance of the remote requests to retrieve information is not adequate, (3) the availability of the remote information node is not convenient, or (4) the information node hosting the information collection is not able to take on the additional workload to supply this information either because of cost or spare capacity.

Example

Each of MCHS Trading's order-processing applications needs up-to-date product information. MCHS wants to maintain product information in one place. It introduces a new application called Product Hub that provides the central place where product details can be maintained. The Product Hub has a master usage information collection for product details with information services that can be accessed by remote information processes. However, E-Shop, Mail-Shop, Stores, Shipping, and Invoicing are applications that need the product details in their own databases in their local format. It would take a huge investment to re-write them to support the Product Hub information services. The case for Reporting Hub is slightly different. It is maintaining a historical perspective about the products. Product Hub only contains the current product details. Reporting Hub needs regular feeds from Product Hub that contain the changes to the product catalog to add to its historical information collection.

Forces

- Every copy of an information collection that is created and distributed adds to the cost of maintaining the information supply chain.
- Retrieving information from a remote information node takes more processing than retrieving information from the local information node.

Solution

Create a read-only copy of the information from an appropriate information collection and locate it where it is accessible to the information process.

An information collection that is a read-only copy of another information collection is said to be playing the reference usage in the information supply chain. Specifically, only the information processes responsible for provisioning it should update such an information collection. All other information processes (that is, the ones that caused this copy of the information to be made) should only retrieve information from it. This is reflected in the reference usage information services because they will only include retrieve operations for the information collection. If these information processes do update the information with the reference information collection, it becomes a master information collection and such updates may have to be synchronized back to the original information collection.

Information collections playing a reference usage are typically located in the same information node as the information processes that are using it. Its contents will be refreshed from the original copy as appropriate. See Figure 5.19.

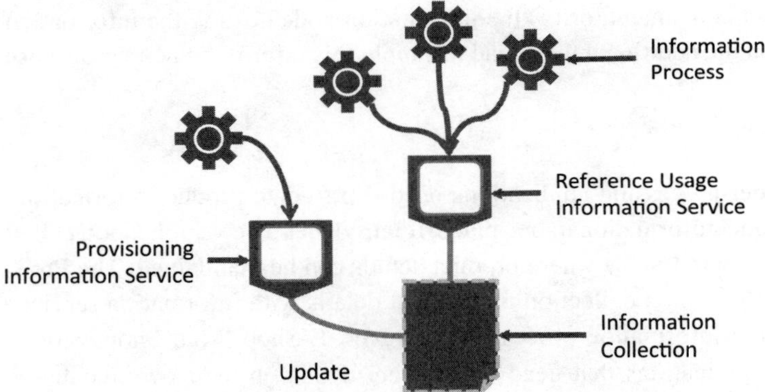

Figure 5.19 Reference usage information collection.

Consequences

Benefits:

- This pattern provides a read-only, purpose-built information collection to one or more information processes to directly support their needs.

Liabilities:

- This information collection needs to be continuously synchronized with the original information collection; otherwise, the information processes using it will be working with obsolete information. Any information processes that are capable of updating a reference usage information collection should be disabled.

Example Resolved

Each order-processing application is sent a read-only copy of the product details. See Figure 5.20. These information collections are provisioned from the Product Hub application, which has the information processes that maintain the master information collection.

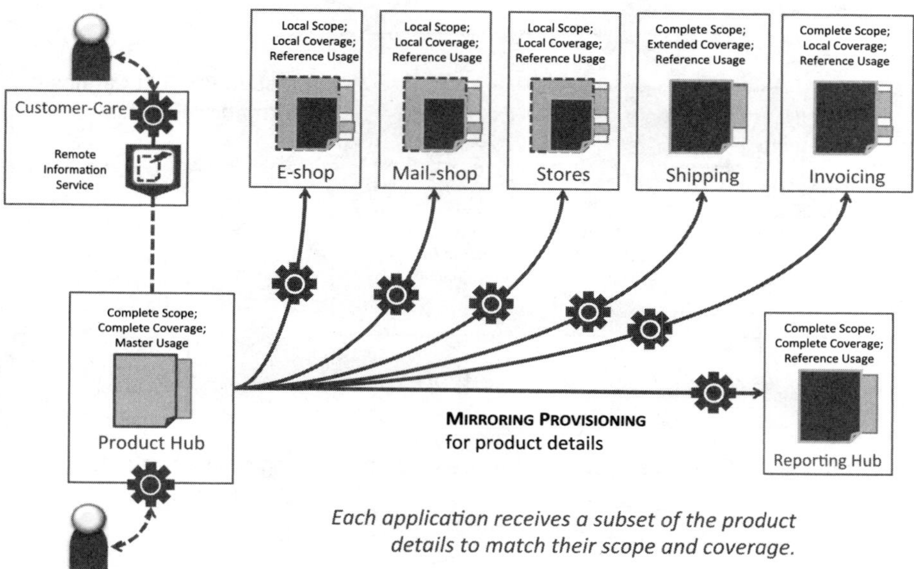

Figure 5.20 Distributing reference copies of product information.

Any information processes implemented in the order-processing applications that would change the product details are either modified or disabled to ensure the product details remain consistent with the master copy in the Product Hub application. For example, Figure 5.21 shows E-Shop's Maintain Product Catalog information process is disabled.

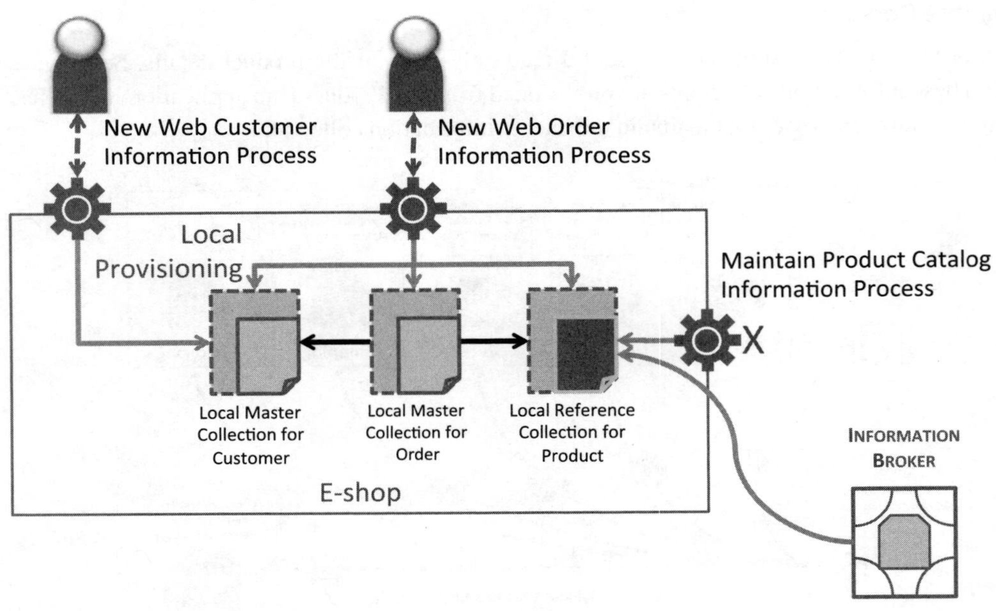

Figure 5.21 Disabling the E-Shop's information process for maintaining product details.

Known Uses

Reference information collections are used extensively throughout many IT systems particularly for lookup tables, which are constantly referred to by the information processes, but can be maintained elsewhere.

Related Patterns

Reference information collections are created and maintained by the **M**IRRORING **P**ROVISIONING pattern. Reference collections can have **C**OMPETE **S**COPE or **L**OCAL **S**COPE. They can have any type of coverage.

Hybrid Usage

Context

Information collections are storing information throughout the information supply chain. Some information collections will store the same type of information and need to be synchronized. You want to understand the best way to keep them synchronized. This is dependent on the behavior of the information processes using it.

Problem

A group of related information processes requires access to information about a subject area that is broader than the attributes it is able to manage locally.

The need for multiple information collections may be for performance, technical, or political reasons. Each information collection is located in a different information node. The information processes running on each information node are maintaining a different subset of values from the information processes on the other nodes.

Example

MCHS Trading plans to introduce an **I**NFORMATION **A**SSET **N**ODE called Customer Hub to provide a single view of its current customers. This single view resides in an information collection located in the Customer Hub. Values from E-Shop, Stores, and Mail-Shop will be synchronized with it. In addition, new applications, such as Customer-Care, will use it as their principle information collection for customer data. There will be analytical insight that classifies each customer added from the analytics team. All in all, many information nodes claim ownership to different parts of each entry in the information collection.

Forces

If each of these information collections plays a master usage, they will have to be synchronized using **P**EER **P**ROVISIONING. This could allow information nodes to change values they do not officially own and have them distributed to the other information collections.

Solution

Create an information collection that supports all of the attributes needed by the local information node. Maintain as many attributes as possible through local processing and synchronize the other attributes though the information supply chain.

This type of information collection is said to be playing the hybrid usage. In this type of collection, some of the attributes are directly changeable through the hybrid usage information services, and others are read-only. The read-only attributes are copies that are updated through a regular provisioning process. See Figure 5.22.

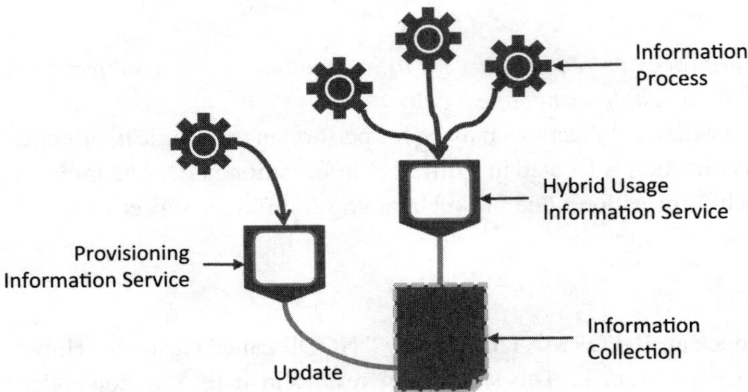

Figure 5.22 Hybrid usage information collection.

Example Resolved

The customer details information collection in the Customer Hub is maintained directly by some information processes and also fed to these collections through both **M**IRRORING **P**ROVISIONING and **P**EER **P**ROVISIONING.

Consequences

Benefits:

- The hybrid information collection is directly supporting a decentralized approach to managing shared data. For many organizations, this can help to break down the resistance to sharing information because the ability to update information and extend it with local attributes is retained.

Liabilities:

- The integration logic to synchronize the information with a hybrid collection can become complex. It is also necessary to maintain governance on how the information is changed, exchanged, and used across the different information collections that are synchronized with the hybrid collection.

Known Uses

This type of information collection is typically found in Master Data Management (MDM) hubs that are operating in a decentralized organization.

Related Patterns

Information collections playing the hybrid usage are synchronized with other information collections using either the **P**EER **P**ROVISIONING or the **H**IERARCHICAL **I**NFORMATION **S**UPPLY **C**HAIN patterns.

Sandbox Usage

Context

Information collections are storing information throughout the information supply chain. Some information collections will store the same type of information and need to be synchronized. You want to understand the best way to keep them synchronized. This is dependent on the behavior of the information processes using it.

Problem

A group of related information processes used for a project needs to make experimental changes to the organization's information.

Example

MCHS Trading would like to do some what-if analysis on the mix of products available through each channel. It wants a set of information collections that covers its customers, the products they buy, through which channel, and when. The Reporting Hub has this information but the structure of the data is not ideal for this type of analysis. In addition, MCHS Trading wants to make changes to some of this data to understand how changes in its product offerings could affect sales.

Forces

When information is shared among multiple information processes, each information process is affected by the work of the others. While an information process is partway through a set of related updates, the affected information entries are typically locked so the other information processes do not see the partially completed changes. This works well for changes that take a few seconds. Anything longer than that needs an alternative approach.

Solution

Commission and provision a set of information collections that is suited to support the needs of the project. During the project, the team is able to run the workloads and make the changes to the information as and when they need to. At the end of the project, these information collections are deleted.

Information collections that are provisioned for a specific experimental project are playing the sandbox usage. These information collections help to isolate the project's information processes, which may be creating fluctuating workloads, from the regular production workloads. See

Figure 5.23. It is not possible to detect sandbox usages from the information services that access the information collection. These information services may include create, update, and delete operations as well as retrieve and may not look any different from master usage information services. It is the management policy associated with the information collection that determines that it is an information collection populated for experimental purposes for a specific project.

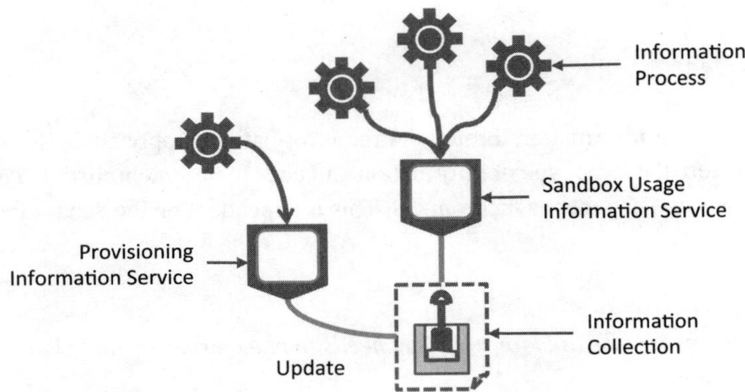

Figure 5.23 Sandbox usage information collection.

Example Resolved

MCHS Trading uses SNAPSHOT PROVISIONING to create linked information collections to support this analysis project. The team is able to change the channels that products are available through and understand how these changes could affect sales based on the knowledge of the channels that its customers work on.

Consequences

Benefits:

- Creating dedicated information collections that are optimized to support a particular project will improve the efficiency of the project.

Liabilities:

- Every copy of an information collection that is created and distributed adds to the cost of maintaining the information supply chain. Ideally, the availability of the sandbox should be time boxed so the information can be properly disposed of and the storage freed up once the project is complete.

Known Uses

Sandbox information collections are often used for analytics such as data mining. They are also test data sets when testing new information processes and services.

Related Patterns

SNAPSHOT PROVISIONING is often used to populate information collections acting as sandboxes.

INFORMATION MART, INFORMATION CUBE, and INFORMATION MINING STORE are specialized types of information nodes for hosting sandbox usage information collections.

Scope of an Information Collection

Information collections are storing information throughout the information supply chain. The existence or absence of an information instance in a specific information collection will depend on the information processes that maintain it. For example, the E-Shop application only maintains details of customers who are registered for Internet shopping, whereas the Customer Hub has details of all of MCHS Trading's customers, irrespective of the channel they use.

When we are looking to provision a new information process with an information collection, or we want to synchronize the information between two information collections, it is important to understand the scope of the information instances within it, to ensure it is compatible.

There are three patterns shown in Table 5.6 that classify the scope of the information entries within an information collection.

Table 5.6 Information Collection Scope Patterns

Icon	Pattern Name	Problem	Solution
	COMPLETE SCOPE	An information process needs to perform an activity once for each instance of a particular subject area (such as a customer, product, order, invoice, shipment, etc.) that occurs within the information supply chain.	The information process needs to use an information collection that stores a single information entry for each instance of the subject area that occurs within the information supply chain. Such an information collection is said to have a complete scope.

Icon	Pattern Name	Problem	Solution
	LOCAL SCOPE	The implementations of the information processes hosted within an information node assume they are in complete control of changes to the information they use.	Provide information collections within the information node for the sole use of its information processes. These information collections will then only have information entries that are created by the locally hosted information processes. These types of information collections are said to have a local scope.
	TRANSIENT SCOPE	An information node needs to provide temporary storage for information entries that are being continuously added and removed by the information processes.	Create an information collection to temporarily store the information entries in the information node. From time to time, the information entries stored in this information collection will change, and so we say this collection has transient scope.

Complete Scope

Context

Information collections are storing information throughout the information supply chain. The existence or absence of an information instance in a specific information collection will depend on the information processes that maintain it. How do we classify the scope of the information entries within an information collection?

Problem

An information process needs to perform an activity once for each instance of a particular subject area (such as customer, product, order, invoice, shipment, ...) that occurs within the information supply chain.

To do this, it needs a list of these instances.

Example

MCHS Trading wants to send a letter to every one of its customers to advertise some special offers it has.

Forces

In many organizations, it is common for information about the same subject area to be duplicated and distributed among multiple information collections. These information collections are used by different subsets of information processes and have become inconsistent over time. In these circumstances, without deliberate **I**NFORMATION **P**ROVISIONING, not all instances will appear in each of these information collections.

Solution

Connect the information process to an information collection that stores a single information entry for each instance of the subject area that occurs within the information supply chain. Such an information collection is said to have a complete scope.

For example, for a collection of customers to have complete scope, it would include all customers for the organization.

Information collections with complete scope are very valuable in an information supply chain because they provide a place were information processes can work with a complete list of information entries for a subject area and they are an excellent place to distribute information from.

Example Resolved

Customer information in MCHS Trading's original set of applications is located in information collections hosted in the E-Shop and Stores applications. However, each of these information collections has local scope—covering only the customers who used the particular channel. Of course, some customers used both channels, and will appear in both information collections. Others may only use the Mail-Shop channels, which means their details are buried in the orders they have made in the past. The result is that there is no easy way to generate a list of people to send the letter to.

MCHS Trading adds a new information node called Customer Hub. This information node is an **I**NFORMATION **A**SSET **H**UB. Its responsibility is to maintain the authoritative source of customer details. As such, it hosts an information collection for customer details that has one entry for each of the individuals who has done at least one of the following:

- Registered on the E-Shop website
- Bought something through mail order or by calling the customer service number
- Registered for a store card

This information collection has complete scope and is suitable to act as the list of customers to receive the letter.

Consequences

Benefits:

- When an information collection has complete scope, it can be used to drive many information processes where the activity should be once and once only for each instance of a subject area.

Liabilities:

- Information collections with complete scope are typically provisioning from multiple information collections. There is an opportunity for duplicate entries to occur. These need to be regularly matched and consolidated to maintain the value of having the complete scope.

Known Uses

You will see information collections with complete scope in either of the following situations:

- In an application that is exposed to every possible instance known to the organization as part of normal business
- Where **I**NFORMATION **P**ROVISIONING is used to explicitly introduce all known instances from the information supply chain to a specialized information node, such as an **I**NFORMATION **A**SSET **H**UB or **I**NFORMATION **W**AREHOUSE

Related Patterns

Compare the complete scope with the **L**OCAL **S**COPE pattern.

An information collection with complete scope may play the **M**ASTER **U**SAGE, **R**EFERENCE **U**SAGE, **H**YBRID **U**SAGE, or **S**ANDBOX **U**SAGE.

Local Scope

Context

Information collections are storing information throughout the information supply chain. The existence or absence of an information instance in a specific information collection will depend on the information processes that update it. How do we classify the scope of the information entries within an information collection?

Problem

The implementations of the information processes hosted within an information node assume they are in complete control of changes to the information they use.

Example

The E-Shop application has information processes that need to store information about the people who have registered to use the E-Shop website. These details include their account identifier, password, default delivery address, and privacy preferences.

Forces

Many of the values used by these information processes are also required by other information processes, which may also be implemented as if they were the only activity updating the information.

Solution

Provide information collections within the information node for the sole use of its information processes. These information collections will then only have information entries that are created by the locally hosted information processes. These types of information collections are said to have a local scope.

Periodically review and prune the information that is retained by the information node to keep it appropriately scoped.

Example Resolved

The E-Shop application has an information collection for customer details. Each entry in this information collection represents a customer who has registered to use the E-Shop website. Customers who only use the mail-order service are not listed in this information collection.

Consequences

Benefits:

- The information collection only contains information that is relevant to the information processes that are using it.

Liabilities:

- The information collection will not reflect a complete picture from an organization's point of view.
- Information provisioning must be used with great care to synchronize new values stored in the local information collection with other parts of the information supply chain.

Known Uses

Most applications host information collections with a local scope.

Related Patterns

Compare local scope to the **C**OMPLETE **S**COPE.

An information collection with complete scope may play the **M**ASTER **U**SAGE, **R**EFERENCE **U**SAGE, **H**YBRID **U**SAGE, or **S**ANDBOX **U**SAGE.

Transient Scope

Context

Information collections are storing information throughout the information supply chain. The existence or absence of an information instance in a specific information collection will depend on the information processes that update it. How do we classify the scope of the information entries within an information collection?

Problem

An information node needs to provide temporary storage for information entries that are being continuously added and removed by the information processes.

Example

New orders need to be passed from E-Shop, Mail-Shop, and Stores to Shipping. As part of the transfer process, the structure of the orders needs to be transformed to fit with the way Shipping expects to receive these orders.

Forces

- Transferring data between two information nodes requires them to both be available at the same time.
- How do you ensure information added to temporary storage is on there temporarily?

Solution

Create an information collection to store the information entries in the information node.

This information collection should implement an ordering mechanism for the information entries so that it is easy for the information processes to ensure complete handling of the transient information.

Example Resolved

A **Q**UEUE **M**ANAGER is used to pass orders from E-Shop, Mail-Shop, and Stores to Shipping. It uses transient scope information collections that contain the orders that are partway through the transfer process between the applications.

Consequences

Benefits:

- With an information collection of transient scope, it easy to see how many information entries are yet to be processed.

Liabilities:

- Care must be taken to ensure information entries are added and removed with integrity to avoid losing or duplicating information entries. The information entries should also be processed in a timely manner.

Known Uses

Information collections with transient scope typically occur as part of the implementation of **I**NFORMATION **P**ROVISIONING. These collections may be stored, for example, in memory, as a message, in a temporary spreadsheet, or in **S**TAGING **A**REAS during the life of an extract, transform, load (ETL) process.

Related Patterns

Information collections with transient scope are typically located in an **I**NFORMATION **S**TORE or **I**NFORMATION **B**ROKER. The **I**NFORMATION **Q**UEUING **P**ROCESS uses an information collection with a transient scope to implement the "queue."

Coverage of an Information Collection

The information collections that store information for a subject area will each support a different subset of the attributes. The coverage patterns shown in Table 5.7, Table 5.8, Table 5.9, and Table 5.10 characterize these subsets.

Complete Coverage

Complete coverage supports all of the attributes defined in the subject area. For example, MCHS Trading's Customer Hub is considered to have complete coverage as it incorporates all attributes about each customer, as defined for the subject area.

Note: A given subject area may have far more potential attributes than an organization can reasonably work with or even obtain. It is not the expectation that complete coverage addresses all possible attributes—just the ones that the organization considers relevant for its business.

Table 5.7 Complete Coverage Pattern

Icon	Pattern Name	Problem	Solution
	COMPLETE COVERAGE	An organization needs an information collection that can store all attributes that are known about a subject area.	Create an information collection that supports all of the attributes for the subject area.

Core Coverage

Core coverage contains just enough information to identify the instance. It is typically used to correlate information entries from different information collections together and so will contain all of the known information keys for the instance. For example, in order to consolidate customer information from the E-Shop and Stores applications, there is a minimal set of attributes required by the consolidation process, including the customer's name and address, phone, and possibly email and date of birth.

Table 5.8 Core Coverage Pattern

Icon	Pattern Name	Problem	Solution
	CORE COVERAGE	An organization needs an index of the instances of a particular subject area.	Create an information collection that supports the minimal set of attributes necessary to understand the critical values that identify each unique instance within the subject area.

Extended Coverage

Extended coverage provides the key attributes for a subject area that are most widely used in the organization as well as the additional attributes needed by those information processes that use the information (these attributes often include: processing dates, status flags, relevant code values, and similar information elements).

Table 5.9 Extended Coverage Pattern

Icon	Pattern Name	Problem	Solution
	EXTENDED COVERAGE	An organization needs an information collection that can store all of the attributes required by a diverse range of information processes.	Create an information collection that supports the minimal set of attributes necessary to understand the essence of each instance within the subject area plus any additional attributes needed by the consuming information processes.

Local Coverage

Local coverage describes an information collection that is needed by the local information processes. For example, the E-Shop only requires some basic information regarding the customer: name, address, phone, email, and credit card information for the order.

Table 5.10 Local Coverage Pattern

Icon	Pattern Name	Problem	Solution
	LOCAL COVERAGE	An information node needs to store the attributes used by its locally hosted information processes.	Create an information collection that just has the attributes to support the consuming information processes.

It should be noted that a given information collection's coverage may change over time based on new requirements and the evolution of the information supply chain, the business and information strategies, and the IT landscape.

Summary of Information Collections

The information collection pattern group describes how to classify and characterize stored information from the point of view of where it is located, how it is used, and what it contains. These classifications help you make design choices for how information should flow between the information nodes owned by the organization. The classifications offered by each of the pattern groups are complementary and can be combined to build up a picture of the role of an information collection in an information supply chain. The icons for these patterns can also be combined to show how an information collection has been categorized. Figure 5.24 illustrates combination icons for usage, scope, and coverage.

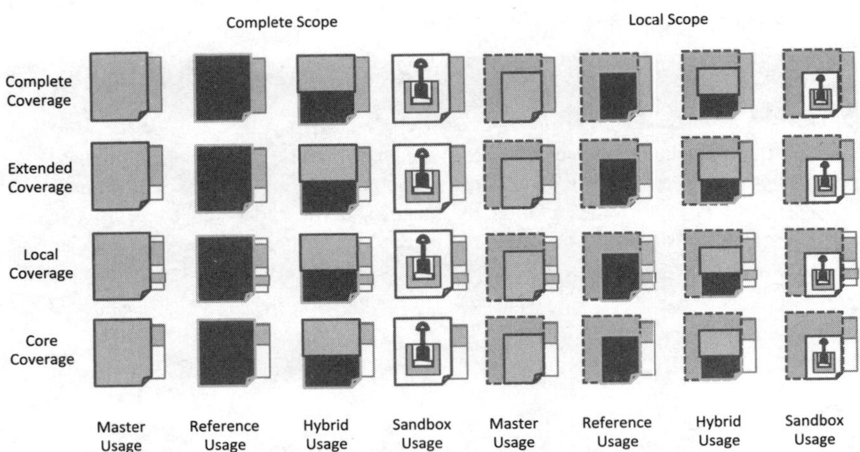

Figure 5.24 Icon combinations for an information collection.

Information Entry Patterns

The INFORMATION COLLECTION pattern group introduced the notion that an organization's information should be divided into logical groups, or collections. This section focuses on information collections that contain structured information. This means that the information within the collection is organized according to a well-known structure.

These structured information collections typically hold information from a single subject area. Customer details are an example of a subject area.

Within a subject area, there are distinct instances that must be recorded. For example, MCHS Trading has a customer called Alistair Steiff and another customer called Daisy Steiff. The information about Alistair represents one instance of the customer details and the information about Daisy represents another instance of customer details.

The information entry patterns consider different design choices for how distinct instances are structured within an information collection. There are many choices and so this pattern group is further subdivided in nested pattern groups covering identity, structure, locking, and behavior.

The lead pattern of the entire group is shown in Table 5.11. This is followed by summaries of some variations on this pattern.

Table 5.11 Information Entry Pattern Summary

Icon	Pattern Name	Problem	Solution
	INFORMATION ENTRY	Distinct instances of a subject area need to be stored in an information collection.	Organize the information collection so each instance is stored as a distinct entry that can be retrieved and maintained independently through the information collection's information services.

Information Entry

Context

An information collection is a logical grouping of related information.

Problem

Distinct instances of a subject area need to be stored in an information collection.

Each instance of a subject area will have multiple information values associated with them. These values are characterized by attributes. The attributes define the types of the information values that are to be stored.

Example

The MCHS Trading E-Shop application stores information about its customers in its customer details information collection. How is information about each individual customer organized to ensure information about different people is not mixed together?

Forces

- **Unique instances of information must be distinct**—Information about each individual instance of a subject area needs to be kept distinct while managed in a consistent manner with the other instances.
- **Instances must be identifiable**—An individual instance needs to be identifiable from other instances.
- **Instances must have correct values**—An individual instance needs to contain valid values.
- **Same change may require propagation to all instances**—Sometimes the same change needs to be made to all instances within a subject area.
- **Distinct instances may need to be grouped or summed**—Sometimes it is important to know how many distinct instances are known about so they may be either counted or categorized.

- **Support may be necessary to meet service agreements**—Large, complex, and highly valuable information requires special support to ensure it can be accessed within agreed service levels.
- **Majority of information is unstructured**—Most electronic information today is unstructured data such as documents, images, and video.
- **Different processes may use the same information instance**—The same instance of a subject area may be used by information processes on different information nodes. This can result in it being stored multiple times and the values becoming out of synchronization.

Solution

Organize the information collection so each instance is stored as a distinct entry that can be retrieved and maintained independently through the information collection's information services.

There are a number of ways to structure an entry within an information collection. Some of them are covered by the STATIC STRUCTURE, DYNAMIC STRUCTURE, ENTRY-LEVEL STRUCTURE, and TAGGED MEDIA STRUCTURE patterns. Whatever the approach, the structure provides some constraints on what can be stored in the entry. These constraints can be quite strict, forcing an information process that is creating or updating the values to conform to predefined standards.

The information collection then supports LOCAL INFORMATION SERVICES that provide the operations that can be performed on the information entries. Operations would typically include the following:

- Retrieving a subset of information entries that match a certain criteria
- Retrieving, creating, updating, or deleting a specific information entry
- Iterating over the whole collection, or a subset, to perform an operation

When an information process is updating an information entry, it should lock it while the update is in progress. Approaches to locking an information entry are described by the LOCAL LOCKING, DISTRIBUTED LOCKING, and OPTIMISTIC LOCKING patterns.

In addition, the other information entry patterns define some more specialized operations. These patterns are LIFECYCLE STATES, UNIQUE ENTRIES, DEFERRED UPDATE, SOFT DELETE, PROXY, PROVENANCE, HISTORICAL VALUES, and RELATIONSHIPS.

Consequences

Benefits:

- Well-defined structured information entries with strong enforcement of valid values within them simplify the work of an information process that is consuming the information because they can make assumptions about the meaning and quality of the information.

Liabilities:

- Over time, the requirements covering the types of information that should be stored will change, and as a result, the implementation of the information collection will have to be updated and the existing information migrated to the new structure.

Example Resolved

The MCHS Trading E-Shop application requires that a given customer create an account name and password when ordering as well as a shipping address, phone number, email address, and credit card information. Each customer account name serves as a unique INFORMATION KEY, and a given customer account name can only occur once—other customers attempting to create an account with the same account name are informed that they must create a different account name.

MCHS Trading realizes that a given customer may, in fact, use another family member's account name or create multiple account names (often because they forgot they already created one). They do not attempt to resolve this in the E-Shop application, but deliver all customer account names and information to the Customer Hub for resolution and consolidation, if appropriate.

Known Uses

The information entry pattern describes how structured information stores are organized. For example,

- When a database table is being used to store an information collection, an entry is stored in a row in that table.
- When a file is used to store an information collection, a record (or row) is often used to represent an information entry.

Related Patterns

The information entry is located in an INFORMATION COLLECTION.

An INFORMATION KEY is an attribute in an information entry that is its unique identifier within the information collection.

A SUBJECT AREA DEFINITION records what should be stored about a subject area.

An INFORMATION MODEL describes the structure of an information entry.

A VALID VALUES DEFINITION defines rules for the values stored within an information entry.

An INFORMATION VALUES PROFILE assesses and compares the values stored in the information entries of an information collection.

The MASTER USAGE, REFERENCE USAGE, HYBRID USAGE, and SNAPSHOT USAGE define how the information processes operate on the information entries.

The COMPLETE SCOPE, LOCAL SCOPE, and TRANSIENT SCOPE patterns describe the scope of the information entries stored in the information collection relative to the total number of unique instances for the subject area.

The COMPLETE COVERAGE, CORE COVERAGE, EXTENDED COVERAGE, and LOCAL COVERAGE patterns describe the coverage of the attributes within the information entries of an information collection relative to the subject area definition.

A LOCAL INFORMATION SERVICE provides the interface for information processes to call the operations that manipulate the information entries.

Identifying Information Using the Information Key

The information key patterns are a subgroup within the information entry pattern group. They describe how an information entry could be uniquely identified within an information collection. This is usually a simple matter within a single information node. However, as information is distributed, how should the information entries in the copies be identified? What if two independent information collections exist for the same subject area, but are located on different information nodes and updated using different information processes? The unique identifiers for the information entries within these collections are not going to match. When information about the same subject area is consolidated from different information collections, how will the different instances be recognized as distinct?

These are the questions covered by the information key pattern group. It starts with the lead pattern shown in Table 5.12.

Table 5.12 Supplementary Patterns for Information Entry—the Information Key

Icon	Pattern Name	Problem	Solution
	INFORMATION KEY	An information entry needs a unique identifier.	Either use one (or more) of the attributes of the information entry or add a new attribute and assign a unique value to it.

The patterns in Table 5.13 describe some approaches to defining information keys within a single information collection. These patterns are in common use in applications.

Table 5.13 Information Key Patterns for Single Information Collections

Icon	Pattern Name	Problem	Solution
	LOCAL KEY	An information node needs to uniquely identify each entry in an information collection for its own internal use.	Assign a unique identifier as an additional attribute in the information entry using a local counter or a time-based value.
	RECYCLED KEY	An information node is running out of unique keys to assign to new information entries in an information collection.	Reuse keys previously allocated to information entries that have since been deleted, starting with the oldest first.
	NATURAL KEY	When is it safe to use externally generated identifiers for the information key of an information collection?	It is safe to use this existing identifier to solely identify an information entry if it can be guaranteed to always be both stable and unique into the future.

Providing a unique identifier that is scoped within a single information collection is not difficult. However, as information is distributed, synchronized, and merged between information collections, the keys are no longer unique or universal, creating some interesting challenges. For example,

- When an information collection is created from a copy of another information collection, how will the information entries in the copy be identified?
- When information entries in an information collection are being merged to remove duplicates, what is the identifier of the resulting merged information collection? If an information collection in a remote information node is storing INFORMATION LINKS to these information entries, how are the links resolved to the new merged information entry?
- What if two independent information collections each located on different information nodes are merged together? The information keys for the corresponding information entries within these collections are not going to match. How should the consolidated information entries be identified?

The mirror key pattern shown in Table 5.14 is often used for a copy of an information collection—particularly one that is being kept synchronized using MIRRORING PROVISIONING.

Table 5.14 The Mirror Key Pattern for Copies of Information Collections

Icon	Pattern Name	Problem	Solution
	MIRROR KEY	What is the appropriate scheme for identifying the information entries in a new information collection that is provisioned from an existing information collection?	Use the same keys as the source.

The remaining key patterns shown in Table 5.15 are for hubs such as the INFORMATION ASSET HUB. The aggregate key is used for their internal identifier. The caller's key is used for matching entries from source systems and simplifying the use of the information services. The stable key enables other information collections to store it as a reliable link to the information entries even when the hub is merging duplicate instances.

Table 5.15 Information Key Patterns for Information Hubs

Icon	Pattern Name	Problem	Solution
	AGGREGATE KEY	What should be the identity of an information entry that is derived by dynamically combining information values from multiple sources, all of which use different key values?	Assign a new unique key value to the aggregated record.
	CALLER'S KEY	When the unique identifiers for a collection of information entries change because they are moved to a new information collection, how are the references to them (which use the original unique identifiers and are stored in related information collections) reconciled with the unique identifiers in the new source of information?	For each entry, store the appropriate key from the remote information collection along with the identifier of the remote information collection.
	STABLE KEY	What should be the identity of information entries that are being merged and restructured on an ongoing basis?	Ensure an information entry that has been formed from the merging of two other entries is still returned with either one of the keys from the merged records.

Information Key

Context

An INFORMATION ENTRY typically represents something discrete—for example, a concept, person, thing, event, or activity—that is also documented in other information collections owned by the organization. Customers, suppliers, external publications, and other sources often refer to it outside of the organization, too.

Problem

An information entry needs a unique identifier.

Most pieces of information, though not necessarily all, have some form of identification. We recognize people by name; where names are the same, we look for additional identifications, such as date and place of birth, national or tax IDs, or place of residence. People can make this adjustment. IT systems are less flexible.

Ensuring each information entry has a unique identifier speeds up retrieval and ensures links between information entries are definitive.

Example

MCHS Trading must have a unique identifier for each order it takes so it can coordinate the processing of the order, and answer questions about it from the customer.

Forces

- **Multiple ways to identify a particular piece of information often exist in the real world**—These are often not completely unique. For example, there are many people who have the same name—particularly those in the same family, possibly at the same address.
- **Many information collections use their own scheme for identifying their information entries**—These are rarely globally unique. This is particularly true of information collections implemented in applications where LOCAL PROVISIONING is assumed.
- **Incomplete or incorrect data may result in incorrect identification and labeling of information entries.**

Solution

Either use one (or more) of the attributes of the information entry or add a new attribute and assign a unique value to it.

The information key consists of one or more attributes in the information entry that together will uniquely identify the information entry. See Figure 5.25.

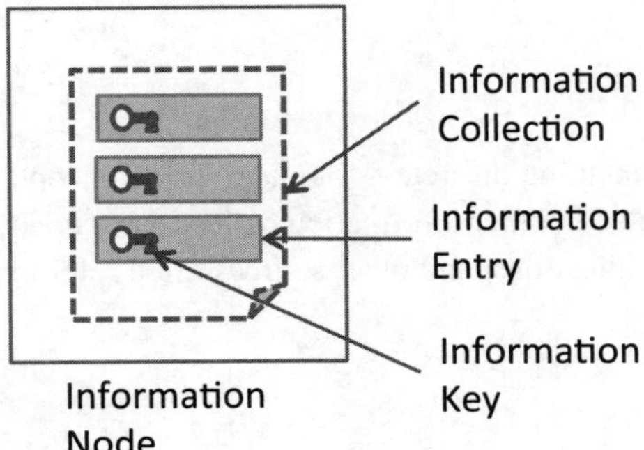

Figure 5.25 The information key uniquely identifies the information entry within the information collection.

Consequences

Benefits:

- Information keys provide a unique identifier for an information entry. Having a unique identifier is useful to be sure that people and systems are referring to the same instance, both for retrieving the right stored information or linking between information entries.

Liabilities:

- Unique keys are typically generated based on a local counter or using the system clock and as a result, most keys are only unique within the scope of a single information collection. This can create an interesting challenge when matching up information from different information collections.

Example Resolved

Each of the MCHS Trading order-taking systems (E-Shop, Mail-Shop, and Stores) will assign a locally unique identifier to an order when it is created. This identifier is only unique within the scope of the originating application. When the order is sent from the order-taking systems to Shipping, a code name of the source information node is added to the information keys to guarantee they are unique across the enterprise. In addition, Mail-Shop uses a recycled key and so its keys must be augmented with a time stamp before being sent to Shipping.

Known Uses

Unique identifiers are typically termed *keys*, which is where the name of this pattern comes from. For example, database systems use a particular nomenclature of *primary*, *foreign*, and *natural* keys. These terms refer to the style of key in use in an information entry:

- Primary key is the unique key that identifies an information entry.
- Foreign key is the unique identifier of another information entry that this information entry is linked to.
- Natural key refers to the use of existing attributes as the information key. This is described in the NATURAL KEY pattern.

Related Patterns

The INFORMATION VALUES PROFILE pattern can provide information on the information key(s) in each information collection.

Linking information entries is covered in more detail in the INFORMATION LINK pattern from the information elements pattern group.

Where information collections contain the same or similar information but do not have common INFORMATION KEYS, an INFORMATION REENGINEERING PROCESS including a LINK ENTRIES step may be needed to connect the information together.

Local Key

Context

An INFORMATION ENTRY typically represents something discrete—for example, a concept, person, thing, event, or activity—that is also documented in other information collections owned by the organization. Customers, suppliers, external publications, and other sources often refer to it outside of the organization, too. Having a unique identifier for each information entry is useful to be sure that people and systems are referring to the same instance, both for retrieving the right stored information or linking between information entries.

Problem

An information node needs to uniquely identify each entry in an information collection for its own internal use.

Example

The E-Shop application needs to assign a unique identifier to an order when the order is created.

Forces

- **Multiple ways to identify a particular piece of information often exist in the real world**—These are often not completely unique. For example, there are many people who have the same name—particularly those in the same family, possibly at the same address.
- **Many information collections use their own scheme for identifying their information entries**—This is particularly true of information collections implemented in applications where LOCAL PROVISIONING is assumed.
- **Incomplete or incorrect data may result in incorrect identification and labeling of information entries.**
- **Many applications are designed with only local scope in mind**—This can cause issues in ensuring unique identifiers when information is distributed beyond its original scope.

Solution

Assign a unique identifier as an additional attribute in the information entry using a local counter or a time-based value.

This is stored as an additional attribute in the information entry. It may simply be a counter, or something that includes a time stamp or local machine identifier. The information node assigns the local key when the information entry is created and it is always bound to that information entry. The value of the key bears no relationship to other values in the information entry. It will be unique within the information collection and meaningful only while the information entry exists. When the information entry is deleted, the key value is never reused. Because of this, it is possible to pass local keys across the information service interface and even store them on other information collections to show a relationship (or link) to the information entry. See Figure 5.26.

Every entry in the information collection must use the same attributes to represent its information key. If there is an INFORMATION SCHEMA for the information entry structure, it often indicates which attributes are used for the key.

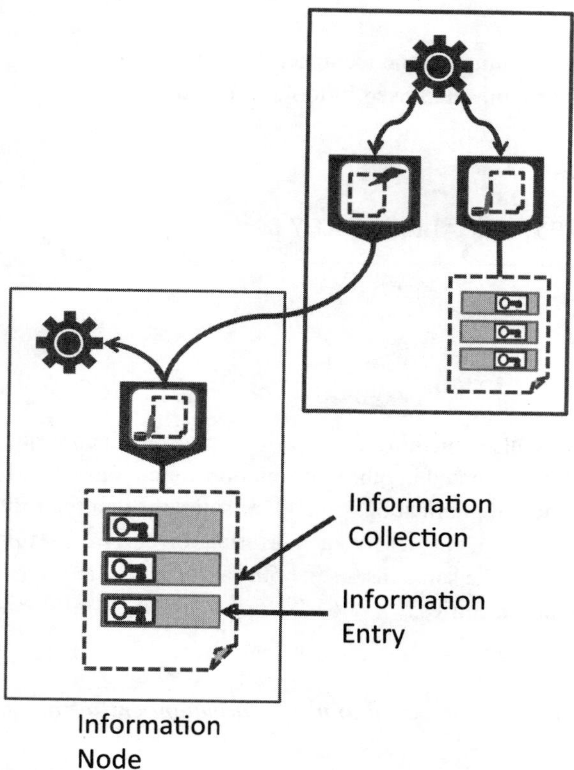

Figure 5.26 Local Key solution.

Consequences

Benefits:

- Local keys allow specific applications or processes to uniquely identify an information entry within the scope of an information collection.

Liabilities:

- Local keys are not unique outside the scope of the information collection.

Example Resolved

E-Shop uses the next number in a sequence as a unique identifier for each new order.

Known Uses

Local keys are the most common approach to creating unique identifiers for information entries. They may be stored in cross-reference files or tables and used in lookup functions by multiple applications, systems, or services.

Related Patterns

Local keys are used in the **A**GGREGATE **K**EY and **C**ALLER'S **K**EY patterns.

Recycled Key

Context

An **I**NFORMATION **E**NTRY typically represents something discrete—for example, a concept, person, thing, event, or activity—that is also documented in other information collections owned by the organization. Customers, suppliers, external publications, and other sources often refer to it outside of the organization, too. Having a unique identifier for each information entry is useful to be sure that people and systems are referring to the same instance, both for retrieving the right stored information or linking between information entries.

Problem

An information node is running out of unique keys to assign to new information entries in an information collection.

This is particularly common in older systems where the data structure used to store the information key is of limited size.

Example

MCHS Trading's Mail-Shop application is its first application. It was developed in-house with a limited budget when the company was starting up. Each order it records is given the next order number in sequence. The order number is stored in a 3-byte field. When the next order number will overflow this 3-byte field, the sequence starts again at 1. As a result, every couple of months or so, the order numbers recycle.

Forces

- **Multiple ways to identify a particular piece of information often exist in the real world**—These are often not completely unique. For example, there are many people who have the same name—particularly those in the same family, possibly at the same address.

- **Many information collections use their own scheme for identifying their information entries**—This is particularly true of information collections implemented in applications where LOCAL PROVISIONING is assumed.
- **Incomplete or incorrect data may result in incorrect identification and labeling of information entries.**
- **Many applications are designed with only local scope in mind**—This can cause issues in ensuring unique identifiers when information is distributed beyond its original scope.

Solution

Reuse keys previously allocated to information entries that have since been deleted, starting with the oldest first.

A recycled key is similar to a LOCAL KEY, except that it is reused. At any one time, each key uniquely identifies an information entry. However, a historical view shows multiple information entries mapping to the same recycled key value. See Figure 5.27.

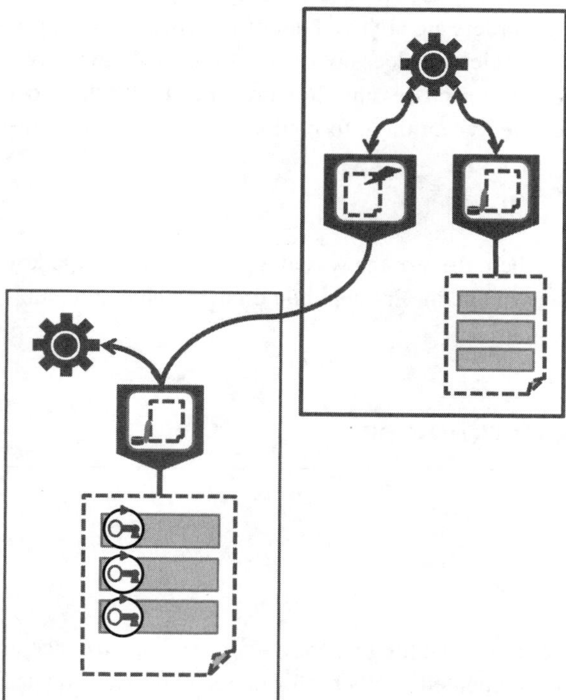

Figure 5.27 Recycled Key solution.

Consequences

Benefits:

- The life of the application is extended because it does not run out of unique key values. The alternative is often an expensive redesign of the key management capability of the application to extend the range of the information key values.

Liabilities:

- This scheme is manageable in the local information node. However, when this key is distributed, it *must* be extended with a time stamp or similar counter so that an information entry can be distinguished from previous, and future, uses of the same key value.
- It is important to monitor how frequently the key recycles to ensure the information node does not run out of free keys. Obsolete information entries need to be removed frequently enough to maintain plenty of free slots.

Example Resolved

The Mail-Shop application is recycling its information keys for orders fairly rapidly. Its INFRASTRUCTURE OPERATORS ensure that older orders are archived out of its order details information collection on a regular basis so that the application does not run out of unused key values. Then the order is sent to the Shipping application for processing; it is prepended with the order date and time to ensure it is globally unique, even when the information key is recycled in the Mail-Shop application.

Known Uses

Recycled keys are used in older applications where the storage was at a premium and large key values would have been expensive to store and maintain. In the public domain, telephone numbers are recycled keys.

Related Patterns

Recycled keys are typically used in an APPLICATION NODE.

Natural Key

Context

An INFORMATION ENTRY typically represents something discrete—for example, a concept, person, thing, event, or activity—that is also documented in other information collections owned by the organization. Customers, suppliers, external publications, and other sources often refer to it outside of the organization, too. Having a unique identifier for each information entry is useful to be sure that people and systems are referring to the same instance, both for retrieving the right stored information or linking between information entries.

Problem

An information entry being created by an information process represents an object that already has one or more unique identifiers by which it is known in the real world.

Is it possible to make use of one of these unique identifiers as the information key for an information collection? This would make it easy to locate the information entry when the request comes from an external party.

Example

MCHS Trading's E-Shop application needs to create an information entry to store the account details of a customer registered with its online shopping website. Each customer must have his or her own unique account name (as well as an email address) for confirming orders and other related communication.

Forces

- **Multiple ways to identify a particular piece of information often exist in the real world—**These are often not completely unique. For example, there are many people who have the same name—particularly those in the same family, possibly at the same address.
- **Many information collections use their own scheme for identifying their information entries—**This is particularly true of information collections implemented in applications where LOCAL PROVISIONING is assumed.
- **Incomplete or incorrect data may result in incorrect identification and labeling of information entries.**
- **Information may be overloaded with local data—**Organizations may reuse natural keys for specific local processing purposes, resulting in incorrect identification of information entries.
- **Many applications are designed with only local scope in mind—**This can cause issues in ensuring unique identifiers when information is distributed beyond its original scope.

Solution

Use the existing unique identifier as the information key for entries in this collection.

This unique identifier may already be stored in the information entry as one or more attributes. See Figure 5.28.

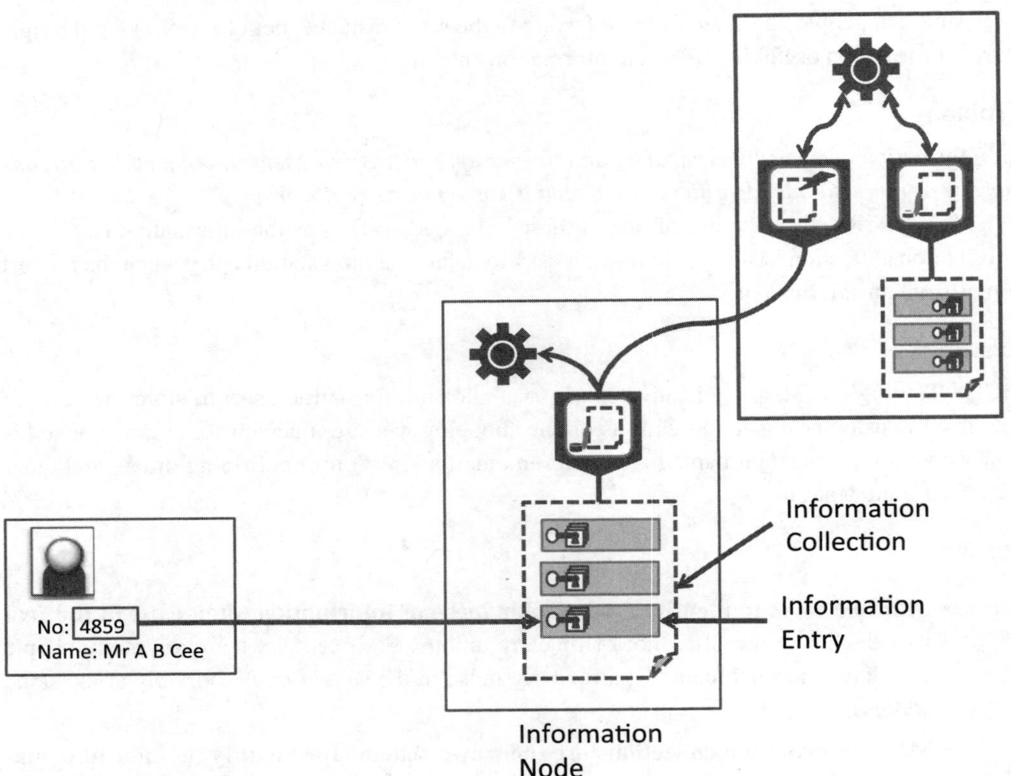

Figure 5.28 Natural Key solution.

Consequences

Benefits:

- The implementation of a natural key makes it easier to retrieve the right information entry based on information from an external system or person. For example, natural keys are useful when interacting with members of the public because it is easier for them to remember the number.

Liabilities:

- Natural keys are often outside the control of the organization and may be prone to change or incorrect usage leading to duplicate information entries for the same piece of information or incorrectly linked information entries for distinct pieces of information.

Example Resolved

MCHS Trading decides to use the customers' email addresses as their login names. This has the advantage that it is unique and the customer should be able to remember it easily. The disadvantage is that many customers change email addresses frequently (as they change providers or use new services), and some customers use the same email address for multiple members of a household, reducing its uniqueness.

Known Uses

Examples of natural keys are as follows:

- **For people**—Their name, email address, passport number, driver's license number, tax identification number, and (sometimes) physical address or mobile phone number (though these latter are recycled in the context of individuals so must be treated with caution as natural keys)
- **For organizations**—The DUNS number, the legal entity name
- **For products**—Universal Product Code (UPC), stock-keeping unit (SKU), International Standard Book Number (ISBN)
- **For assets**—Serial number, make + model + date purchased
- **For locations**—Physical address, geospatial coordinates (latitude/longitude)

Related Patterns

The INFORMATION PROFILE REPORT pattern can provide information on the information key(s) in each information collection.

Mirror Key

Context

An INFORMATION ENTRY typically represents something discrete—for example, a concept, person, thing, event, or activity—that is also documented in other information collections owned by the organization. Customers, suppliers, external publications, and other sources often refer to it outside of the organization, too. Having a unique identifier for each information entry is useful to be sure that people and systems are referring to the same instance, both for retrieving the right stored information or linking between information entries.

Problem

What is the appropriate scheme for identifying the information entries in a new information collection that is provisioned from an existing information collection?

Example

MCHS Trading's Shipping application is receiving orders from E-Shop, Mail-Shop, and Stores. What key value should it use for each product in an order?

Forces

- **Multiple ways to identify a particular piece of information often exist in the real world—**These are often not completely unique. For example, there are many people who have the same name—particularly those in the same family, possibly at the same address.
- **Many information collections use their own scheme for identifying their information entries—**This is particularly true of information collections implemented in applications where LOCAL PROVISIONING is assumed.
- **Incomplete or incorrect data may result in incorrect identification and labeling of information entries.**
- **Many applications are designed with only local scope in mind—**This can cause issues in ensuring unique identifiers when information is distributed beyond its original scope.

Solution

Use the same keys as the source.

Consequences

Benefits:

- The mirror key is a simple approach that avoids the need to store mappings between the source and destination information keys.

Liabilities:

- If the source information node supports multiple keys per information entry (because, for example, it is supporting STABLE KEY or CALLER'S KEY), then the destination information node may need to do one of the following if the information keys from the destination are saved in other information collections:
  - Support multiple keys per information entry.
  - Duplicate information entries so that there is a copy for each key.
  - Pick one of the keys to use.

Example Resolved

Shipping uses the key value located in the "order-id" attribute of the order INFORMATION PAYLOAD it receives from the order-taking applications. This is based on the key value used when the order was created in the originating application. The initial key value is augmented in the INFORMATION FLOW with a code value that indicated which order-taking application created the order. In addition, the Mail Shop's key value is also augmented with a time stamp because Mail-Shop uses a RECYCLED KEY.

Known Uses

Mirror key is a common pattern used when information is being distributed.

Related Patterns

Mirror keys are useful when a copy of an information collection is being synchronized using MIRRORING PROVISIONING.

Aggregate Key

Context

An INFORMATION ENTRY typically represents something discrete—for example, a concept, person, thing, event, or activity—that is also documented in other information collections owned by the organization. Customers, suppliers, external publications, and other sources often refer to it outside of the organization, too. Having a unique identifier for each information entry is useful to be sure that people and systems are referring to the same instance, both for retrieving the right stored information or linking between information entries.

Problem

What should be the identity of an information entry that is derived by dynamically combining information values from multiple sources, all of which use different key values?

Example

MCHS Trading's Customer Hub is receiving customer details from a variety of systems. What should it use as an information key for the customer details information entries it stores?

Forces

- **Multiple ways to identify a particular piece of information often exist in the real world**—These are often not completely unique. For example, there are many people who have the same name—particularly those in the same family, possibly at the same address.

- **Many information collections use their own scheme for identifying their information entries—**This is particularly true of information collections implemented in applications where LOCAL PROVISIONING is assumed.
- **Incomplete or incorrect data may result in incorrect identification and labeling of information entries.**
- **Many applications are designed with only local scope in mind—**This can cause issues in ensuring unique identifiers when information is distributed beyond its original scope.

Solution

Assign a new unique key value to the aggregated record.

This unique key has no relationship to the information keys used in the source information nodes. This is because the information keys from the sources are likely to be LOCAL KEYS and not unique beyond the scope of their information collection. See Figure 5.29.

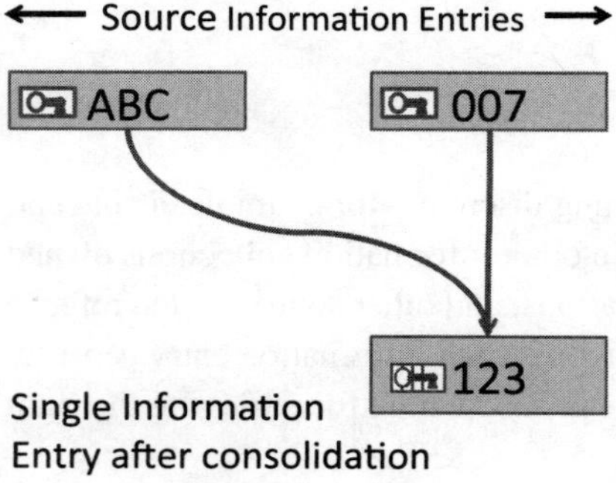

Figure 5.29 Aggregate Key solution.

Consequences

Benefits:

- All of the information entries in the destination information collection have consistent unique identifiers.

Liabilities:

- If the original source information nodes send updates, the hub needs to be able to map the information to their local version of the information entry because the key value will be different. Supporting CALLER'S KEY as well as aggregate key provides the mapping from the aggregate key to the incoming key.

Example Resolved

Customer Hub assigns its own unique identifier to each of its customer details information entries. This key is private to its internal operation. Information processes in other information nodes reference these information entries through the CALLER'S KEY or the STABLE KEY because neither of these keys is affected by the merges and splits of the information entries.

Figure 5.30 shows customer information from E-Shop (top left) and Stores (top right) being consolidated into a single information entry in Customer Hub (bottom middle) with a new unique identifier (called Customer Id or CID) of 25802823.

Figure 5.30 Consolidating customer information from E-Shop and Stores.

Known Uses

Aggregate keys are used in a hub where information is being consolidated from multiple sources. They are sometimes known as surrogate keys if they are never exposed outside of the information collection and caller's key and/or stable keys are being used to provide externally accessible information keys. Aggregate keys are commonly used in Electronic Data Interchange (EDI) where each involved party needs appropriate links to its local information collections as well as keys that identify the other party.

Related Patterns

The aggregate key is built using a LOCAL KEY. We call it out as a separate pattern because the problem is different.

The keys from the other sources may be stored as additional attributes in the information entry. This enables them to be used in searches. This is an example of the CALLER'S KEY pattern.

Caller's Key

Context

An INFORMATION ENTRY typically represents something discrete—for example, a concept, person, thing, event, or activity—that is also documented in other information collections owned by the organization. Customers, suppliers, external publications, and other sources often refer to it outside of the organization, too. Having a unique identifier for each information entry is useful to be sure that people and systems are referring to the same instance, both for retrieving the right stored information or linking between information entries.

Problem

A remote information node needs to retrieve an information entry using its own local key.

Example

MCHS Trading's Customer Hub is receiving customer details from a variety of systems. What should it use as an information key for the customer details information entries it stores?

Forces

- **Multiple ways to identify a particular piece of information often exist in the real world—**These are often not completely unique. For example, there are many people who have the same name—particularly those in the same family, possibly at the same address.
- **Many information collections use their own scheme for identifying their information entries—**This is particularly true of information collections implemented in applications where LOCAL PROVISIONING is assumed.
- **Incomplete or incorrect data may result in incorrect identification and labeling of information entries.**
- **Many applications are designed with only local scope in mind—**This can cause issues in ensuring unique identifiers when information is distributed beyond its original scope.

Solution

For each entry, store the appropriate key from the remote information collection along with the identifier of the remote information collection.

This key then acts as an alternative unique identifier for the entry. See Figure 5.31.

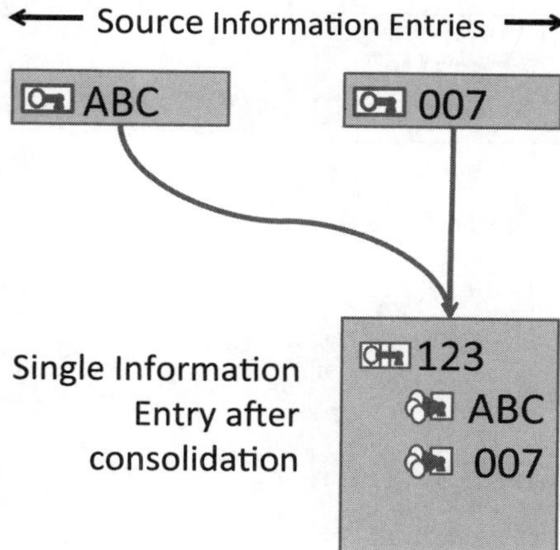

Figure 5.31 Caller's Key solution.

Consequences

Benefits:

- Caller's keys allow a remote information node to use its own unique key to access equivalent information in the local information collection.

Liabilities:

- Caller's keys require a mechanism to associate the keys from the calling systems with the keys from the local system. This should be done dynamically when each remote information node shares information.

Example Resolved

In addition to its locally assigned customer ID, the Customer Hub also stores the information keys from the E-Shop and Stores applications when it receives information about a customer from them. Figure 5.32 shows the consolidated information in information entry 25802823. This information entry can be accessed either using 25802823 or using either of the account numbers as long as the account type is also supplied.

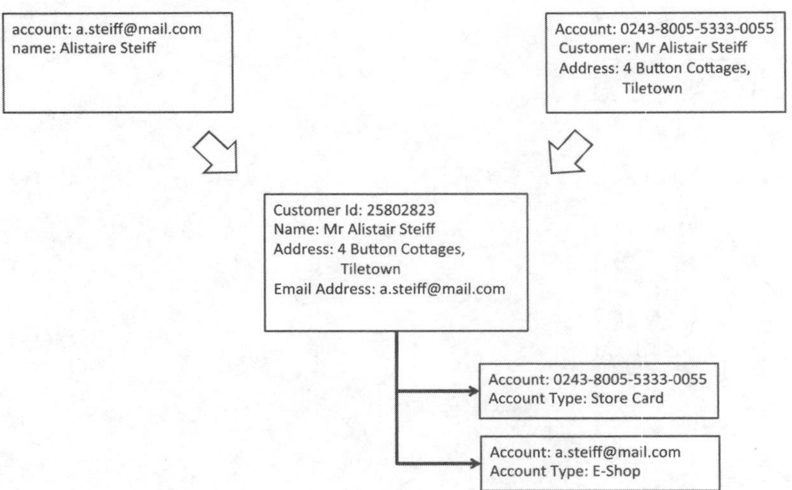

Figure 5.32 Retaining the E-Shop and Stores keys in a customer record.

Known Uses

Master Data Management (MDM) hubs should support caller's keys to simplify the retrieval of the information it manages from remote information nodes. Information exchanges with external third parties typically need caller's keys.

Related Patterns

INFORMATION ASSET HUBS using caller's key typically have an AGGREGATE KEY for their own internal use. This provides faster access to the information because it is possible to implement the aggregate key with the database primary key support.

Stable Key

Context

An INFORMATION ENTRY typically represents something discrete—for example, a concept, person, thing, event, or activity—that is also documented in other information collections owned by the organization. Customers, suppliers, external publications, and other sources often refer to it outside of the organization, too. Having a unique identifier for each information entry is useful to be sure that people and systems are referring to the same instance, both for retrieving the right stored information or linking between information entries

Problem

An information node is merging and restructuring information entries while remote information nodes are retrieving specific information entries.

What information key should a remote information process use to retrieve information after the information entry has been merged with another?

Example

MCHS Trading wants to have a single information entry in its Customer Hub for each individual customer. The customer information is supplied from E-Shop, Mail-Shop (in new orders), and Stores. Details about an individual customer may come in independently from each of these three applications and be stored in separate information entries. Subsequent processing in the Customer Hub may detect these duplicate entries and merge them together. What is the customer's identifier (CID) before and after the merge?

Forces

- **Multiple ways to identify a particular piece of information often exist in the real world**—These are often not completely unique. For example, there are many people who have the same name—particularly those in the same family, possibly at the same address.
- **Many information collections use their own scheme for identifying their information entries**—This is particularly true of information collections implemented in applications where LOCAL PROVISIONING is assumed.
- **Incomplete or incorrect data may result in incorrect identification and labeling of information entries.**
- **Many applications are designed with only local scope in mind**—This can cause issues in ensuring unique identifiers when information is distributed beyond its original scope.

Solution

Ensure an information entry that has been formed from the merging of two other entries is still returned with either one of the keys from the merged records.

The consolidation (or subsequent splitting) of multiple information entries requires consistent access to any of the individual entries over time, as seen in Figure 5.33.

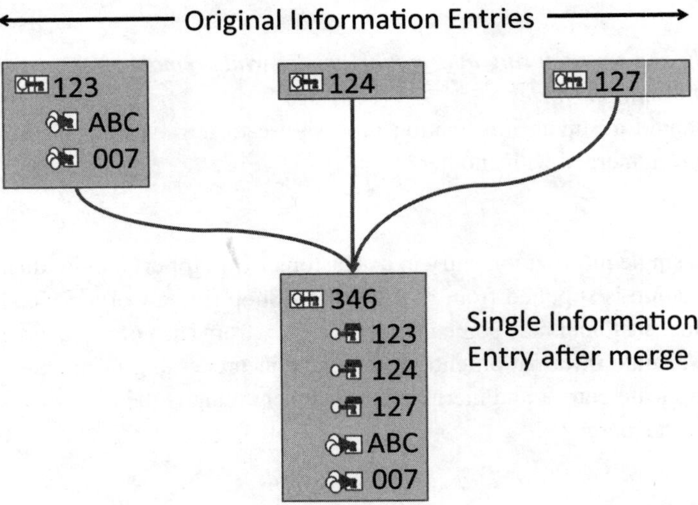

Figure 5.33 Stable Key solution.

Consequences

Benefits:

- Stable keys enable an information node that is accessing the information collection through its information services to save the key in another collection as a method of linking together related information entries in different information collections.

Liabilities:

- Because stable keys must be maintained over time in a consistent fashion, it can be expensive to change or introduce stable keys. Where stable keys cannot be introduced, other keys must be translated, mapped, and linked to simulate stable key support, usually in cross-reference files. Maintenance of such cross-references can be time consuming and prone to error.

Example Resolved

When information entries in the Customer Hub are consolidated, the consolidated information entry is given a new unique information key and the keys from the original information entries are associated with the new information entry as stable keys. An information process can retrieve the new information entry using either the new key or the stable keys.

Figure 5.34 shows the merging of two customer records: 57293200 and 25802823. A new information entry called 75828499 is created, which can be accessed using any of these keys: 57293200, 25802823, or 75828499. Because the Customer Hub supports caller's key, it can also be accessed using the account identifiers as long as the account type is also supplied.

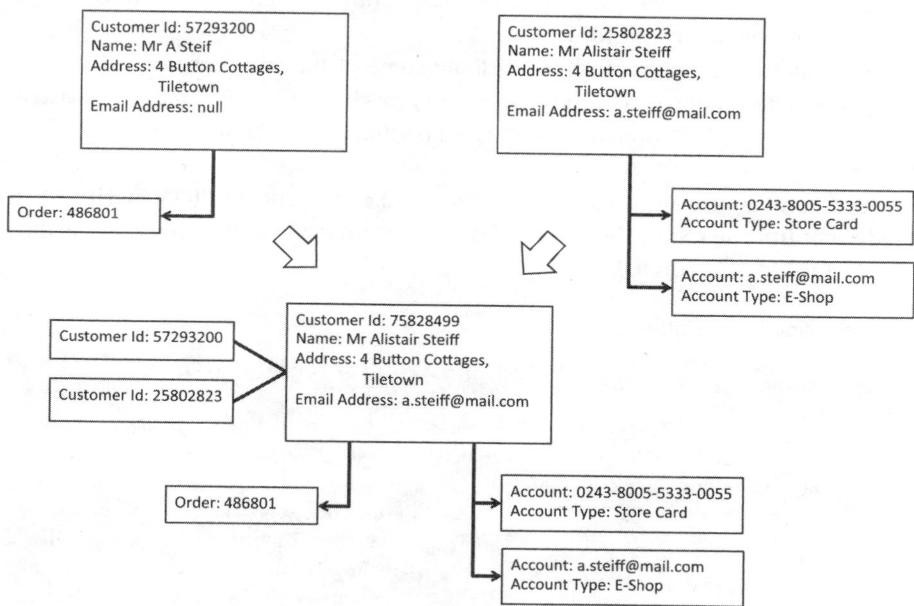

Figure 5.34 Merging information entries in Customer Hub.

Known Uses

Stable keys are typically stored in Master Data Management (MDM) hubs that are merging and splitting information entries.

Related Patterns

The MERGE ENTRIES and SEPARATE ENTRIES patterns in the information reengineering steps pattern group describes how information entries are merged together and split apart.

An INFORMATION ASSET HUB supports stable keys to reduce the impact on other information nodes when it merges or splits an information entry.

Structures for an Information Entry

When we talk about the different types of information, we often use the terms *structured data* and *unstructured data*. These classifications are a little misleading because most, if not all, digital data has some structure to it (even if it is merely binary); otherwise, it would not be possible for it to be read and processed. However, there is a difference in how fine-grained the structuring is and how rigorously the structure is enforced.

The patterns summarized in Table 5.16 illustrate some of the approaches to structuring information within an information entry. The choice of approach is dependent on how consistent the attributes are between each information entry and how frequently the number and types of attributes change.

The structure of an information entry is typically called an INFORMATION SCHEMA. It is often derived either from an INFORMATION MODEL or through configuration administered by the hosting INFORMATION NODE.

Table 5.16 Information Entry Patterns—Structure

Icon	Pattern Name	Problem	Solution
	STATIC STRUCTURE	The values stored in an information entry need to be accessed with minimum processing.	Use a predefined static data schema that governs how the values in an information entry are formatted. Use the schema consistently for all entries. Embed the data schema in the information store and use it for all access to the information collection.
	DYNAMIC STRUCTURE	The structure of the information entries in an information collection must expand over time without requiring development effort.	Provide an interface on the information node to add new optional attributes to an information collection's data schema. Use self-describing data structures on external interfaces with the ability to query the schema.
	ENTRY-LEVEL STRUCTURE	Each entry in an information collection must be structured differently.	Enable an INFORMATION SCHEMA to be associated with one or a group of information entries within an information collection.
	TAGGED MEDIA STRUCTURE	Each entry in an information collection contains what is called unstructured data, for example, text, documents, audio, or video. We call this information unstructured, but it does have some structure to it.	Create a set of structured "tags" that describe the characteristics of the unstructured data.

Locking for an Information Entry

Often an information process needs to make multiple calls to an information entry when it is updating it. An information node can provide locking services to enable an information process to ensure the values don't change while it is working with it. There are different approaches to locking that are well understood. Table 5.17 summarizes some of the more popular ones in use.

Table 5.17 Information Entry Patterns—Locking

Icon	Pattern Name	Problem	Solution
	LOCAL LOCKING	An information node needs to ensure each process it is performing in parallel works with consistent information during its lifetime.	Provide the ability for an information process to lock information entries locally within the information collection.
	DISTRIBUTED LOCKING	An information node needs to coordinate changes to information in multiple information nodes.	Provide a pessimistic locking scheme in each of the called information nodes that can be controlled by the calling information node.
	OPTIMISTIC LOCKING	When an occasional change is made to an information entry, it should have minimal performance impact on the frequently occurring read operations.	Use an optimistic locking scheme where the update() operation passes in the time stamp of the information entry when it retrieved it. If no changes have been made since then, the update() succeeds. Otherwise, it is rejected.

Specialized Operations for an Information Entry

The patterns in Table 5.18 describe specialized capabilities that an information node can support to manage the quality of information entries within its locally hosted information collections. These capabilities are typically available in an INFORMATION ASSET HUB.

Table 5.18 Information Entry Patterns—Specialized Operations

Icon	Pattern Name	Problem	Solution
	LIFECYCLE STATES	Not all operations on an information entry are valid all of the time.	Use a state machine to model the life cycle of an archetypal information entry in the information collection. For each entry, record its current state. When an operation is issued against an entry, its state is checked to ensure the operation is allowed at this time.

Icon	Pattern Name	Problem	Solution
	UNIQUE ENTRIES	An organization does not want duplicate entries in an information collection.	Add a search function to the add() and update() operations to determine if the entry already exists in the information collection.
	DEFERRED UPDATE	Changes need to happen to an information entry at a certain point in time.	Prepare the changes in the information collection and program them to become active at the required date and time.
	SOFT DELETE	An entry is no longer needed operationally but must be kept for legal or reporting reasons.	Mark the entry as deleted so it no longer appears in normal operational queries. Keep the entry in the information collection, or move it to a separate information collection for the required retention period.
	PROXY	Some of the values for an information entry are located in a remote information node.	Use an information service to retrieve the remote values whenever the entry is requested.
	PROVENANCE	Where did the values from an information entry come from?	Record details of the originating source, provisioning mechanism, and time of creation or update with the entry.
	HISTORICAL VALUES	What were the values of an information collection at a certain point in time in the past?	Keep all versions of the data and provide temporal queries to be able to access the values for any point in time.
	RELATIONSHIPS	How are the groups and relationships between individuals, organizations, things, and events represented in the information supply chain?	Create relationship services and information collections to support different patterns of grouping and linking information entries together.

Summary of Information Entries

We have skipped very lightly over some of the information entry patterns. There are many more patterns in this area, and many have been covered in the numerous pattern languages around data persistence design.

The information key patterns are one subgroup of patterns that we have paid special attention to. Getting the identity right for information instances that are distributed and copied into many information collections is not easy. It is not possible to have a global scheme for information keys because so many information nodes implement their own schemes. And so it is necessary to create mechanisms that correlate information keys together. The information key pattern group provides useful approaches for managing the correlation of information keys.

Information Node Patterns

An information node provides an environment to host related INFORMATION PROCESSES and INFORMATION COLLECTIONS. In its simplest terms, an information node can be thought of as a server. However, in today's world of high-powered and virtualized hardware, it is possible that

- More than one information node may reside on a single physical server.
- An information node may be distributed over multiple physical servers.

So it is hard to be too precise on exactly how an information node relates to the IT infrastructure. However, from an operational point of view, it is an identifiable "system," "subsystem," or "application" that can be stopped, started, and upgraded by the IT operations staff. It must be operational for its information processes and information collections to be available to the organization.

The information node patterns describe the capabilities of such a "server" with respect to the management of information. These patterns are used during the design of an information supply chain:

- When assessing an existing system to determine its potential role in the information supply chain. If there is a good match, the existing system's characteristics are represented as an information node in the appropriate place in the information supply chain.
- When identifying new collections, because these new collections typically need an information node to host or support them.
- When designing the implementation of information provisioning, additional information nodes and information flows may be inserted to simplify the processing or to add resiliency to the information supply chain.

The information node patterns describe the different types of information nodes in an information supply chain. First, there is the overview pattern for an INFORMATION NODE that describes the basic characteristics of an information node. This is shown in Table 5.19. The rest of the patterns describe specialized types of information nodes, including the following:

- **Business information nodes—**For running information processes that directly support the organization's INFORMATION WORKERS
- **Integration information nodes—**For moving information along an information supply chain

- **Big data information processing nodes—**For storing and managing large volumes of information
- **Analysis information nodes—**Specialized nodes for analytics

These pattern descriptions also include suggestions for appropriate types of middleware (computer software that provides some level of capability beyond the basic computer operating system) to implement the information node. Middleware plays an important role in the success of an information supply chain. It simplifies the work to support resilience, quality, recoverability, scalability, and security of individual components such as information nodes and information flows, freeing up the development team to focus on delivering the end-to-end business value of the information supply chain.

Table 5.19 Information Node Patterns Summary

Icon	Pattern Name	Problem	Solution
	INFORMATION NODE	What is the appropriate IT infrastructure to host information collections and information processes?	Related information processes and information collections should be hosted together in a server.

Information Node

Context

You are designing an information supply chain and have a view on the information processes and information collections that are involved. The next question to consider is what type of IT infrastructure they should run on. This may be IT infrastructure that already exists or new.

This pattern language does not go into depth on how to design IT infrastructure for an information supply chain, but it does cover the basic notions of where information and the processes that operate on it are located because it affects the availability and efficiency of the information supply chains.

Problem

What is the appropriate IT infrastructure to host information collections and information processes?

Example

MCHS Trading is creating new customer care information processes that provide support for its customer-facing staff across all of the sales channels. Where should these new information processes run?

Forces

- **IT infrastructure takes resources—**Needed resources include the power, space, and human effort to maintain the IT infrastructure.
- **IT infrastructure is not always available—**The IT infrastructure fails at inopportune moments and is also taken out of service from time-to-time for maintenance.
- **Ownership of IT infrastructure is distributed—**The IT infrastructure for an organization may be split up and managed by different groups, each providing different levels of service.
- **IT infrastructure is specialized—**The type of IT infrastructure required will depend on the type of workload the information processes are performing against the information collections.
- **IT infrastructure needs specialists—**Each type of IT infrastructure typically needs a specialist to maintain it.

Solution

Related information processes and information collections should be hosted together in a server.

The server provides the execution environment for the information processes and collections. It also supports the INFORMATION NODE MANAGEMENT PROCESS to enable INFRASTRUCTURE OPERATORS to control the availability of the server (and, hence, the availability of the information processes and collections).

The server also provides the implementations of the INFORMATION SERVICE capabilities that enable an information process to access the information collections that are either in the local information node or remote from it.

Figure 5.35 is a schematic of a typical information node. A specialized type of information node may contain a subset of these components, or specialize on a particular type of process or information.

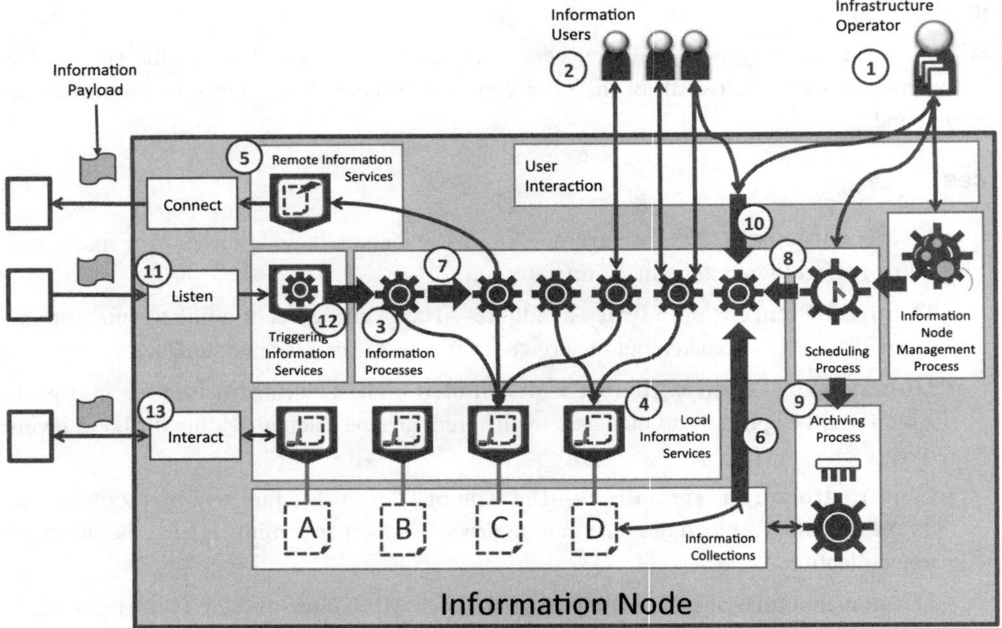

Figure 5.35 Schematic of a typical information node.

The numbers on the diagram refer to these notes:

1. An infrastructure operator has user interfaces and command-line capability to manage the information node (through the information node management process); to schedule information processes for later, or periodic, execution (through the **S**CHEDULING **P**ROCESS) and run any other locally hosted information processes they have permission to use.
2. Other types of information users are also interacting through user interfaces with information processes running on the information node.
3. The information processes are accessing information through information services.
4. The **L**OCAL **I**NFORMATION **S**ERVICES provide interfaces to the information collections hosted on the local information node.
5. The **R**EMOTE **I**NFORMATION **S**ERVICES call **I**NFORMATION **R**EQUESTS to connect to information services on other information nodes.
6. When a local information collection is changed, it may be configured with an **I**NFORMATION **C**HANGE **T**RIGGER that initiates an information process locally. This new process may simply call a **R**EMOTE **I**NFORMATION **S**ERVICE to notify another

information node that the change occurred. This could be part of an INFORMATION SUPPLY CHAIN.

7. This shows an information process using an INFORMATION TRIGGER to start another information process on the information node.
8. The SCHEDULING PROCESS uses the SCHEDULED INFORMATION TRIGGER when it is time to initiate an information process.
9. The ARCHIVING PROCESS is responsible for removing unwanted information values from the local information collections. The scheduling process initiates this process at regular intervals.
10. Whenever the information users want to start a new information process, they may type in a command or select an option from the user interface and this results in a MANUAL INFORMATION TRIGGER starting the desired information process.
11. An information process in another information node may use a remote information service to call a TRIGGERED INFORMATION SERVICE hosted locally.
12. The triggered information service will use the INFORMATION SERVICE TRIGGER to start the requested information process.
13. A remote information service may alternatively call a local information service to access one of the local information collections.

As you can see, most of the work of the information node is in triggering information processes and providing access to information. The distinguishing features of each of the variations of the information node patterns are the type of information processes that they support and the type of information they store in the information collections.

Consequences

Benefits:

- Related information processes and information collections may be collocated, giving efficient operation. The server infrastructure around them enables their availability to be managed.

Liabilities:

- An information node takes effort to maintain, so there is often savings to be made by consolidating as many information processes and collections together into a single information node. However, this will increase the criticality of this node and so the cost of change can become high.

Note: Multiple information nodes can be hosted on a single physical machine, or split across a cluster of networked machines.

Example Resolved

Because the existing order-taking applications are only focused on a single channel, and their customer information collections only cover the customer using that channel, they are not suitable places for the new customer care information processes. MCHS Trading decides to install a new information node called Customer-Care to host these information processes. These information processes use **R**EMOTE **I**NFORMATION **S**ERVICES to access the customer information in the Customer Hub information node.

Known Uses

Examples of information nodes include application servers, bespoke applications, database servers, data warehouses, workflow engines, Master Data Management servers, ETL engines, enterprise service buses, search engines, and many more.

Related Patterns

Information nodes run **I**NFORMATION **P**ROCESSES. All types of **I**NFORMATION **T**RIGGERS start these processes.

The information node stores information in **I**NFORMATION **C**OLLECTIONS. The information is supplied to the information processes from the information collections via **I**NFORMATION **S**ERVICES. The mechanism for doing this is called **I**NFORMATION **P**ROVISIONING.

Information nodes often support the **A**RCHIVING **P**ROCESS to maintain the information entries in its information collections. Many information nodes also support the **S**CHEDULING **P**ROCESS to trigger information processes at the appropriate times.

The **O**PERATIONAL **H**EALTH **M**ONITORING **P**ROCESS is used to ensure the information nodes are operating correctly.

The **N**EW **I**NFORMATION **N**ODE and **I**NFORMATION **N**ODE **U**PGRADE solutions cover how information nodes are set up and connected to the **I**NFORMATION **S**UPPLY **C**HAINS.

Business Information Nodes

The business information nodes, shown in Table 5.20, host the information processes that are directly supporting the organization's business. Each node tends to support a particular function within the business, for example, sales, marketing, finance, distribution, human resources, and more. The information hosted by an information node tends to reflect the needs of the business function only.

Business information nodes are a major source of new information for the organization and will produce many of the information products that drive the business.

INFORMATION **W**ORKERS are the principal users of these information nodes and they require the availability of these information nodes to be in line with business hours. For some companies, this is a normal working week. However, for global companies, or Internet-based operations, this is approaching twenty-four hours a day, seven days a week (24/7) operation.

The business information nodes are critical systems. They need to be an integral part of an organization's information supply chains. However, due to their restricted focus, they are often the most difficult systems to work with from an information architecture point of view.

Table 5.20 Information Node Patterns—Business Information Nodes

Icon	Pattern Name	Problem	Solution
	APPLICATION NODE	What is the appropriate IT infrastructure to host information collections and information processes that collectively support a particular aspect of the business?	Host these information processes and information collections together in their own server. Ensure the server is available when the information users supporting this part of the business need it.
	INFORMATION CONTENT NODE	What is the appropriate infrastructure for managing large collections of documents and other types of media files?	Use a specialized information node that is able to maintain an index and related metadata around the documents and media files.
	SEARCH NODE	What is the appropriate infrastructure to enable an organization to locate information on an ad hoc basis?	Create a server to host the processes that crawl through the information sources creating a search index, and then provide access to the search index through a user interface.
	INFORMATION STORE	What is the appropriate infrastructure to store information that does not have a natural home with the information processes that make use of it?	Design a file/directory structure or database schema to act as a store for the information. Information processes running in different information nodes are responsible for consuming and maintaining this information.
	INFORMATION MART	A group within an organization needs its own source of historical information to match its reporting needs.	Create a dimensional view of the historical information to suit the reporting and/or analytical needs of the group.
	INFORMATION CUBE	An information user needs to analyze multiple dimensions of correlated information.	Create a snapshot of the desired information and store it in a cube structure where the information attributes can be referenced as a point or a series of related points.

Application Node

Context

A set of information processes, and their related information collections, provides support for a particular aspect of an organization's core business. These information processes must all be available when the information users need them and they need to be managed and maintained consistently.

Problem

What is the appropriate infrastructure to host information collections and information processes that collectively support a particular aspect of the business?

Example

MCHS Trading has an online shopping website that allows people to create an online account, browse and search the product catalog, and make orders. All of the information processes that support this website need to be available all of the time.

Forces

- **Information processes, and the information collections they depend on, must be available when their users need them**—For example, if office workers in a single location are the only people to use a group of information processes, then these information processes may only be required during office hours. If, however, the information processes, or the information collections, are used by people all over the world, then they must be available 24 hours each day, and given the weekend varies from country to country, they may be needed 6–7 days a week as well.
- **The logic inside an information process can be complex and require specialized knowledge to create**—If this knowledge is outside of the core competency of an organization, the organization may choose to buy the implementation of these information processes as a software package. Such a software package will typically include the required information collections together with the information processes.

Solution

Host the information processes and information collections together on their own server. Ensure the server is available when the information users supporting this part of the business need it.

Figure 5.36 shows the structure of an application node. You can see it follows the information node very closely.

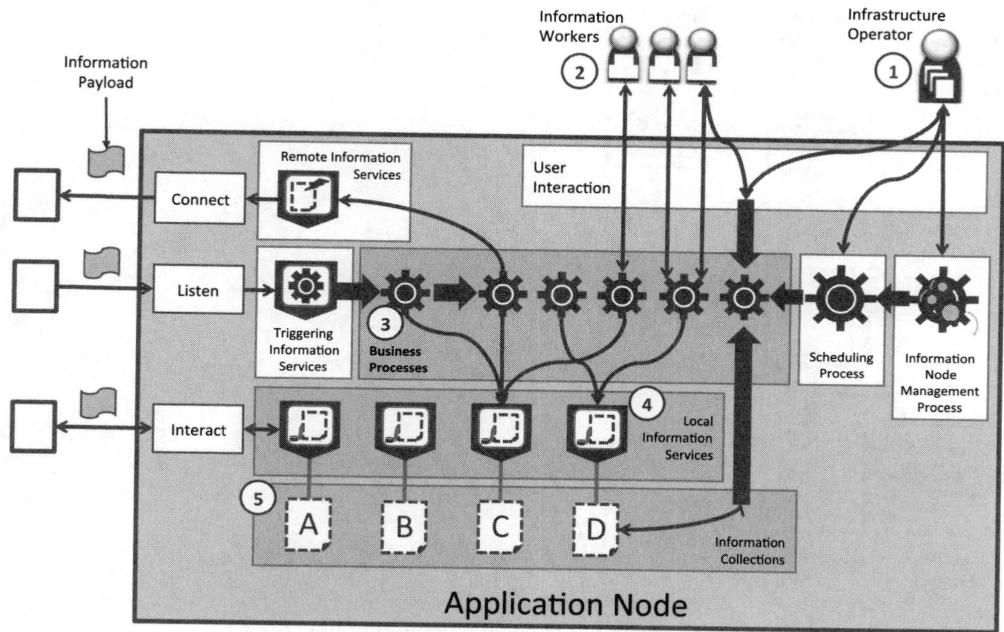

Figure 5.36 Schematic of an application node.

The numbers on the diagram in Figure 5.36 refer to these notes:

1. Application nodes are managed by the **I**NFRASTRUCTURE **O**PERATORS using the **I**NFORMATION **N**ODE **M**ANAGEMENT **P**ROCESS.
2. The users of the majority of information processes running on the application node are used by **I**NFORMATION **W**ORKERS.
3. The information processes are focused on one function of the business.
4. Much of the information in use is locally hosted on the application node.
5. The information collections typically have **M**ASTER **U**SAGE, **L**OCAL **S**COPE, and **L**OCAL **C**OVERAGE.

Figure 5.37 shows the interaction of an application node with other information nodes.

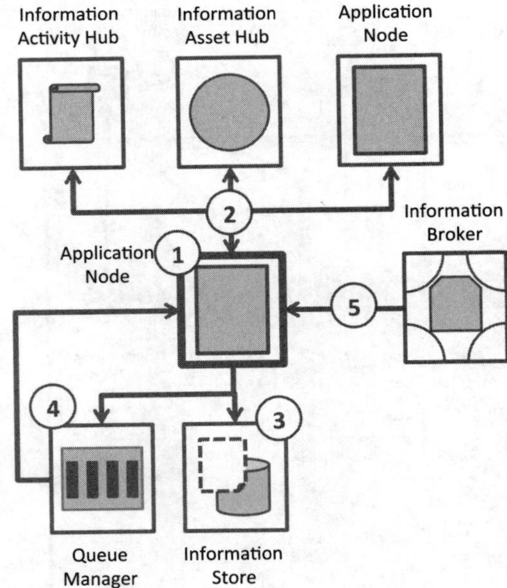

Figure 5.37 Interaction of an application node with other information nodes.

The numbers on the diagram in Figure 5.37 refer to these notes:

1. This is the application node itself.
2. There are other information nodes exchanging information with it using information services.
3. The application node may export or import information to/from an information store. Other information nodes could use this information store as an information-sharing mechanism.
4. The application node may pass messages to/from a **Q**UEUE **M**ANAGER information node. The queue manager may distribute these messages further. This is a useful approach to distribute updates and alerts as they happen.
5. Information may be passed in an out of the application node via an **I**NFORMATION **B**ROKER that is implementing an **I**NFORMATION **F**LOW.

Consequences

Benefits:

- A separate application node supporting a localized group of people, specialized for their needs, can be managed and made available to them with a high degree of reliability because the needs are well defined.

Liabilities:

- The people using an application node typically have a very localized view of the organization. The information collections managed by the application node typically require synchronization with other information collections to keep them in line with the rest of the organization.

Example Resolved

The information processes and information collections that support the online shopping website are all hosted in an application node called E-Shop.

Known Uses

This pattern is a very common approach for grouping and managing related processes together. For example,

- A packaged application is an application node, running information processes that follow the **P**ACKAGED **A**PPLICATION **P**ROCESS pattern, with **L**OCAL **P**ROVISIONING of information collections that have a **M**ASTER **U**SAGE.
- A homegrown application is very similar. It consists of an application node running information processes that follow the **B**ESPOKE **A**PPLICATION **P**ROCESS pattern, with **L**OCAL **P**ROVISIONING of information collections that have a **M**ASTER **U**SAGE.
- If you are using a workflow, or business process management software, then its runtime environment is an application node running information processes that support information processes following the **A**GILE **B**USINESS **P**ROCESS, **S**TATE **D**RIVEN **P**ROCESS, and/or **C**OLLABORATIVE **E**DITING **P**ROCESS patterns.
- If you are an information user who is using either the **I**NFORMATION **M**ONITORING **P**ROCESS or **O**PERATIONAL **H**EALTH **M**ONITORING **P**ROCESS, then these processes will be hosted on an application node that has information collections containing the **I**NFORMATION **E**VENTS that describe what is going on in the information supply chains.
- If you are an information user who is browsing business reports, an **I**NFORMATION **R**EPORTING **P**ROCESS running on an application node would have produced these reports.

Related Patterns

Most application nodes manage information collections that support a **M**ASTER **U**SAGE with **L**OCAL **C**OVERAGE and **L**OCAL **S**COPE—that is, they only store what they need in order to process the work they have. This is true for the E-Shop and Stores application, which only have information about customers they serve directly—rather than all customers of MCHS Trading.

Information Content Node

Context

The fastest growing type of information is what is called unstructured. This includes documents, web pages, text files, video and audio files, and images. It requires different approaches to manage it because the information values within it are dispersed and hard to identify.

Problem

What is the appropriate infrastructure for managing large collections of documents and other types of media files?

Example

MCHS Trading needs to maintain documents relating to its contracts and other agreements plus images of products and services that are used in a variety of places. How does it catalog and manage these files?

Forces

- **Documents and media files are unstructured**—Specific information values have to be discovered through parsing or inference.
- **Documents and media files have limited useful lifetime**—They need to be managed from creation to destruction.
- **Documents and media files take up a lot of storage**—Reducing the number of copies of the files and destroying them once they are no longer needed helps to minimize the amount of storage.
- **Regulations define retention period**—Some information must be retained for a defined period based on governmental or legal regulations. Keeping information longer than required is a liability.

Solution

Use a specialized information node that is able to maintain an index and related metadata around the documents and media files.

This node is called the information content node. It stores the unstructured information and assigns classifications, such as tags and keywords, owners, descriptions, and a life cycle to each document/file to control how it is managed.

What makes this type of node special is that the information collections are structured following the TAGGED MEDIA STRUCTURE pattern and each stored document can support the LIFECYCLE STATES pattern. This enables the storage of the tags, the management of the life cycle of the document, and the proper assignment of ownership and responsibilities for the document throughout its life cycle.

Figure 5.38 shows the interaction of an information content node with other information nodes. As you can see, the integration of an information content node is very similar to an application node. The difference is in the types of **I**NFORMATION **P**AYLOADS that are transmitted. The content of the document or media file is rarely transformed as it flows through an information supply chain; however, the tagging and other descriptive information is structured information and may be transformed as it flows between information nodes.

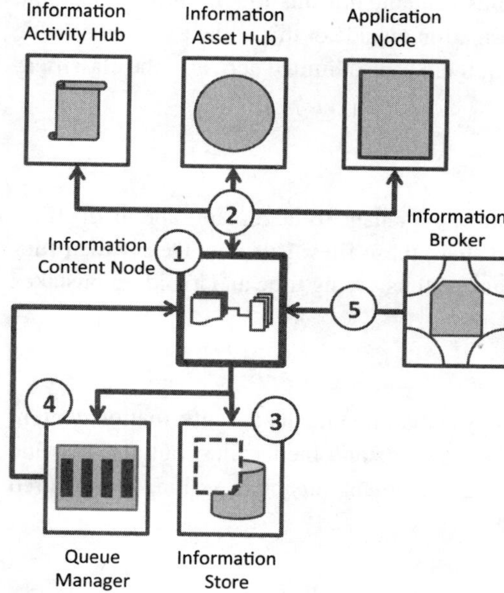

Figure 5.38 Interaction of an information content node with other information nodes.

The numbers on the diagram in Figure 5.38 refer to these notes:

1. This is the information content node itself.
2. There are other information nodes exchanging information with it using information services.
3. The information content node may export or import information to/from an information store. Other information nodes could use this information store as an information-sharing mechanism.
4. The information content node may pass messages to/from a **Q**UEUE **M**ANAGER information node. The queue manager may distribute these messages further. This is a useful approach to distribute updates and alerts as they happen.
5. Information may be passed in an out of the information content node via an **I**NFORMATION **B**ROKER that is implementing an **I**NFORMATION **F**LOW.

Consequences

Benefits:

- The information content node provides an organizing framework around documents and media files so they can be located when needed and destroyed once they are not needed.

Liabilities:

- The information content node typically holds valuable information for the organization, but it is often hard to make use of this information outside of this node. Partly this is due to the nature of the information it stores, but there is also limited access to the classification and descriptive metadata.

Example Resolved

MCHS Trading installs a new information content node to manage its documents and media files. This gives them a centralized place to manage and share these files. It is now clear which files are the latest approved copies of documents and images, thus saving time and avoiding mistakes caused by using the wrong version of a file.

Known Uses

A class of middleware called content management systems implements the information content node pattern. These systems not only manage the documents and media files, but also provide AGILE BUSINESS PROCESSES to provide case management capabilities along with search and text analytics capability.

Related Patterns

A good implementation of an information content node will support LINKED INFORMATION PROVISIONING to enable remote references to the documents and files to be stored in related information collections on other information nodes.

Search Node

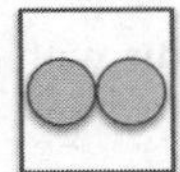

Context

An organization needs to be able to locate information on an ad hoc basis.

Problem

What is the appropriate infrastructure to enable an organization to locate information on an ad hoc basis?

Example

Employees of MCHS Trading need to make ad hoc queries for information stored in documents and files.

Forces

- Information is distributed across multiple information nodes.
- It is not possible to anticipate all of the types of information queries an organization will need.
- Information is not always consistent or perfectly correlated.

Solution

Create a server to host the processes that crawl through the information sources creating a search index, and then provide access to the search index through a user interface.

The search node breaks the problem of locating information into the following parts:

- **Locating and indexing information—**This is a batch operation, run at least once a day to scan through the information, picking out the presence of keywords and tags.
- **Matching the user's search request with the relevant content from the index—**When a person requests information, the keywords from the request are matched against the index and a list of relevant documents that match the keyword are returned.

Figure 5.39 shows the search node interacting with other information nodes that contain information worthy of searching.

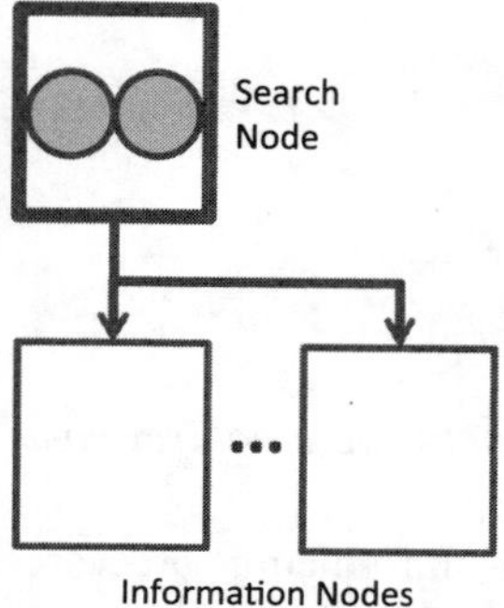

Figure 5.39 Interaction of a search node with other information nodes.

Consequences

Benefits:

- The search node provides an approach to locating information in the organization without requiring change to the existing information nodes.

Liabilities:

- The processing necessary to crawl through the information sources and create the search index can take a large amount of processing power. If the indexes are not refreshed regularly, the search locates missing, or incomplete, information.

Example Resolved

MCHS Trading deploys a search node to create and manage a search index that represents the content of these documents and files. This search node also has a web user interface, which is embedded into the company's home page so employees can access the search index and link to the required information.

Known Uses

This type of information node is also known as a search engine.

Related Patterns

The search node hosts the **I**NFORMATION **C**RAWLING **P**ROCESS, **I**NFORMATION **I**NDEXING **P**ROCESS, and **I**NFORMATION **S**EARCH **P**ROCESS.

Information Store

Context

Some information does not seem to belong to any specific information node.

Problem

What is the appropriate infrastructure to store information that does not have a natural home with the information processes that make use of it?

This information may need to be kept independently from the information processes because:

- The information node where the information processes reside is not able to host this information.
- Information processes hosted on multiple information nodes share the information. None of the existing information nodes has the quality of service to support the needs of all of these information processes.

- The information is only required for a short period of time and an implementation that does not impact the existing information node is required.

Example

One of MCHS Trading's managers needs to create documents and presentation to support his or her role. He or she needs somewhere to store them with the related information that is supporting his or her work.

Forces

- **Ownerless information**—Information that does not have an owner is rarely managed properly.
- **Shared information needs broader availability**—Information nodes may be available at different times of the day. An information node must be available whenever any of the information processes (local or remote) need it.

Solution

Design a file/directory structure or database schema to act as a store for the information. Information processes running in different information nodes are responsible for consuming and maintaining this information.

The information store is a very flexible and simple information node that is not able to run information processes beyond those needed to manage the information node itself. Its schematic is shown in Figure 5.40.

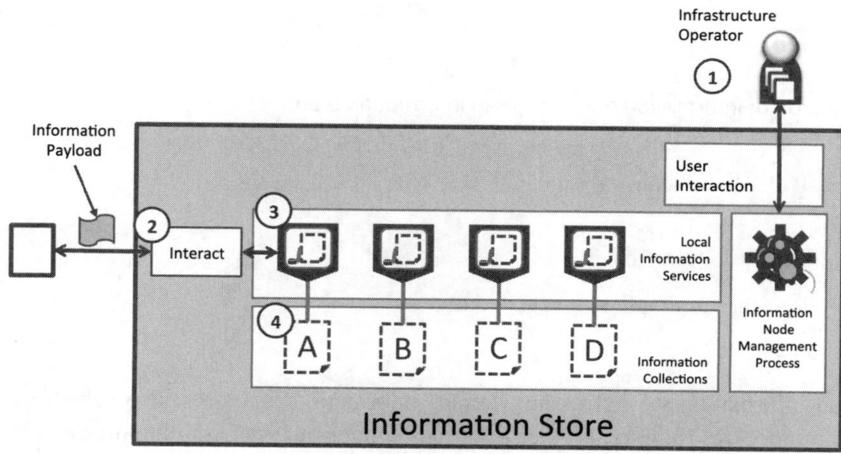

Figure 5.40 Schematic of an information store.

The numbers on the diagram in Figure 5.40 refer to these notes:

1. The infrastructure operation is able to start and stop the information store using the information node management process.
2. Remote information processes are able to access the information through remote information services.
3. The remote information services call the local information services of the information store. These information services reflect the structure in which they are stored in the information collections.
4. The information collections are responsible for the storage and retrieval of the information.

Although the information store cannot run its own information processes to work with its information, the information services make the information available to a wide range of remote information processes—see Figure 5.41.

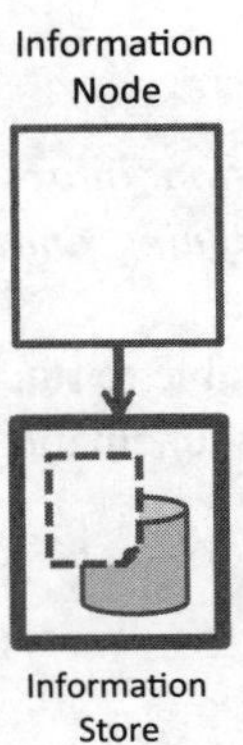

Figure 5.41 Interaction of information nodes with an information store.

Consequences

Benefits:

- An information store is simple to create and use.

Liabilities:

- Because an information store does not support information processes, it is reliant on information processes running in other information nodes to maintain the information collections it stores.

- There are many packages that create information stores. The result is that information workers can create private information stores that are unmanaged. This is fine for non-critical or information for personal use. But there is always a danger that parts of the organization may become dependent on this private information store that could be vulnerable to loss or theft. See the USER PRIVATE PROVISIONING pattern for more details on this liability.

Example Resolved

The MCHS manager has a private information store to keep the draft documents. They are added to a shared repository when they are ready to be shared.

Known Uses

Information stores are typically implemented using database servers or file systems.

Related Patterns

The INFORMATION MART, INFORMATION CUBE, STAGING AREA, LOOK-UP TABLE NODE, INFORMATION MIRROR STORE, INFORMATION EVENT STORE, OPERATIONAL STATUS STORE, and INFORMATION MINING STORE are all specialized forms of information store.

Information Mart

Context

An organization requires an information process to support one of its activities. This information process is using information.

Problem

A group within an organization needs its own source of historical information to match its reporting needs.

Example

MCHS Trading's Reporting Hub maintains the relationships between customers and the products they buy. Some of the management reports need to see customers by segment and the products they buy. Others need to focus on product categories and the buying trends within these categories. Essentially, the information behind each of these reports is the same. However, the way the values are rolled up and structured is very different.

Forces

- **Specialized information collections are the fastest**—Information collections designed specifically for an information process, and stored locally in the same information node as the information process, typically provide the fasted access to the information for the information process.
- **Information copies add cost**—Every copy that is made of some information values costs money to store and maintain.
- **Inline transformation is transient**—If transformed information is not stored, then the transformation must be redone each time the information is needed in that format. This makes sense if the information values are changing rapidly. However, when the information values are fairly static, collating and reformatting the set of information values on the fly over and over again is inefficient.
- **Inconsistent terminology for the same information**—Different parts of an organization may use inconsistent terminology from each other. This terminology difference may derive from a different heritage, skill sets, or decentralized operation.

Solution

Create a dimensional view of the historical information to suit the reporting needs of the group.

A dimensional view is one particularly suited to reports. It stores the main facts of the report in the core database table and then links off to tables that provide supporting information.

For example, an information mart for reports about orders would have a core table where each row contained the essential information about an order. This row would include the customer identifier, number of items, value, date of the order, date it was fulfilled, identifier of warehouse that shipped the goods, and so on. Linking off of this core table would be customer details relating to each referenced customer identifier. Similarly, there would be a table of warehouse details for each warehouse identifier.

Figure 5.42 shows how the information mart interacts with other information nodes.

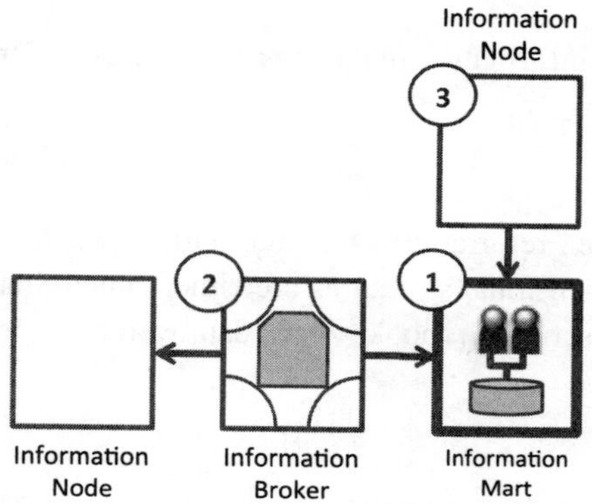

Figure 5.42 Interaction of an information mart with other information nodes.

The numbers on the diagram in Figure 5.42 refer to these notes:

1. This is the information mart.
2. An INFORMATION BROKER provisions the information mart from other information nodes such as an INFORMATION WAREHOUSE. The information broker will extract the appropriate subset of the information and transform it into the desired format for the consumers of the information.
3. One or more information nodes (running, for instance, the INFORMATION REPORTING PROCESS) use the information from the information mart.

Consequences

Benefits:

- The information mart provides information to the information workers in the form they need it. It can also serve as a historical record for the organization if it does not have an INFORMATION WAREHOUSE.

Liabilities:

- The information workers should not update the information mart. It should have reference usage by the business processes and only be updated via the information provisioning processes of the information supply chain.

Example Resolved

The Reporting Hub has information marts that store the information in the appropriate format for each of the reports.

Known Uses

The information mart pattern is describing what is often referred to as a data mart, a structure related to an information (or data) warehouse. The dimensional structures are either called Star Schemas or Snowflake Schemas and are commonly described in books about data warehousing and business intelligence.

Related Patterns

Information marts have information collections with **R**EFERENCE **U**SAGE (that is, they are read-only). They are refreshed periodically using **M**IRRORING **P**ROVISIONING.

INFORMATION **C**UBES are specialized information marts for ad hoc analysis.

Information marts often store subsets of information extracted from an **I**NFORMATION **W**AREHOUSE.

Information Cube

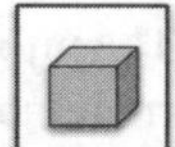

Context

Some activities require thought and ad hoc analysis. An individual needs to look at the evidence and come to a conclusion. Often information that is correlated in multiple dimensions is needed to fully understand the situation.

Problem

An information user needs to analyze multiple dimensions of correlated information.

Example

MCHS Trading would like to do some what-if analysis on the mix of products available through each channel. It wants a set of information collections that covers its customers, the products they buy, through which channel, and when. The Reporting Hub has this information, but the structure of the data is not ideal for this type of analysis. In addition, MCHS Trading wants to make changes to some of this data to understand how changes in its product offerings could affect sales.

Forces

- **Correlating information requires quality information—**Particularly when it comes from multiple sources.

- **Specialized information collections are the fastest—**Information collections designed specifically for an information process, and stored locally in the same information node as the information process, typically provide the fasted access to the information for the information process.
- **Information copies add cost—**Every copy that is made of some information values costs money to store and maintain.

Solution

Create a snapshot of the desired information and store it in a cube structure where the information attributes can be referenced as a point, or a series of related points.

An information cube node hosts the cube structure and also provides analytics capabilities to enable an information user to experiment with different views of the information.

Figure 5.43 shows the information cube interacting with other information nodes.

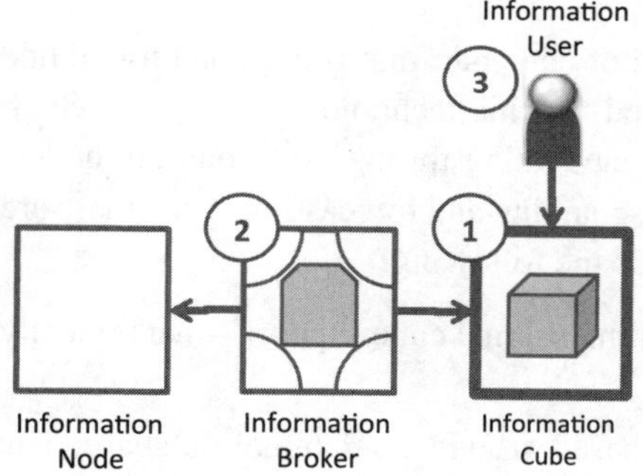

Figure 5.43 Interaction of an information cube with other information nodes.

The numbers on the diagram in Figure 5.43 refer to these notes:

1. This is the information cube.
2. An information broker provisions the information cube from information that typically comes from an INFORMATION WAREHOUSE or an INFORMATION MART.
3. The information user can access and experiment with the information once it is loaded.

Consequences

Benefits:

- The user of the information cube is able to quickly extract information from different perspectives to understand a complex situation.

Liabilities:

- This is, of course, another copy of the information. Every copy of an information collection that is created and distributed adds to the cost of maintaining the information supply chain. Ideally, the availability of the information cube should be time boxed so the information can be properly disposed of and the storage freed up once the project is complete.
- Information cubes require complex information transformations to populate it.

Example Resolved

MCHS Trading uses SNAPSHOT PROVISIONING to create linked information collections to support this analysis project. It is stored in an INFORMATION CUBE. The team is able to change the channels that products are available though and understand how these changes could affect sales based on the knowledge of the channels that its customers work on.

Known Uses

The pattern we have described here is a specialized type of data mart that is designed for ad hoc analysis by an individual. The generic term that is used for this technology is OLAP, which stands for Online Analytical Processing. It is used for navigating through information, understanding aggregates, and relationships. It is also used for planning and forecasting. Then there are specialized types of OLAP technology. Examples include the following:

- **MOLAP—**Another name for traditional multidimensional cube support—that typically loads information into memory to process.
- **ROLAP—**This is an OLAP implementation based around a relational database. The multidimensional structures are represented directly in the database tables.
- **HOLAP—**This is hierarchical OLAP that used both the relational database and in-memory calculations.

To understand more about this type of technology, refer to books about data warehousing and business intelligence.

Related Patterns

The INFORMATION MART is similar to an information cube in that it holds multidimensional data. However, the information mart is much more geared to supporting the type of queries on the information that is commonly issued by reporting and other business intelligence tools, whereas the information cube is more for ad hoc requests from a single user.

Integration Nodes

This next group of information nodes shown in Table 5.21 supports the movement and integration of information along the information supply chains. They are designed to work with a wide range of different types of technology and support the reengineering of information so different information nodes can consume it.

Table 5.21 Information Node Patterns—Integration Nodes

Icon	Pattern Name	Problem	Solution
	INFORMATION BROKER	What is the appropriate infrastructure to support the information processes that proactively move information between different information nodes?	Use a specialized information node called an information broker to host these information processes.
	QUEUE MANAGER	An organization wants operational independence between their applications, allowing information to flow reliably between them even though they may not always be available at the same time.	Use an intermediary information node that is able to reliably store and forward information payloads from one application and deliver them to the intended recipients when they are available.
	STAGING AREA	An information node needs a temporary store to hold information that is in the process of being provisioned into a different information collection.	Create a dedicated information store to hold one or more information collections that have **TRANSIENT USAGE** by the provisioning information processes.
	LOOK-UP TABLE NODE	An information process needs to look up the code value to classify or describe some information.	Provide a lookup table that translates between the descriptive information values and the code values.
	EVENT CORRELATION NODE	What is the appropriate infrastructure to host the real-time analysis and correlation of disparate events?	Consolidate the events into a single information node in real time and perform complex event processing on them.

Information Broker

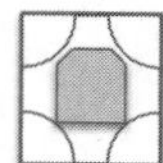

Context

The transfer of information between existing information nodes is implemented by **INFORMATION FLOWS**. Often, these information flows add additional information processes to the information supply chain to perform the transfer of information.

Problem

What is the appropriate infrastructure to support the information processes that proactively move information between different information nodes?

These information processes are typically added after the source and destination information nodes are in place and are designed to minimize the impact on them.

Example

Where should the processes that move MCHS Trading's product details from the Product Hub application to the downstream order-taking systems, such as E-Shop, Stores, and Mail-Shop, be located?

Forces

- **Varying formats—**Information stored in different systems is not likely to be the same format—nor will the information values be consistent.
- **Limited availability—**It is possible that the source and destination information nodes are not always available at the same time.
- **Expensive to change—**Changing the source and/or destination information nodes may be expensive and disruptive on the existing business.
- **Limited integration capability—**Application nodes, particularly, are designed to support their business function and don't typically have specialized capability needed to transform and transport information.
- **Dynamic environment—**The provisioning support needs to be flexible to allow the organization to continuously improve the integration and synchronization or the organization's systems.
- **Limited capacity—**The source and/or destination nodes may be running at full capacity performing their primary role.

Solution

Use a specialized information node called an information broker to host these information processes.

An information broker is designed to provide a server environment for hosting provisioning information processes (also known as integration jobs), such as the INFORMATION DEPLOYMENT PROCESS.

It supports the dynamic creation and maintenance of these types of information processes and maintains information collections of metadata described in the information identification patterns to help pinpoint the types of information located in each of the information nodes.

The provisioning information processes make extensive use of the INFORMATION REENGINEERING STEP patterns to reconcile the differences between the information in the source(s) and the intended destination systems.

Figure 5.44 shows the information broker interacting with other information nodes and using a LOOK-UP TABLE NODE and STAGING AREA to manage the transformation of information as it moves from the source to the destinations.

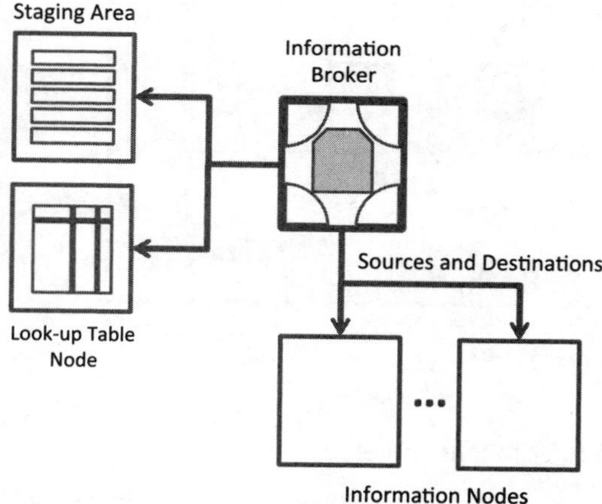

Figure 5.44 Interaction of an information broker with other information nodes.

Information brokers do not provide any facilities in which to store an organization's business information. Its information collections are for its internal use. As such, information brokers typically use INFORMATION STORES, LOOK-UP TABLE NODE, and other types of information nodes to acquire the information used by the provisioning information processes.

Figure 5.45 summarizes the structure of the information broker.

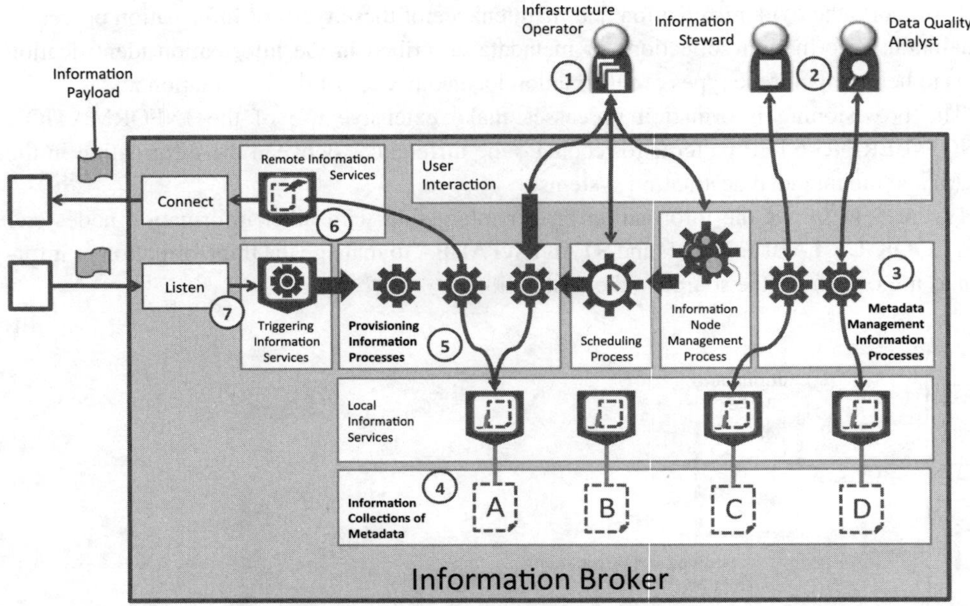

Figure 5.45 Schematic of an information broker node.

The numbers on the diagram in Figure 5.45 refer to these notes:

1. The information broker is started and maintained by the INFRASTRUCTURE OPERATOR.
2. The information broker hosts information collections of metadata that are maintained and used by information management users such as the INFORMATION STEWARD and DATA QUALITY ANALYST.
3. The metadata management processes are supporting many of the information identification patterns, such as SUBJECT AREA DEFINITION, INFORMATION LOCATION, VALID VALUES DEFINITION, INFORMATION VALUES PROFILE, INFORMATION LINEAGE, SEMANTIC TAGGING, and SEMANTIC MAPPING.
4. The metadata information stores support the information provisioning processes with knowledge of the information to be provisioned.
5. When the information provisioning processes run, they access the metadata to locate the information to process and reengineer in the information. They work with REMOTE INFORMATION SERVICES to access the information in the sources and destinations.
6. The remote information services are responsible for the network communication to access the information in the sources and destinations.

7. Information provisioning processes can be started in the information broker by invoking **T**RIGGERING **I**NFORMATION **S**ERVICES.

Consequences

Benefits:

- The information broker makes it easy to update the provisioning information processes that support the movement of information along the information supply chain.

Liabilities:

- This is another server to manage and ensure it is available.

Example Resolved

The information processes that move the product details are part of a **P**ARTITIONED **D**ISTRIBUTION information flow. They are hosted together in an information broker. This solution is also using a **S**TAGING **A**REA to hold the intermediate results and **L**OOK-UP **T**ABLE **N**ODE for translating code values from the source code values to the destination code values. This is illustrated in Figure 5.46.

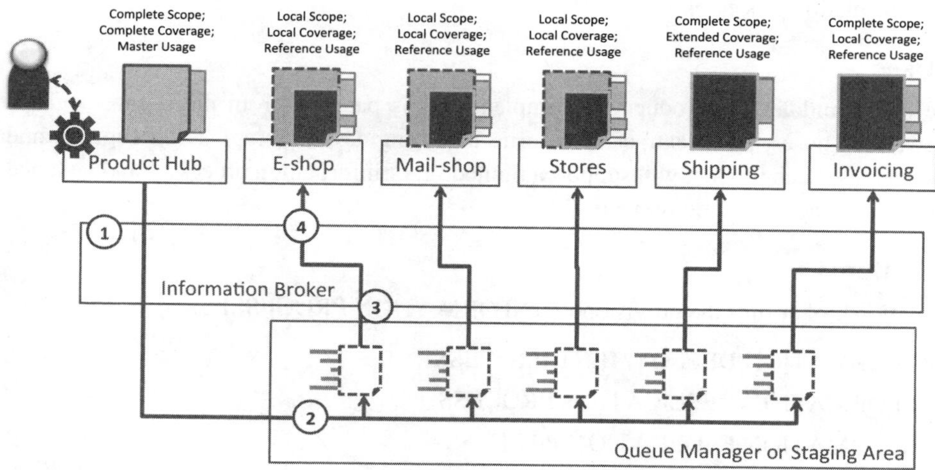

Figure 5.46 Distribution of information through an information broker.

The numbers on the diagram in Figure 5.46 refer to these notes:

1. The first information process receives details of a product in an **I**NFORMATION **P**AYLOAD. It is responsible for deciding which of the downstream information nodes needs to receive details about a particular product.

2. There is a staging area for each of the destination information nodes. The first information process places a copy of the payload into each of the appropriate staging areas. This type of selection is required when the destination information nodes have different scopes. In effect, this information process must understand the differing scopes in the downstream information nodes in order to select which payloads to put in each staging area.
3. The payloads in the staging area have **C**OMPLETE **C**OVERAGE and are in the source systems format (although they could have been converted to a canonical format). Information is taken out of each staging area by a dedicated information process that selects the appropriate attributes from each payload to match the coverage of the destination and transforms them to match the destination's format.
4. The transformed payload is passed to the destination information node and used to update the appropriate information details.

To perform this information flow, the provisioning information processes needed to know the internal details of the information collections within the source and destinations. This logic will have to be modified any time the usage, scope, or coverage of the information collections within these information nodes changes. This maintenance effort is simplified by hosting the provisioning information processes in an information broker because it is designed to make it easy to change its information processes.

Known Uses

There are many middleware products that implement this pattern—from messaging engines, enterprise service buses, ETL (extract, transform, load) engines, data replication engines, and workflow engines. Each product will support a limited set of information processes and be tuned for particular nonfunctional requirements.

Related Patterns

The information broker runs the provisioning **I**NFORMATION **P**ROCESSES:

- **I**NFORMATION **D**EPLOYMENT **P**ROCESS
- **I**NFORMATION **R**EPLICATION **P**ROCESS
- **I**NFORMATION **F**EDERATION **P**ROCESS
- **I**NFORMATION **R**ELOCATION **P**ROCESS
- **I**NFORMATION **Q**UEUING **P**ROCESS
- **I**NFORMATION **B**ROADCASTING **P**ROCESS
- **I**NFORMATION **S**CAVENGING **P**ROCESS
- **I**NFORMATION **S**UMMARIZING **P**ROCESS

Queue Manager

Context

Information is changing all of the time. How do we keep the information collections synchronized across multiple information nodes?

Problem

An organization wants operational independence between its information nodes, allowing information to flow reliably between them even though they may not always be available at the same time.

Example

MCHS Trading's order-taking information nodes—E-Shop, Mail-Shop, and Stores—need to pass new orders to the Shipping information node, which is responsible for order fulfillment. Shipping needs a daily maintenance cycle where it is not available to receive new orders. What happens to the new orders that are received when Shipping is not available?

Forces

- **Information nodes fail unexpectedly**—Even the best-run infrastructure may fail from time to time. It is necessary to have some contingency to minimize the impact of a component failing.
- **Polling is inefficient**—Polling is when an activity connects to a resource to look for a change of status, or a piece of work to do. This is wasteful of resources, particularly when there is often nothing to do.
- **Diversity of formats**—Each information node typically uses its own private format for the information it works with. When information is moved between information nodes, it must be transformed from the source's format to the destination's format.

Solution

Use an intermediary information node that is able to reliably store information payloads from a source information node and deliver them to the intended recipients when they are available.

We call this information node a queue manager as it uses a queuing paradigm to manage the sequence of information payloads that need to be transmitted. Figure 5.47 shows its logical structure.

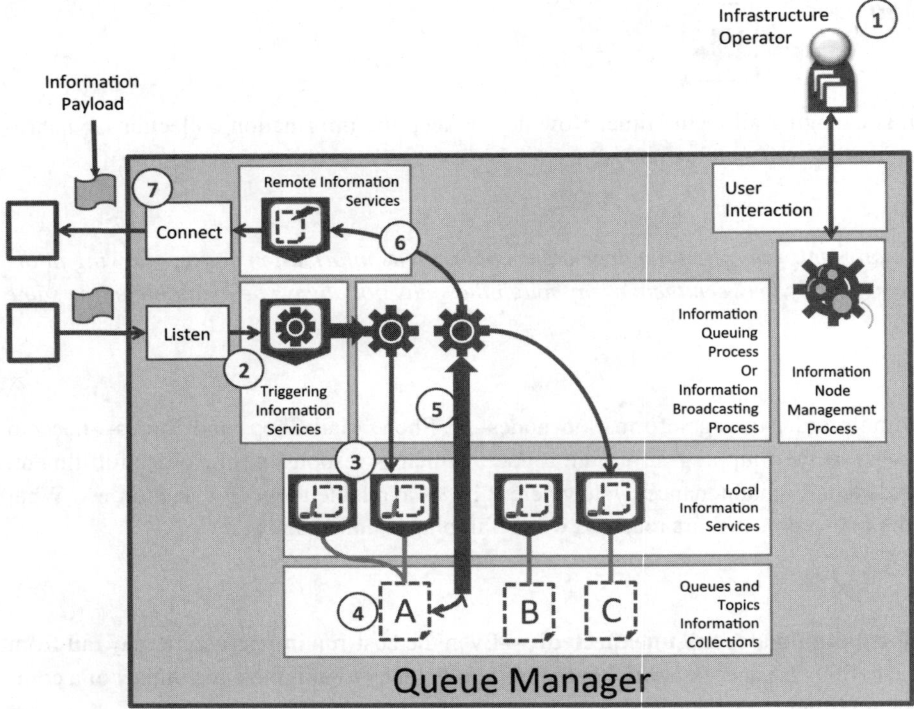

Figure 5.47 Schematic of a queue manager node.

The numbers on the diagram in Figure 5.47 refer to these notes:

1. The queue manager is started and stopped through the **I**NFORMATION **N**ODE **M**ANAGEMENT **P**ROCESS.
2. Either an **I**NFORMATION **Q**UEUING **P**ROCESS or an **I**NFORMATION **B**ROADCASTING **P**ROCESS receives an information payload that must be safely delivered.
3. The information payload is passed to a local information service that represents a queue.
4. The information service stores the information payload.
5. The result of storing the information payload triggers an attempt to deliver it to the intended recipient(s).
6. The intended recipient could be registered with the queue manager, providing the queue manager with an information service to call to deliver the information payload.

7. If the queue manager successfully delivers the information payload, then it is deleted from the information collection. If not, it remains in the information collection until (1) the recipient registers, in which case the stored payloads are passed to it and removed from the information collection, or (2) an information node requests an information payload explicitly.

The queue manager is able to support the delivery of information payloads between many different information nodes. This is illustrated in Figure 5.48.

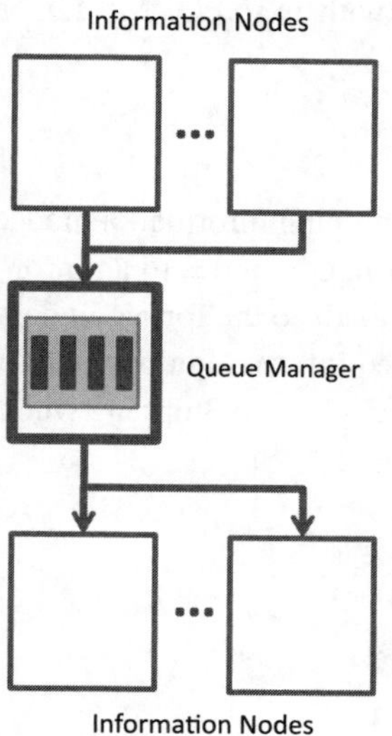

Figure 5.48 Interaction of a queue manager with other information nodes.

Consequences

Benefits:

- The queue manager increases the resiliency of an information flow by ensuring information is delivered even if one of the destinations is not available when the information payload is sent. The queue manager logic can be implemented in the source, destination, or information broker nodes. However, the simplicity of the queue manager's behavior makes it easier to keep it running at high availability.

Liabilities:

- The queue manager must be configured for as close to continuous availability as possible. This is typically achieved by having a cluster of queue managers supporting the information supply chain so the service continues even if one of the queue managers is unavailable.
- Neither the information queuing process nor the information broadcasting process can perform transformation on the information payloads that pass through the queue manager. Because most information nodes implement their own private information format, the queue manager often needs to be used in conjunction with an INFORMATION BROKER.

Example Resolved

As seen in Figure 5.49, a queue manager is installed "in front" of the Shipping information node. Orders are passed in information payloads from the order-taking information nodes to an information broker that is responsible for transforming the information payloads to the format understood by Shipping. The information broker then passes the transformed information payload to the queue manager. The queue manager delivers the order information payload to Shipping when it is next available.

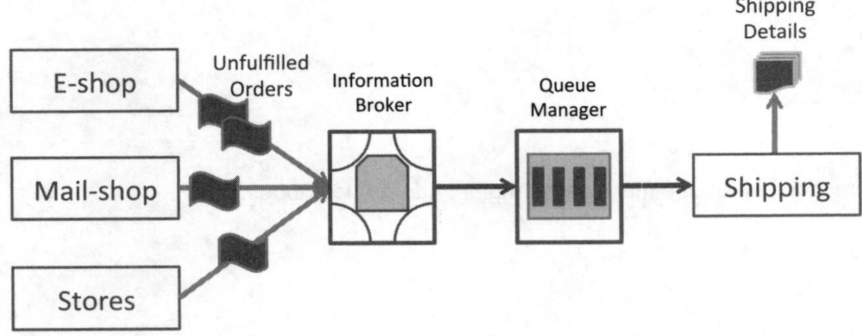

Figure 5.49 Implementation of a queue manager to buffer orders when Shipping is unavailable.

The queue manager is able to buffer new orders whether Shipping is unavailable due to a planned outage or an unexpected failure. It can also throttle back the delivery of new orders during peak demand so Shipping does not get overloaded.

Known Uses

The queue manager is a common component of message-oriented middleware. It is capable of supporting many more patterns than we have described here. However, we have focused on its use in the distribution of information. Its function is covered in greater detail in works on information integration technologies.

Related Patterns

The **I**NFORMATION **B**ROKER is a complementary capability. It is able to extract information, transform it, and deliver it to the recipients. It does not have native capability to reliably store information for later delivery. However, the queue manager and information broker working together enable **I**NFORMATION **P**AYLOADS to be reliably transformed and delivered when the source and destinations are not always available.

Staging Area

Context

Information needs to flow between information nodes.

Problem

An information node needs a temporary store to hold information that is in the process of being provisioned into a different information collection.

Example

Product details need to be distributed from MCHS Trading's Product Hub to the order-taking applications.

Forces

- **Different formats**—There are differences in the way information is stored in each information node.
- **Insufficient quality**—Information from one information node may be of such poor quality that it needs a lot of work to bring it up to standards before it can be distributed to other information nodes. As such, it may be necessary to introduce information collections with transient scope to store intermediate results.
- **Different processing needs**—The processing required on some **I**NFORMATION **P**AYLOADS might be different from others. As such, they may need to take a different route in an **I**NFORMATION **F**LOW.

Solution

Create a dedicated information store to hold one or more information collections that have TRANSIENT USAGE by the provisioning information processes.

The information store is an information node dedicated to hosting temporary information collections that are needed to store the intermediate results while moving and transforming information.

Figure 5.50 shows the workings of a staging area.

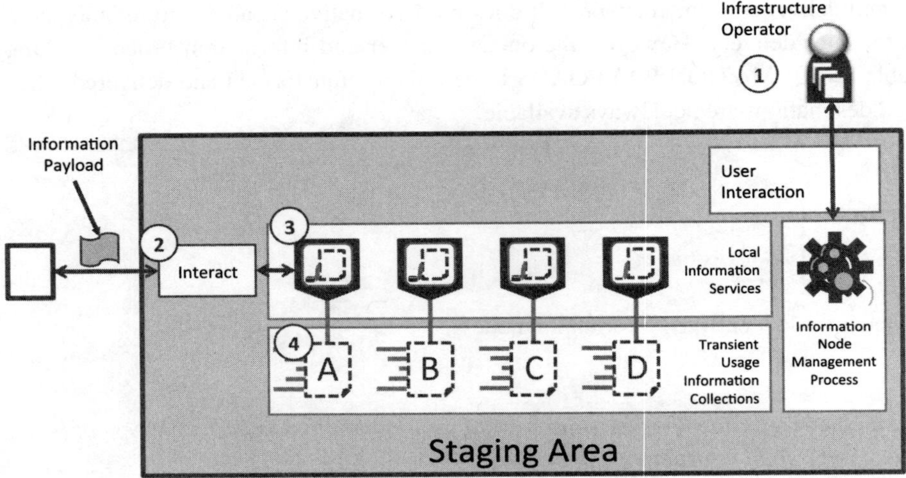

Figure 5.50 Schematic of a staging area information node.

The numbers on the diagram in Figure 5.50 refer to these notes:

1. As with any information node, the staging area must be running for the information collections it hosts to be available.
2. The provisioning information processes read and write **I**NFORMATION **P**AYLOADS to staging areas using information services.
3. The information services provide access to the information collections.
4. The information collections have **T**RANSIENT **U**SAGE, for information payloads are typically being added and deleted, but rarely updated.

Consequences

Benefits:

- Provisioning information processes need to store intermediate results and use temporary files and database tables. Having a well-defined place to store these intermediate results ensures the content of these temporary files can be protected and, if there is an error in the logic of a provisioning information process, abandoning information payloads in one of these temporary stores, the condition can be checked for and rectified.

Liabilities:

- The staging area needs naming conventions for the information collections to be able to trace back and discover which information process created it.

Example Resolved

The staging area provides information collections that are used as post boxes for the information processes running in the information broker. The numbers on the diagram in Figure 5.51 refer to these notes:

1. The staging area has an information collection for each destination information node. The information payloads are written to these information collections as required.
2. When an information payload is retrieved and processed, it is deleted from the information collection in the staging area.

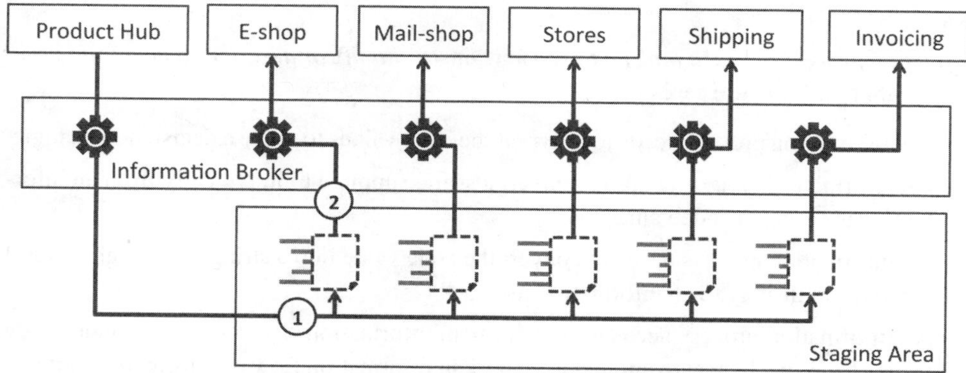

Figure 5.51 Incorporation of a staging area for distribution of information.

Known Uses

The staging area is a common approach used to provide temporary storage for integration logic. Sometimes files are used, or database tables. If database tables are used, the database features, such as triggers, can be used to implement INFORMATION PROBES that monitor the flow of information.

Related Patterns

In the example above, the staging area could be replaced by a QUEUE MANAGER running an INFORMATION QUEUING PROCESS for each of the destination information nodes. This is because each information payload is processed independently. The queue manager would handle the deletion of payloads from the queues once they were processed, making the information processes easier to write. However, staging areas are necessary if information payloads are not processed independently—for example, when combining payloads from multiple sources. So if staging areas were already used in other provisioning information processes, then they would be a good choice here, to simplify the management of the operational environment.

Look-Up Table Node

Context

Many systems use code values to represent a fixed set of values that can be stored in an attribute within an information collection. (This is known as an enumeration.) The information processes that use the information collection need to understand the code values used.

Problem

An information process needs to look up the code value to classify or describe some information.

There are four basic use cases:

- An information process needs to interpret the code values to make a decision in its logic.
- An information process needs to convert a string supplied to it, typically from an information user, into a code value.
- An information process needs to convert the code value into a string of the right natural language to display to an information user.
- An information process needs to transform an information structure that includes code values from one format to another as part of an information flow or information service.

Example

When a MCHS Trading customer submits an order, he or she has three delivery options:

- To have it delivered to his or her home address
- To have it delivered to a store
- To have it delivered to an alternative address

The attribute in the order details that stores the delivery option uses a code value. There is one code value for each option. The E-Shop application can operate in English or French. Also, the code values used for the delivery option are different in the Shipping application.

Forces

- **No standards for code values**—The code values used by each information collection are typically different. When information is distributed to other information collections, the code values from the source must be transcoded to the code values for the destination. The information process that is choreographing the distribution must understand the mapping between the two code value sets. Errors in code value mapping are the largest source of errors in information supply chains.
- **Sets of code values need to be maintained**—New code values will need to be added to the list—and very occasionally, values need to be deleted.

Solution

Provide a lookup table that translates between the descriptive information values and the code values.

This may be a simple lookup table supporting a single information collection, or one that supports the transcoding of code values from one information collection to another.

Consequences

Benefits:

- Using code values for enumerations makes it easier to validate that a new value is acceptable; it saves storage and makes it easier to support text representations in different languages for display in messages and on user interfaces.
- Using lookup tables that can be shared with many information processes reduces the cost of maintaining the sets of code values.

Liabilities:

- Lookup tables are passive stores and need external information processes to maintain the values.

Example Resolved

In this example, there are two lookup tables:

- Within E-Shop, there is a code table that maps the three code values to their French and English strings.
- For the information broker that transforms orders from E-Shop, Mail-Shop, and Stores, there is a lookup table that maps between the code values used in E-Shop, Mail-Shop, and Stores to the code values from Shipping, as seen in Table 5.22. Notice that the mappings are not 1-1 as there are different options offered by each of the order-taking applications.

Table 5.22 Differences in Code Values Used in Different Applications

Meaning	Code Values from E-Shop	Code Values from Mail-Shop	Code Values from Stores	Code Values from Shipping
Home	0	H	CA	A
Store	1	-	SA	B
Alternate	2	A	-	C
Unknown	-	U	-	C

If a new delivery option is added, both code tables must be updated.

Known Uses

Lookup tables are used within the implementation of applications and as standalone database tables for use by INFORMATION BROKERS. They can be simple database tables, or a most sophisticated solution that offers authoring of code tables; mapping between them; information services for import, export, and transcoding; along with provisioning information flows to maintain consistent values in all of the copies. This type of solution is called a Reference Data Management (RDM).

Related Patterns

An INFORMATION ASSET HUB can be used to manage the master copy of the code values and the mapping between them. The code values can be distributed from the hub to the lookup tables.

The INFORMATION CODE pattern describes these INFORMATION ELEMENTS. INFORMATION VALUE PROFILES store details about the codes used for use in designing new applications or understanding transformations through the INFORMATION SUPPLY CHAIN.

Event Correlation Node

Context

The activity within an organization is complex, with many things happening at once. As an individual person, or information process, it is hard to recognize that a series of seemingly disparate events that have recently occurred indicate something significant has happened.

Problem

What is an appropriate infrastructure to host a complete picture of the enterprise with a historical perspective?

Example

MCHS Trading knows that the sales of certain products can be affected by a variety of events, such as weather, marketing offers, an item in the news, fashion, and public opinion. They do historical analysis of buying patterns, which gives them the overall trends in demand, but does not warn them of unexpected spikes in demand. How should they tackle this issue?

Forces

- **The events can come from multiple sources**—They need to be brought together in real time.
- **The timing of events affects their significance**—For example, if an individual's address has changed 5 times in the last 10 minutes, then that suggests the individual might have been the victim of identity theft—but if an address changes 5 times in 20 years, then that is not so significant.

Solution

Consolidate the events into a single information node in real time and perform complex event processing on them.

This information node is called the event correlation node. It is a specialized piece of software comprising state machines, timers, mapping, and correlation processing. Each event is processed as it arrives. This processing classifies it and groups it with related events. Each group is being monitored to see if it matches a pattern. When/if the pattern is confirmed, a new event is published, recording that a significant complex event has occurred. This new event is passed to other information nodes to handle the situation.

Consequences

Benefits:

- The event correlation node detects when events from multiple sources together indicate that something significant has occurred.

Liabilities:

- The complex event processing logic is difficult to write and needs constant evaluation and tuning to ensure it continues to be accurate.

Example Resolved

MCHS Trading adds an event correlation node to detect weather and media events and correlate them with unusual levels of sales through its channels. If it looks like a product has a spike in popularity, it contacts its suppliers to acquire more stock.

Known Uses

Event correlation nodes are used to detect unusual demand from customers, potential fraudulent activity, and potential opportunities to sell something to a client.

Related Patterns

Simple event correlation can be achieved with a **S**TATE **D**RIVEN **P**ROCESS.

Operational Data Stores and Hubs

The information nodes in Table 5.23 provide consolidated views of information to support your organization's operations.

Most organizations have many applications (see **A**PPLICATION **N**ODE). Each provides specialized information processes to support an aspect of the business. Sometimes the role of an application is historical, based on how the organization grew, or the sequence of mergers and acquisitions that formed the organization as it is today. The result is a fragmented information landscape, with each application representing a scoped point of view of the organization.

Many organizations struggle to provide a consolidated view of operational information when it is dispersed among applications with different information keys, scope, coverage, quality standards, and terminology differences. It may be possible to use **I**NFORMATION **S**ERVICES to create a federated view of the information, on demand. However, in many cases, the amount of transformation and complex correlation that would be required is too high to make this practical.

This next set of patterns describes specialized information nodes that support consolidated operational information. The patterns with "Store" in their name provide storage and information services to access the information. They rely on remote information processes to maintain their information. The patterns with "Hub" in their name have additional information processes to maintain the information they store.

Table 5.23 Information Node Patterns—Operational Data Stores and Hubs

Icon	Pattern Name	Problem	Solution
	INFORMATION MIRROR STORE	An organization needs to support queries against information located in either a closed or overloaded information node.	Provide a replica set of information collections that are hosted together on a different information node.
	INFORMATION EVENT STORE	An organization needs an audit trail of who did what, why, where, and when.	Create an information node where information event records can be consolidated.

Icon	Pattern Name	Problem	Solution
	OPERATIONAL STATUS STORE	An organization needs a consolidated view of the operational state of an aspect of its day-to-day business.	Create a set of linked information collections that can store the required information and host them together on an information node.
	INFORMATION ASSET HUB	An organization needs a consolidated and consistent view of the information assets that are central to its operation.	Create a specialized information node where the information assets can be consolidated and managed, plus providing a base from which to synchronize the values in other information nodes.
	INFORMATION ACTIVITY HUB	An organization needs a consolidated real-time view of the activity relating to a business transaction that is dispersed among multiple information nodes.	Create an information node where consolidated information activity records can be stored and then accessed in real time.

Information Mirror Store

Context

An organization has many information nodes supporting its day-to-day business.

Problem

An organization needs to support queries against information located in either a closed or overloaded information node.

An existing information node contains valuable information required by other parts of the information supply chain. However, this information node is not able to support remote queries of its information collections from other information nodes.

Example

The MCHS Trading application called Stores is responsible for providing order management support for the physical stores (shops) located in various cities. It is a mainframe application that uses application files to manage information about each store's capability, where they are located, employees, stock, and the customer store card. The stock information covers both the orders they are making either for the shelves, or for individual customers, and the deliveries they receive.

The developers of the Stores application have been totally focused on the needs of the stores themselves. When the stores are open for business, this application is running at full capacity and is not able to handle additional workload. However, head office needs information about the operation of the stores.

Forces

- **Applications are valuable**—An application represents a significant investment and its usefulness makes it hard to change.
- **Overloaded information node**—Calls to an information node's services create a processing load on the information node.
- **Information formatted for original use**—One of the reasons the original source information may be hard to query is that it is formatted to suit its primary local use cases and this is not compatible with the remote queries.
- **Information is constantly changing**—If a copy of some operational information is taken, the copy must be kept synchronized with the original or it will become increasingly worthless.

Solution

Provide a replica set of information collections that are hosted together on a different information node.

The information mirror node is an information store that hosts the replica information collections as seen in Figure 5.52. These information collections can be populated as follows:

- Regular SNAPSHOT PROVISIONING that takes a fresh copy of the information from the original information node and completely replaces the replica information collections.
- After an initial load of the original information, the replica is kept up to date with delta updates using MIRRORING PROVISIONING. This approach can only be used if it is easy to detect which values have changed since the last time the information mirror node was refreshed.

The approach used will depend on how frequently each of the values in the information is changing. In either case, however, the information collections in the mirror information store have REFERENCE USAGE.

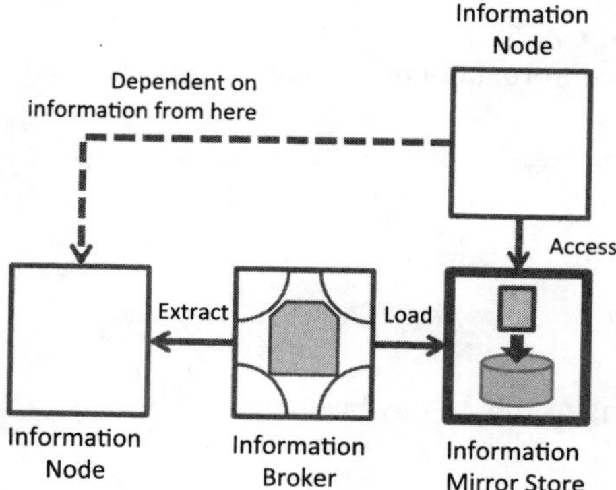

Figure 5.52 Interaction of an information mirror store with other information nodes.

Consequences

Benefits:

- The information mirror store is able to support information services that provide access to the information without impacting the original information node. The information can be reformatted as it is synchronized into the information mirror store to better support the queries.

Liabilities:

- The information mirror store takes additional storage and needs to be kept synchronized with the original information node.

Example Resolved

MCHS Trading creates an information mirror store for a replica of the Stores information. It is replicated once a day once the processing is completed for the physical store's daily trading. The frequency that it is updated is a compromise between the capacity of the Stores application and the information needs of the rest of the organization.

Known Uses

This is a simple operational data store. You would use this to off-load the query traffic from the application either because the application does not have a query interface, or it is overloaded, or it is not always available.

Related Patterns

An INFORMATION BROKER is necessary to host the information processes that will maintain the information in the information mirror store.

Information Event Store

Context

An organization has many information nodes supporting its day-to-day business.

Problem

An organization needs an audit trail of who did what, why, where, and when.

Example

MCHS Trading needs to monitor the information flow along its information supply chains.

Forces

- **Auditors require proof**—It is not enough for an organization to comply with a regulation—it needs to be able to demonstrate that it is compliant.
- **Events happen in many places**—It is necessary to capture the event type, time, location, and the context in which it occurred.

Solution

Create an information node where information event records can be consolidated.

This information node is called an information event store—see Figure 5.53. It is a specialized information store that is designed for inserting new records. It hosts a number of local information collections that each store a particular type of information event as an information entry. The information event record provides information services to receive new information events. These services are used most of the time. There are also information services for retrieving sets of information events for reports and audit, which are called occasionally. There are no facilities for changing the events that are recorded.

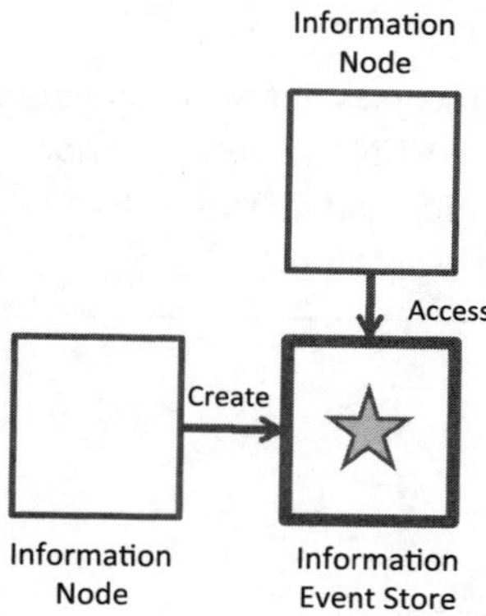

Figure 5.53 Interaction of an information event store with other information nodes.

Consequences

Benefits:

- The information event store provides a reliable store for information events. It can be used as a local store for an information probe and it can be used to store information events in a centralized monitoring node and console.

Liabilities:

- The information event store takes additional storage and needs to be kept with the latest activity from the original information nodes.

Example Resolved

MCHS Trading uses INFORMATION PROBES throughout its information supply chains to monitor particular aspects of its operation. These probes use information event stores to record their readings. The information events are consolidated through a consolidating information supply chain to a central operations console where unexpected events are reviewed and action taken.

See the INFORMATION MONITORING solution pattern for more information about this use case.

Known Uses

This type of store is used for diagnostic logs and audit trails.

Related Patterns

An **I**NFORMATION **B**ROKER is necessary to host the information processes that will maintain the information in the information event store. The **I**NFORMATION **E**VENT pattern describes the life cycle of an event. The **I**NFORMATION **M**ONITORING solution and **C**ONSOLIDATING **I**NFORMATION **S**UPPLY **C**HAIN make use of the information event store.

Operational Status Store

Context

An organization has many information nodes supporting its day-to-day business.

Problem

An organization needs a consolidated view of the operational state of an aspect of its day-to-day business.

This requires consolidating and linking the most recent values from the information activity records and information assets spread throughout the information supply chains.

Example

MCHS Trading has three main physical warehouses that goods are shipped from. When they run out of stock, the Shipping application must order more from the supplier. Meanwhile, customer orders are not being fulfilled. How does MCHS Trading coordinate the ordering of new supplies with the management of the customers with waiting orders?

Forces

- **Applications have limited scope and coverage**—An application contains information that represents the interests of a business function within an internal organizational unit.
- **Inconsistent distributed information**—Information assets are distributed across multiple information nodes, duplicated, and inconsistent.

Solution

Create a set of linked information collections that can store the required information and host them together on an information node.

This information node is implemented as an information store (typically a database) that provides a place to marshal and correlate information from different information nodes to support complex queries.

Information processes hosted in an information broker maintain the information within the operational status store. Information is accessed through its information services (typically as SQL queries). See Figure 5.54.

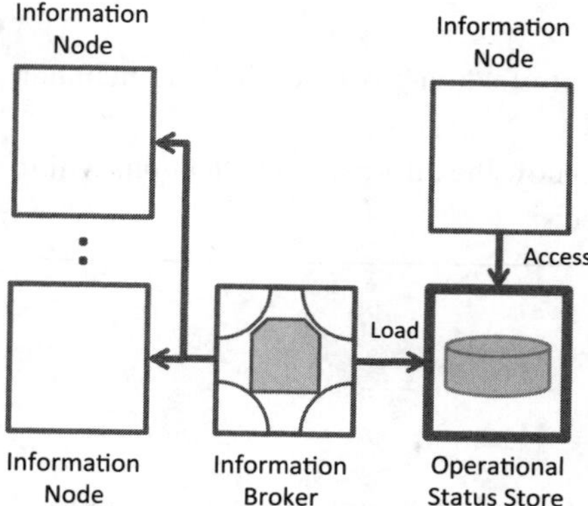

Figure 5.54 Operational status store loaded by information broker and accessed via information node(s).

Consequences

Benefits:

- The operational status store may be used to provide a consolidated view of the organization's activity and/or to provide a consolidated information collection that can be used as a source for distributing this information to other information nodes.

Liabilities:

- The operational status store takes additional storage and needs to be kept up to date with the latest activity from the original information nodes.

Example Resolved

MCHS Trading introduces a Re-Stocking operational status store. This information node maintains information about the orders to suppliers being handled by the Supplier-net application and the customer orders being handled by the Shipping application.

Re-Stocking is used by the Customer-Care application that is managing queries from customers. It also feeds the Reporting Hub on the impact of out-of-stock conditions on customer orders and which product lines these occur in.

Known Uses

This is a type of operational data store that has normalized and correlated operational data. It is used to support use cases where information needs to be correlated from multiple systems. It could also be a feed for a data warehouse (INFORMATION WAREHOUSE) or data mart (INFORMATION MART).

Related Patterns

An **INFORMATION BROKER** is necessary to host the information processes that will maintain the information in the operational status store.

Use the **INFORMATION FLOW** patterns to design how the information collections within an operational status store should be provisioned and used.

Information Asset Hub

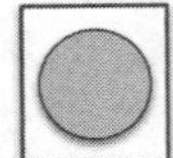

Context

INFORMATION ASSETS such as customer and product details are central to an organization's operations. As a result, this information tends to be replicated in many information nodes.

Problem

An organization needs a consolidated and consistent view of the information assets that are central to its operation.

This consolidated view can be used to enable new capabilities and can act as a hub from which to distribute updates.

Example

MCHS Trading needs a consolidated view of its customers' details for operational use. At the moment, customer details are stored in E-Shop (for customers who use the Internet shopping service), Stores (for customers who have a store card), and they are entered into each order in Mail-Shop. There is a consolidated list of customers in the Reporting Hub, but that information node is not suitable for an operational load.

Forces

- **Slowly changing**—Information assets do change, but it tends to be updates each week/month rather than every few minutes.
- **Widely used**—Information assets contain information that is core to the organization's work and, as a result, they are needed in many of the business information nodes.
- **Difficult to identify**—Information assets often represent people, concepts, objects, and organizations in the real world. They do not come with a unique identifier and so many information nodes assign an identifier. In fact, each node assigns a different identifier when it stores information about the asset. Information nodes are often not good at ensuring they haven't already stored information about the asset, and so may store it twice, resulting in it having two identifiers in one information node. The result is that an information asset has many identifiers.

- **Disconnected information**—An information node receives new information about an asset, for example, through its user interface. It stores the update locally. Because there is no linkage to the other information entries about this asset that are stored in various information collections dotted among the organization's information nodes, there is no easy way to propagate this update to the other copies. The result is that, over time, the copies become inconsistent.

Solution

Create a specialized information node where the information assets can be consolidated and managed, plus providing a base from which to synchronize the values in other information nodes.

This information node is called an information asset hub. It becomes the authoritative source of these information assets.

Figure 5.55 shows the internals of the information asset hub.

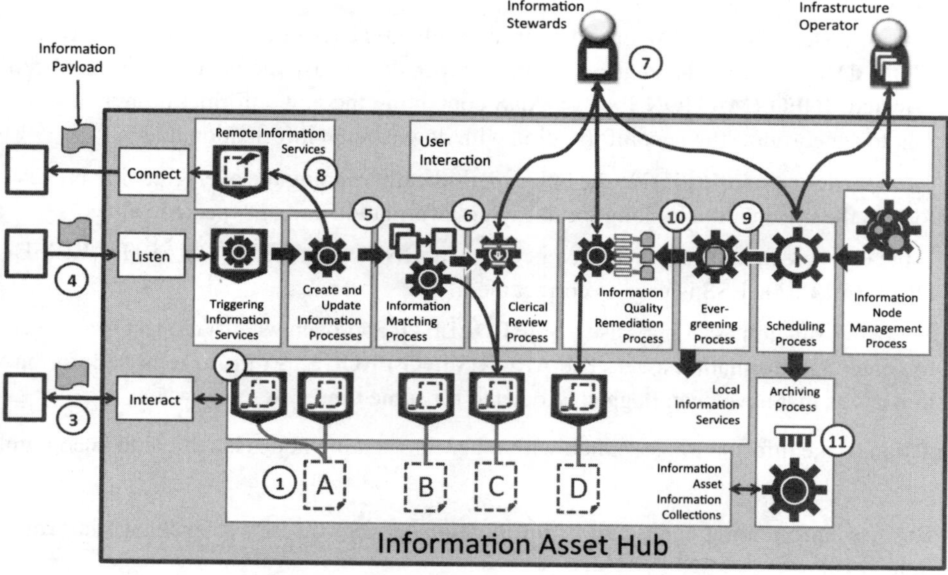

Figure 5.55 Schematic of an information asset hub.

The numbers on the diagram in Figure 5.55 refer to these notes:

1. Most information collections contain information assets, although there may be references and summaries of relevant INFORMATION EVENTS and INFORMATION ACTIVITIES.

2. The information collections are accessed through **I**NFORMATION **S**ERVICES. The hub may offer different views over the same information asset to service different consumers.
3. The information stored in the information asset hub can be retrieved directly through the information services.
4. When a change is to be made to information in the hub (create, update, delete), the request goes through a **T**RIGGERED **I**NFORMATION **S**ERVICE where a variety of validation rules can be checked.
5. For create and update requests, an **I**NFORMATION **M**ATCHING **P**ROCESS is run to make sure the new information is not going to create duplicate entries.
6. If a match is found that is fairly close, a **C**LERICAL **R**EVIEW **P**ROCESS may be triggered to involve an **I**NFORMATION **S**TEWARD in the decision.
7. The information steward may use its domain knowledge, additional information, or persona inquiry to make the decision.
8. Once the status of the new information is resolved, alerts in the form of **I**NFORMATION **E**VENTS may be sent out if an unexpected or suspicious condition has been detected. **I**NFORMATION **P**AYLOADS containing the new information may also be sent to synchronize the new information with downstream information nodes.
9. The scheduling process inside the hub is periodically running the ever-greening process to scan the information looking for decaying information and unexpected values.
10. If the ever-greening process discovers errors, an **I**NFORMATION **Q**UALITY **R**EMEDIATION **P**ROCESS is used to correct them.
11. Many information asset hubs use a **S**OFT **D**ELETE approach when a request is received to delete an information asset. The **A**RCHIVING **P**ROCESS runs to remove information assets that have been flagged as deleted for some time.

The interaction of the information asset hub with other information nodes is critical to keep it up to date:

- Business information nodes call its information services directly to exchange information.
- Information brokers call the information services to synchronize information in and out of the hub as part of an information supply chain.
- The information processes within the information asset hub call remote information services to send out alerts and data synchronization requests.

Consequences

Benefits:

- The information asset hub is a central place to manage, protect, and apply quality standards and governance to information. The canonical form of the information often can be used to provision new information processes—saving time and money by avoiding supporting another set of information collections.

Liabilities:

- This is another information node to manage containing another copy of the information for a subject area.
- The hub is merging information entries that the information matching process has flagged as duplicates. Information nodes downstream of the information asset hub in an information supply chain may need to merge their copies of these information entries as well. If at a later time, the merge is found to be invalid, all merged information entries need to be split apart again, and any decisions made using the merged versions may need to be revisited.

Example Resolved

MCHS Trading deploys an information asset hub called Customer Hub, as seen in Figure 5.56. This information node provides a central location to manage its customer details.

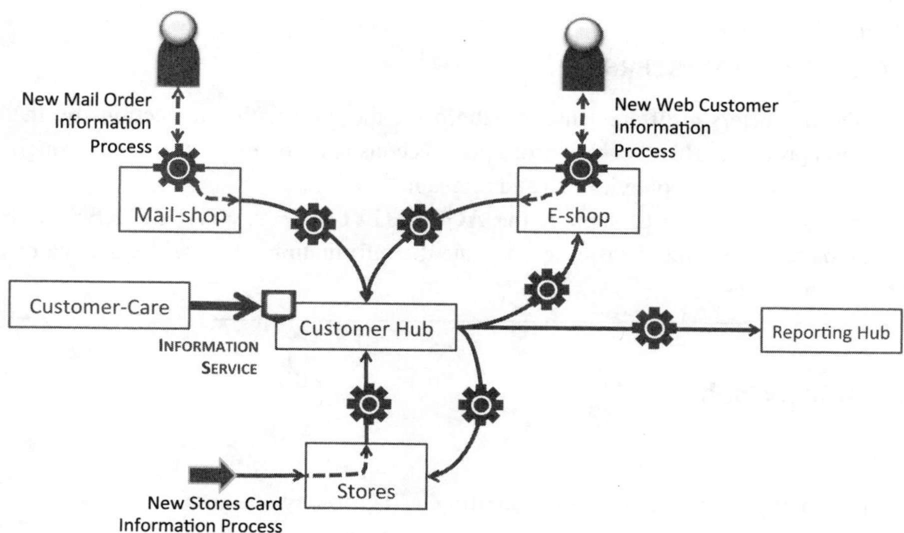

Figure 5.56 Customer Hub acting as an authoritative source of customer details.

Known Uses

The information asset hub is a description of a Master Data Management (MDM) hub that manages information assets such as customer details, product details, asset details, and account/contract details.

Related Patterns

The **I**NFORMATION **A**SSET pattern describes the characteristics of the information managed by an information asset hub.

The **I**NFORMATION **A**CTIVITY **H**UB is a companion information node to the information asset hub that can provide activity information that is relevant to the information asset.

The **C**OLLABORATIVE **E**DITING **P**ROCESS may be added to an information asset hub to enable new instances of information assets to be created by a team of people.

The information asset hub may also be managing the master copies of code tables used within the information asset. This could include the canonical version used in the local information collections and master copies of these code tables used in other information nodes.

The following information solutions cover different configurations of an information asset hub:

- **S**HARED **M**ASTER
- **C**ENTRALIZED **M**ASTER
- **I**NFORMATION **R**EGISTRY
- **G**OLDEN **R**EFERENCE
- **G**OLDEN **H**YBRID
- **S**YNCHRONIZED **M**ASTERS

Each of these solutions offers a different usage pattern for the information collections by the business information processes. In all cases, information is constantly being provisioned through the information supply chains, keeping it fresh and relevant.

Information asset hubs tend to support the **A**GGREGATE **K**EY, **S**TABLE **K**EY, and **C**ALLER'S **K**EY patterns to make it easier to correlate the information assets with information from other information nodes.

Information Activity Hub

Context

An organization has many information nodes supporting its day-to-day business.

Problem

An organization needs a consolidated real-time view of the activity relating to a business transaction that is dispersed among multiple information nodes.

Multiple information processes are performing a particular type of activity. These information processes are distributed across different information nodes. Each of these information nodes has a local information collection to document the progress of the work occurring locally. This information needs to be consolidated in some way so it can be located and retrieved in real time, often in the context of an information asset.

Example

MCHS Trading's order-processing capability is dispersed among its E-Shop, Mail-Shop, Stores, Shipping, and Invoicing applications. How does MCHS Trading discover the status of a customer's order?

Forces

- **Applications have limited scope and coverage**—An application contains information that represents the interests of a business function within an internal organizational unit.
- **Real-time information sharing**—Information about an activity piece of work needs to be shared in real time.
- **Real-time decisions**—Predictive analytics needs consolidated real-time information to provide recommendations as part of a business transaction.

Solution

Create an information node where consolidated information activity records can be stored and then accessed in real time.

This type of information node is called an information activity hub. Within it are two types of information collections:

- An event information collection where each information entry is an INFORMATION EVENT that describes a change or action performed on behalf of an activity
- An activity information collection where each information entry is an INFORMATION ACTIVITY

The information activity hub has information services that enable information events to be received. The arrival of an information event causes a STATE DRIVEN PROCESS to start. It is responsible for storing the information event in a local information collection and updating the status of the related information activity. Together, the information collections and state driven process provide the current status and an audit trail of the activity.

Figure 5.57 shows the internals of the information activity hub.

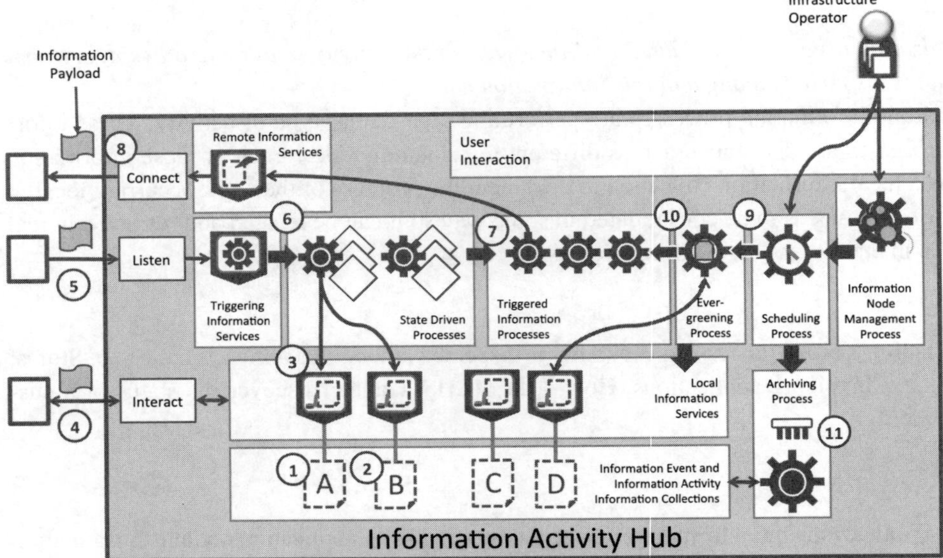

Figure 5.57 Schematic of an information activity hub.

The numbers on the diagram in Figure 5.57 refer to these notes:

1. The information collections in the information activity hub operate in pairs. One of the information collections contains information activities.
2. The second information collection in the pair contains information events.
3. The information collections are accessed by information services.
4. The information services offer the ability to retrieve the activity status of collections of events.
5. When a new event is received, it is processed by a triggering information service that initiates the correct state driven process for the corresponding activity.
6. The state driven process retrieves the appropriate information activity and determines the new state based on the event. It updates and stores the information activity and inserts the event into the information event collection.
7. For some state changes, the state driven process may trigger an additional information process.
8. This triggered information process may invoke information services to send alerts, or initiate some related processing.

9. The scheduler will periodically kick off an **I**NFORMATION **E**VER-GREENING **P**ROCESS.
10. The information ever-greening process is looking for information activities that have stalled, or are in unlikely states, or have missing information.
11. When activities have been completed for a while, they are archived.

Consequences

Benefits:

- The information activity hub may be used to provide a consolidated view of the organization's activity. It supports information processes that understand the significance of events occurring across multiple information nodes.
- It provides information services that support the current status of related activity that is occurring in distributed information nodes.
- It can detect when an event has not occurred—suggesting a silent failure.
- It can provide additional situational information relating to an information asset.
- It can be used as a source for distributing this information to other information nodes.

Liabilities:

- The information activity hub takes additional storage and needs to be kept up to date with the latest activity from the original information nodes.
- When changes occur in the information nodes that are performing the business transaction, the information activity node may be affected because it may start to receive different events.

Example Resolved

MCHS Trading deploys an information activity hub called Order-Tracking that is responsible for maintaining the state of the customers' orders as seen in Figure 5.58. It receives events from E-Shop, Mail-Shop, Stores, Shipping, Invoicing, and Re-Stocking. It is used by the Customer-Care system for discovering the status of orders. It also feeds the Reporting Hub.

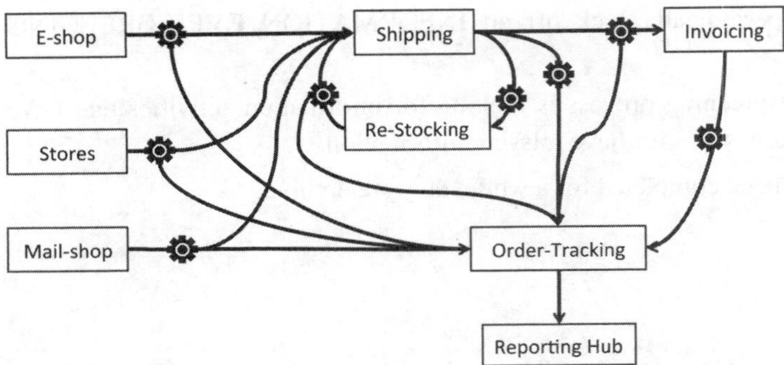

Figure 5.58 Order tracking using an information activity hub.

Known Uses

This type of information node is a useful supplementary store to a Master Data Management (MDM) hub (INFORMATION ASSET HUB) because it keeps volatile information that is related to the information asset in a form that can be accessed in real time. The information activity hub may be hosted on the same physical server as the information asset hub, if the performance load allows—otherwise, they may be deployed separately.

Related Patterns

The information activity hub and the INFORMATION ASSET HUB often act as key frontline nodes for a SINGLE VIEW INFORMATION SUPPLY CHAIN.

The INFORMATION ACTIVITY pattern describes the characteristics of information that describes a business activity. The DISTRIBUTED ACTIVITY STATUS pattern uses an information activity hub.

Big Data Information Processing Nodes

The information nodes shown in Table 5.24 are specialized to handle very large quantities of information. Their information collections are so large that the information processes they host need to be specialized to handle the volume of information, variety of information, and/or velocity of information.

Table 5.24 Information Node Patterns—Big Data Information Processing

Icon	Pattern Name	Problem	Solution
	INFORMATION WAREHOUSE	What is an appropriate infrastructure to host a complete picture of the enterprise with a historical perspective?	Create a set of linked information collections that supports the full scope of the information that is required by the organization to know the full scope of its operations.
	MAP-REDUCE NODE	An organization wants to perform analytics over a large collection of unstructured files.	Use an information node that supports distributed map-reduce processing on a file system.
	STREAMING ANALYTICS NODE	How do you introduce data from real-time monitors and sensor devices into the information supply chain?	Use streaming technology to collect and collate data from various monitoring devices and publish summaries of this data into the information supply chain.

Information Warehouse

Context

An organization needs to understand what the state of its business is and how it is changing over time. This is necessary to improve the performance of the business, understand the history and context of specific events, and meet regulatory requirements.

Problem

What is an appropriate infrastructure to host a complete picture of the enterprise with a historical perspective?

Example

MCHS Trading needs a historical record of its customers and the products they are buying. This is to enable it to understand the trends in its business. For example, which products are selling well and which are in decline? This helps MCHS Trading plan new product offerings.

Forces

- **Change is inevitable**—Any historical record needs to take into account that structures change. This could be a reorganization of the organization, acquisition, or expansion of the scope of the business; changing priorities; and markets affecting what data are collected. Individual facts must be considered within the structure, or context, in which they were gathered.

- **Information decays at different rates**—Over time, the value of keeping information about individual events may diminish.
- **Foresight**—When selecting the information to preserve, how do you know what information you will need in the future?
- **Volume**—Organizations create a lot of data. Keeping it all for indefinite periods of time takes a lot of storage.
- **Seeing the wood for the trees**—Too much information can be overwhelming, causing you to miss the critical facts.
- **Regulators need proof**—It is not enough to comply with a regulation; an organization must prove it is doing so.

Solution

Create a set of linked information collections that supports the full scope of the information that is required by the organization to know the full scope of its operations.

These information collections will store not only the current state of the organization's information, but also the values that were used in the past. They are hosted together in a specialized server called an information warehouse. The information processes within this node are focused solely on the accumulation, management, and delivery of this information.

An information warehouse has to accommodate change, both in terms of how the information is structured and the relationships between the information entries and values within them. It must also represent the notion of time and the state of the business at a particular moment in time.

The information warehouse is a highly connected system that is fed from the majority of the organization's information supply chain. This keeps the information warehouse current, while being able to provide a historical perspective on the organization's performance.

Consequences

Benefits:

- **The information warehouse creates an information repository that contains the facts about how your organization is running**—This information is necessary for demonstrating compliance with regulation, understanding what is working well and what needs changing, and detecting trends and changes in the market.
- **The art and science of building information warehouses is well understood**—There are many books, best practices, and skilled technical professionals who understand how to construct these systems so they deliver value over many years.

Liabilities:

- **The temptation is to store everything, just in case**—An information warehouse needs to be carefully planned, with a good understanding of where the information is coming from and how it will be consumed. If people do not have confidence in the quality and usefulness of the information, then it will fall into disuse—and become an expense rather than an asset.
- **The information warehouse is designed for structured information**—Increasingly, an organization's information is unstructured and information warehouses need to be coupled with MAP-REDUCE NODES and INFORMATION CONTENT NODES to manage the full breadth of information.

Example Resolved

MCHS Trading creates an information warehouse that is part of the Reporting Hub. The information warehouse hosts the historical record of its business. It includes the following:

- Details of all of its customers, the channels they use, the orders they make, how they pay, what offers they were given, and which were accepted
- Details of all of its products, the suppliers, how well it is selling, through which channels it is selling, the effectiveness of delivery, levels of profit from the products, levels of customer satisfaction, issues, and returns

Known Uses

Powerful database systems called data warehouses have been developed to cope with the volume of data—and the complex structures and operations—that are necessary for historical information. These systems support both relational and dimensional structures, along with the capability called extract, load, transform (ELT) to transform and move data between internal storage areas.

Related Patterns

An information warehouse is typically part of a broader ecosystem that is managing both the consolidation of information into its information collections and the distribution/consumption of this information afterward. The HISTORICAL SYSTEM OF RECORD solution pattern describes the whole ecosystem around an information warehouse.

The INFORMATION BROKER information node is typically responsible for hosting the information processes that load information into the information warehouse.

Streaming Analytics Node

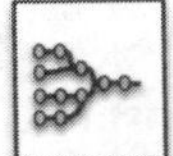

Context

Sensor-based data represents a growing sector of information typically of high volume. It contains useful information for the information supply chain, but its format and content can be challenging to use directly in an information supply chain.

Problem

How do you introduce data from real-time monitors and sensor devices into the information supply chain?

Data received from real-time monitors and sensor devices may be unpredictable in terms of its arrival rates, of mixed quality, and of very high volume. From a nonfunctional point of view, this data is very different from the other types of data in the supply chain. As such, there needs to be some sort of analysis and consolidation of the data before it is introduced into the information supply chain.

Example

MCHS Trading has three large physical warehouses from where its goods are shipped. Many of the goods in its product line are valuable, or require a special license to purchase. There have been some incidents of theft which MCHS Trading has been ordered to stop by its regulator.

Forces

If an information process needs to react to events as they are happening, the information gathering and processing must be as close to real time as possible.

Solution

Use streaming technology to collect and collate data from various monitoring devices and publish summaries of this data into the information supply chain.

Streaming technology is able to perform real-time data collection, analysis, and transformation of device information as the device is producing it. On its own, it could be used to pump summarized information directly into the information supply chain. However, this would introduce values into the information supply chain that are difficult to audit and it could be difficult to repair the effects of a rogue device.

The information streaming process consolidated the results of the streaming processing into one or more information collections. Information can then be passed into the information supply chain from these information collections. Figure 5.59 shows streaming technology in action.

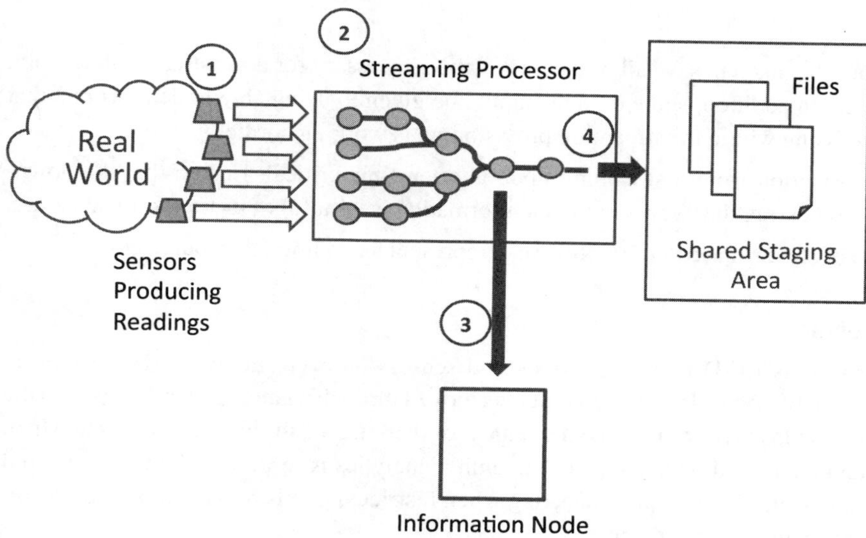

Figure 5.59 Streaming Analytics Node solution.

The numbers on the diagram in Figure 5.59 refer to these notes:

1. Data from sensors is being received at a tremendous velocity. The information within these readings has a very short lifetime where it is useful.
2. The readings are fed into the streaming processor. It runs many parallel threads, trying to process each reading on its own as much as possible, and then starting to classify, group, and consolidate the information that has been extracted.
3. Some facts that are discovered must be acted on immediately and these are turned into an information event and passed to another information node for processing using a remote information service.
4. All of the information that is extracted is stored. It is shown here as being written to a staging area, but it could be passed to a queue manager, information broker, or information store.

Consequences

Benefits:

- Sensors allow organizations to capture new information that may be related or correlated with other standard information sources. This pattern supports the processing of huge quantities of incoming data, which is extremely vital for managing information from real-world sensors and networks.

Liabilities:

- Care must be taken to save all of the information necessary for downstream information processes. In addition, some thought should be given to being able to demonstrate that the processing within the streaming provisioning is working correctly.
- The information from a streaming node is often time critical. Ensure that the downstream processing that works with this information is mindful of its time-critical nature.
- Storage of stream-based information may represent an additional resource cost.

Example Resolved

MCHS Trading installs RFID tags on its stock and sensors on every doorway. These sensors detect the movement of goods. If a restricted item is moved through a gate, an alert is raised to the security team. This helps them restrict the movement of these goods through a single gate where the manifests can be checked manually. The streaming analytics is responsible for tracking and recording the movement of goods plus detecting when restricted goods move out of their designated area through an unauthorized exit.

Known Uses

Information streaming processes are beginning to appear in larger organizations that need to constantly monitor input from specific sensors. Examples of this type of processing include traffic analysis, electronic device input, and automatic maintenance checks. For more examples, see recent works on "Big Data."[1]

Related Patterns

An information streaming process is often used in conjunction with analytical processes, such as the **I**NFORMATION **P**ATTERN **D**ETECTING or **I**NFORMATION **P**ATTERN **D**ISCOVERY process patterns.

The **E**VENT **C**ORRELATION **N**ODE provides a similar function, but not at the scale of input provided by streaming processing because it does not have the ability to exploit parallel processing.

Map-Reduce Node

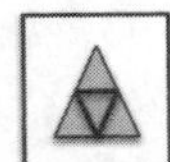

Context

The fastest-growing type of information is unstructured information, particularly documents, web pages, social media, images, and video.

1. Paul Zikopoulos, Chris Eaton, et al., *Understanding Big Data: Analytics for Enterprise Class Hadoop and Streaming Data* (New York: McGraw-Hill Osborne Media, 2011).

Problem

An organization wants to perform analytics over a large collection of unstructured files.

How is this type of information assembled and processed?

Example

MCHS Trading wants to understand the sentiment around a product line that it is considering adding to its product catalog.

Forces

- **The processing must come to the information**—When a collection of information gets very large, it is no longer viable to copy it around.
- **Unstructured information does not fit well in a database**—Databases are better at handling structured information.

Solution

Use an information node that supports distributed map-reduce processing on a file system.

Map-reduce processing breaks down the processing of the files into a mapping process that looks for patterns in the information, and a reduce process where the results detected are combined and consolidated. The map processing in particular is highly parallelized, enabling this technology to scan vast quantities of information to perform an analysis as seen in Figure 5.60.

This technology is new and the best practices around its use are still evolving, so the pattern details are light at this stage, but there are increasing numbers of successful deployments that suggest it should be included in the pattern language.

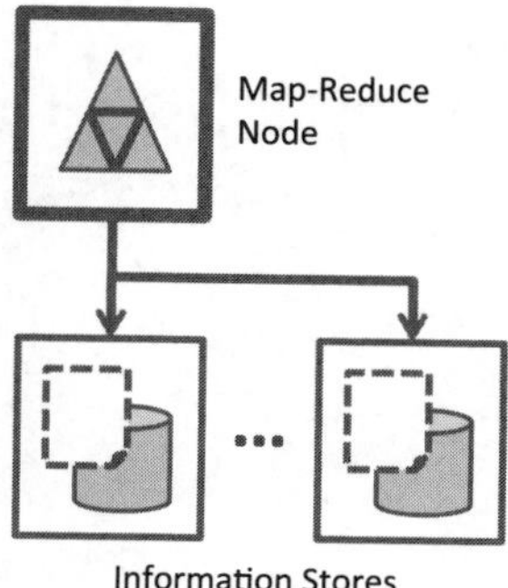

Figure 5.60 The map-reduce node solution.

Consequences

Benefits:

- This type of processing is very powerful at performing the same operation on information spread across multiple distributed file systems.

Liabilities:

- The tools and programming languages for this type of processing are still evolving and so you need to expect some churn and rework around the use of this technology. There is also a shortage of people skilled at using the technology.

Example Resolved

MCHS Trading takes daily downloads from the social media sites and uses map-reduce processing to detect and extract comments about products in its product line. These are fed through to the Marketing Department.

Figure 5.61 summarizes the processing.

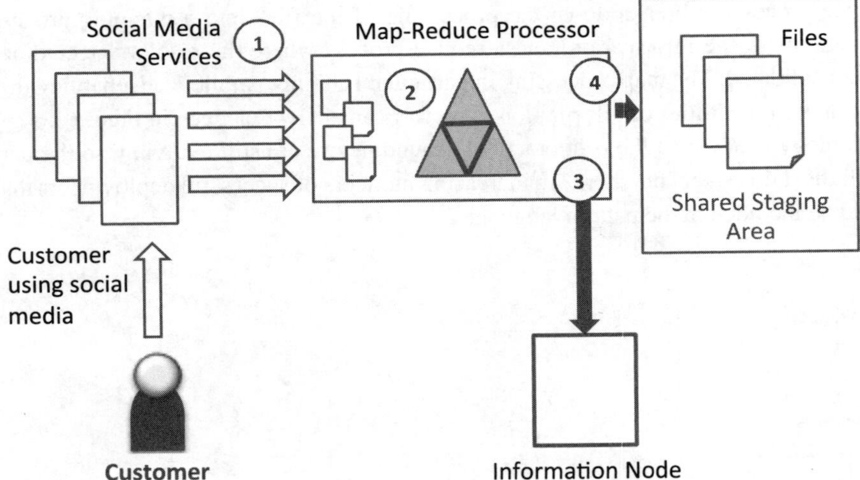

Figure 5.61 A map-reduce node processing social media.

The numbers on the diagram in Figure 5.61 refer to these notes:

1. Downloads from social media are taken regulary and stored in files.
2. The map-reduce process runs, looking for discussons about products that MCHS Trading sells. When a reference is dicovered, the text around it is analyzed to discover the sentiment.

3. References to dangerous or illegal attributes of a product are sent as a high-priority alert to the marketing team to investigate and potentially withdraw the product.
4. All of the references to the products, with the surrounding text and sentiment classification are stored to files. These are picked up by an information broker and stored as additional attributes about the product in the Product Hub.

The analysis could be extended to look for positive references to products that MCHS Trading does not sell but are similar to MCHS Trading's product line. This could provide suggestions for new products to add to the catalog.

Known Uses

The most well-known distributed map-reduce engine is Apache™ Hadoop™.[2] It is a new technology and there are many experimental systems being built with it. Some are operating on unstructured data as the pattern suggests, whereas others are working on a mixture of structured and unstructured information. Two popular usage patterns are exploratory analytics, where new information sources are analyzed to discover interesting facts, and a queryable archive, where information is archived to the distributed map-reduce engine (which will run on commodity hardware) and can then be searched and analyzed at a later date. For more examples, see recent works on "Big Data."[3]

Related Patterns

Large quantities of structured information can be handled by the INFORMATION WAREHOUSE. If information is arriving too fast to store, then the STREAMING ANALYTICS NODE is an option.

Analysis Information Nodes

Analytics is a growth area for information management. The growth in computing power, the availability of powerful information processing nodes, and the reduction in the cost of storage all make the analysis of more types of information economically viable.

Analytics typically runs in batch on historical information or in real time during normal business activity. The analytics logic may be one of the following:

- **An analytics model**—Created by an INFORMATION PATTERN DISCOVERY PROCESS

2. See http://hadoop.apache.org.
3. Paul Zikopoulos, Chris Eaton, et al., *Understanding Big Data: Analytics for Enterprise Class Hadoop and Streaming Data*. (New York: McGraw-Hill Osborne Media, 2011).

- **A decision model**—Created by an INFORMATION DECISION DEFINITION PROCESS

These models are built offline using specialized software. The patterns in this section describe the information nodes that support these offline processes. There are two patterns. The information analysis node provides the tools for DATA SCIENTISTS and BUSINESS ANALYSTS to build the models. The information mining store supplies the information. See Table 5.25.

Table 5.25 Information Node Patterns—Analysis Information Nodes

Icon	Pattern Name	Problem	Solution
	INFORMATION ANALYSIS NODE	What is the appropriate infrastructure to support the information pattern discovery process (mining)?	Provide a dedicated information node to manage the demanding workloads created by information pattern discovery.
	INFORMATION MINING STORE	An organization needs to create an effective source of information for analytical pattern discovery (mining).	Create an information store that has flat structures in its information collections to allow the pattern discovery process to work most effectively.

Information Analysis Node

Context

An organization wants to use information-based decisions for particular aspects of its business. Information-based decisions use analytics and business rules that use the information stored in their information nodes to make a decision. This decision is embedded in an information process and affects the subsequent steps that the information process takes.

Problem

What is the appropriate infrastructure to support the development of analytics models and decision models?

Analytics models and decision models are created using the INFORMATION PATTERN DISCOVERY PROCESS and the INFORMATION DECISION DEFINITION PROCESS, respectively. These processes need access to the organization's information to operate. They perform large information manipulation and computational operations and need to visualize subsets of information in a variety of ways.

Example

MCHS Trading wants to implement a **N**EXT **B**EST **A**CTION solution. This uses analytics to offer its customers relevant offers, information, and services depending on their individual interests. MCHS Trading needs to analyze information about its customers' interests, buying patterns, and channel usage along with the pipeline of new and existing products. This information is dispersed among MCHS Trading's production systems. Which information node should MCHS Trading use to develop the models that will drive the next best action analytics?

Forces

- **High performance requirement**—The **I**NFORMATION **P**ATTERN **D**ISCOVERY **P**ROCESS searches for patterns of values in one or more information collections. This processing can take considerable computing resources (memory, CPU, and disk IO) to perform this activity.
- **Disparate sources of information**—The information to be analyzed often originates from a variety of sources.
- **Specialized tools**—Specialized information users called data scientists and business analysts build these models. They need specialized tools that examine, analyze, and visualize the information to allow them to experiment with different algorithms.

Solution

Provide a dedicated information node to host the specialized analytics tools, and information users, that build analytics models and decision models.

Because existing information nodes are unlikely to support the processing load of the analytical processes, nor have the information stored in an efficient structure for their operation, it is typical to set up a new information node that is dedicated to the analytics processing. This information node is called the information analytics node.

The information analytics node supports two primary information users: the data scientist and the business analyst. Figure 5.62 shows its operation.

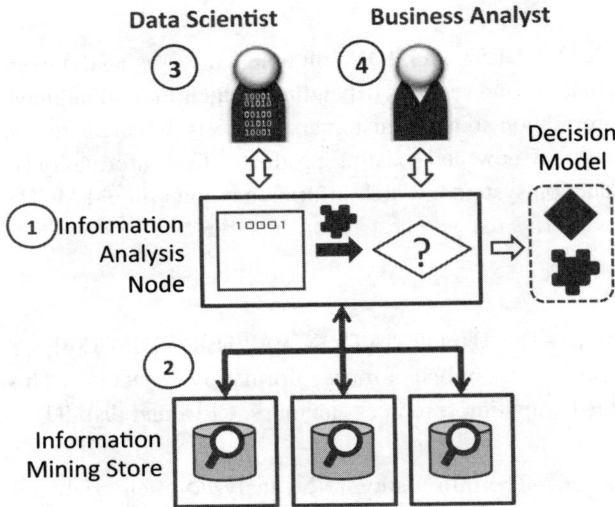

Figure 5.62 Information Analysis Node solution.

The numbers on the diagram in Figure 5.62 refer to these notes:

1. This is the information analysis node.
2. It is supplied information through a **S**INGLE **V**IEW **I**NFORMATION **S**UPPLY **C**HAIN. Typically, the frontline information nodes are information mining stores that are fed from a big data information node such as an **I**NFORMATION **W**AREHOUSE.
3. The data scientist uses the **I**NFORMATION **P**ATTERN **D**ISCOVERY **P**ROCESS to extract, sample, visualize, and experiment with different algorithms to build an analytics model. This can be used as is in an **I**NFORMATION **P**ATTERN **D**ETECTION **P**ROCESS. It may also be passed to a business analyst to incorporate in a decision model.
4. The business analyst builds a decision model using the **I**NFORMATION **D**ECISION **D**EFINITION **P**ROCESS by combining analysis models with business rules and policies to create a piece of logic that is based on the evidence of the organization's information but tempered with its policies and rules. The completed decision model may also be executed in an information pattern detection process.

Consequences

Benefits:

- The information analytics node keeps the specialized tools with their high workload cost in a segregated environment where the ad hoc nature of the workload will not impact other users.

Liabilities:

- This information node relies on its information supply chain to ensure it has good information to work with.

Example Resolved

MCHS Trading buys a high-quality analytics package that supports both the information pattern discovery process and the information decision definition process. This is run as an information analytics node. It is fed using an INFORMATION MINING STORE that is the root node of a single view information supply chain.

Known Uses

The information analysis node represents an analytics package that is bought and installed as a separate system. Such a package can offer sophisticated capabilities for understanding and manipulating information in pursuit of the perfect model. It is called out as a special type of information node in the pattern language because it uses information supplied to it to develop logic that will drive the organization's business. As such, it needs to be supplied with information through a well-defined information supply chain; otherwise, the models created by the package will probably be incorrect.

Related Patterns

The INFORMATION MINING STORE is designed to supply information to the information analysis node.

Information Mining Store

Context

Analytics processing, such as the INFORMATION PATTERN DISCOVERY PROCESS, requires huge quantities of correlated, but highly denormalized information, both current and historical, to allow the analytics software to explore and discover the patterns in the information values that can be used to report on past events and predict future events.

Problem

An organization needs to create an effective source of information for information pattern discovery (data mining).

Example

MCHS Trading wants to implement a next best action solution. This uses analytics to offer its customers relevant offers, information, and services depending on their individual interests. MCHS Trading needs to analyze information about its customers' interests, buying patterns, and channel usage along with the pipeline of new and existing products. This information is dispersed among MCHS Trading's production systems.

How should this information be made available to the analysis processes?

Forces

- **High processing requirement**—The INFORMATION PATTERN DISCOVERY PROCESS searches for patterns of values in one or more information collections. This processing can take considerable computing resources (memory, CPU, and disk I/O) to perform this activity.
- **Disparate sources of information**—The information to be analyzed often originates from a variety of sources.

Solution

Create an information store that has flat structures in its information collections to allow the information pattern discovery process to work most effectively.

This information store is called an information mining store. Figure 5.63 shows how it is used.

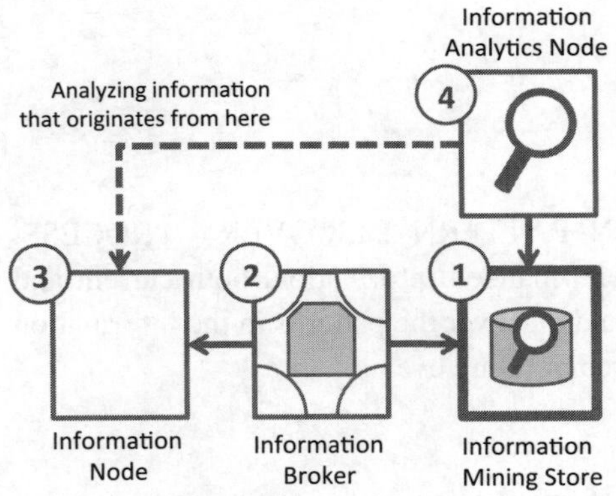

Figure 5.63 Information Mining Store solution.

The numbers on the diagram in Figure 5.63 refer to these notes:

1. This is the information mining node.
2. It is provisioned using an information broker.
3. The information collections in this new node are provisioned as required from other information nodes. Typically, the source of information would be one of the big data nodes such as the INFORMATION WAREHOUSE. However, it may be provisioned from INFORMATION MARTS or operational information nodes such as the OPERATIONAL STATUS STORE or INFORMATION ASSET HUB.
4. Once provisioned, the information analysis node uses the information mining store as a source of information to analyze. It makes direct INFORMATION SERVICE calls on the information mining store to retrieve the information.

The information mining store can be used in two modes:

- The analytics may be part of an ongoing solution where the analytics models are in production, driving an aspect of the business. In this case, the information mining store must be kept up to date with the latest information to ensure the analysis is working on good information. The information broker should provision the information mining store using MIRRORING PROVISIONING and the analytics processing should access the information using REFERENCE USAGE only.
- The analytics may be part of an ad hoc project with a short lifetime. In this case, the information broker uses SNAPSHOT PROVISIONING to populate the information mining store. If the analytics processing makes changes to the information, for example, to understand the effect of particular changes to the information, the information broker can repopulate the affected information collections by rerunning the snapshot provisioning.

Consequences

Benefits:

- The analysis processing is not affecting the performance of the production systems.
- The data scientists do not need to be given access to the production systems.
- The analysis can start with a small subset of the information and grow the sample size as confidence in the analytics model increases.

Liabilities:

- The information mining store may be provisioned with sensitive or valuable information. This must be properly safeguarded.
- The information stored in an information mining store gradually decays and needs refreshing at regular intervals for the results to remain relevant.

Example Resolved

MCHS Trading creates two information mining stores for the analysis of its customer, order, and product information as seen in Figure 5.64.

For the next best action solution, MCHS Trading creates an information mining store called Next Best Action Analysis Store. It is refreshed regularly from the Reporting Hub using **M**IRRORING **P**ROVISIONING to ensure the analysis continues to use the latest information.

From time to time, MCHS Trading also has an information mining store called Marketing Analysis Store that is used for ad hoc analysis of product sales to plan marketing campaigns. This node is provisioned from the Reporting Hub using **S**NAPSHOT **P**ROVISIONING whenever it is needed.

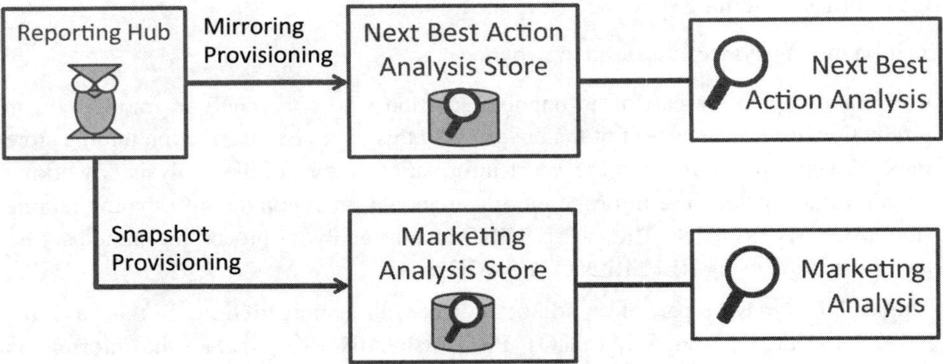

Figure 5.64 Information mining stores in MCHS Trading.

Known Uses

Using an information mining store to work on a local copy of an organization's information is a common approach for analysis. Often, it is implemented as a directory of files, or a database or data mart. This is also known as a type 4 operational data store (ODS) that is supporting data mining or related processes.

Related Patterns

The **I**NFORMATION **A**NALYSIS **N**ODE runs the information processes that will analyze the information hosted by the information mining store.

Summary of Information Nodes

The information node pattern group provides some insight into the wide variety of systems that an organization may deploy. Some are applications, directly supporting the business. These systems are the source of new information for most information supply chains. They may also be the destination—particularly as more operations become real time. In between them, there are the provisioning, consolidating, and managing information nodes that connect, transform, consolidate, and redistribute information between the applications. Many of these nodes are supported by basic middleware software, such as databases and application servers. What we have tried to capture in these patterns are the roles these information nodes play in the end-to-end management of an organization's information.

The sophistication of the nodes that link the applications has grown steadily over time. The integration and consistency of an organization's operation is necessary for financial, regulatory, and market reasons. Customers expect to be treated as individuals and, at the same time, expect an organization to act as a single coherent unit toward them. As a result, these nodes have become business critical to the organization.

Information nodes such as the OPERATIONAL STATUS STORE, INFORMATION WAREHOUSE, and INFORMATION ASSET HUB are well established in many organizations today. We also included some newer kinds of information nodes, though their roles are still evolving. These are the MAP-REDUCE NODE and STREAMING ANALYTICS NODE. They are designed to handle new sources of information, such as high-velocity external sensor/device readings and huge volumes of textual and other types of media information. This information is available to the organization from external sources. It seems relevant, but needs a different approach to process it. Existing enterprise information is purposefully collected and reflects activity within the organization. The efforts are around collecting it, maintaining it, and getting value from all of it. These new sources of information reflect a wide variety of activity, and contain values that are largely irrelevant, or of dubious quality. However, hidden within them are nuggets of very valuable information. Finding these nuggets requires more of an opportunistic, prospecting approach to be continuously applied and, when they are found, to act on them immediately, typically by feeding them into the information supply chains of the existing systems.

The next few years are going to be very exciting as we learn how best to handle this enormous influx of data. No doubt new information node patterns will emerge as our understanding and experience evolves.

Summary

This chapter focused on what is called *information at rest*. It covered:

- **The INFORMATION SERVICE pattern group**—The interfaces to information.
- **The INFORMATION COLLECTION pattern group**—The stores of information.
- **The INFORMATION ENTRY pattern group**—The organization of information within the information collections, including how information is identified (the INFORMATION KEY pattern group).
- **The INFORMATION NODE pattern group**—The servers that host all these capabilities along with the INFORMATION PROCESS pattern group (Chapter 7, "Information Processing") that manipulates the information.

The next chapter, Chapter 6, "Information in Motion," is about *information in motion*. This describes the mechanisms for moving information between the information collections in different information nodes.

Chapter 6

Information in Motion

This chapter discusses the patterns that cover how information is shared between the organization's information nodes. There are two pattern groups:

- The information requests patterns cover how information is accessed directly from a remote information node.
- The information flow patterns cover how information is copied between information nodes.

Figure 6.1 shows where these pattern groups fit in the pattern language.

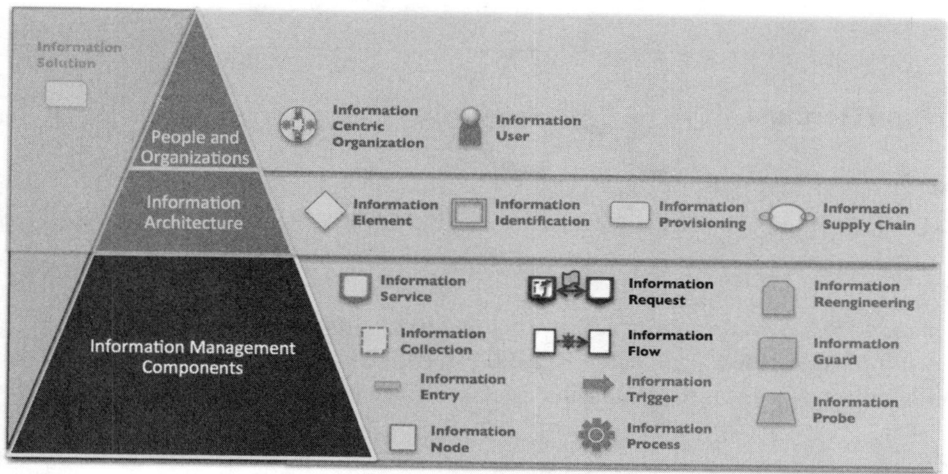

Figure 6.1 The information in motion pattern groups within the context of the pattern language.

Information Request Patterns

Information processes need to access stored information while they are running. This needs to be retrieved synchronously as part of the information process's logic. The information it needs may be in an information collection that is local (that is, running in the same information node as the information process) or remote (residing in a different information node).

The information request pattern group covers the basic mechanism for requesting information from a remote information collection. Information requests are the underpinning of the **R**EMOTE **I**NFORMATION **S**ERVICE because they enable an information process to interact with an information collection on a remote information node as if it were local.

The lead information request pattern is shown in Table 6.1 and covers the basic mechanism of an information request. This is followed by summaries of more specialized interactions that cover different operations, such as create, update, and delete.

Table 6.1 Information Request Pattern Summary

Icon	Pattern Name	Problem	Solution
	INFORMATION **R**EQUEST	An information process needs to work with information located on a remote information node.	Open a communication link with the remote information node and exchange the information and associated commands using an agreed-upon protocol.

Information Request

Context

An organization's information is distributed among its **I**NFORMATION **N**ODES.

Problem

An information process needs to work with information located on a remote information node.

The information process will call a **R**EMOTE **I**NFORMATION **S**ERVICE to access the information collection. How is the remote information service implemented?

Example

MCHS Trading's Customer-Care application needs to work with customer details that are stored in the Customer Hub application.

Forces

- Multiple information processes often work with the same stored information. This information may be located on a different information node.

- An information node is not always running.
- The structure in which information is stored is not always the most convenient structure for a consuming information process.
- If the structure of an information collection is changed, it may affect all information processes that use it.

Solution

Open a communication link with the remote information node and exchange the information and associated commands using an agreed-upon protocol.

The full exchange is described below and it is illustrated in Figure 6.2 that follows:

1. The information process makes a request to the remote information service, passing parameters that described the request.
2. The remote information service formats the request and its parameters into an **I**NFOR-MATION **P**AYLOAD and sends it to the information node where the information collection resides.
3. The information payload is received, unpacked, and the parameters are used to invoke a local information service.
4. The results of the local information service are formatted into another information payload and sent back to the originator to be returned to the information process.

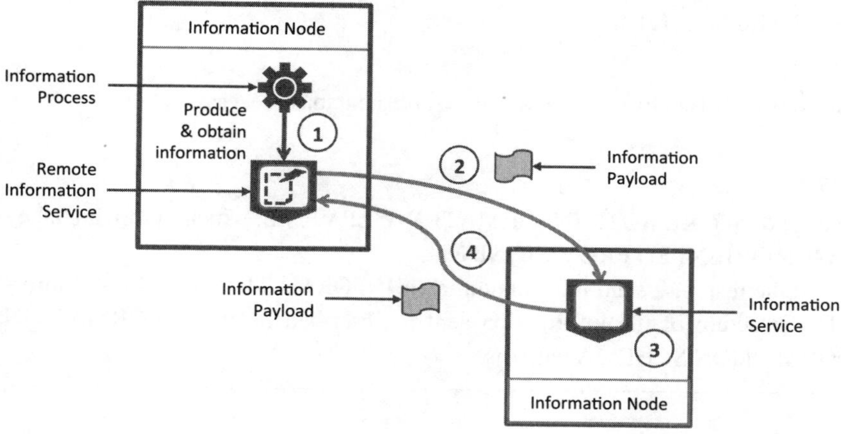

Figure 6.2 Information Request solution.

Consequences

Benefits:

- The information request pattern provides up-to-date information to information processes located in different information nodes and reduces the need to make copies of information.

Liabilities:

- The information node where the information collection is located must be operational whenever the information process needs information. In addition, the information service, or information process, may need to reformat the information to support the processing needs of the calling information process.

Example Resolved

The Customer-Care application uses an information request to access the customer details stored in the Customer Hub.

Known Uses

The information request pattern is used for most types of remote procedure calls. These are available through the following types of technology:

- Web services technology
- Remote procedure calls (such as Enterprise Java Beans) supported by standards such as Java Enterprise Edition (JEE)
- REST
- ODBC and JDBC calls between an application and a database server

Related Patterns

Information requests underpin **R**EMOTE **I**NFORMATION **S**ERVICES, which in turn are a key capability of **S**ERVICE **O**RIENTED **P**ROVISIONING.

The request and the response send information in an **I**NFORMATION **P**AYLOAD information element. The structure of the information sent is described by the **I**NFORMATION **M**ODEL and **I**NFORMATION **S**CHEMA patterns.

Variations of the Information Request Pattern

The pattern summaries in Table 6.2 describe more specialized types of information requests. They describe how information that an information process has produced is distributed. Notice that the information for distribution is sent in the request.

Table 6.2 Information Request Patterns—Distribution

Icon	Pattern Name	Problem	Solution
	CREATE INFORMATION REQUEST	An information process needs to create an information entry in an information collection located on a remote node.	Send the information to the remote information node. The information node will store the information and return an acknowledgment as possibly the key value of the new information.
	DELETE INFORMATION REQUEST	An information process needs to delete an information entry in an information collection located on a remote node.	Send enough data to identify the information that should be removed to the remote information node. The remote information node will remove the requested information and send an acknowledgment that it has gone.
	UPDATE INFORMATION REQUEST	An information process needs to update an information entry in an information collection located on a remote node.	Send the new values, and enough details to identify the information to be updated to the remote information node. The remote information node will update the requested information and send an acknowledgment that it has completed the task.

Table 6.3 shows how information is retrieved from a remote information collection. Notice that the information being distributed is sent in the response.

Table 6.3 Information Request Patterns—Remote Retrieval

Icon	Pattern Name	Problem	Solution
	RETRIEVE ONE INFORMATION REQUEST	An information process needs an information entry on a remote information node.	Send enough details to the remote information node to describe the information that is required. The remote information node will send the information as a response.
n	RETRIEVE CURSOR INFORMATION REQUEST	An information process needs to step through a selection of information entries one at a time. These information entries are located on a remote information node.	Send enough details to the remote information node to describe the information that is required. The remote information node will respond with a cursor. The cursor can be used to retrieve each piece of information using the **R**ETRIEVE **O**NE **I**NFORMATION **R**EQUEST pattern.

Icon	Pattern Name	Problem	Solution
	RETRIEVE COLLECTION INFORMATION REQUEST	An information process needs to retrieve a group of related information entries located on a remote information node.	Send enough details to the remote information node to describe the information that is required. The remote information node will send the information in a data batch as a response.

Table 6.4 lists information requests that trigger information processes in a remote information node. This is useful when some processing in the remote information node can reduce the amount of information that must be sent over the network.

Table 6.4 Information Request Patterns—Triggering

Icon	Pattern Name	Problem	Solution
	EVENT INFORMATION REQUEST	Information describing an event needs to be passed between information nodes.	A description of the event is packaged into a payload and a one-way information flow is used to send it to the destination(s).
	RUN PROCESS INFORMATION REQUEST	An information process needs to run another information process located in a different information node.	Send details to the remote information node to run the information process and return the results synchronously.
	INITIATE PROCESS INFORMATION REQUEST	An information process needs to initiate work in a different information node.	Send details of the information process to the remote information node. The remote information node replies with an acknowledgment that it has received the request.
	BATCH INFORMATION REQUEST	An information node has accumulated a number of required changes to one or more information collections located on a remote information node. How can these changes be executed?	Send the requests as a data batch to the remote information node.

Summary of Information Requests

The information request patterns describe the typical synchronous call-response operations that are made between different information nodes. They assume both information nodes are running, and the information is returned in real time so it can be used immediately in the calling information process.

For some information transfer, it is not practical to copy the information between information nodes on demand because there is either too much processing required for the response to be timely, or the same processing would be required many times as the information request is made repeatedly.

The information flow pattern group describes how information is copied and transformed between information collections. This has the effect of performing the transformation once only, in anticipation of the information process requesting it.

Information Flow Patterns

Your existing systems (**I**NFORMATION **N**ODES) maintain valuable information. How do you tap into them to provide a flow of this information to other information nodes with minimal disruption to their current deployment?

The simple answer is to use an **I**NFORMATION **B**ROKER as an external agent to take the information from one or more information nodes (called the source information nodes), transform it and deliver it to the information nodes that need it (see Figure 6.3). The recipients of the information are called the destination information nodes.

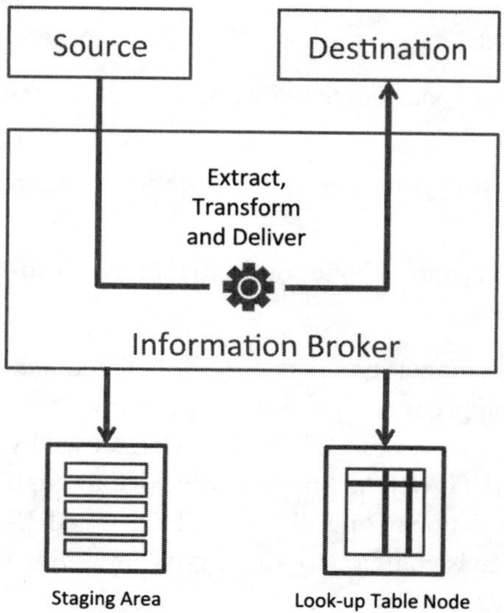

Figure 6.3 The role of an information broker.

Information flows define patterns of provisioning information processes that move information between information nodes. The movement of information using an information flow is typically asynchronous and often involves multiple information processes to complete the transfer. These processes manage the filtering, routing, and transformation of the information, and often include the use of **S**TAGING **A**REA information nodes to store intermediate results and **L**OOK-UP **T**ABLES to translate between different code values.

Using information flows tends to increase latency of the transfer of information. However, the use of the staging areas can increase resiliency for the situation where either the source or the destination is temporarily unavailable for some reason and keeping the integration logic external to the information nodes running the business enables the information supply chain to be reconfigured with minimal impact to the core business systems.

The lead pattern for the information flow pattern group is shown in Table 6.5.

Table 6.5 Information Flow Pattern Summary

Icon	Pattern Name	Problem	Solution
	INFORMATION **F**LOW	Information needs to flow between information nodes with minimal impact to their current operation.	Use an information trigger to start an information process to control the movement of information. This information process is responsible for extracting the required information from the appropriate sources, re-engineering it, and delivering it to the destination information nodes.

The rest of the patterns are divided into three groups:

- **Routing patterns**—For moving information from one source to one destination information node
- **Consolidating patterns**—For moving information from multiple source information nodes to a single destination
- **Distributing patterns**—For moving information from a single source to multiple destination information nodes

Note that multiple information flows may be sequenced to support complex provisioning requirements or address situations where multiple information supply chains cross. For instance, a **S**YNCHRONIZED **C**ONSOLIDATION information flow may feed into a **S**TAGING **A**REA used by a **P**ARTITIONED **R**OUTING pattern to another **S**TAGING **A**REA, which is processed through an **O**RDERED **D**ISTRIBUTION pattern to deliver information to an **I**NFORMATION **W**AREHOUSE. This complex type of information flow sequence is common to extract, transform, load (ETL) processing and underlies **I**NFORMATION **P**ROVISIONING.

Information Flow

Context

An organization is designing how information should flow between information collections located in different information nodes.

Problem

Information needs to flow between information nodes with minimal impact to their current operation.

An organization is designing the implementation of a flow of information between information nodes. The source of the information is an existing information node. The destination may be a new information node, or an existing one, too. Neither information node currently has the capability to flow the information because it is not core to their operation.

This movement needs to be reliable, predictable, and asynchronous.

Example

Orders need to be transferred from the order-taking systems, such as E-Shop, to the Shipping system. Customers can order from E-Shop at all hours of the day. However, the order-processing component of the Shipping system is not continuously available—it is offline at certain times of the night to feed order information to the inventory system.

Forces

- **Availability differs**—The availability of the source and destination information nodes may differ.
- **Processing limitations**—Processing capability may be limited in the source or destination information node whether due to system criticality, information volume, or platform limitations.
- **Transformation required**—Additional processing is required to transform the information before the destination can receive it.
- **Complexity impacts design**—As more information flows handling more information collections and more information processing are introduced, it becomes more difficult to design optimal information flows and reuse existing information flows.

Solution

Use an INFORMATION TRIGGER to start an INFORMATION PROCESS to control the movement of information. This information process is responsible for extracting the required information from the appropriate sources, reengineering it, and delivering it to the destination information nodes.

The information trigger that starts an information flow may be initiated from the source or destination information node, or from another information node such as an **I**NFORMATION **B**ROKER. Refer to the information trigger patterns for more information on how each approach works.

The information process that is started is typically a provisioning information process. It may run in either the source or destination information nodes. However, it is more usual for it to run in an information broker. See Figure 6.4.

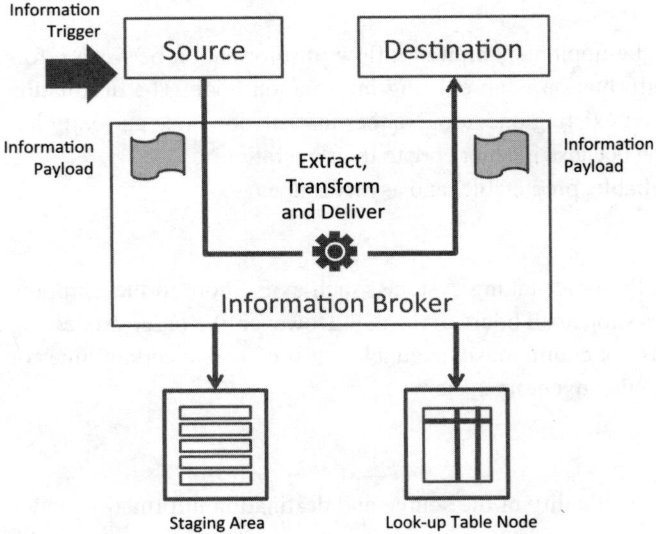

Figure 6.4 Information Flow solution.

The provisioning information process often includes **I**NFORMATION **R**EENGINEERING **S**TEPS to transform the information into the required format for the destination. It may also include appropriate **I**NFORMATION **G**UARDS and **I**NFORMATION **P**ROBES to protect and monitor the flow of information, respectively.

The **I**NFORMATION **(RE)D**EPLOYMENT **P**ROCESS is the most commonly used information process for implementing information flows because it offers the most flexible capabilities for transforming the information as it flows between the source and destination.

Consequences

Benefits:

- Complexity is reduced in the source and destination information nodes.
- Information flows can be standardized and reused in multiple conditions.
- Variability in access to information nodes can be accommodated.

Liabilities:

- Information flows can increase latency between information nodes, particularly as the components within the information flows grow more complex.
- Information flows may require additional storage capacity for new staging nodes.

Example Resolved

In the case of MCHS Trading's order information from E-Shop, a staging node is used to receive all incoming orders. The orders are collected until a specific information trigger starts a subsequent process to batch the information payloads in a standard format and deliver them to the Shipping system.

Known Uses

Information flows describe how information moves from one information collection to another. The technology that supports them may be an ETL engine, a messaging engine, or an Enterprise Service Bus (ESB). Usage includes the following:

- Synchronizing multiple applications that store the same type of information
- Acquiring and merging or consolidating information collections
- Distributing or broadcasting information to multiple destination information collections
- Populating and maintaining information collections stored in an INFORMATION WAREHOUSE, INFORMATION MART, or INFORMATION ASSET HUB
- Transforming and delivering messages from incoming information nodes to operational applications

Related Patterns

Information flows are used to implement INFORMATION PROVISIONING and different information flows may be connected together to support a specific provisioning process. They work with INFORMATION PAYLOADS and include provisioning INFORMATION PROCESSES that execute in an INFORMATION BROKER. These information processes may store intermediate results in a STAGING AREA and use LOOK-UP TABLES to transform values. The information processes may also include INFORMATION REENGINEERING, INFORMATION GUARD, and INFORMATION PROBE patterns as steps within their implementation.

The INFORMATION IDENTIFICATION patterns can provide details on the information structures in each information node used in the information flows to ensure that the information flows are correctly constructed with the right steps.

Where no changes to information are required between a source and a target and both are available at the same time, the information flow can use an INFORMATION REPLICATION process pattern. If the information in the source needs to be read and removed, use an **I**NFORMATION **R**ELOCATION process pattern instead. Specialized information flows support more complex process requirements.

Routing Information Flows

The routing information flows in Table 6.6 cover the sending of information from a single source to a single destination information node.

Table 6.6 Routing Information Flow Pattern Summaries

Icon	Pattern Name	Problem	Solution
	STAGED **R**OUTING	Information needs to flow between two information nodes that are not always able to participate in the transfer at the same time, or an information node is unable to take responsibility for distributing information to a downstream node.	Insert a staging area in between the source and destination node to act as a temporary store for the information that is passing between them.
	PARTITIONED **R**OUTING	Some of the information that is flowing between two information nodes needs additional processing before the downstream information node can accept and handle the data.	Identify which information needs the additional processing at the point it is sent. Route this information via an intermediate information collection, which feeds the additional processing, before forwarding it on to the downstream node.
	BUFFERED **R**OUTING	Large quantities of information are arriving continuously and need to be captured, filtered, and organized.	Divide the problem into two parts: storing the information as it arrives into rolling time-based buffers and processing batches of information from each buffer when it is full.
	FILTERED **R**OUTING	A downstream information collection does not require or cannot consume all information from the upstream information collection.	Filter the information collection to send only the information required in the downstream information collection.

Icon	Pattern Name	Problem	Solution
	SUMMARIZED ROUTING	A downstream information collection cannot consume detailed information or requires summarized or aggregated information from the upstream information collection.	Summarize the information collection to send only the information required in the downstream information collection.

Staged Routing

Context

An organization is designing how information should flow between information collections located in different information nodes.

Problem

Information needs to flow between two or more information nodes that are not always able to participate in the transfer at the same time; or an information node is unable to take responsibility for distributing information to a downstream node.

Example

MCHS Trading needs to provide its Customer-Care operations with faster access for order tracking to address customer complaints and missing orders.

Forces

- **Processing must be done external to the source or target**—Information must be staged for additional processing from a source information node before it can be used in the destination information node.
- **Timeliness varies**—Where latency must be minimized, processing must occur immediately; where less critical, data may be batched for processing.

Solution

Insert a staging area in between the source and destination node to act as a temporary store for the information that is passing between them.

Divide any processing required into the following:

1. An information process for extracting information from the source information node and storing it in the staging area

2. An information process for retrieving the information from the staging area and passing it to the destination

Reengineering the information for the destination can be the responsibility for either of these information processes. It is shown in the second process in Figure 6.5.

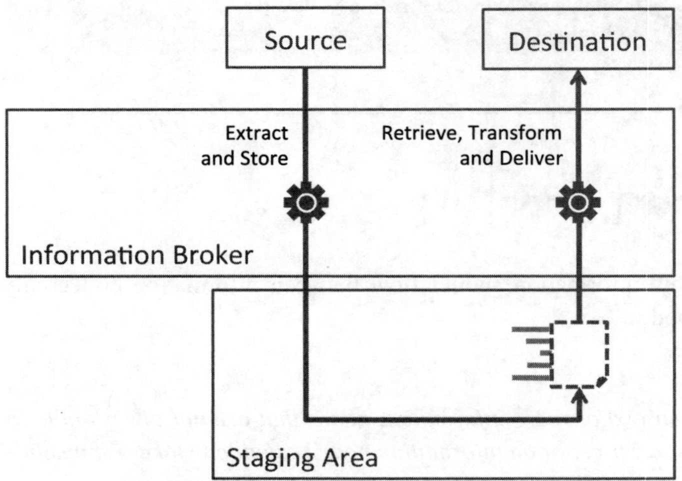

Figure 6.5 Staged Routing solution.

Consequences

Benefits:

- Complexity is reduced in the source and destination information nodes.
- Information flows can be standardized and reused in multiple conditions.
- Variability in access to information nodes can be accommodated.

Liabilities:

- Information flows can increase latency between information nodes, particularly as the components within the information flows grow more complex.
- Information flows may require additional storage capacity for new staging nodes.

Example Resolved

In the case of MCHS Trading's Customer-Care application, a new staging node is introduced after the order information processing queue, which serves the purpose of linking the order flow directly to the Customer-Care process. Customer-Care now has immediate access to all order information, reducing customer complaints and missing orders.

Known Uses

Staged routing is most common in ETL engines or messaging engines. Where transformation of information is needed, the former is more likely. Where timely delivery on an ongoing basis is necessary, the latter is more likely.

Usage includes the following:

- Synchronizing multiple applications that store the same type of information in APPLICATION NODES
- Acquiring and merging or consolidating information collections
- Distributing or broadcasting information to multiple destination information collections
- Populating and maintaining information collections stored in an INFORMATION WAREHOUSE, INFORMATION MART, or INFORMATION ASSET HUB
- Transforming and delivering messages from incoming information nodes to operational applications

Related Patterns

Staged routing is one form of information flow used to implement INFORMATION PROVISIONING. It works with INFORMATION PAYLOADS and includes provisioning INFORMATION PROCESSES that execute in an INFORMATION BROKER. Staged routing flows store intermediate results in a STAGING AREA. The information processes may also include INFORMATION REENGINEERING, INFORMATION GUARD, and INFORMATION PROBE patterns as steps within their implementation.

The INFORMATION IDENTIFICATION patterns can provide information on the structure of information in each information node, including that of the STAGING AREA.

Where data volumes are high, use the PARTITIONED ROUTING or BUFFERED ROUTING pattern to control or divide up the workload. If not all data is required, use the FILTERED ROUTING pattern to minimize processing requirements and time to process.

Where information must be processed as soon as it is available and needs minimal or no transformation, then an INFORMATION QUEUING process pattern may be used. If information needs significant transformation and timing is less of an issue, an INFORMATION (RE)-DEPLOYMENT process pattern may be a better option.

Partitioned Routing

Context

An organization is designing how information should flow between information collections located in different information nodes.

Problem

Some of the information that is flowing between two information nodes needs additional processing before the downstream information node can accept it.

Example

MCHS Trading needs different processing for customer name and address information than for order information coming from E-Shop that is simply passed through to the Shipping system.

Forces

- **Some data needs extra processing**—Some information must be partitioned for additional processing from a source information node before it can be used in the destination information node.
- **Computationally intensive processing**—Some processing steps require dedicated information nodes to achieve the computations required in the necessary time frame.
- **Timeliness is critical**—The processing time must be minimized.

Solution

Identify which information needs the additional processing at the point it is sent. Route this information via an intermediate information collection, which feeds the additional processing, before forwarding it on to the downstream node.

Partitioning allows multiple computational activities to occur simultaneously, reducing the overall processing time. It can be extended to include more than one partition depending on specific requirements. As long as sets of information can be segmented, multiple partitions may perform the same or different steps.

See Figure 6.6.

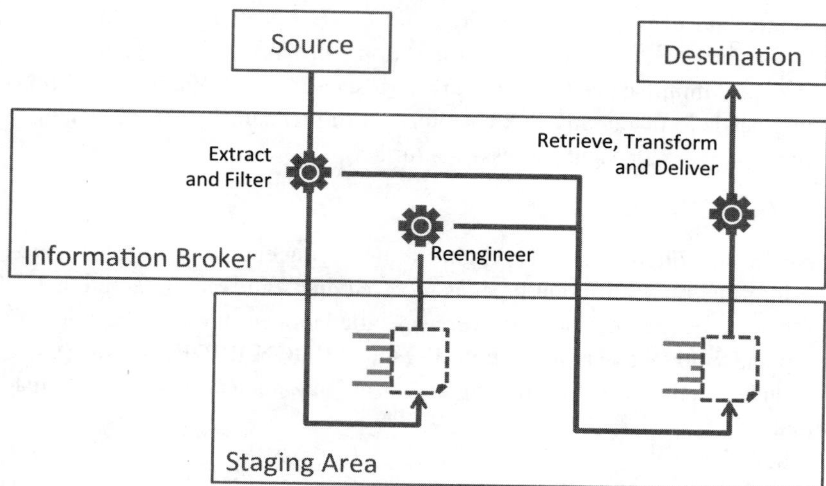

Figure 6.6 Partitioned Routing solution.

Consequences

Benefits:

- Complexity is reduced in the source and destination information nodes.
- Information flows can be standardized and reused in multiple conditions.
- Variability in access to information nodes can be accommodated.
- Processing time for all information may be reduced.
- Only information requiring additional processing needs to be partitioned reducing the volume of information through that information node.

Liabilities:

- Information flows can increase latency between information nodes, particularly if some information must wait for the processing of partitioned information to complete.
- Information flows may require additional storage capacity for new staging nodes.
- Rules for partitioning must be maintained and may not readily respond to changing business conditions.

Example Resolved

MCHS Trading introduces a partitioned routing through a new information node to handle the additional processing needed for name and address information on E-Shop orders. This includes specialized **I**NFORMATION **R**EENGINEERING steps to **S**TANDARDIZE **D**ATA, **E**NRICH

DATA with demographics and geospatial information, and LINK ENTRIES to existing customer details in the Customer Hub. They add distinct partitions for North American and European customers as they expect minimal need to link data across sales regions. Within each region, because MCHS Trading needs to potentially link customers with nicknames or maiden names, they do not partition the customer name and address data further.

Known Uses

Partitioned routing may be supported by an ETL engine, a messaging engine, or an ESB. Partitioning is used where information of different types is received and some require additional or different processing (such as account transactions over a specified monetary value). Partitioning may also be used to spread workload across multiple INFORMATION BROKERS such as in parallel processing engines—in this case, partitioning may occur automatically as new information nodes are identified.

Usage includes the following:

- Synchronizing multiple applications that store the same type of information in APPLICATION NODES
- Acquiring and merging or consolidating information collections
- Populating and maintaining information collections stored in an INFORMATION WAREHOUSE, INFORMATION MART, or INFORMATION ASSET HUB
- Transforming and delivering messages from incoming information nodes to operational applications

Related Patterns

Information flows are used to implement INFORMATION PROVISIONING. They work with INFORMATION PAYLOADs and include provisioning INFORMATION PROCESSES that execute in an INFORMATION BROKER. Partitioned routing may store intermediate results in a STAGING AREA. The information processes may also include INFORMATION REENGINEERING, INFORMATION GUARD, and INFORMATION PROBE patterns as steps within their implementation.

The INFORMATION IDENTIFICATION patterns can provide information on the structure of information in each information node, including that of any STAGING AREA. Partitioning may be based on an INFORMATION KEY, a specific INFORMATION ELEMENT, or may need to be derived through another INFORMATION REENGINEERING step.

Use the BUFFERED ROUTING pattern if data volumes are high and unpredictable and where you cannot readily divide the workload based on an INFORMATION ELEMENT, or where latency must be minimized for near-real-time processing.

If the partitioned information goes to a separate, independent target information node, use a DISTRIBUTING INFORMATION FLOW pattern.

Buffered Routing

Context

An organization is designing how information should flow between information collections located in different information nodes.

Problem

Large quantities of information are arriving continuously that needs to be captured, filtered, and organized.

Sometimes there is a mismatch in the volume of information being produced by a source information node and the ability of the destination node to consume it. The information flow that links these information nodes together must balance the ability of the source information node to produce information against the ability of the destination to consume it.

Example

MCHS Trading started collecting social media data about the products its customers were interested in. The purpose was to understand and anticipate which products would sell well to different groups of people. There were two use cases for this data. The first was an immediate, operational use of the information to anticipate required stock levels and identify potential candidate products for promotions. This is covered in the **S**TREAMING **A**NALYTICS **N**ODE pattern.

The second use was to create a historical record of the correlation of the social media content with the actual buying patterns of their customers. This second use of information requires summarized information from the social media data to be fed and correlated into their **H**ISTORICAL **S**YSTEM OF **R**ECORD called the Reporting Hub. The issue they faced was how to organize the processing required to translate the insight from the social media data into the data warehouse structures at a fast enough rate to keep up with the incoming data.

Forces

- **Data is constantly arriving**—Data generated from the real-world activity, such as social media data, or sensor data, continuously arrives. It is necessary to process it at the rate it is captured because otherwise you never get an opportunity to catch up.
- **Data value degrades rapidly**—This data contains a huge amount of detail about individual **I**NFORMATION **E**VENTS. The value of this level of detail tends to degrade fairly rapidly. To get the maximum value out of it, it is necessary to make use of the detail as soon as possible. Summarized versions of this data, when aggregated together, can provide interesting perspectives with longer-term value.

Solution

Divide the problem into two parts: storing the information as it arrives into rolling time-based buffers and processing batches of information from each buffer when it is full.

See Figure 6.7. The objective of this solution is twofold:

- To minimize the contention on the storage media by only having one information process accessing it at any one time
- To balance the processing power given to the computing intensive work of summarizing and collating information into the destination

The information broker working with the source is focused on filling the staging areas with information. It fills one then moves on to the next. When it has filled them all, it starts again, filling the first one.

In the meantime, one or more information brokers are unloading the filled staging areas. They must complete their processing before the source's information broker starts to reuse their staging area. They are responsible for summarizing and collating the raw information from the source and transferring the results to the destination.

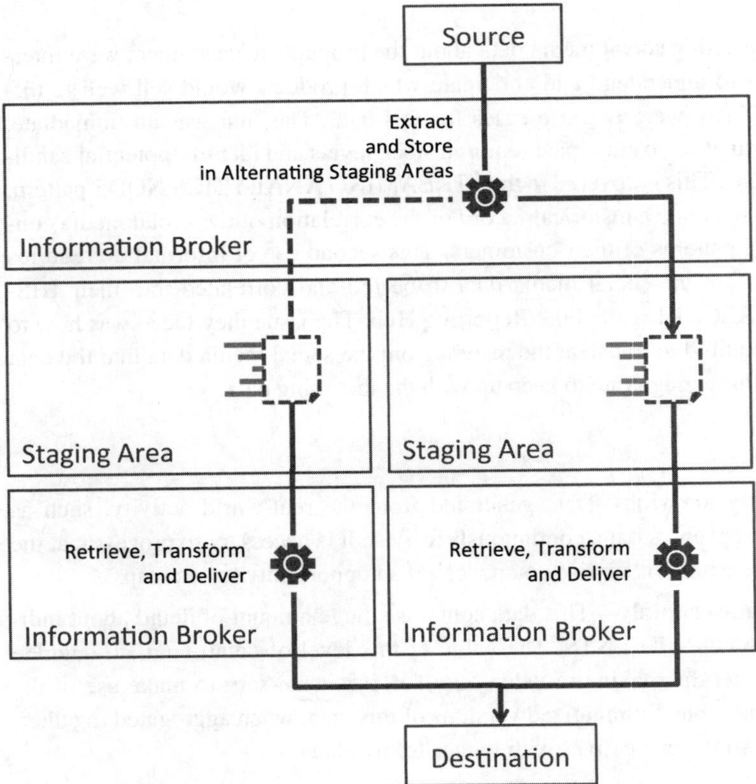

Figure 6.7 Buffered Routing solution.

Consequences

Benefits:

- By separating the process of capturing the information into chunks and then processing each chunk, it is possible to scale out the computing intensive work of the destination information brokers. The result is a flexible implementation that can adapt to changes (usually increases) in data volume.

Liabilities:

- The trick when using this pattern is to have sufficient destination information brokers to handle the velocity of the incoming data. It is also important to have a contingency, or spare capacity, in the staging areas, for when the destination is not available—for example, during maintenance.

Example Resolved

MCHS Trading use the buffered routing pattern to handle the summarization and collating of the insight from the social media data into its Reporting Hub.

Known Uses

This pattern is often used when loading large volumes of operational data into an INFORMATION WAREHOUSE. Buffered routing may also be applied when handling widely varying volumes of messages to ensure that message queues are not filled up.

Related Patterns

This pattern is useful when moving data from a STAGING AREA into a HISTORICAL SYSTEM OF RECORD NODE.

Information flows, in general, are used to implement INFORMATION PROVISIONING. They work with INFORMATION PAYLOADs and include provisioning INFORMATION PROCESSES that execute in an INFORMATION BROKER. These information processes using buffered routing store intermediate results in a STAGING AREA. The information processes may also include INFORMATION REENGINEERING, INFORMATION GUARD, and INFORMATION PROBE patterns as steps within their implementation.

The INFORMATION IDENTIFICATION patterns can provide information on the structure of information in each information node used in the information flows.

Use the PARTITIONED ROUTING pattern if data volumes are high but predictable and you can readily divide the workload based on an INFORMATION KEY or INFORMATION ELEMENT.

Filtered Routing

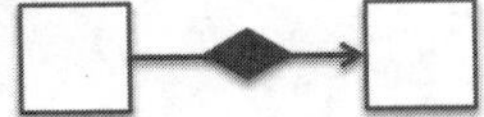

Context

An organization is designing how information should flow between information collections located in different information nodes.

Problem

A downstream information collection does not require or cannot consume all information from the upstream information collection.

Example

MCHS Trading cannot distinguish the types of customers used in its reporting processes.

Forces

- **Not all data is needed**—Information must be filtered from a source information node before it can be used in the destination information node.
- **Processing resources are limited**—The cost to increase processing capability is not justified versus the work that must be done.

Solution

Filter the information collection to send only the information required in the downstream information collection.

See Figure 6.8.

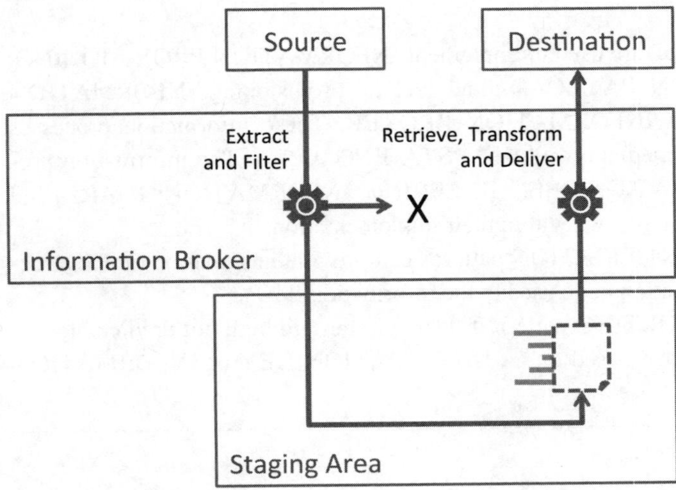

Figure 6.8 Filtered Routing solution.

Consequences

Benefits:

- Complexity is reduced in the source and destination information nodes.
- Information flows can be standardized and reused in multiple conditions.
- Only required information needs to be filtered and passed to the destination information node, reducing the volume of delivered information.
- Timeliness of delivery is improved as processing volume is reduced.
- Variability in access to information nodes can be accommodated.

Liabilities:

- Information flows can increase latency between information nodes, particularly as the components within the information flows grow more complex.
- Rules for filtering must be maintained and may not readily respond to changing business conditions.

Example Resolved

In the case of MCHS Trading's reporting process, only certain customers should be reported so customer information flowing to the Reporting Hub is filtered to address this consideration.

Known Uses

Filtered routing may be supported by an ETL engine, a messaging engine, or an ESB, particularly where the source system cannot segregate outgoing information. Usage includes the following:

- Acquiring and merging or consolidating information collections
- Populating and maintaining information collections stored in an INFORMATION WAREHOUSE, INFORMATION MART, APPLICATION NODE, or INFORMATION ASSET HUB
- Transforming and delivering messages from incoming information nodes to operational applications
- Reporting on information stored in specific information collections

Related Patterns

Information flows are used to implement INFORMATION PROVISIONING. They work with INFORMATION PAYLOADs and include provisioning INFORMATION PROCESSES that execute in an INFORMATION BROKER. Filtered routing stores selected intermediate results in a STAGING AREA. The information processes may also include INFORMATION REENGINEERING, INFORMATION GUARD, and INFORMATION PROBE patterns as steps within their implementation.

The **I**NFORMATION **I**DENTIFICATION patterns can provide information on the structure of information in each information node used in filtered routing. Filtering may be based on an **I**NFORMATION **K**EY, a specific **I**NFORMATION **E**LEMENT, or may need to be derived through another **I**NFORMATION **R**EENGINEERING step such as **S**AMPLE **D**ATA.

If the filtering of information is based on aggregation of specific factors (**I**NFORMATION **K**EYS or **E**LEMENTS), use the **S**UMMARIZED **R**OUTING pattern instead.

Where timeliness is critical and filtering will only remove a small percentage of information, other information flow patterns may be required after filtering (e.g., a **P**ARTITIONED **R**OUTING pattern).

Summarized Routing

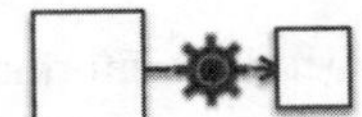

Context

An organization is designing how information should flow between information collections located in different information nodes.

Problem

A downstream information collection cannot consume detailed information or requires summarized or aggregated information from the upstream information collection.

Example

MCHS Trading currently dumps all transactional information into the Reporting Hub. This has significant impact on the ability to generate reports pertaining to customer orders for key product lines as well as performing subsequent analysis.

Forces

- **Information must be summarized**—Information must be summarized from a source information node before it can be used in the destination information node.

Solution

Summarize the information collection to send only the information required in the downstream information collection.

See Figure 6.9.

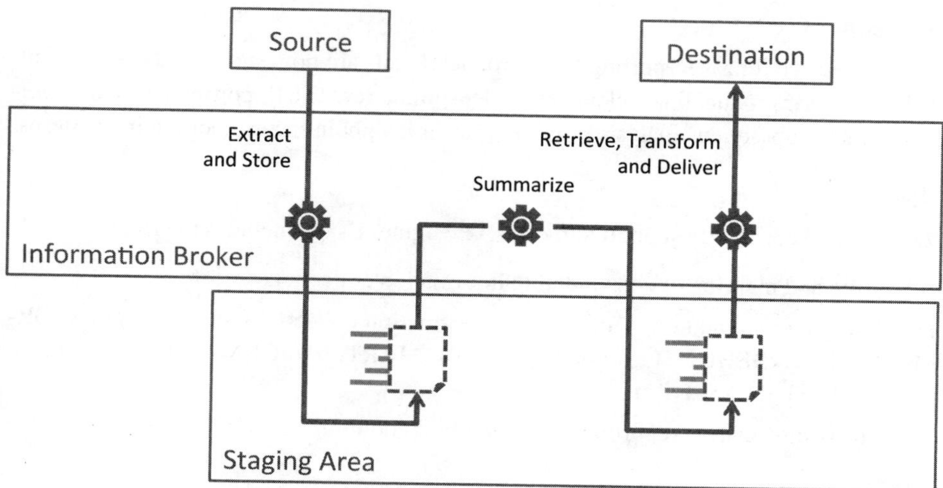

Figure 6.9 Summarized Routing solution.

Consequences

Benefits:

- Complexity is reduced in the source and destination information nodes.
- Information flows can be standardized and reused in multiple conditions.
- Only required information needs to be summarized and passed to the destination information node.
- Variability in access to information nodes can be accommodated.

Liabilities:

- Information flows can increase latency between information nodes, particularly as the components within the information flows grow more complex.
- Rules for summarization must be maintained and may not readily respond to changing business conditions.
- Changes to summarization levels can dramatically impact downstream dependencies (e.g., reporting).

Example Resolved

In the case of MCHS Trading's Reporting Hub, product details are now summarized in the routing process into broader product lines relevant to order summaries. The Reporting Hub can generate reports faster and subsequent analysis provides greater insight into customer buying patterns.

Known Uses

Summarized routing is primarily supported by an ETL engine. Usage includes the following:

- Acquiring and merging or consolidating information collections
- Populating and maintaining summarized information collections stored in an INFORMATION WAREHOUSE, INFORMATION MART, INFORMATION CUBE, or INFORMATION ASSET HUB
- Supporting information reporting and analytics solutions

Related Patterns

Summarized routing is used to implement INFORMATION PROVISIONING. It works with INFORMATION PAYLOADs and includes provisioning INFORMATION PROCESSES that execute in an INFORMATION BROKER. These information processes may store intermediate results in a STAGING AREA and use LOOK-UP TABLES to transform values for summarization. Summarization includes INFORMATION REENGINEERING and may included INFORMATION GUARD and INFORMATION PROBE patterns as steps.

The INFORMATION IDENTIFICATION patterns can provide information on the structure of information in each information node used in the information flows. Summarization may be based on an INFORMATION KEY or a specific INFORMATION ELEMENT, and usually requires a DERIVE VALUES step.

If subset rather than summary information is needed, use a FILTERED ROUTING pattern. In many cases, detail and summary information must be delivered to a target information node. The PARTITIONED ROUTING pattern can support special processing for the summary information while delivering detail as is. Where summary and detail information must be delivered to separate target information nodes, consider following the summarized routing pattern with a specific DISTRIBUTING INFORMATION FLOW pattern such as SYNCHRONIZED DISTRIBUTION if the target updates must occur together.

Consolidating Information Flows

The consolidating information flows in Table 6.7 cover how information from multiple information nodes is consolidated into a single destination information node.

Table 6.7 Consolidating Information Flows Pattern Summaries

Icon	Pattern Name	Problem	Solution
	SYNCHRONIZED CONSOLIDATION	Consistent values need to be consolidated from multiple information nodes.	Use a provisioning information process to extract and assemble the information from the source information nodes and send it on to the downstream information node(s).
	FILTERED CONSOLIDATION	Information from multiple information nodes must be consolidated through specific filters for use by one or more downstream nodes.	Use a provisioning information process to extract and filter the information from the source information nodes and send it on to the downstream information node(s).
	ORDERED CONSOLIDATION	Information needs to be reliably obtained and consolidated from multiple information nodes in a predefined order.	Use a provisioning information process that is able to sequence and process the information from multiple nodes in a given order even in the event of a failure and restart.
	INDEPENDENT CONSOLIDATION	An information node requires information from multiple information nodes as soon as it is available.	Flow the information from each information node independently as soon as it is available. Consolidate their values within the receiving information node.

Synchronized Consolidation

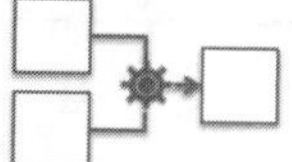

Context

An organization is designing how information should flow between information collections located in different information nodes.

Problem

Consistent values need to be consolidated from multiple information nodes.

Example

MCHS Trading's Customer-Care services requires consolidated information from both the Shipping system for orders and the Customer Hub for customer detail in order to effectively respond to customer service requests. The lack of consistent and timely information from the Shipping system has significantly impacted the quality of customer service.

Forces

- **Consumption of information must be synchronized**—Information must be synchronized between multiple source information nodes before it can be consumed in the destination information node.
- **When information is updated, the changes must be synchronized with all copies**—Without this synchronization, the copies become inconsistent.
- **Information must be consolidated from multiple sources**—Information must be grouped or consolidated from multiple source information nodes before it can be used in the destination information node.
- **Time delays must be minimized**—Latency must be minimized or nonexistent between source and destination information nodes.
- **Timing is different between information sources**—Information must be processed from multiple source information nodes on differing schedules.

Solution

Use a provisioning information process to extract and assemble the information from the source information nodes and send it on to the downstream information node(s).

With a synchronized consolidation, all the data that either system knows about specific information values is sent at the same time.

See Figure 6.10.

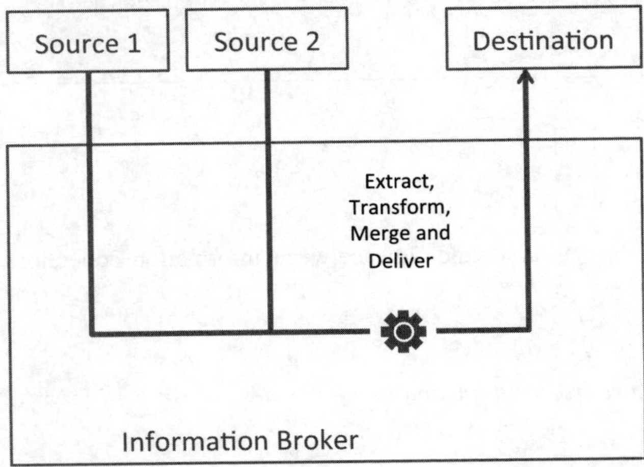

Figure 6.10 Synchronized Consolidation solution.

Consequences

Benefits:

- Consolidation from all sources occurs at the same time, minimizing discrepancies to downstream destinations.
- Synchronization ensures that consistent information is available across the information flow.
- Complexity is reduced in the source and destination information nodes.
- Information flows can be standardized and reused in multiple conditions.
- Variability in access to information nodes can be accommodated.

Liabilities:

- Information flows can increase latency between information nodes, particularly as the components within the information flows grow more complex.
- Synchronization requires coordinated timing across the information flow.
- The synchronization process needs to understand the format of each of the sources and the destination system and the scope of information required.
- Recoding of the processes in the flow may be required every time a change is introduced to the information collection or a new source is added to the information supply chain.

Example Resolved

In the case of MCHS Trading's customer data processing, the introduction of an Order Tracking process allows earlier capture of customer order information. However, it still requires a synchronized consolidation to ensure that the right customer information is available and connected to the order information in a timely manner for Customer-Care services to respond appropriately.

Known Uses

Information flows describe how information moves from one information collection to another. The technology that supports them may be an ETL engine, a messaging engine, or an ESB. Usage includes the following:

- Synchronizing information from multiple sources into an APPLICATION NODE or an OPERATIONAL STATUS STORE
- Acquiring and merging or consolidating information collections
- Populating and maintaining information collections stored in an INFORMATION WAREHOUSE, INFORMATION MART, or INFORMATION ASSET HUB
- Transforming and delivering messages, particularly those entered as multiple parts (e.g., a header, some number of line item details, and a trailer), from incoming information nodes to operational applications

Related Patterns

Information flows are used to implement INFORMATION PROVISIONING. They work with INFORMATION PAYLOADs and include provisioning INFORMATION PROCESSES that execute in an INFORMATION BROKER. These information processes may store intermediate results in a STAGING AREA and use LOOK-UP TABLES to transform values. The information processes may also include INFORMATION REENGINEERING, INFORMATION GUARD, and INFORMATION PROBE patterns as steps within their implementation.

The INFORMATION IDENTIFICATION patterns can provide information on the structure of information in each information node used in the information flows. Synchronized consolidation may be based on an INFORMATION KEY or a specific set of INFORMATION ELEMENTS.

Where the order of information acquisition (i.e., when the values from one system determine which values to pull from another) is critical to consolidation, use an ORDERED CONSOLIDATION pattern instead.

Filtered Consolidation

Context

An organization is designing how information should flow between information collections located in different information nodes.

Problem

Information from multiple information nodes must be consolidated through specific filters for use by one or more downstream nodes.

Example

MCHS Trading's Product Hub application generates and sends out all product catalog information. The Stores only care about product information for those products that they stock on shelves and receive a filtered collection. However, this approach has inhibited the Stores from keeping up with current buying trends, resulting in business shifts to the E-Shop, Mail-Shop, or other companies.

Forces

- **Not all data is needed**—Information must be filtered from multiple source information nodes before it can be consumed in the destination information node.
- **Some information is more valuable than others**—It makes sense to focus on the most valuable and delete the information that has no value at all.

- **Information is spread across multiple sources**—Information must be grouped or consolidated from multiple source information nodes before it can be used in the destination information node.
- **Timing may be distinct in different sources**—Information must be processed from multiple source information nodes on differing schedules.

Solution

Use a provisioning information process to extract and filter the information from the source information nodes and send it on to the downstream information node(s).

See Figure 6.11.

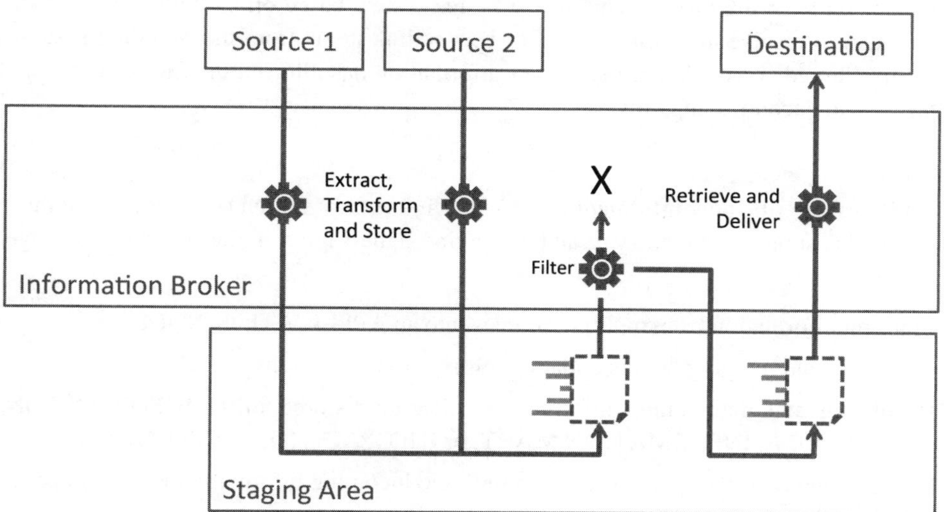

Figure 6.11 Filtered Consolidation solution.

Consequences

Benefits:

- Only required information needs to be filtered and passed to the destination information node, reducing the volume of consolidated and delivered information.
- Complexity is reduced in the source and destination information nodes.
- Information flows can be standardized and reused in multiple conditions.
- Variability in access to information nodes can be accommodated.

Liabilities:

- Information flows can increase latency between information nodes, particularly as the components within the information flows grow more complex.
- Recoding of the processes in the flow may be required every time a change is introduced to the information collection or a new source is added to the information supply chain.
- Rules for filtering must be maintained and may not readily respond to changing business conditions.

Example Resolved

In the case of MCHS Trading's Stores system, the application is enhanced to not only filter the product catalog from the Product Hub to the Stores system based on individual store stock requests, but also to receive an additional list of best-selling items from the Shipping system. This additional filtered consolidation of product information has allowed the Stores to change stocking patterns to become competitive.

Known Uses

Information flows describe how information moves from one information collection to another. The technology that supports them may be an ETL engine, a messaging engine, or an ESB. Usage includes the following:

- Filtering information from multiple sources into an APPLICATION NODE
- Acquiring and merging or consolidating information collections
- Populating and maintaining information collections stored in an INFORMATION WAREHOUSE, INFORMATION MART, or INFORMATION ASSET HUB
- Filtering and delivering messages from multiple incoming information nodes to operational applications

Related Patterns

Information flows are used to implement INFORMATION PROVISIONING. They work with INFORMATION PAYLOADs and include provisioning INFORMATION PROCESSES that execute in an INFORMATION BROKER. These information processes may store intermediate results in a STAGING AREA and use LOOK-UP TABLES to transform values. The information processes may also include INFORMATION REENGINEERING, INFORMATION GUARD, and INFORMATION PROBE patterns as steps within their implementation.

The INFORMATION IDENTIFICATION patterns can provide information on the structure of information in each information node used in the information flows. Filtered consolidation may be based on an INFORMATION KEY or a specific set of INFORMATION ELEMENTS.

Filtered consolidation assumes filtering *during* consolidation. If filtering is to occur independently from the sources *before* consolidation, apply one or more **F**ILTERED **R**OUTING patterns before a consolidating information flow to reduce data volume and processing time. If filtering is based on outcomes *from* the consolidating process, then apply a **F**ILTERED **R**OUTING pattern after a consolidating information flow to reduce data volume to the target information node or a **P**ARTITIONED **D**ISTRIBUTION pattern if different information needs to go to different targets.

Ordered Consolidation

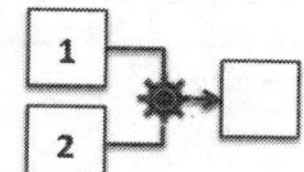

Context

An organization is designing how information should flow between information collections located in different information nodes.

Problem

Information needs to be reliably obtained and consolidated from multiple information nodes in a predefined order.

Example

MCHS Trading's Reporting Hub receives unordered transaction information from the Shipping and Invoicing systems. However, this has created reporting issues as invoices and payments are not correctly linked to the associated orders.

Forces

- **Information must be ordered**—Information must be ordered or sequenced before it can be consumed in the destination information node.
- **Information must be brought from different sources**—Information must be grouped or consolidated from multiple source information nodes before it can be used in the destination information node.
- **Timing of delivery varies**—Information must be delivered from multiple source information nodes on differing schedules.

Solution

Use a provisioning information process that is able to sequence and process the information from multiple nodes in a given order even in the event of a failure and restart.

Ordering can be supported by specific sequencing in retrieving or triggering requests of information from the sources, or by processes that subsequently order the information within the information flow. Ordered consolidation is needed when the values from one system determine which values to pull from another. See Figure 6.12.

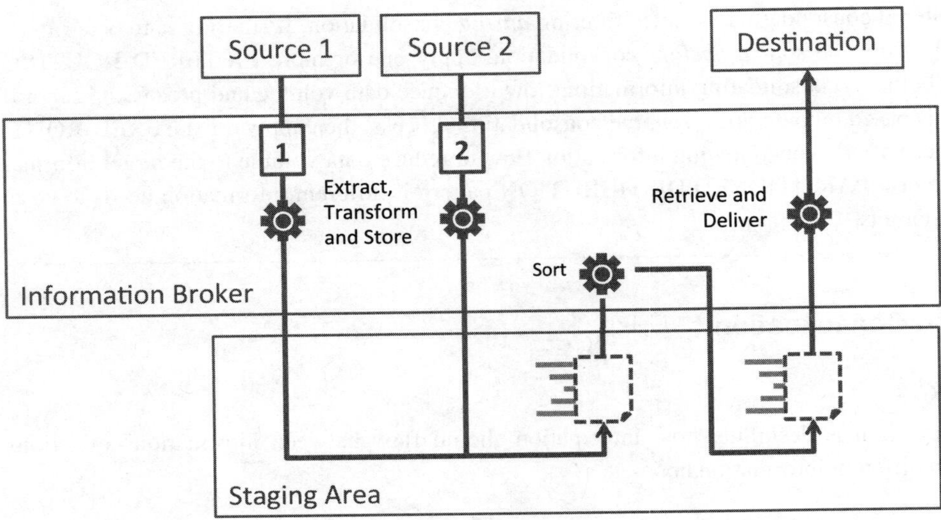

Figure 6.12 Ordered Consolidation solution.

Consequences

Benefits:

- Ordering ensures that information is appropriately sequenced and available across the information flow.
- Complexity is reduced in the source and destination information nodes.
- Information flows can be standardized and reused in multiple conditions.
- Variability in access to information nodes can be accommodated.

Liabilities:

- Ordered information flows increase latency between information nodes as information must wait for specific sequencing, particularly as the number of incoming components within the information flow grows more complex.
- Ordering requires coordinated timing across the information flow particularly in the source information nodes.
- Recoding of the processes in the flow may be required every time a change is introduced to the information collection or a new source is added to the information supply chain.
- Rules for ordering must be maintained and may not readily respond to changing business conditions.

Example Resolved

MCHS Trading's Reporting Hub is modified to support an ordered consolidation where it receives and processes transactions in a specific sequence of order, invoice, and payment.

Known Uses

Information flows describe how information moves from one information collection to another. The technology that supports them may be an ETL engine, a messaging engine, or an ESB. Usage includes the following:

- Sequencing information from multiple sources into an APPLICATION NODE or an EVENT CORRELATION NODE
- Acquiring and merging or consolidating information collections
- Populating and maintaining information collections stored in an INFORMATION WAREHOUSE, INFORMATION MART, or INFORMATION ASSET HUB
- Transforming and delivering messages from incoming information nodes to operational applications particularly where sequence of messages must be understood and maintained (e.g., create order before update or cancel order)

Related Patterns

Information flows are used to implement INFORMATION PROVISIONING. They work with INFORMATION PAYLOADs and include provisioning INFORMATION PROCESSES that execute in an INFORMATION BROKER. These information processes may store intermediate results in a STAGING AREA and use LOOK-UP TABLES to transform values. The information processes may also include INFORMATION REENGINEERING, INFORMATION GUARD, and INFORMATION PROBE patterns as steps within their implementation.

The INFORMATION IDENTIFICATION patterns can provide information on the structure of information in each information node used in the information flows.

Where you need to consolidate based on all the current available information from multiple systems (and the values in one system do not constrain or determine the values provided from another), use a SYNCHRONIZED CONSOLIDATION pattern instead.

Independent Consolidation

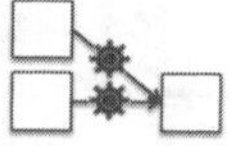

Context

An organization is designing how information should flow between information collections located in different information nodes.

Problem

An information node requires information from multiple information nodes as soon as it is available.

Example

MCHS Trading needs to fulfill orders from the E-Shop and Mail-Shop as soon as they are received in order to ensure timely entry of customer orders and to maintain accurate inventory levels.

Forces

- **Information consolidated from multiple sources**—Information must be grouped or consolidated from multiple source information nodes before it can be used in the destination information node.
- **Timing varies**—Information must be processed from multiple source information nodes on differing schedules.
- **Time delays must be minimized**—Latency must be minimized or nonexistent between source and destination information nodes.

Solution

Flow the information from each information node independently as soon as it is available. Consolidate their values within the receiving information node.

See Figure 6.13.

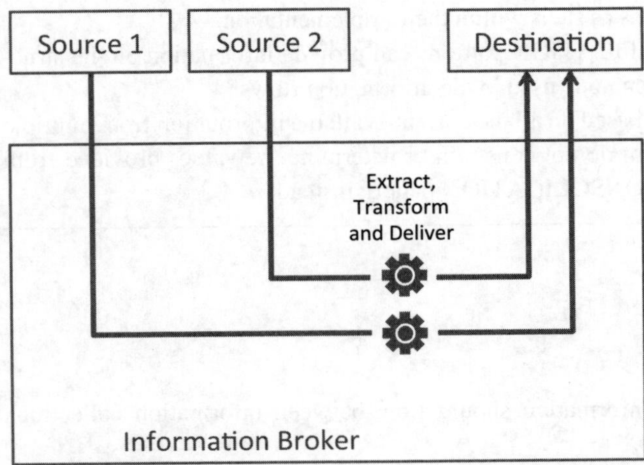

Figure 6.13 Independent Consolidation solution.

Consequences

Benefits:

- Independent consolidation removes synchronization and ordering requirements across the information flow.
- Independent information flows can minimize latency between information nodes.
- Information flows can be standardized and reused in multiple conditions.
- Variability in access to information nodes can be accommodated.

Liabilities:

- Information flows can increase latency between information nodes, particularly as the components within the information flows grow more complex.
- Complexity may be increased in the source and destination information nodes to handle independent processing.
- Recoding of the processes in the flow may be required every time a change is introduced to the information collection or a new source is added to the information supply chain.
- Rules for handling each information source must be maintained and may not readily respond to changing business conditions.

Example Resolved

In the case of MCHS Trading's Order Transaction system, all order transactions are delivered independently from the E-Shop and Mail-Shop as they are received. The Order Transaction system has processes to read these transactions from an information broker that queues all incoming requests.

Known Uses

Information flows describe how information moves from one information collection to another. The technology that supports them may be an ETL engine, a messaging engine, or an ESB. Usage includes the following:

- Acquiring and merging or consolidating information collections into an APPLICATION NODE
- Populating and maintaining information collections stored in an INFORMATION WAREHOUSE, INFORMATION MART, or INFORMATION ASSET HUB
- Transforming and delivering messages from multiple incoming information nodes to specific operational applications or APPLICATION NODES

Related Patterns

Information flows are used to implement INFORMATION PROVISIONING. They work with INFORMATION PAYLOADs and include provisioning INFORMATION PROCESSES that execute in an INFORMATION BROKER. These information processes may store intermediate results in a STAGING AREA and use LOOK-UP TABLES to transform values. The information processes may also include INFORMATION REENGINEERING, INFORMATION GUARD, and INFORMATION PROBE patterns as steps within their implementation.

The INFORMATION IDENTIFICATION patterns can provide information on the structure of information in each information node used in the information flows.

If all information values must be collected together for accurate consolidation from multiple sources, use a SYNCHRONIZED CONSOLIDATION pattern. If the order or sequence of the values is critical for consolidation, use an ORDERED CONSOLIDATION pattern.

Distributing Information Flows

The final group of information flow patterns in Table 6.8 cover how information is distributed to multiple information nodes from a single source.

Table 6.8 Distributed Information Flows Pattern Summaries

Icon	Pattern Name	Problem	Solution
	SYNCHRONIZED DISTRIBUTION	Information needs to be reliably distributed to multiple downstream information nodes.	Use a provisioning information process that is able to send the information to multiple nodes even in the event of a failure and restart.
	PARTITIONED DISTRIBUTION	Information from an information node must be distributed among multiple downstream information nodes according to a classification rule.	Extract and store the appropriate information into transient information collections, one per destination. Transform and deliver to each destination from the appropriate information collection.
1 2	ORDERED DISTRIBUTION	Information needs to be reliably distributed to multiple downstream information nodes in a predefined order.	Use a provisioning information process that is able to send the information to multiple nodes in a given order even in the event of a failure and restart.
	INDEPENDENT DISTRIBUTION	Information needs to be distributed to different downstream nodes on different schedules.	Use independent INFORMATION REQUESTS, or INFORMATION FLOWS, to transmit the information from each of the nodes.

Icon	Pattern Name	Problem	Solution
	BROADCAST DISTRIBUTION	An information node needs to distribute information to an arbitrary number of downstream information nodes.	Use an **I**NFORMATION **B**ROADCAST **P**ROCESS running in a **Q**UEUE **M**ANAGER to broadcast to destination adapters that can transform and deliver the information to the destination.

Synchronized Distribution

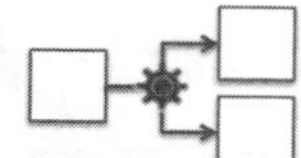

Context

An organization is designing how information should flow between information collections located in different information nodes.

Problem

Information needs to be reliably distributed to multiple downstream information nodes.

Example

Customers of MCHS Trading find that the products available in the E-Shop and Mail-Shop are not consistently available. This creates customer confusion and frustration when trying to order goods.

Forces

- **Delivery must be synchronized**—Information must reach multiple destination information nodes at the same time.
- **When information is updated, the changes must be synchronized with all copies**—Without this synchronization, the copies become inconsistent.
- **Timing is critical**—Latency must be minimized or nonexistent between source and destination information nodes.

Solution

Use a provisioning information process that is able to send the information to multiple nodes even in the event of a failure and restart.

With synchronized distribution, all the data about specific information values is sent to and stored at all destinations simultaneously.

See Figure 6.14.

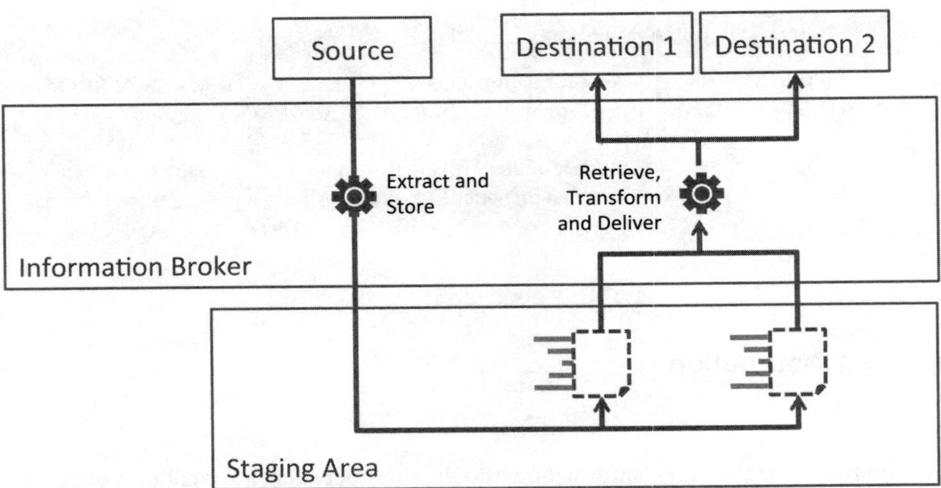

Figure 6.14 Synchronized Distribution solution.

Example Resolved

In the case of MCHS Trading's Product Hub application, the distribution of product catalog details was not synchronized across the different customer shopping channels. By introducing a new integration process, MCHS Trading can now synchronize distribution to both the E-Shop and Mail-Shop applications.

The processes in the information flow control the distribution to all of the destinations in a consistent and simultaneous fashion. In the synchronized distribution pattern, the process needs to understand the formats of each system and which subset of the information is required.

Consequences

Benefits:

- Distribution to all destinations occurs at the same time, minimizing discrepancies between downstream destinations.
- Synchronization ensures that consistent information is available across the information flow.
- Synchronization is handled outside the source or destination information collections, reducing processing complexity.
- Removal of information in all information nodes is supported when deliveries to one or more information nodes fail.
- Complexity is reduced in the source and destination information nodes.

- Information flows can be standardized and reused in multiple conditions.
- Variability in access to information nodes can be accommodated.

Liabilities:

- Information flows can increase latency between information nodes, particularly as the components within the information flows grow more complex.
- Synchronization requires coordinated timing across the information flow and must be able to remove previously delivered information if other information nodes fail to receive the same information.
- The synchronization process needs to understand the format of the source and each destination system and which subset of the information is required.
- Recoding of the processes in the flow may be required every time a change is introduced to the information collection or a new destination is added to the information supply chain.

Known Uses

Synchronizing information flows describe how information moves from one information collection to another and stay consistent with one another. The technology that supports them may be an ETL engine or an ESB. Usage includes the following:

- Synchronizing multiple applications that store the same type of information
- Distributing information to multiple destination information collections
- Populating and maintaining information collections stored in an **I**NFORMATION **W**AREHOUSE, **I**NFORMATION **M**ART, or **I**NFORMATION **A**SSET **H**UB

Related Patterns

Information flows are used to implement **I**NFORMATION **P**ROVISIONING. They work with **I**NFORMATION **P**AYLOADs and include provisioning **I**NFORMATION **P**ROCESSES that execute in an **I**NFORMATION **B**ROKER. These information processes may store intermediate results in a **S**TAGING **A**REA and use **L**OOK-UP **T**ABLES to transform values. The information processes may also include **I**NFORMATION **R**EENGINEERING, **I**NFORMATION **G**UARD, and **I**NFORMATION **P**ROBE patterns as steps within their implementation.

The **I**NFORMATION **I**DENTIFICATION patterns can provide information on the structure of information in each information node used in the information flows.

Where the order of information delivery (i.e., when the values from one system determine which values to deliver to another) is critical to distribution, use an **O**RDERED **D**ISTRIBUTION pattern instead.

Partitioned Distribution

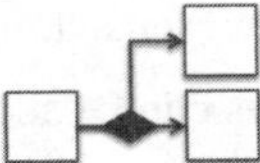

Context

An organization is designing how information should flow between information collections located in different information nodes.

Problem

Information from an information node must be distributed among multiple downstream information nodes according to a classification rule.

Partitioning allows multiple computational activities to occur simultaneously, reducing the overall processing time. It can be extended to include more than one partition depending on specific requirements. As long as sets of information can be segmented, multiple partitions may perform the same or different distribution steps.

Example

MCHS Trading's Product Hub application is used to create the approved descriptions of the products that the company sells. Once the product details are approved, they must be sent to the appropriate order-processing systems: E-Shop, Mail-Shop, Stores, Shipping, and Invoicing. Each order-processing system has its own format for storing product details. Because not all products are sold through every channel, each of the order-taking systems (E-Shop, Mail-Shop, and Stores) needs a different subset of the product details.

Forces

- **Information must be segmented**—Information must be partitioned for delivery across multiple destination information nodes.
- **Timeliness is critical**—The processing time must be minimized.

Solution

Extract and store the appropriate information into transient information collections, one per destination. Transform and deliver to each destination from the appropriate information collection.

Partitioning allows multiple computational activities to occur simultaneously, reducing the overall processing time. It can be extended to include more than one partition depending on specific requirements. As long as sets of information can be segmented, multiple partitions may perform the same or different distribution steps.

See Figure 6.15.

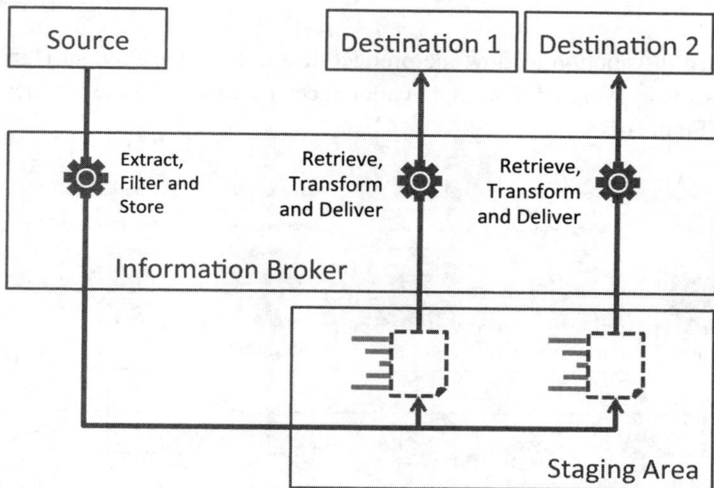

Figure 6.15 Partitioned Distribution solution.

Consequences

Benefits:

- Only required information needs to be partitioned and passed to the destination information nodes, reducing the volume of distributed information.
- Processing time for all information may be reduced.
- Complexity is reduced in the source and destination information nodes.
- Information flows can be standardized and reused in multiple conditions.
- Variability in access to information nodes can be accommodated.

Liabilities:

- Information flows can increase latency between information nodes, particularly as the components within the information flows grow more complex.
- Recoding of the processes in the flow may be required every time a change is introduced to the information collection or a new destination is added to the information supply chain.
- Rules for partitioning must be maintained and may not readily respond to changing business conditions.

Example Resolved

MCHS Trading uses partitioned distribution to flow the product details from the Product Hub application to the order-processing application. Each application receives a subset of the product details to match its scope. See Figure 6.16.

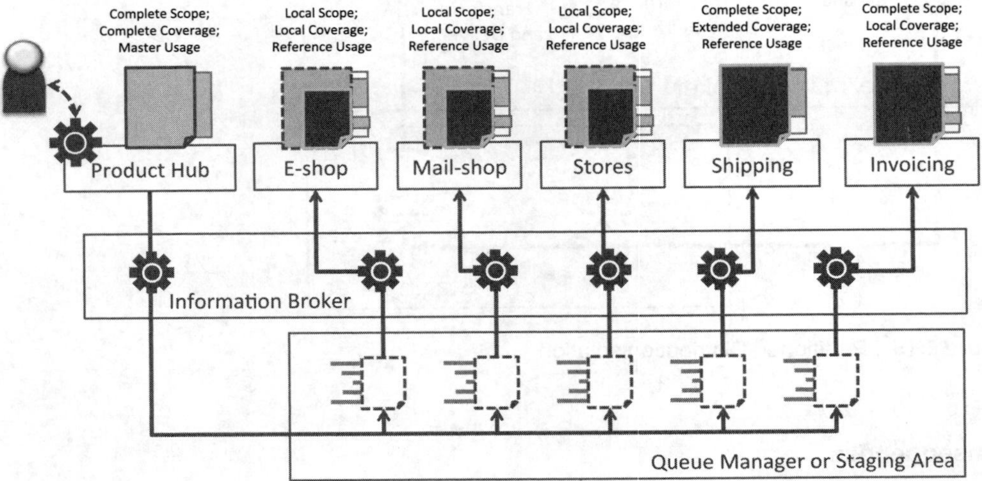

Figure 6.16 Distributing product details.

Known Uses

Information flows describe how information moves from one information collection to another. The technology that supports them may be an ETL engine, a messaging engine, or an ESB. Usage includes the following:

- Distributing or broadcasting information to multiple destination information collections
- Populating and maintaining information collections stored in an INFORMATION WAREHOUSE, INFORMATION MART, or INFORMATION ASSET HUB
- Transforming and delivering messages from incoming information nodes to operational APPLICATION NODES

Related Patterns

Information flows are used to implement INFORMATION PROVISIONING. They work with INFORMATION PAYLOADs and include provisioning INFORMATION PROCESSES that execute in an INFORMATION BROKER. These information processes may store intermediate results in a **S**TAGING **A**REA and use **L**OOK-UP **T**ABLES to transform values. The information processes may also include **I**NFORMATION **R**EENGINEERING, **I**NFORMATION **G**UARD, and **I**NFORMATION **P**ROBE patterns as steps within their implementation.

The **I**NFORMATION **I**DENTIFICATION patterns can provide information on the structure of information in each information node used in the information flows.

Where the information targets have the same data requirements and information must be delivered at the same time or based on specific order (usually supporting removal of the information in all information nodes in case of failure in one), use a **S**YNCHRONIZED **D**ISTRIBUTION or an **O**RDERED **D**ISTRIBUTION pattern.

Ordered Distribution

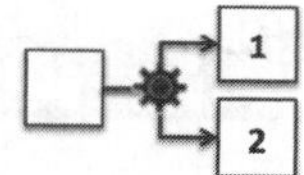

Context

An organization is designing how information should flow between information collections located in different information nodes.

Problem

Information needs to be reliably distributed to multiple downstream information nodes in a predefined order.

Example

MCHS Trading's Stores system generates new loyalty cards and must ensure accuracy for customer accounts. However, the customer and loyalty card information are delivered directly to the Accounting system without correctly creating or updating the Customer Hub first. As a consequence, the Accounting system stores the loyalty card information but in many instances links to the wrong or no customer records. Customers are upset that they encounter issues trying to use their loyalty cards.

Forces

- **Sequencing is critical**—Information must be delivered across multiple destination information nodes in a specific order or sequence.
- **Availability may impact ordering**—Information must be delivered to multiple destination information nodes on differing schedules.

Solution

Use a provisioning information process that is able to send the information to multiple nodes in a given order even in the event of a failure and restart.

See Figure 6.17.

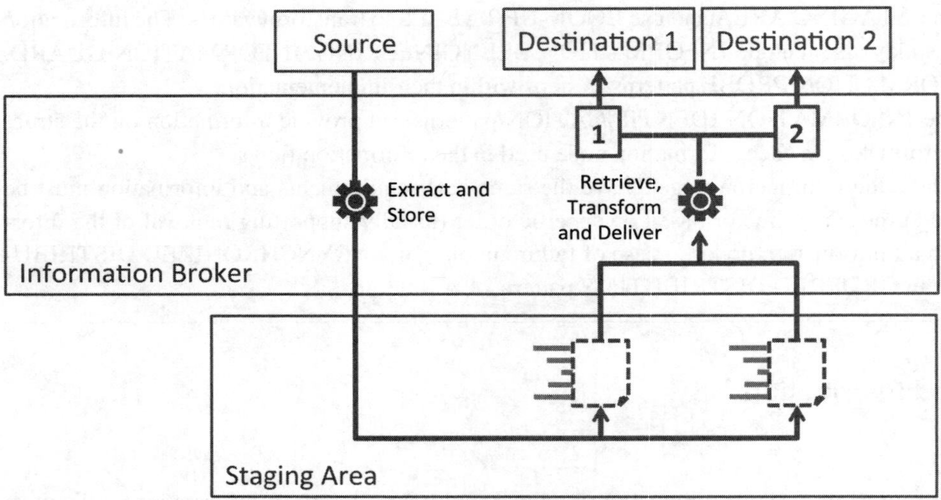

Figure 6.17 Ordered Distribution solution.

Consequences

Benefits:

- Ordering ensures that information is appropriately sequenced and available across the information flow.
- Complexity is reduced in the source and destination information nodes.
- Removal of information in initial information nodes is supported when deliveries to subsequent information nodes fail.
- Information flows can be standardized and reused in multiple conditions.
- Variability in access to information nodes can be accommodated.

Liabilities:

- Ordered information flows increase latency between information nodes as information must wait for specific sequencing, particularly as the number of outgoing destinations within the information flow grows more complex.
- Ordering requires coordinated timing across the information flow particularly in the destination information nodes and must be able to remove previously delivered information if other subsequent information nodes fail to receive the same information.
- Recoding of the processes in the flow may be required every time a change is introduced to the information collection or a new destination is added to the information supply chain.

- Rules for ordering must be maintained and may not readily respond to changing business conditions.

Example Resolved

In the case of MCHS Trading's Stores system, the distribution is modified to perform an ordered sequence of events: first, generating the customer information in the Customer Hub; then, generating the loyalty card information in the Accounting system. This resolves the issues in the Accounting system.

Known Uses

Information flows describe how information moves from one information collection to another. The technology that supports them may be an ETL engine, a messaging engine, or an ESB. Usage includes the following:

- Distributing or broadcasting information to multiple destination information collections such as APPLICATION NODES
- Populating and maintaining information collections stored in an INFORMATION WAREHOUSE, INFORMATION MART, or INFORMATION ASSET HUB
- Transforming and delivering messages from incoming information nodes to operational APPLICATION NODES

Related Patterns

Information flows are used to implement INFORMATION PROVISIONING. They work with INFORMATION PAYLOADs and include provisioning INFORMATION PROCESSES that execute in an INFORMATION BROKER. These information processes may store intermediate results in a STAGING AREA and use LOOK-UP TABLES to transform values. The information processes may also include INFORMATION REENGINEERING, INFORMATION GUARD, and INFORMATION PROBE patterns as steps within their implementation.

The INFORMATION IDENTIFICATION patterns can provide information on the structure of information in each information node used in the information flows.

Independent Distribution

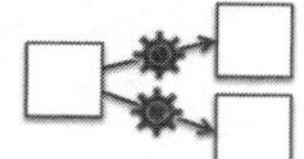

Context

An organization is designing how information should flow between information collections located in different information nodes.

Problem

Information needs to be distributed to different downstream nodes on different schedules.

Example

MCHS Trading has encountered a high level of customer duplication between their E-Shop and Mail-Shop, and the lack of a Customer Hub means that customers often must reenter their information to place new orders, increasing customer frustration.

Forces

- **Delivery time is critical**—Latency must be minimized or nonexistent between source and destination information nodes.
- Information must be delivered to multiple destination information nodes on differing schedules.

Solution

Use independent INFORMATION REQUESTS or INFORMATION FLOWS to transmit the information from each of the nodes.

See Figure 6.18.

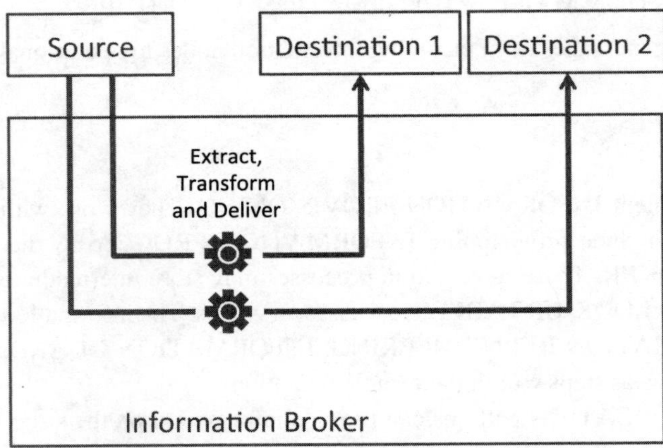

Figure 6.18 Independent Distribution solution.

Consequences

Benefits:

- Independent distribution removes synchronization and ordering requirements across the information flow.

- Independent information flows can minimize latency between information nodes.
- Information flows can be standardized and reused in multiple conditions.
- Variability in access to information nodes can be accommodated.

Liabilities:

- Information flows can increase latency between information nodes, particularly as the components within the information flows grow more complex.
- Complexity may be increased in the source and destination information nodes to handle independent processing.
- Recoding of the processes in the flow may be required every time a change is introduced to the information collection or a new source is added to the information supply chain.
- Rules for handling each information destination must be maintained and may not readily respond to changing business conditions.

Example Resolved

When MCHS Trading introduced its Customer Hub, one of its goals was to ensure that existing customers did not have to reenter their information to place new orders in either the E-Shop or Mail-Shop. By establishing an independent distribution from the Customer Hub, updated customer information is made available to the E-Shop and Mail-Shop at the points when those applications can apply it.

Known Uses

Information flows describe how information moves from one information collection to another. The technology that supports them may be an ETL engine, a messaging engine, or an ESB. Usage includes the following:

- Distributing or broadcasting information to multiple destination information collections
- Populating and maintaining information collections stored in an INFORMATION WAREHOUSE, INFORMATION MART, or INFORMATION ASSET HUB
- Transforming and delivering messages from incoming information nodes to operational APPLICATION NODES

Related Patterns

Information flows are used to implement INFORMATION PROVISIONING. They work with INFORMATION PAYLOADs and include provisioning INFORMATION PROCESSES that execute in an INFORMATION BROKER. These information processes may store intermediate results in a STAGING AREA and use LOOK-UP TABLES to transform values. The information processes may also include INFORMATION REENGINEERING, INFORMATION GUARD, and INFORMATION PROBE patterns as steps within their implementation.

The **I**NFORMATION **I**DENTIFICATION patterns can provide information on the structure of information in each information node used in the information flows.

If all information values must be delivered into multiple sources simultaneously, use a SYNCHRONIZED **D**ISTRIBUTION pattern. If the order or sequence of the values is critical for distribution, use an **O**RDERED **D**ISTRIBUTION pattern. If different information must be routed to different information nodes, use the **P**ARTITIONED **D**ISTRIBUTION pattern. If multiple information destinations need to control whether they receive specific information, use the **B**ROADCAST **D**ISTRIBUTION pattern instead.

Broadcast Distribution

Context

An organization is designing how information should flow between information collections located in different information nodes.

Problem

An information node needs to distribute information to an arbitrary number of downstream information nodes.

Example

MCHS Trading is finding it difficult to ensure that product inventory levels are consistently updated from the Shipping system across their E-Shop and Mail-Shop applications (the Stores maintain their own product inventories) in a timely fashion impacting customer satisfaction.

Forces

- **Only interested parties want the information**—Information is distributed only to destination information nodes with an interest in the information.
- **Process as quickly as targets demand**—Latency must be minimized or nonexistent from the source but may vary based on the destination information nodes.
- **Targets operate independently**—Information must be delivered to multiple destination information nodes on differing schedules.

Solution

Use an INFORMATION BROADCAST PROCESS running in a QUEUE MANAGER to broadcast to destination adapters that can transform and deliver the information to the destination.

If a destination is able to consume the information from the source, then the destination adapter is not needed. Also, if the information broker is able to host the information broadcast process, the queue manager node would not be required. See Figure 6.19.

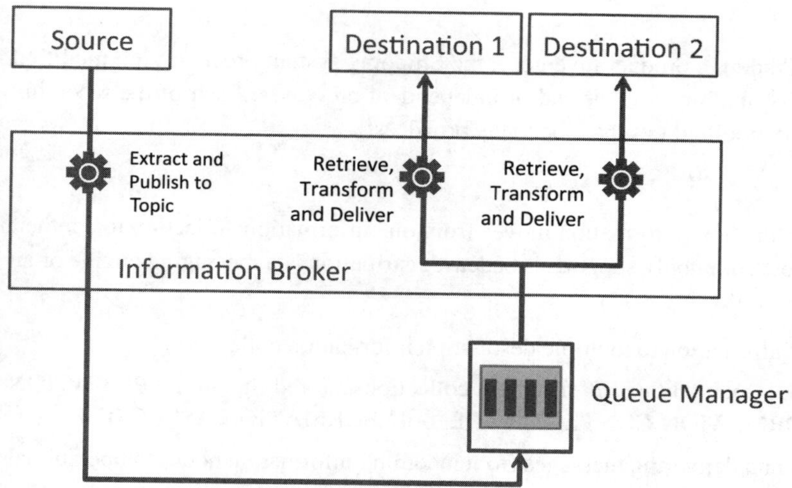

Figure 6.19 Broadcast Distribution solution.

Consequences

Benefits:

- Broadcast distribution removes synchronization and ordering requirements across the information flow.
- Complexity is minimized in the source and destination information nodes, as all processing is independent and disconnected.
- Broadcast distribution flows can minimize latency to destination information nodes.
- Recoding of the processes in the flow is not required when new destinations are added to the information supply chain.
- Information flows can be standardized and reused in multiple conditions.
- New target information nodes can be easily added.
- Variability in access to information nodes can be accommodated.

Liabilities:

- Broadcast distribution flows can increase latency between information nodes, when destination information nodes cannot increase their speed of processing.
- There is a limited ability to ensure that target information nodes pick up the new information.
- Recoding of the processes in the destination information nodes may be required every time a change is introduced to the broadcast information collection.

Example Resolved

In the case of MCHS Trading's product inventory, the Shipping system processes are modified to utilize a broadcast distribution flow instead of independent processes. Each of the receiving application nodes is also modified to subscribe to the broadcast.

Known Uses

Information flows describe how information moves from one information collection to another. The technology that most commonly supports broadcast distribution is a messaging engine or an ESB. Usage includes the following:

- Broadcasting information to multiple destination information collections
- Populating and maintaining information collections stored in an **A**PPLICATION **N**ODE, **I**NFORMATION **C**ONTENT **N**ODE, or **I**NFORMATION **A**SSET **H**UB
- Transforming and delivering messages from incoming information nodes to operational **A**PPLICATION **N**ODES

Related Patterns

Information flows are used to implement **I**NFORMATION **P**ROVISIONING. They work with **I**NFORMATION **P**AYLOADs and include provisioning **I**NFORMATION **P**ROCESSES that execute in an **I**NFORMATION **B**ROKER. These information processes may store intermediate results in a **S**TAGING **A**REA and use **L**OOK-UP **T**ABLES to transform values. The information processes may also include **I**NFORMATION **R**EENGINEERING, **I**NFORMATION **G**UARD, and **I**NFORMATION **P**ROBE patterns as steps within their implementation.

The **I**NFORMATION **I**DENTIFICATION patterns can provide information on the information structures in each information node used in the information flows.

Where all information values are needed in target information nodes and either synchronization or ordering of delivery is critical, use the **S**YNCHRONIZED or the **O**RDERED **D**ISTRIBUTION patterns instead. If delivery can occur independently, but the delivery must occur to the target, use the **P**ARTITIONED or the **I**NDEPENDENT **D**ISTRIBUTION patterns instead.

Summary of Information Flow Patterns

The information flow patterns describe how to copy information between information collections that are located on different information nodes. These patterns address most of the situations where information is being copied between information collections. They show the optimal place to select and transform information as it is routed between the information collections. These patterns can be composed together by inserting staging areas to act as intermediaries where information from multiple sources needs to be combined and copied to multiple destinations.

Summary

This chapter covered the information in motion pattern groups. These patterns describe how information is moved between information processes and information collections located on different information nodes. The information request patterns copy information on demand, as part of an information service request. The information flow patterns copy information between information collections so information processes have the information they need on their local information node.

Chapter 7, "Information Processing," introduces two pattern groups for the processing of information. The information trigger pattern group describes how information processes are initiated. The information processes pattern group describes the different kinds of information processes.

CHAPTER 7

Information Processing

The information processing pattern groups describe how an organization produces and consumes information:

- **I**NFORMATION **T**RIGGERS describe how information processes are initiated.
- **I**NFORMATION **P**ROCESSES describe the types of automated processes to be found in an organization and how they use information.

These patterns provide some of the base information management components for the organization, as shown in Figure 7.1.

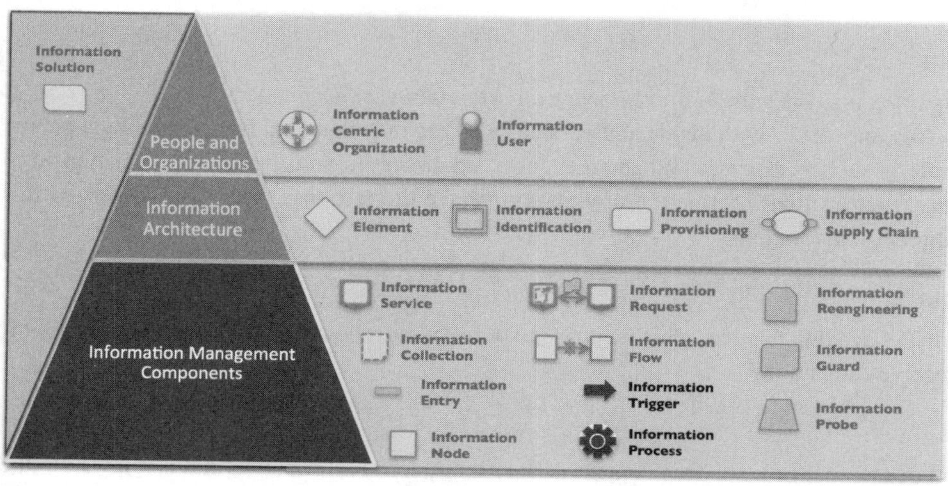

Figure 7.1 Information processing pattern groups in the context of the pattern language.

Information Trigger Patterns

The information trigger pattern group describes the ways a new instance of an information process is initiated. Although these patterns are simple, the choices they describe have a profound effect on how an information supply chain operates because they determine where and when activity occurs.

The basic concept of an information trigger is described by the **I**NFORMATION **T**RIGGER pattern shown in Table 7.1. It is followed by specialized variations.

Table 7.1 Information Trigger Pattern Summary

Icon	Pattern Name	Problem	Solution
	INFORMATION TRIGGER	An information process must be started when a particular event occurs.	When the event is detected, trigger a mechanism that is able to request the initiation of the information process on an appropriate information node.

Information Trigger

Context

Information processes support the activities of the organization. These activities are triggered when particular events occur.

Problem

An information process must be started when a particular event occurs.

Events may occur both inside and outside of an organization, and be detected by a person or technology such as a sensor. When an event is significant to an organization, it is typical to create an instance of an information process to manage the response to the event. How is this information process started?

Example

When MCHS Trading receives a payment for an order, it must be processed to ensure the organization receives the money.

Forces

An event occurs in a context. This context defines the specific information that is relevant to the activity. This context must be captured and passed to the information process.

Solution

When the event is detected, trigger a mechanism that is able to request the initiation of the information process on an appropriate information node.

This mechanism is called an information trigger. It is responsible for monitoring for a particular type of event, capturing details of the event, and the context in which it occurred, into an INFORMATION EVENT structure and initiating a new instance of an appropriate information process. The information event is used to pass the context onto the information process as the information process starts up. This is shown in Figure 7.2.

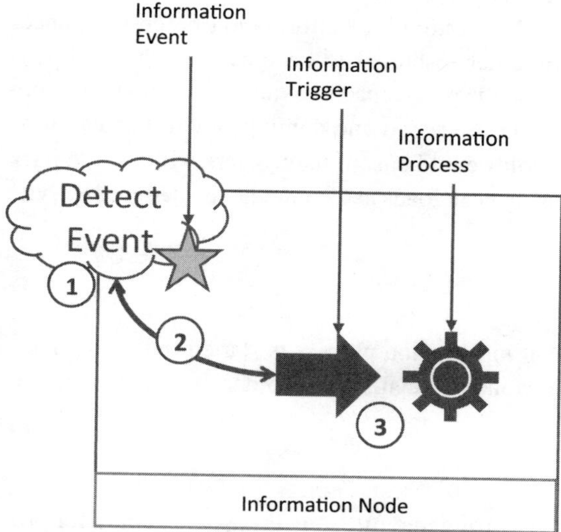

Figure 7.2 Information Trigger solution.

The numbers on the diagram in Figure 7.2 refer to these notes:

1. The information trigger detects the event.
2. The information trigger gathers information about the event into an information event structure.
3. The information trigger initiates the information process and passes the information event to it.

Consequences

Benefits:

- Information triggers provide well-defined mechanisms for capturing events and initiating new processes. Recording the associated information event defines why the processing was initiated. This is the responsibility of an **I**NFORMATION **P**ROBE.

Liabilities:

- Information triggers react to events that are often happening outside the control of the organization. In unusual circumstances, there may be a sudden increase in the number of events. This results in an unusually high number of information process instances being started, which in turn can cause other resources to become overwhelmed. It is good practice to ensure that there is enough spare capacity available to handle reasonable peaks in the number of events being processed and contingency to handle unexpected high loads. For example, thresholds could ensure the triggers will throttle back on the number of processes created during peak loads and complete the deferred activity once the peak subsides.

Example Resolved

When a payment is received, a Process Payment information process is started in the Invoicing application. The information event it is passed contains details of the order that the payment is for, and how much it covers.

Known Uses

IT systems are essentially passive. They need to be triggered by "something" happening for processing to start. This triggering is an example of an information trigger. There are many types of implementations of information triggers from buttons on user interface menus to command lines, environmental sensors, triggers in databases, timers, and many more. The other patterns in this pattern group cover further examples.

Related Patterns

An information trigger initiates an **I**NFORMATION **P**ROCESS. The **I**NFORMATION **E**VENT describes the record of the event (its type, time stamp, content, etc.) that is passed to a newly started information process.

The information trigger, and information process that it starts, execute in the same **I**NFORMATION **N**ODE. The information process may use a **R**EMOTE **I**NFORMATION **S**ERVICE to pass the work to another information process located in a different information node. The remote information service will use a **T**RIGGERING **I**NFORMATION **S**ERVICE to create an **I**NFORMATION **S**ERVICE **T**RIGGER that will initiate the second process. This is described in the **D**AISY **C**HAIN **P**ROVISIONING pattern.

Variations of the Information Trigger Pattern

The pattern summaries shown in Table 7.2 describe more specialized types of information triggers. They are named after the component that creates the event.

Table 7.2 Information Trigger Specialist Patterns

Icon	Pattern Name	Problem	Solution
	MANUAL INFORMATION TRIGGER	There is no simple way to automatically detect the event and trigger the appropriate information process.	Provide a command line or user interface to enable an INFORMATION USER to initiate the information process.
	SCHEDULED INFORMATION TRIGGER	An information process needs to run to a regular timetable—such as once an hour.	Use a SCHEDULING PROCESS to initiate the information process at the required time.
	INFORMATION SERVICE TRIGGER	An information process needs to be triggered on a remote information node.	Trigger a local information process to use a REMOTE INFORMATION SERVICE to call the appropriate information trigger in the remote information node.
	INFORMATION CHANGE TRIGGER	An information process needs to be started whenever information arrives at a certain location, is accessed, is changed, or is removed.	Set up a monitoring mechanism to watch for the change in information. Trigger the appropriate information process as required.
	EXTERNAL SENSOR TRIGGER	A sensor has detected an event or made a measurement that needs to be processed.	The sensor's data is packaged into an information event and passed to an appropriate information process.

Manual Information Trigger

Context

INFORMATION PROCESSES support the activities of the organization. These activities are triggered when particular events occur. Events may occur both inside and outside of an organization, and be detected by a person or technology such as a sensor. When an event is significant to an organization, it is typical to create an information process to manage the response to the event.

Problem

There is no simple way to automatically detect the event and trigger the appropriate information process.

This is often the case where the event is initiated outside the control of the organization.

Example

A customer phones the MCHS Trading call center to notify the company that she has changed her address.

Forces

- **People initiate processes**—An information process needs to be started at an appropriate time, on the right INFORMATION NODE, and must be passed the appropriate context in an INFORMATION EVENT.
- **Volume of events may overwhelm individuals**—People can only process so many items in a given span of time.
- **Insufficient information**—There may not be sufficient information for an individual to trigger a process. This may be due to lack of training, misunderstanding of the content, issues with timing of information delivery, or other factors. This can result in significant process delays.

Solution

Provide a command line or user interface to enable an INFORMATION USER to initiate the information process.

The information user must manually enter the description of the event to provide the context for the information process. This is shown in Figure 7.3.

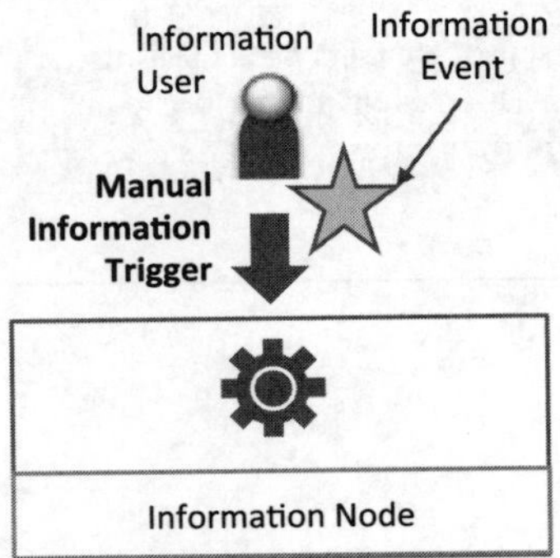

Figure 7.3 Manual Information Trigger solution.

Consequences

Benefits:

- This pattern is effective at handling ad hoc activities—particularly those driven by events coming from outside of the organization.

Liabilities:

- The manual information trigger needs to have appropriate INFORMATION GUARDS protecting it to ensure only authorized and appropriate information processes are started up.

Example Resolved

The customer service representative clicks on a menu option on his or her user interface to invoke the **Change of Customer Address** information process. This guides him or her through a series of steps to validate the identity of the customer and update the address if appropriate.

Known Uses

Manual information triggers are typically implemented via user interfaces (menus, buttons, mouse clicks, or similar prompts) or via operating system scripts or commands. The user interface may request additional information before creating the information process. This is passed to the information process in the information event.

Related Patterns

Manual information triggers are invoked by INFORMATION USERS.

If the information process needs to be triggered in a different information node, the information process triggered by the information user should act as a simple proxy to the required information process and use the INFORMATION SERVICE TRIGGER to start it.

Scheduled Information Trigger

Context

Information processes support the activities of the organization. These activities are triggered when particular events occur. Events may occur both inside and outside of an organization, and be detected by a person or technology such as a sensor. When an event is significant to an organization, it is typical to create an information process to manage the response to the event.

Problem

An information process needs to run to a regular timetable—such as once an hour.

Example

The orders made by MCHS Trading's outlet stores are accumulated in the Stores application. At the end of the trading day, they must be transmitted to the Shipping application for processing.

Forces

- **People are not always present**—People cannot be relied on to always perform an activity to a fixed timetable because they may be distracted by other work. Therefore, the triggering mechanism for this problem must be automated.
- **Expected conditions must be met**—Information processes are implemented using particular assumptions on the location and state of the information they are working with. If these conditions are not met, the information process may appear to execute successfully but produce incorrect results.
- **Volume may exceed processing capacity**—When a process is triggered, if it lacks the capacity to complete its task before the next trigger occurs, there may be significant processing issues (e.g., contention for resources, locking of information collections).

Solution

Use a **S**CHEDULING **P**ROCESS to initiate the information process at the required time.

Information may be passed to the scheduling process when the information trigger is set up. This is added to the **I**NFORMATION **E**VENT created by the scheduling process when it triggers the new information process. See Figure 7.4.

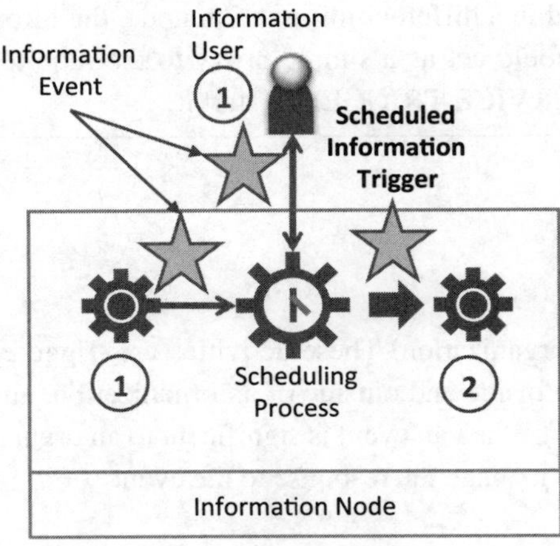

Figure 7.4 Scheduled Information Trigger solution.

The numbers on the diagram refer to these notes:

1. An information user or an information process sets up the schedule for the triggering mechanism in a scheduling process.
2. Whenever the schedule requires it, the scheduling process creates a timer event and passes it to the information trigger to initiate the appropriate information process.

Consequences

Benefits:

- This pattern automates the initialization of regular processing.

Liabilities:

- The scheduled information process is started independently of all other activity in the information nodes. It must be written defensively to validate that any processing that should have run before it has happened. Otherwise, it may fail to produce the correct results because, for example, the information that it should process has not been copied in the information collection it uses.

Example Resolved

The Stores application accumulates orders into an INFORMATION COLLECTION hosted in a STAGING AREA during each trading day. There is an INFORMATION PROCESS that is scheduled to run each evening that moves the orders to the Shipping application.

Known Uses

Scheduling information processes is a common practice in information provisioning where a batch of information must be transmitted at regular intervals. The information to send is accumulated in an information collection and the scheduled information process retrieves the information and moves it to the required destination.

Related Patterns

The SCHEDULING PROCESS initiates the information process. This pattern is used for batched INFORMATION PROVISIONING.

Information Service Trigger

Context

Information processes support the activities of the organization. These activities are triggered when particular events occur. Events may occur both inside and outside of an organization, and be detected by a person or technology such as a sensor. When an event is significant to an organization, it is typical to create an information process to manage the response to the event.

Problem

An information process needs to be triggered on a remote information node.

This situation arises when the event is detected on a different information node to where it will be processed.

Example

The **New Product Introduction** information process running in MCHS Trading's Product Hub application needs to distribute new product details to the order-processing application once they have been approved.

Forces

- **Changes to the location of information**—The most appropriate information node to host the information process may change over time. It is a balance between placing the information process close to the information it uses, while ensuring the information node it is hosted on has both the functionality and the capacity to support it.
- **Availability of remote information nodes**—Changes in the availability of information nodes impacts triggering and delivery of information.
- **Volume of requests may exceed processing capacity**—When a process is triggered, if the information node lacks the capacity to support the volume of triggered requests, there may be significant processing issues (e.g., contention for resources, locking of information collections, delays in information delivery).

Solution

Trigger a local information process to use a REMOTE INFORMATION SERVICE to call the appropriate information trigger in the remote information node.

See Figure 7.5.

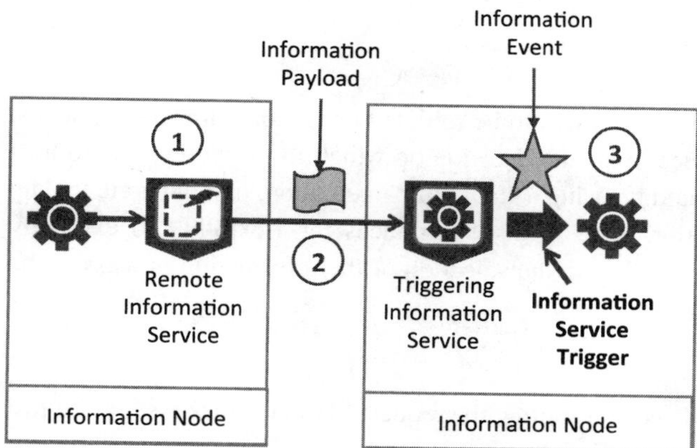

Figure 7.5 Information Service Trigger solution.

The numbers on the diagram refer to these notes:

1. The remote information service is called.
2. It creates an INFORMATION PAYLOAD to hold the parameters passed to it and calls an INFORMATION REQUEST to invoke a TRIGGERING INFORMATION SERVICE. The specific information request may be:
   - **EVENT INFORMATION REQUEST**—When the caller does not know which process to initiate, so the decision is delegated to the triggering information service.
   - **RUN PROCESS INFORMATION REQUEST**—When a specific information process is to be called and the caller will wait for the process to complete in order to get its results. This is for short-running information processes that have no user interaction.
   - **INITIATE PROCESS INFORMATION REQUEST**—When a specific process is to be started and the caller just needs an acknowledgment that it has started successfully.
3. The triggering information service creates an INFORMATION EVENT from the information payload and initiates the appropriate information process, passing the event. It creates a response to the information request and returns it to the caller.

Consequences

Benefits:

- This pattern allows information processes to be initiated on remote information nodes. The remote information service owns the decision on which information node to host the information process. It could be using a static implementation, or a dynamic lookup to locate the target information node. It also introduces the flexibility to explicitly request a particular process, or delegate the selection of the information process to the target information node.

Liabilities:

- If the remote information node is not running, the request to run the process may be lost without special coding in the calling information node.

Example Resolved

When the **New Product Introduction** information process detects that some product details have been approved, it calls a remote information service to trigger the **Distribute Product Details** information process in an **I**NFORMATION **B**ROKER. This is a type of **I**NFORMATION **D**EPLOYMENT **P**ROCESS that is the initial information process in the **P**ARTITIONED **D**ISTRIBUTION information flow.

Known Uses

This approach is used in workload management systems to distribute work across a number of information nodes. It is also used in Service-Oriented Integration (SOI) to request that information processes are run by remote systems.

Related Patterns

The **W**ORKLOAD **O**FFLOAD pattern uses this approach to move work off of an overloaded information node.

Information Change Trigger

Context

Information processes support the activities of the organization. These activities are triggered when particular events occur. Events may occur both inside and outside of an organization, and be detected by a person or technology such as a sensor. When an event is significant to an organization, it is typical to create an information process to manage the response to the event.

Problem

An information process needs to be started whenever information arrives at a certain location, is accessed, is changed, or is removed.

Example

Whenever new product details are available for the E-Shop application, they are posted in an INFORMATION COLLECTION located in a STAGING AREA. They need to be transformed and loaded into E-Shop's internal product details information collection as soon as they are available.

Forces

- **Multiple sources of change**—There may be many information processes that are updating the same information. This can result in many events that could be processed by a single information process.
- **Volume of change**—The number of changes occurring against a particular piece of information may hamper response if processing capacity is insufficient or may obscure what changes have occurred.

Solution

Set up a monitoring mechanism to watch for the change in information. Trigger the appropriate information process as required.

The INFORMATION EVENT that is passed to the triggered information process describes the nature of the change to the information. See Figure 7.6.

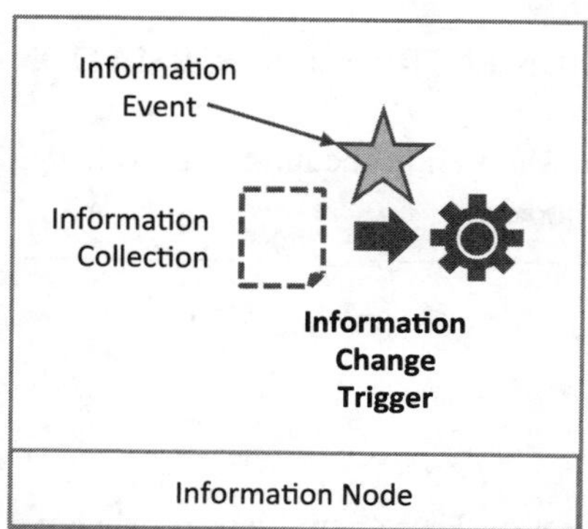

Figure 7.6 Information Change Trigger solution.

Consequences

Benefits:

- With this pattern, every change to the information collection results in an information trigger—irrespective of the information process that made the change.

Liabilities:

- The context information passed to the triggered information process can be pretty limited because there is no knowledge of the business reason for the information change at this level of the architecture.

Example Resolved

New product details are created by the Product Hub application. When they are approved, the **Distribute Product Details** information process copies the product details into the information collection in the staging area.

Known Uses

Database triggers follow this pattern, as do operating system processes that are triggered when files change.

Often, when the triggering mechanism runs in a database, the work to trigger the information process runs under the same transaction as the work to make the change to the information. The positive effect of this approach is that if the change is rolled back, the new information process is not triggered. The downside is that it can slow down the information process making the original update.

Related Patterns

Information change triggers typically monitor INFORMATION ENTRIES in INFORMATION COLLECTIONS.

The description of the INFORMATION NODE pattern shows how the information change trigger fits in with the rest of the function in an information node.

External Sensor Trigger

Context

Information processes support the activities of the organization. These activities are triggered when particular events occur. Events may occur both inside and outside of an organization, and be detected by a person or technology such as a sensor. When an event is significant to an organization, it is typical to create an information process to manage the response to the event.

Problem

A sensor has detected an event, or made a measurement that needs to be processed.

How is this processing initiated (bearing in mind that there will probably be many sensors and/or many measurements coming from an individual sensor)?

Example

The warehouses have sensors on its exits that detect the movement of particular goods that either have very high value or require regulatory control. These sensors detect the RFID tag stuck to these types of goods and record which goods left a particular exit and when this occurred. This information must be checked to ensure the movement of these goods is authorized. The check has to be made immediately so the truck containing the goods can pass through the final security gate.

Forces

- **Large volumes of information**—Sensors can generate a huge amount of information—particularly in moments of crisis, or when unusual situations arise. When this happens, the events need to be triaged very quickly to ensure the most important events are processed first.
- **All events look the same**—The events produced by sensors are undistinguished until an INFORMATION PROCESS organizes and distinguishes them.

Solution

The sensor's data is packaged into an information event and passed to an appropriate information process.

The sensor is part of a small processor that is connected to the network. It takes a reading and then sends the data to a collection point. The collection point triggers the information process when the reading is received. See Figure 7.7.

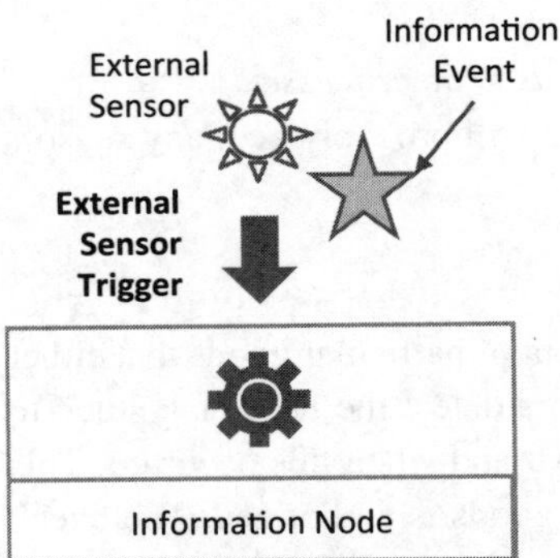

Figure 7.7 External Sensor Trigger solution.

Consequences

Benefits:

- Using external sensors can improve the reaction time of the organization to external events.

Liabilities:

- External sensor triggers must be able to handle sudden peaks of events appropriately, ensuring the most important are processed first.

Example Resolved

The sensors in the warehouse doors trigger an information process that checks the RFID tag data against orders that are due for dispatch.

Known Uses

Examples of external sensors include RFID tag sensors, audio and video monitoring, liquid levels, digital metering, bar code sensors, and infrared beams. In general, the price of these sensors is reducing, along with their associated tags. In addition, the price of hardware to process the information generated from these sensors is also reducing, making it affordable for many organizations to collect information from the environment. The result is that external sensor triggers and the related processing are becoming more common.

Related Patterns

The STREAMING ANALYTICS NODE running INFORMATION STREAMING PROCESSES is able to process sensor events at very high speed because it processes them in memory. This means it can act as the collection point for sensor data and make an initial assessment of the sensor data as it receives it. Only significant events and other insight are stored or passed to other information processes. Any additional processing can be initiated using another type of trigger.

Summary of Information Triggers

The information triggers describe the different mechanisms for starting an information process. This includes people clicking on a user interface or running a command script or program, external sensors, database triggers, schedulers, and calls to information services. They are the means by which activity is initiated and linked together.

The information processes pattern group describes the kinds of processing that the information triggers can start.

Information Process Patterns

Information processes describe the automated processing being performed within the INFORMATION NODES. It is the information processes that drive changes to the information throughout the information supply chain. Each is focused on supporting a particular type of activity within the information supply chain. Some are supporting the business activities directly, others are just managing information, and others are running the information nodes themselves.

The INFORMATION PROCESS pattern shown in Table 7.3 describes the general concepts around an information process. The remaining information process patterns in the group cover the more specialized behaviors. They are organized as follows:

- **Business processes**—Directly supporting the organization's primary activity
- **Quality information processes**—Managing the quality of the organization's information
- **Provisioning information processes**—Moving information from one information collection to another
- **Analytics processes**—Supporting fact-based decisions
- **Search processes**—Locating information based on ad hoc requests
- **IT service management processes**—Managing the IT infrastructure, such as the information nodes

Table 7.2 Information Process Pattern Summary

Icon	Pattern Name	Problem	Solution
	INFORMATION PROCESS	An organization has to process information to support one of its activities.	Formally define and implement the processing for that activity in an information node. Ensure this information node has access to the information it needs.

Information Process

Context

An organization performs activities to fulfill its purpose.

Problem

An organization has to process information to support one of its activities.

This processing involves the retrieval, creation, updating, and deleting of information.

Example

MCHS Trading needs to maintain a product catalogue. This involves the following:

- Introducing new products, including assessing the market need, describing the product for the catalog, finding suitable suppliers, and deciding on the price
- Retiring products that are either not popular or are no longer manufactured
- Reviewing pricing and defining special offers
- Improving product descriptions

Forces

- **Activities are complicated by the real world—**The activities of a business are often complicated by the inconsistencies in the organization and the world beyond.
- **An activity may involve contributions from multiple people.**
- **An activity may involve complex or specialized processing.**
- **An activity takes time (minutes, days, weeks, or years)**—Any IT infrastructure supporting the activity may fail, or be replaced or upgraded during the lifetime of an activity.

Solution

Formally define and implement the processing for that activity and host it in an information node. Ensure this processing has access to the information it needs.

The implementation of the processing for such an activity is called an information process. An information process is made up of a number of logical steps. There may be decisions, calculations, or loops in the process, but there will always be a well-defined starting point and one or more ending points.

Often the behavior of an information process is described using a flowchart, use case model, or other diagram that shows the steps and decision points. These flowcharts or diagrams can be used simply as a documented description of the information process, or, as in the case of an AGILE BUSINESS PROCESS, form part of the information process's implementation itself. See Figure 7.8.

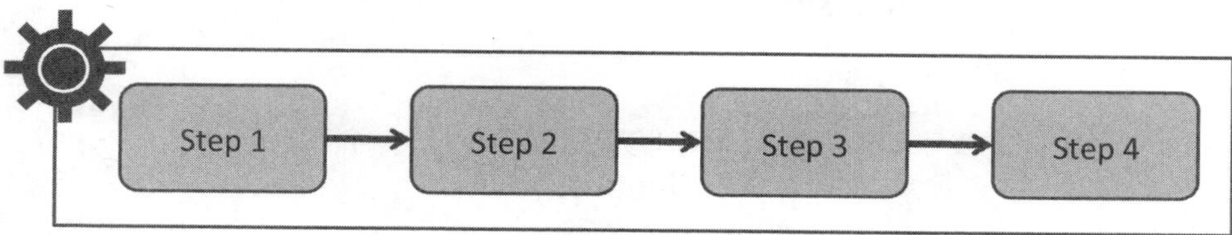

Figure 7.8 Information process steps.

Information is made available to an information process via a number of routes, as shown in Figure 7.9. An information process is started by an INFORMATION TRIGGER. The trigger may pass the information process some information to give it some context for its work. This information is in the form of an INFORMATION EVENT. An information process may return some information values to the trigger once it is completed.

The information process may both obtain and produce additional information. Specifically, an information process may receive a supply of information either from users interacting directly with it, or from stored information. Stored information is available to the information process through the INFORMATION SERVICES.

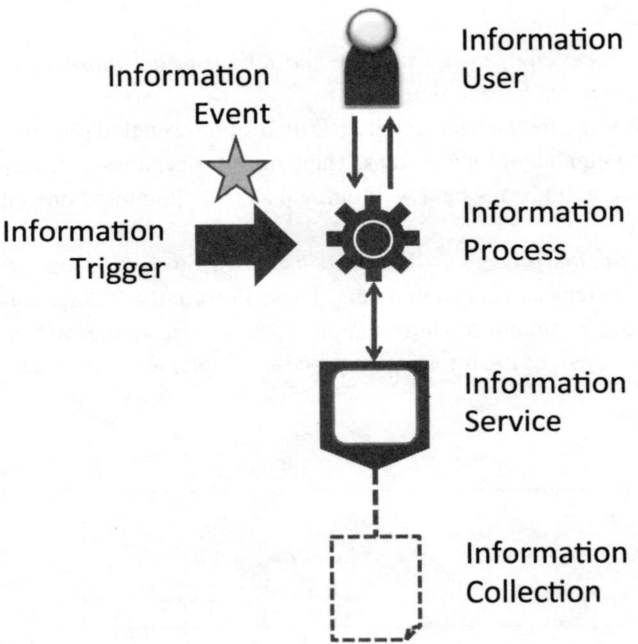

Figure 7.9 Information process sources of information.

The **I**NFORMATION **P**ROVISIONING pattern provides more detail on the working of these mechanisms.

An information process works with all types of information (called **I**NFORMATION **E**LEMENTS). For example, it maintains its in-memory working variable in an **I**NFORMATION **P**ROCESSING **V**ARIABLES element. It creates an **I**NFORMATION **A**CTIVITY to store details of the work it is performing. This information activity serves as a permanent record of the work performed by the information process.

The information process will also use **I**NFORMATION **A**SSETS during its processing. Often, the relevant information assets will be referred to in the information record. For example, customer details may be referred to in an order record. This linking provides valuable business context to the information record, enabling the organization to understand who or what is involved in the most valuable work going on in the organization.

Consequences

Benefits:

- Information processes provide repeatable capability. They organize the work between people and provide a record of the work of the organization and help to normalize many aspects of the work.

Liabilities:

- Because the behavior of an information process is hard-coded, it can be expensive to change. The business process implementation must be flexible enough to handle the unusual cases.

Example Resolved

In the case of MCHS Trading's product catalog, the bulleted activities are each implemented as a different information process in the Product Hub application. More details for this example are shown in the specialized pattern COLLABORATIVE EDITING PROCESS.

Known Uses

Information processes provide the core IT capabilities for an organization. There are many implementation approaches from direct coding to model-driven processes and declarative systems. There are more detailed descriptions of implementation approaches in the more specific information processes that follow.

Related Patterns

The major information process types related to an information supply chain are described by the information process patterns that follow:

- Information processes are started by INFORMATION TRIGGERS.
- Information processes access information via INFORMATION SERVICES.
- Information processes are hosted in INFORMATION NODES.
- Information processes typically involve people. The information process needs to provide user interfaces for these people with appropriate INFORMATION GUARDS to protect the information supply chain either from mistakes when entering new information or inappropriate use of information.

Business Processes

Over the years, an organization will accumulate many different types of systems. The systems that implement the set of information processes that support the primary activity of the organization are referred to as applications (see APPLICATION NODE pattern) and the processes that run in them are called business processes. Most of the people interacting with these processes are INFORMATION WORKERS.

The purpose of the business process patterns in this section is to characterize the different ways that the processes inside applications manage information, and how easy it is to incorporate them into an INFORMATION SUPPLY CHAIN. They provide a useful classification scheme for both existing and new applications for use at the start of an INFORMATION SOLUTION project. See Table 7.4.

Table 7.4 Business Process Pattern Summaries

Icon	Pattern Name	Problem	Solution
	BESPOKE APPLICATION PROCESS	An information process needs highly specialized behavior to support an activity in an organization.	Implement the information process using an in-house or consultant team ensuring it meets the needs of the organization.
	PACKAGED APPLICATION PROCESS	All or part of an information process is too expensive or too complex for the organization to implement.	Buy a software package to support the information process. This will either come as a standalone application or a software library that needs to be integrated into an application.
	AGILE BUSINESS PROCESS	An information process needs to be regularly updated to meet the changing needs of the business.	Implement the information process in a workflow engine that is interpreting a business process model. The model can be updated as the business changes and redeployed to the workflow engine.
	STATE DRIVEN PROCESS	An information process must be driven by events in other information processes.	Create a state machine that defines the behavior of the information process for each event it has to react to.
	COLLABORATIVE EDITING PROCESS	Introducing a new entry in an information collection needs values from a variety of individuals.	Define an information process that coordinates the collection of the information values from the relevant individuals and then stores the combined results in an information collection.
	INFORMATION REPORTING PROCESS	The business needs reports that report on past performance and possible projected performance.	Use a variety of visualization approaches to display the information so that the information users can understand the trends, exceptions, and relationships in the information.

Bespoke Application Process

Context

An organization requires an **INFORMATION PROCESS** to support one of its activities.

Problem

An information process needs highly specialized behavior to support an activity in an organization.

In many large organizations, it is necessary to divide the teams into autonomous groups and provide IT services to them that are specialized to their needs. Some of these teams need bespoke function for areas that are critical to its success, particularly if it gives them a competitive advantage or it is supporting fast-changing regulations or business environment.

Example

When MCHS Trading was first started, the organization needed an application to manage the orders coming in from its clients, either via the telephone or mail order. This order processing was central to the business and, the organization believed this had to be specially tailored to its needs.

Forces

- **Many organizations believe they are special and unique**—This leads to the internal development of more function than is strictly necessary.
- **Applications affect behavior**—The way an application is implemented will have a profound influence on the way the organization operates around it. It is often hard to separate those operational aspects that are dictated by the existing applications and those that are requirements of the organization's business.
- **Workarounds are common**—Where an application does not completely meet the needs of an organization, the people using it find ways to work around it. This can involve putting information into attributes designed for different purposes, or changing values in files/databases after the application has finished processing. Often this creates inconsistencies in recording the current state of processing.

Solution

Implement the information process using an in-house or consultant team ensuring it meets the needs of the organization.

Such bespoke information processes are typically self-contained, running in their own information node with their own user interfaces and all of the information they use managed in local information collections. They are often implemented and maintained by in-house staff.

Change to these applications happens slowly because it is costly to the organization. However, provided the IT team has retained the source code and appropriate documentation, the behavior of the information processes it supports is both understood and can be changed to meet new business needs.

Consequences

Benefits:

- The information process is tailored to the needs of the organization.

Liabilities:

- Creating software may not be the core competency of the organization and so these applications may not be best-of-breed.

Example Resolved

MCHS Trading implemented its own Mail-Shop application to take orders from customers received either though the post (mail), or through the call center. This application is efficient at entering new orders. It requires the customer details to be entered for each order and does not keep a history of an individual's orders longer than a month.

Known Uses

This pattern represents the many types of business application built by organizations to support their business.

Related Patterns

A bespoke application process resides in an **A**PPLICATION **N**ODE. It uses information collections that have a **M**ASTER **U**SAGE, with **L**OCAL **S**COPE and **L**OCAL **C**OVERAGE.

Packaged Application Process

Context

An organization requires an **I**NFORMATION **P**ROCESS to support one of its activities.

Problem

All or part of an information process is too expensive or too complex for the organization to implement.

Example

When MCHS Trading wanted to create an Internet-based shop, it had no in-house experience with web technology. They needed a professional website that was secure and easy to use.

Forces

- **Many organizations believe they are special and unique—**This leads to the internal development of more function than is strictly necessary.
- **Applications affect behavior—**The way an application is implemented will have a profound influence on the way the organization operates around it. It is often hard to separate those operational aspects that are dictated by the existing applications and those that are requirements of the organization's business.
- **Workarounds are common—**Where an application does not completely meet the needs of an organization, the people using it find ways to work around it. This can involve putting information into attributes designed for different purposes, or changing values in files/databases after the application has finished processing. Often this creates inconsistencies in recording the current state of processing.

Solution

Buy a software package to support the business process.

This will either come as a standalone application or a software library that needs to be integrated into an application.

Consequences

Benefits:

- Specialized expertise is encoded in the function of the package that would be too expensive for the organization to write itself. This is particularly valuable if the subject area is evolving rapidly and is not part of the organization's differentiating or core capability.

Liabilities:

- The function, and to some extent, the information, within a packaged application is opaque to the organization. When changes are needed, the organization will typically need the help of the package supplier. Also a package imposes a business operations model on the organization. It is typically most cost effective to adopt the package's assumed business operations model rather than modify the package to the organization's existing model.

Example Resolved

MCHS Trading bought a specialist e-commerce package that was used to create the E-Shop application. This software provided the catalog web pages for browsing and selecting goods, a shopping basket, secure customer account, and management of payment details. This package also offered an external interface for loading product information and working with the customer and order data.

Known Uses

Packaged applications are used extensively in the IT industry today. They are often called "Custom off-the-shelf" (COTS) packages.

Related Patterns

A packaged application process resides in an **A**PPLICATION **N**ODE. It typically uses information collections that have a **M**ASTER **U**SAGE, with **L**OCAL **S**COPE and **L**OCAL **C**OVERAGE.

Agile Business Process

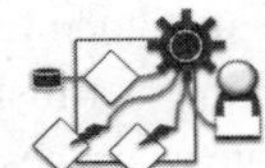

Context

An organization requires an **I**NFORMATION **P**ROCESS to support one of its activities.

Problem

An information process needs to be regularly updated to meet the changing needs of the business.

Example

MCHS Trading wants to improve its customer service. It is aware that its customers want more information and control over the progress of their orders. However, the precise details of the capabilities that its customers will appreciate are still a little hazy. MCHS Trading is looking for an approach that will allow it to experiment with new features without incurring too much cost.

Forces

- **Many organizations believe they are special and unique**—This leads to the internal development of more function than is strictly necessary.
- **Applications affect behavior**—The way an application is implemented will have a profound influence on the way the organization operates around it. It is often hard to separate those operational aspects that are dictated by the existing applications and those that are requirements of the organization's business.
- **Workarounds are common**—Where an application does not completely meet the needs of an organization, the people using it find ways to work around it. This can involve putting information into attributes designed for different purposes, or changing values in files/databases after the application has finished processing. Often this creates inconsistencies in recording the current state of processing.

Solution

Implement the information process in a workflow engine that is interpreting a business process model. The model can be updated as the business changes and redeployed to the workflow engine.

A business process model describes the steps and decisions that implement the required behavior. Each step is implemented by a web service or local procedure. Some steps may involve displaying user interface screens to selected people to provide information or review a proposed change.

Consequences

Benefits:

- Using business process modeling enables the organization to review how the information process will behave. Some business people may even be involved in the creation of the definition. When the business needs change, the model can be changed and redeployed.

Liabilities:

- An agile business process may run slower than a hard-coded one. These types of processes also work with information from remote information nodes. The information collections and information processes that originally supported it need to be checked to make sure the new use case introduced by the agile business process is not going to impact the existing operation.

Example Resolved

MCHS Trading introduces a new application called Customer-Care that is implemented with a workflow engine. The workflow engine runs a number of agile business processes that implement the new customer service capability.

Figure 7.10 shows a sample process definition for canceling an order.

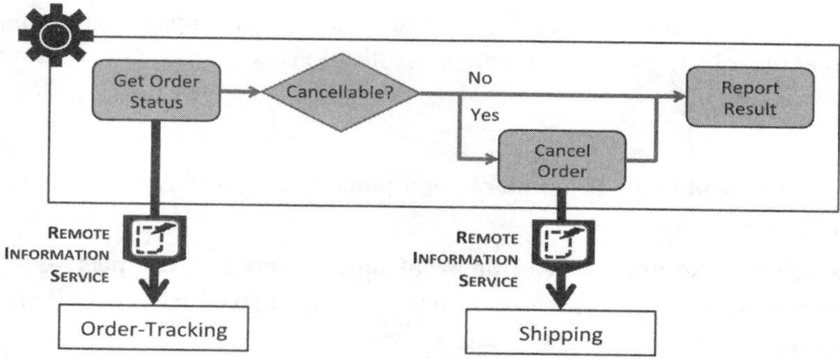

Figure 7.10 Cancel Order process for MCHS Trading.

The agile business process makes calls to the other applications to find out the status of the order and cancel the order if necessary. This includes a new application called Order-Tracking (which contains a **S**TATE **D**RIVEN **P**ROCESS that monitors the state of the orders as they flow between the applications). The Shipping application is responsible for actually canceling the order. This cancellation request may arrive before the original order arrives, in which case the cancel request is stored and matched with the order request when it arrives.

Known Uses

Workflow and business process management engines support this pattern. The business process flows are typically models in BPMN2.0 or UML.

Related Patterns

An agile business process resides in an **A**PPLICATION **N**ODE. An agile business process may incorporate an **I**NFORMATION **D**ECISION **D**EFINITION **P**ROCESS for complex business decisions.

State Driven Process

Context

An organization requires an **I**NFORMATION **P**ROCESS to support one of its activities.

Problem

An information process must be driven by events in other information processes.

This information process is passive, dependent on the calling information processes to pass it information. It is responsible for reacting to the events as they arrive.

Example

MCHS Trading would like to maintain the current state of each order as the orders pass between the applications. This information is not currently maintained by any of the applications. It is implicit in how far the order record has progress through the applications.

Forces

- **No activity may be a problem**—If an information process fails, it may not send an event to the state driven process.
- **The correct action to take may depend on what has occurred in the past**—For example, if a business transaction is canceled, then the work to undo what has been done so far will depend on how far the processing had reached.

- **The order in which events occur may vary in a distributed environment**—When work is split between information nodes, it is sometimes hard to be sure of the exact sequence of activity.

Solution

Create a state machine that defines the behavior of the information process for each event it has to react to.

The state driven process is responsible for maintaining a state value. This is stored as an attribute in an information entry within an information collection.

Typically, an information service is called to trigger the state driven process. This service passes the process an INFORMATION EVENT and the INFORMATION KEY for the state machine. The information key is used to retrieve the information entry with the current state attribute in it. The event and the current state are fed into the state machine to determine the new current state. The new current state is saved into the information entry and returned to the caller.

Extensions to this can include the following:

- Calls to the state driven process are scheduled to check that it has not been in the same state too long. If no state change has occurred since the last time check, then an alert is raised. If the state change occurred, then the time check is ignored.
- The state driven process may invoke information services to save data or to initiate another information process when a particular state change, or state, occurs.
- The events may be logged in an information collection for future reference—particularly auditing or troubleshooting.
- Additional information in the information events, such as links to related information activities and information assets, can be added to the information entry. This is useful for events that can occur at any time prior to a certain state transition.

Consequences

Benefits:

- Consolidation of state changes increases the consistency and reliability of applications that must make decisions based on the state of the information. Changes to the behavior of specific states can be consolidated, reducing the management cost.

Liabilities:

- The number of states in the state machine can become large if events can happen in a nondeterministic order. One way to combat this is to supplement the state value stored in the local information collection with additional information that is received in the events that count occurrences, record activity, and point to related INFORMATION ACTIVITIES and INFORMATION ASSETS.

Example Resolved

MCHS Trading introduced a new application called Order-Tracking that manages the state of all orders as they pass through other applications. The other applications use specific information services available from Order-Tracking to pass information events as they occur.

Figure 7.11 shows the state machine. The labels on the arcs (such as Payment Made, Order Canceled, etc.) represent the types of events that the state driven process can receive. The ellipses represent the state of the order.

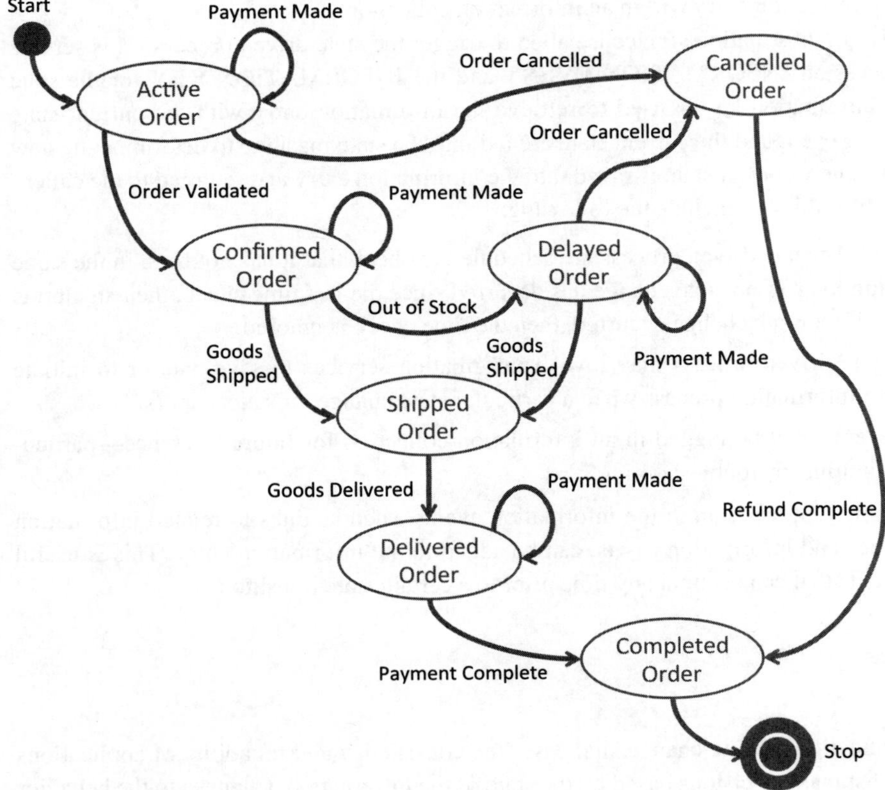

Figure 7.11 Order-Tracking's state machine.

There are a couple of interesting points to notice:

- The state machine restricts when certain events are permitted. For example, Order Canceled is only permitted if the current state is Active Order or Delayed Order.

- Payment Received can occur in many states, and does not cause a state change. The Payment Received event includes the amount received. The state driven process is accumulating the payments and will not transition to Completed Order until the payments match the order value.

Known Uses

State machines are particularly useful when monitoring DAISY CHAIN PROVISIONING, or for case management systems where a case has to pass through particular states to be resolved.

Related Patterns

The INFORMATION EVENT pattern describes the event that drives a state driven process.

The INFORMATION ACTIVITY HUB makes use of state driven processes to record the current state of a distributed activity.

Collaborative Editing Process

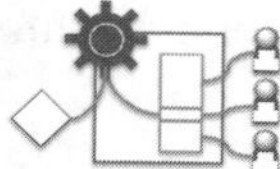

Context

An organization requires an INFORMATION PROCESS to support one of its activities.

Problem

Introduction of a new entry in an information collection needs values from a variety of individuals.

These individuals may be from different parts of the organization and have different skill sets and vocabularies. This requirement is common when either introducing or making significant changes to instances of INFORMATION ASSETS—for example, products, employees, suppliers, or a new account for a customer.

Example

Introducing a new product into the MCHS Trading catalog requires a market to be identified, suppliers to be identified and contacted, pricing and advertising to be worked out, relevant regulatory provision to be enabled, and entries to be coordinated into the information collections that require the product details.

Forces

- **The way an application is implemented will have a profound influence on the way the organization operates around it**—It is often hard to separate those operational aspects that are dictated by the existing applications and those that are requirements of the organization's business. This can make it hard to change the implementation of information processes, particularly when previously independent teams need to coordinate their activities.

- **Information growth requires new approaches**—Increasing volumes of information can dramatically impact the ability to process information through human interaction points.

Solution

Define a business process that coordinates the collection of the information values from the relevant individuals and then stores the combined results in an information collection.

Each step in the process creates a task for an individual to provide the information values he or she is responsible for, or to approve information values that have already been provided. As the process progresses, more of the attributes in the new information entry are filled in and approved.

With this approach, people from different teams are able to contribute and control the subset of the attributes that are relevant to their work. Behind the scenes, the information is assembled, validated, and consolidated into one or more information entries in one or more information collections.

Consequences

Benefits:

- This pattern coordinates the collection of new information values for an information entry from independent teams, along with the necessary approval cycles, while automating validation and distribution of the resulting information entry to one or more information collections. The result is coherent information capture. It enables the creation of shared information collections with broader coverage in organizations where the independent teams would naturally elect to have private information collections.

Liabilities:

- The collaborative editing process must take into account that people have vacations, sick leave, and change jobs. It must enable the reallocation and delegation of work when individuals are not available so that work is not halted when someone is absent.

Example Resolved

The Product Hub information processing for adding a new product is an automated business process that assigns and coordinates the work of the teams involved.

Figure 7.12 shows the steps involved. For each product to be defined, the Product Hub application assigns a task to an appropriate individual to supply information or approve some of the information that has already been provided.

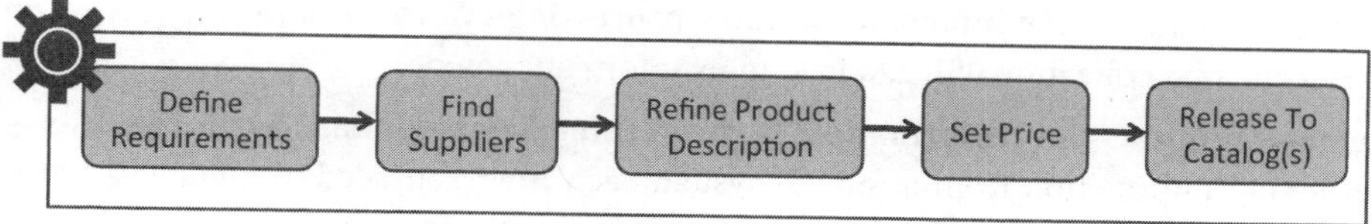

Figure 7.12 New product introduction process.

Known Uses

Most common are business processes that incorporate human input, editing, and review around the creation of new entities. These are sometimes called human-centric workflows. Examples include the introduction of new products as shown in the example, the introduction of new employees, the creation of a new account for a customer, or the tracking and update of customer service calls.

Related Patterns

A collaborative editing process resides in an **A**PPLICATION **N**ODE.

It is typically used when introducing or making a significant change to an **I**NFORMATION **E**NTRY that represents an **I**NFORMATION **A**SSET.

Information Reporting Process

Context

An organization requires an **I**NFORMATION **P**ROCESS to support one of its activities.

Problem

The business needs reports that present information on past performance and possible projected performance.

Example

When management at MCHS Trading wanted to get more insight into the trends in customer purchases across specific demographics and geographies, it found that the reporting within its existing applications was not sufficient to provide this view and custom programming to collect the diverse information did not provide timely or consistent reporting.

Forces

- **Information growth requires new approaches—**Increasing volumes of information can dramatically impact the amount of resources and time required to process it.

- **Servicing requests for information takes processing effort**—Additional queries on an information collection will add load to its information node.
- **Remote requests for information have greater latency than local requests**—Retrieving information from a remote system each time you need to include it introduces a delay and puts extra load on the system hosting the information.
- **Additional copies of information add cost**—Copying information so it is local to the processing reduces latency in retrieving information but takes additional storage and adds a requirement to synchronize the copies.
- **Variety of formats**—Information is not stored in the same format in every information node.

Solution

Use a variety of visualization approaches to display the information so that the information users can understand the trends, exceptions, and relationships in the information.

The information reporting process is responsible for the effective display of complex sets of information. It must support a variety of visualization techniques to allow a person to review the information from different perspectives and levels of detail.

An industry model can define a best-practice structure for consolidating information from multiple information supply chains to support a particular report. Information elements from the differing supply chains can be deployed, replicated, or federated into the modeled structure at detailed and summarized levels to support and optimize reporting queries and dashboards.

Consequences

Benefits:

- Consolidated and consistent views across multiple information supply chains can be established, providing greater insight into business results.

Liabilities:

- An information reporting process is likely to require additional information collections to be established with the associated costs.
- The quality of the reports and dashboards produced by this process is only as good as the information supply chains provisioning it.

Example Resolved

MCHS Trading introduces a new information node called Decision-Center that supports specialized information reporting processes to generate and display standardized daily, weekly, monthly, and annual reports, as well as dashboard views for management. The Decision-Center is provisioned with information from the Reporting Hub. This is a **H**ISTORICAL **S**YSTEM OF **R**ECORD solution where customer, product, orders and sales, shipping, and inventory information are collected and synchronized.

Known Uses

Information reporting processes are found in applications and in business intelligence and reporting packages. They are able to visualize information in many different ways. Examples of visualizations can be found at http://www-958.ibm.com/software/data/cognos/manyeyes/page/Visualization_Options.html.

Related Patterns

INFORMATION **W**ORKERs are the users of an information reporting process.

The **P**ERFORMANCE **R**EPORTING solution is built using information reporting processes.

Information reporting processes are hosted in an **A**PPLICATION **N**ODE. Their information is typically provisioned through **I**NFORMATION **S**ERVICES accessing an **I**NFORMATION **M**ART.

Quality Information Processes

The information processes in Table 7.5 are focused on improving the quality of an organization's information, either through direct action or through reporting on the state of the information's quality. The aim with these processes is to use as much automation as possible to maintain a cadence around information quality so that it becomes a regular part of running the business. Over time, these activities embed care of information into the organization's culture, resulting in an improvement of information quality.

Table 7.5 Quality Information Processes Pattern Summaries

Icon	Pattern Name	Problem	Solution
	INFORMATION PROFILE TRACKING PROCESS	An organization does not understand the profile of its information or know when the profile of one of its critical information collections changes.	Periodically run an information process to create an **I**NFORMATION **V**ALUES **P**ROFILE report and compare the values from the recent profile with those of previous runs. Report on the changes.
	CLERICAL REVIEW PROCESS	An information process is not able to complete the processing of a request without input from an information steward.	Create a task to inform the information steward that its assistance is required. This task is populated with details of the work that needs to be completed.

Icon	Pattern Name	Problem	Solution
	INFORMATION REMEDIATION PROCESS	Errors in the organization's information are being detected all of the time but never fixed.	Gather together errors and then triage and remediate them, focusing on the most critical errors first.
	INFORMATION VALIDATION PROCESS	An organization does not know whether its information conforms to the validation rules it has defined.	Run an information process to step through the information and execute the appropriate validation rules. Report on the errors found.
	INFORMATION MATCHING PROCESS	An information process needs to combine related information entries that have come from multiple sources.	Use matching technology to score the similarity between the information entries from the different sources and combine them as appropriate.
	INFORMATION EVER-GREENING PROCESS	Information about the real world decays over time. The existing information processes are not able to guarantee that the contents of an information collection are correct and up to date.	Set up a regular process that steps through the entries in the information collection and runs various validation checks against them, raising alerts where information values are found to be incorrect or stale.
	INFORMATION ARCHIVING PROCESS	Eventually, entries in an information collection are no longer needed operationally, but must be retained for reference.	Set up a regular archiving process to move the information that is no longer needed operationally to an archive store where it can be retrieved if necessary.

Information Profile Tracking Process

Context

An organization wants to automate the quality management of its information.

Problem

An organization does not understand the profile of its information or know when the profile of one of its critical information collections changes.

The profile of an information collection describes the information values that it contains. This includes the range of values in an attribute, the frequency that a particular value occurs in an attribute, and the relationships between information values in different attributes. This is useful to know when assessing the quality of the information within the collection.

Example

In an initial test of its new Customer Hub, MCHS Trading wants to understand the characteristics of its customers.

Forces

- **The information explains how the information processes are really working**—Most information collections have an information schema that describes the structure of the information attributes stored in each information entry and the relationships between them. There may also be design documents that describe what type of information is stored in each attribute. However, the software developer can receive late requests to support new functions and find they need to manage and store information in attributes that were intended for different purposes. It is not until the information processes are running, and the information values in the information collections are checked, that these expediencies come to light.
- **The profile of an information collection changes over time**—This may be because the quality is improving, or simply that the characteristics of the world it is describing are changing. This changing profile may affect the information processes that are using the information because they are coded with assumptions about the information they are using.
- **Information growth requires new approaches**—Increasing volumes of information can dramatically impact the amount of resources and time required to process it. Statistical sampling or other approaches may be needed to support ongoing tracking.
- **Cost to store/track full profile**—Information profiling requires dedicated processing time and storage to maintain and track.
- **Cost to correct may not be cost-justified**—The cost to fix specific errors in the information vales must be measured against the cost to the business in increased risk, added business costs, or loss of revenue.

Solution

Periodically run an information process to create an INFORMATION VALUES PROFILE report and compare the values from the recent profile with those of previous runs. Report on the changes.

The frequency of evaluation and review corresponds to the criticality and volatility of the information. New sources of information should be evaluated at the point of acquisition. Old information value profiles need to be regularly archived or purged, striking a balance between usefulness and relevance.

Consequences

Benefits:

- Using information profile tracking enables the organization to identify, understand, and track the information values with a goal of delivering effective information processes that work with and move data, reducing risk during project implementation or migration of new data into existing information collections. Such understanding also becomes a foundational aspect of a broader **I**NFORMATION **G**OVERNANCE **P**ROGRAM.

Liabilities:

- Many information values have a business context that requires business knowledge to interpret—review can be labor-intensive particularly if the information profile is applied to too many information collections without appropriate focus. There is also a cost to storing and retaining information value profiles.

Example Resolved

MCHS Trading runs an information profile tracking process on the customer information used in the initial Customer Hub test. They find that the customer tax ID stored in the Stores' Sales Account collection includes hyphens in the values, whereas the tax ID stored in the E-Shop Customer collection does not. They determine that an **I**NFORMATION **R**EENGINEERING **S**TEP, specifically a **S**TANDARDIZE **D**ATA step, is needed in the **I**NFORMATION **D**EPLOYMENT **P**ROCESS to ensure correct loading of the new customer information collection in the Customer Hub.

MCHS Trading schedules a monthly refresh of the **I**NFORMATION **V**ALUE **P**ROFILES to maintain trust in the Customer Hub.

Known Uses

Advanced information profiling tools offer the capability to schedule profiling and validation jobs so that they run against critical information collections on a regular basis. Where the information profiling tools do not offer this facility, it may be possible to schedule a script or program to manage the invocation of the profiling process and analysis of the results.

Related Patterns

An **I**NFORMATION **R**EMEDIATION **P**ROCESS may be implemented to correct issues in the information collection that have been detected by the information profile tracking process.

Clerical Review Process

Context

An organization wants to automate the quality management of its information.

Problem

An information process is not able to complete the processing of a request without input from an information steward.

The role of the information steward in this process is often to simply confirm a proposed change to the information (such as the enrichment of information). However, there are other circumstances where the information steward needs to make a decision (such as whether two records should be merged) or select some information values (such as which values to use from two information entries that are being merged).

Example

MCHS Trading implements its new Customer Hub incorporating processes to match and merge information entries that relate to the same person. (See the **I**NFORMATION **M**ATCHING **P**RO-CESS for more information on this type of processing.) Subsequent calls to the Customer-Care center indicate that some customers' orders were sent to the wrong individuals because some customer records were inappropriately merged together. Examples of incorrect customer record merging include the following:

- "Thomas Jones, 104 W. Elm St., Black Rock, WI" merged with
  "Thomas Jonas, 104 Elm Ave., Black Rock, WI"
- "Wm Holden, 128A Maine Sq, Carmelton, Il" merged with
  "Will Holden, 128 Main Sq, Carmelton, IL" and
  "Willa Holden, 128C Maine Sq, Carmelton, IL"

Subtle differences in spelling and location, errors, or a lack of sufficient information values can impact the reliability of such automated processes.

Forces

- **Manual processes add latency—**The time for an information steward to review a case adds latency into the process.
- **Manual correction of issues are limited by volume—**High volumes of information or a high proportion of issues in the information will require prioritization of which changes are reviewed, and when.

- **Automated correction of issues is limited by data complexity**—The complexity of the information or requirements for specialized knowledge may preclude automated remediation or ever-greening options.
- **Cost to correct may not be cost-justified**—The cost to review specific types of clerical records must be measured against the cost to the business in increased risk, added business costs, or loss of revenue.

Solution

Create a task to inform the information steward that his or her assistance is required. This task is populated with details of the work that needs to be completed.

The information steward regularly reviews the tasks on his or her list and processes each in turn. When he or she selects a task, details of the proposed change are displayed and the information steward is able to make updates and accept or reject the changes. The decision the information steward makes is recorded and may be passed to another information steward or supervisor for review/approval.

Once the change is approved, it is applied to the information collection. It is important that these changes are applied as soon as possible before new updates to the affected information entries are made.

Not all information collections, even those within the same subject area, require the same level of manual review. For example, duplicate customer information for a marketing campaign may be merged automatically without a clerical review as the consequences of a mistake are minimal, whereas customer information used for orders must be kept distinct to ensure that the right goods reach the right person.

Consequences

Benefits:

- Using clerical review enables the organization to verify and approve changes that information processes are proposing to make to an information collection.

Liabilities:

- Clerical review requires dedicated resources to resolve issues. The people involved must understand the information values and business context. Clerical review may be perceived as expensive, particularly if they are not directed to information nodes of high value to the organization from a revenue, cost, or risk standpoint.

Example Resolved

MCHS Trading modifies the thresholds on the **I**NFORMATION **M**ATCHING **P**ROCESS in the Customer Hub to include a clerical review whenever information entries are to be merged that are only a close match rather than an exact match. This clerical review helps to prevent the erroneous merging of information going forward.

MCHS Trading also uses clerical review to check the merges that have already taken place, so information entries can be split apart again if they were merged in error. This is possible because the Customer Hub keeps archived copies of the original information entries and creates a new information entry for the merged result.

Known Uses

Clerical review processes are often a key component of Master Data Management (MDM) hubs that are continuously validating and matching new information as it is received. The clerical review process provides a rapid confirmation of changes that are proposed by the hub information processes that have a certain level of doubt to them.

Related Patterns

The **I**NFORMATION **M**ATCHING **P**ROCESS and **I**NFORMATION **E**VER-GREENING **P**ROCESS often invoke clerical review processes.

The process of merging information entries is described in the **M**ERGE **E**NTRIES pattern. The process for splitting merged information entries apart is described in the **S**EPARATE **E**NTRIES pattern. Both the merge entries and separate entries patterns are from the **I**NFORMATION **R**EENGINEERING **S**TEP pattern group.

Information Remediation Process

Context

An organization wants to automate the quality management of its information.

Problem

Errors in the organization's information are being detected all of the time but never fixed.

This is because the organization needs a person with knowledge of the subject area to review the information values, perform some investigation, and make changes. How is this manual correction of information managed?

Example

The MCHS Trading Mail-Shop application is used by the call center to enter new customer orders. It is an older system that has limited validation of the information that is entered. The result is that the Shipping application sometimes receives order details with errors in them. Examples of these errors include customer name spelled incorrectly, incomplete or incorrect address, or an order for an unknown product. How does MCHS Trading process these orders?

Forces

- **Manual processes add latency—**The time to remediate an issue adds latency into the process—remediation may have to be applied after the fact.
- **Manual correction of issues are limited by volume—**High volume of data or a high proportion of issues in the data will preclude manual remediation of information.
- **Automated correction of issues is limited by data complexity—**The complexity of the information or requirements for specialized knowledge may preclude automated remediation or ever-greening options.
- **Cost to correct may not be cost-justified—**The cost to fix specific types of data errors must be measured against the cost to the business in increased risk, added business costs, or loss of revenue.

Solution

Gather together errors, and then triage and remediate them, focusing on the most critical errors first.

When errors are detected, they should be flagged and added to the list of errors that need correcting. An individual, or a team, must be responsible for processing the errors found. The errors should be prioritized and processed in the most cost-effective order. The person working on an error needs to investigate why the value is wrong, find the correct value, change the information so the correct values are introduced into the information supply chain, and record what was changed and why. This explanation provides an audit trail of changes being made to the information.

From time to time, the records from the remediation process should be reviewed to determine if there are changes that could be made to the information supply chain to reduce the chances of similar errors being introduced in the future.

Consequences

Benefits:

- Using information remediation processes enables the organization to identify and respond to errors with a goal of improving the overall quality of its information (and rules and processes applied to the data). Such corrective action becomes an aspect of a broader INFORMATION GOVERNANCE PROGRAM.

Liabilities:

- Information remediation requires dedicated resources to resolve issues. These resources may be perceived as expenses or costs to the organization, particularly if they are not directed to information nodes of high value to the organization from a revenue, cost, or risk standpoint.

Example Resolved

An **I**NFORMATION **V**ALIDATION **P**ROCESS situated in the **I**NFORMATION **F**LOW that moves new orders from E-Shop, Mail-Shop, and Stores is used to check all orders before they are passed to Shipping. Most orders are correct and they are passed directly to Shipping. Orders that have errors in them are moved to a **S**TAGING **A**REA. They are corrected by the Shipping team who focus on high-value orders and orders from high-value customers first before processing the rest. The Shipping team keeps detailed records of the changes that they are making to the incorrect orders, and may call the customer to verify the order. These details of the changes and comments from the Shipping team are fed into the Customer Hub so the Customer-Care center can answer questions from a customer if the order is not what they expected.

Known Uses

Information quality and information governance initiatives incorporate information remediation processes at all levels of maturity, though at lower levels the approach is reactive rather than preventative. ETL, messaging, or ever-greening processes and any other information management routines that incorporate information validation processes to identify errors often feed remediation processes.

The software that supports a remediation process may simply maintain the list of outstanding errors; support the triaging of these errors and the recording of the remediation action taken. More sophisticated systems may also incorporate **A**GILE **B**USINESS **P**ROCESSES to coordinate the correction, review, and approval of changes made to the information.

Related Patterns

A process that includes a **C**HECK **D**ATA step, an **I**NFORMATION **V**ALIDATION **P**ROCESS, or an **I**NFORMATION **R**EPORTING **P**ROCESS can trigger an information remediation process.

Information Validation Process

Context

An organization wants to automate the quality management of its information.

Problem

An organization does not know whether its information conforms to the validation rules it has defined.

How do you understand how well an information supply chain is working when its processing is so varied and distributed?

Example

MCHS Trading uses specific product categories in its **I**NFORMATION **R**EPORTING **P**ROCESSES to identify broad sales and buying trends. For each category, there are specific **V**ALID **V**ALUES **D**EFINITIONS that are supposed to be adhered to. The buyers notice unexpected sales trends in one product category, with sales much lower than expected in another. How do they determine if the reports are correct?

Forces

- **Rapidly changing content**—Changes in information quality rules can result in incorrect information validation results if such changes are not properly synchronized across the entire information supply chain.
- **Some information must always be processed**—Errors found in the information values cannot always halt the information from further processing.
- **Acquired information may have different context or format**—New or acquired information may not be based on the same criteria or be structured in the same manner.
- **Business context poorly understood**—Old systems, lack of knowledgeable personnel, or lack of documentation may significantly limit the understanding of what rules to apply to the data.

Solution

Run an information process to step through the information and execute the appropriate validation rules. Report on the errors found.

The information process will iterate through the information values, using a **V**ALIDATE **D**ATA step to check that it conforms to the appropriate valid values definitions. It will record the errors discovered for later remediation.

Consequences

Benefits:

- Validating the completeness, consistency, reliability, and quality of information will improve the information used by an organization for key decision making, resulting in cost savings, mitigated risk, or potential revenue opportunity. Such information validation becomes an aspect of a broader **I**NFORMATION **G**OVERNANCE **P**ROGRAM.

Liabilities:

- Information validation is only useful if the results are acted upon through an **I**NFORMATION **R**EMEDIATION **P**ROCESS. This takes time, qualified people, and resources.

- Information validation processes must be kept in sync with changes to business processes and rules, potentially adding time and cost to implement such changes. Having centralized management of validation rules can minimize this work because the information verification processes will pick up the changes immediately.

Example Resolved

Based on discoveries from an INFORMATION VALUES PROFILE pattern, MCHS adds an INFORMATION VALIDATION PROCESS to check the consistency of products and product categories between the Stores system and the Product Hub. MCHS Trading looks to identify the most problematic items in the Store system and establish tighter information controls on entering and changing product categories in the Stores.

Known Uses

Information quality and information governance initiatives incorporate information validation processes at various levels of maturity. ETL and other data integration routines incorporate information monitoring to ensure that required information has been received and that the same information is not processed multiple times.

Related Patterns

The INFORMATION PROFILE TRACKING PROCESS is used to identify the INFORMATION VALUES PROFILE from which some validation rules are derived.

The INFORMATION DEPLOYMENT PROCESS, as well as most business process patterns, incorporates the CHECK DATA patterns for specific validations to catch issues before they move further along the information supply chain. The INFORMATION REMEDIATION PROCESS pattern is used to resolve issues found by an INFORMATION VALIDATION PROCESS.

Information Matching Process

Context

An organization requires an information process to support the provisioning of information along an INFORMATION SUPPLY CHAIN.

Problem

An information process needs to combine related information entries that have come from multiple sources.

These information entries represent the same person, organization, place, account, object....

Example

MCHS Trading has customer information arriving from its E-Shop, Mail-Shop, and Stores systems. Review of the Customer Hub shows many similar names with common addresses or email addresses as well as addresses that match but have distinct names.

Multiple instances of the same or similar records in the Customer Hub cause inconsistent customer views as well as generating customer care issues.

Forces

- **Insufficient information to match together**—There may be insufficient information values to support the matching of information entries.
- **Information is time sensitive**—Time dependencies may require that incorrect or unlinked information be loaded into the target information node and matched after that point.
- **Information volatility may impact matching**—The addition of differing "population" groups to a given subject area may significantly impact matching processes.

Solution

Use matching technology to score the similarity between the information entries from the different sources and combine them as appropriate.

This process is implemented using the following steps:

- Certain INFORMATION REENGINEERING STEPS, such as ENRICH DATA and STANDARDIZE DATA, may be needed to improve the accuracy of matching.
- The information entries to be matched are compared and their similarity is scored against a variety of criteria and weightings.
- Based on the score, the match is classified into one of three groups. The thresholds for these groups are typically configurable values:
  1. **Weak match**—The score is too low, which means the information entries are for different "things."
  2. **Close match**—The score indicates the match is close, but not close enough to be sure. This pair is passed to a CLERICAL REVIEW PROCESS.
  3. **Strong match**—The information entries are matched and should either be linked together (see LINK ENTRIES) or merged into a single information entry (see MERGE ENTRIES).
- Finally, the new and updated information is saved into the destination.

Consequences

Benefits:

- The information matching process provides the mechanism to effectively link and consolidate related information together.

Liabilities:

- Individuals familiar with the requirements of the subject area must tune this process to ensure appropriate grouping and consolidation of data. Incorrect grouping can have significant ramifications and risks to an organization because the matching is typically applied to core subject areas, such as Customer, Account, or Product.

Example Resolved

MCHS Trading uses an **I**NFORMATION **E**VER-GREENING **P**ROCESS to trawl through the existing information entries in the Customer Hub and call the information matching process to detect information entries that should be merged. Some entries are automatically merged; others are merged after a **C**LERICAL **R**EVIEW **P**ROCESS.

The process of adding and updating information entries in the Customer Hub is also changed to use an information matching process to detect if new information is in fact an update of an existing information entry rather than a creation of a new information entry. This enhancement is called the unique entries pattern that is part of the information entry pattern group.

Known Uses

Information matching is a core component of Master Data Management (MDM) solutions particularly for core subject areas, such as Person, Party, Location, and Product. Information matching processes may be incorporated into business processes, information provisioning processes, and information quality processes.

Related Patterns

Information entries that are potential match candidates are linked together using the **L**INK **E**NTRIES information reengineering step. Information entries that need to be merged are combined using the **M**ERGE **E**NTRIES information reengineering step and information entries that have been merged in error can be split apart again using the **S**EPARATE **E**NTRIES information reengineering step.

Information Ever-Greening Process

Context

An organization wants to automate the quality management of its information.

Problem

Information about the real world decays over time. The existing information processes are not able to guarantee that the contents of an information collection are up to date.

Example

MCHS Trading wants to send promotional emails to its customers from time to time. When a new customer registers with E-Shop, he or she is asked to provide an email address, which will be used when sending the promotional material. In the United States, it is estimated that people change contact information, such as email addresses, on average about once every 3 months. This means that over time, the email addresses in the customer details in E-Shop are gradually becoming obsolete.

Forces

- **Unused information is out of date**—It is typically the information that is not being accessed that is the most likely to be out of date.
- **There is an increasing load on information nodes**—Additional queries on an information collection will add load to its information node.
- **Information is time sensitive**—Time dependencies may require that incorrect or unlinked data be loaded into the target information node and linked and merged after that point.
- **Many conditions cannot be automated**—Issues from upstream in the information supply chain and some validation checks cannot be handled automatically and must be remediated through manual review.

Solution

Set up a regular process that steps through the entries in the information collection and runs various validation checks against them, raising alerts where information values are found to be incorrect or stale.

An information ever-greening process provides continuous patching of the values within an information collection. It typically runs on the information node where the information collection is located, or in an INFORMATION BROKER that has access to the information collection.

Consequences

Benefits:

- The ever-greening process detects and flags information that is potentially out of date.

Liabilities:

- There may be some latency introduced by the information ever-greening process to the information supply chain. It can result in additional processing load to the information node that hosts the information collections, affecting all information processes that use the information. The information ever-greening process should be throttled back to minimize the impact.

Example Resolved

MCHS Trading has an integration job that systematically scans the customer details entries in the E-Shop application and flags those entries where the email address has not been verified for over 2 months. When a customer connects to the E-Shop, the flag is checked for his or her entry and if it is set, the customer is asked to verify that the email and phone number are correct.

Known Uses

Ever-greening is typically supported by Master Data Management (MDM) products for detecting data decay and duplicate suspects. Ever-greening may trigger other automated processes such as requesting that customers provide updated address and phone information.

Related Patterns

The information ever-greening process may detect errors that it cannot correct automatically. It will notify an **I**NFORMATION **R**EMEDIATION **P**ROCESS to correct it. Similarly, the information ever-greening process may propose changes to make that must be submitted to a **C**LERICAL **R**EVIEW **P**ROCESS.

Information Archiving Process

Context

An organization wants to automate the quality management of its information.

Problem

Eventually, entries in an information collection are no longer needed operationally, but must be retained for reference.

Once this happens, their presence in the information collection can start to impact the performance of the information processes using it.

Example

The E-Shop application stores details of each customer's orders. Three months after the order has been completed, this information is likely to be obsolete.

Forces

- **Increasing volume degrades query performance**—Additional volume of data and queries on an information collection will degrade the performance of an information node.
- **Regulations and policies set retention requirements**—For some types of information, there are legal regulations that require an organization to retain information for many years. This retention period may be longer than the useful life of the originating application.

Solution

Set up a regular archiving process to move the information that is no longer needed operationally to an archive store where it can be retrieved if necessary.

The information archiving process may run on the information node where the information collection is hosted, or on a remote information node (for example, where the information archive is located).

Consequences

Benefits:

- The information collection that receives regular housekeeping, such as archiving of obsolete information, benefits from improved processing time and reduced online storage costs.

Liabilities:

- Information that has been archived needs to be associated with descriptive information that records where the information came from, how to read it, how long to keep it, and what level of security it should be given. If archived information must be kept for a long time, it must be read back and rearchived from time to time to refresh the media and ensure it is located on viable hardware for retrieval.

Example Resolved

Due to tax reporting requirements, MCHS Trading cannot simply delete the details of each customer's orders for several years. However, to save storage costs and reduce processing time, MCHS Trading implements an archiving process to move the order details to an offline archive store once it has been complete for 3 months.

Known Uses

Information archiving is widely used by IT departments to remove older information to cheaper storage once the information processes running the business no longer need it. The archive repository provides a safeguard against an unusual circumstance where the old information is required.

Related Patterns

A SCHEDULED INFORMATION TRIGGER will typically initiate an information archiving process.

Provisioning Information Processes

The information processes shown in Table 7.6 support the implementation of INFORMATION PROVISIONING by providing different approaches to integrating and distributing information. They execute as information processes within an INFORMATION FLOW or within an INFORMATION NODE that is actively managing the receipt, distribution, and quality of the information in its care. The INFORMATION ASSET HUB is an example of this type of information node.

Table 7.6 Provisioning Information Process Pattern Summaries

Icon	Pattern Name	Problem	Solution
	INFORMATION REPLICATION PROCESS	An exact copy of an information collection needs to be maintained.	Create an information process that is monitoring changes to the information collection and replicating them to the copy.
	INFORMATION DEPLOYMENT PROCESS	Information must be proactively transformed and either (1) introduced into the information supply chain or (2) copied between two or more information collections within the information supply chain.	Create a process that is able to extract the required information, perform any necessary reengineering on it, and send it to the destination information collection(s).
	INFORMATION RELOCATION PROCESS	Information must be moved from one location to another.	Create a recoverable process that is able to read and delete information from the source location and write it to the target system.
	INFORMATION FEDERATION PROCESS	An information process needs up-to-date information that is stored in multiple information collections.	Create an information process that is able to retrieve and combine information from multiple information collections on demand.

Icon	Pattern Name	Problem	Solution
	INFORMATION QUEUING PROCESS	Information must be reliably passed between two information nodes even though they are not always available at the same time.	Use a recoverable queue to store the information and pass it on to the downstream information node.
	INFORMATION BROADCASTING PROCESS	Information must be broadcast to a varying group of information nodes.	Use a recoverable publish/subscribe mechanism to provide a topic that source information nodes can post to and other information nodes can subscribe to.
	INFORMATION SUMMARIZING PROCESS	Keeping the fine-grained detailed information created by the operational systems uses a lot of storage for the value it delivers.	Summarize the important information into a new information collection, enabling the fine-grained detail to be archived or deleted.
	INFORMATION SCAVENGING PROCESS	What is the appropriate approach to introduce information extracted from a huge corpus of unstructured information?	Use text analytics to extract facts from the corpus of unstructured information and store them in an information collection that can feed the information supply chain.

Information Replication Process

Context

An organization requires an information process to support the provisioning of information along an INFORMATION SUPPLY CHAIN.

Problem

An exact copy of an information collection needs to be maintained.

This copy is kept in a different information collection, which may be on the same information node or a different one.

Reasons for creating this copy include the following:

- For use as a backup in case a system error or loss of facility destroys the original information collection
- To bring the information closer to one or more information processes that need reliable, high-speed access to the information.

Example

The information collections stored in the Customer Hub need to be copied to a set of information collections located in MCHS Trading's disaster recovery facility.

Forces

- **Retrieval adds delay**—Retrieving information from a remote system each time you use it introduces a delay and puts extra load on the system hosting the information.
- **Local copies reduce delay, but require synchronization**—Copying information so it is local to the processing reduces latency in retrieving information but adds a requirement to synchronize the copies.
- **Transfer of information may be interrupted**—Network and system failures may interfere with the transfer of information. These disruptions must be recovered from once the failing components have been recovered.

Solution

Create a process that is monitoring changes to the information collection and replicating them to the copy.

The process of replicating an information collection can be thought of in two parts. First, there is the initial load. This is where the existing contents of the information collection are copied into the replica information collection. Then there is the ongoing trickle feed of updates that must be copied across to keep the replica synchronized with the original. This requires the following:

- A mechanism for monitoring for updates in the original information collection. For example, using a database trigger, or even better, monitoring the transaction log of the database. These are examples of INFORMATION CHANGE TRIGGERS.
- The ability to extract the information values that have changed.
- An information flow to move the information values to the replica information collection(s).

Consequences

Benefits:

- This information process provides a simple mechanism for maintaining an exact copy of an information collection.

Liabilities:

- Inevitably there is some latency introduced by the replication process.

- The information replication process may impact the performance of the information node where the original information collection resides. However, this impact is likely to be lower than having remote information processes access it directly.
- The replica information collection should have **R**EFERENCE **U**SAGE or **S**ANDBOX **U**SAGE because changes to it are not reflected back into the original copy.

Example Resolved

A replication process is set up to monitor changes to the Customer Hub information collections and then sends them to the disaster recovery site.

Known Uses

Replication can be used for many purposes. There is the disaster recovery scenario as described in the example. It may also be used to replicate code tables or other types of reference data to systems on different premises or in different countries.

Related Patterns

Consider the **I**NFORMATION **D**EPLOYMENT **P**ROCESS where information needs to be transformed, or filtered, before it is added to the downstream information collection. A replication process initiates a simple **I**NFORMATION **F**LOW pattern.

Information Deployment Process

Context

An organization requires an information process to support the provisioning of information along an **I**NFORMATION **S**UPPLY **C**HAIN.

Problem

Information must be proactively transformed and either (1) introduced into the information supply chain or (2) copied between two or more information collections within the information supply chain.

Example

When new products are defined in the Product Hub application, they need to be distributed to MCHS Trading's order-processing applications and the Reporting Hub.

Forces

- **Retrieval adds delay**—Retrieving information from a remote system each time you use it introduces a delay and puts extra load on the system hosting the information.
- **Local copies reduce delay, but require synchronization**—Copying information so it is local to the processing reduces latency in retrieving information but adds a requirement to synchronize the copies.
- **Information collections have differing structures**—The structure of the information that needs to be deployed is not necessarily the same as the destination(s).
- **Quality may be an issue**—The level of quality of the information may not be sufficient for the destination information collection(s).
- **Not all information is needed**—A destination might only need a subset of the information that is available.

Solution

Create a process that is able to extract the required information, perform any necessary reengineering on it, and send it to the destination information collection(s).

This process is implemented using the following steps:

- The information to be deployed is copied into some form of staging area.
- Working from the staging area, it performs the following types of INFORMATION REENGINEERING STEPS where required:
  1. STANDARDIZE DATA—For the complex structures such as addresses
  2. VALIDATE DATA—Using lookups to ensure values conform to known values
  3. ENRICH DATA—To add values that are missing
  4. RESTRUCTURE DATA—To modify the structure of the information to match the destination
- Finally, the reengineered information is saved into the destination.

Consequences

Benefits:

- The information deployment process provides the mechanism to provide information to new processes by transforming it and placing it in a more convenient location.

Liabilities:

- This process has created one or more copies of the information. These copies need to be managed in an appropriate manner. This includes updating it at appropriate points and deleting it when it is no longer needed.

Example Resolved

See Figure 7.13. Product details in the Product Hub application include details of the channels through which the product will be sold. There is a STAGING AREA for each of the applications that will receive product details. When the Product Hub application has new product information to distribute, it pushes a copy of it into the appropriate staging areas. There is an integration job dedicated to each of the staging topics. When product details are added into a topic, it triggers the integration job to transform and deliver them to the appropriate application.

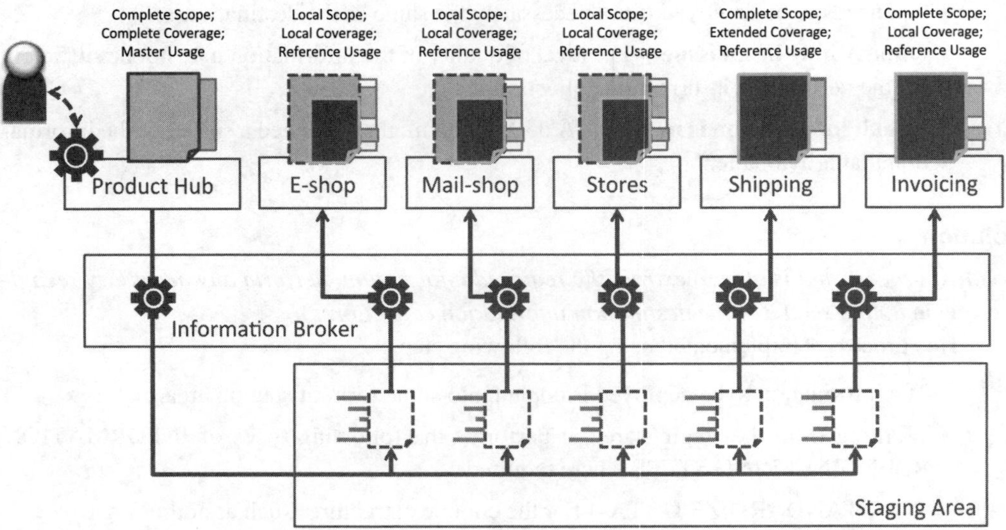

Figure 7.13 Deploying new product details.

Note: In this example, the Product Hub application supplies information that is sufficient quality that it only needs to be restructured for the target application.

Known Uses

This is the most common process that is used to flow information between nodes in the information supply chain—primarily because it is the most versatile and caters for the differences in the information support offered by each information node. The typical implementation of the integration job is an extract, transform, load (ETL) process. However, it may be performed by an extract, load, transform (ELT) process.

Related Patterns

This pattern is used in the implementation of many of the INFORMATION PROVISIONING patterns that are implemented using INFORMATION FLOWS. It typically runs in an INFORMATION BROKER and has no interaction with information users.

If the information does not need transforming as it is passed to the destination information collection(s), consider the INFORMATION REPLICATION PROCESS.

Information Relocation Process

Context

An organization requires an information process to support the provisioning of information along an INFORMATION SUPPLY CHAIN.

Problem

Information must be moved from one location to another.

The information needs transforming, enriching, or validating as part of the transfer.

Example

When the Mail-Shop application is in the process of being decommissioned in favor of the new M-Shop application, details of the employees in the customer call center have to be moved to M-Shop when they transfer between the two applications. MCHS Trading wants to ensure that when an employee transfers over to M-Shop, he or she can no longer log in to Mail-Shop.

Forces

- **Coordination of updates can be challenging**—It is difficult to coordinate the updating of information across multiple information nodes.

Solution

Create a recoverable process that is able to read and delete information from the source location and write it to the target location.

Typically, this process runs in the source information node and moves (create in the new and then delete from the old) the information to an intermediary information node that supports distributed transactions. The information is then retrieved from the intermediary node, transformed, and stored in the target information node. Once it is in the target information node, it is removed from the intermediary.

The purpose of the intermediary is to safely remove it from the source information node to prevent any more updates to it until it is safely installed in the target information node. The intermediary can be used to stage any information reengineering or remediation that is required before the information can be added to the target node.

Consequences

Benefits:

- This type of process moves information from one part of the supply chain to another without duplicating information. It is also able to transform the information as it moves it.

Liabilities:

- It is very hard to make sure all of the timing windows and failure scenarios are covered, particularly when the technology involved cannot be included in a two-phase commit (distributed transaction).

Example Resolved

When an employee is ready to transfer over to M-Shop, his or her profile is removed from Mail-Shop and stored in a **Q**UEUE **M**ANAGER using an **I**NFORMATION **Q**UEUING **P**ROCESS. The profile is immediately picked up from the queue manager, transformed, and inserted into M-Shop. The employee can now log on to M-Shop and his or her preferences will have been transferred over. The employee will no longer be able to log on to Mail-Shop.

Known Uses

This type of process is used where information must move between two information collections without duplication.

Related Patterns

The **I**NFORMATION **N**ODE **U**PGRADE solution uses the information relocation process to move information from the old version of the information node to the new one. The information relocation process uses a **S**TAGED **R**OUTING **I**NFORMATION **F**LOW. If information is to remain in the originating information node, consider either the **I**NFORMATION **R**EPLICATION **P**ROCESS or the **I**NFORMATION **D**EPLOYMENT **P**ROCESS.

Information Federation Process

Context

An organization requires an information process to support the provisioning of information along an INFORMATION SUPPLY CHAIN.

Problem

An information process needs up-to-date information that is stored in multiple information collections.

Due to either the volume of information, or the frequency it is updated, it is not practical to keep a local copy of the information.

Example

The Customer-Care application needs to retrieve information about a product and its current stock level. The product details are available from the Product Hub application. The current stock level is available from the Shipping application.

Forces

- **Retrieval adds delay**—Retrieving information from a remote system each time you use it introduces a delay and puts extra load on the system hosting the information.
- **Availability of remote information varies**—If remote information is not consistently available, work and decisions may be impacted.
- **Local copies reduce delay, but require synchronization**—Copying information so it is local to the processing reduces latency in retrieving information but adds a requirement to synchronize the copies.
- **Information collections have differing structures and keys**—Information is not stored in the same format in every information node and differences in keys may limit the ability to connect together.
- **The information context varies**—Information retrieved from one system may be needed to formulate the request to a subsequent system.

Solution

Create an information process that is able to retrieve and combine information from multiple information collections on demand.

A TRIGGERING INFORMATION SERVICE initiates the information federation process. Once started, the information federation process makes calls to other information services to extract and assemble information from multiple information collections. It must be able to perform the following:

- Break the request into parts that each correspond to a request for information from a separate location.
- For each part request, use an information service to retrieve the required information.
- Transform and correlate the received information together.
- Return it to the requesting information process.

Consequences

Benefits:

- The information federation process is able to combine information from different information collections together without creating copies of it. This is particularly important when the information collections are large or changing rapidly because maintaining copies of them would be expensive.

Liabilities:

- Retrieving information using federation is likely to be slower than working with a pre-joined and formatted local copy. Therefore, it is not suitable where there are a large number of requests for information on a fairly static collection.

Example Resolved

The product availability process uses an information service to extract the product details and supplier information from the Product Hub application. It then retrieves the current stock levels from the Shipping application using another information service. The results are combined together to provide details of current stock levels and how long each supplier would need to get more.

Known Uses

There are several of ways of approaches to implementing this pattern:

- **Using federated database queries**—The database is able to split up the query and push down parts of the request to other databases. It then combines the results to satisfy the original query.
- **Using a composite service**—The federation process runs on an INFORMATION BROKER. It is invoked via an INFORMATION SERVICE. It extracts information from service interfaces of various applications, combines the information, and returns the results to the caller.
- **Using a local procedure**—Implement the federation process on the local information node. This is useful when the retrieve information is also to be combined with local information.

Related Patterns

The information federation process is the enabling capability in a VIRTUAL INFORMATION COLLECTION and SINGLE VIEW INFORMATION SUPPLY CHAIN. It can run in many types of information nodes but is most frequently found in INFORMATION BROKER nodes.

Where information needs to be available locally, consider using the INFORMATION REPLICATION PROCESS. Where INFORMATION KEYS are not common, an INFORMATION DEPLOYMENT PROCESS that includes a LINK ENTRIES step should be utilized.

Information Queuing Process

Context

An organization requires an information process to support the provisioning of information along an INFORMATION SUPPLY CHAIN.

Problem

Information must be reliably passed between two information nodes even though they are not always available at the same time.

This means they need to use an intermediary information node that is always available that they can use to act as a reliable place to put information and retrieve it later. This intermediary node must pass the information payloads to the destination in the same order that the source sent them and be careful not to lose any of them, or send them more than once.

Example

New orders can be raised on the E-Shop at any time because its website is available twenty-four hours a day, seven days a week (24/7). The Shipping application needs 2 hours downtime each evening for backups and maintenance. What happens to orders from E-Shop when Shipping is down?

Forces

- **Information can arrive at any time**—When some information nodes are available and others are not, information still needs to be processed.
- **Information collections have differing structures**—Information is not stored in the same format in every information node.
- **Issues in one node can impact others**—A source information node must not hang when another information node is not available, or underperforming. Otherwise, a situation called sympathy-sickness occurs where an issue in one of the information nodes spreads to others. If a target information node is not available, the source information node will have to save the information payload and retry.

Solution

Use a recoverable queue to store the information and pass it on to the downstream information node.

An information queuing process runs on a queue manager. The queue manager is a robust information node with very high availability. Each instance of an information queuing process either puts an information payload onto a first in, first out (FIFO) queue or takes an information payload out of a queue. The information payloads in the queue are written to storage so they are not lost in the unlikely event of a failure.

Consequences

Benefits:

- The queuing mechanism is easy to use, understand, and implement.

Liabilities:

- The queuing process offers no opportunity to reformat the information payload being sent.
- The applications using the queue have to be modified to put information payloads on the queue and get the information payloads from it.

Example Resolved

See Figure 7.14. The E-Shop application (along with the Mail-Shop and Stores applications) writes the order into a distributed queue whenever they have a new order. When the Shipping application is available, it is listening for orders from the queue and processing them.

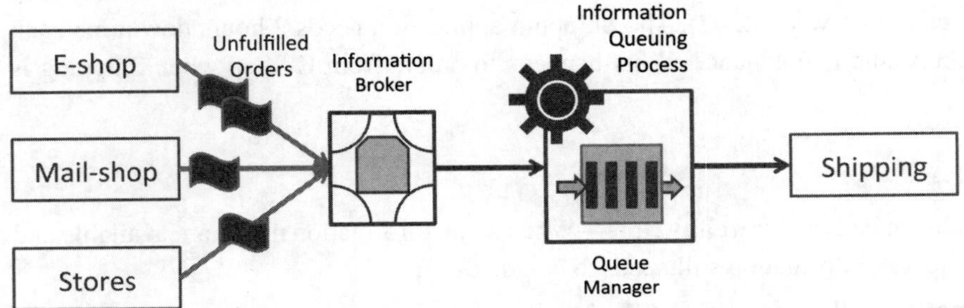

Figure 7.14 Information queuing process for Shipping.

Known Uses

Information queuing processes are implemented by message-oriented middleware. This style of information passing is used extensively in Enterprise Application Integration (EAI).

Related Patterns

The information queuing process runs on a **Q**UEUE **M**ANAGER. The information queuing process may be used to support **I**NDEPENDENT **C**ONSOLIDATION or **I**NDEPENDENT **D**ISTRIBUTION **I**NFORMATION **F**LOWS. If the format or structure of the information must be changed to meet the needs of the target destination, an **I**NFORMATION **D**EPLOYMENT **P**ROCESS may be placed ahead of or after the information queuing process. It does not interact with any information users.

Information Broadcasting Process

Context

An organization requires an information process to support the provisioning of information along an **I**NFORMATION **S**UPPLY **C**HAIN.

Problem

Information must be broadcast to a varying group of information nodes.

This information must be sent to all information nodes that are registered to receive it. The list of registered information nodes will vary over time.

Example

The MCHS Trading order-taking applications exchange order records with the Shipping application using an information queuing process. This works well until the new orders need to also be distributed to the Reporting Hub via an **I**NFORMATION **A**CTIVITY **N**ODE.

If the queuing mechanism is retained, new order records will either go to Shipping or to the information activity node but never both.

Forces

- **Interest in certain types of information varies**—The number of information processes interested in information payloads passing through a certain point in the information supply chain may vary over time.

Solution

Use a recoverable publish/subscribe mechanism to provide a topic that source information nodes can post to and other information nodes can subscribe to.

A publish/subscribe mechanism has three parts to it:

1. The ability to define a set of topics that information can be published to. These topics can be thought of as letterboxes where INFORMATION PAYLOADS can be posted.
2. The ability for an information node to subscribe to one or more topics and nominate an information process to call when an information payload is posted to it.
3. The ability for an information process to post an information payload to a topic by calling an INFORMATION SERVICE.

Consequences

Benefits:

- Using topics means another information node could subscribe and receive the information payloads without updating the source or other destination information nodes.

Liabilities:

- Similar to the information queuing process, the information broadcast process offers no opportunity to provide the payloads in different formats for different consumers. This is why, for information supply chains that make heavy use of this type of information integration, there are canonical payload formats that are used throughout the information supply chain. This means every information node has to understand the canonical payloads, but a payload can be distributed to multiple destinations and be understood.

Example Resolved

In Figure 7.15, the information queuing process shown in Figure 7.14 is replaced with an information broadcasting process. The Shipping application is updated to listen for the payloads on the "New Order" topic rather than the "New Order" queue. The information process that transfers new orders to the operational snapshot store also listens on the "New Order" topic.

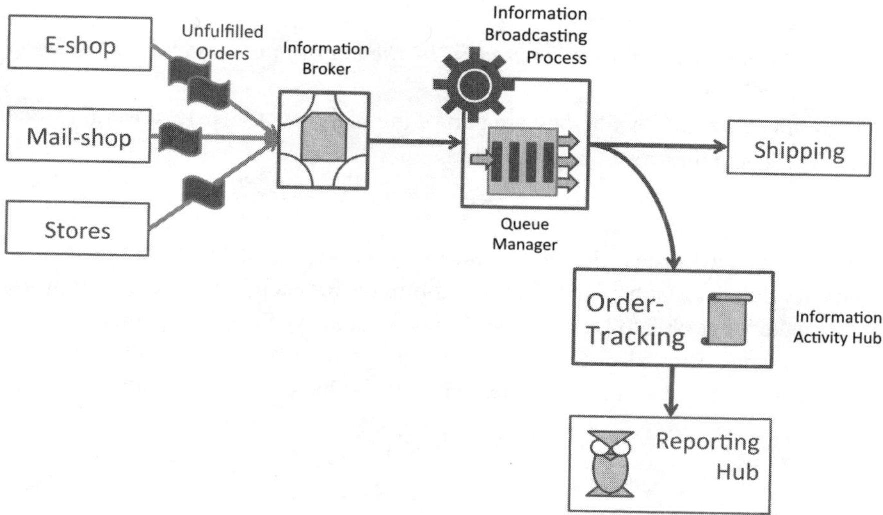

Figure 7.15 Broadcasting orders to Shipping and the Reporting Hub.

Known Uses

The use of publish/subscribe technology is used to provide very loose coupling between multiple sources and multiple destinations. It is implemented in message-oriented middleware and is commonly referred to as a pub-sub engine.

Related Patterns

The information broadcast process runs on a **Q**UEUE **M**ANAGER. The information broadcast process is used to implement a **B**ROADCAST **D**ISTRIBUTION **F**LOW pattern. If the format or structure of the information must be changed to meet the needs of the target destination, an **I**NFORMATION **D**EPLOYMENT **P**ROCESS may be placed ahead of the information broadcast process.

Information Summarizing Process

Context

An organization requires an information process to support the provisioning of information along an **I**NFORMATION **S**UPPLY **C**HAIN.

Problem

Keeping the fine-grained detailed information created by the operational systems uses a lot of storage for the value it delivers.

This information is necessary while they are part of the current activity. It is useful for the first few reporting cycles, and then its value diminishes.

Example

In MCHS Trading, when a package is shipped, details of the packaging style, truck, batch, drivers, route, intermediary depots, weather, and a full set of timings for each stage of the journey are recorded. This is to make it possible to locate a lost shipment, or prove the goods were delivered, or similar types of incidents. They also use it to monitor the effectiveness of the delivery companies they use. However, once the package is delivered, the value of this information starts to diminish.

Forces

- **It is hard to know what information you might need in the future**—The temptation is to keep it all just in case.
- **The value of information can diminish over time**—As such, it may not be cost effective to keep it forever.
- **Information must be viewed in context for it to be understood correctly**—Not everyone in an organization will use the same terminology, precision, or validation rules or have the same expectations for information quality and timeliness.
- **Storing information that is never going to be used is wasteful**—Storage costs money to buy and power to operate.

Solution

Summarize the important information into a new information collection, enabling the fine-grained details to be archived or deleted.

Consequences

Benefits:

- Summarizing information will reduce the storage necessary for keeping historical information. More important, designing information summary information elements for this purpose means the information kept includes the context in which it was created.

Liabilities:

- It is possible that information needed in the future was not anticipated and is discarded in the summary process. Also, the summarizing logic requires an additional information process to be maintained and run.

Example Resolved

The detailed shipping information is summarized into two INFORMATION SUMMARY information elements as follows:

- A summary of the package shipment, including order number, package number, shipment date/time, delivery date/time, and shipping company
- A summary of each shipping incident, including incident number, order number, package number, incident raise date/time, incident type, incident description, incident resolution type, and incident completion date/time

These two types of summaries cover the minimal information about a shipment for most packages that are delivered without incident. When issues occur, additional information is kept about the shipping incident.

Related Patterns

The result of an information summarizing process is an INFORMATION SUMMARY. This information process typically runs in an INFORMATION WAREHOUSE or in an INFORMATION BROKER that is manipulating the information in the information warehouse's INFORMATION COLLECTIONS. Information summaries are used in the HISTORICAL SYSTEM OF RECORD solution.

If the format or structure of the information must be changed or information with different keys must be linked to achieve the right summarization, an INFORMATION DEPLOYMENT PROCESS should be used instead.

Information Scavenging Process

Context

An organization requires an information process to support the provisioning of information along an INFORMATION SUPPLY CHAIN.

Problem

What is the appropriate approach to introduce information extracted from a huge corpus of unstructured information?

Example

MCHS Trading is interested in understanding the feedback of people who have bought the types of products that MCHS Trading sells. This information is located in various support forums and social media sites.

Forces

- **Unstructured data is difficult to use directly**—Unstructured data such as pictures, video, websites, and documents are the largest growing sector of information. They contain useful information for the information supply chain, but their format, and the informal way they are typically created and managed, makes it hard to use them directly in an information supply chain.

Solution

Use text analytics to extract facts from the corpus of unstructured information and store them in an information collection that can feed the information supply chain.

The facts that are extracted include direct references to the subject matter of interest and relationships to other things.

Consequences

Benefits:

- Business processes can respond faster to emerging feedback about the organization, its products, or its processes.

Liabilities:

- Information scavenging processes must revalidate their data continuously and ensure they are still targeting the best sources of unstructured data.
- Unstructured information generally ages quickly (often in hours or days).
- The volumes of unstructured data have storage and processing costs that must be addressed.

Example Resolved

MCHS Trading implements an information scavenging process to scan popular social media sites looking for instances where customers are discussing MCHS Trading. This information is collated and analyzed to understand if there are any issues in general that should be addressed.

Known Uses

Information scavenging processes are beginning to appear in larger organizations that need to extract value from unstructured information. Examples of this type of processing include sentiment analysis, social network analysis, and financial relationships of public companies.

Related Patterns

An information scavenging process is often used in conjunction with analytical processes such as the **I**NFORMATION **P**ATTERN **D**ETECTING or **I**NFORMATION **P**ATTERN **D**ISCOVERY process patterns.

Analytics Processes

The patterns in Table 7.7 cover the analytical processes associated with the information supply chain. Analytics information processes can be thought of in two groups:

- There are the offline information processes that are for creating the models that execute the analytics.
- There are the online processes that run the models against the organization's information to produce the results.

In Table 7.7, there are three analytics information process patterns:

- The **I**NFORMATION **P**ATTERN **D**ISCOVERY **P**ROCESS describes an offline process for creating an analytics model. This is a model that looks for patterns in the organization's information that predict a particular outcome. Analytics models are typically used for scoring and classifying information.
- The **I**NFORMATION **D**ECISION **D**EFINITION **P**ROCESS describes another offline information process for creating decision models. These models combine analytics models and business rules to create a step in a process that can make a decision, or prediction, about the next step to take in an information process.
- **T**HE **I**NFORMATION **P**ATTERN **D**ETECTION **P**ROCESS is the online information process that is able to run either an analytics model or a decision model. It may run in a batch mode, using historical information, or operate in real time as activities are occurring.

Table 7.7 Analytics Information Process Patterns Summary

Icon	Pattern Name	Problem	Solution
	INFORMATION PATTERN DISCOVERY PROCESS	What are the key predictive indicators within the information that the organization is collecting?	Use data mining and other analytical techniques to discover the patterns in the information that seems to coincide with a predicted outcome.
	INFORMATION DECISION DEFINITION PROCESS	An organization needs to improve the consistency and quality of its operational decision-making process.	Combine business rules with the results of data mining to create an automated decision process that can be included in operational activities.
	INFORMATION PATTERN DETECTING PROCESS	Where are the key predictive indicators occurring in the information collected by the organization?	Run either an analytics model or a decision model against the organization's information to detect when patterns occur in the organization's information that predicts a particular outcome.

Information Pattern Discovery Process

Context

An organization requires an information process to discover new patterns or trends about its business.

Problem

What are the key predictive indicators within the information that the organization is collecting?

Predictive indicators are combinations of information values that suggest either a particular event is about to occur or the person, object, place, activity, or asset that the information values are about should be classified and processed in a particular way. If an organization understands which information values are key predictive indicators and what the different combinations of values predict, it is able to react to situations before they arise or discover new opportunities in time to act on them.

Example

MCHS Trading is interested in discovering what types of products its individual customers like to buy so it can make personal product recommendations to them.

Forces

- **Difficult to correlate certain information**—Different information sources hold related pieces of information that may contain useful information but their content is not easily correlated.
- **Many possible combinations of information**—There are a lot of information values to consider, in many combinations.
- **Some relevant information may be external**—Information that may be necessary to make specific correlations and pattern discoveries may not be available through existing systems (e.g., customer demographics, geographic or regional-based characteristics). Often this information must be acquired from third parties.

Solution

Use data mining and other analytical techniques to discover the patterns in the information that seems to coincide with a predicted outcome.

Data mining tools are designed to hunt out patterns in information (see Figure 7.16). They typically work on information stored in INFORMATION MINING STORES. The result is an analytics model that can be used to analyze the organization's information. (See INFORMATION PATTERN DETECTING PROCESS for more information on using an analytics model.)

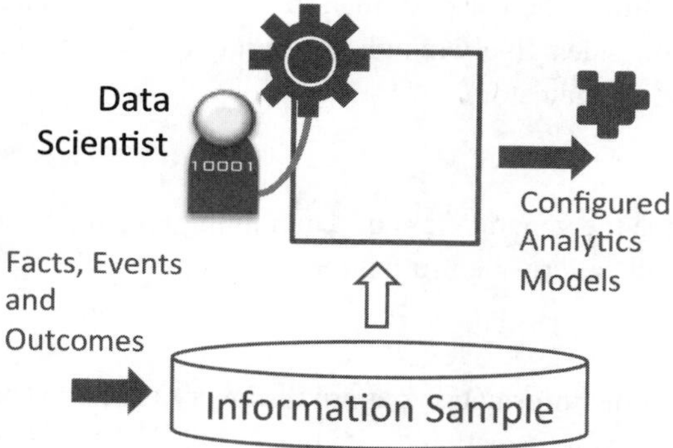

Figure 7.16 Information Pattern Discovery Process solution.

Consequences

Benefits:

- When an organization understands its key predictive indicators, it can be more proactive in how it manages its business and interaction with customers and suppliers.

Liabilities:

- Information pattern discovery processes must reassess the models regularly to ensure that the previously discovered patterns are still correlated.
- Information pattern discovery processes use **D**ATA **S**CIENTISTS to establish the right tests or evaluate the results properly.

Example Resolved

MCHS Trading creates an information mining store that hosts correlated information collections covering customer demographics, the orders each customer has made, when they make them, and the types of products they buy. MCHS Trading then uses the information pattern discovery process to understand the following:

- Which products the same person typically buys
- Whether there is a common sequence in the purchase order of these products
- Whether there are common traits associated with people who bought the same products

This knowledge enables MCHS Trading to classify its customers into groups based on their characteristics and make meaningful product recommendations both through E-Shop and through direct mail (post).

Over time, fashion and consumer taste change and so these key predictive indicators will change, too. MCHS Trading continuously monitors whether customers buy the recommended products and checks that this process is increasing sales. Every month they rerun the information pattern discovery process to tune the key predictive indicators.

Known Uses

Information pattern discovery processes describe the general class of data mining tools that use statistical models and other techniques to seek out patterns in information.

Related Patterns

The **I**NFORMATION **A**NALYSIS **N**ODE hosts the information pattern discovery process. The information pattern discovery process typically uses information located in an **I**NFORMATION **M**INING **S**TORE. The information collections in the information mining store are **S**ANDBOX **U**SAGE and are populated using either **S**NAPSHOT **P**ROVISIONING or **M**IRROR **P**ROVISIONING.

Information Decision Definition Process

Context

An organization requires an information process to support one of its activities.

Problem

An organization needs to improve the consistency and quality of its operational decision-making process.

The organization wants to insert business rules into the operational information processes.

Example

MCHS Trading believes that contact details for its customers should be checked about once every six months. Some contact details are fairly stable, such as home address, whereas email addresses tend to change more rapidly.

MCHS Trading has used an **I**NFORMATION **P**ATTERN **D**ISCOVERY **P**ROCESS to create an analytics model to detect if contact details are likely to have changed. This model uses knowledge about when the contact details were last checked—and the types of orders the customer is making—to indicate which of the contact details of the customer should be validated. MCHS Trading decides that this analytics model should be run no more than once every 3 months when the customer uses any of the channels.

Forces

- **People forget to do ancillary tasks**—Most people are busy, focused on their main tasks. They often skip additional tasks that get in the way of their main task—particularly if it will not be noticed. Therefore, it is often necessary to automate these tasks, or the prompts to ask a person to do them.
- **Certain decisions are complex**—Decisions may follow many steps with many possible branches to get to the end result.

Solution

Combine business rules with the results of data mining to create an automated decision process that can be included in operational activities.

Data mining (or information pattern discovery process) tools enable a **D**ATA **S**CIENTIST to produce an analytics model. Combining the analytics model with business rules created by a **B**USINESS **A**NALYST results in a decision model that can be inserted as a decision step in the operational information processes. See Figure 7.17.

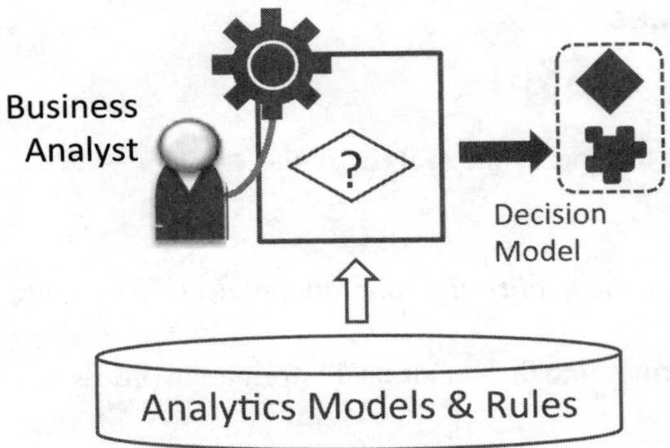

Figure 7.17 Information Decision Definition Process solution.

Consequences

Benefits:

- Consistent decisions can be deployed across multiple channels and lines of business. The business rules can easily be updated and redeployed as necessary.

Liabilities:

- The results of the decision model should be captured and regularly assessed to ensure they are delivering the best results. It is likely that both the analytics model and the decision model will need to be refined over time.

Example Resolved

MCHS Trading designs a decision model that combines the analytics model with a business rule that ensures the customer is only asked at most once every 3 months to verify that his or her contact details are still correct.

Known Uses

Decision models may be incorporated into operational business processes. Decision models that combine rules and analytics are a common approach for real-time predictive analytics. The analytics typically give better results than rules alone, and the business rules define the policies that control when the analytics should run.

Related Patterns

The **I**NFORMATION **P**ATTERN **D**ISCOVERY **P**ROCESS creates analytics models. The **I**NFORMATION **P**ATTERN **D**ETECTING **P**ROCESS runs either an analytics model or a decision model. The information decision definition process runs in an **I**NFORMATION **A**NALYTICS **N**ODE.

Information Pattern Detecting Process

Context

An organization requires an information process to support one of its activities.

Problem

Where are the key predictive indicators occurring in the information collected by the organization?

Predictive indicators are combinations of information values that suggest an event is likely to occur in the near future. The sooner they are detected and acted upon, the more effective the organization will be.

Example

MCHS Trading is interested in understanding how the availability and timeliness of phone responses affects its Mail-Shop business and customer call center service.

Forces

- **Key predictive indicators are forever changing**—They need to be constantly monitored and tuned to meet the current operational needs.

Solution

Run either an analytics model or a decision model against the organization's information to detect when patterns occur in the organization's information that predicts a particular outcome.

The information pattern detecting process (see Figure 7.18) takes the context passed to it from the information trigger and combines it with information in the information collection to invoke either an analytics model or a decision model. The results of the model and the information used to call it are stored in an information collection for later analysis. The results are passed back to trigger for action. The results of the action are saved at a later date with the results of the model when they are known.

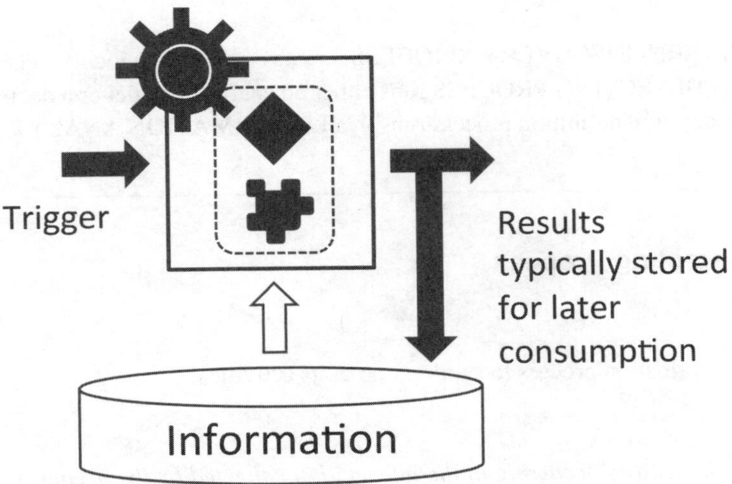

Figure 7.18 Information Pattern Detecting Process solution.

Consequences

Benefits:

- The organization can respond faster and more consistently to situations that can be detected and resolved before a problem occurs, or an opportunity is lost.

Liabilities:

- The models that detect the predictive indicators must be regularly assessed to ensure they are still accurate. It is often necessary to tune these models as the predictive indicators change over time.

Example Resolved

MCHS Trading adds an information pattern detecting process in association with its new information streaming process. By analyzing new information on the length of time to answer and place a call in the queue, to route a call, and to engage a service representative, MCHS Trading can identify the frequency with which issues in customer response result in lost or canceled orders.

Known Uses

Information pattern detecting processes are beginning to appear in larger organizations that need to extract value from their existing information. Examples of this type of processing include event prediction, such as traffic analysis, disease, or network virus spread.

Related Patterns

The analytics model used by the information pattern detecting process is created and configured by the **I**NFORMATION **P**ATTERN **D**ISCOVERY **P**ROCESS and the **I**NFORMATION **D**ECISION **D**EFINITION **P**ROCESS. It is designed to run in many types of **I**NFORMATION **N**ODES and although information users do not directly interact with this information process, they do use its results.

Search Processes

The processes described in Table 7.8 cover search technology. Searching operates over a dispersed and disparate set of information collections that are hosted by a variety of information nodes. The aim of a search capability is to locate potentially relevant information about a topic or a question specified by an information user.

The search processing is roughly sequential:

- The **I**NFORMATION **C**RAWLING **P**ROCESS is a batch process that reviews the information that is to be searchable and builds a map of where the information is located and what it is about. This is run frequently to keep up to date with changes in the information.
- The **I**NFORMATION **I**NDEXING **P**ROCESS takes the output from the information crawling process and creates an index that maps potential topics to the located information.
- The **I**NFORMATION **S**EARCH **P**ROCESS is the process that offers the user interface to the information user to enter the topic or question. It uses the search index to return a list of potentially relevant information to the user. The user then manually reviews the returned list and decides what to make use of and what to ignore.

Table 7.8 Search Information Process Pattern Summaries

Icon	Pattern Name	Problem	Solution
	INFORMATION CRAWLING PROCESS	Where is all of the interesting information located?	Run search crawlers to build a map of where information is located.
	INFORMATION INDEXING PROCESS	What type of information does the organization store on each topic?	Build an index that links topic to file/location.
	INFORMATION SEARCH PROCESS	Where is a particular type of information?	Provide a user interface to allow an individual to request a list of files that cover a particular topic.

Search typically operates on documents and media files, but it may consider structure information, too. An individual information node may offer search facilities over its own local information collections, or search capabilities may be hosted in a specialized SEARCH NODE and cover a broad range of information collections hosted in other information nodes. All types of INFORMATION USERS use the information search process.

IT Service Management Processes

The final set of information processes, shown in Table 7.9, manages the IT infrastructure that supports the information supply chain. Operating IT infrastructure is a complicated business that has been well documented in IT service management standards such as Information Technology Infrastructure Library (ITIL).[2] These three information processes on their own are not sufficient to manage IT infrastructure but have been included because they are directly relevant in the management of an organization's information.

Table 7.9 Operational Management Information Process Pattern Summaries

Icon	Pattern Name	Problem	Solution
	OPERATIONAL HEALTH MONITORING PROCESS	Is the information infrastructure that supports the information supply chain working?	Add operational health probes to the information infrastructure to detect when systems and networks fail or experience problems.
	INFORMATION NODE MANAGEMENT PROCESS	What ensures an information node is available and operating correctly?	At the heart of an information node is a controlling information process that is responsible for starting and stopping the information node and monitoring its operation while it is running.
	SCHEDULING PROCESS	Information processes need to run at regular time intervals.	Create an information process that can trigger other processes according to a schedule.

2. http://www.itil-officialsite.com

Operational Health Monitoring Process

Context

An organization requires an information process to support one of its activities.

Problem

Is the information infrastructure that supports the information supply chain working?

The information processes that support the information supply chain, and the information collections they use, are hosted by information nodes. These information nodes must be operating correctly for the information supply chain to function. How does an organization ensure all of its critical information nodes are working correctly?

Example

MCHS Trading relies heavily on its order-processing systems such as Mail-Shop, E-Shop, and Shipping. Failures in these key information processes disrupt order fulfillment and have a high impact on customer satisfaction and retention.

Forces

- **Issues in IT impact the business**—The issues in the IT infrastructure often complicate the activities of a business.
- **An activity takes time**—Any IT infrastructure supporting the activity may fail during that processing time.
- **Issues incur cost and time**—Addressing issues after failure incurs higher costs in problem determination and resolution, and adds time to the information process.

Solution

Add OPERATIONAL HEALTH PROBES to the information infrastructure to detect when systems and networks fail or experience problems.

These information probes are checking that the information nodes are operating correctly. They will check that each node is processing work and has enough resources (CPU, memory, disk) to continue to do so. It also looks for failing information processes because they may indicate that the information node is incorrectly configured.

Consequences

Benefits:

- This monitoring will detect when an information node is not running correctly, or has failed completely. It has the information to determine why the information node failed so that the infrastructure operators can correct the problem and restart the information node.

Liabilities:

- Information health monitoring can generate a huge amount of information to monitor. When a catastrophic event occurs, such as a power outage, the number of alerts raised can be overwhelming for the infrastructure operators.

Example Resolved

MCHS Trading adds operational health monitoring processes through these key information processes to ensure that orders are not lost or remain unfulfilled.

Known Uses

Operational monitoring processes are present in IT infrastructure monitoring software. This software collects information from probes and analyzes it, looking for significant situations. When information nodes are found to be down, or not operating correctly, they raise alerts for infrastructure operators to take action.

Related Patterns

An operational health monitoring process analyzes information from **I**NFORMATION **P**ROBES. If an information node has failed, it is restarted using an **I**NFORMATION **N**ODE **M**ANAGEMENT **P**ROCESS. It is found in many kinds of **I**NFORMATION **N**ODES and is operated typically by an **I**NFRASTRUCTURE **O**PERATOR.

Information Node Management Process

Context

An organization requires an information process to support one of its activities.

Problem

What ensures an information node is available and operating correctly?

An information node is a server that must be started before it can run any information processes. It must be configured with the computing resources it needs and when it is not needed, it should be shut down so it does not waste power.

Example

MCHS Trading notices that orders are not being received by the Shipping application.

Forces

- **Issues in IT impact the business**—The issues in the IT infrastructure often complicate the activities of a business.
- **An activity takes time**—Any IT infrastructure supporting the activity may fail during that processing time.
- **Issues incur cost and time**—Addressing issues after failure incurs higher costs in problem determination and resolution, and adds time to the information process.

Solution

At the heart of an information node is a controlling information process that is responsible for starting and stopping the information node and monitoring its operation while it is running.

The information node management process is present in every information node. It provides a command line and user interface for a person to start, stop, and configure an information node. Calls to this information process may be made from a script to automate the management of the information node.

Consequences

Benefits:

- This process provides the mechanism to manage and configure an information node so its availability and use of resources can be managed.

Liabilities:

- There is very little standardization of information node management processes between different types of information nodes. The result is that individual infrastructure operators tend to need to specialize on one or two particular types of information nodes. It makes it hard to standardize the operations of a large and varied IT operation.

Example Resolved

MCHS Trading discovers that the **I**NFORMATION **B**ROKER responsible for transferring orders from E-Shop and Mail-Shop to Shipping is not running. It uses the information broker's information node management process to start it up and very quickly the new orders start to flow to the Shipping application.

Known Uses

Any information node (server) will have commands and menu options to start and stop its server and to configure it with settings. The information node management process implements these commands and property sheets.

Related Patterns

An information node management process is present in each INFORMATION NODE and is operated by an INFRASTRUCTURE OPERATOR. It is started with a MANUAL INFORMATION TRIGGER.

Scheduling Process

Context

An organization requires an information process to support one of its activities.

Problem

Information processes need to run at regular time intervals.

Example

MCHS Trading generated invoices based on received orders. This created inefficiencies and customer dissatisfaction as canceled orders, insufficient inventory to complete shipments, and other events required generation of offsetting or credit invoices.

Forces

- **The real world impacts the business's activities—**The activities of a business are often complicated by the inconsistencies in the organization and the world beyond.
- **An activity may involve contributions from multiple processes.**
- **An activity may involve complex or specialized processing.**
- **An activity takes time (minutes, days, weeks, or years)**—Any IT infrastructure supporting the activity may fail.

Solution

Create an information process that can trigger other processes according to a schedule.

This information process makes use of the operating system services to regularly check the time and trigger information processes at the time that has been specified in its configuration.

Consequences

Benefits:

- Activities or events prior to the scheduled process can be consolidated, ensuring that specific sequences are handled or outside changes are incorporated.
- Scheduling may potentially reduce the cost of running specific processes by reducing frequency of occurrence.

Liabilities:

- Scheduling introduces latency into an information supply chain, which may result in missed opportunities.

Example Resolved

MCHS Trading introduces a scheduling process to run invoice generation once per day after daily shipments are complete. This allows MCHS Trading to achieve tighter control over invoice processing and more accurate invoices, improving customer satisfaction.

Known Uses

Scheduling is used to initiate processing that must be performed at regular intervals. Most ETL platforms and application servers incorporate some form of scheduler for this purpose. The scheduling may be part of some polling logic, looking for work to do, or as a means to initiate new processing.

Related Patterns

The scheduling process creates SCHEDULED INFORMATION TRIGGERS. It is used to initiate other information processes, such as an INFORMATION DEPLOYMENT PROCESS or an INFORMATION EVER-GREENING PROCESS. It is found in many kinds of INFORMATION NODES and is operated typically by an INFRASTRUCTURE OPERATOR.

Summary of Information Processes

Information processes are the means by which information changes. They are responsible for the transformation of information as it is received by the organization, the recording of activities within the organization, and the production of information outputs (or products). There are many kinds of information processes and our patterns have tried to reflect the different ways that an organization's information is maintained. The chapter started with the business processes that are directly supporting the organization's lines of business (LOBs). Then it covered those processes that manage the quality of information, the processes that copy and transform information between information collections, and finally the search, analytical, and infrastructure management processes.

Each of the process patterns runs on a particular kind of INFORMATION NODE. The information nodes group related information processes for particular kinds of INFORMATION USERS together with the INFORMATION COLLECTIONS these processes are working with.

Summary

This chapter covered the different kinds of information processes and how they are initiated.

Chapter 8, “Information Protection,” introduces the information protection pattern groups. This includes the information reengineering pattern group for transforming and improving the quality of information. Then there is the information guard pattern group for security of the information. Finally, there is the information probe pattern group for monitoring and measuring the information supply chain.

CHAPTER 8

Information Protection

Information is a valuable resource that needs protection. Locked doors keep unauthorized people away from an organization's physical servers, but the information within them must be accessible to a wide range of people. Protecting information involves the following:

- The INFORMATION REENGINEERING STEPS protect the quality of the information and ensure it is formatted to match the needs of the consumers—reducing the likelihood that it is misinterpreted.
- The INFORMATION GUARDS test that authorized people and systems are using the organization's information.
- The INFORMATION PROBES monitor the information processes and the infrastructure that supports them to ensure they are functioning correctly.

These patterns appear in the information management components part of the pattern language, as shown in Figure 8.1.

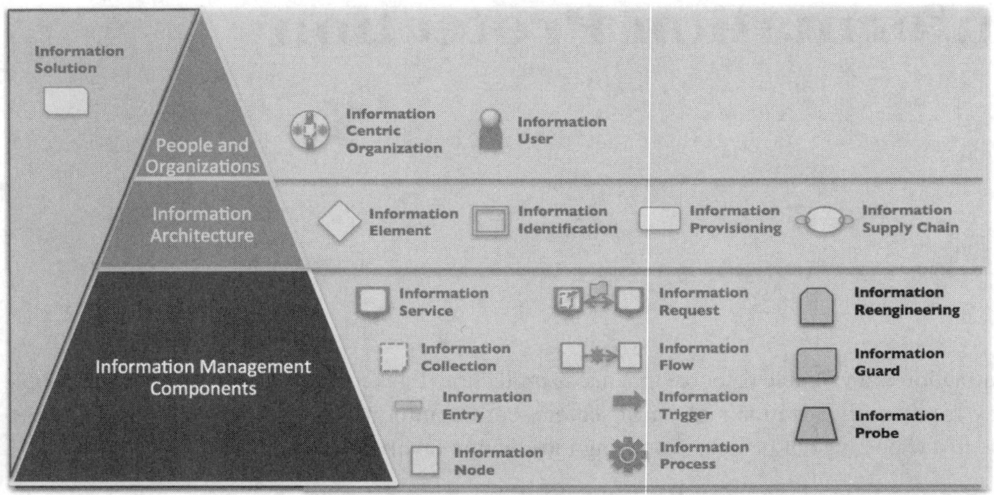

Figure 8.1 Information protection pattern groups in the context of the pattern language.

Information Reengineering Step Patterns

The information reengineering step patterns describe how information is transformed and improved. An information reengineering step is deployed as a step in an **I**NFORMATION **P**ROCESS. The pattern is summarized in Table 8.1.

Table 8.1 Information Reengineering Step Summary

Icon	Pattern Name	Problem	Solution
	INFORMATION **R**EENGINEERING **S**TEP	An information process is not able to consume the information it needs, as currently exists.	Insert capability to transform the information so it is consumable by the information process.

Information Reengineering Step

Context

An organization is designing how information collected for one purpose can be used for new purposes.

Problem

An information process is not able to consume the information it needs, as it currently exists.

This may be for structural or quality reasons.

Example

MCHS Trading's Stores application maintains details of customers with a store card. These customer details must be synchronized with the Customer Hub. However, there are significant differences between the way customer details are stored in the Stores and Customer Hub information collections. For example,

- The Stores application stores date fields in a character string format, whereas the Customer Hub uses a standard database date format.
- Similarly, the tax identifier is stored in a format with hyphens in the Stores application, but the Customer Hub uses only numeric data.
- The Stores application stores the customer name and address in single free-form fields, which are difficult to use to link customer records unlike the Customer Hub where the data is stored in parsed and well-defined fields.

Forces

- **Implementations differ**—The information structures used with each information node cannot be changed (this is particularly true when the information originates from or is flowing to third parties, such as government agencies or existing or packaged applications).
- **Information validation is sporadic**—Not all information processes validate new information entered via its user interfaces or imported from external sources.

Solution

Insert capability to transform the information so it is consumable by the information process.

This capability is called an information reengineering step. It executes as a step in an information process. This step may be in the original information process that needs the information, or in another information process that is preparing information in advance. See Figure 8.2.

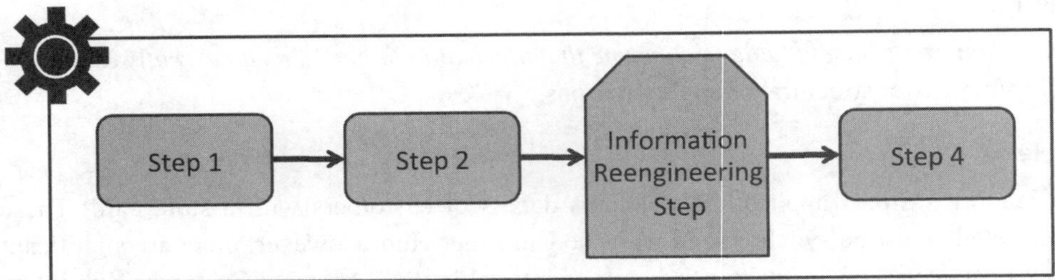

Figure 8.2 An information reengineering step in an information process.

Consequences

Benefits:

- Information can be shared and synchronized between different information nodes.
- Information collections are enriched with associated and relevant information.
- Reengineering information dynamically whenever it is moved along the information supply chain means the information nodes are free to structure their information collections to suit their internal needs.

Liabilities:

- In reengineering information, there is the possibility that information may be lost, incorrectly transformed, or misapplied in the destination information node. The INFORMATION IDENTIFICATION patterns provide valuable guidance to the developer of an information reengineering step on how to work with the information.
- If there are many different information flows within the information supply chain, the burden of information reengineering can be high.

Example Resolved

In the case of MCHS Trading's movement of Stores Account information into the Customer Hub, the bulleted activities are implemented as part of an INFORMATION PROCESS that is implementing an INFORMATION FLOW.

- Customer information, including name, address, and tax ID must be extracted from the Stores information collection.
- The customer name and address must be parsed and standardized to useful formats with separate fields, including first name, middle name, last name; and house number, directional value, street name, and street type using a STANDARDIZE DATA pattern.

- Where multiple names are found on the same record, such as spouses holding a joint Stores account, a SEPARATE ENTRIES pattern is used to create one record per individual.
- The dates and tax ID fields are transformed into the appropriate structure and format for the customer information collection through a RESTRUCTURE DATA pattern.
- The customer information has an ENRICH DATA pattern that adds information from a third-party source with demographic data, such as date of birth and gender, and with geospatial data from another third-party source.
- Customer information entries representing the same person are connected through a LINK ENTRIES pattern on common criteria of standardized name, address, tax ID, date of birth, and gender.
- Where multiple representations of the same person are identified, the customer information uses a MERGE ENTRIES pattern with a preference given to the most complete and most recent data.
- The consolidated customer information entries are then loaded into the Customer information collection in the target information node.

Known Uses

Information reengineering is a primary activity in moving information from one information collection to another (extract, transform, load, or ETL, technologies being one example). Usage includes the following:

- Synchronizing multiple applications that host similar information collections
- Acquiring and merging (or consolidating) new information sources
- Populating and maintaining information collections stored in an INFORMATION WAREHOUSE, INFORMATION MART, INFORMATION ACTIVITY HUB, or INFORMATION ASSET HUB
- Transforming and receiving INFORMATION PAYLOADS from external systems

If no alteration of data is required, then INFORMATION REENGINEERING patterns are not required (as in Messaging technology).

Related Patterns

The INFORMATION VALUES PROFILE describes the characteristics of the values within an information collection.

The SEMANTIC TAGGING and SEMANTIC MAPPING patterns can provide information on the relationship between source and destination information structures.

Information reengineering occurs as a step in an **I**NFORMATION **P**ROCESS. This step may be implemented in the information process that needs to consume the information, in an information process implementing an **I**NFORMATION **F**LOW, or in an information process that is part of a **T**RIGGERING **I**NFORMATION **S**ERVICE.

Specialist Information Reengineering Steps

The remaining information reengineering step patterns describe specific types of reengineering. These patterns are summarized in Table 8.2.

Table 8.2 Specialist Information Reengineering Steps

Icon	Pattern Name	Problem	Solution
	**R**ESTRUCTURE **D**ATA	An information process is not able to consume information that is structured differently from the intended information collection.	Use a mapping between the current structure and the intended structure to transform the information.
	**S**TANDARDIZE **D**ATA	An information process is not able to consume some information because the values are not correctly stored in the information structure.	Analyze and categorize the values in the information. Move them to the correct slots in the information structure.
	**E**NRICH **D**ATA	An information process is not able to consume some information because the values are incomplete.	Use either an authoritative source or an algorithm to add the missing information.
	**C**LASSIFY **D**ATA	Information values need to be grouped according to a business rule, analytics model, or decision model.	Step through the information values running the business rule, analytics model, or decision model against each group as appropriate. Record the classification based on the business rule.
	**C**HECK **D**ATA	An information node must not store incorrect information.	Review the information values and flag those that are incorrect for remediation.
	**C**ORRECT **D**ATA	Information values are incorrect.	Use either an authoritative source or an algorithm to correct the information. This may require human intervention.

Icon	Pattern Name	Problem	Solution
	LINK ENTRIES	Information entries in different information collections represent the same person, object, event, place, or activity.	Link these information entries together so they can easily be retrieved as a group.
	MERGE ENTRIES	Multiple information entries in the same information collection represent the same person, event, object, place, or activity.	Create a new information entry that contains the best values from the information entries to be merged. Archive the previous information entries in case the merge needs to be reversed at a later time.
	SEPARATE ENTRIES	A single information entry contains information about multiple people, objects, places, or activities.	Separate out the values into new information entries, one for each person, object, place, or activity. Archive the original information entry in case the split needs to be reversed or corrected at a later time.
	DERIVE RELATIONSHIP	Are two or more information entries related in some way?	Use analytics to detect common values that suggest a relationship.
	DERIVE VALUE	Values within an information entry need to be consistent.	Only store the essential details and derive the other values when they are needed. (For example, age is derived from date of birth.)
	SMOOTH DATA	A stream of information contains outlier values due to errors in the data capture.	Use a moving average to smooth out the effect of the outliers.
	SAMPLE DATA	The volume of data is large; containing very similar values takes a lot of capacity to process.	Use information values profiling to understand the variability in the information and extract subsets of the information with the same characteristics.

Restructure Data

Context

An organization is designing how information collected for one purpose can be used for new purposes.

Problem

An information process is not able to consume information that is structured differently from the intended information collection.

Although two information nodes contain information collections for the same information subject area, there is no guarantee that the information nodes will store the information collections in the same format as each other. When information flows between the information nodes, this difference must be reconciled.

Example

MCHS Trading must move customer data from a Sales Account information collection to a Customer information collection and needs to restructure the data format:

- A tax ID is stored in the Sales Account collection as a character string consisting of three numbers, a hyphen, two numbers, a hyphen, and four numbers. The tax ID is stored in the Customer collection as a nine-digit integer.

Forces

- **Information structures cannot be changed**—The structures used with each information collection cannot be changed (this is particularly true when the information originates from or is flowing to third parties, such as government agencies or existing or packaged applications).
- **Information cannot be modified where it resides**—The information nodes cannot restructure or modify the information directly (e.g., direct replication of the information cannot be applied).

Solution

Use a mapping between the current structure and the intended structure to transform the information.

This restructuring could be done directly between the information nodes' structures or via a canonical information structure. The choice depends on how much other processing needs to be done in addition to the restructuring.

Develop common restructuring routines for known types of data to ensure consistent application of the transformation.

Consequences

Benefits:

- Consistent representation of information collections is achieved in the target information node without requiring modification of the source information node.

- Restructuring data dynamically whenever it is moved along the information supply chain means the information nodes are free to structure their information collections to suit their internal needs.

Liabilities:

- In restructuring information, there is the possibility that information may be lost, incorrectly transformed, or misapplied in the target information node.
- Changes made to content or format of the source information node may be missed or unhandled in the established data restructuring flow.
- If there are many different information flows within the information supply chain, the burden of data restructuring can be high.

Example Resolved

In the case of MCHS Trading's movement of Sales Account information into the Customer Hub, for each field where there are inconsistent formats, convert the data to the target format:

- For the tax ID field, use functions to first trim any extraneous spaces from the Sales Account data, then remove all hyphens or other special characters from the data, and finally cast the remaining string of numeric values into an integer matching the format of the target information node.

Known Uses

Restructuring data is a component of information reengineering and is achieved in technologies such as extract, transform, load (ETL) software and application programs.

Usage includes any situation where two different sources maintain different structural formats (e.g., character strings instead of integers) for the same information content, such as the following:

- Synchronizing information between multiple information nodes
- Acquiring and merging (or consolidating) new data sources
- Populating and maintaining information collections stored in an INFORMATION WAREHOUSE, INFORMATION MART, or INFORMATION ASSET HUB
- Transforming and delivering messages from incoming information nodes to operational applications

Related Patterns

The SEMANTIC TAGGING and SEMANTIC MAPPING patterns can provide information on the relationship between source and destination information structures. The CHECK DATA pattern can be used to confirm the right structure.

RESTRUCTURE DATA occurs as a step in an INFORMATION PROCESS. This step may be implemented in the information process that needs to consume the information, in an information process implementing an INFORMATION FLOW, or in an information process that is part of a TRIGGERING INFORMATION SERVICE.

For complex information content that requires separation or parsing, use the STANDARDIZE DATA pattern. Where the data content needs to be replaced with related content (e.g., date of birth instead of age), use the DERIVE VALUES pattern.

Standardize Data

Context

An organization is designing how information must flow and integrate from one information collection or node to another.

Problem

An information process is not able to consume some information because the values are not correctly stored in the information structure.

This is particularly common when the data originates from a user interface and it is entered with little validation. Names, addresses, and other free-form descriptive text typically suffer from this problem.

Example

MCHS Trading must move customer data from a Sales Account information collection to the Customer Hub and needs to standardize the data to make it consumable for additional reengineering purposes as well as the target information node:

- The customer name stored in the Sales Account collection is a free-form 50-character text field.
- The name may contain personal or organizational names.
- Personal names may include first name (actual, nickname, or initial), middle name, last name, salutation, title, and generational identifier (e.g., Dr. Anna M. Bowen, Mr. James Green Jr.).
- Organizational names may include company name, trading names (e.g., DBA, C/O), franchise information, division or department information, and contact details.

Forces

- **Information structures cannot be changed**—The information structures used with each information node cannot be changed (this is particularly true when the information originates from or is flowing to third parties, such as government agencies or existing or packaged applications).

- **Information cannot be modified where it resides**—The information nodes cannot standardize or modify the information directly (e.g., direct replication of the information cannot be applied).
- **Delays in delivery may occur**—The information may not reach the target information node in a timely manner.
- **Lack of understanding of the information**—Contents of each information collection and node may not be understood, preventing standardization from being applied appropriately.
- **Different requirements through the information supply chain**—There may be differing requirements for standardization for the information flow (such as linking data for which highly parsed data is preferred) and the information node (for which a structured format may be needed).
- **Too many patterns of data to handle**—The total number of possible data format patterns or the presence of unrecognizable data format patterns in the source information node may preclude standardization of all information successfully.

Solution

Analyze and categorize the values in the information. Move them to the correct slots in the information structure.

Parse the data and break it into its atomic parts, standardize the atomic values, and move/reassemble the parts consistently back into the information structure.

Save and deliver the original data content if legal or organization requirements indicate this must be maintained.

This process requires domain knowledge to properly segment the data into atomic parts.

Establish reusable standardization routines to ensure consistent application to common data elements.

Consequences

Benefits:

- Consistent representation of information collections is achieved in the target information node without requiring modification of the source information node.
- Standardizing data dynamically whenever it is moved along the information supply chain means the information nodes are free to structure their information collections to suit their internal needs.
- This pattern simplifies other information reengineering work, particularly linkage,

enrichment, and merging of information, and should be done as early as possible in the information supply chain.

Liabilities:

- In standardizing information, there is the possibility that information may be lost, incorrectly standardized, or misapplied in the target information node.
- If there are many different information flows within the information supply chain, the burden of data standardization can be high.
- If there are many different formats of data within the source information node, the time to correctly identify standardization routines can be high and the processing time to standardize the data can be lengthy.

Example Resolved

In the case of MCHS Trading's movement of Sales Account information into the Customer Hub, the customer name information must be parsed and standardized to ensure correct usage later in the information supply chain:

- Identify and separate personal from organizational names.
- For personal names, separate (parse) the first, middle, and last names as well as title and generational values using known data patterns.
- Standardize the title and generational values.
- Identify a standardized first name based on common nickname values.
- Store the parsed and standardized values with the customer record for subsequent processing.

Known Uses

Standardizing information is used in ETL processing typically as a precursor to linking or matching data. Standardization functions may be used in web services to ensure a canonical form, particularly after data entry of free-form text whether in operational applications or Master Data Management.

Related Patterns

Apply the ENRICH **D**ATA, SEPARATE **E**NTRIES, and LINK **E**NTRIES patterns to standardized data to achieve optimal results. The CHECK **D**ATA pattern can be used to identify problematic standardization. Use the **R**ESTRUCTURE **D**ATA pattern if the only requirement is to transform the structure of the data (e.g., from character string to integer).

STANDARDIZE **D**ATA occurs as a step in an **I**NFORMATION **P**ROCESS. This step may be implemented in the information process that needs to consume the information, in an information process implementing an INFORMATION FLOW, or in an information process that is part of a TRIGGERING INFORMATION SERVICE.

Enrich Data

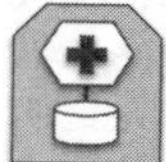

Context

An organization is designing how information collected for one purpose can be used for new purposes.

Problem

An information process is not able to consume some information because the values are incomplete.

This is particularly common where specific types of data such as postal verification files, geospatial data, government or industry standard data, or third-party, value-added information are from sources external to the organization.

Example

When new customer details are added to MCHS Trading's Customer Hub, they need to be enriched with geospatial coordinates used in regional customer marketing campaigns.

Forces

- **Information structures must be changed in order to enrich the data**—Information may require restructuring or standardization before enrichment can be applied successfully.
- **External sources are required**—Information that cannot be calculated or derived from the originating information node must be acquired from external reference sources.

Solution

Use either an authoritative source or an algorithm to add the missing information.

This may require human intervention if the missing information is unknown.

Consequences

Benefits:

- The destination information collection in the information supply chain will contain additional information unavailable in the originating information stores.

Liabilities:

- In enriching information, there is the possibility that information may be incorrectly enriched with the wrong information or misapplied in the target information node.
- If there are many different information flows within the information supply chain, data enrichment may be applied from differing "authoritative" sources.

Example Resolved

The customer details do not contain geospatial data, but do contain address information, including street address, city, state, postal code, and country code. MCHS Trading has purchased a third-party geospatial data file. An enrich data reengineering step is added to the information process that accepts new customer details into the Customer Hub. This step will use the customer's address to look up and add the geospatial details to the appropriate information entry for this new customer.

Known Uses

Enriching information is used when redeploying information to a different information node, and throughout its lifetime within an information node as more information attributes are discovered. Data enrichment may occur within ETL processing, through application programs, or through the use of web services.

Related Patterns

Apply the STANDARDIZE **D**ATA and **R**ESTRUCTURE **D**ATA patterns to achieve optimal enrichment results. The CHECK **D**ATA pattern can be used to confirm whether correct enrichment of data occurred.

Classify Data

Context

An organization is designing how information collected for one purpose can be used for new purposes.

Problem

Information values need to be grouped according to a business rule, analytics model, or decision model.

How do you segment data within an information collection or an information payload?

Example

MCHS Trading must standardize and organize product data from multiple organizations before adding to the Product Hub but standardization and display requirements differ by type of product:

- The E-Shop and Mail-Shop Order applications distinguish five main categories (clothing, accessories, appliances, entertainment products, and grocery products) of products for purchase as well as additional subcategories.
- The product descriptions for each of these five main categories have unique requirements for standardization.
- There are particular rules based on a combination of UPC code, product name, and product description elements that determine the product category.

Forces

- **Information structures cannot be changed**—The information structures used with each information node cannot be changed (this is particularly true when the information originates from or is flowing to third parties, such as government agencies or existing or packaged applications).
- **Classification based on original information**—Classification values must be calculated, retrieved, or derived from the data in the originating information store.
- **Values need to be stored**—Classification values may need to be stored in a reference collection if they change regularly for ease of maintenance.
- **Lack of understanding of the information**—Contents of each information collection and node may not be understood, preventing appropriate enrichment from occurring.

Solution

Step through the information values running the business rule, analytics model, or decision model against each group as appropriate. Record the classification based on the business rule.

Evaluate and classify the values in the information nodes.

This process requires domain knowledge to properly segment the data into appropriate classifications.

Establish reusable classification routines to ensure consistent application to common data elements.

Consequences

Benefits:

- The destination information collection in the information supply chain will contain additional information unavailable in the originating information stores.

Liabilities:

- In classifying information, there is the possibility that information may be incorrectly classified with the wrong information or misapplied in the target information node, if the classification algorithms are not kept in sync with the incoming data.

- If there are many different information flows within the information supply chain, data classification may be applied from differing "authoritative" sources.

Example Resolved

In the case of MCHS Trading's Product Hub, the products must be classified to ensure correct usage later in the information supply chain:

- Identify the category of the UPC code by deriving the value from a reference source.
- Parse the product name and description for specific code attributes.
- Classify the product data into the current five categories by evaluating specific combinations of UPC category, product name attributes, and description attributes.
- Store the product classification for use on each product record.

Known Uses

Information classification is used to determine how information should be governed and managed. Classification is also used in ETL processing, in application programming, in web services, and in information reporting as a means to categorize data for subsequent use.

Related Patterns

The information may require the **S**TANDARDIZE **D**ATA and **R**ESTRUCTURE **D**ATA patterns to be applied before classification because the necessary values for classification are embedded in free-form content or must be mapped to a consistent form. The **E**NRICH **D**ATA and **D**ERIVE **V**ALUES patterns may be needed to add sufficient data to make the right classification. The **C**HECK **D**ATA pattern can be used to confirm the right classification.

Check Data

Context

An organization is designing how information collected for one purpose can be used for new purposes.

Problem

An information collection must not store incorrect information.

How do you ensure the validity of information values within an information collection, or an information payload, or typed in by an information user?

Example

MCHS Trading has attempted to standardize the addresses on data from the Stores Account system to pass into the Customer Hub:

- The standardized addresses should have a combination of City, State, and Postal Code that are valid based on an authoritative postal reference source.
- The street address must be populated to ensure that invoices and mailings can be delivered to the customer.

Forces

- **Inconsistent validation—**Different parts of an organization may have different definitions of the values that are valid for an attribute, and at which point in the processing the value must be in place. These differences may be because different silos of the organization developed them independently, or due to very different perspectives on how these values will be used. Either way, establishing consistent validation rules will require negotiation, compromise, and change—a common theme when setting up shared information resources.

Solution

Review the information values and flag those that are incorrect for remediation.

Validation rules are defined in a VALID VALUES DEFINITION. Step through the information values and check them against the valid values definition. Flag those that are incorrect for remediation.

This process requires domain knowledge to properly assign business rules for validation against the data.

Establish reusable validation routines to ensure consistent application to common information attributes.

Consequences

Benefits:

- The destination information collection in the information supply chain will contain valid information.

Liabilities:

- In validating information, there is the possibility that information may be incorrectly validated if the valid values definitions are not kept in sync with the incoming data content.
- If there are many different information flows within the information supply chain, data validation may be applied from differing "authoritative" sources.

Example Resolved

In the case of MCHS Trading's Stores Account address data, the addresses must be validated to ensure correct usage later in the information supply chain:

- Identify the valid values definition.
- Parse and standardize the addresses using the **S**TANDARDIZE **D**ATA pattern to get optimal validation results.
- Check the combination of City, State, and Postal Code.
- Check the parsed Street Address for completeness.
- Mark the records with indicators where the rules were not passed and what rule violations occurred.
- Use the violation markings to classify the data as valid or invalid.
- Route the invalid data to a **S**TAGING **A**REA against which the **C**ORRECT **D**ATA pattern can be applied.

Known Uses

Validation of information should be used wherever information is received into an information node. It is typically applied in user interfaces or information services—either by its user interfaces or **I**NFORMATION **S**ERVICES.

Related Patterns

Information may require the **S**TANDARDIZE **D**ATA, **C**LASSIFY **D**ATA, **E**NRICH **D**ATA, and **R**ESTRUCTURE **D**ATA patterns to be applied before validation can be effective because the necessary values for validation are calculated or drawn from external sources.

The **C**ORRECT **D**ATA and **I**NFORMATION **Q**UALITY **R**EMEDIATION **P**ROCESS patterns provide approaches for handling correction of information values.

Correct Data

Context

An organization is designing how information collected for one purpose can be used for new purposes.

Problem

Information values are incorrect.

Information values need to be corrected based on one or more business rules relevant to the data, often requiring human intervention.

Example

MCHS Trading has attempted to standardize the addresses on data from the Stores Account system to pass into the Customer Hub:

- In using the CHECK DATA pattern against the standardized addresses, 1% of the records have an incorrect combination of City, State, and Postal Code.
- Further, 100 records have no usable Street Address data.
- These records cannot be passed into the Customer Hub until the value issues are corrected.
- The incorrect records must be resolved and reprocessed.

Forces

- **Validation needed before use**—The data content entering the information supply chain requires validation prior to loading into the target information node.
- **Assessment based on original information**—Valid data values, formats, and data combinations must be assessed from the data in the originating information store or from data standardized, enriched, or otherwise reengineered in the information supply chain.
- **Information is time sensitive**—Time dependencies may require that incorrect data be loaded into the target information node and corrected after that point.
- **Invalid data must be stored and resolved**—When incorrect data cannot be loaded into the target information node, the incorrect data must be held in a staging area or corrected in the originating information node.

Solution

Use either an authoritative source or an algorithm to correct the information. This may require human intervention.

Check and evaluate the values in the information supply chain using the CHECK DATA pattern.

Step through the information values reviewing the business rule that the data violated as appropriate. Record the correction based on the business rule.

If the incorrect records must flow into the target information node, then apply correction to the data at that point. The correction will likely require human intervention.

If the incorrect records cannot flow into the target, but can be captured in a staging area for review and correction, then apply correction to the data at that point. This may utilize algorithms where the appropriate correction can be system-generated or may need human intervention. This may be part of an INFORMATION REMEDIATION PROCESS pattern. Corrections may be routed back to the originating system as updates or may be recycled into the same or distinct INFORMATION FLOW patterns.

Consequences

Benefits:

- The destination information collection in the information supply chain will contain corrected data content.

Liabilities:

- If the volume of incorrect data is too high, particularly where manual review is required, data correction can be very costly.
- If there are many different information flows within the information supply chain, data correction may be applied from differing "authoritative" sources, resulting in further data quality issues across the information supply chain.

Example Resolved

In the case of MCHS Trading's incorrect address data from the Stores Account information node, the addresses are first validated using the **C**HECK **D**ATA pattern:

- Identify the rule that the address data violated.
- Where the City, State, and Postal Code were not valid combinations, apply the **E**NRICH **D**ATA pattern to provide the correct data and update the record. Recycle the record into the information supply chain.
- Where the City, State, and Postal Code were not valid combinations and could not be resolved through data enrichment or the address information cannot be resolved, manually review the data. Send a report or request to the Stores system to contact the customer and update the address.
- Once a record has been automatically resolved or manually reviewed, remove the record from the **S**TAGING **A**REA.

Known Uses

Information should be corrected as soon at it is found to be invalid because it may cause confusion and mislead decision makers if it remains in its current state. Applications may incorporate steps to correct data. Data stewardship functions, particularly within Master Data Management, may include data correction. Web services and business processes may include steps to address and correct information.

Related Patterns

The **I**NFORMATION **Q**UALITY **R**EMEDIATION **P**ROCESS pattern coordinates information values correction where human intervention is required. The **C**HECK **D**ATA pattern can be used to reassess the data after corrections are applied. **C**ORRECT **D**ATA occurs as a step in an **I**NFORMATION **P**ROCESS.

Link Entries

Context

An organization is designing how information collected for one purpose can be used for new purposes.

Problem

Information entries in different information collections represent the same person, object, place, event, or activity.

The organization wants to document how the information entries in these information collections relate to one another.

Example

MCHS Trading is consolidating the customer account information from E-Shop and Stores along with details of recent orders from all of the order-taking applications together in Customer Hub. How should this information that related to a single person be brought together?

Forces

- **Information structures cannot be changed—**The information structures used with each information collection often cannot be changed. This is particularly true when the information originates from or is flowing to third parties, such as government agencies or existing or packaged applications.
- **Insufficient information to identify matching data—**There may be insufficient information values stored in some of the information collections to determine which information entities should be linked together.
- **Assessment based on original information—**Information values in the different information collections may be inconsistent due to differences in the input validation, how well the information is kept up to date by the information processes managing the information collection, or human error.

Solution

Link these information entries together so they can easily be retrieved as a group.

This linkage is recorded using INFORMATION LINKS. The information entries may be linked directly with one another, or a new information entry, possibly in a different information collection, is linked to the original information entries. Figure 8.3 illustrates the direct linking of information entries together. For an information entry to be linked to another, it needs to record the location and INFORMATION KEY for the target information entry.

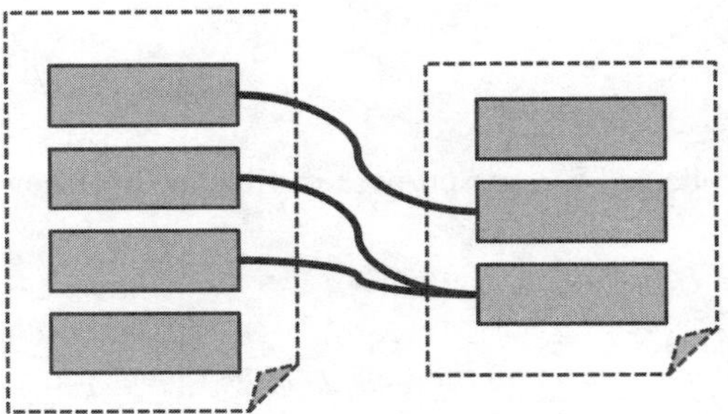

Figure 8.3 Direct linking of information entries.

Figure 8.4 shows an alternative approach where a third information collection is used to hold the information links. This has the advantage that the linking does not impact the original information collections, although it is a bit more involved to navigate between the links.

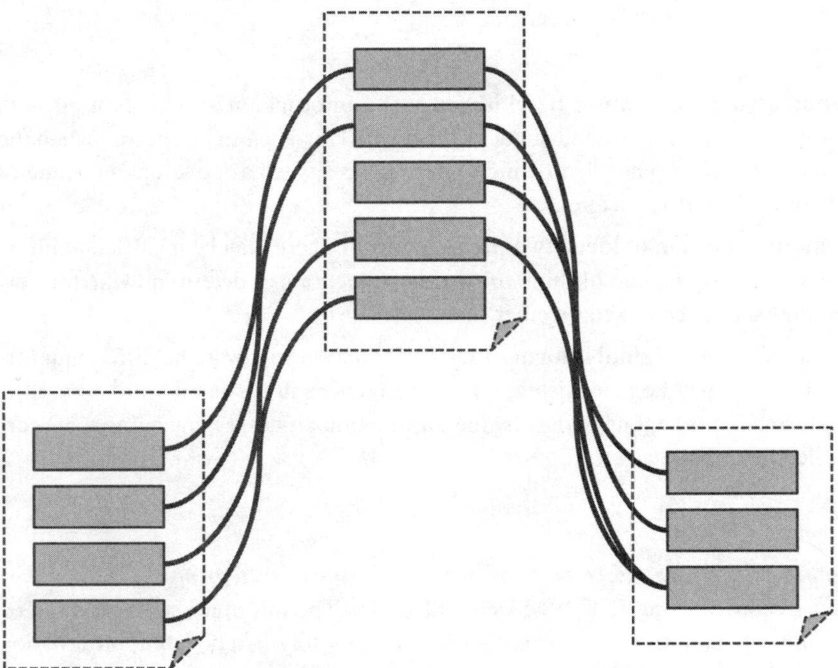

Figure 8.4 Indirect linking of information entries.

Consequences

Benefits:

- The relationship between the information elements is recorded and can be used by new information processes that need a more complete picture of the subject area than can be supplied by any one of the original information collections.

Liabilities:

- The information entries in the different information collections must be matched together accurately to ensure the right information entries are linked together. (See INFORMATION MATCHING PROCESS.)
- The information links need to be maintained because information entries in any of the information collections may be updated or deleted, invalidating one or more links.

Example Resolved

MCHS Trading elects to use the linking approach shown in Figure 8.4. The information collection that maintains the links contains customer details. It links to the account information and recent orders that comes from E-Shop, Mail-Shop, and Stores. (See Figure 8.5.)

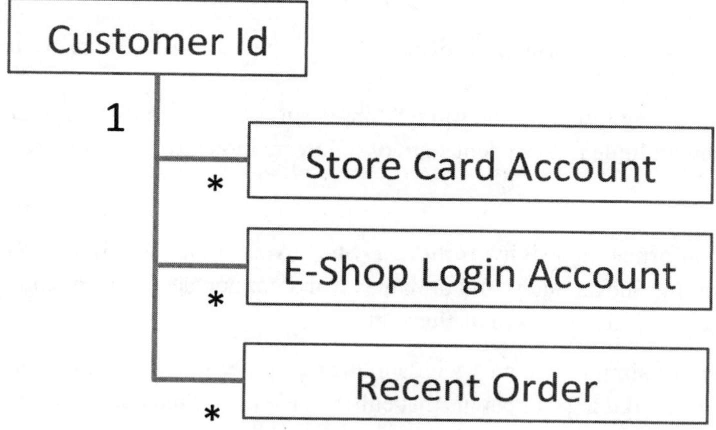

Figure 8.5 Linking customer, account, and order information together.

Known Uses

Linking of related information entries is the philosophy of the linked data standards such as the Open Services Lifecycle and Collaboration (OSLC)[1] standard. Data linkage or matching is utilized in ETL processing and Master Data Management (MDM) to connect related information entries and information payloads for subject areas such as Customer, Person, or Product.

Related Patterns

Links between information entries follow the **I**NFORMATION **L**INK life cycle defined in the **I**NFORMATION **E**LEMENTS pattern group.

Information links are used in the **I**NFORMATION **R**EGISTRY and **S**EMANTIC **I**NTEGRATION solutions found in the **I**NFORMATION **S**OLUTION pattern group.

Merge Entries

Context

An organization is designing how information collected for one purpose can be used for new purposes.

Problem

Multiple information entries in the same information collection represent the same person, event, object, place, or activity.

Multiple information entries representing the same "thing" can occur when there is ineffective input validation or when multiple independent sources of information have been merged.

Example

MCHS Trading has customer information arriving from its E-Shop, Mail-Shop, and Stores systems. Review of the Customer Hub shows many similar names with common addresses or email addresses as well as addresses that match but have distinct names:

- The multiple instances of similar or same records in the Customer Hub result in inconsistent customer views, marketing campaigns that either send out too much mail or miss likely customer targets.
- The multiple records for the same people also require more data storage and make information integration more complex.

1. **http://open-services.net**

Forces

- **Insufficient information to connect together**—There may be insufficient information values to support matching of the information entries.
- **Assessment based on original information**—Information values in the different information collections may be inconsistent due to differences in the input validation, how well the information is kept up to date by the information processes managing the information collection, or human error.

Solution

Create a new information entry that contains the best values from the information entries to be merged. Archive the previous information entries in case the merge needs to be reversed at a later time.

The best values to use in the merged information entry are determined by survivorship rules. These define rules for each attribute that may favor, say, the most recent value, or the value from the most reliable information node, or the value that is most commonly occurring in the information entries to be merged.

Consequences

Benefits:

- Duplicated information is eliminated and a complete, coherent information entry is created.

Liabilities:

- If the merge happened in error, the information entries will need to be split apart again (see SEPARATE ENTRIES).

Example Resolved

MCHS Trading uses an Information Matching Process to establish which information entries should be merged together. The information stewards decide the survivorship rules and these information entries are merged into new information entries. The original information entries are archived in case any information entries are merged in error. An example of the merging of information entries is shown in Figure 8.6.

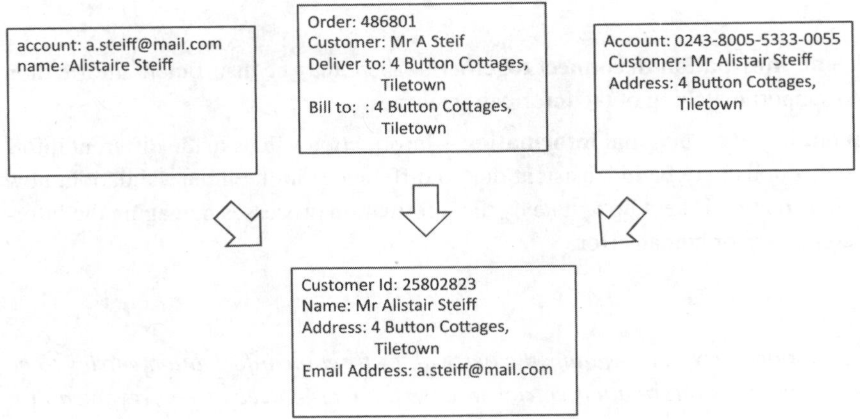

Figure 8.6 Merging information entries for Alistair Steiff.

Known Uses

Matching and merging information entries occurs when information is consolidated from multiple sources into a single information collection. Merging of data may occur in ETL processing or Master Data Management (MDM) solutions to consolidate related records in subject areas such as Customer, Person, or Product.

Related Patterns

The INFORMATION MATCHING PROCESS determines which information entries to merge. The CLERICAL REVIEW PROCESS pattern uses MERGE ENTRIES under the control of an information user to merge information entries. The SEPARATE ENTRIES pattern will split information entries that have been incorrectly merged.

Separate Entries

Context

An organization is designing how information collected for one purpose can be used for new purposes.

Problem

A single information entry contains information about multiple people, objects, places, or activities.

How do you separate those data values and ensure correct content is reestablished within or across information collections or information payloads?

Example

MCHS Trading implements its new Customer Hub incorporating processes to match and merge information entries that relate to the same person. (See the INFORMATION MATCHING PROCESS for more information on this type of processing.) Subsequent calls to the Customer-Care center indicate that some customers' orders were sent to the wrong individuals because some customer records were inappropriately merged together. Examples of incorrect customer record merging include the following:

- "Thomas Jones, 104 W. Elm St., Black Rock, WI" merged with "Thomas Jonas, 104 Elm Ave., Black Rock, WI"
- "Wm Holden, 128A Maine Sq, Carmelton, Il" merged with "Will Holden, 128 Main Sq, Carmelton, IL" and "Willa Holden, 128C Maine Sq, Carmelton, IL"

Subtle differences in spelling and location, errors, or a lack of sufficient information values can impact the reliability of such automated processes.

Forces

- **Re-creation of information may be required in the sources**—When incorrectly merged data is already loaded into the target information node without the possibility of correctly separating the data, the incorrect data must be deleted in the target, and correct entries be re-created from the originating sources.

Solution

Separate out the values into new information entries, one for each person, object, place, or activity. Archive the original information entry in case the split needs to be reversed or corrected at a later time.

Consequences

Benefits:

- The destination information collection in the information supply chain will contain correctly segmented/separated data content.

Liabilities:

- If the volume of incorrectly merged data is too high, particularly where manual review is required, data separation can be very costly and could require a reload/remerge from the original sources.
- If there are many different information flows within the information supply chain, data separation may be applied from differing "authoritative" sources with differing merging and separation rules, resulting in further data quality issues across the information supply chain.

Example Resolved

MCHS Trading modifies the thresholds on the **I**NFORMATION **M**ATCHING **P**ROCESS in the Customer Hub to include a clerical review whenever information entries are to be merged that are only a close match rather than an exact match. This clerical review helps to prevent the erroneous merging of information going forward.

MCHS Trading also uses clerical review to check the merges that have already taken place, so information entries can be split apart again if they were merged in error. This is possible because the Customer Hub keeps archived copies of the original information entries and creates a new information entry for the merged result.

Known Uses

Separating entries is required wherever they are being actively merged because mistakes occasionally happen. This capability is usually only found in Master Data Management (MDM) hubs.

Related Patterns

Use the **L**INK **E**NTRIES pattern to connect multiple records together that may hold related or unrelated information for subsequent merging and separation. Use the **M**ERGE **E**NTRIES pattern to merge data that is to be consolidated. Where records are separated, additional steps to **D**ERIVE **V**ALUES for recalculating numeric aggregations may be required.

The **C**LERICAL **R**EVIEW **P**ROCESS pattern provides approaches for handling information entry separation review as part of a distinct information governance approach that consolidates separation issues and incorporates steps for identifying, responding, and addressing data separation activities. **S**EPARATE **E**NTRIES occurs as a step in an **I**NFORMATION **P**ROCESS.

Derive Value

Context

An organization is designing how information collected for one purpose can be used for new purposes.

Problem

Values within an information entry need to be consistent.

How do you ensure that those data values are consistent within or across information collections or data payloads?

Example

MCHS Trading has an array of customer information arriving from its E-Shop, Mail-Shop, and Stores systems that is subsequently passed to the Customer Hub, including the date of birth. The

Reporting Hub does not require the demographic information for regular reports, but Marketing campaigns periodically require customer segmentation based on age (a value which changes over time).

Forces

- **Different levels of information required—** Applications and information processes do not require the same level of information for specific information entries. Further, retention of information in multiple points increases both storage costs and the likelihood that synchronization issues will occur, resulting in incorrect information used or passed into subsequent processes.

Solution

Only store the essential details and derive the other values when they are needed. (For example, age is derived from date of birth.)

Consequences

Benefits:

- Related attributes are kept consistent and use minimal storage.

Liabilities:

- If either the volume of data is high or the derivation of content is lengthy, then the timeliness of delivery in the information supply chain may not be sufficient to meet requirements.
- The algorithm used to derive the value must be the same throughout the information supply chain to ensure consistency.

Example Resolved

Only store a customer's demographic data, such as date of birth, in the Customer Hub. When a marketing campaign targets a specific customer segment based on age, retrieve the customers based on date of birth from the Customer Hub. Derive the value of customer age from the date of birth provided by the Customer Hub.

Known Uses

This type of processing is used in many systems to minimize the information that is stored and to ensure information entries are self-consistent. Examples of use can be found in application programming, information warehouses, and information reporting.

Related Patterns

The **S**UBJECT **A**REA **D**EFINITION and **I**NFORMATION **V**ALUES **P**ROFILE describe the characteristics of the values within an information collection so that derivations can be identified.

An **I**NFORMATION **M**ETRIC is an example of a derived value.

DERIVE **V**ALUES occurs as a step in an **I**NFORMATION **P**ROCESS. The **R**ESTRUCTURE **D**ATA, **S**TANDARDIZE **D**ATA, **E**NRICH **D**ATA, or **C**LASSIFY **D**ATA patterns may be necessary to ensure appropriate value derivation.

Derive Relationship

Context

An organization is designing how information collected for one purpose can be used for new purposes.

Problem

Are two or more information entries related in some way? How do you identify whether those information entries are connected when common keys or values are not present within or across information collections or data payloads?

Applications and information processes may need to associate information that is not related or not connected by common keys or values.

Example

MCHS Trading has an array of customer and order information in its E-Shop, Mail-Shop, and Stores systems that are subsequently passed to the Customer Hub. Which customers are parts of the same household?

Forces

- **Information structures cannot be changed**—The information structures used with each information node cannot be changed (this is particularly true when the information originates from or is flowing to third parties, such as government agencies or existing or packaged applications).
- **Insufficient data to determine relationships**—There may be insufficient data to support derivation of relationships in the information nodes, requiring further enrichment or data collection.

Solution

Use analytics to detect common values that suggest a relationship.

Consequences

Benefits:

- The information supply chain will derive or contain relationships otherwise unexpected in the original data sources.

Liabilities:

- The rules that derive relationships need to be carefully defined, and the results used with care, particularly when working with information about people, organizations, and external events because there are many exceptions in the real world.

Example Resolved

MCHS Trading uses analysis of customer addresses to determine which individuals are in the same household.

Known Uses

Deriving additional relationships occurs in information nodes where information is being aggregated and cross-referenced. Examples of use can be found in application programming, information warehouses, business analytics, and information reporting.

Related Patterns

The INFORMATION ASSET HUB and INFORMATION WAREHOUSE are information nodes where new relationships are derived.

Where relationships cannot be readily identified, use a LINK ENTRIES or an INFORMATION PATTERN DISCOVERY PROCESS pattern to identify the closest potential relationships.

DERIVE RELATIONSHIPS occurs as a step in an INFORMATION PROCESS. The RESTRUCTURE DATA, STANDARDIZE DATA, ENRICH DATA, or CLASSIFY DATA patterns may be necessary to ensure appropriate relationship derivation.

Smooth Data

Context

An organization is designing how information collected for one purpose can be used for new purposes.

Problem

A stream of information contains outlier values due to errors in data capture or initial data conditions.

How do you handle those data values within or across information collections or data payloads?

Example

MCHS Trading tracks customer order information arriving from its E-Shop, Mail-Shop, and Stores systems on a daily, weekly, and annual basis. Because the weeks are not consistent from year to year due to moving holidays and yearly start/end dates, certain anomalies occur, which skew inventory planning.

Can the customer order information be adjusted to compensate for the anomalies in data conditions at the time of information capture to correctly compare daily and weekly volumes from year to year?

Forces

- **Too costly to fix errors or outliers at initial input—**For certain information, it is not possible or is too costly to fix errors or outliers introduced at the time of data capture. To smooth a data set is to create an approximating function that attempts to capture important patterns in the data, while leaving out noise or other fine-scale structures/rapid phenomena. Many different algorithms are used in smoothing such as the *moving average*.

Solution

Use algorithms such as a moving average to smooth out the effect of data outliers or certain initial data conditions.

Consequences

Benefits:

- The information supply chain will provide more consistent information that compensates for data outliers or differing initial data conditions.
- Smoothed data can be subsequently used for better reporting and analysis in the information supply chain.

Liabilities:

- Smoothed data only approximates possible data conditions and may mask important data anomalies or data conditions, which may not be understood at the time of reporting and analysis, and may result in inaccurate information products and delivery.

Example Resolved

In the case of MCHS Trading's customer order statistics, any aggregated information occurring during weeks with moving holidays must be smoothed:

- Identify the days and weeks that require smoothing across prior and subsequent days and weeks.
- Define and store algorithms to smooth data based on the targeted results.
- Smooth the data utilizing the established algorithms.
- Save the smoothed data in an information node if this is to be a regular process or in a report if this is a periodic request.

Known Uses

Information smoothing is useful in monitoring of sensor data. Smoothing may also be used on data stored in the information warehouse or data marts to improve business intelligence and analytics results.

Related Patterns

The **I**NFORMATION **S**TREAMING **N**ODE may use this type of information reengineering. **I**NFORMATION **P**ATTERN **D**ISCOVERY **P**ROCESS and **I**NFORMATION **P**ATTERN **D**ETECTION **P**ROCESS patterns may require smoothing to resolve outliers or normalize the data sufficiently to identify patterns against background noise.

Sample Data

Context

An organization is designing how information collected for one purpose can be used for new purposes.

Problem

The volume of data is large, which requires a lot of capacity to process.

Example

MCHS Trading needs a representative sample of its customer details to support its **I**NFORMATION **P**ATTERN **D**ETECTION **P**ROCESS to create a predictive analytics model for its **N**EXT **B**EST ACTION solution.

Forces

- **Timeliness of information is important**—More data results in longer processing time.
- **Difficult to identify a good sample**—What is a representative sample of an information collection?

Solution

Use information values profiling to understand the variability in the information and extract subsets of the information with the same characteristics.

Consequences

Benefits:

- The information processes using the sampled information will execute quicker because they have less information to process.

Liabilities:

- If the sampling is not perfect, the resulting information collection will not represent a representative subset of the original information collections. An **I**NFORMATION **V**ALUES **P**ROFILE will provide guidance on the range and frequency of information values within an information collection.

Example Resolved

The Information Pattern Detection Process will use a private information collection of customer details and their related activities (**S**ANDBOX **U**SAGE). This information collection is populated from existing information collections in the Reporting Hub using **S**NAPSHOT **P**ROVISIONING. The **I**NFORMATION **F**LOW that implements the snapshot provisioning has a sample data step to select the information entries that will be added to the destination information collection.

Known Uses

Data sampling is a commonly used statistical technique for information analysis to reduce the volume of information required and the processing time necessary to perform the analysis.

Related Patterns

Sampling information is particularly useful in **S**NAPSHOT **P**ROVISIONING. It is frequently used in **I**NFORMATION **I**DENTIFICATION to quickly find patterns, relationships, or issues in data. **I**NFORMATION **P**ATTERN **D**ISCOVERY **P**ROCESSES and **I**NFORMATION **P**ATTERN **D**ETECTION **P**ROCESSES traditionally used sampling techniques, though that is changing with the advent of new techniques for handling extremely high data volumes.

Information Guard Patterns

The information guard patterns cover the mechanisms for information security and privacy. The generic **I**NFORMATION **G**UARD pattern is shown first in Table 8.3 and followed by summaries of more specialist guards.

Table 8.3 Information Guard Pattern Summary

Icon	Pattern Name	Problem	Solution
	INFORMATION GUARD	The organization's information needs to be protected from inappropriate use and theft.	Insert mechanisms into the information supply chain to verify that the right people are only using information for authorized purposes.

Information Guard

Context

Information has value to an organization. It is vulnerable to theft, loss, and damage; inappropriate use; and corruption.

Problem

The organization's information needs to be protected from inappropriate use and theft.

Information would be perfectly safe if no one could access it. It would also be irrelevant. So an organization creates access points in its IT systems to allow people and other systems to access the information.

The Internet has been a driving force and an enabler in terms of opening up the access to IT systems and linking them together. There is now a lot more information available and a higher expectation that an organization will make its information available to its customers, regulators, investors, the media, and the government.

Technology has become more sophisticated and organizations are able to put a variety of mechanisms in place to protect their information. At the same time, this sophistication means that the organization may not understand all of the capability it has running, creating loopholes for hackers and viruses.

How is an organization's information protected from theft, loss, and inappropriate use?

Example

MCHS Trading stores information about its customers. How can it be sure that this personal information is used appropriately?

Forces

- **Multiple copies of information**—Valuable information is often needed by many information processes and so may be copied to multiple information nodes. Each copy represents a point of vulnerability.

- **Selected users need access**—Selected users will need different types of access to the information. It is unlikely that everyone will need all information.
- **Appropriate protection**—The level of protection given to information should be commensurate with its value or the harm it will do if it is compromised.
- **Copying leaves no mark**—When information is copied, the original is not affected. Therefore, copying has to be detected in the act as it is not possible to know that the information has been copied.

Solution

Insert mechanisms into the information supply chain to verify that the right people are only using information for authorized purposes.

Information security must be deployed to every entry point to the systems. There are two basic underpinnings to information security:

- **Authentication**—Validating that a person or a system is who or what they claim to be. Typically, this is achieved through a user account that provides a user identifier and password. The password is secret to the individual (or system) and so it is assumed that anyone who knows the password is the person named in the user account. Alternatively, biometric information such as fingerprints and retinal scans may be used for high-security situations. Authentication is determined when a user or system first connects and remains active until they disconnect—or a time limit is reached.
- **Authorization**—Ensuring that an authenticated user is only given access to the resources that he or she is supposed to access. Typically, the resource owner manages authorization. The resource owner maintains a list of the users, or groups of users, that may have access to the resources and the level access permitted. Authorization is performed on every access to a resource. Once you know who a person or system is, and what they have access to, it is possible to enforce security around information, and audit that authorized users are using information appropriately.

Because information can be morphed and copied, there are additional techniques that can be applied to reduce its sensitivity and make it suitable for broader uses. This includes the following:

- **Masking**—Blanking out information values that are sensitive, leaving other values intact so other people can use them.
- **Anonymizing**—Ensuring an individual cannot be identified from the information, while preserving the referential integrity of the information. For example, if the information showed details of five people living at a particular address, after anonymization, you would still know there were five people living at an address—but you would not

know who they where or which address it was. This type of information is useful for research and trend analysis where the individual details are not significant.

- **Encryption**—This is the hiding of information using an algorithm that can only recover the information if a security key is provided. The intention is that only the originator and the intended recipients can read the information.

Security and the protection of information take constant vigilance because the IT systems are constantly changing, and as a result, new points of vulnerability are being opened up.

Consequences

Benefits:

- The information guard pattern provides mechanisms to ensure information is only available to the individuals who are authorized to use it.

Liabilities:

- Information guards take time to set up and maintain. They need constant maintenance to adapt to the changing user community and business use of the information. Using these mechanisms should not be too difficult for users or they will find ways to circumvent them. Examples of impractical security policies include the following:
  - Setting password policies that are too complex results in users writing their passwords down (because no one can remember his or her password), and creates vulnerability.
  - Making it too difficult to create a new user when a new person is brought into a team encourages the sharing of user accounts.
  - Failing to delete a user account for an individual who has left the organization creates an opportunity for that user to continue to access the systems.

Example Resolved

MCHS Trading has a number of mechanisms to protect customer information:

- All employees of MCHS Trading have their own user account (user ID/password) that they are not allowed to share. This means all use of information is attributable.
- A customer using the E-Shop has to log on to the site with his or her own user ID and password to review the customer details that the E-Shop stores or to place an order.
- Whenever payment details from a customer are displayed to an employee, or printed out, the account details are always masked with XXXXX so they cannot be read.
- None of the information nodes will accept a request for customer details unless the request comes from an authenticated source (system/user).

Known Uses

The information guard patterns describe security and privacy features that are provided in the majority of commercial software, including applications, databases, and network systems. These include user logon credentials, encryption, anonymization and masking of data, physical security, detection of unusual patterns of use, and special procedures to ensure information is protected.

Related Patterns

The **I**NFORMATION **P**ROBE patterns describe how to monitor the activity in the information supply chain.

Variations of the Information Guard Pattern

The pattern summaries in Table 8.4 below describe more specialized types of guards that can be used in the information supply chain.

Table 8.4 Information Guard Specialist Pattern Summary

Icon	Pattern Name	Problem	Solution
	IDENTITY VERIFICATION	It is necessary to identify who is performing actions on local information.	Provide a unique electronic identifier for each person using the information systems and a mechanism, such as a password or biometric reader, to enable each individual to prove who he or she is.
	IDENTITY PROPAGATION	It is necessary to identify who is performing actions on remote information.	When a request is made for information from a remote information node, flow the identity of the requesting person and/or process to the remote node to enable it to verify and record the request.
	TRUSTED NODE	It is necessary to ensure an information node is legitimately part of the information supply chain.	Provide each information node with an identity that it is able to use to prove to the information nodes it is communicating with that it is an authorized member of the information supply chain.
	FUNCTION-CENTRIC ACCESS	It is necessary to control who is able to perform a particular activity.	Maintain lists of the actions each individual is able to perform and check these lists when the activity is requested.
	DATA-CENTRIC ACCESS	It is necessary to control who is able to see certain types of information.	Maintain lists of who is able to access each type of data and remove values that the caller is not authorized to see whenever he or she accesses the information.

Icon	Pattern Name	Problem	Solution
	SEPARATION OF DUTIES	It is necessary to ensure that certain activities are performed, reviewed, and approved by independent people.	Keep track of who is performing certain activities and the relationships between individuals. When a review or approval is required, ensure the person assigned to do it is not related to the original worker.
	ENCRYPT DATA	It is necessary to prevent third parties from seeing information as it flows through the information supply chain.	Use an encryption algorithm to transform information to make it unreadable to anyone except those possessing special knowledge, usually referred to as a key.
	MASK DATA	It is necessary to hide certain data values as they are transmitted to parts of the information supply chain.	Use masking algorithms to obfuscate these values.
	ANONYMIZE DATA	It is necessary to hide the identity of an individual who is referenced in information flowing between information nodes. The information values still need to be valid values—but must hide the identity of the individual.	Use algorithms to consistently replace real values with pseudonyms and securely record the mapping so the transformation can be applied consistently over time.
	PHYSICAL SECURITY ZONE	It is necessary to prevent unauthorized people from accessing the hardware of the information supply chain.	Keep the hardware in secure locations with access restricted to authorized people.
	COLLECTION CONTROL	It is necessary to prevent collections of information from leaking outside of the information supply chain.	Create information processes to control how collections of information are handled once they are exported outside of the care of the information supply chain.
	INTERACTION ANALYSIS	It is necessary to detect fraudulent use of the information within the information supply chain.	Record the activity within the information supply chain and analyze for unexpected patterns as they are happening.

Information Probe Patterns

The information probe patterns cover how an information supply chain and its supporting infrastructure can be monitored. The parts of an information supply chain are distributed and heterogeneous. Monitoring is achieved by adding information probes throughout the infrastructure to monitor the activity (or lack of activity) at a particular point and writing information events to local information collections.

An information probe can be monitoring:

- All activity
- Unexpected situations

The information events can be read either (1) through a local user interface, or (2) through a remote information service, and/or (3) they are consolidated and sent to a central monitoring information node.

The generic information probe pattern is shown first in Table 8.5 and followed by summaries of more specialist probes.

Table 8.5 Information Probe Pattern Summary

Icon	Pattern Name	Problem	Solution
	INFORMATION PROBE	The operation of an information supply chain needs to be monitored to ensure it is working properly.	Insert probes into key points in the information supply chain to gather measurements for further analysis.

Information Probe

Context

An information centric organization is concerned with the efficient and accurate use of information.

Problem

The operation of an information supply chain needs to be monitored to ensure it is working properly.

Example

MCHS Trading wants to be sure that its information supply chains are working properly. For example, it wants to know that orders are being fulfilled on time, that its product descriptions are correct, and that its customer information is up to date. How does MCHS Trading achieve this?

Forces

- **Failures can occur at any time**, in any place, for many reasons.
- **Failures can ripple through the information supply chain**—If a failure in an information supply chain is not detected and resolved in time, further failures can occur downstream as a consequence. For example, if information about monthly sales figures from one region is not loaded in time, the report that aggregates the sales figures for the whole organization will be wrong.
- **Local knowledge is often required**—It takes local knowledge to understand how a particular information process should be operating.
- **Indiscriminant monitoring can generate a lot of data**—The useful information is often buried within large volumes of data.

Solution

Insert information probes into key points in the information supply chain to gather measurements for further analysis.

An information probe is a component that is called at key points in an information process. It is passed relevant information by the information process. It may simply store the information it is passed in an information collection, or perform some processing on it and then store the results, or perform some action, such as call a remote information service. Because it is operating in the mainline of the information process, it is designed to impose minimum overhead on the calling information process.

The information node that is hosting the information probe may offer facilities to configure the information probe. This configuration may control how much information is stored and any preprocessing that should be performed on the information passed to the information probe.

Consequences

Benefits:

- Information probes provide a flexible approach to extracting information about the internal behavior of an information process.

Liabilities:

- The processing within an information probe may slow down the operation of the calling information process.

Example Resolved

MCHS Trading inserted information probes in each information process that supported its information supply chain and used the information from them to detect failures that would impact the quality of its information and operations.

Known Uses

Information probes represent sensors, diagnostics tracing, monitoring probes, and other devices that generate information about the internal workings of an information process or information node.

The **Common Base Event** standard provides a comprehensive view of the type of information that should be emitted from an information probe:
http://www.eclipse.org/tptp/platform/documents/resources/cbe101spec/CommonBaseEvent_SituationData_V1.0.1.pdf

In particular, it describes the following situation types that cover most of the situations that a probe could report on:

- **Start Situation—**A component (such as an information node, information process, information service, or information trigger) is starting.
- **Stop Situation—**A component is stopping.
- **Connect Situation—**A component has connected to another. This means an information request has completed and the information guards in place have allowed the request.
- **Configure Situation—**A configuration has changed for a component.
- **Request Situation—**An information request has completed, either successfully or not.
- **Feature Situation—**An information process (or group of related information processes) is available, or no longer available.
- **Dependency Situation—**A component's dependency has either been met, or not.
- **Create Situation—**Something has been created, such as an information entry.
- **Destroy Situation—**Something has been deleted.
- **Report Situation—**A component is making a report about its current state or a subcomponent's state. This could be PERFORMANCE, SECURITY, HEARTBEAT, STATUS, TRACE, DEBUG, or LOG.
- **Available Situation—**A component has completed its initialization and is available for work.
- **Other Situation—**Something else.

Related Patterns

An information probe may use an INFORMATION EVENT STORE to record the events it detects.

The INFORMATION MONITORING information solution pattern illustrates the use of information probes.

The CONSOLIDATING INFORMATION SUPPLY CHAIN pattern describes how to bring information from the information probes into a monitoring application.

Variations of the Information Probe Pattern

The pattern summaries in Table 8.6 below describe more specialized types of probes that can be used in the information supply chain.

Table 8.6 Information Probe Specialist Pattern Summary

Icon	Pattern Name	Problem	Solution
	SUBJECT AREA PROBE	How consistent are the values between a set of information collections from the same subject area?	Compare the values from all, or a representative subset, of the related information entries in each information collection.
	PROFILING RULE PROBE	What is the quality of the values in an information collection?	Regularly run validation rules against all, or a representative subset, of the information values.
	INFORMATION FLOW PROBE	How much information is flowing between two information nodes?	Record details such as the number of payloads and amount of data and time, each time a data flow is initiated.
	ENTRY UNIQUENESS PROBE	How much duplicated information is located in an information collection?	Record the number of information entries that represent the same "thing" within the information collection.
	ACCESS AUDITING PROBE	Who is accessing and changing information?	Record the identity of who is accessing information and what activity he or she is performing from which information node.
	OPERATIONAL HEALTH PROBE	Is a part of the information infrastructure operating successfully?	Record operation health checks, such as availability, memory usage, CPU usage, and response times.
	SAMPLE DATA PROBE	What are the types of information values flowing between two information nodes?	Occasionally record samples of the values that are flowing between two nodes and analyze.
	ENVIRONMENT PROBE	When the state of the environment is changing, how do we incorporate its state into the information supply chain?	Use sensors located at appropriate places in the environment and pipe the measurements they record into the information supply chain.

Summary

This chapter covered the protection of information. This is something that must be designed holistically, considering the welfare of key information at all stages of it lifetime. It is then implemented through the deployment of small components throughout the systems, where each is responsible for protecting an aspect of the information. The patterns of information management break down the aspects of information protection into three pattern groups:

- **INFORMATION REENGINEERING STEP**—These patterns focus on maintaining the quality and format of information.
- **INFORMATION GUARD**—These patterns ensure authorized people and processes are using information for authorized purposes.
- **INFORMATION PROBE**—These patterns are used to monitor the use and movement of information. With these patterns, it is possible to detect issues in the management of information and correct it.

The information protection patterns are used as processing steps in both the information process and information service pattern groups where they transform, protect, or monitor information as it enters the organization, when it is stored, when it is sent between systems, retrieved, updated, and eventually archived and deleted. Individually, they protect a single point in the processing—collectively, they protect the organization's information throughout its entire life cycle.

Chapter 9, "Solutions for Information Management," builds on the pattern groups in previous chapters to describe complete information solutions.

CHAPTER 9

Solutions for Information Management

Information solutions are the projects that an organization implements to improve the management of its information. These information solutions build upon the underlying patterns that we have discussed in the prior chapters and pull them together in new patterns. The case studies presented in Chapter 2, "The MCHS Trading Case Study," are examples of information solutions and illustrate ways in which the pattern groups fit together.

The lead pattern that describes the general structure of an information solution is called INFORMATION SOLUTION, which is highlighted in Figure 9.1.

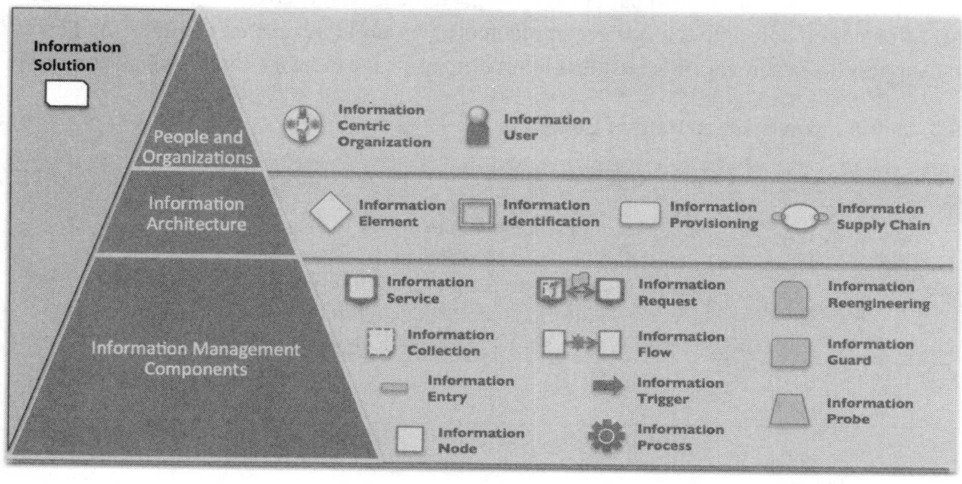

Figure 9.1 Where the patterns from Chapter 9 fit in the pattern language.

Each kind of information solution focuses on a specific aspect of information management.

There are a wide range of options—and hence patterns. We have grouped a selection of information solutions as follows:

- **Solutions for changing information nodes—**Introduces or upgrades information nodes
- **Solutions for integrating information nodes—**Improves the flow of information between applications
- **Master Data Management solutions—**Describes approaches for introducing a master data management hub to improve the management of shared operational information
- **Big data and warehouses solutions—**Adds the ability to manage large quantities of information
- **Business intelligence and analytics solutions—**Describes solutions for reporting and analytics
- **Information protection solutions—**Improves the protection, life cycle, and quality of information

Descriptions of these specific solutions follow the description of the information solution lead pattern.

Information Solution Patterns

Table 9.1 is the summary of the lead pattern for this group, called INFORMATION SOLUTION.

An information solution is a project implemented by an IT team that changes the IT systems that support the organization's business in order to improve the way it manages information.

Table 9.1 Information Solution Pattern Summary

Icon	Pattern Name	Problem	Solution
	INFORMATION SOLUTION	An organization recognizes there is a missing capability, or a major issue with the way it manages an aspect of its information.	Create a project, or series of projects, to transform the way the information is managed by the organization's people and information systems.

Information Solution

Context

An information centric organization is concerned with the efficient and accurate use of information.

Problem

An organization recognizes there is a missing capability, or a major issue with the way it manages an aspect of its information.

The organization wants to invest in a solution to find a reliable and repeatable resolution to this issue.

Example

In MCHS Trading, order records are created in the order-taking applications (E-Shop, Mail-Shop, and Stores) and passed to the Shipping application. The Shipping application controls the dispatch of goods. When all of the goods on the order are sent to the customer, a copy of the order record is sent to the Invoicing application. The Invoicing application maintains the accounts and controls the process for invoicing the customer and collecting the payment. This is shown in Figure 9.2.

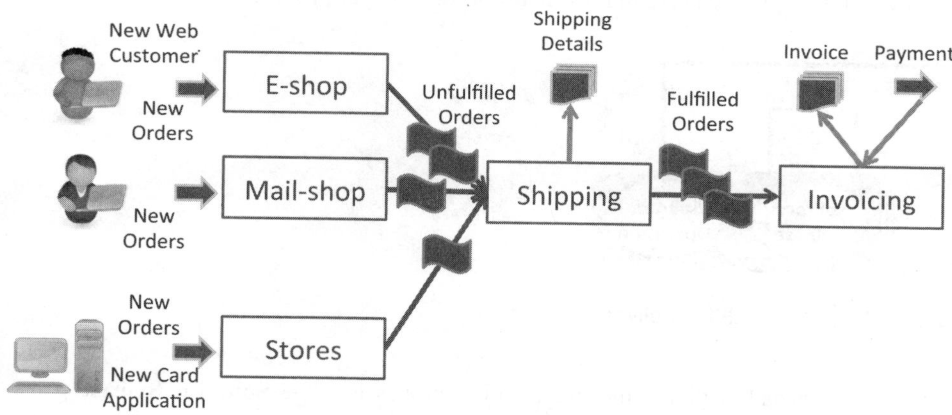

Figure 9.2 Order processing at MCHS Trading.

Although this arrangement works—customers and the stores can order goods, they are delivered, and payment is received, MCHS Trading realizes its existing order-processing systems are not delivering the customer-centric service it wants to offer. It requires a consolidated view of its customers, the channels they use, the types of products they buy, and the results of the purchases (both good and bad).

Forces

- **The effects of changes are often widespread**—Changes to information systems tend to affect the procedures that people use around them.

- **Information is duplicated and inconsistent**—Information that is duplicated across multiple systems is often stored in different formats with different validation rules and currency.
- **Ownership without responsibility**—It is not uncommon to find that parts of an organization feel they own a particular type of information but they are unwilling to invest in an organizationwide solution.

Solution

Create a project, or series of projects, to transform the way the information is managed by the organization's people and information systems.

Information solutions typically go through the three high-level phases shown in Figure 9.3. First is the **Solution Outline** phase. This may involve protracted discussions internally, and with software and services vendors. Often prototypes or proof of concept projects are run to understand any new technology or change in information-processing approach.

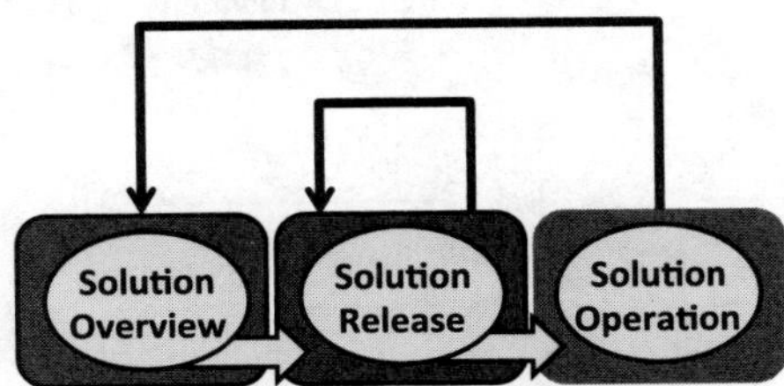

Figure 9.3 Information solution delivery phases.

When the go-ahead is given, the organization moves into the **Solution Release** phase. Development teams use a variety of methods during this phase. However, they need to accomplish five major activities:

- Analysis of affected systems and the information they use. This analysis feeds the design process and is a key activity to ensure the new solution will integrate successfully with the existing systems.
- Design of the information solution.
- Configuration, coding, and testing of the new capability.
- Deployment of the new capability into the production environment.
- Operations handover.

These activities are, of course, coordinated using project management techniques. Once the new capability is developed and tested, it moves to the **Solution Operation** phase.

An information solution will have changed the way information is managed going forward. Often, as the organization is using the information, there is an ability to monitor and improve the information it is using through information governance and stewardship processes. The success of the information solution will hopefully lead to further investment in additional information solutions.

This is summarized in Figure 9.4.

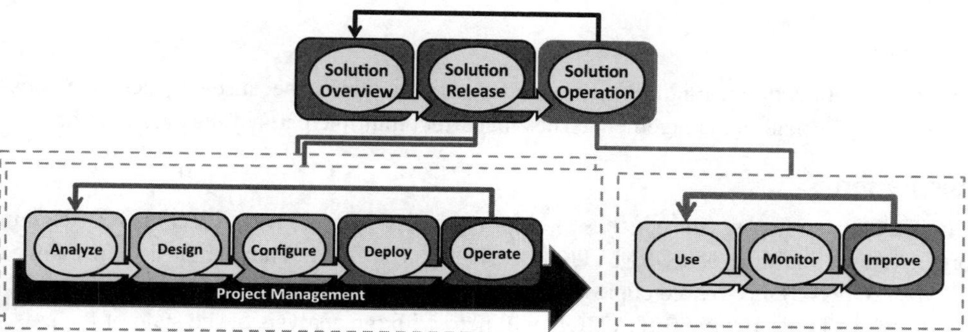

Figure 9.4 Information solution delivery activities within phases.

The specialized information solution patterns cover more detail of the types of capability that are often created by an information solution.

Consequences

Benefits:

- Implementing information solutions will change the IT infrastructure to improve the management of information.

Liabilities:

- In general, the information needs of an organization are relatively stable and this investment can deliver value for many years. However, recent developments are opening up new sources of information through social media and real-world sensors. An organization should continually look for new opportunities to augment this information with new insight.

Example Resolved

MCHS Trading implements a series of information solutions to improve its management of information. This includes the following:

- **C**ENTRALIZED **M**ASTER for product details
- **S**YNCHRONIZED **M**ASTERS for customer details
- **M**ANAGED **A**RCHIVE for completed order details
- **P**ERFORMANCE **R**EPORTING for monitoring the performance of the organization

Refer to these patterns to understand the work that MCHS Trading needed to do for each of these solutions.

Known Uses

The enterprise architecture team initiates most information solutions because they describe holistic solutions to information management issues that affect multiple parts of the organization.

Related Patterns

Most information solutions introduce some form of **I**NFORMATION **P**ROVISIONING in support of one or multiple **I**NFORMATION **S**UPPLY **C**HAINS. They often use specialized **I**NFORMATION **N**ODES to hold copies of the information that is being managed.

INFORMATION **I**DENTIFICATION will help with the analysis of the state of the existing information and the impact that the issues with it are causing the organization. In particular, **I**NFORMATION **V**ALUES **P**ROFILES will understand the state of the information values in an information collection and the **S**UBJECT **A**REA **D**EFINITION can formalize the definition of the affected subject areas. The **I**NFORMATION **G**OVERNANCE **P**ROGRAM pattern can help with establishing governance practices for the new capability.

Patterns for Changing Information Nodes

An organization typically has many applications, each performing a unique role for a particular group of information users. The implementation of these applications is typically focused on performing the business activity, and less concerned with the management of the information they hold beyond that end. The information solutions in Table 9.2 covers additional types of projects to supplement the behavior of an organization's applications.

Table 9.2 Information Solutions Patterns Summary—Changing Information Nodes

Icon	Pattern Name	Problem	Solution
	NEW INFORMATION NODE	What are the information implications of deploying a new information node and how should the organization handle them?	Initialize, protect, and synchronize the new information node's information collections.

Icon	Pattern Name	Problem	Solution
	INFORMATION NODE UPGRADE	When an information node is upgraded, how will the new information node reflect the processing that has occurred in the past when the existing information node is decommissioned?	Migrate, refresh, and reconnect the information from the existing information node to the new one.

New Information Node

Context

An organization needs to deploy a new information node.

Problem

What are the information implications of deploying a new information node and how should the organization handle them?

The new information node may be supporting a new business, or improving an existing business, or be required to comply with a new regulation, or be part of an information supply chain's mechanism that keeps the organization's information synchronized. Whatever the reason, once it is up and running, the information node becomes important to the success of the organization. How should it be set up to become an integrated part of the business?

Example

MCHS Trading wants to replace its old Mail-Shop application with a new application called M-Shop. How should M-Shop be provisioned with information?

Forces

- **Operational criticality—**For new information nodes supporting critical operational processes, the new information node and other existing information nodes may require parallel operation to ensure the new information node performs as expected.
- **Initial load—**A new information node has empty information collections. Unless this is a brand-new business, the organization needs to load the new information node with details of the relevant information assets.
- **Ongoing synchronization—**The information collections within the new information node will need to be synchronized with the other information collections used by the organization.

- **Ensuring quality**—New information nodes need to be evaluated for information quality from the point when they are initially loaded and on an ongoing basis to ensure they meet the expectations of all consumers of the information.
- **Tracking performance**—The new information node must be monitored to ensure adequate performance against data volumes, delivery times, and other key measurements.
- **Limiting access**—The new information node needs to be secured and only provide access to authorized people and information processes.
- **Surviving disaster**—An information node (even a new one) can fail. This could be caused by a hardware failure, software bug, operator error, or malicious attack. The result might be a failure of a single operation, the loss of a business transaction, the loss of the information node for a period of time, or the permanent loss of the system and/or location where it was sited. How does the organization continue after this has happened?

Solution

Initialize, evaluate, protect, and synchronize the new information node's information collections.

When the information collections are located in the same information node as the information processes that are using them, it is called LOCAL PROVISIONING. These information collections may need to be initialized with existing information. This is called the initial load.

Once the initial load is completed and evaluated for appropriate quality, the information node is ready for new work (though in operational systems, it may operate in parallel to other existing information nodes for a period of time to ensure it functions as expected). However, if it remains disconnected from the rest of the organization, its local information will become inconsistent with other information nodes. It needs to be connected to the organization's INFORMATION SUPPLY CHAINS.

Many of the other types of provisioning around an information node that connect it to the information supply chains are shown in Figure 9.5.

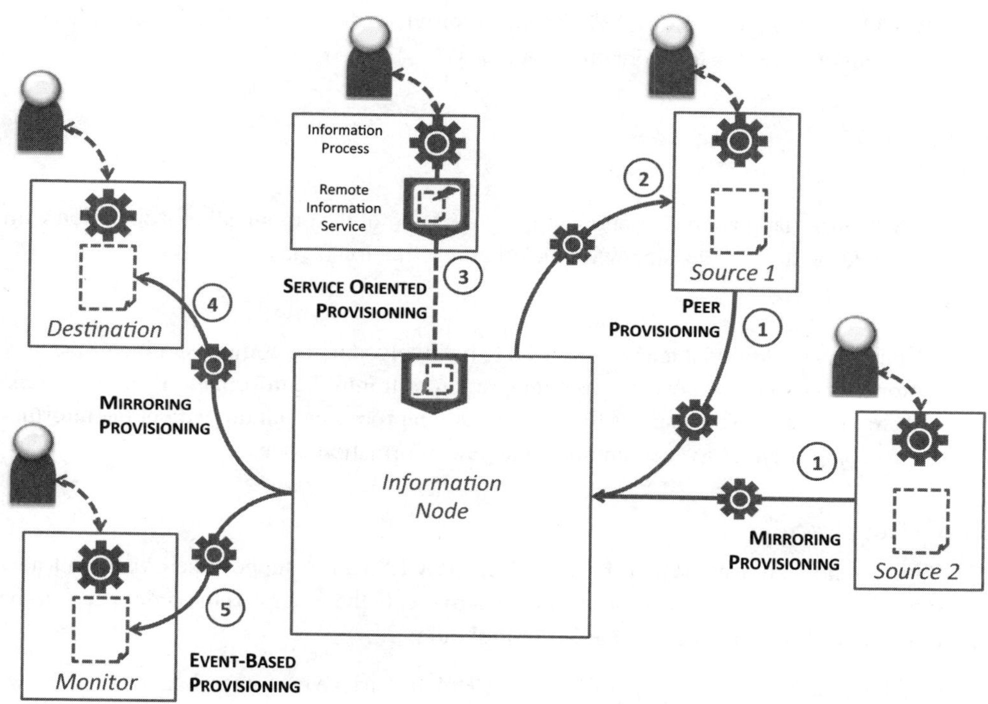

Figure 9.5 Provisioning an information node.

The numbers on the diagram refer to these notes:

1. New information can be fed into the information node using MIRRORING PROVISIONING, PEER PROVISIONING, or SNAPSHOT PROVISIONING (not shown above, though commonly used when a new information node will run in parallel with an existing information node for an initial period of time).
2. When new information is passed into the information node, peer provisioning replicates it to other connected information nodes.
3. Information can be supplied or retrieved using SERVICE ORIENTED PROVISIONING.
4. New information can be distributed to other information nodes using mirroring provisioning.
5. Alerts for unusual situations can be distributed using EVENT-BASED PROVISIONING.

6. **R**ECOVERY **P**ROVISIONING should be provided for every information collection that cannot be re-created from other methods.

Consequences

Benefits:

- A new information node becomes an integrated part of the organization's operation with information that is consistent with the other information nodes.

Liabilities:

- A number of additional teams may need to be involved in the commissioning of the new information node to coordinate the integration of it into the information supply chains. There may need to be changes to the information processes that implement the information supply changes to accommodate the new information node.

Example Resolved

The M-Shop application uses AGILE **B**USINESS **P**ROCESSES to support the creation of new orders. It needs customer details and product details to create the order and the order needs to be stored somewhere. The team decides that M-Shop should:

- Call the information services of Customer Hub to retrieve customer details.
- Have a read-only local version of the product details.
- Have a local information collection for storing orders.

M-Shop needs to join two information supply chains: It needs to receive changes to product details from the product information supply chain and to feed new orders into the order details information supply chain.

M-Shop needs **R**ECOVERY **P**ROVISIONING of its user registry and configuration. If the M-Shop information node was completely destroyed, it would be reinstalled on new hardware and the information collections reloaded as if it were newly commissioned. Any partial orders not published from M-Shop would be lost but that is a risk that MCHS Trading is prepared to take. They plan to advise customers to use E-Shop while M-Shop is unavailable, or to try again later.

Known Uses

New information nodes are commissioned all of the time in a vibrant organization. In many cases, the team will use information from an existing information node for the initial load. If the new information node is critical to the organization's operation, it will be backed up and have some disaster recover contingency. If the organization is focused on synchronizing the type of information that the new information node has stored locally, then it will connect it to its information supply chains.

Related Patterns

INFORMATION NODE describes the internal mechanisms of an information node. INFORMATION SUPPLY CHAIN covers how information is synchronized between information nodes. The RECOVERY PROVISIONING pattern covers backup/restore and disaster recovery capabilities.

INFORMATION IDENTIFICATION will help with the analysis of the state of the existing information and the design of the new information node. In particular, INFORMATION VALUES PROFILES will understand the state of the information values in an information collection and the SUBJECT AREA DEFINITION can formalize the definition of the affected subject areas. These help identify differences in content and structure between the existing and new information node designs.

INFORMATION NODE UPGRADE covers the migration of information into a new information node.

Information Node Upgrade

Context

An organization is upgrading or consolidating one or more information nodes.

Problem

When an information node is upgraded, how will the new information node reflect the processing that has occurred in the past when the existing information node is decommissioned?

Most information nodes host information collections. When an information node is decommissioned, the information in its local information collections is lost. Does this matter or should the organization do something to preserve the information?

Example

When MCHS Trading launched its new loyalty card, it needed to migrate all of the existing Stores cardholders to the new loyalty program.

Forces

- **Existing dependencies**—There may be information processes in other information nodes that are dependent on the existing information node's information services and the information collections behind them.
- **Limited capacity to support parallel information nodes**—There may be limits on whether the organization can run two parallel environments simultaneously.
- **New user interfaces and terminology**—The new version of the information node will have new capability and some of the existing capability will have changed. This will be reflected in the user interfaces and user messages that are produced.

- **New information structures and relationships—**The new version of the information node will probably have new implementations of the information collections that have the information formatted differently from the existing information collections. These new collections may have different relationships or dependencies across information elements.
- **Private information collections—**Information processes may have many of the integrity rules and interpretation logic for their information collections hard-coded in their logic so it is difficult for new information processes to interpret the contents of the information collections through its information services.
- **Legal or other obligations—**Obligations to maintain information for a specified period of time may require that the information collection from the old information node be saved and available in a specific state.
- **Obsolete information—**If an information node is no longer used for everyday business, its information becomes out of date or stale.

Solution

Migrate, refresh, and reconnect the information from the existing information node to the new one.

To prepare the new version for operation, extract a copy of the information from the existing information node, reengineer it to the requirements of the new information node, and store it in the upgraded information node. Repeat the process with any changes made to the information in the existing information node until the new information node starts processing work.

If the new information node is to be run in parallel with the old information node, both should be set up to process the same work and the information in their information collections should remain logically consistent. Checks should be made to ensure it is the case.

When it is time for the old information node to discontinue operation, the provisioning of downstream information supply chains will be swapped over to the upgraded information node.

Note: If the existing information node has failed and there are no plans to put it into production, use **R**ECOVERY **P**ROVISIONING to load the latest information it processed and transfer it to the new information node.

Consequences

Benefits:

- Migrating information from an obsolete information node to one that will be actively involved in the organization's operations enables the complete shutdown and decommissioning of the obsolete information node. Using this approach enables the new information node to be prepared in advance of the shutdown of the old information node so the cutover time is as short as possible.

Liabilities:

- All information users of the obsolete information node will need to be trained on how to use the new information processes supported by the new information node.

Example Resolved

The existing store card scheme is managed by the Stores application. The information around the loyalty card scheme will be maintained in the Customer Hub. The first step in migrating over is to use MIRRORING PROVISIONING from Stores to the Customer Hub to ensure information about all customers with a store card are represented in the Customer Hub and are allocated a new loyalty card. The new loyalty cards are sent out to the store card customers. There is a period of a couple of months where they may use either card. Any usage of the store cards—or updates to them—is mirrored to the Customer Hub. Usage of the loyalty cards is fed directly to the Customer Hub. When the store cards become obsolete, the information processes in Stores are decommissioned and the mirroring stops.

Known Uses

This pattern is implemented in three circumstances:

- **Application migration**—When the capability of one application is replaced by a new application. This may be a later version of the application or a completely different application.
- **Application consolidation**—When multiple deployments of an application are consolidated into one instance of the application.
- **Middleware upgrade**—When middleware software, such as an INFORMATION BROKER or INFORMATION ASSET HUB, is upgraded to a newer version.

Related Patterns

INFORMATION NODE describes the internal mechanisms of an information node. INFORMATION SUPPLY CHAIN covers how information is synchronized between information nodes. The RECOVERY PROVISIONING pattern covers backup/restore and disaster recovery capabilities, though depending on obligations and recovery requirements, a SNAPSHOT PROVISIONING pattern may be sufficient to save the prior information collection in an archived format.

INFORMATION IDENTIFICATION will help with the analysis of the state of the existing information and the quality of the upgraded information node. In particular, INFORMATION VALUES PROFILES will help measure the consistency between the information nodes.

NEW INFORMATION NODE covers the setting up and integration of any newly installed information node.

Patterns for Integrating Information Nodes

This group of solutions shown in Table 9.3 will integrate information nodes together. The aim is to provide access to broader and more consistent information to the information processes.

Table 9.3 Information Solutions Pattern Summary—Integrating Information Nodes

Icon	Pattern Name	Problem	Solution
	DISTRIBUTED ACTIVITY STATUS	An organization needs to understand the status of a business activity that spans multiple information processes distributed among a variety of information nodes.	Create an information collection to manage the status that is fed by each of the information processes involved in the business activity.
	SEMANTIC INTEGRATION	An organization needs to ask questions at multiple levels of abstraction about information located in a variety of information collections.	Create an ontology model to describe the question subject area and map it to the information collections using information services. Use the ontology to identify the information required to answer the questions.
	PARTNER COLLABORATION	An organization wants to collaborate electronically with a business partner.	Set up a managed gateway between the two organizations where information can be exchanged in a controlled manner.

Distributed Activity Status

Context

An information centric organization is concerned with the efficient and accurate use of information.

Problem

An organization needs to understand the status of a business activity that spans multiple information processes distributed among a variety of information nodes.

Example

MCHS Trading needs to store information about the state of the orders it has taken from its customers in order to resolve queries about them and to monitor efficiency.

Forces

- **No fixed order of execution**—The order that events occur may vary when processing is distributed, particularly when different parts of an activity can run in parallel.
- **An information process may fail**—An information process that is part of a distributed activity may fail partway through before it has initiated other parts of the activity. The effect is that the distributed activity stalls until someone notices and restarts the appropriate information process.

Solution

Create an information collection to manage the status that is fed by each of the information processes involved in the business activity.

Managing distributed activity status requires each information process that is involved in the business activity to generate and send events to a common information node. This information node uses the information events to piece together the current status of the activity.

There are three possible types of information node that could be used to determine the distributed status:

- An INFORMATION ACTIVITY HUB would use a state machine to track the status of the activity.
- If the event relationships are complex, it may be necessary to use an EVENT CORRELATION NODE rather than an INFORMATION ACTIVITY HUB.
- If the events are arriving very rapidly, it may be necessary to use a STREAMING ANALYTICS NODE in place of the information activity hub.

Consequences

Benefits:

- This solution enables an organization to track the status of a distributed activity to understand the current status, determine how long each step has taken, and detect that an activity has stalled, has failed partway through, is behaving in an unexpected way, or is just taking too long.

Liabilities:

- The definition of the state machine needs to be changed in line with changes in the participating information nodes because it may need to handle different events or a different sequence of events.

Example Resolved

MCHS Trading creates a new information node called Order-Tracking, which is an **I**NFORMATION **A**CTIVITY **H**UB. This has an information collection that records the order status. The order-processing information processes use the information services provided by Order-Tracking to record the work they are doing to process an order.

Figure 9.6 shows the calls into Order-Tracking as orders are processed. New orders from E-Shop, Stores, and Mail-Shop are passed to Order-Tracking. It synchronizes the customer details with the Customer Hub before passing the request on to the Shipping application. Shipping sends the goods on to the customer and, once the order is complete, sends the request on to Invoicing. When the status of the order changes in either Shipping or Invoicing, these applications call Order-Tracking to record the latest status.

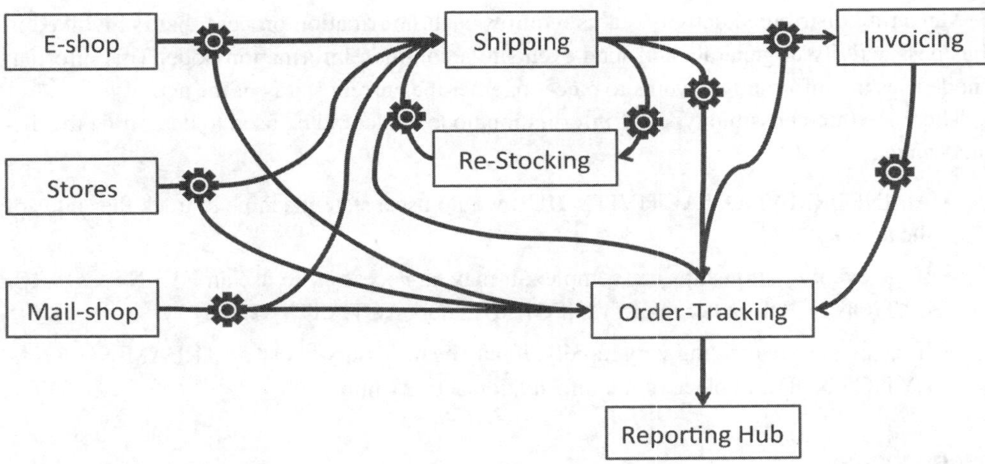

Figure 9.6 Tracking the status of a customer's order.

Once the Order-Tracking information node is in place, it is possible to support new information processes such as Cancel Order, which is located in the Customer-Care information node. See Figure 9.7.

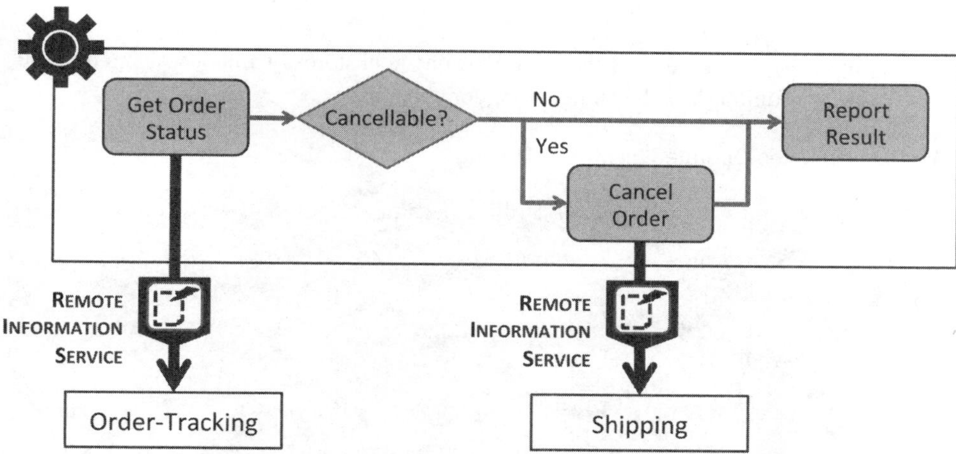

Figure 9.7 Cancel Order implementation calling Order-Tracking.

Known Uses

Status tracking using state machines is a common approach to understand a distributed activity that is being coordinated with messages—for example, in an Enterprise Application Integration (EAI) approach.

Related Patterns

The INFORMATION ACTIVITY pattern describes the characteristics of information that describes a business activity. The INFORMATION EVENT pattern describes the characteristics of an event. The distributed activity status pattern is useful for monitoring a business transaction that is implemented with DAISY CHAIN PROVISIONING.

Semantic Integration

Context

An information centric organization is concerned with the efficient and accurate use of information.

Problem

An organization needs to ask questions at multiple levels of abstraction about information located in a variety of information collections.

They need the ability to make ad hoc queries using keywords from the problem domain and have them translated into queries on the distributed information.

Example

MCHS Trading has many physical sites. These are the physical stores, warehouses, and distribution centers. Table 9.4 summarizes the United Kingdom operation.

Table 9.4 Physical Sites Operated by MCHS Trading

Headquarters	Warehouses	Distribution Centers	Stores
Milton Keynes	Birmingham	Aberdeen	Aberdeen
	Edinburgh	Bristol	Bath
	Reading	Glasgow	Cambridge
		Leeds	Chichester
		Nottingham	Edinburgh
		Plymouth	Glasgow
			Guildford
			Liverpool
			London, Islington
			London, Knightsbridge
			Manchester
			York

The sites vary in size and each site will have appropriate types of facilities depending on their use. Most sites operate reasonably autonomously with local IT systems supporting their work. There is a small team at headquarters that is responsible for the management of these sites. How does this team manage the information it needs about these physical sites? Examples of their information requirements include questions such as which sites are close to one another, or could share facilities, or provide back up if something fails?

Forces

- **Information is stored for a particular purpose**—This purpose provides a specialized context for the information that is typically reflected in the information services that surround it.

- **Information about the same subject area may be distributed**—The information services around each specific information collection may not be consistent with one another because they are probably targeted for different groups of information processes.
- **Distributed information may be inconsistent**—This makes it hard to match values from different information collections.

Solution

Create an ontology model to describe the question subject area and map it to the information collections using information services. Use the ontology to identify the information required to answer the questions.

An ontology model is a description of the concepts in a subject area, the relationships between these concepts, and links to instances of the concepts. The ontology includes "composed-of" relationships and "is-a" relationships, plus concepts can have attributes associated with them.

At the leaf nodes of the ontology model are the instances—the actual information. These can be

- Literal values, enabling the ontology to include information not stored elsewhere.
- Information values copied from existing INFORMATION COLLECTIONS. These need to be kept synchronized with the changing information values in the original information collections.
- INFORMATION LINKS to individual INFORMATION ENTRIES in existing information collections. The information values are extracted in real time when the ontology instance is accessed. The links must be kept up to date as information entries are added and removed.
- A query to dynamically retrieve the information values from the existing information collections when the ontology instance is accessed.

The information values are needed in the ontology model to enable inferencing to take place. That is, the navigation of the ontology model to locate instances that match a complex query. The approach on how these values are supplied depends on the volume and volatility of the information values in the organization's other information collections.

Figure 9.8 illustrates this solution.

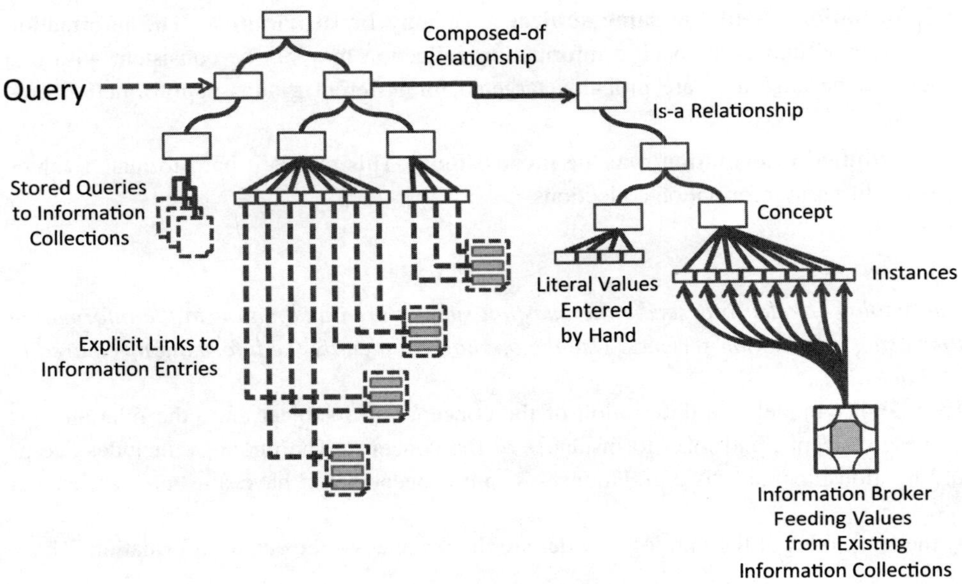

Figure 9.8 The ontology model and how it relates to information values.

Consequences

Benefits:

- This approach provides a rich and flexible query interface to distributed information. It is effectively adding relationships between disparate information collections based in knowledge of the subject area.

Liabilities:

- This solution does not fix incorrect and incomplete information values. It is just linking them together.
- Ontology models can quickly become incomprehensible. The successful ones are very targeted to a single subject area.
- The semantic layer must be kept synchronized with the information collections it is federating together. This task grows as more information values are copied into the ontology to enrich the query capability.

Example Resolved

MCHS Trading creates an ontology model that describes the physical sites, where they are located, the facilities they contain, and the different government agencies and business partners engaged for different regions and aspects of their operation.

With this ontology, MCHS Trading is able to ask questions such as:

- Which of our physical sites do the South East England Health and Safety Authority regulate and what type of site are they?
- Which of our Scottish sites have a backup generator?

The ontology locates the instances of interest and then queries are made on the other information collections to drill into more detail.

Known Uses

This approach to integration is experimental. There are a small number of implementations in progress that are showing good results over small ontology models. The w3 standards, Web Ontology Language (OWL)[1] and Resource Description Framework (RDF),[2] are the most common languages used for specifying the ontology model. Queries are expressed in the SPARQL query language.[3] Open Services for Lifecycle and Collaboration (OSLC)[4] links are often used to implement information links in the ontology instance when OWL/RDF are in use because OSLC provides a URL reference for the information entry it refers to, plus operations to extract the values from the information entry.

Related Patterns

The ontology model in this solution is an example of a sophisticated **V**IRTUAL **I**NFORMATION **C**OLLECTION. The **S**UBJECT **A**REA **D**EFINITION pattern describes how to document a subject area. The **S**INGLE **V**IEW **I**NFORMATION **S**UPPLY **C**HAIN pattern describes a useful approach to supply information to this solution. The **I**NFORMATION **L**INK pattern describes the linking of information entries from different information collections.

Partner Collaboration

Context

An information centric organization is concerned with the efficient and accurate use of information.

1. http://www.w3.org/TR/owl-features/
2. http://www.w3.org/TR/rdf-primer/
3. http://www.w3.org/TR/rdf-sparql-query/
4. http://open-services.net/resources/tutorials/oslc-primer/what-is-oslc/

Problem

An organization wants to collaborate electronically with a business partner.

Example

MCHS Trading wants to be able to improve the exchange of product details and orders with its suppliers. Simply introducing electronic INFORMATION FLOWS between MCHS Trading and its suppliers does little to improve its existing manual solution—mostly a reduction in transportation cost—as the INFORMATION FLOWS retain the same point-to-point characteristic.

Forces

- **Different organizations are often independent legal entities—**They have a duty to protect their own organization's assets and to report on their activities.
- **Competition law—**In many countries, competition law requires large organizations that are dominant in their sector to ensure that they deal fairly with business partners.

Solution

Set up a managed gateway between the two organizations where information can be exchanged in a controlled manner.

This type of gateway is a specialized type of INFORMATION BROKER that supports Electronic Data Interchange (EDI).

Consequences

Benefits:

- Business partners can collaborate as effectively as internal parts of a single organization.

Liabilities:

- The organizations that are collaborating must maintain clear definitions of the information that is to be exchanged, under which conditions and with what security, and the level of service each guarantees to the other.

Example Resolved

MCHS Trading sets up a gateway information node called Supplier-net that is responsible for managing orders with the suppliers and introducing product details into the product information supply chain. The first focal area for MCHS Trading is collaboration in Order Management, Invoice Reconciliation, and Payment Processing, where each specific set of information is delivered as an INFORMATION PAYLOAD. The sets of information in each payload are defined by INFORMATION CODES.

See the "Connecting MCHS Trading into a B2B Trading Partnership" section in Chapter 2 for more discussion of this solution.

Known Uses

This type of solution is used in many manufacturing and distribution companies where delivering good customer service in a cost-effective manner requires all organizations in the physical supply chain to coordinate their activities. Partner collaboration can incorporate many aspects of interaction, including purchase orders, invoices, inventory levels, shipment tracking, and payments.

Interaction with such Electronic Data Interchange (EDI) systems is often handled by enterprise resource planning (ERP) software, an example of a PACKAGED APPLICATION PROCESS. The EDI information broker most commonly sends and delivers messages that define the type of content.

Related Patterns

This pattern introduces an external organization into the INFORMATION SUPPLY CHAINS of the organization. INFORMATION FLOW patterns describe the delivery of information to and from the INFORMATION BROKER. To avoid point-to-point solutions with each and every external organization, there need to be appropriate INFORMATION KEYS established for each involved party. Typically, these are AGGREGATE KEYS that incorporate a LOCAL KEY and a CALLER'S KEY.

An APPLICATION NODE with a PACKAGED APPLICATION PROCESS could support such processing and distribution of information to suppliers and incorporate more specialized processing. However, such an application may be expensive to build or buy and subsequently maintain.

An INFORMATION BROKER most commonly supports this activity providing an effective transfer mechanism without adding more processing. This approach is less expensive to build or buy than an APPLICATION NODE, but is reliant on other INFORMATION NODES to incorporate the appropriate INFORMATION TRIGGERS and to perform necessary processing of the INFORMATION PAYLOADS.

Patterns for Master Data Management

The solutions shown in Table 9.5 describe different configurations of the INFORMATION ASSET HUB pattern.

The choice between each of these information solution patterns is dependent on which information nodes need to maintain the master copy (or copies) of the information. Ideally, the information asset hub holds the only master copy and all other information nodes access the information directly (see SHARED MASTER), or have their own reference copy (see CENTRALIZED MASTER). However, that is not always practical and so the other patterns exist...

Table 9.5 Master Data Management (MDM) Solutions

Icon	Pattern Name	Problem	Solution
	SHARED MASTER	Information processes distributed across a number of information nodes need access to the same up-to-date information.	Create a single master collection of the information and use information services in each information node to connect to this information collection.
	CENTRALIZED MASTER	The same updates need to be manually entered into multiple information processes to maintain consistency between the multiple stored copies of the same information.	Centralize all updates to a single MASTER USAGE copy of the information. Distribute these information values to other information nodes to use as local reference (read-only) copies.
	INFORMATION REGISTRY	An organization needs a consolidated list of the unique information instances for a subject area, despite the fact that this information is distributed and duplicated across many information collections.	Create a centralized information registry to combine the best of the core values from all of the information collections on demand. When the information service for the registry is called, it dynamically matches the values from the different sources to return the unique instances.
	GOLDEN REFERENCE	An organization needs a complete, read-only view of the information it stores about a subject area that is currently maintained in multiple disparate systems.	Create an information collection for this information that has COMPLETE SCOPE and COMPLETE COVERAGE. Distribute and combine relevant information from the existing information collections into this new information collection.
	SYNCHRONIZED MASTERS	An organization needs to provide a remotely accessible complete master information collection for a subject area that is synchronized with other existing information collections.	Monitor for changes in any of the master information collections and distribute to the other copies, taking particular care to handle incompatible simultaneous changes.

To best illustrate the differences in this approach, we have used the same sample problem in each of the pattern descriptions: How does MCHS Trading support a consolidated information collection of its customer details when none of its existing information nodes can host it?

The answer is to deploy a new information node called Customer Hub. This information node is an INFORMATION ASSET HUB and it will be commissioned as described by the NEW INFORMATION NODE solution pattern. The following patterns cover different configurations of the Customer Hub and illustrate how that affects the way the information is managed and controlled.

Shared Master

Context

An information centric organization is concerned with the efficient and accurate use of information. It is focused on the management of shared information—in particular, its INFORMATION ASSETS. It believes it needs Master Data Management (MDM) but are not sure how to use it.

Problem

Information processes distributed across a number of information nodes need access to the same up-to-date information.

Example

MCHS Trading needs a consolidated view of its customers' details for operational use. At the moment, customer details are stored in E-Shop (for customers who use the Internet shopping service), Stores (for customers who have a Store card), and they are entered into each order in Mail-Shop. There is a consolidated list of customers in the Reporting Hub, but that information node is not suitable for an operational load.

MCHS Trading decides to introduce an INFORMATION ASSET HUB called Customer Hub to host the consolidated customer details information collection. How should the Customer Hub integrate with the other information nodes?

Forces

- **Repetitive work**—Even with the best will in the world, people are not good at making the same edits to multiple copies of information.
- **Remote access to information adds latency to an information service**—An **information request** takes a finite amount of time to execute.
- **Copied data needs to be synchronized**—Mirroring information that is changing rapidly can create a lot of network traffic and it may be that the copies never truly reflect the most up-to-date values.
- **Many information nodes are implemented with local information collections**—Changing this to enable the information node to use remote information services would require extensive alteration to the information node and could be very expensive.

- **Information is duplicated and inconsistent**—Information assets are central to the organization's business, which means they appear in many information nodes. Each information node typically uses it own INFORMATION KEY scheme and there is little attempt to keep the information about the information assets. The result is duplicated and inconsistent information that is hard to correlate.

Solution

Create a single master collection of the information and use information services in each information node to connect to this information collection.

Create a MASTER USAGE information collection and use information services in each information node to connect to this information collection.

Provide information services for the information collection to enable information processes to access it, irrespective of the information node they are located in. This is shown in Figure 9.9.

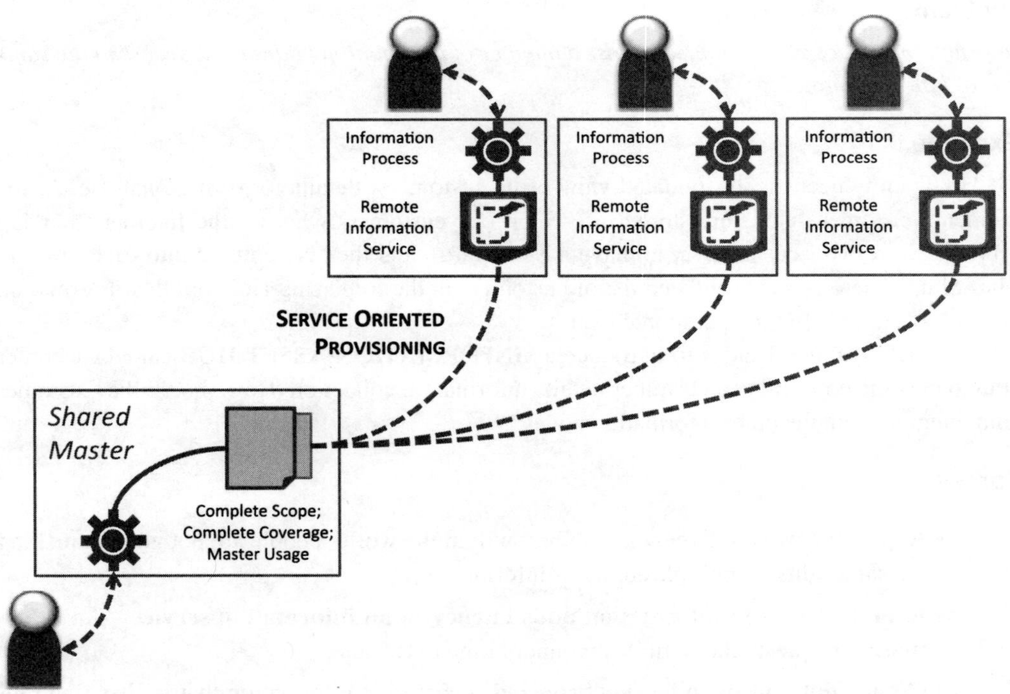

Figure 9.9 Shared Master solution.

The shared master information node hosts an information collection with MASTER USAGE, COMPLETE COVERAGE, and COMPLETE SCOPE. As a result, it supports all of the information needed by the information process for a particular subject area. The information services that provide access to this information collection present appropriate views of the information to the consuming information processes.

Consequences

Benefits:

- This approach results in a single copy of the information—which is efficient in terms of storage and effort to maintain.
- With a single copy, it is simple to expand the attributes stored and hence expand the information processes that can be supported.

Liabilities:

- A shared master can easily become a single point of failure that affects many parts of the organization's operations if it is unavailable.
- Often this solution is not possible because existing information nodes hold this information already and it would be too expensive to change them to use the shared master.
- When the shared master is introduced, it often needs to be loaded with an initial set of values. The source of these initial values and the work that will be needed to clean and transform these values needs to be included in the project plan.

Example Resolved

If MCHS Trading used this approach to support its customer details, each of the order-taking information nodes would have to be changed so that they extracted their customer information from Customer Hub, rather than having their customer details stored locally. This would affect the majority of the information processes on these information nodes, which is why this would be an expensive solution to implement.

Known Uses

This approach is used when an organization is adding support for a new type of information or is focused only on a small subset of the organization's information processes.

Related Patterns

The shared master pattern is using SERVICE ORIENTED PROVISIONING to provide information to the information processes.

The shared master information collection is typically hosted in either an INFORMATION ASSET HUB or an APPLICATION NODE.

Centralized Master

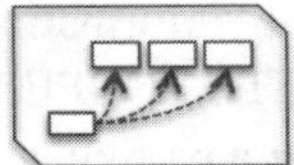

Context

An information centric organization is concerned with the efficient and accurate use of information. It is focused on the management of shared information—in particular, its INFORMATION ASSETS. It believes it needs Master Data Management (MDM) but are not sure how to use it.

Problem

The same updates need to be manually entered into multiple information processes to maintain consistency between the multiple copies of the same information.

Example

MCHS Trading needs a consolidated view of its customers' details for operational use. At the moment, customer details are stored in E-Shop (for customers who use the Internet shopping service), Stores (for customers who have a Store card), and they are entered into each order in Mail-Shop. There is a consolidated list of customers in the Reporting Hub, but that information node is not suitable for an operational load.

MCHS Trading decides to introduce an INFORMATION ASSET HUB called Customer Hub to host the consolidated customer details information collection. How should the Customer Hub integrate with the other information nodes?

Forces

- **Repetitive work**—Even with the best will in the world, people are not good at making the same edits to multiple copies of information.
- **Storage costs money**—Every copy that is made of information costs money to store and maintain. An information collection may be too large to make it cost effective to make copies of it.
- **Inconsistent copies**—Different copies of the same information located in different information nodes are typically inconsistent unless they are actively synchronized.
- **Copied data needs to be synchronized**—Mirroring information that is changing rapidly can create a lot of network traffic and it may be that the copies never truly reflect the most up-to-date values.
- **Remote access to information adds latency to an information service**—An **information request** takes a finite amount of time to execute. Collating and reformatting the same piece of information on the fly, over and over again, is inefficient.
- **Many information nodes are implemented with local information collections**—Changing this to enable the information node to use remote information services would require extensive alteration to the information node and could be very expensive.

- **Information is duplicated and inconsistent**—Information assets are central to the organization's business, which means they appear in many information nodes. Each information node typically uses it own **I**NFORMATION **K**EY scheme and there is little attempt to keep the information about the information assets. The result is duplicated and inconsistent information that is hard to correlate.

Solution

Centralize all updates to a single master copy of the information. Distribute these information values to other information nodes to use as local reference (read-only) copies.

This is shown in Figure 9.10.

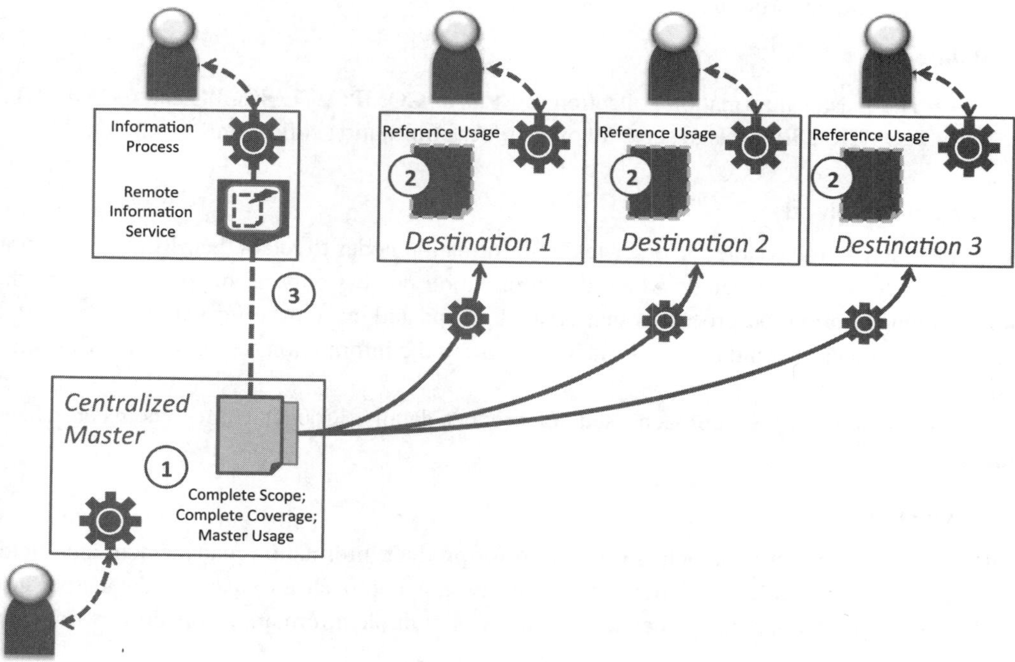

Figure 9.10 Centralized Master solution.

The numbers on the diagram refer to these notes:

1. Nominate or create an information node to host the information collection that will be used to assemble, maintain, and coordinate the synchronization of the values for this type of information. This information collection will have **M**ASTER **U**SAGE, **C**OMPLETE **S**COPE, and **C**OMPLETE **C**OVERAGE to be sure to support all destination systems.

2. When updated information is ready, distribute it to other information nodes using **M**IRRORING **P**ROVISIONING. These destination information nodes store this information and use it as local reference (read-only) copies.
3. The centralized master can be made available for update to other information processes through **S**ERVICE **O**RIENTED **P**ROVISIONING.

Consequences

Benefits:

- People are only involved in the maintenance of one copy of the information, which is then automatically duplicated to the other information collection copies. This reduces cost and opportunities for human error.

Liabilities:

- The master information collection must have **C**OMPLETE **S**COPE and **C**OMPLETE **C**OVERAGE if it is to serve all of the other information collections.

Example Resolved

This approach would enable the order-taking information nodes to retain their local information collections for customer details where the information process only needed read access to the information. Information processes that created or updated customer information (such as the New Order process) would need to be modified to call the information services on the Customer Hub.

This pattern is the approach used for product details. Product Hub is their centralized master.

Known Uses

The centralized master approach is often used for product information management and maintaining employee details. It is often difficult to use this approach for customer details because updates come in through many channels, resulting in multiple information collections with master usage.

Related Patterns

The centralized master information collection is normally hosted in an **I**NFORMATION **A**SSET **H**UB and often uses **C**OLLABORATIVE **E**DITING **P**ROCESSES to make changes to the master copy of information.

If more than one master information collection is required, consider the following patterns: **I**NFORMATION **R**EGISTRY, **G**OLDEN **R**EFERENCE, and **S**YNCHRONIZED **M**ASTERS.

The **I**NFORMATION **A**SSET pattern provides more details on this type of information.

Information Registry

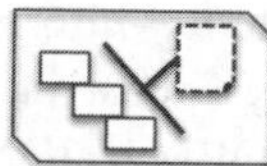

Context

An information centric organization is concerned with the efficient and accurate use of information. It is focused on the management of shared information—in particular, its INFORMATION ASSETS. It believes it needs Master Data Management (MDM) but are not sure how to use it.

Problem

An organization needs a consolidated list of the unique information instances for a subject area, despite the fact that this information is distributed and duplicated across many information collections.

Example

MCHS Trading needs a consolidated view of its customers' details for operational use. At the moment, customer details are stored in E-Shop (for customers who use the Internet shopping service), Stores (for customers who have a Store card), and they are entered into each order in Mail-Shop. There is a consolidated list of customers in the Reporting Hub, but that information node is not suitable for an operational load.

MCHS Trading decides to introduce an INFORMATION ASSET HUB called Customer Hub to host the consolidated customer details information collection. How should the Customer Hub integrate with the other information nodes?

Forces

- **Storage costs money**—Every copy that is made of information costs money to store and maintain. An information collection may be too large to make it cost effective to make copies of it.
- **Inconsistent copies**—Different copies of the same information located in different information nodes are typically inconsistent unless they are actively synchronized.
- **Copied data needs to be synchronized**—Mirroring information that is changing rapidly can create a lot of network traffic and it may be that the copies never truly reflect the most up-to-date values.
- **Remote access to information adds latency to an information service**—An **information request** takes a finite amount of time to execute. Collating and reformatting the same piece of information on the fly, over and over again, is inefficient.
- **Many information nodes are implemented with local information collections**—Changing this to enable the information node to use remote information services would require extensive alteration to the information node and could be very expensive.

- **Information is duplicated and inconsistent**—Information assets are central to the organization's business, which means they appear in many information nodes. Each information node typically uses it own INFORMATION KEY scheme and there is little attempt to keep the information about the information assets. The result is duplicated and inconsistent information that is hard to correlate.

Solution

Create a centralized information registry to combine the best of the core values from all of the information collections on demand.

When the information service for the registry is called, it dynamically matches the values from the different sources to return the unique instances. Figure 9.11 illustrates how the information registry works.

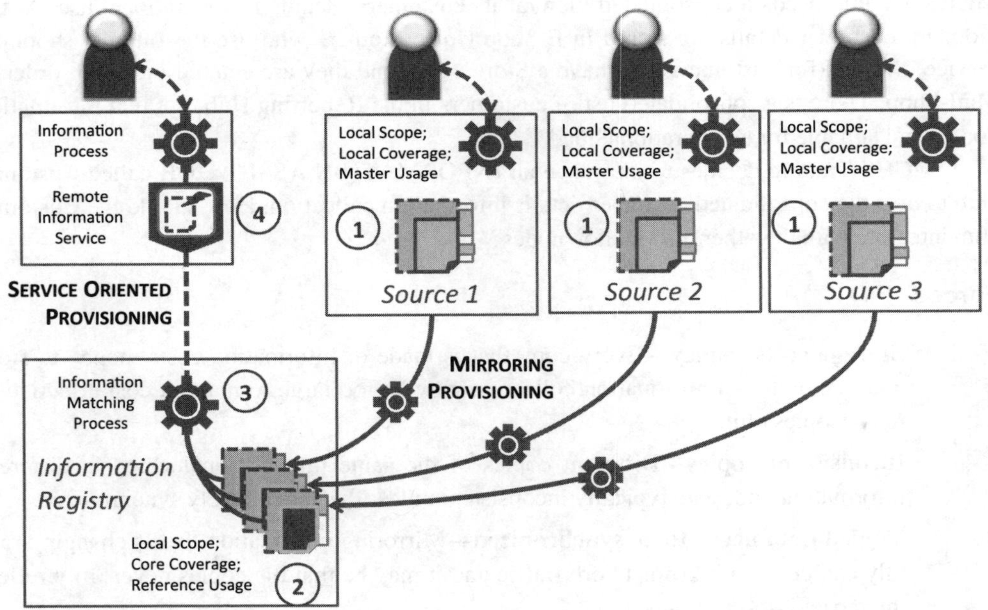

Figure 9.11 Information Registry solution.

The numbers on the diagram refer to these notes:

1. A supply of information about the subject area it is covering. This comes from selected information nodes that host information collections for the subject area. For each relevant information collection, the hosting information node sends the CORE COVERAGE attributes for all of the information entries it stores using MIRRORING PROVISIONING.

2. An **I**NFORMATION **A**SSET **H**UB to host the information registry. This has one or more information collections to host the information coming from the source information nodes.
3. An **I**NFORMATION **M**ATCHING **P**ROCESS to combine the values from related information entries that originate from the different source information collections.
4. **I**NFORMATION **S**ERVICES enable information processes to request the results of the information matching process.

To the calling information processes, the information registry appears to be hosting an **I**NFORMATION **C**OLLECTION for the subject area with **C**OMPLETE **S**COPE and **C**ORE **C**OVERAGE that supports the **R**EFERENCE **U**SAGE role.

Consequences

Benefits:

- The information registry is able to create a read-only information collection with complete scope and core coverage, with very little disruption to the original source systems.

Liabilities:

- The information registry creates the combined view of an information entry on demand. If an information entry is requested many times, it may be more efficient to use the **G**OLDEN **R**EFERENCE pattern, which creates the combined view once and stores it.

The information registry typically stores only the **C**ORE **C**OVERAGE attributes because they are all that is necessary to do the matching. It is possible to extend the coverage of the attributes that the information registry holds. This creates a richer set of information that can be returned on the registry's information services, but may increase the synchronization traffic between the source systems and in the information registry.

Example Resolved

MCHS Trading implements an information registry for its customer details as a first step to having a consolidated master copy of its customer details. This information registry was used to identify how many individual customers it has and the channels each uses.

However, ultimately MCHS Trading wants to be able to manage customer details in a centralized manner and so it moves to the **S**YNCHRONIZED **M**ASTER solution.

Related Patterns

An information registry requires special matching technology to implement the dynamic combining of records. As such, it is typically implemented in an **I**NFORMATION **A**SSET **H**UB that has the registry processing built in. The **I**NFORMATION **A**SSET pattern provides more details on this type of information.

Golden Reference

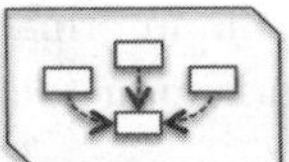

Context

An information centric organization is concerned with the efficient and accurate use of information. It is focused on the management of shared information—in particular, its **I**NFORMATION **A**SSETS. It believes it needs Master Data Management (MDM) but are not sure how to use it.

Problem

An organization needs a complete, read-only view of the information it stores about a subject area.

Unfortunately, this information is distributed and duplicated across a number of disconnected information nodes.

Example

MCHS Trading needs a consolidated view of its customers' details for operational use. At the moment, customer details are stored in E-Shop (for customers who use the Internet shopping service), Stores (for customers who have a Store card), and they are entered into each order in Mail-Shop. There is a consolidated list of customers in the Reporting Hub, but that information node is not suitable for an operational load.

MCHS Trading decides to introduce an **I**NFORMATION **A**SSET **H**UB called Customer Hub to host the consolidated customer details information collection. How should the Customer Hub integrate with the other information nodes?

Forces

- **Storage costs money**—Every copy that is made of information costs money to store and maintain. An information collection may be too large to make it cost effective to make copies of it.
- **Inconsistent copies**—Different copies of the same information located in different information nodes are typically inconsistent unless they are actively synchronized.
- **Copied data needs to be synchronized**—Mirroring information that is changing rapidly can create a lot of network traffic and it may be that the copies never truly reflect the most up-to-date values.
- **Remote access to information adds latency to an information service**—An **information request** takes a finite amount of time to execute. Collating and reformatting the same piece of information on the fly, over and over again, is inefficient.
- **Many information nodes are implemented with local information collections**—Changing this to enable the information node to use remote information services would require extensive alteration to the information node and could be very expensive.

- **Information is duplicated and inconsistent**—Information assets are central to the organization's business, which means they appear in many information nodes. Each information node typically uses it own **I**NFORMATION **K**EY scheme and there is little attempt to keep the information about the information assets. The result is duplicated and inconsistent information that is hard to correlate.

Solution

Create an information collection for this information that has COMPLETE SCOPE and COMPLETE COVERAGE. Distribute and combine relevant information from the existing information collections into this new information collection.

The resulting Golden Reference is primarily for **R**EFERENCE **U**SAGE; however, it may be **H**YBRID **U**SAGE enabling additional, new attributes to be stored in the golden reference and distributed to downstream information nodes. This is shown in Figure 9.12.

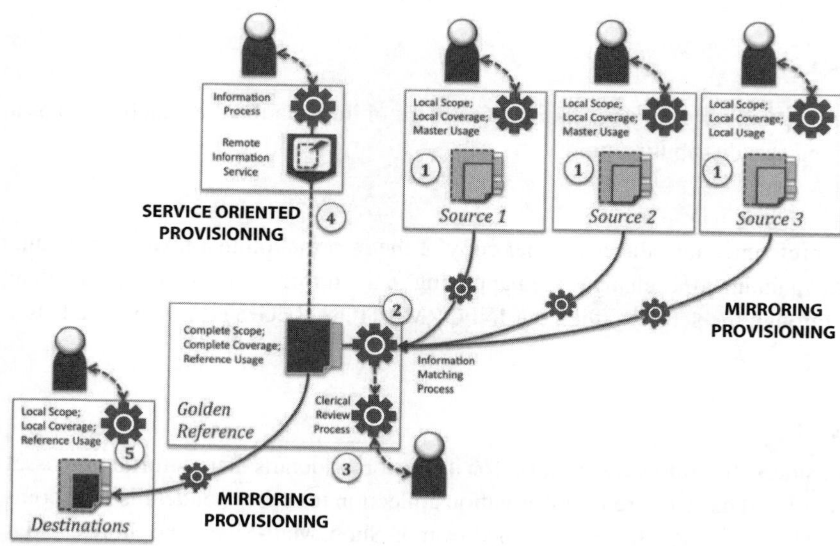

Figure 9.12 Golden Reference solution.

The numbers on the diagram refer to these notes:

1. All changes to the information collections in the source systems are sent to the golden reference.
2. The golden reference has an **I**NFORMATION **M**ATCHING **P**ROCESS that compares the incoming information with that information already stored.
3. If the matching is close but not good enough to automatically combine, it is sent with the close matches to a **C**LERICAL **R**EVIEW **P**ROCESS to enable an **I**NFORMATION **S**TEWARD to decide where to store the new information.
4. The golden reference offers information services to allow other information processes to read the consolidated information collection.
5. Attributes from the golden reference can be distributed to other information nodes for reference usage.

Consequences

Benefits:

- This solution provides a single authoritative source of information that can be used as a reference and as a distribution point.

Liabilities:

- The golden reference introduces another copy of the information that takes storage and needs to be maintained. If changes are happening to the information at a faster rate than it is used through the services, then the **I**NFORMATION **R**EGISTRY may be a better solution.

Example Resolved

MCHS Trading considers the following solution for its customer details. The information asset hub (called Customer Hub) has a reference information collection for customer details with complete scope and complete coverage. It is provisioned from E-Shop, Mail-Shop, and Stores, and it is used, in turn, to provision the Reporting Hub. The Customer Hub is also supporting **S**ERVICE **O**RIENTED **P**ROVISIONING for another new application called Customer-Care. This application is reading customer details through web services. See Figure 9.13.

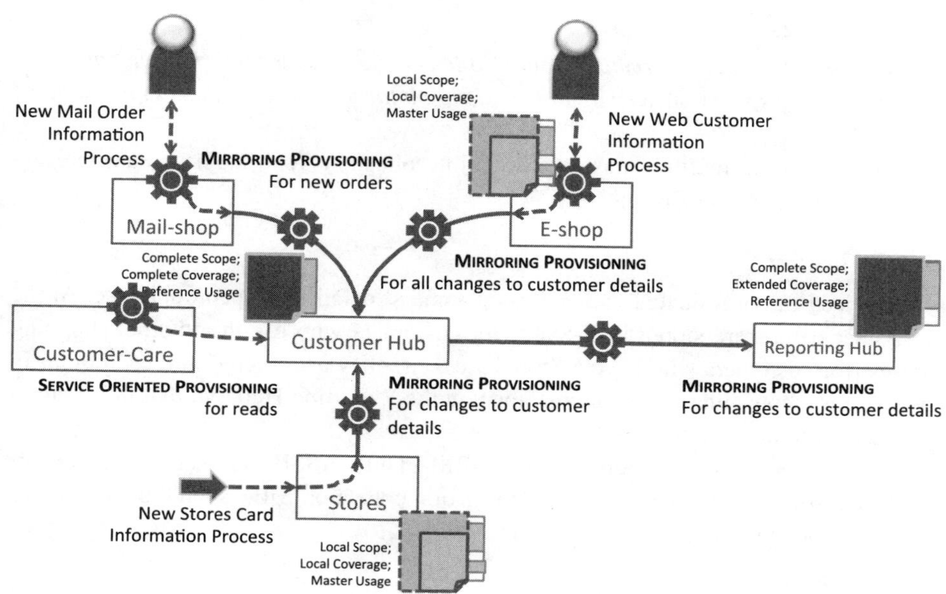

Figure 9.13 Managing customer details at MCHS Trading with a Golden Reference.

Known Uses

This style of solution is often used to consolidate information for distribution.

Related Patterns

The golden reference is implemented using the INFORMATION ASSET HUB pattern. The INFORMATION ASSET pattern provides more details on this type of information.

The consolidation process requires incoming information to be matched against what is stored already. This uses the INFORMATION MATCHING PROCESS. If incoming information is a good match, but not close enough to automatically combine it, the information asset hub may invoke a CLERICAL REVIEW PROCESS.

Synchronized Masters

Context

An information centric organization is concerned with the efficient and accurate use of information. It is focused on the management of shared information—in particular, its INFORMATION ASSETS. It believes it needs Master Data Management (MDM) but are not sure how to use it.

Problem

An organization needs to provide a remotely accessible complete master information collection for a subject area that is synchronized with other existing information collections that also have master usage.

An organization needs multiple master information collections for a subject area where any attribute may change at any time, in any copy.

Example

MCHS Trading needs a consolidated view of its customers' details for operational use. At the moment, customer details are stored in E-Shop (for customers who use the Internet shopping service), Stores (for customers who have a Store card), and they are entered into each order in Mail-Shop. There is a consolidated list of customers in the Reporting Hub, but that information node is not suitable for an operational load.

MCHS Trading decides to introduce an **I**NFORMATION **A**SSET **H**UB called Customer Hub to host the consolidated customer details information collection. How should the Customer Hub integrate with the other information nodes?

Forces

- **Inconsistent copies**—Different copies of the same information located in different information nodes are typically inconsistent unless they are actively synchronized.
- **Copied data needs to be synchronized**—Mirroring information that is changing rapidly can create a lot of network traffic and it may be that the copies never truly reflect the most up-to-date values.
- **Remote access to information adds latency to an information service**—An **information request** takes a finite amount of time to execute. Collating and reformatting the same piece of information on the fly, over and over again, is inefficient.
- **Many information nodes are implemented with local information collections**—Changing this to enable the information node to use remote information services would require extensive alteration to the information node and could be very expensive.
- **Information is duplicated and inconsistent**—Information assets are central to the organization's business, which means they appear in many information nodes. Each information node typically uses it own **I**NFORMATION **K**EY scheme and there is little attempt to keep the information about the information assets. The result is duplicated and inconsistent information that is hard to correlate.

Solution

Monitor for changes in any of the master information collections and distribute to the other copies, taking particular care to handle incompatible simultaneous changes.

This is shown in Figure 9.14.

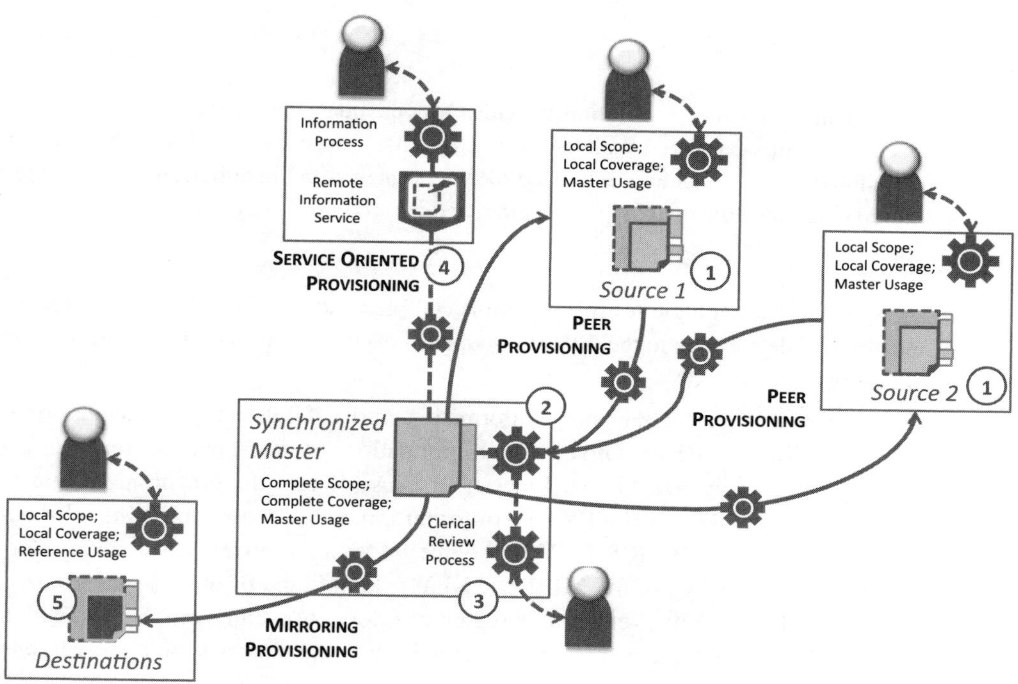

Figure 9.14 Synchronized Master solution.

The numbers on the diagram refer to these notes:

1. Information from master usages information collections is exchanged with the synchronized master using peer provisioning.
2. New information entries, or updates to existing information entries, cause an INFORMATION MATCHING PROCESS to run that checks for duplicate entries.
3. If duplicate entries are found, they may require a CLERICAL REVIEW PROCESS where an INFORMATION STEWARD can review and collapse similar information entries together.

4. The synchronized master may be queried and updated using INFORMATION SERVICES.
5. Information from the synchronized master may be distributed to information nodes that are downstream in the information supply chain.

Consequences

Benefits:

- The synchronized master solution provides a consolidated master usage information collection with centralized maintenance. The other information nodes with a master usage information collection only need to synchronize with the hub, which can be configured to manage the matching, enriching, and correcting of the information.

Liabilities:

- The synchronization logic for this pattern is complex and may be different for creates, updates, and deletes due to the different scopes of each of the master usage information collections.
- The synchronized master may merge information entries if it detects duplicate information entries. This can be disruptive to other information nodes that may be storing information keys from the synchronized master. Because of this, the synchronized master should support the STABLE KEY pattern for information processes using its information services and CALLER'S KEY for source information nodes. Destination information nodes typically use the MIRROR KEY pattern based of off the synchronized master's stable key. However, if the merging of information entries in the destination causes problems, multiple copies of the merged information entry should be sent, one for each of the resulting stable keys associated with the merged information entry.

Example Resolved

This is the solution that MCHS Trading chose for its customer details. At the same time, it moved the store card to a loyalty card that covered all of its sales channels. Support for the loyalty card was implemented across Customer-Care and the Customer Hub. This meant that the Stores application no longer needed to store information about the customers. The resulting flow of information between the information nodes is shown in Figure 9.15.

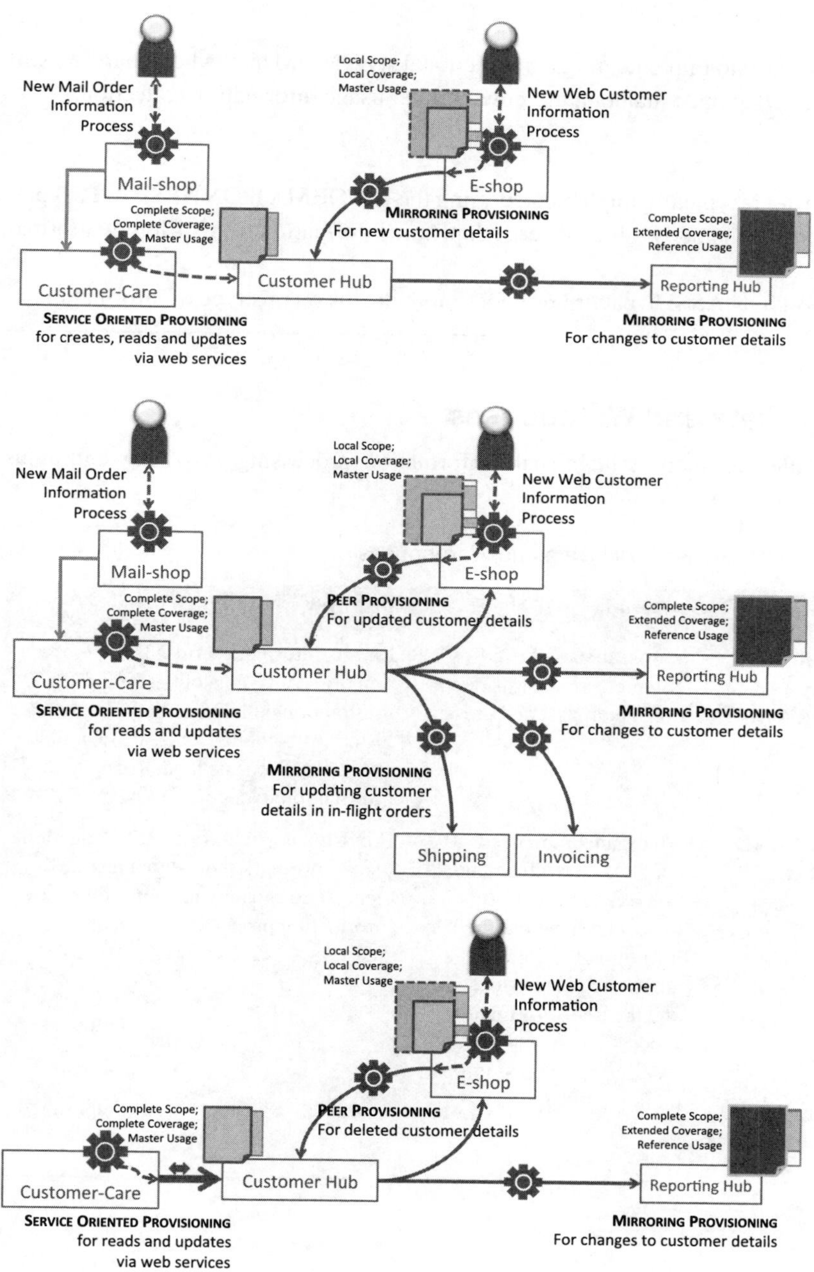

Figure 9.15 Create, update, and delete flows for the synchronized masters.

Known Uses

This is a common approach to implementing a transactional style MDM hub, where there are still other information nodes that must maintain their own master usage information collection.

Related Patterns

The synchronized master is typically implemented using the **I**NFORMATION **A**SSET **H**UB pattern because this information node is able to merge duplicate information from different information nodes.

The **I**NFORMATION **A**SSET pattern provides more details on this type of information.

Patterns for Big Data and Warehouses

The solutions in Table 9.6 support large-scale information processing involving enormous amounts of information.

Table 9.6 Information Solutions for Big Data and Warehouses

Icon	Pattern Name	Problem	Solution
	HISTORICAL **S**YSTEM OF **R**ECORD	An organization needs a complete view of its operations, both past and present.	Extract information from the operational systems; consolidate it into information collections that maintain a history of how the values are changing over time. Reformat and distribute this information to decision makers.
	WORKLOAD **O**FFLOAD	An organization needs to enable a new information process but the information node where the required information collections are located is overloaded and the new information process needs to work with locally provisioned information.	Provision a new information collection on an information node that has sufficient spare capacity to support the new information process.

Historical System of Record

Context

An information centric organization is concerned with the efficient and accurate use of information. It is focused on understanding how the organization is performing holistically.

Problem

An organization needs a complete view of its operations, both past and present.

Operational systems focus on the current state of the day-to-day detail. An overseer (manager, executive, auditor) needs to understand the aggregated results compared against different criteria (cost, profitability, popularity, and many more).

Example

MCHS Trading cares about how well its business is performing and how it is changing over time so it can plan changes and improvements. The key driver for the business is the orders made by customers. The operational systems focus on the detailed and effective management of these orders.

Once an order is complete, it is no longer of interest to the operational systems. However, it contains valuable information for running the business—but not in the same form that the operational systems need it.

For example, by the time the order is complete, it contains details of who the customer was, what the customer ordered, how the customer paid, which warehouse the goods came from, how many packages were shipped, how long it took to complete the order, which employees worked on the order, how long the goods were in the warehouse before the goods were shipped, any issues that occurred and how they were resolved, who the suppliers were, what the profitability of the order was, ... and much more.

Each element of information listed above is an indicator of how well the business is performing—but it needs to be aggregated with similar information from other orders. For example,

- The warehouse team needs to know, on average, how long goods are stored in the warehouse and how long it takes to fulfill the order. The team also needs to know what factors impact the team's effectiveness—is it time of year, weather, public holidays, suppliers, location of customer, location of warehouse, type of product, or mix of products in an order?
- The merchandising team needs to understand which products are selling well, which suppliers are reliable, and where the most profitable product lines are for each season.
- The managers of employees need to know who is performing the best.
- The accountants need to know where the revenue and costs originate.

It is the same information but is it separated out and regrouped to satisfy the needs of each part of the business.

Forces

- **Usefulness of detailed information changes over time**—Detailed information that is collected and used in the short term has decreasing value as time passes.
- **Averages matter**—Aggregated information gives a clear impression of the overall effectiveness of a part of the business.
- **Outliers matter**—Unusual events, the behavior of the few highly profitable customers, or an unusual transaction may well indicate a risk, opportunity, or start of a new trend. These outliers can be missed if you only use aggregated information.
- **Information needs change over time**—The world is constantly changing—in many ways, it is becoming more complex and sophisticated. The information used by the organization must evolve with the times.
- **Organizations are complex**—They have many different systems, activities, departments, and information collections. The detail is too much for any one person to comprehend.
- **Trends matter**—To understand how well you are doing, it is necessary to understand the current situation and how that compares with past performance.
- **Operational systems maintain the current state of the business**—How is the past represented?

Solution

Extract information from the operational systems; consolidate it into information collections that maintain a history of how the values are changing over time. Reformat and distribute this information to decision makers.

The historical system of record solution consists of a number of specialized information nodes that are responsible for storing, managing, and transforming information. At the core is an information warehouse. This holds most of the information.

The historical system of record solution is fed using STAGING AREAS and QUEUE MANAGERS. It begins by collecting together the detailed operational information. This includes INFORMATION ACTIVITY information elements that need to be correlated with INFORMATION ASSET information elements. For example, details of an order need to be correlated with details of the customer who made the order and the products selected in the order. This correlation links together the information activities that relate to a particular information asset—because, typically, it is information assets that represent the areas of interest to the management team.

Once correlated, it is possible to generate detailed reports about the activity related to key information assets. These reports have great value in the short term but are too detailed for longer-term views of trends and averages. Information processes create INFORMATION SUMMARY and INFORMATION METRIC information elements from the detailed information and also link them to the appropriate information assets—or to information summaries of groups of related information assets. These information elements are used for the longer-term analysis.

An information warehouse feeds **I**NFORMATION **M**ARTS and **I**NFORMATION **C**UBES. These information nodes provide different consumers with different views of the information. Some will need the fine-grained detail and others will need summaries.

As time passes, the detailed information elements are deleted, or more typically archived, to clear space for new information.

Figure 9.16 shows some of the typical connections you would see with other types of information nodes.

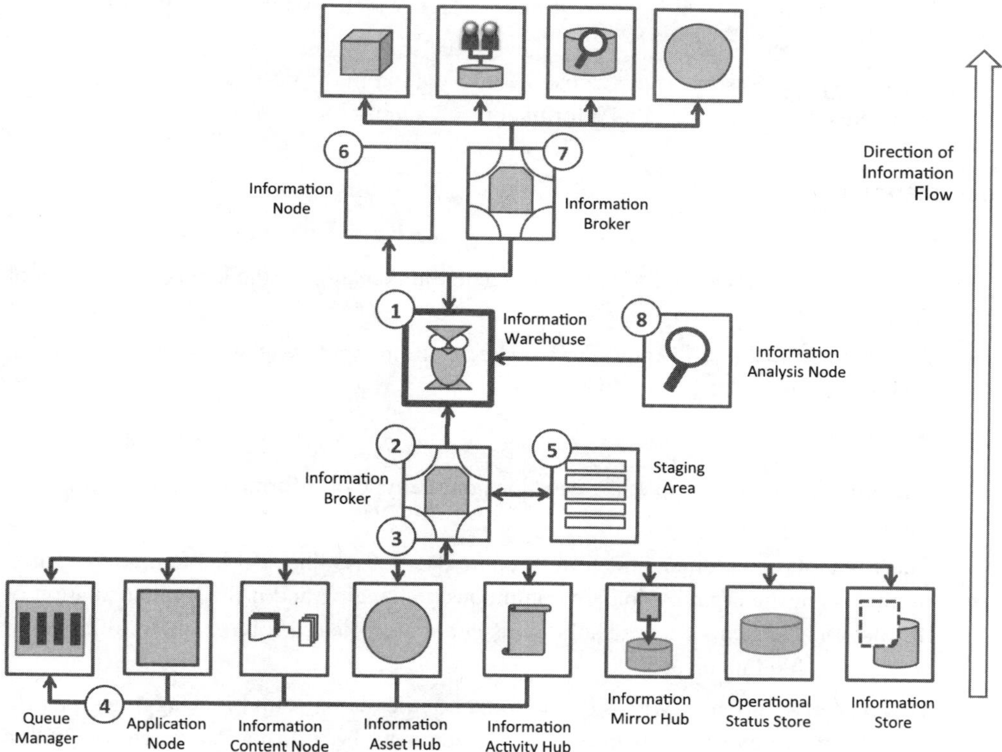

Figure 9.16 Historical system of record solution.

The numbers on the diagram refer to these notes:

1. This is the information warehouse.
2. It is fed from operational systems.

3. Information from the operational systems is transformed, consolidated, and correlated by an INFORMATION BROKER.
4. Some of the transformations are complex and the information may use a STAGING AREA for intermediate results.
5. Updates may be extracted directly from the operational systems by the information broker, or they may be fed to it through a QUEUE MANAGER.
6. Any information node may query information in the information warehouse.
7. However, it is more likely that subsets of the information are extracts by an information broker and passed to a variety of consuming information nodes, where the consolidated information can be used by the organization for reporting and other types of decision making.
8. Analytics processes may run against the information in the information warehouse and the results stored directly in its information collections.

Consequences

Benefits:

- This solution delivers high-quality aggregated information to the key control points of the organization.
- It attempts to make efficient use of storage by slimming down the amount of detail that is kept over time.

Liabilities:

- The organization needs to make decisions on the type of information it needs for management purposes.
- There is a lot of implementation effort required to deliver this information. The information needs of the organization are continuously changing and if the implementation of the historical system of record solution is not continuously evolving, the information it creates will fall into disuse.
- This type of solution may miss the important outliers as a result of the aggregation process. There are experiments in progress to augment the information warehouse with a MAP-REDUCE NODE to manage the accumulation of the original detailed operational information, augmented with information gathered from the Internet, to provide alternative forms of analysis.
- This type of information supply chain relies on the ability to correlate the information activities with the information activities. This can be tricky if the information activities come from multiple sources that use different INFORMATION KEY values to identify the information assets. It often calls for an INFORMATION ASSET HUB supporting the CALLER'S KEY pattern.

Example Resolved

The historical system of record solution is implemented in MCHS Trading's Reporting Hub, which is a subsystem made up of a **S**TAGING **A**REA, an **I**NFORMATION **W**AREHOUSE, and a number of **I**NFORMATION **M**ARTS. This is illustrated in **Figure 9.17**.

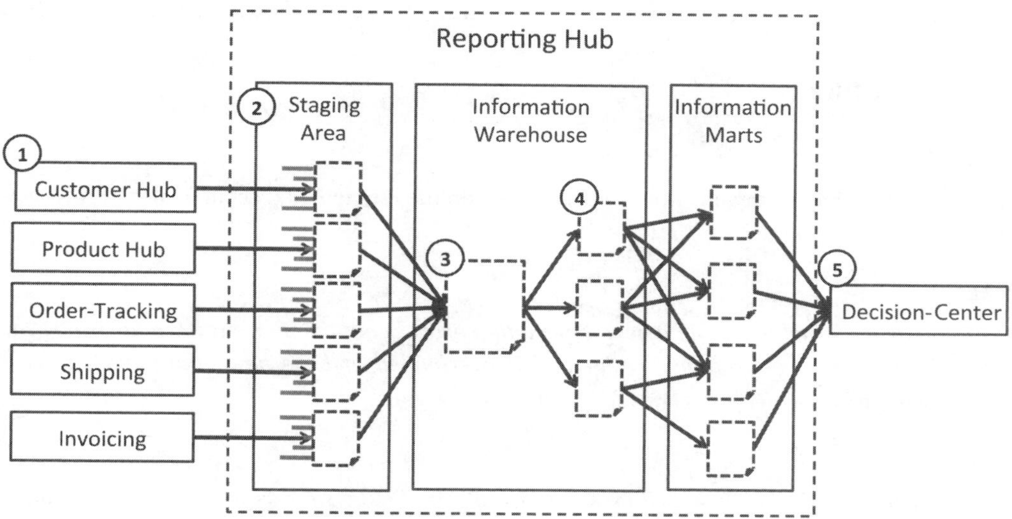

Figure 9.17 MCHS Trading's historical system of record solution.

The numbers on Figure 9.17 refer to these notes:

1. The operational systems regularly send information to the Reporting Hub.
2. This information is initially added to a staging area ready for processing.
3. The information is retrieved from the staging area, correlated, transformed, and consolidated into the main system of record information collections.
4. Over time, the order records become less useful and they are summarized. They retain information about the customer, the products that were ordered, how much was spent, the supplier, and the delivery data. Information such as the delivery route, product batch, and driver are eliminated at this point.
5. Both the full record and the summaries are used to populate the information marts that serve the reporting in the Decision-Center.

Known Uses

This type of information solution is often implemented as an enterprise data warehouse that is supporting business intelligence.

Related Patterns

The **P**ERFORMANCE **R**EPORTING solution is a consumer of a historical system of record.

The **M**ANAGED **A**RCHIVE solution works well with the historical system of record because it moves older detailed information entries that have been summarized and are no longer needed to cheaper storage and then eventual removal.

Workload Offload

Context

An information centric organization is concerned with the efficient and accurate use of information.

Problem

An organization needs to enable a new information process but the information node where the required information collections are located is overloaded and the new information process needs to work with locally provisioned information.

Example

As part of its **N**EXT **B**EST **A**CTION solution, MCHS Trading needs to analyze information about its customers' interests, buying patterns, and channel usage along with the pipeline of new and existing products. The analysis places a heavy strain on the information node that hosts either the **I**NFORMATION **C**OLLECTIONS and/or **I**NFORMATION **P**ROCESSES. The information is consolidated into the Reporting Hub.

Forces

- **Usefulness of the form**—Information is not always captured in the form that is useful for processing.
- **Impacts on other processing**—Analytical processes require resources that may be needed for other processing.
- **Additional resource costs**—Adding copies of information collections and more information nodes costs money.

Solution

Provision a new information collection on an information node that has sufficient spare capacity to support the new information process.

Typically, this uses **S**NAPSHOT **P**ROVISIONING if this information process is only needed for a short period of time or **M**IRRORING **P**ROVISIONING if it will run for an extended period of time and needs up-to-date information.

Consequences

Benefits:

- A processing-hungry information process can be isolated so it does not impact the operation of other information processes.

Liabilities:

- This solution requires investment in additional infrastructure to support the off-loaded information process and the information collections it uses.

Example Resolved

MCHS Trading creates two information mining stores for the analysis of its customer, order, and product information. This is shown in Figure 9.18.

For the next best action solution, they create an information mining store called Next Best Action Analysis Store. It is refreshed regularly from the Reporting Hub using **M**IRRORING **P**ROVISIONING to ensure the analysis continues to use the latest information.

From time to time, they also have an information mining store called Marketing Analysis Store that is used for ad hoc analysis of product sales to plan marketing campaigns. This node is provisioning from the Reporting Hub using **S**NAPSHOT **P**ROVISIONING whenever it is needed.

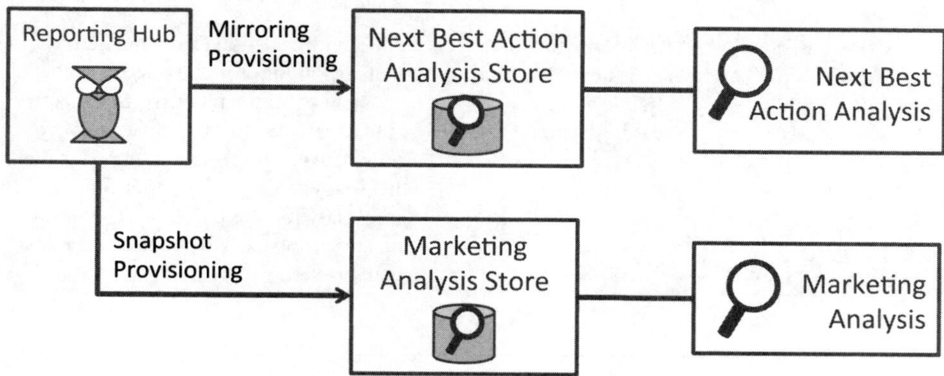

Figure 9.18 Workload offload of analytics at MCHS Trading.

Known Uses

This solution is often used to offload analytics modeling, which can invoke large queries as it searches out patterns in the information collections.

Related Patterns

INFORMATION ANALYSIS NODE is often used to off-load analytics modeling. It is provisioning with an INFORMATION MINING STORE.

Patterns for Business Intelligence and Analytics

The solutions shown in Table 9.7 covers business intelligence and analytics.

Table 9.7 Information Solutions for Business Intelligence and Analytics

Icon	Pattern Name	Problem	Solution
	PERFORMANCE REPORTING	An organization needs to understand how well its business is operating.	Provide decision makers with consolidated and summarized information about their organization's activity that covers the current state and how this state has been achieved over time.
	OPERATIONAL ANALYTICS	An organization wants to classify and react to patterns of use that suggest an opportunity or a threat to the organization.	Using historical data, determine the patterns of events and actions that preceded either a good or bad outcome. Add monitors to the information processes to detect these patterns and take the appropriate actions.
	NEXT BEST ACTION	An information user needs immediate and reliable advice on the next best action to take.	The advice is derived from predictive analytics. It must be delivered in real time to the information user. Some part of the analytics can run inline. However, behind it is an information supply chain that is assembling information and running analytics ahead of time. The results are stored and used to augment the inline analytics.

Performance Reporting

Context

An information centric organization is concerned with the efficient and accurate use of information.

Problem

An organization needs to understand how well its business is operating.

Example

MCHS Trading needs to know the characteristics of its high-valued customers to plan its investments and sale campaigns going forward.

Forces

- **Organizations are complex**—They have many different systems, activities, departments, and information collections. The detail is too much for any one person to comprehend.
- **Different views provide insight**—A decision maker often needs to see the same information summarized and visualized in different ways to fully understand a complex situation.
- **Trends matter**—To understand how well you are doing, it is necessary to understand the current situation and how that compares with past performance.
- **Operational systems maintain the current state of the business**—How is the past represented?

Solution

Provide decision makers with consolidated and summarized information about their organization's activity that covers the current state and how this state has been achieved over time.

This information can be extracted and visualized in multiple ways, allowing the decision maker to explore and understand the current state of the business and how it is changing over time. This capability is provided to the decision maker using an INFORMATION REPORTING PROCESS running in an APPLICATION NODE. Typically, the information that the information reporting process is using is provisioned through an INFORMATION MART.

Consequences

Benefits:

- Performance reporting provides a view on how the organization is operating today with a historical perspective that shows whether particular aspects of the business are trending up or down.

Liabilities:

- The performance reporting solution is dependent on the information that is supplied to it. If this is inaccurate, out of date, or incomplete, then the results will be misleading.

Example Resolved

MCHS Trading introduces a new information node called Decision-Center to provide management reports. This includes the high-value customer report. Because this report is used many times, there is a monthly Information Movement process that extracts the relevant information from the Reporting Hub and builds a new entry in an information collection for the high-value customer report. The MCHS Trading employees can retrieve the high-value customer report for the current month or preceding months through the Reporting Hub's user interface, which is responsible for ensuring that the requesting person is authorized to access it.

Known Uses

Performance reporting solutions are typically provided through business intelligence packages.

Related Patterns

The **H**ISTORICAL **S**YSTEM OF **R**ECORD solution provides summarized information about an organization's operation.

The **I**NFORMATION **M**ART provides information formatted to support performance reporting.

Operational Analytics

Context

An information centric organization is concerned with the efficient and accurate use of information.

Problem

An organization wants to classify and react in real time to patterns of use that suggest an opportunity or a threat to the organization.

Example

MCHS Trading wants to detect when its stock of each type of product should be replenished. The time interval and order size is different for every product and demand fluctuates based on season, weather, and fashion. Currently, MCHS Trading relies on the skill of its buyers to determine when to reorder more stock before it runs out.

Forces

- **Outcomes are caused by many events intersecting events**—Often. it takes information about the events and likely causes and effect to be collected over time to be able to detect the key predictive indicators.

Solution

Using historical data, determine the patterns of events and actions that preceded either a good or bad outcome. Add monitors to the information processes to detect these patterns and take the appropriate actions.

Consequences

Benefits:

- Operational analytics can handle a volume of decisions far beyond the capacity of an organization's employees. This means they can be far more granular in their treatment of each business transaction.

Liabilities:

- The hardest part of operational analytics is building an effective analytics model. This requires the right information to be collected, for long enough for the patterns to emerge, plus a skilled DATA SCIENTIST to tease these patterns out.

Example Resolved

MCHS Trading uses the data from the Reporting Hub to work out which factors affect the demand for each of its products. They then set a reorder threshold for each product in the Shipping application. It generates a request to purchase more stock when this threshold is reached when fulfilling an existing order. The threshold is a combination of how often the product is ordered and how long it takes to restock.

Known Uses

Operational analytics is sometimes called real-time analytics, or predictive analytics. The results or insights may be incorporated into user dashboards or reports to support operational business processes.

Related Patterns

The INFORMATION PATTERN DISCOVERY PROCESS describes an offline process for creating an analytics model. This is a model that looks for patterns in the organization's information that predict a particular outcome. Analytics models are typically used for scoring and classifying information.

The INFORMATION DECISION DEFINITION PROCESS describes another offline information process for creating decision models. These models combine analytics models and business rules to create a step in a process that can make a decision, or prediction, about the next step to take in an activity.

The INFORMATION PATTERN DETECTION PROCESS is the online information process that is able to run either an analytics model or a decision model. It may run in a batch mode, using historical information or operating in real time as activities are occurring.

Next Best Action

Context

An information centric organization is concerned with the efficient and accurate use of information. In particular, it wants to provide exemplary service to its customers.

Problem

An information user needs immediate and reliable advice on the next best action to take.

Typically, an information user is in a situation where he or she has to make a decision in a very short period of time and the information needed to investigate the alternatives is diverse and voluminous, making it impractical to perform detailed research manually.

Example

When a customer contacts the MCHS Trading call center, the customer service representative needs to quickly establish why the customer is calling, what has happened recently in the customer's dealings with the organization, and, as a consequence, the next best action to take to increase the customer's satisfaction and loyalty in MCHS Trading—and ultimately increase the amount this person is spending with the company.

Forces

- **Satisfaction and loyalty are affected by many factors**—The factors that affect customer satisfaction and loyalty are complex and changing.
- **Multiple contact points within an organization**—An individual may interact with an organization through multiple contact points and on different levels. From an IT point of view, details of customer interactions are dispersed in multiple systems (information nodes).

Solution

The advice is derived from predictive analytics. It must be delivered in real time to the information user. Some part of the analytics can run inline. However, behind it is an information supply chain that is assembling information and running analytics ahead of time. The results are stored and used to augment the inline analytics.

Figure 9.19 is the logical view of the predictive analytics decision loop that is executed in real time. It is passed the context of the request (such as who the customer is and why he or she is calling). This context is augmented with stored information to drive the decision model. The results of the decision model are fed back to the caller. Once the suggested actions have either been used or rejected, feedback on the actual outcome is stored and fed back into the information used to configure and tune the decision model.

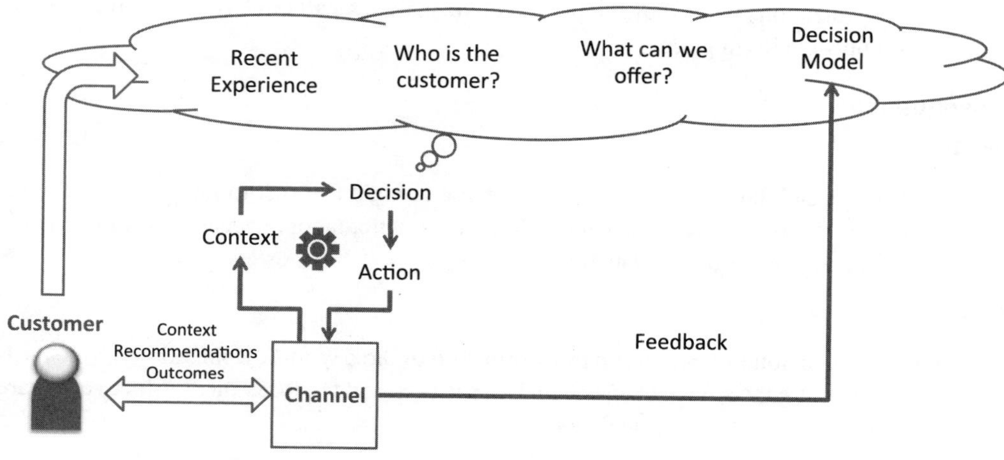

Figure 9.19 The decision loop.

Figure 9.20 shows the information supply chains that support this process. There are two high-level flows: first, the supply of information to the model to configure and tune it for use; second, the flow of information into the operational systems that are needed to augment the context when the decision model is run.

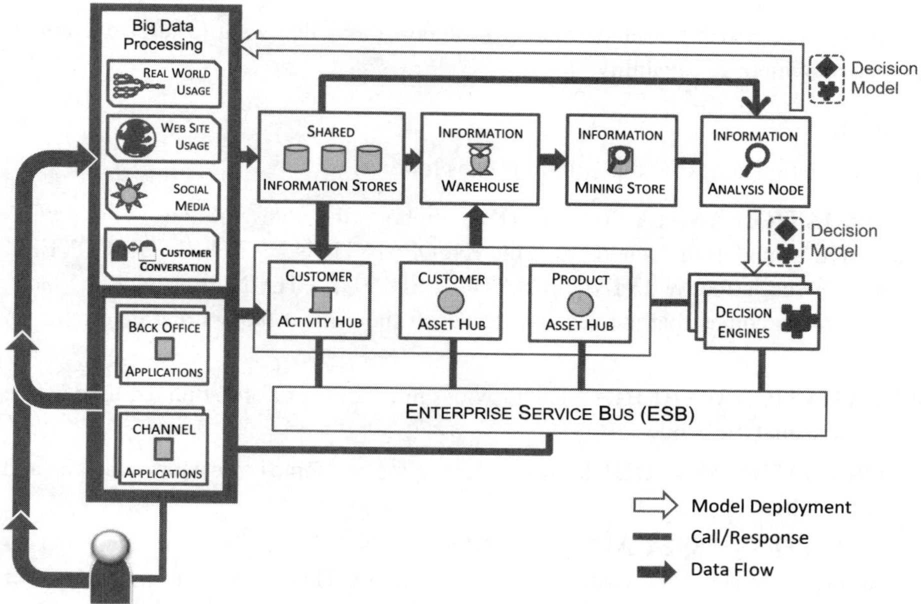

Figure 9.20 Next best action information solution.

Many organizations when they adopt predictive analytics will already have some of these information supply chains in place.

Consequences

Benefits:

- Analytics and the appropriate information are brought together to influence the day-to-day operations of the organization. Without this automation, decisions would be made with incomplete or out-of-date information.

Liabilities:

- This type of solution requires a transformation of the day-to-day operations of the business to ensure the advice from the analytics is used and feedback on its effectiveness are collected to tune the analytical models.

Example Resolved

Prescriptive analytics models are deployed into the Customer-Care application to support the customer service representative. The customer information supply chain supports these models both in terms of tuning the models and providing real-time information required to execute the model for a particular customer.

Known Uses

Prescriptive analytics is growing in importance for organizations that want to offer exemplary customer service or diagnostic capability.

Related Patterns

The principle information nodes for this solution are as follows:

- **INFORMATION ANALYTICS NODE**—Supports the configuration of the predictive analytics models. This node runs the **I**NFORMATION **P**ATTERN **D**ISCOVERY **P**ROCESS and is fed by an **I**NFORMATION **S**UPPLY **C**HAIN to provide the facts, events, and outcomes that are required to detect the critical factors that determine an outcome.
- **INFORMATION WAREHOUSE**—Provides much of the information required by the information analytics node.
- **INFORMATION ASSET HUB**—Provides the master copies of customer details and product details.
- **INFORMATION ASSET ACTIVITY NODE**—Extends the customer details master with information about the customer's recent activity. This is fed from multiple other systems.

- **INFORMATION STORE**—Provides the enterprise system integration layer that is used to store the unstructured and semistructured raw information about the customer's activity.
- **INFORMATION BROKER**—Various instantiations of the information broker are used to support the information supply chains that connect the information nodes together. These supply chains are using a variety of provisioning styles. For example,
  - **MIRRORING PROVISIONING**—To pull information from the enterprise system integration layer into the system of record node
  - **SANDBOX PROVISIONING**—To transfer information from the system of record node, and other information nodes, into the information analytics node
  - **MIRRORING PROVISIONING**—To synchronize the system of record node with the latest information from the operational systems

Patterns for Information Protection

This last group of patterns supports information protection. Information protection has three technical parts to it:

- Managing the life cycle of information
- Protecting information with security and privacy techniques
- Actively managing its quality throughout the information supply chain

The three patterns following Table 9.8 enhance an organization's information management capability to support its INFORMATION GOVERNANCE PROGRAM.

Table 9.8 Information Solution Patterns for Information Protection

Icon	Pattern Name	Problem	Solution
	MANAGED ARCHIVE	An organization is not meeting its information retention obligations.	Create an archiving service that manages and acts on retention policies defined for each of the effected information collections.
	INFORMATION ACCESS AUDIT	An organization needs to know who is accessing its information.	Monitor and record every access to an information collection and validate that the use is approved.
	INFORMATION MONITORING	Is the information supply chain working?	Add information probes at key points in the information supply chain and analyze the measurements they bring back to detect gaps, abnormal patterns, or deteriorating quality in the information.

Managed Archive

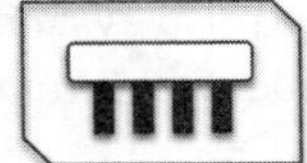

Context

An information centric organization is concerned with governing information throughout its lifetime.

Problem

An organization is not meeting its information retention obligations.

In many industries, it is necessary to retain certain records for a long period of time in case there are investigations that are necessary in the future. Keeping these records in the operational systems can slow them down and be expensive in terms of online storage.

Example

MCHS Trading needs to keep records of who bought some of the more sensitive products that it sells. There is a small chance that they will need to retrieve this information if a problem occurs.

Forces

- **Bloated information collections**—Access to an information collection that has a lot of information that is no longer needed may be slowed down due to excessive size of the collection.
- **Obsolete technology**—The corollary of the rapid advancement of technology is that it also rapidly becomes obsolete. Often information has value well beyond the life of the technology on which it resides.
- **Expensive or unavailable skills**—Obsolete technology also requires skills that become increasingly expensive or hard to find to keep functioning.
- **Decommissioning applications**—An organization is often unable to decommission an application even though it is not being used because it may need the information it contains.

Solution

Create an archiving service that manages and acts on retention policies defined for each of the effected information collections.

The managed archive solution has the following parts to it:

- A metadata description of the subject areas that need archiving, which information collections hold the information, how frequently archiving should run, how it identifies the information entries that are ready to be archived, and how long the information should be retained.

- An archiving agent that is scheduled to run and move the appropriate information entries from the information collections into the archive. This archiving agent needs access to an information service that allows it to locate, read, and delete these information entries. It must create a record of what was archived and where it was located. This record is added to the archive catalog that is used by the organization to locate and retrieve information when it needs to.
- An archive housekeeping process that removes information entries from the archive once their retention period has been reached.

Consequences

Benefits:

- The managed archive moves obsolete information to cheaper storage while keeping a record of what has been archived and when.

Liabilities:

- For long retention periods, the managed archive solution needs to ensure there is a system available that can still read the information that has been archived. There are two parts to this:
  1. Can the device used to store the archived information still be read?
  2. Can the contents be understood from a business point of view—particularly if the application that created the information has subsequently been decommissioned?

Example Resolved

MCHS Trading implements a managed archive process in its Reporting Hub. All of the orders received by MCHS Trading are copied into the Reporting Hub, so the information is complete. The open format used by the Reporting Hub makes it easy to recover and interpret the information in the archive.

Known Uses

Managed archiving is used in industries where there are regulations that require the organization to retain certain types of information for long periods of time, for example, policy records in the insurance industry. It is sometimes referred to as records retention or it is part of information lifecycle management (ILM).

Related Patterns

The INFORMATION ARCHIVING PROCESS provides the archiving mechanism.

The **I**NFORMATION **I**DENTIFICATION pattern describes the types of metadata that is necessary to locate and classify the information to archive. The **I**NFORMATION **M**ANAGEMENT **O**BLIGATION pattern describes what external regulations may impact requirements for archiving, ongoing access, and retention.

The **S**OFT **D**ELETE pattern is used by information nodes that want to mark an information entry as logically deleted as far as the business is concerned, but is still available in storage to allow the information archiving process to access the entries and copy them to archive storage.

The **R**OLL UP **I**NFORMATION **S**UPPLY **C**HAIN creates summaries of information entries that are ready for archiving. This means that critical aspects of the information can be retained for reporting, while the detailed information is archived to cheaper storage, and eventually deleted.

Archiving is typically focused on the removal of **I**NFORMATION **E**VENTS and **I**NFORMATION **A**CTIVITIES.

Information Access Audit

Context

An information centric organization is concerned with governing information throughout its lifetime.

Problem

An organization needs to know who is accessing its information.

This is particularly important for personal information and information that is competitively sensitive.

Example

MCHS Trading wants to be sure that its Customer Hub is only being used for legitimate purposes.

Forces

- **Access security defines maximum access rights**—The traditional access security mechanisms define all of the resources that an individual should have access to. Once the access is given, the individual can access the information for any purpose.
- **Inappropriate use**—An individual may be given access rights to some data for a very specific task. That individual then may use this information for other purposes—including copying it to portable storage.
- **Copying or replicating information adds risk**—Sensitive information is often useful or critical for many functions. Wherever it resides, it is at risk and controls must exist in all places, not just central storage locations.

- **The inclusion of access controls is not sufficient**—It is not enough to just monitor for access violations after the fact.
- **Monitoring access controls is time sensitive**—Its value diminishes over time, and it must be processed as soon as possible.
- **Access control monitoring can generate a huge volume of information**—There must be capabilities available to find critical events and circumstances.

Solution

Monitor every access to an information collection and validate that the use is approved.

In this solution, the monitoring is correlating the data access with the task being performed and the time (occasion) it is being performed. The purpose is to uncover unexpected uses of information.

Consequences

Benefits:

- This type of monitoring provides additional proof that only authorized people are using the critical information collections. The level of monitoring can be adapted to meet the changing needs and threats to the organization over time.

Liabilities:

- The monitoring adds additional processing load to the information supply chain. Also, it must be someone's role to review, investigate, and action any alerts raised; otherwise, the monitoring is a waste of time and resources.

Example Resolved

MCHS Trading adds a monitoring solution that records every access to the Customer Hub database that is not authorized, or is requesting particularly sensitive information.

Known Uses

Data privacy laws and regulations, particularly around Personally Identifiable Information (PII) and Payment Card Industry (PCI) information, describe specific information elements that must be protected, secured, and guarded.

This type of monitoring can be implemented by simple database triggers or user-defined functions. However, that tends to add a large additional load on the database. There are specialized network monitoring solutions that are able to monitor information requests as they flow into the network.

Related Patterns

The INFORMATION GUARD patterns cover different types of information security. The INFORMATION MANAGEMENT OBLIGATION pattern describes what external regulations may impact requirements for protecting specific types of information. The SUBJECT AREA DEFINITION pattern may describe the obligations around a particular piece of business information. The INFORMATION IDENTIFICATION pattern may incorporate sensitive data classifications for specific INFORMATION ELEMENTS.

Information Monitoring

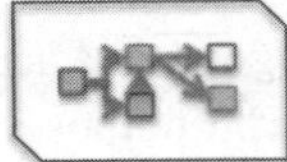

Context

An information centric organization is concerned with the efficient and accurate use of information.

Problem

Is the information supply chain working?

For example,

- Is the correct information being transferred between the information nodes in a timely manner? Is the information passed to the destination semantically equivalent to the information in the source?
- Is the information stored in each information collection complete, up to date, and protected?
- Are invalid values being detected and corrected—both within the information collections and during information provisioning?
- Is information being used appropriately?

Example

MCHS Trading wants to be sure that its information supply chains are working properly. For example, it wants to know that orders are being fulfilled on time, that its product descriptions are correct, and that its customer information is up to date. How does it achieve this?

Forces

- **Failures can occur at any time, any place for many reasons.**
- **The absence of activity may indicate a problem—**It is not sufficient just to monitor for errors.

- **Where an application does not completely meet the needs of an organization, the people using it find ways to work around it**—This can involve putting information into attributes designed for different purposes, or changing values in files/databases after the application has finished processing.
- **Network and system failures may interfere with the transfer of information**—These disruptions must be recovered from once the failing components have been recovered to ensure that correct information content has been transferred with the correct relationships to other information.
- **If a failure in an information supply chain is not detected, and resolved in time, further failures can occur downstream as a consequence**—For example, if information about monthly sales figures from one region is not loaded in time, the report that aggregates the sales figures for the whole organization will be wrong.
- **It takes local knowledge** to understand how a particular information process should be operating.
- **It takes holistic knowledge** of the information supply chain to understand the impact of any incident.
- **Monitoring information is context sensitive**—Its meaning is lost if the location and circumstances under which the monitoring information was gathered is lost.
- **Monitoring information is time sensitive**—Its value diminishes over time, and it must be processed as soon as possible.
- **Monitoring can generate a huge volume of information**, causing resource shortages for other activity running within an information node.

Solution

Add information probes at key points in the information supply chain and analyze the measurements they bring back to detect gaps, abnormal patterns, or deteriorating quality in the information.

The processing of this information is time critical. Its aim is to gather information from a wide range of sources and consolidate them into a central location where the values can be monitored in near real time, while also allowing historical analysis of the information.

The leaf nodes of this information solution are typically INFORMATION PROBES that are continuously pumping out events. These events are stored either in an information collection that is hosted in the same information node as the information probe, or in an INFORMATION EVENT STORE. Whichever approach is used, the events are periodically extracted and sent, either directly, or via intermediary nodes, to a central information node for analysis.

This is shown in Figure 9.21.

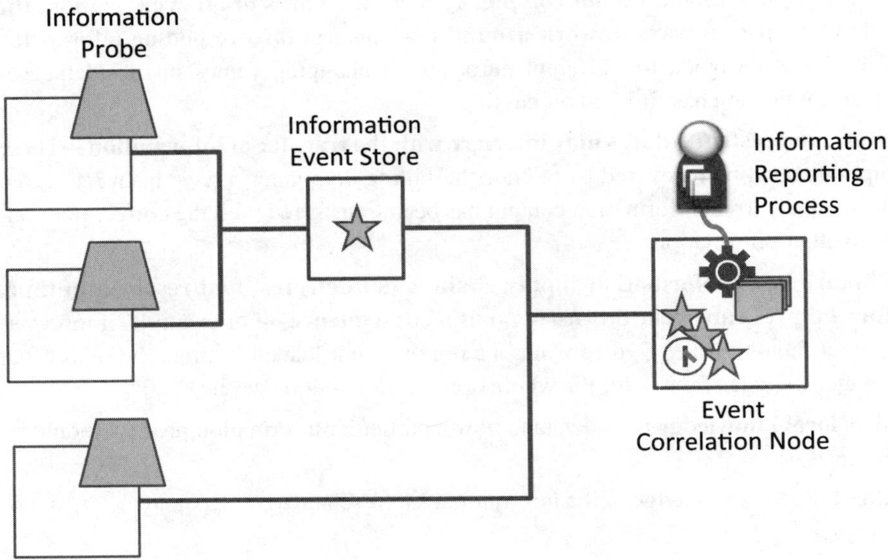

Figure 9.21 Information Monitoring solution.

Information events in the original source information nodes need to be purged as part of the information supply chain's function. This may be as part of the information flow that sends the events toward the centralized information node, or via a regularly scheduled INFORMATION ARCHIVING PROCESS. Using an information archiving process leaves the events in place for a short period of time to enable a local INFRASTRUCTURE OPERATOR to monitor what is occurring in the local information node while still enabling the centralized monitoring.

Each information probe writes the events they detect to a local INFORMATION EVENT STORE to provide a historical view of the events. This store can be accessed through a REMOTE INFORMATION SERVICE to enable a CASCADING INFORMATION SUPPLY CHAIN to consolidate the interesting events into information event stores in a central monitoring information node. This node hosts information processes that review and action the events that are received.

Consequences

Benefits:

- Monitoring the consistency, reliability, and quality of information improves the information used by an organization for key decision making, resulting in cost savings, mitigated risk, or potential revenue opportunity. Such monitoring action becomes an aspect of a broader INFORMATION GOVERNANCE PROGRAM.
- This approach enables detailed information to be collected from a wide range of sources.

Liabilities:

- An information node that is experiencing failures, or a shortage of resources, may not be able to forward on the information it has gathered at a fast enough rate to avoid being swamped by incoming information.
- There is a time delay between capturing information and processing it. This may be significant for time-sensitive events, in which case it will be better to query the event information directly from the source rather than use information flows to move them into a consolidated information collection.
- Monitoring processes must be kept in sync with changes to business processes and rules, potentially adding time and cost to implement such changes.

Example Resolved

MCHS Trading sets up INFORMATION PROBES at each of its information nodes to monitor the information processes that contribute to its information supply chains:

- Each information node is monitored for availability.
- Each information node monitors that its information processes complete successfully.
- Every information flow contains an information probe that counts the information payloads it has processed.
- The Order-Tracking information node monitors that orders are being processed in a timely manner.

Each information probe writes the events it detects to a local INFORMATION EVENT STORE. These are consolidated into event stores in the main operator console for MCHS Trading's systems. The availability of the information nodes, and any unexpected event any of them detect is sent to the operator console for review and action. The operator console is an EVENT CORRELATION NODE and is able to filter events and detect common patterns, reducing the load on the infrastructure operator.

Known Uses

Information monitoring is normally implemented by organizations that have a strong business need (such as regulatory requirements or customer service) to be sure particular types of information are correct. In these environments, it is not sufficient to just monitor for errors. The monitoring must positively demonstrate that all of the right information has been included, from authoritative sources, and it is not contaminated with inappropriate values.

Related Patterns

The INFORMATION PROBE patterns detail the type of information that could be gathered with store-and-forward provisioning.

The **B**UFFERED **R**OUTING information flow pattern describes a mechanism for transferring large amounts of information between information nodes.

The **C**ONSOLIDATING **I**NFORMATION **S**UPPLY **C**HAIN pattern describes how to bring information in to the monitoring application.

The **E**VENT **C**ORRELATION **N**ODE running the **I**NFORMATION **M**ONITORING **P**ROCESS provides an effective implementation for the centralized monitoring hub.

Summary of Information Solutions

The information solutions described above should be considered as a starter set—there are many more! The important point to remember is that information solutions are always implemented in a brown field environment: So they must integrate with, enhance, or incorporate existing systems and information. Buy-in is often required from a broad range of stakeholders and the state of the existing systems must be carefully considered early in the project to avoid nasty surprises. Most information owners believe their information is better than it actually is. The cause of any information quality problems could be the practices of the information users, poor implementation in the information processes, or an unreliable/missing supply of information. The earlier you know about these issues, the more likely you are able to fix them rather than allowing them to derail the information solution.

Final Thoughts

Information management is a complex topic. It is deeply routed in every part of IT, and every person, program, and component plays its part in the correct processing and use of information. A single book cannot capture its richness and variety, but we hope we have provided a framework to think about the issues and to formulate approaches that will deliver value to your organization.

Over time, new patterns will emerge, and we will develop more experience with the existing patterns. To stay in touch with the latest developments, visit us at:
https://www.ibm.com/developerworks/mydeveloperworks/groups/service/html/communityview?communityUuid=8b999d32-11d5-4f68-a06e-6825f3c78233

> "Nothing in life is to be feared, it is only to be understood. Now is the time to understand more, so that we may fear less."
> —**Marie Curie**

APPENDIX 1

Glossary

Topic	Description	Related Patterns
Activity	A piece of work that is being performed by a person, an IT system, or both. Many activities within an organization are well defined—someone has defined how that type of work will be performed. Well-defined activities have well-defined information needs and are often cost effective to support with IT systems. However, there are always unexpected events and circumstances that need to be handled by people through ad hoc activities.	INFORMATION PROCESS
Adapter	An additional piece of software used to either extract or load information in or out of an information node.	INFORMATION BROKER, INFORMATION TRIGGER
Analytics	The use of algorithms and information to characterize a situation.	INFORMATION ANALYTICS NODE
Application	A collection of information processes and related information that is supporting an aspect of an organization's activity.	APPLICATION NODE
Attribute	A type of property that can be recorded about something. For example, attributes for MCHS Trading's customers could include the customer's name, the customer's address, the customer's demographic details, and so on.	INFORMATION ELEMENT, INFORMATION ENTRY
Authoritative source	An information collection that is known to be the best source of a particular type of information.	INFORMATION GOVERNANCE PROGRAM
Big data	Large quantities of data that need specialist servers to process because of its volume (amount), velocity (arrival rate), variety (different topics—often unstructured and mixed up), and veracity (quality).	HISTORICAL SYSTEM OF RECORD, MAP-REDUCE NODE, STREAMING ANALYTICS NODE

Topic	Description	Related Patterns
Business information	Information required to operate your organization.	INFORMATION ELEMENT, SUBJECT AREA DEFINITION
Business intelligence	Information required to understand and improve how well an organization is operating. It typically combines reporting and analytics.	INFORMATION REPORTING, NEXT BEST ACTION
Business transaction	An execution of a request or short-term contract for an external party.	INFORMATION ACTIVITY, DAISY CHAIN PROVISIONING
Code Value	A number or letter combination that is short-hand for a phrase, or option. Code Values are used to create consistency in how attribute values are recorded, enabling decision making, validation, and language translation around the attribute.	LOOKUP TABLES, INFORMATION CODE, INFORMATION VALUES PROFILE
Consolidation	The collecting together of information from multiple sources.	INFORMATION FLOW
Context	A description of the relevant aspects of the environment from where information is collected. This may include details of the people involved, what activity they were performing, where and when it happened, and the assumptions that were made.	INFORMATION CONTEXT
Coverage	The set of attributes that are supported by an information collection, relative to the possible attributes that an organization believes is useful for that subject area.	LOCAL COVERAGE, CORE COVERAGE, EXTENDED COVERAGE, COMPLETE COVERAGE
Data	A set of facts that has not yet been understood, classified, correlated, and stored within an organization's information collections.	INFORMATION ELEMENT
Data mart	A collection of information organized in a dimensional structure to support a specific use case, or related use cases. It can be thought of as a subset of a data warehouse that has been extracted for a specific purpose.	INFORMATION MART
Data set	A logical collection of information.	INFORMATION COLLECTION
Data warehouse	A database that is configured to support large set–based queries that are typical of business intelligence activities such as analytics and reporting.	INFORMATION WAREHOUSE
Database	A collection of related tables of information stored in a special-purpose server—called a database server.	INFORMATION STORE

Topic	Description	Related Patterns
Destination	An information node or information collection that will receive information from an information supply chain.	INFORMATION SUPPLY CHAIN
Distribution	The delivery of information from one information collection to others, typically located on different information nodes.	INFORMATION FLOW
Downstream	An information collection that receives information from another information collection directly or indirectly via an information supply chain.	INFORMATION SUPPLY CHAIN
Element	A set of related attributes that describe something.	INFORMATION ELEMENT
Federation	Consolidation and correlating information from different information collections on request.	INFORMATION FEDERATION PROCESS
File	Related information stored on a disk. Each file has a name. It must be opened to access the information inside and closed once it is no longer being used.	INFORMATION STORE
Format	The structure in which information is represented, as it is stored or passed around. A schema describes the format.	INFORMATION SCHEMA
Information	Facts, records, and opinions that have been categorized, organized, and stored.	INFORMATION ELEMENT, INFORMATION IDENTIFICATION
Infrastructure	Hardware, operating system, and middleware installed to support an aspect of an organization's business.	INFORMATION NODE
Instance	Refers to an occurrence of something. This may be a person, an object, an activity, an event, or a result.	INFORMATION ENTRY
Integration	The consolidation of information from multiple sources.	INFORMATION FLOW
Integration job	An information process that runs in an information broker.	INFORMATION BROKER
IT system	Hardware, operating system, middleware, and application that is installed and managed together to support an aspect of the organization's work.	INFORMATION NODE
Knowledge	A coherent understanding of a subject area. Understanding what to do with the information at hand based on experience, practice, and education.	SUBJECT AREA DEFINITION, INFORMATION CENTRIC ORGANIZATION

Topic	Description	Related Patterns
Life cycle	The time period from when a piece of information is created to when it is eventually destroyed. In between, it may be retrieved, updated, reformatted, summarized, copied, and archived.	INFORMATION ELEMENT
Master data	High-value operational information that needs to be maintained and shared in a consistent and managed way.	INFORMATION ASSET
Master Data Management	Master Data Management (MDM) is the discipline of managing master data.	INFORMATION ASSET HUB
Metadata	Information that is used to understand and manage the organization's IT systems. Its use can reduce the effort to create new capability, increase opportunities to reuse existing capability, and speed up the resolution of issues. For it to remain useful, it needs active management to keep it up to date.	INFORMATION IDENTIFICATION
OLAP cube	Online Analytical Processing store designed for multidimensional information that is used by an individual to explore and experiment with.	INFORMATION CUBE
Operational data store	A specialized database that stores consolidated information for operational use.	INFORMATION MIRROR NODE, INFORMATION ACTIVITY NODE, OPERATIONAL STATUS NODE, INFORMATION ASSET ACTIVITY NODE
Organization	A group of people working together to achieve a common goal.	INFORMATION CENTRIC ORGANIZATION
Payload	Information that is structured to send between information nodes.	INFORMATION PAYLOAD
Predictive Analytics	The use of analytics in operational systems that uses information about past events and outcomes to predict/advise how the current activity should proceed.	NEXT BEST ACTION
Provisioning	The supply of information to an information process.	INFORMATION PROVISIONING
Real-world entity	A person, concept, organization, event, or object in the physical world.	INFORMATION USER, INFORMATION ASSET
Reference data	A set of code values and related meanings.	LOOKUP TABLES, INFORMATION CODE

Topic	Description	Related Patterns
Reference data management (RDM)	The management of sets of code values and the relationship between them.	INFORMATION ASSET HUB
Replication	The copying of information from one information collection to another—typically preserving all of the content.	INFORMATION REPLICATION PROCESS
Routing	The copying of information from one information node to another.	INFORMATION FLOW
Schema	Formal definition for how information should be formatted into a well-understood structure. This schema guides an information process when it is parsing the structure. It is also used to validate information as it is being placed into the structure.	INFORMATION SCHEMA
Scope	The number of instances that an information collection stores when compared with the total number of instances that the organization knows about.	LOCAL SCOPE, COMPLETE SCOPE, TRANSIENT SCOPE
Server	A hardware or software system that can be managed and controlled. It typically performs a well-defined capability for the owning organization.	INFORMATION NODE
Service	A well-defined interface to information.	INFORMATION SERVICE
Source	A supply of information that is being used by an information process.	INFORMATION SERVICE
Structured information	Information that is organized into distinctly defined and formatted fields, called attributes. Using structured information allows rapid identification, processing, delivery, and subsequent storage of the information.	INFORMATION MODEL, INFORMATION SCHEMA, INFORMATION ENTRY
Subject area	A topic that is of sufficient interest to an organization that it wants to store information about it.	SUBJECT AREA DEFINITION
System	A generic term for people, processes, and technology working together for a common goal.	
Target	*See* Destination.	

Topic	Description	Related Patterns
Transcoding	The conversion of one code value to another code value of the same meaning. This occurs when information is being extracted from an information collection and is being transformed for use in a different context. The transcoding takes the code value used in the original collection and converts it to a code value used in the new context.	LOOKUP TABLES
Unstructured information	Documents and media information, including text, audio, video, and images.	INFORMATION CONTENT NODE
Upstream	An information node that has provided information to the local information node.	INFORMATION SUPPLY CHAIN
Usage	The types of operations that are performed on information.	MASTER USAGE, REFERENCE USAGE, HYBRID USAGE, SANDBOX USAGE
Visualization	The display of information to a person. This includes text, tables, charts, graphs, annotated maps, three-dimensional models, dashboards, graphical indicators—such as traffic lights and many more.	INFORMATION REPORTING PROCESS
Web service	A well-defined interface specified in XML that can be called from a remote information node.	REMOTE INFORMATION SERVICE
Wisdom	The combination of knowledge with experience that leads to knowing when the existing practices are good, or this is a new situation and some innovation is required.	

APPENDIX 2

Summary of MCHS Trading's Systems

System	Description
Accounts Payable	Accounts Payable is an **A**PPLICATION **N**ODE that receives information on the purchase orders sent to suppliers and the invoices from suppliers, and triggers payments to suppliers.
Customer Activity Hub	Customer Activity Hub is an **I**NFORMATION **A**CTIVITY **H**UB that provides information on the activity of customers.
Customer-Care	Customer-Care is an **A**PPLICATION **N**ODE that provides a single view of the customer, using information from the Customer Hub and the Customer Activity Hub.
Customer Hub	Customer Hub is an **I**NFORMATION **A**SSET **H**UB for managing and coordinating the synchronization of customer details.
Decision-Center	Decision-Center is MCHS Trading's business intelligence application. It supports reporting and some analytics. The information it manages is located in information marts that are fed from the Reporting Hub.
E-Shop	E-Shop is a packaged application (**A**PPLICATION **N**ODE) that supports MCHS Trading's Internet shopping business. The Internet shopping business is MCHS Trading's most profitable channel and so this application is their top priority when it comes to investment, maintenance and disaster recovery.
Inventory	The inventory systems exist in the three physical warehouses that MCHS Trading uses. Users at the warehouses receive actual products (and the associated bills of lading) and enter the stock information into these systems, which, in turn, send updates to the Shipping application.
Invoicing	Invoicing is an **A**PPLICATION **N**ODE that sends invoices and collects outstanding payments for orders from customers.
M-Shop	M-Shop is a new **A**PPLICATION **N**ODE that uses **A**GILE **B**USINESS **P**ROCESSES to support the mail order and telephone ordering businesses. It uses information services to retrieve customer details from Customer Hub.
Mail-Shop	Mail-Shop is the first **A**PPLICATION **N**ODE that MCHS Trading owned. It supports their mail order and telephone ordering businesses. It is homegrown and a little bit inflexible. There is no customer details information collection so customer information has to be entered by hand on every order. MCHS Trading has a desire to decommission this application and replace it with a new application called M-Shop.

System	Description
Order-Tracking	Order-Tracking is an **I**NFORMATION **A**CTIVITY **H**UB that determines the status of orders as they flow between the order-processing applications.
Predictive Analytics	MCHS Trading introduces an **I**NFORMATION **N**ODE that facilitates an **O**PERATIONAL **A**NALYTICS solution. This includes a highly specialized set of analytics processes that are fed by multiple information supply chains.
Product Hub	Product Hub is a specialized application for managing product details, primarily by the Merchandising Department. It is the centralized master for product details and read-only copies of product details are sent to the other systems that need them.
Purchasing	Purchasing is an **A**PPLICATION **N**ODE that coordinates the acquisition of products to be sold from suppliers (as well as for MCHS Trading itself). It receives input from the Product Hub (among other sources) in the form of purchase order requests and creates purchase orders for suppliers.
Re-Stocking	Re-Stocking is an **O**PERATIONAL **S**TATUS **S**TORE that helps provide information from the Shipping application to handle customer orders that are delayed waiting for new stock to arrive from the suppliers.
Reporting Hub	Reporting Hub is a **H**ISTORICAL **S**YSTEM **o**F **R**ECORD solution for maintaining a complete picture of the enterprise.
Shipping	Shipping is an **A**PPLICATION **N**ODE that ensures goods are shipped to customers as part of order processing. It is working with the inventory systems in the three physical warehouses to determine the best place to ship the goods from.
Stores	Stores is an **A**PPLICATION **N**ODE that supports the physical stores (shops). When the stores are open, this application is running at full capacity, which is why it has the Stores-Mirror to provide access to its information.
Stores-Mirror	Stores-Mirror is an **I**NFORMATION **M**IRROR **S**TORE that replicates information from the Stores application.
Supplier-net	Supplier-net is an **I**NFORMATION **B**ROKER that is managing the exchanges of product details and orders for new stock to suppliers.

APPENDIX 3

Related Pattern Languages

As noted in Chapter 1, "Introduction," different technologies have emerged over the past two to three decades to address different aspects of information management. These technologies include relational database management systems (RDBMS); data warehouse models and approaches; Service Oriented Architectures (SOA); messaging technology; extract, transform, load (ETL) technology; and many others.

Along with the introduction and adoption of these technologies have come pattern languages (and user communities) to help architects and designers establish effective and consistent approaches for the use of the specific technology.

One of the forerunners in software and application patterns was *Design Patterns: Elements of Reusable Object-Oriented Software*.[1] This work provides core design principles for object-oriented programming through creational, structural, and behavioral patterns. These patterns are key considerations in the design of the BESPOKE APPLICATION PROCESS.

Martin Fowler's *Patterns of Enterprise Application Architecture*[2] is another key work in the development of patterns supporting information technologies.

Enterprise Integration Patterns: Designing, Building, and Deploying Messaging Solutions[3] targets the area of information integration through message-based techniques, providing depth to topics described within this text, such as the INFORMATION QUEUING PROCESS, QUEUE MANAGER, and DAISY CHAIN PROVISIONING.

More recently, *SOA Design Patterns*[4] addresses the domain of Service Oriented Architectures (SOA) and the details of constructing INFORMATION SERVICES.

1. Erich Gamma and others, *Design Patterns: Elements of Reusable Object-Oriented Software* (Reading, MA, Addison-Wesley, 1994).
2. Martin Fowler, *Patterns of Enterprise Application Architecture* (Boston, MA, Addison-Wesley, 2002).
3. Gregor Hohpe and Bobby Woolf, *Enterprise Integration Patterns: Designing, Building, and Deploying Messaging Solutions* (Boston, MA, Addison-Wesley, 2003).
4. Thomas Erl, *SOA Design Patterns* (Prentice Hall/PearsonPTR, 2009).

And pattern work has been brought into other related domains such as analysis,[5] data modeling,[6] and IT management.[7]

For active areas of pattern research, the Pattern Languages of Programs (PLoP) conferences (particularly in the United States and Europe, but also occasionally elsewhere) provide active support and mentoring in developing and writing patterns.[8]

See these works and Appendix 4, "Bibliography," for additional pattern references.

5. Martin Fowler, *Analysis Patterns: Reusable Object Models* (Boston, MA, Addison-Wesley, 1997).

6. David C. Hay, *Data Model Patterns: A Metadata Map* (San Francisco, CA, Elsevier, 2006).

7. Charles T. Betz, *Architecture & Patterns for IT* (Waltham, MA, Morgan Kaufmann, 2011).

8. For a summary of the different Pattern Languages of Programs (PLoP) Conferences as well as patterns and works produced from the conferences, see The Hillside Group at: http://hillside.net/conferences.

APPENDIX 4

Bibliography

The subject of information management covers such a broad range of topics and focused disciplines that we cannot make a comprehensive or exhaustive reference of the literature. What we do offer here are starting points into the literature across a number of common themes, works which can in turn bring the reader into the broader set of materials in each theme.

Information Centric Organization

Information strategy may be considered from a business perspective (e.g., How can information be utilized to drive maximum advantage for the organization?) or a more focused information technology (IT) perspective (e.g., How can we best run the systems and applications to support business operations and processes?). In the existing literature, there is an array of material addressing a range of topics from using information to drive business to using information as a business asset to outlining approaches for managing information in IT.

Recent works that touch on the information centric organization include the following:

Aitkin, Iain. *Value-Driven IT Management: Commercializing the IT Function*. Oxford: Butterworth-Heinemann, 2003.

Benson, Robert J., and Tom Bugnitz. *From Business Strategy to IT Action: Right Decisions for a Better Bottom Line*. New York: John Wiley and Sons, 2004.

Betz, Charles T. *Architecture & Patterns for IT*. Waltham, MA: Morgan Kaufmann, 2011.

High, Peter A. *World Class IT: Why Businesses Succeed When IT Triumphs*. New York: Wiley Press/Jossey-Bass, 2009.

Hillard, Robert. *Information-Driven Business*. New York: John Wiley and Sons, 2010.

Enterprise Architecture

In the early 1980s, John Zachman of IBM developed the initial conceptions of what first formalized Information System Architecture, and subsequently Enterprise Architecture, beyond what had been focal points on systems analysis and design. What subsequently emerged was the Zachman Framework for describing a set of views or perspectives in enterprise architecture. Other frameworks have been subsequently developed, such as that of The Open Group (TOGAF).

Broadly, enterprise architecture addresses the context, scope, and material used by an organization to define its approaches for business and technology optimization. See:

DAMA International. *The DAMA Guide to the Data Management Body of Knowledge*. Bradley Beach, NJ: Technics Publications, LLC, 2010.

Lankhorst, Marc. *Enterprise Architecture at Work: Modelling, Communication and Analysis*. 3rd ed. Heidelberg, Germany: Springer, 2012.

The Open Group Architecture Framework (TOGAF). http://pubs.opengroup.org/architecture/togaf8-doc/arch/.

Zachman, John A. "A Framework for Information Systems Architecture." *IBM Systems Journal* 26, no. 3 (1987). IBM Publication G321-5298.

Zachman International. http://www.zachman.com/about-the-zachman-framework.

Enterprise Application Architecture

With the rise of distributed client/server applications and object-oriented programming in the mid-1990s, there developed a greater focus on the architecture of such systems for both performance and process in the handling of information. Enterprise application architecture can be applied from website design to complex packaged enterprise resource planning (ERP) systems. Although technologies have shifted, the use of unified methods, common patterns, and modeling has helped standardize the development of enterprise applications. See:

Brown, Kyle, Gary Craig, David Pitt, Russell Stinehour, Mark Weitzel, Jim Amsden, Peter M. Jakab, and Daniel Berg. *Enterprise Java Programming with IBM WebSphere*. 2nd ed. Boston, MA: Addison-Wesley, 2003.

Evans, Eric. *Domain-Driven Design: Tackling Complexity in the Heart of Software*. Boston, MA: Addison-Wesley, 2003.

Fowler, Martin. *Patterns of Enterprise Application Architecture*. Boston, MA: Addison-Wesley, 2002.

Fowler, Martin. *UML Distilled: A Brief Guide to the Standard Object Modeling Language*. 3rd ed. Boston, MA: Addison-Wesley, 2003.

Fowler, Martin, Kent Beck, John Brant, William Opdyke, and Don Roberts. *Refactoring: Improving the Design of Existing Code*. Boston, MA: Addison-Wesley, 1999.

Jacobson, Ivar, Grady Booch, and James Rumbaugh. *The Unified Software Development Process*. Boston, MA: Addison-Wesley, 1999.

Kroll, Per, and Philippe Kruchten. *The Rational Unified Process Made Easy: A Practitioner's Guide to the RUP*. Boston, MA: Addison-Wesley, 2003.

Service-Oriented Architecture and Web Services

Following the advent of client/server technologies and object-oriented programming, service-oriented architectures sought to increase the ability to reuse and standardize common information actions through sets of callable services, both within an organization and across organizations (through the World Wide Web). Approaches developed to establish models and associated modeling languages, as well as best practices in the form of design patterns. Service-oriented architectures now form the foundation for enterprise software as well as application development and Software-as-a-Service offered by specific technology vendors. See:

Cerami, Ethan. *Web Services Essentials*. Sebastopol, CA: O'Reilly Media, 2002.

Daigneau, Robert. *Service Design Patterns: Fundamental Design Solutions for SOAP/WSDL and RESTful Web Services*. Boston, MA: Addison-Wesley, 2011.

de Bruijn, Jos, Mick Kerrigan, Uwe Keller, Holger Lausen, and James Scicluna. *Modeling Semantic Web Services: The Web Service Modeling Language*. Heidelberg, Germany: Springer, 2008.

Erl, Thomas. *SOA Design Patterns*. Prentice Hall, 2009.

Erl, Thomas, Benjamin Carlyle, Cesare Pautasso, and Raj Balasubramanian. *SOA with REST: Principles, Patterns & Constraints for Building Enterprise Solutions with REST*. Indianapolis, IN: Prentice Hall, 2012.

Josuttis, Nicolai M. *SOA in Practice: The Art of Distributed System Design*. Sebastopol, CA: O'Reilly Media, 2007.

Papazoglou, Michael. *Web Services: Principles and Technology*. Prentice Hall, 2007.

Woods, Dan, and Thomas Mattern. *Enterprise SOA: Designing IT for Business Innovation*. rev. ed. Sebastopol, CA: O'Reilly Media, 2006.

Information Architecture

Information architecture provides the information-centric view within the larger enterprise architecture. It addresses the aspects of standards, governance, and use of information to ensure effective information technology decisions. At a high level, see:

Godinez, Mario, Eberhard Hechler, Klaus Koenig, Steve Lockwood, Martin Oberhofer, and Michael Schroeck. *The Art of Enterprise Information Architecture: A Systems-Based Approach for Unlocking Business Insight*. IBM Press, 2010.

O'Rourke, Carol, Neal Fishman, and Warren Selkow. *Enterprise Architecture Using the Zachman Framework*. Independence, KY: Course Technology, 2003.

Data Models

Data models have existed in some fashion since data storage was introduced. A sequential file designed for a COBOL program contains a data model, though focused on the needs of that specific program or the outputs it must produce. With the advent of relational databases, particularly as introduced by E. F. Codd and C. J. Date, the need to model the *relationships* across data structures increased dramatically and the role of data modeler emerged. Object-oriented programming in the mid- to late-1990s led to further advancements and refinements in data modeling such as the Unified Modeling Language introduced by G. Booch, I. Jacobson, and J. Rumbaugh. And more recently, developments with patterns and focus on Service Oriented architectures and business semantics has led to works on data model patterns, standard industry models, and models of the semantic web. See:

Blaha, Michael. *Patterns of Data Modeling (Emerging Directions in Database Systems and Applications)*. Boca Raton, FL: CRC Press, 2010.

Booch, Grady, James Rumbaugh, and Ivar Jacobson. *The Unified Modeling Language User Guide*. 2nd ed. Boston, MA: Addison-Wesley, 2005.

Date, C. J. *An Introduction to Database Systems*. 7th ed. Boston, MA: Addison-Wesley, 2000.

Fowler, Martin. *UML Distilled: A Brief Guide to the Standard Object Modeling Language*. 3rd ed. Boston, MA: Addison-Wesley, 2003.

Hay, David C. *Data Model Patterns: A Metadata Map*. San Francisco, CA: Elsevier, 2006.

Olive, Antoni. *Conceptual Modeling of Information Systems*. Heidelberg, Germany: Springer, 2007.

Silverston, Len. *The Data Model Resource Book, Vol. 1: A Library of Universal Data Models for All Enterprises*. John Wiley and Sons, 2001.

Silverston, Len. *The Data Model Resource Book, Vol. 2: A Library of Data Models for Specific Industries*. John Wiley and Sons, 2001.

Silverston, Len, and Paul Agnew. *The Data Model Resource Book, Vol. 3: Universal Patterns for Data Modeling*. John Wiley and Sons, 2009.

Metadata Management

Metadata, or the data about the data, has become a critical component of information architectures. Metadata repositories allow the capture and management of business terminology, logical and physical models, database schemas, report designs, integration processes, and web services. By capturing the metadata, greater understanding of both the existing and future information landscape can be achieved. An emerging focus given the breadth of information through the World Wide Web is on information taxonomies and the associated structure of information. See:

Heddon, Heather. *The Accidental Taxonomist*. Medford, NJ: Information Today, Inc., 2010.

Inmon, William H., Bonnie O'Neil, and Lowell Fryman. *Business Metadata: Capturing Enterprise Knowledge*. Burlington, MA: Morgan Kaufmann, 2007.

Lambe, Patrick. *Organising Knowledge: Taxonomies, Knowledge and Organisational Effectiveness*. Cambridge, England: Chandos, 2007.

Marco, David. *Building and Managing the Meta Data Repository: A Full Lifecycle Guide*. New York: John Wiley and Sons, 2000.

Marco, David, and Michael Jennings. *Universal Meta Data Models*. Indianapolis, IN: John Wiley and Sons, 2004.

Tozer, Guy. *Metadata Management for Information Control and Business Success*. Norwood, MA: Artech House, 1999.

Turco, Carl. *Enterprise Architecture & Metadata Modeling: A Guide to Conceptual Data Model, Metadata Repository, Business and Systems Re-engineering*. Infinity Publishing, 2009.

Wegener, Hans. *Aligning Business and IT with Metadata: The Financial Services Way*. Chichester, England: John Wiley and Sons, 2007.

Zeng, Marcia Lei, and Jian Qin. *Metadata*. Chicago, IL: Neal-Schuman, 2008.

Information Warehouse

Increasing numbers of databases supporting enterprise applications led to increasing challenges by the early- to mid-1990s to organize and structure information for effective use. Differences in information context created barriers in understanding the business of the organization, even where data was modeled. New approaches to collecting and storing information in the form of the data (or now commonly termed information) warehouse, associated data marts, and operational data stores emerged. More recently, standard industry models for information warehouses have been developed based on years of practical implementation expertise (see additional references in the "Data Models" section found earlier in this appendix). See:

Adamson, Christopher. *Star Schema The Complete Reference*. McGraw-Hill Osborne, 2010.

Brackett, Michael H. *The Data Warehouse Challenge*. New York: John Wiley and Sons, 1996.

Inmon, W. H. *Building the Data Warehouse*. 2nd ed. New York: John Wiley and Sons, 1992.

Inmon, W. H., Claudia Imhoff, and Greg Battas. *Building the Operational Data Store*. New York: John Wiley and Sons, 1996.

Inmon, W. H., Claudia Imhoff, and Ryan Souza. *Corporate Information Factory*. New York: John Wiley and Sons, 1998.

Kimball, Ralph. *The Data Warehouse Toolkit*. 2nd ed. New York: John Wiley and Sons, 2002.

Kimball, Ralph, Margy Ross, Warren Thornthwaite, Joy Mundy, and Bob Becker. *The Data Warehouse Lifecycle Toolkit*. 2nd ed. Indianapolis, IN: Wiley Publishing Inc., 2008.

Laberge, Robert. *The Data Warehouse Mentor: Practical Data Warehouse and Business Intelligence Insights*. McGraw-Hill Osborne, 2011.

Information Integration

With the requirement to move information from multiple applications to common data stores such as information warehouses, easier integration techniques were needed than point-to-point programmed interfaces. Messaging; federation or virtualization; and extract, transform, load (ETL) technologies are among the core capabilities in this space. See:

Davis, Judith, and Robert Eve. *Data Virtualization: Going Beyond Traditional Data Integration to Achieve Business Agility*. Nine Five One Press, 2011.

Doan, AnHai, Alon Halevy, and Zachary Ives. *Principles of Data Integration*. Waltham, MA: Morgan Kaufmann, 2012.

Giordana, Anthony David. *Data Integration Blueprint and Modeling: Techniques for a Scalable and Sustainable Architecture*. IBM Press, 2011.

Hohpe, Gregor, and Bobby Woolf. *Enterprise Integration Patterns*. Boston: Addison-Wesley, 2004.

Kimball, Ralph, and Joe Caserta. *The Data Warehouse ETL Toolkit: Practical Techniques for Extracting, Cleaning, Conforming, and Delivering Data*. Indianapolis, IN: Wiley Publishing Inc., 2004.

van der Lans, Rick. *Data Virtualization for Business Intelligence Systems: Revolutionizing Data Integration for Data Warehouses*. Waltham, MA: Morgan Kaufmann, 2012.

Information Quality

Information (or data) quality emerged as a discipline in the early 1990s, though the objective of providing quality data through information processes has existed since information technology was introduced. As organizations extended the number of information systems in their environments, particularly moving information across systems to support new business initiatives, the challenges of maintaining information quality became increasingly difficult.

Changes to the structure, format, value content, and semantic context as information is delivered to downstream consumers often results in issues of completeness, integrity, and consistency. Questions about the provenance and lineage of specific pieces of information emerge. Issues with information quality can result in business risk, customer dissatisfaction, failed projects, manual costs to correct, and, in some cases, fines due to failure to meet regulatory requirements.

From a pattern language perspective, the information identification pattern group focuses in part on the aspects of understanding the information and its level of information quality. In the information process patterns, there are another group of patterns that focus on how information quality is handled and supported. And at a low level, specific information reengineering step patterns focus on how to check, standardize, match, and correct data. All of these patterns form part of all the information solution patterns, not just information monitoring.

A substantial literature has developed on practices and approaches of incorporating information quality as a core facet of business and information processes. See:

English, Larry P. *Improving Data Warehouse and Business Information Quality*. John Wiley and Sons, 1999.

Lee, Yang, L. Pipino, J. Funk, and R. Wang. *Journey to Data Quality*. Cambridge, MA: MIT Press, 2006.

Loshin, David. *Enterprise Knowledge Management: The Data Quality Approach*. San Francisco, CA: Morgan Kaufmann, 2001.

McGilvray, Danette. *Executing Data Quality Projects: Ten Steps to Quality Data and Trusted Information*. Burlington, MA: Morgan Kaufmann, 2008.

Olson, Jack E. *Data Quality: The Accuracy Dimension*. San Francisco, CA: Morgan Kaufmann, 2003.

Redman, Thomas C. *Data Quality for the Information Age*. Artech House, 1996.

Redman, Thomas C. *Data Quality: The Field Guide*. Woburn, MA: Digital Press, 2001.

Master Data Management

All organizations work with core pieces of data whether about people, places, products, or other components necessary to the business. With increased complexity in the applications collecting and delivering this information, there has emerged over the last 10 years a strong focus on connecting and managing this core master data. See:

Benson, Alex, and Larry Dubov. *Master Data Management and Data Governance*. 2nd ed. McGraw-Hill Osborne, 2010.

Dreibelbis, Allen, Eberhard Hechler, Ivan Milman, Martin Oberhofer, Paul van Run, and Dan Wolfson. *Enterprise Master Data Management: An SOA Approach to Managing Core Information*. IBM Press, 2008.

Big Data

With the rapid growth of incoming information into an organization—whether sensor-based, social media, customer calls, or other often unstructured content—new technologies have emerged to provide up-front analytics on real-time, in-motion data. Collectively, these technologies, and the problems they seek to solve, are commonly termed "Big Data." (Note more references on data analytics can be found later in this appendix in the "Analytics and Reporting" section.) See:

Franks, Bill. *Taming the Big Data Tidal Wave: Finding Opportunities in Huge Data Streams with Advanced Analytics*. Hoboken, NJ: John Wiley and Sons, 2012.

Isson, Jean-Paul, and Jesse Harriott. *Win with Advanced Business Analytics: Creating Business Value from Your Data*. New York: John Wiley and Sons, 2012.

Russell, Matthew A. *Mining the Social Web: Analyzing Data from Facebook, Twitter, LinkedIn, and Other Social Media Sites*. Sebastopol, CA: O'Reilly, 2011.

Soares, Sunil. *Big Data Governance: An Emerging Imperative*. Boise, ID: MC Press, 2013.

Zikopoulos, Paul, Dirk DeRoos, Krishnan Parasuraman, Thomas Deutsch, David Corrigan, and James Giles. *Harness the Power of Big Data*. New York: McGraw-Hill, 2013.

Analytics and Reporting

As long as there has been information processing, there has been reporting. Paper output has given way to user interfaces and dashboards delivered through web portals, but operational systems continue to generate reports of what they have processed. As long as the information sources for reports remained relatively homogenous and the processes using the information remained segregated, reporting could be confined within specific application systems. As organizations added more heterogeneous information sources and sought to bring together diverse information sets, reporting became significantly harder. Information warehouses and marts, information integration, data federation, and specialized business intelligence and reporting technologies were among the solutions to this challenge. With the integration of diverse sets of information came the opportunity to mine and analyze the data and find hidden patterns whether to increase revenue opportunities, decrease risk, or decrease costs. The rapid expansion of data visualization and predictive analytic capabilities is a consequence. See:

Few, Stephen. *Show Me the Numbers: Designing Tables and Graphs to Enlighten*. 2nd ed. Burlingame, CA: Analytics Press, 2012.

Han, Jiawei, and Micheline Kamber. *Data Mining: Concepts and Techniques* (2nd ed). San Francisco, CA: Morgan Kaufmann, 2006.

Laursen, Gert H. N., and Jesper Thorlund. *Business Analytics for Managers: Taking Business Intelligence Beyond Reporting*. Hoboken, NJ: John Wiley and Sons, 2010.

Milton, Michael. *Head First Data Analysis: A Learner's Guide to Big Numbers, Statistics, and Good Decisions*. Sebastopol, CA: O'Reilly, 2009.

Moss, Larissa T., and Shaku Atre. *Business Intelligence Roadmap: The Complete Project Lifecycle for Decision-Support Applications*. Addison-Wesley, 2003.

Stubbs, Evan. *The Value of Business Analytics: Identifying the Path to Profitability*. Hoboken, NJ: John Wiley and Sons, 2011.

Taylor, James. *Decision Management Systems: A Practical Guide to Using Business Rules and Predictive Analytics*. IBM Press, 2011.

Tufte, E. R. *Envisioning Information*. Cheshire, CT: Graphics Press, 1990.

Turban, Efraim, Ramesh Sharda, Dursun Delen, and David King. *Business Intelligence: A Managerial Approach*. 2nd ed. Prentice Hall, 2012.

Witten, Ian H., Eibe Frank, and Mark A. Hall. *Data Mining: Practical Machine Learning Tools and Techniques*. 3rd ed. Morgan Kaufmann, 2011.

Information Security and Privacy

There are many recent examples of security breaches in organizations worldwide, particularly focused on issues of customer data privacy. As more and more information is collected, analyzed, connected, and shared, the risks and penalties associated with improperly secured information grow. Technologies have advanced to provide data encryption and obfuscation, as well as basic access controls, network security, and so on. See:

Anderson, Ross. *Security Engineering: A Guide to Building Dependable Distributed Systems*. John Wiley and Sons, 2008.

Andress, Jason. *The Basics of Information Security: Understanding the Fundamentals of InfoSec in Theory and Practice*. Waltham, MA: Syngress, 2011.

Ben Naten, Ron. *Implementing Database Security and Auditing: Includes Examples for Oracle, SQL Server, DB2 UDB, Sybase*. Burlington, MA: Elsevier Digital Press, 2005.

Hayden, Lance. *IT Security Metrics: A Practical Framework for Measuring Security & Protecting Data*. McGraw-Hill Osborne, 2010.

Kenan, Kevin. *Cryptography in the Database: The Last Line of Defense*. Addison-Wesley, 2005.

Litchfield, David, Chris Anley, John Heasman, and Bill Grindlay. *The Database Hacker's Handbook: Defending Database Servers*. John Wiley and Sons, 2005.

Matwyshyn, Andrea. *Harboring Data: Information Security, Law, and the Corporation*. Stanford, CA: Stanford University Press, 2009.

Nissenbaum, Helen. *Privacy in Context: Technology, Policy, and the Integrity of Social Life*. Stanford, CA: Stanford University Press, 2009.

Stamp, Mark. *Information Security: Principles and Practice*. John Wiley and Sons, 2011.

Vacca, John R. *Computer and Information Security Handbook*. Burlington, MA: Morgan Kaufmann, 2009.

Information Life-Cycle Management

Information traverses a life cycle from initial collection through regular use and change to eventual archival or removal. Literature on applications, database systems, information warehouses, and storage technologies may include sections on life-cycle management in those specific contexts. This is also a core discipline in information governance models. See:

EMC Education Services. *Information Storage and Management: Storing, Managing, and Protecting Digital Information in Classic, Virtualized, and Cloud Environments*. John Wiley and Sons, 2012.

Hill, David. *Data Protection: Governance, Risk Management, and Compliance*. Boca Raton, FL: CRC Press, 2009.

IBM Redbooks. *Implementing an Infosphere Optim Data Growth Solution*. Vervante, 2011.

Matthews, David. *Electronically Stored Information: The Complete Guide to Management, Understanding, Acquisition, Storage, Search, and Retrieval*. Boca Raton, FL: CRC Press, 2012.

Soares, Sunil. *The IBM Data Governance Unified Process: Driving Business Value with IBM Software and Best Practices*. Ketchum, ID: MC Press, 2010.

Patterns Index

E

F

G

H

I-J-K

L

M

T

U

V

W-X-Y-Z

Index

D

E

F

K

L

Q

R

T

U

V

W-X-Y-Z